IMPORT

HERE IS YOUR REGISTRATION

YOUR PREMIUM McGRAW-HILL ONLINE RESOURCES.

MW01124716

For key premium online resources you need THIS CODE to gain access. Once the code is entered, you will be able to use the Web resources for the length of your course.

If your course is using **WebCT** or **Blackboard**, you'll be able to use this code to access the McGraw-Hill content within your instructor's online course.

Access is provided if you have purchased a new book. If the registration code is missing from this book, the registration screen on our Website, and within your WebCT or Blackboard course, will tell you how to obtain your new code.

Registering for McGraw-Hill Online Resources

TO gain access to your McGraw-Hill web resources simply follow the steps below:

(1) USE YOUR WEB BROWSER TO GO TO: **www.mhhe.com/wu**

(2) CLICK ON **FIRST TIME USER**.

(3) ENTER THE REGISTRATION CODE* PRINTED ON THE TEAR-OFF BOOKMARK ON THE RIGHT.

(4) AFTER YOU HAVE ENTERED YOUR REGISTRATION CODE, CLICK **REGISTER**.

(5) FOLLOW THE INSTRUCTIONS TO SET-UP YOUR PERSONAL UserID AND PASSWORD.

(6) WRITE YOUR UserID AND PASSWORD DOWN FOR FUTURE REFERENCE.
KEEP IT IN A SAFE PLACE.

TO GAIN ACCESS to the McGraw-Hill content in your instructor's **WebCT** or **Blackboard** course simply log in to the course with the UserID and Password provided by your instructor. Enter the registration code exactly as it appears in the box to the right when prompted by the system. You will only need to use the code the first time you click on McGraw-Hill content.

Thank you, and welcome to your McGraw-Hill online Resources!

REGISTRATION CODE

T9EK-NT94-I8O8-6U0U-K934

Mc Graw Hill **Higher Education**

* YOUR REGISTRATION CODE CAN BE USED ONLY ONCE TO ESTABLISH ACCESS. IT IS NOT TRANSFERABLE.

0-07-292006-8 T/A WU: AN INTRODUCTION TO OBJECT-ORIENTED PROGRAMMING WITH JAVA, 3E

An Introduction to Object-Oriented Programming with Java™

updated third edition

C. Thomas Wu
Naval Postgraduate School

Higher Education

Boston   Burr Ridge, IL   Dubuque, IA   Madison, WI   New York   San Francisco   St. Louis
Bangkok   Bogotá   Caracas   Kuala Lumpur   Lisbon   London   Madrid   Mexico City
Milan   Montreal   New Delhi   Santiago   Seoul   Singapore   Sydney   Taipei   Toronto

 **Higher Education**

AN INTRODUCTION TO OBJECT-ORIENTED PROGRAMMING WITH JAVA™
UPDATED THIRD EDITION

Published by McGraw-Hill, a business unit of The McGraw-Hill Companies, Inc., 1221 Avenue of the Americas, New York, NY 10020. Copyright © 2004, 2001, 1999 by The McGraw-Hill Companies, Inc. All rights reserved. No part of this publication may be reproduced or distributed in any form or by any means, or stored in a database or retrieval system, without the prior written consent of The McGraw-Hill Companies, Inc., including, but not limited to, in any network or other electronic storage or transmission, or broadcast for distance learning.

Some ancillaries, including electronic and print components, may not be available to customers outside the United States.

This book is printed on acid-free paper.

1 2 3 4 5 6 7 8 9 0 VNH/VNH 0 9 8 7 6 5 4

ISBN 0–07–304095–9

Publisher: *Elizabeth A. Jones*
Sponsoring editor: *Kelly H. Lowery*
Managing developmental editor: *Emily J. Lupash*
Marketing manager: *Dawn R. Bercier*
Senior project manager: *Sheila M. Frank*
Lead production supervisor: *Sandy Ludovissy*
Coordinator of freelance design: *Rick D. Noel*
Cover/interior designer: *Elise Lansdon*
Cover image: *©GettyImages-Stone, Zen Buddhist rock garden, stone set in raked sand, close-up, Peter Samuels*
Compositor: *Interactive Composition Corporation*
Typeface: *10.5/12 Times Roman*
Printer: *Von Hoffmann Corporation*

Library of Congress Cataloging-in-Publication Data

Wu, C. Thomas.
    An introduction to object-oriented programming with Java™ / C. Thomas Wu. — Updated 3rd ed.
        p.   cm.
    Includes bibliographical references and index.
    ISBN 0–07–304095–9 (hard copy : alk. paper)
    1. Object-oriented programming (Computer science). 2. Java™ (Computer program language). I. Title.

QA76.64.W78   2004b
005.13'3—dc22   2004007673
                                                                                 CIP

www.mhhe.com

To my family

Contents

7 Event-Driven Programming and Basic GUI Objects   381

8 Exceptions and Assertions   461

9 Characters and Strings   515

Preface

We have made a number of improvements in this third edition of the book, but the main objectives remain the same. This book is intended as an introductory text on object-oriented programming, suitable for use in a one-semester CS1 course, and assumes no prior programming experience from the students. We only assume basic computer skills and some background in algebra and trigonometry to solve certain chapter exercises. Those who already have experience in traditional non-object-oriented programming languages such as C, BASIC, and others also can use this book as an introduction to object-oriented programming, graphical user interface, and event-driven programming. The two main objectives of this book are to teach

- object-oriented programming, and
- the foundations of real-world programming.

Object-orientation has become an important paradigm in all fields of computer science, and it is important to teach object-oriented programming from the first programming course. Teaching object-oriented programming is more than teaching the syntax and semantics of an object-oriented programming language. Mastering object-oriented programming means becoming conversant with the object-oriented concepts and being able to apply them effectively and systematically in developing programs. The book teaches object-oriented programming, and students will learn how to develop object-oriented programs.

The second objective of this book is to prepare students for real-world programming. Knowing object-oriented concepts is not enough. Students must be able to apply that knowledge to develop real-world programs. Sample programs in many introductory textbooks are too simplistic, and they do not teach students techniques to develop large object-oriented programs. In this book, we teach students how to use classes from the class libraries from Chapter 2 and how to define their own classes from Chapter 4. We emphasize foremost the teaching of effective object-oriented design and necessary foundations for building large-scale programs. We will discuss this point further in the Features section of this preface.

New Features in the Third Edition

We would like to take this opportunity to thank the adopters of the earlier editions. Numerous suggestions we received from the adopters and their students helped us tremendously in improving the texbook. For this edition, we focused on improving the strengths of the earlier editions, updating and adding the materials by incorporating capabilities of Java 2 SDK 1.4 and 1.5 class libraries, and removing the materials that have less relevance and significance today. Before we get into the features of the book, we will highlight briefly the changes we made in the third edition:

1. **Full-color pages.** We started with one color in the first edition. We introduced the second color in the second edition to enhance the illustrations and the overall presentation of the materials. We took it one step further and decided to use full-color pages in this edition. The result is dramatic. Different sections are clearly identified, syntax coloring is used in code listings, illustrations are more lucid, and the overall flow of the pages is very attractive and appealing. Pedagogy has been greatly enhanced by the use of full-color pages.

   In addition to the use of full color, the page layout is completely redesigned, with new icons to highlight the helpful reminders and design guidelines. We adopted the Japanese rock garden as our design theme.

2. **No reliance on the javabook classes.** In the earlier versions of Java systems, we did not have an easy way to perform input and output. To work around this shortcoming, many authors provided their own classes which the students can use to perform input and output. To that end, we provided a GUI (graphical user interface) based collection of classes organized into a package named javabook. The situation has improved with the introduction of new Swing classes, most notably the JOptionPane class. In this edition, we will be using the standard classes exclusively for input and output. The javabook package is still available, however, for those who wish to use them. We will discuss more on this in the Features section of this preface.

3. **Short sample programs.** Many reviewers and adopters requested more short sample programs that illustrate the concepts in a succint manner. We now have numerous short sample programs throughout the chapters. At the end of many sections, we provide one or two short sample programs to illustrate the main concept taught in that section. A complete list of all sample classes (programs) is given in Appendix B.

4. **Java 2 SDK 1.4 and 1.5 materials.** We teach newly added features of versions 1.4 and 1.5. For example, pattern matching capabilities and

assertion features from version 1.4 are covered in Chapter 9 and Chapter 8, respectively. The Scanner class from version 1.5 that simplifies the standard input is covered in Chapter 3.

5. **No applets.** We no longer teach applets in this textbook. After students cover Chapter 7 and a portion of Chapter 14, they can easily master applets on their own. A short handout on applets is available from our website.

6. **Swing classes for GUI.** For teaching GUI and event-driven programming, we use Swing classes exclusively. There will be no discussion on AWT-based GUI components.

7. **UML notations.** UML diagrams are used to document the relationships of the classes in the sample programs. Other diagrams (such as state-of-memory diagrams) will also use UML notations for consistency. Notice that although UML notations are used in these diagrams, these illustrative diagrams are not strictly speaking UML diagrams.

Features

There are many pedagogical features that make this book attractive. We will describe the defining features of this book.

Java

We chose Java for this book. Unlike C++, Java is a pure object-oriented language, and it is an ideal language to teach object-oriented programming because Java is logical and much easier to program when compared to other objectoriented programming languages. Java's simplicity and clean design make it one of the most easy to program object-oriented languages today. Java does not include language features that are too complex and could be a roadblock for beginners in learning object-oriented concepts. Although we use Java, we must emphasize that this book is not about Java programming. It is about object-oriented programming, and as such, we do not cover every aspect of Java. We do, however, cover enough language features of Java to make students competent Java programmers.

Standard Classes for Input and Output

In this edition, we decided to use the standard classes exclusively for both GUI and console input and output. We still make the author-defined javabook classes available for use, but there will be no discussion on their use in the textbook. Also, some exercises may still suggest the use of certain javabook classes, but its use is not mandatory in solving them.

With the advent of Swing classes, specifically the JOptionPane class, the practical reason for using the javabook classes is eliminated for the most part. Moreover, we can achieve most of the pedagogical reasons for providing the javabook classes by using appropriate standard classes such as String, Date, and others instead. We, therefore, decided to drop the javabook classes in this edition.

Full-Immersion Approach

We wrote a series of articles in 1993 on how to teach object-oriented programming in the *Journal of Object-Oriented Programming* (Vol. 6, No. 1; Vol. 6, No. 4; and Vol. 6, No. 5). The core pedagogic concept we described in the series is that one must become an object user before becoming an object designer. In other words, before being able to design one's own classes effectively, one first must learn how to use predefined classes. We adopt a full-immersion approach in which students learn how to use objects from the first program. It is very important to ensure that the core concepts of object-oriented programming are emphasized from the beginning. Our first sample program from Chapter 2 is this:

```
/* Chapter 2 Sample Program: Displays a Window
    File: Ch2Sample1.java
*/

import javax.swing.*;

class Ch2Sample1 {

    public static void main( String[] args ) {

        JFrame myWindow;

        myWindow = new JFrame();

        myWindow.setSize(300, 200);
        myWindow.setTitle("My First Java Program");
        myWindow.setVisible(true);
    }
}
```

This program captures the most fundamental notion of object-oriented programming. That is, an object-oriented program uses objects. As obvious as it may sound, many introductory books do not really emphasize this fact. In the program, we use a JFrame object called myWindow to display a generic window. Many introductory textbooks begin with a sample program such as

```
/*
   Hello World Program
*/
class HelloWorld
{

    public static void main(String args[])
    {
        System.out.println("Hello World");
    }
}
```

or

```
/*
    Hello World Applet
*/
import java.applet.*;
import java.awt.*;

public class HelloWorld extends Applet
{
    public void paint( Graphics g)
    {
        g.drawString("Hello World", 50, 50);
    }
}
```

Both programs have problems. They do not illustrate the key concept that object-oriented programs use objects. The first program does indeed use an object System.out, but the use of System.out does not illustrate the object declaration and creation. Beginners normally cannot differentiate classes and objects. So it is very important to emphasize the concept that you need to declare and create an object from a class before you can start using the object. Our first sample program does this.

The second HelloWorld program is an applet, which, as its name suggests, is a mini-application with a very specific usage. Applets are specific to Java, and our objective is to teach object-oriented programming, not to teach the specific features of the Java language.

Illustrations

We believe a picture is worth a thousand words. Difficult concepts can be explained nicely with lucid illustrations. Diagrams are an important tool for designing and documenting programs, and no programmers will develop real-world software applications without using some form of diagramming tools. We use UML diagrams for the sample programs, and UML notations are used consistently in all types of illustrations.

This book includes numerous illustrations that are used as a pedagogic tool to explain core concepts such as inheritance, memory allocation for primitive data types and objects, parameter passing, and others. Representative illustrations can be found on pages 38, 155, 196, 197, 585, 604, 653, 743, and 835.

Incremental Development

We teach object-oriented software engineering principles in this book. Instead of dedicating a separate chapter for the topic, we interweave program development principles and techniques with other topics. Every chapter from Chapter 2 to Chapter 14 includes a sample development to illustrate the topics covered in the chapter, and we develop the program using the same design methodology consistently.

This book teaches a software design methodology that is conducive to object-oriented programming. All sample developments in this book use a technique we characterize as incremental development. The incremental development technique is based on the modern iterative approach (some call it a spiral approach), which is a preferred methodology of object-oriented programmers.

Beginning programmers tend to mix the high-level design and low-level coding details, and their thought process gets all tangled up. Presenting the final program is not enough. If we want to teach students how to develop programs, we must show the development process. An apprentice will not become a master builder just by looking at finished products, whether they are furniture or houses. Software construction is no different.

The problem with other textbooks is that the authors often dedicate a single chapter to discuss and preach effective software development methodologies, but they never actually show how to put these methodologies into practice. They only show and explain the finished products. But without putting what they preach into practice by showing the development process, students will not learn how to develop programs. And it is not enough to show the development process once. We must show the development process repeatedly. In this book, we develop every sample development program incrementally to show students how to develop programs in a logical and methodical manner.

Feature 6

Design Guidelines, Helpful Reminders, and Quick Checks

Throughout the book, we include design guidelines and helpful reminders. Almost every section of the chapters is concluded with a number of Quick Check questions to make sure that students have mastered the basic points of the section.

Design guidelines are indicated with a bonsai icon like this:

Design Guidelines

Design a class that implements a single well-defined task. Do not overburden the class with multiple tasks.

Helpful reminders come in different styles. The first style is indicated with a stone lantern icon like this:

Helpful Reminder

Watch out for the off-by-one error (OBOE).

The second style is a Take My Advice box:

On occasions, programming can be very frustrating because no amount of effort on your part would make the program run correctly. You are not alone. Professional programmers often have the same feeling, including this humble self. But, if you take time to think through the problem and don't lose your cool, you will find a solution. If you don't, well, it's just a program. Your good health is much more important than a running program and a good grade.

Interesting pieces of background information are presented in the You Might Want to Know box:

There's a reason behind choosing a Japanese rock garden as a design theme. The famous rock garden at Ryoan-ji temple in Kyoto, Japan has 15 stones. It is told that viewing the rock garden from any angle you can see only 14 of these stones, but when you master Zen, you can "see" the 15th stone with your mind's eye. Likewise, when you study object-oriented programming with this book, you can visualize objects easily with your mind's eye while developing programs.

When we refer to materials available on websites that are related to the topic covered in the book, we indicate this availability with the following icon:

How-to documents on how to compile and run Java programs with different development tools are available from our website at **www.drcaffeine.com.**

Quick Check questions appear at the end of the sections with the following banner:

1. How many stones are there at Ryoan-ji's rock garden?
2. Name the purpose of the bonsai and lantern icons.

Graphical User Interface and Event-Driven Programming

Since modern real-world programs are GUI-based and event-driven, we cannot skirt around them if we want to teach the foundation of real-world programming. Although we teach console input and output and use them in many sample programs, the large sample programs in this book are GUI-based. We introduce Swing-based GUI components in Chapter 7 and present advanced GUI topics in Chapter 14. We feel strongly that GUI and event-driven programming must be taught in CS1, but those instructors who wish to keep the discussion on user interface to a minimum can omit the entire Chapter 14.

Assertions and Pattern Matching

Two of the new features added to Java 2 SDK 1.4 are pattern matching and assertions. Pattern matching is a very powerful and flexible tool in manipulating strings, and we teach pattern matching with many examples in Chapter 9. Assertion is one of the software engineering techniques to ensure the program reliability, and finally, the assertion feature is added to Java. In Chapter 8, we explain two key language features—exception handling and assertion—which we can use to improve program reliability.

Walk Through

This guided tour is designed to walk you through the features of the chapters and the supplements. As you examine them, note the following

- Each chapter begins by orienting you to what you will learn.
- A variety of examples are used to demonstrate concepts.
- A large number of colorful diagrams intuitively explains concepts.
- Excellent pedagogy keeps students motivated.
- Each chapter reinforces concepts in numerous ways.

Chapter openers orient students to what they will learn

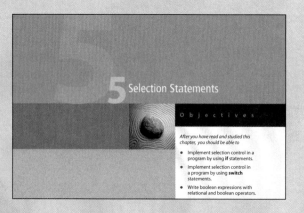

Chapter Objectives detail what students will be able to accomplish when they have worked through the chapter.

The Introduction motivates the material to be covered in the chapter and often relates the topics to be learned to what has already been covered.

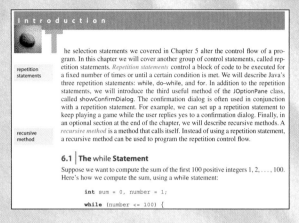

Introduction

repetition statements

recursive method

he selection statements we covered in Chapter 5 alter the control flow of a program. In this chapter we will cover another group of control statements, called repetition statements. *Repetition statements* control a block of code to be executed for a fixed number of times or until a certain condition is met. We will describe Java's three repetition statements: while, do–while, and for. In addition to the repetition statements, we will introduce the third useful method of the JOptionPane class, called showConfirmDialog. The confirmation dialog is often used in conjunction with a repetition statement. For example, we can set up a repetition statement to keep playing a game while the user replies yes to a confirmation dialog. Finally, in an optional section at the end of the chapter, we will describe recursive methods. A *recursive method* is a method that calls itself. Instead of using a repetition statement, a recursive method can be used to program the repetition control flow.

6.1 | The while **Statement**

Suppose we want to compute the sum of the first 100 positive integers 1, 2, . . . , 100. Here's how we compute the sum, using a while statement:

```
int sum = 0, number = 1;

while (number <= 100) {
```

Teaching By Example

```
public boolean equals(Ch5Weight wgt) {

    boolean result;                        The use of this is
                                           optional here.
    double thisGram  = this.getGram();
    double otherGram = wgt.getGram();

    if (thisGram == otherGram) {
        result = true;
    } else {
        result = false;
    }

    return result;
}
...
}
```

This if statement can be written succinctly as

result
  = thisGram == otherGram:

Code with comments is found throughout the text. This annotated code helps students to understand how the various lines of code work.

The equals method is called in the following manner:

```
Ch5Weight wgt1, wgt2;
wgt1 = new Ch5Weight();
wgt2 = new Ch5Weight();
...
if (wgt1.equals(wgt2)) {
```

Short Example Programs scattered throughout each chapter demonstrate how to implement concepts being learned.

```
/*
    Chapter 3 Sample Program: Compute Area and Circumference
                              using standard input and output

    File: Ch2Circle4.java
*/
import java.io.*;                              Don't forget to
import java.text.*;                            add this clause

class Ch3Circle4 {

    public static void main( String[] args ) throws IOException {

        final double PI = 3.14159;

        String radiusStr;
        double radius, area, circumference;
        BufferedReader bufReader;

        DecimalFormat df = new DecimalFormat("0.000");

        bufReader = new BufferedReader(
                        new InputStreamReader( System.in ) );

        //Get input
        System.out.print("Enter radius: ");
        radiusStr = bufReader.readLine();

        radius = Double.parseDouble(radiusStr);

        //Compute area and circumference
        area          = PI * radius * radius;
        circumference = 2.0 * PI * radius;

        //Display the results
        System.out.println("");
        System.out.println("Given Radius: " + radius);
        System.out.println("Area: " + df.format(area));
        System.out.println("Circumference: " + df.format(circumference));
    }
}
```

Longer Sample Programs at the end of each chapter walk students through larger examples, giving students a framework for building programs incrementally.

Problem Statement—presents the goal of the program to be designed.

Overall Plan—at this stage the problem is broken down into tasks and a plan is developed.

Development: Then for each component to the program that needs to be developed the student is walked through the steps of design, coding and testing, then finalizing the program.

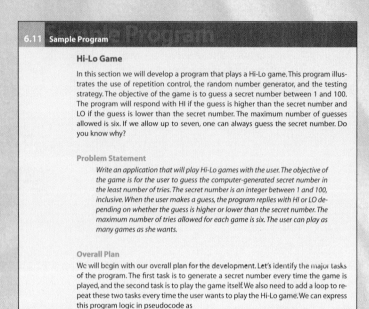

6.11 Sample Program

Hi-Lo Game

In this section we will develop a program that plays a Hi-Lo game. This program illustrates the use of repetition control, the random number generator, and the testing strategy. The objective of the game is to guess a secret number between 1 and 100. The program will respond with HI if the guess is higher than the secret number and LO if the guess is lower than the secret number. The maximum number of guesses allowed is six. If we allow up to seven, one can always guess the secret number. Do you know why?

Problem Statement

Write an application that will play Hi-Lo games with the user. The objective of the game is for the user to guess the computer-generated secret number in the least number of tries. The secret number is an integer between 1 and 100, inclusive. When the user makes a guess, the program replies with HI or LO depending on whether the guess is higher or lower than the secret number. The maximum number of tries allowed for each game is six. The user can play as many games as she wants.

Overall Plan

We will begin with our overall plan for the development. Let's identify the major tasks of the program. The first task is to generate a secret number every time the game is played, and the second task is to play the game itself. We also need to add a loop to repeat these two tasks every time the user wants to play the Hi-Lo game. We can express this program logic in pseudocode as

Visual Approach

Diagrams give visual representation to concepts and help to explain the relationships of classes and objects.

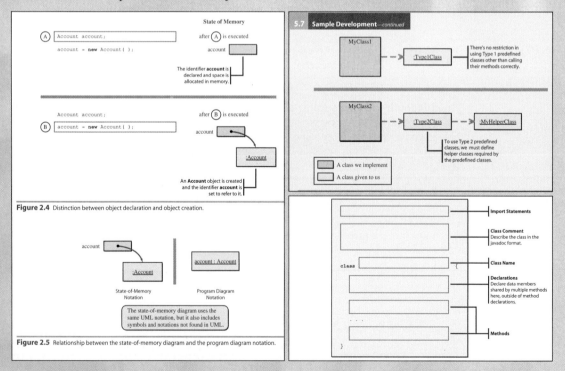

Figure 2.4 Distinction between object declaration and object creation.

Figure 2.5 Relationship between the state-of-memory diagram and the program diagram notation.

Excellent Pedagogy

Helpful Reminders provide tips for students to help them become more effective programmers.

 Helpful Reminder

To draw geometric shapes on the content pane of a frame window, remember that

1. The content pane is declared as a **Container**, for example,

```
Container contentPane;
```

2. The frame window must be visible on the screen before we can get the content pane's **Graphics** object.

 To show you just how common the off-by-one error occurs in everyday life, consider the following two questions. When you want to put a fence post every 10 ft, how many posts do you need for a 100-ft fence? If it takes 0.5 seconds for an elevator to rise one floor, how long does it take to reach the fourth floor from the ground level? The answers that come immediately are 10 posts and 2 seconds, respectively. But after a little more thought, we realize the correct answers are 11 posts (we need the final post at the end) and 1.5 seconds (there are three floors to rise to reach the fourth floor from the ground level).

You Might Want to Know boxes give students interesting bits of information

Take My Advice boxes give students advice on coding from an experienced programmer perspective.

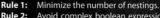 It takes some practice before you can write well-formed **if** statements. Here are some rules to help you write the **if** statements.

Rule 1: Minimize the number of nestings.
Rule 2: Avoid complex boolean expressions. Make them as simple as possible. Don't include many ANDs and ORs.
Rule 3: Eliminate any unnecessary comparisons.
Rule 4: Don't be satisfied with the first correct statement. Always look for improvement.
Rule 5: Read your code again. Can you follow the statement easily? If not, try to improve it.

 Design Guidelines

Always define a constructor and initialize instance variables fully in the constructor so an object will be created in a valid state.

Design Guidelines provide tips on good program design techniques.

Tools That Reinforce the Concepts

Key Terms are highlighted in the margin, so students can find them easily when studying.

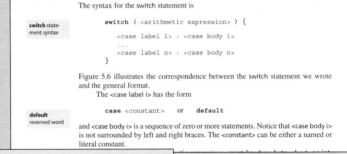

switch statement syntax

default reserved word

The syntax for the switch statement is

```
switch ( <arithmetic expression> ) {
    <case label 1> : <case body 1>
    ...
    <case label n> : <case body n>
}
```

Figure 5.6 illustrates the correspondence between the switch statement we wrote and the general format.
The <case label i> has the form

```
case <constant>    or    default
```

and <case body i> is a sequence of zero or more statements. Notice that <case body i> is not surrounded by left and right braces. The <constant> can be either a named or literal constant.

Quick **CHECK**

1. Translate the following while loop to a loop-and-a-half format.

```
int sum = 0, num = 1;
while (num <= 50) {
    sum += num;
    num++;
}
```

Quick Check exercises at the end of sections allow students to test their comprehension of concepts.

End of Chapter Summary provides a bulleted explanation of important topics explained in the chapter.

The **Key Concepts** section lists the important terms that the students should know after finishing the chapter.

Summary

- A selection control statement is used to alter the sequential flow of control.
- The if and switch statements are two types of selection control.
- A boolean expression contains conditional and boolean operators and evaluates to true or false.
- Three boolean operators in Java are AND (&&), OR (‖), and NOT (!).

Key Concepts

selection control
if statements
boolean operators and expressions
precedence rules for boolean
    expressions

nested-if statements
switch statements
break statements
graphics
content pane of a frame

Exercises at the end of each chapter give students a chance to practice what they are learning.

Exercises

1. Indent the following if statements properly.
    a. if (a == b) if (c == d) a = 1; else b = 1; else c = 1;
    b. if (a == b) a = 1; if (c == d) b = 1; else c = 1;
    c. if (a == b) {if (c == d) a = 1; b = 2; } else b = 1;
    d. if (a == b) {
        if (c == d) a = 1; b = 2; }
        else {b = 1; if (a == d) d = 3;}
        else c = 1;

2. Which two of the following three if statements are equivalent?
    a. if (a == b)
        if (c == d) a = 1;
        else b = 1;
    b. if (a == b) {

Development Exercises
For the following exercises, use the incremental development methodology to implement the program. For each exercise, identify the program tasks, create a design document with class descriptions, and draw the program diagram. Map out the development steps at the start. Present any design alternatives and justify your selection. Be sure to perform adequate testing at the end of each development step.

29. Write an application that draws nested *N* squares, where *N* is an input to the program. The smallest square is 10 pixels wide, and the width of each successive square increases by 10 pixels. The following pattern shows seven squares whose sides are 10, 20, 30, . . . , and 70 pixels wide.

Development Exercises give students an opportunity to use the incremental development methodology to implement programs.

Supplements for Instructors and Students

For Instructors

- Complete set of **PowerPoints,** including lecture notes and figures.

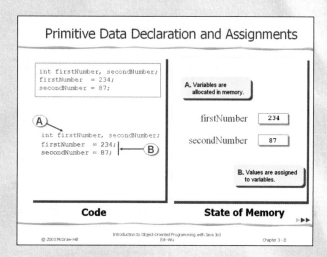

- **Complete solutions** for the exercises
- **Example Bank**—Additional examples, which are searchable by topic, are provided online in a "bank" for instructors.
- **Homework Manager/Test Bank**—Conceptual review questions are stored in this electronic question bank and can be assigned as exam questions or homework.
- **Online labs** which accompany this text, can be used in a closed lab, open lab, or for assigned programming projects.

For Students

- **Compiler How Tos** provide tutorials on how to get up and running on the most popular compilers to aid students in using IDEs.

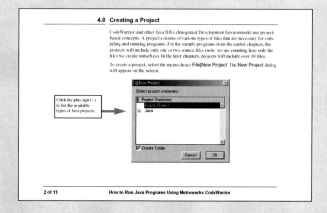

- **Source code** for all example programs in the book.
- **Answers** to quick check exercises.
- **Glossary** of key terms.
- **Recent News** links relevant to computer science.
- **Additional Topics** such as more on swing and an introduction to data structures.

Book Organization

There are 16 chapters in this book, numbered from 0 to 15. There are more than enough topics for one semester. Basically the chapters should be covered in linear sequence, but nonlinear sequence is possible. We show the dependency relationships among the chapters at the end of this section.

Here is a short description for each chapter:

- **Chapter 0** is an optional chapter. We provide background information on computers and programming languages. This chapter can be skipped or assigned as an outside reading if you wish to start with object-oriented programming concepts.

- **Chapter 1** provides a conceptual foundation of object-oriented programming. We describe the key components of object-oriented programming and illustrate each concept with a diagrammatic notation using UML.

- **Chapter 2** covers the basics of Java programming and the process of editing, compiling, and running a program. From the first sample program presented in this chapter, we emphasize object-orientation. We will introduce the standard classes String, JOptionPane, Date, and SimpleDateFormat so we can reinforce the notion of object declaration, creation, and usage. Moreover, by using these standard classes, students can immediately start writing practical programs.

- **Chapter 3** introduces variables, constants, and expressions for manipulating numerical data. We explain the standard Math class from java.lang and introduce more standard classes (GregorianCalendar and DecimalFormat) to continually reinforce the notion of object-orientation. We describe and illustrate console input and output (System.in and System.out) so the students can see the use of non-GUI I/O. The optional section explains how the numerical values are represented in memory space.

- **Chapter 4** teaches how to define and use your own classes. The key topics covered in this chapter are constructors, visibility modifiers (public and private), local variables, parameter passing, and value-returning methods. We explain and illustrate parameter passing and value-returning methods using both primitive data types (int, double, etc.) and reference data types (objects). Through these explanations and illustrations, we clearly distinguish the primitive and reference data types. By the end of this chapter, students will have a solid understanding of object-orientation.

- **Chapter 5** explains the selection statements if and switch. We cover boolean expressions and nested-if statements. We explain how objects are compared by using equivalence (==) and equality (the equals and compareTo methods). Illustrative and meaningful examples are provided to make the distinction between the equivalence and equality clear. Drawing 2-D graphics is introduced, and a screensaver sample development program is developed.

- **Chapter 6** explains the repetition statements while, do–while, and for. Pitfalls in writing repetition statements are explained. The use of confirmation dialog with the showConfirmDialog method of JOptionPane is shown. The optional last section of the chapter introduces recursion as another technique for repetition.

- **Chapter 7** covers basic GUI components and event-driven programming. Only the Swing-based GUI components are covered in this chapter. This chapter provides a first glimpse of using inheritance. We limit the discussion to defining a subclass of a standard class (JFrame) as a nice foundation for a fuller coverage of inheritance in Chapter 13. GUI components introduced in this chapter are JButton, JLabel, ImageIcon, JTextField, JTextArea, and menu-related classes. Our main focus for this chapter is event-driven programming, so we keep the discussion on GUI components at the basic level. For instance, we defer the discussion on layout managers and mouse events until Chapter 14. For those who wish to cover more GUI topics can teach a portion of Chapter 14 before continuing to Chapter 8.

- **Chapter 8** teaches exception handling and assertions. The focus of this chapter is the construction of reliable programs. We provide a detailed coverage of exception handling in this chapter. In the previous edition, we presented exception handling as a part of discussing file input and output. In this edition, we treat it as a separate topic. We introduce an assertion, a newly added Java 2 SDK 1.4 feature, and show how it can be used to improve the reliability of finished products by catching logical errors early in the development.

- **Chapter 9** covers nonnumerical data types: characters and strings. Both the String and StringBuffer classes are explained in the chapter. An important application of string processing is pattern matching. We describe pattern matching and regular expression in this chapter. We introduce the Pattern and Matcher classes, newly added to Java 2 SDK 1.4 and show how they are used in pattern matching.

- **Chapter 10** teaches arrays. We cover arrays of primitive data types and of objects. An array is a reference data type in Java, and we show how arrays are passed to methods. We describe how to process two-dimensional arrays and explain that a two-dimensional array is really an array of arrays in Java. Lists and maps are introduced as more general and flexible ways to maintain a collection of data. The use of ArrayList and HashMap classes from the java.util package is shown in the sample programs. Also, we show how the WordList helper class used in Chapter 9 sample development program is implemented with another map class called TreeMap.

- **Chapter 11** presents searching and sorting algorithms. Both N^2 and $N \log_2 N$ sorting algorithms are covered. The mathematical analysis of searching and sorting algorithms can be omitted depending on the students' background.

- **Chapter 12** explains the file I/O. Standard classes such as File and JFile-Chooser are explained. We cover all types of file I/O, from a low-level byte I/O to a high-level object I/O. We show how the file I/O techniques are used to implement the helper classes—Dorm and FileManager—in Chapter 8 and 9 sample development programs.

- **Chapter 13** discusses inheritance and polymorphism and how to use them effectively in program design. The effect of inheritance for member accessibility and constructors is explained. We also explain the purpose of abstract classes and abstract methods.

- **Chapter 14** covers advanced GUI. We describe the effective use of nested panels and layout managers. Handling of mouse events is described and illustrated in the sample programs. A capstone sample development program that uses a modified Model-View-Controller design pattern is constructed in this chapter.

- **Chapter 15** covers recursion. Because we want to show the examples where the use of recursion really shines, we did not include any recursive algorithm (other than those used for explanation purposes) that really should be written nonrecursively.

Chapter Dependency

For the most part, chapters must be read in sequence, but some variations are possible, especially with the optional chapters. Chapters 0, 14, 15 and Section 6.12 are optional. Section 8.6 on assertions can be considered optional. Here's a simplified dependency graph (optional chapters are shown in green):

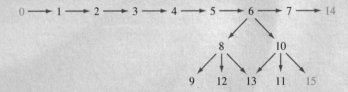

More detailed information on chapter dependency and suggested sequences for different audiences can be found at our website.

Acknowledgments

I would like to thank the following reviewers and the focus group participants for their comments, suggestions, and encouragement.

Focus Group Attendees
Roger Ferguson, *Grand Valley State University*
Gerald Gordon, *Depaul University*
Susan Haller, *University of Wisconsin, Parkside*
Eliot Jacobson, *University of California, Santa Barbara*
Marian Manyo, *Marquette University*
Thaddeus Pawlicki, *University of Rochester*
Paul Tymann, *Rochester Institute of Technology*

Reviewers:

Ken Brown, *University of Aberdeen, UK*

Robert Burton, *Brigham Young University*

Michael Crowley, *University of Southern California*

Adrienne Decker, *University of Buffalo*

Deborah Deppeler, *University of Wisconsin, Madison*

Julian Dermoudy, *University of Tasmania, Australia*

Roger Ferguson, *Grand Valley State University*

Mark Fienup, *University of Northern Iowa*

H.J. Geers, *Technical University Delft, Netherlands*

John Hamer, *University of Auckland, New Zealand*

Sherri Harms, *University of Nebraska, Lincoln*

Joseph D. Hurley, *Texas A & M University*

Eliot Jacobson, *University of California, Santa Barbara*

Saroja Kanchi, *Kettering University*

Andrew Kinley, *Rose-Hulman Institute of Technology*

Blayne E. Mayfield, *Oklahoma State University*

James McElroy, *California State University, Chico*

Carolyn S. Miller, *North Carolina State University*

Jayne Valenti Miller, *Purdue University*

Thaddeus Pawlicki, *University of Rochester*

Gyorgy Petruska, *Indiana University-Purdue University, Fort Wayne*

David Raymond, *United States Military Academy, West Point*

Donna S. Reese, *Mississippi State University*

Alan Saleski, *Loyola University*

Carolyn Schauble, *Colorado State University*

Ken Slonneger, *University of Iowa*

Howard Straubing, *Boston College*

Alex Thornton, *University of California, Irvine*

David Vineyard, *Kettering University*

Gregory F. Welch, *University of North Carolina*

I would like to thank the following McGraw-Hill staff for their trust in my ability to produce a quality text book and their never-ending support throughout the whole project.

Kelly Lowery
Emily Lupash
Sheila Frank
Dawn Bercier

My Story

In September, 2001, I changed my name for personal reasons. Prof. Thomas Wu is now Prof. Thomas Otani. To maintain continuity and not to confuse people, the third edition is published under my former name. Those who care to find out the reasons for changing the name (they are not dramatic) can do so by visiting my website (www.drcaffeine.com).

0 Introduction to Computers and Programming Languages

After you have read and studied this chapter, you should be able to

- State briefly a history of computers.
- Name and describe five major components of the computer.
- Convert binary numbers to decimal numbers and vice versa.
- State the difference between the low-level and high-level programming languages.

1

Introduction

Before we embark on our study of computer programming, we will present some background information on computers and programming languages in this optional chapter. We provide a brief history of computers from the early days to present and describe the components found in today's computers. We also present a brief history of programming languages from low-level machine languages to today's object-oriented languages.

0.1 | A History of Computers

Humans have evolved from a primitive to a highly advanced society by continually inventing tools. Stone tools, fire powder, wheels, and other inventions have changed the lives of humans dramatically. In recent history, the computer is arguably the most important invention. In today's highly advanced society, computers affect our lives 24 hours a day: class schedules are formulated by computers, student records are maintained by computers, exams are graded by computers, dorm security systems are monitored by computers, and numerous other functions that affect us are controlled by computers.

Although the first true computer was invented in the 1940s, the concept of a

Charles Babbage

computer is actually more than 160 years old. *Charles Babbage* is credited with inventing a precursor to the modern computer. In 1823 he received a grant from the British government to build a mechanical device he called the *Difference*

Difference Engine

Engine, intended for computing and printing mathematical tables. The device was based on rotating wheels and was operated by a single crank. Unfortunately, the technology of the time was not advanced enough to build the device. He ran into difficulties and eventually abandoned the project.

But an even more grandiose scheme was already with him. In fact, one of the reasons he gave up on the Difference Engine may have been to work on his new concept for a better machine. He called his new device the *Analytical Engine*. This de-

Analytical Engine

vice, too, was never built. His second device also was ahead of its time; the technology did not yet exist to make the device a reality. Although never built, the Analytical Engine was a remarkable achievement because its design was essentially based on the same fundamental principles of the modern computer. One principle that stands out was its programmability. With the Difference Engine, Babbage would have been able to compute only mathematical tables, but with the Analytical Engine he would have been able to compute any calculation by inputting instructions on punch cards. The method of inputting programs to computers on punch cards was actually adopted for real machines and was still in wide use as late as the 1970s.

The Analytical Engine was never built, but a demonstration program was

Ada Lovelace

written by *Ada Lovelace,* a daughter of the poet Lord Byron. The programming language *Ada* was named in honor of Lady Lovelace, the first computer programmer.

In the late 1930s John Atanasoff of Iowa State University, with his graduate student Clifford Berry, built the prototype of the first automatic electronic calculator.

One innovation of their machine was the use of binary numbers. (We discuss binary numbers in Section 0.2.) At around the same time, Howard Aiken of Harvard University was working on the *Automatic Sequence-Controlled Calculator,* known more commonly as *MARK I*, with support from IBM and the U.S. Navy. MARK I was very similar to the Analytical Engine in design and was described as "Babbage's dream come true."

MARK I

MARK I was an electromechanical computer based on relays. Mechanical relays were not fast enough, and MARK I was quickly replaced by machines based on electronic vacuum tubes. The first completely electronic computer, *ENIAC I* (*Electronic Numerical Integrator and Calculator*), was built at the University of Pennsylvania under the supervision of John W. Mauchly and J. Presper Eckert. Their work was influenced by the work of John Atanasoff.

ENIAC I

ENIAC I was programmed laboriously by plugging wires into a control panel that resembled an old telephone switchboard. Programming took an enormous amount of the engineers' time, and even making a simple change to a program was a time-consuming effort. While programming activities were going on, the expensive computer sat idle. To improve its productivity, John von Neumann of Princeton University proposed storing programs in the computer's memory. This *stored-program* scheme not only improved computation speed but also allowed far more flexible ways of writing programs. For example, because a program is stored in the memory, the computer can change the program instructions to alter the sequence of the execution, thereby making it possible to get different results from a single program.

stored-program

We characterized these early computers with vacuum tubes as *first-generation computers. Second-generation computers,* with transistors replacing the vacuum tubes, started appearing in the late 1950s. Improvements in memory devices also increased processing speed further. In the early 1960s, transistors were replaced by integrated circuits, and *third-generation computers* emerged. A single integrated circuit of this period incorporated hundreds of transistors and made the construction of minicomputers possible. Minicomputers are small enough to be placed on desktops in individual offices and labs. The early computers, on the other hand, were so huge that they easily occupied the whole basement of a large building.

generations of computers

Advancement of integrated circuits was phenomenal. Large-scale integrated circuits, commonly known as *computer chips* or *silicon chips,* packed the power equivalent to thousands of transistors and made the notion of a "computer on a single chip" a reality. With large-scale integrated circuits, *microcomputers* emerged in the mid-1970s. The machines we call *personal computers* today are descendants of the microcomputers of the 1970s. The computer chips used in today's personal computers pack the power equivalent to several millions of transistors. Personal computers are *fourth-generation computers.*

Early microcomputers were isolated, stand-alone machines. The word *personal* describes a machine as a personal device intended to be used by an individual. However, it did not take long to realize there was a need to share computer resources. For example, early microcomputers required a dedicated printer. Wouldn't it make more sense to have many computers share a single printer? Wouldn't it also make sense to share data among computers, instead of duplicating the same data on

network

Internet

individual machines? Wouldn't it be nice to send electronic messages between the computers? The notion of networked computers arose to meet these needs.

Computers of all kinds are connected into a *network*. A network that connects computers in a single building or in several nearby buildings is called a *local-area network* (LAN). A network that connects geographically dispersed computers is called a *wide-area network* (WAN). These individual networks can be connected further to form interconnected networks called *internets*. The most famous internet is simply called the *Internet*. The Internet makes the sharing of worldwide information possible and easy. The hottest tool for viewing information on the Internet is a *web browser*. A web browser allows you to experience *multimedia information* consisting of text, audio, video, and other types of information. We will describe how Java is related to the Internet and web browsers in Section 0.4.

www

If you want to learn more about the history of computing, there is a wealth of information available on the Web. You can start your exploration from
http://www.yahoo.com/Computers_and_Internet/History
For a nice slide show on the evolution of computing machines, visit
http://www.computer-museum.org
For more information on the pioneers of computers, visit
http://directory.google.com/Top/Computers/History/Pioneers/

Quick
CHECK
√

1. Who was the first computer programmer?
2. Who designed the Difference and Analytical Engines?
3. How many generations of computers are there?

0.2 | Computer Architecture

A typical computer today has five basic components: RAM, CPU, storage devices, I/O (input/output) devices, and communication devices. Figure 0.1 illustrates these five components. Before we describe the components of a computer, we will explain the binary numbering system used in a computer.

Binary Numbers

To understand the binary number system, let's first review the decimal number system in which we use 10 digits: 0, 1, 2, 3, 4, 5, 6, 7, 8, 9. To represent a number in the decimal system, we use a sequence of one or more of these digits. The value that each digit in the sequence represents depends on its position. For example, consider the numbers 234 and 324. The digit 2 in the first number represents 200, whereas the digit 2 in the second number represents 20. A position in a sequence has a value that is an integral power of 10. The following diagram illustrates how the values of

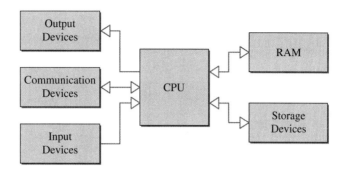

Figure 0.1 A simplified view of an architecture for a typical computer.

positions are determined:

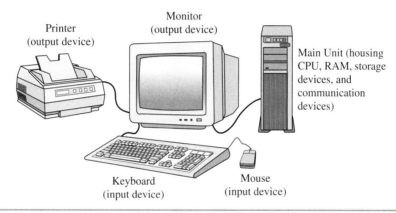

The value of a decimal number (represented as a sequence of digits) is the sum of the digits, multiplied by their position values, as illustrated:

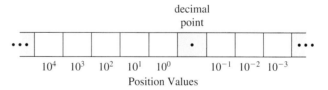

$$= 2 \times 10^2 + 4 \times 10^1 + 8 \times 10^0 + 7 \times 10^{-1}$$

$$= 2 \times 100 + 4 \times 10 \ + 8 \times 1 \ \ + 7 \times 1/10$$

$$= 200 \ \ \ \ + 40 \ \ \ \ + 8 \ \ \ \ \ \ + 7/10 \ \ \ \ \ = 248.7$$

base-2
numbers

bits

   In the decimal number system, we have 10 symbols, and the position values are integral powers of 10. We say that 10 is the *base* or *radix* of the decimal number system. The binary number system works the same as the decimal number system but uses 2 as its base. The binary number system has two digits (0 and 1) called *bits*, and position values are integral powers of 2. The following diagram illustrates how the values of positions are determined in the binary system:

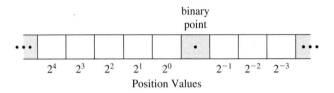

$$2^4 \quad 2^3 \quad 2^2 \quad 2^1 \quad 2^0 \qquad 2^{-1} \quad 2^{-2} \quad 2^{-3}$$

Position Values

   The value of a binary number (represented as a sequence of bits) is the sum of the bits, multiplied by their position values, as illustrated:

1	0	1	•	1

$$2^2 \quad\;\; 2^1 \quad\;\; 2^0 \qquad\;\; 2^{-1}$$

binary-to-
decimal
conversion

$$= 1 \times 2^2 + 0 \times 2^1 + 1 \times 2^0 + 1 \times 2^{-1}$$

$$= 1 \times 4 \;\; + 0 \times 2 \;\; + 1 \times 1 \;\; + 1 \times 1/2$$

$$= 4 \qquad + 0 \qquad + 1 \qquad + 1/2 \qquad = 5.5$$

   So the binary number 101.1 is numerically equivalent to the decimal number 5.5. This illustration shows how to convert a given binary number to the decimal equivalent. How about converting a given decimal number to its binary equivalent?

   The following steps show how to convert a decimal number (only the whole numbers) to the equivalent binary number. The basic idea goes something like this:

decimal-to-
binary
conversion

1. Divide the number by 2.
2. The remainder is the bit value of the 2^0 position.
3. Divide the quotient by 2.
4. The remainder is the bit value of the 2^1 position.
5. Divide the quotient by 2.
6. The remainder is the bit value of the 2^2 position.
7. Repeat the procedure until you cannot divide any further, that is, the quotient becomes 0.

The following diagram illustrates the conversion of decimal number 25.

Division #5	Division #4	Division #3	Division #2	Division #1

$$\begin{array}{ccccc} 0 & 1 & 3 & 6 & 12 \\ 2)\overline{1} & 2)\overline{3} & 2)\overline{6} & 2)\overline{12} & 2)\overline{25} \\ \underline{0} & \underline{2} & \underline{6} & \underline{12} & \underline{24} \\ 1 & 1 & 0 & 0 & 1 \end{array}$$

$$2^4 \qquad 2^3 \qquad 2^2 \qquad 2^1 \qquad 2^0$$

$$16 \quad + \quad 8 \quad + \quad 0 \quad + \quad 0 \quad + \quad 1 \quad = 25$$

The binary system is more suitable for computers than the decimal system because it is far easier to design an electrical device that can distinguish two states (bits 0 and 1) than 10 states (digits 0 through 9). For example, we can represent 1 by turning the switch on and 0 by turning the switch off. In a real computer, 0 is represented by electrical voltage below a certain level and 1 by electrical voltage at or above this level.

You Might Want to Know

When you pay closer attention to the on/off switch on computers and other electronic devices, you should notice an icon like this

This is a stylized representation of binary digits 0 and 1.

RAM

byte

Random access memory (RAM) is a repository for both program instructions and data manipulated by the program during execution. RAM is divided into *cells,* with each cell having a unique address. Typically, each cell consists of 4 *bytes* (B), and a single byte (1 B) in turn consists of 8 *bits*. Each bit, which can be either on or off, represents a single binary digit. RAM is measured by the number of bytes it contains. For example, 128 kilobytes (KB) of RAM contain $128 \times 1024 = 131{,}072$ bytes because 1 KB is equal to $2^{10} = 1024$ bytes. Notice that 1 K is not equal to 10^3, although $10^3 = 1000$ is a close approximation to $2^{10} = 1024$. The first IBM PC introduced in 1981 came with 16 KB of RAM, and the first Macintosh computer introduced in 1984 came with 128 KB of RAM. In contrast, a typical PC today has anywhere from 128 MB to 256 MB of RAM. 1 MB is equal to 1024 KB, so 256 MB means 256×1024 KB $= 262{,}144$ KB $= 262{,}144 \times 1024$ B $= 268{,}435{,}456$ bytes.

CPU

register

The *central processing unit* (CPU) is the brain of a computer. The CPU is the component that executes program instructions by fetching an instruction (stored in RAM), executing it, fetching the next instruction, executing it, and so on until it encounters an instruction to stop. The CPU contains a small number of *registers,* which are high-speed devices for storing data or instructions temporarily. The CPU also contains the *arithmetic-logic unit* (ALU), which performs arithmetic operations such as addition and subtraction and logical operations such as comparing two numbers.

clock speed

CPUs are characterized by their *clock speeds*. For example, in the Intel Pentium 200, the CPU has a clock speed of 200 megahertz (MHz). The *hertz* is a unit of frequency equal to 1 cycle per second. A *cycle* is a period of time between two on states or off states. So 200 MHz equals 200,000,000 cycles per second. The fastest CPU for commercially available personal computers was around 200 MHz in 1997 when the first edition of this textbook was published. But by the beginning of 1998, many vendors started selling 300 MHz machines. And in a mere 6 months, by the middle of 1998, the top-of-the-line personal computers were 400 MHz machines. As of this writing in late 2002, we see computers with 2.0 GHz (2000 MHz) CPU being advertised and sold. The increase of the CPU speed in the last two decades is truly astonishing. The clock speed of the Intel 8080, the CPU introduced in 1974 that started the PC revolution, was a mere 2 MHz. In contrast, the clock speed of the Intel Pentium 4 introduced in 2001 was 2 GHz (2000 MHz). Table 0.1 lists some of the Intel processors.

I/O Devices

Input/output (I/O) *devices* allow communication between the user and the CPU. Input devices such as keyboards and mice are used to enter data, programs, and commands in the CPU. Output devices such as monitors and printers are used to display or print information. Other I/O devices include scanners, bar code readers, magnetic strip readers, digital video cameras, and musical instrument digital interface (MIDI) devices.

Storage Devices

nonvolatile and volatile memory

Storage devices such as disk and tape drives are used to store data and programs. Secondary storage devices are called *nonvolatile memory,* while RAM is called *volatile memory. Volatile* means the data stored in a device will be lost when the power to the device is turned off. Being nonvolatile and much cheaper than RAM, secondary storage is an ideal medium for permanent storage of large volumes of data. A secondary storage device cannot replace RAM, though, because secondary storage is far slower in data access (getting data out and writing data in) compared to RAM.

The most common storage device today for personal computers is a disk drive. There are two kinds of disks: hard and floppy (also known as diskettes). Hard disks provide much faster performance and larger capacity, but are normally not removable; that is, a single hard disk is permanently attached to a disk drive. Floppy

Table 0.1	A table of Intel processors. For some CPUs, several types with different clock speeds are possible. In such case, only the fastest clock speed is shown. For more information on Intel CPUs, visit http://www.intel.com.		
	CPU	**Date Introduced**	**Clock Speed (MHz)**
1970s	4004	11/15/71	0.108
	8008	4/1/72	0.200
	8080	4/1/74	2
	8088	6/1/79	8
1980s	80286	2/1/82	12
	80386SX	6/16/88	16
	80486DX	4/10/89	25
1990s	Pentium	3/22/93	66
	Pentium Pro	11/1/95	200
	Pentium II	5/7/97	300
	Pentium II Xeon	6/29/98	400
	Pentium III	10/25/99	733
2000s	Xeon	9/25/01	2000
	Pentium 4	4/27/01	2000
	Itanium 2	7/8/02	1000

disks, on the other hand, are removable, but their performance is far slower and their capacity far smaller than that of hard disks. As the standard floppy disks can store only up to approximately 1.44 MB, they are becoming less useful in today's world of multimegabyte image and sound files. They are fast becoming obsolete, and hardly anybody uses them anymore. Floppy disks are being replaced by other high-capacity removable storage media such as zip disks (capable of holding 100 to 250 MB of data).

Hard disks can store a huge amount of data, typically ranging from 20 GB (gigabyte; 1 GB = 1024 MB) to 80 GB for a standard desktop PC in 2002. Portable and removable hard disk drives, with performance and capacity that rival those of nonremovable hard disks, are also available, but their use is not widespread.

Compact disks (CDs) are very popular today for storing massive amounts of data, approximately 700 MB. Many software packages we buy today—computer games, word processors, and others—come with a single CD. Before the CD became a popular storage device for computers, some software came with more than 20 floppy diskettes. Because of its massive storage capacity, most computer vendors eliminated printed manuals altogether by putting the manuals on the CD.

Today we see more and more companies are even eliminating CDs and promoting "boxless" online distribution of software. With this scheme, we go to their websites and download the software, after paying for it with our credit card. Maybe someday soon, we may be able to buy textbooks in the same manner and stop carrying 40 lb of dead trees in our backpacks.

Communication Devices

A communication device connects the personal computer to an internet. The most common communication device for computers at home and small offices is the *modem*. A modem, which stands for *modulator-demodulator,* is a device that converts analog signals to digital and digital signals to analog. By using a modem, a computer can send to and receive data from another computer over the phone line. The most critical characteristic of a modem is its transmission speed, which is measured in *bits per second* (bps). A typical speed for a modem is 56,000 bps, commonly called a 56K modem. Under an ideal condition (no line noise or congestion), a 56K modem can transfer a 1 MB file in about 2½ minutes. Frequently, though, the actual transfer rate is much lower than the possible maximum. So called DSL and cable modems are not truly a modem because they transfer data strictly in digital mode, which allows for much faster connection speeds of 144K or above. High-speed satellite connection to the Internet is also available today.

A communication device for connecting a computer to a LAN is a *network interface card* (NIC). An NIC can transfer data at a much faster rate than the fastest modem. For instance, a type of NIC called *10BaseT* can transfer data at the rate of 10 Mbps over the network.

Quick **CHECK**

1. Name five major components of a computer.
2. What is the difference between volatile and nonvolatile memory?
3. What does the acronym *CPU* stand for?
4. How many bytes does the 64 KB RAM have?
5. Which device connects a computer to the Internet using a phone line?

0.3 | Programming Languages

machine language

Programming languages are broadly classified into three levels: machine languages, assembly languages, and high-level languages. *Machine language* is the only programming language the CPU understands. Each type of CPU has its own machine language. For example, the Intel Pentium and Motorola PowerPC understand different machine languages. Machine-language instructions are binary-coded and very low level—one machine instruction may transfer the contents of one memory location into a CPU register or add numbers in two registers. Thus we must provide many machine-language instructions to accomplish a simple task such as finding the average of 20 numbers. A program written in machine language might look like this:

machine code

```
10110011 00011001
01111010 11010001 10010100
10011111 00011001
01011100 11010001 10010000
10111011 11010001 10010110
```

assembly language

One level above machine language is *assembly language*, which allows "higher-level" symbolic programming. Instead of writing programs as a sequence of bits, assembly language allows programmers to write programs by using symbolic operation codes. For example, instead of 10110011, we use MV to move the contents of a memory cell into a register. We also can use symbolic, or mnemonic, names for registers and memory cells. A program written in assembly language might look like this:

assembly code

```
MV   0,   SUM
MV   NUM, AC
ADD  SUM, AC
STO  SUM, TOT
```

assembler

Since programs written in assembly language are not recognized by the CPU, we use an *assembler* to translate programs written in assembly language into machine-language equivalents. Compared to writing programs in machine language, writing programs in assembly language is much faster, but not fast enough for writing complex programs.

high-level languages

High-level languages were developed to enable programmers to write programs faster than when using assembly languages. For example, FORTRAN (FORmula TRANslator), a programming language intended for mathematical computation, allows programmers to express numerical equations directly as

high-level code

```
X = (Y + Z) / 2
```

compiler

COBOL (COmmon Business-Oriented Language) is a programming language intended for business data processing applications. FORTRAN and COBOL were developed in the late 1950s and early 1960s and are still in use. BASIC (Beginners All-purpose Symbolic Instructional Code) was developed specifically as an easy language for students to learn and use. BASIC was the first high-level language available for microcomputers. Another famous high-level language is Pascal, which was designed as an academic language. Since programs written in a high-level language are not recognized by the CPU, we must use a *compiler* to translate them to assembly language equivalents.

The programming language C was developed in the early 1970s at AT&T Bell Labs. The C++ programming language was developed as a successor of C in the early 1980s to add support for object-oriented programming. Object-oriented programming is a style of programming gaining wider acceptance today. Although the concept of object-oriented programming is old (the first object-oriented programming language, Simula, was developed in the late 1960s), its significance wasn't realized until the early 1980s. Smalltalk, developed at Xerox PARC, is another well-known object-oriented programming language. The programming language we use in this book is Java, the newest object-oriented programming language, developed at Sun Microsystems.

0.4 | Java

Java is a new object-oriented language that is receiving wide attention from both industry and academia. Java was developed by James Gosling and his team at Sun Microsystems in California. The language was based on C and C++ and was originally intended for writing programs that control consumer appliances such as toasters, microwave ovens, and others. The language was first called Oak, named after the oak tree outside of Gosling's office, but the name was already taken, so the team renamed it Java.

applet

Java is often described as a *web programming language* because of its use in writing programs called *applets* that run within a web browser. That is, you need a web browser to execute Java applets. Applets allow more dynamic and flexible dissemination of information on the Internet, and this feature alone makes Java an attractive language to learn. However, we are not limited to writing applets in Java.

application

We can write Java applications also. A Java *application* is a complete stand-alone program that does not require a web browser. A Java application is analogous to a program we write in other programming languages. In this book, we place focus on Java applications because our objective is to teach the fundamentals of object-oriented programming that are applicable to all object-oriented programming languages.

We chose Java for this textbook mainly for its clean design. The language designers of Java took a minimalist approach; they included only features that are indispensable and eliminated features that they considered excessive or redundant. This minimalist approach makes Java a much easier language to learn than other object-oriented programming languages. Java is an ideal vehicle for teaching the fundamentals of object-oriented programming.

Summary

- Charles Babbage invented the Difference and Analytical Engines, precursors to the modern computer.
- Ada Lovelace is considered the first computer programmer.
- The first two modern computers were MARK I and ENIAC I.
- John von Neumann invented the stored-program approach of executing programs.
- Computers are connected into a network. Interconnected networks are called internets.

- Binary numbers are used in computers.
- A typical computer consists of five components: RAM, CPU, storage devices, I/O devices, and communication devices.
- There are three levels of programming languages: machine, assembly, and high-level.
- Java is one of the newest high-level programming language in use today. This textbook teaches how to program using Java.

Key Concepts

network	binary numbers
LAN	binary-to-decimal conversion
WAN	machine language
internets and Internet	assembly language
CPU	assembler
RAM	high-level language
I/O devices	compiler
communication devices	Java

Exercises

1. Visit your school's computer lab or a computer store, and identify the different components of the computers you see. Do you notice any unique input or output devices?

2. Visit your school's computer lab and find out the CPU speed, RAM size, and hard disk capacity of its computers.

3. Convert these binary numbers to decimal numbers:

   a. 1010
   b. 110011
   c. 110.01
   d. 111111

4. Convert these decimal numbers to binary numbers:

   a. 35
   b. 125
   c. 567
   d. 98

5. What is the maximum decimal number you can represent in 4 bits? 16 bits? N bits?

6. If a computer has 128 MB of RAM, how many bytes are there?

7. How do high-level programming languages differ from low-level programming languages?

8. Consider a hypothetical programming language *Kona*. Using Kona, you can write a program to compute and print out the sum of 20 integers entered by the user as

```
let sum = 0;

repeat 20 times [
    let X = next input;
    add X to sum;
]

printout sum;
```

Is Kona a high-level language? Why or why not?

Introduction to Object-Oriented Programming and Software Development

Objectives

After you have read and studied this chapter, you should be able to

- Name the basic components of object-oriented programming.

- Differentiate classes and objects.

- Differentiate class and instance methods.

- Differentiate class and instance data values.

- Draw program diagrams using icons for classes, objects, and other components of object-oriented programming.

- Describe the significance of inheritance in object-oriented programs.

- Name and explain the stages of the software life cycle.

efore we begin to write actual programs, we need to introduce a few basic concepts of *object-oriented programming* (OOP), the style of programming we teach in this book. The purpose of this chapter is to give you a feel for object-oriented programming and to introduce a conceptual foundation of object-oriented programming. You may want to refer to this chapter as you progress through the book.

Take my *Advice*

Those of you who have some experience in programming, whether object-oriented or non-object-oriented, will probably find many similarities between Java and the programming languages you already know. This similarity may accelerate your learning process, but in many cases what seems to be similar at first may turn out to be quite different. So please do not jump to any conclusions about similarity prematurely.

Another purpose of this chapter is to introduce the software development process. To be able to write programs, knowing the components of object-oriented programs is not enough. We must learn the process of developing programs. We will present a brief introduction to the software development process in this chapter.

1.1 | Classes and Objects

object

The two most important concepts in object-oriented programming are the class and the object. In the broadest term, an *object* is a thing, both tangible and intangible, that we can imagine. A program written in object-oriented style will consist of interacting objects. For a program to keep track of student residents of a college dormitory, we may have many Student, Room, and Floor objects. For another program to keep track of customers and inventory for a bicycle shop, we may have Customer, Bicycle, and many other types of objects. An object is comprised of data and operations that manipulate these data. For example, a Student object may consist of data such as name, gender, birth date, home address, phone number, and age and operations for assigning and changing these data values. We will use the notation shown in Figure 1.1 throughout the book to represent an object. The notation we used in the book is based on the industry standard notation called *UML*, which stands for Unified Modeling Language. In some of the illustrations, we relax the rules of UML slightly for pedagogy.

Almost all nontrivial programs will have many objects of the same type. For example, in the bicycle shop program we expect to see many Bicycle, Customer, and other objects. Figure 1.2 shows two Bicycle objects with the names Moto-1 and Moto-2 and one Customer object with the name Jon Java.

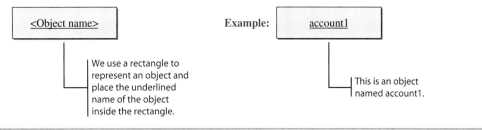

Figure 1.1 A graphical representation of an object.

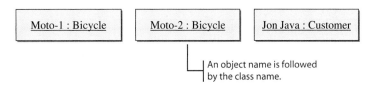

Figure 1.2 Two Bicycle objects with the names Moto-1 and Moto-2 and one Customer object with the name Jon Java.

class

instance

Inside a program we write instructions to create objects. For the computer to be able to create an object, we must provide a definition, called a *class*. A class is a kind of mold or template that dictates what objects can and cannot do. An object is called an *instance* of a class. An object is an instance of exactly one class. An instance of a class *belongs to* the class. The two Bicycle objects Moto-1 and Moto-2 are instances of the Bicycle class. Once a class is defined, we can create as many objects of the class as a program requires.

Helpful Reminder

A class must be defined before you can create an instance (object) of the class.

Figure 1.3 shows a diagram that we will use throughout the book to represent a class.

Quick **CHECK** √

1. Draw an object diagram for a **Person** class and two **Person** objects Ms. Latte and **Mr. Espresso**.
2. What must be defined before you can create an object?

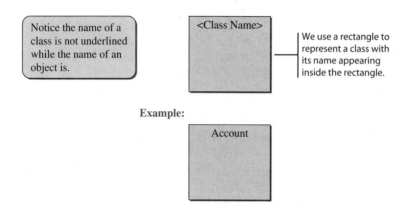

Notice the name of a class is not underlined while the name of an object is.

<Class Name>

We use a rectangle to represent a class with its name appearing inside the rectangle.

Example:

Account

Figure 1.3 A graphical representation of a class.

www

Many beginning programmers may not see the distinction between the class and object as clearly as the more experienced programmers do. It may be helpful to compare the class and object to a woodcut and the prints produced from the woodcut. A woodcut is a block of wood engraved with a design for printing. Once you have a woodcut, you can make as many prints as you wish. Similarly, once you have a class, you can make as many objects from the class. Also, just as you cannot make prints without having a woodcut, you cannot create an object without first defining a class. For sample prints by the 19th-century Japanese artist Hiroshige, visit **http://www.ibiblio.org/wm/paint/auth/hiroshige/**

Another helpful analogy is a robot factory. A factory is a class, and the robots produced from the factory are the objects of the class. To create robots (instances) we need the factory (class) first. Those interested in mobile robots can visit **http://www.ai.mit.edu/projects/mobile-robots/robots.html**

1.2 | Messages and Methods

In writing object-oriented programs we must first define classes, and while the program is running, we use the classes and objects from these classes to accomplish tasks. A task can range from adding two numbers, to computing an interest payment for a college loan, to calculating the reentry angle of a space shuttle. To instruct a

message

class or an object to perform a task, we send a *message* to it. For example, we send a message deposit to an Account object to deposit $100.

For a class or an object to process the message, it must be programmed accordingly. You cannot just send a message to any class or object. You can send a message only to the classes and objects that understand the message you send to them. For a class or an object to process the message it receives, it must possess a

method

matching *method,* which is a sequence of instructions that a class or an object

class and
instance
methods

follows to perform a task. A method defined for a class is called a *class method,* and a method defined for an object is an *instance method.*

Let's look at an example of an instance method first. Suppose a method called walk is defined for a Robot object and instructs the robot to walk a designated distance. With this method defined, we can send the message walk to a Robot object, along with the distance to be walked. A value we pass to an object is called an

argument

argument of a message. Notice that the name of the message we send to an object or a class must be the same as the method's name. In Figure 1.4 we represent the sending of a message.

The diagram in Figure 1.4 illustrates one-way communication; that is, an object carries out the requested operation (it walks the designated distance) but does not respond to the message sender. In many situations we need two-way communication, in which an object responds by returning a value to the message sender. For example, suppose we want to know the distance from a robot to its nearest obstacle. The designer of a robot may include a method getObstacleDistance that returns the desired value. The diagram in Figure 1.5 shows a method that returns a value to the message sender. Instead of returning a numerical value, a method can report back the status of the requested operation. For example, a method walk can be defined to return the status success/fail to indicate whether the specified distance was covered successfully or not (e.g., it fails when the robot bumps into an obstacle).

Now let's look at an example of class methods. The class method getMaximumSpeed shown in Figure 1.6 returns the maximum possible speed of all Robot objects. A method such as getMaximumSpeed that deals with collective information about the instances of a class is usually defined as a class method. So we define an

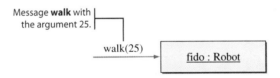

Figure 1.4 Sending the message **walk** to a **Robot** object.

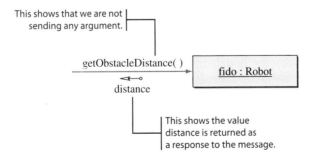

Figure 1.5 The result **distance** is returned to the sender of the message.

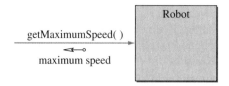

Figure 1.6 The maximum possible speed of all **Robot** objects is returned by the class method **getMaximumSpeed.**

Have you ever left a message on the wrong person's answering machine by mistake? When the machine said, "Hi, I cannot come to the phone right now, but if you leave your message . . . ," you answered, "Hi. It's me. Please come to SP105 right now." Of course, nothing happens, because the receiver of your message does not recognize it.

Similarly, you cannot send a message to a class or an object unless it is programmed to handle the message; that is, it must contain a matching method. Sending a message to a class or an object is the way to execute the matching method, and if there's no matching method, nothing happens (actually, an error will occur).

instance method for a task that pertains to an individual instance and a class method for a task that pertains to all instances.

1. Draw an object diagram of an Account object with instance methods **deposit** and **withdraw.**

2. Is the **getObstacleDistance** method an instance or a class method?

1.3 | Class and Instance Data Values

Suppose the method **deposit** of an Account object instructs the object to add a given amount to the current balance. Where does the object keep the current balance? Remember that an object is comprised of data values and methods. Analogous to defining class and instance methods, we need to define class and instance data values. For example, we define an *instance data value* current balance for Account objects to record the current balance. Figure 1.7 shows three Account objects with their data values current balance. Notice that they all have the same data value current balance. All instances of the same class will possess the same set of data values. The

instance data value

Figure 1.7 Three **Account** objects possess the same data value **current balance,** but the actual dollar amounts differ.

actual dollar amounts for current balance, as the diagram illustrates, differ from one instance to another. Items such as opening balance and account number are other possible instance data values for Account objects.

class data value

A *class data value* is used to represent information shared by all instances or to represent collective information about the instances. For example, if every account must maintain a minimum balance of, say, $100, we can define a class data value minimum balance. An instance can access the class data values of the class to which it belongs, so every Account object can access the class data value minimum balance. Figure 1.8 shows how we represent a class data value. Notice that we underline the class data value. Because the objects of a class are underlined, and the class data values are accessible to all objects of the class, we likewise underline the class data value to show this relationship. Data values are also called *data members*

data member

because they belong to a class or instance of the class.

To appreciate the significance of a class data value, let's see what happens if we represent minimum balance as an instance data value. Figure 1.9 shows

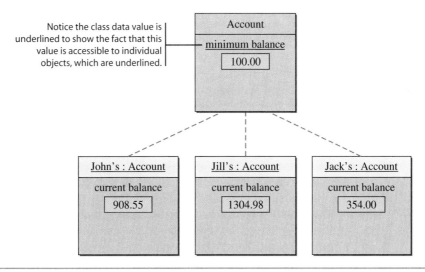

Figure 1.8 Three **Account** objects sharing information (**minimum balance** = $100) stored as a class data value.

Figure 1.9 Three **Account** objects duplicating information (**minimum balance** = $100) in instance data values.

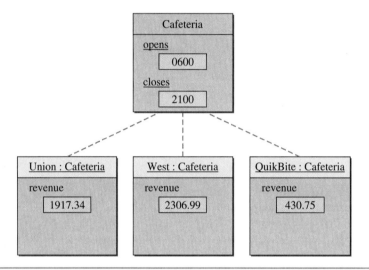

Figure 1.10 Three **Cafeteria** objects sharing the same opening and closing times, stored as class data values.

three Account objects having different dollar amounts for the current balance but the same dollar amount for the minimum balance. Obviously, this duplication of minimum balance is redundant and wastes space. Consider, for example, what happens if the bank raises the minimum balance to $200. If there are 100 Account objects, then all 100 copies of minimum balance must be updated. We can avoid this by defining minimum balance as a class data value. Figure 1.10 shows another example where the opening and closing times are shared by all cafeteria on campus.

There are two types of data values: those that can change over time and those that cannot. A data value that can change is called a *variable* and one that cannot change is a *constant*. Figure 1.11 illustrates how we represent and distinguish between variables and constants. We use the keyword frozen for constants to indicate that they cannot change. Notice that we now have four kinds of data values: class variables, class constants, instance variables, and instance constants.

variable and
constant data
values

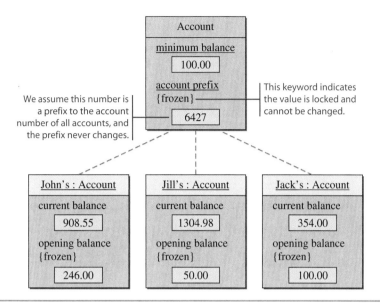

Figure 1.11 Graphical representations for four types of data values: class variable, class constant, instance variable, and instance constant.

1.4 | Inheritance

When we used the Account class and its instances to illustrate object-oriented concepts, some of you were probably thinking about checking accounts, while others may have been thinking about savings accounts. We did not distinguish between the two in the examples. But when we look at the problem a little more carefully, we will realize that in fact these two types of accounts are different, even though they share many features.

In general, using only a single class to model two or more entities that are similar but different is not good design. In object-oriented programming, we use a mechanism called *inheritance* to design two or more entities that are different but share many common features. First we define a class that contains the common features of the entities. Then we define classes as an extension of the common class inheriting everything from the common class. We call the common class the *superclass* and all classes that inherit from it *subclasses*. We also call the

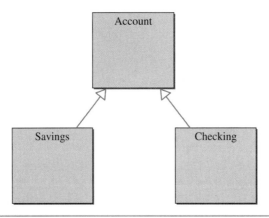

Figure 1.12 A superclass **Account** and its subclasses **Savings** and **Checking.**

superclass an *ancestor* and the subclass a *descendant*. Other names for superclass and subclass are *base class* and *derived class,* respectively. For the bank example, we can define a superclass Account and then define Savings and Checking as subclasses of Account. We represent the superclass and its subclasses as shown in Figure 1.12. Notice that we draw arrows from each subclass to its superclass because a subclass can refer to items defined in its superclass, but not vice versa.

Inheritance is not limited to one level. A subclass can be a superclass of other classes, forming an inheritance hierarchy. Consider the example shown in Figure 1.13. Inheritance is very powerful, and if it is used properly, we can develop complex programs very efficiently and elegantly. The flip side of using a very powerful tool is that if we do not use it correctly, we could end up in a far worse situation than if we did not use it. We will be seeing many examples of inheritance throughout this book. In Chapter 2, for example, we will be introducing many classes that come with the Java system. Most of these classes are defined using inheritance. We will provide an in-depth discussion of inheritance and related topics in Chapter 13.

Quick **CHECK**

1. If Class A inherits from Class B, which is a superclass? Which is a subclass?
2. Draw a diagram that shows Class A is inheriting from Class B.
3. What are the other names for superclass and subclass?
4. If we have Animal, Insect, and Mammal classes, which one will be a superclass?
5. Model different types of vehicles, using inheritance. Include Vehicle, Automobile, Motorcycle, Sports Car, Sedan, and Bicycle.

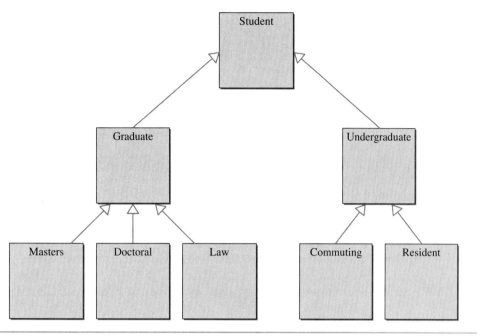

Figure 1.13 An example of inheritance hierarchy among different types of students.

1.5 | Software Engineering and Software Life Cycle

When we say *computer programming,* we are referring not only to writing Java commands, but also to a whole process of software development. Knowing a programming language alone is not enough to become a proficient software developer. You must know how to design a program. This book will teach you how to design programs in an object-oriented manner.

We construct a house in well-defined stages and apply the engineering principles in all stages. Similarly, we build a program in stages and apply disciplined methodology in all stages of program development. The sequence of stages from conception to operation of a program is called the *software life cycle,* and *software engineering* is the application of a systematic and disciplined approach to the development, testing, and maintenance of a program.

There are five major phases in the software life cycle: analysis, design, coding, testing, and operation. Software starts its life from the needs of a customer. A person wants an online address book, for example. In the *analysis* phase, we perform a feasibility study. We analyze the problem and determine whether a solution is possible. Provided that a solution is possible, the result of this phase is a *requirements specification* that describes the features of a program. The features must be stated in a manner that is testable. One of the features for the address book program may be the capability to search for a person by giving his or her first name. We can test this feature by running the program and actually searching for a person. We verify that the program behaves as specified when the first name of a

software life cycle

software engineering

analysis

person in the address book and the first name of a person not in the address book are entered as a search condition. We do this testing in the testing phase, which we will explain shortly.

design

In the *design* phase, we turn a requirements specification into a detailed design of the program. For an object-oriented design, the output from this phase will be a set of classes that fulfill the requirements. For the address book program, we may design classes such as Person, Phone, and others.

coding

In the *coding* phase, we implement the design into an actual program, in our case, a Java program. Once we have a well-constructed design, implementing it into actual code is really not that difficult. The difficult part is the creation of the design, and in this book, we place greater emphasis on the design aspect of the software construction.

testing

When the implementation is completed, we move to the *testing* phase. In this phase, we run the program, using different sets of data to verify that the program runs according to the specification. Two types of testing are possible for object-oriented programs: *unit testing* and *integration testing*. With unit testing, we test classes individually. With integration testing, we test that the classes work together correctly. Activity to eliminate programming error is called *debugging*. An error could be a result of faulty implementation or design. When there's an error, we need to backtrack to earlier phases to eliminate the error.

debugging

operation

Finally, after the testing is successfully concluded, we enter the *operation* phase, in which the program will be put into actual use. The most important and time-consuming activity during the operation phase is *software maintenance*. After the software is put into use, we almost always have to make changes to it. For example, the customer may request additional features, or previously undetected errors may be found. Software maintenance means making changes to software. It is estimated that close to 70 percent of the cost of software is related to software maintenance. So naturally, when we develop software, we should aim for software that is easy to maintain. We must not develop a piece of software hastily to reduce the software development cost. We should take time and care to design and code software correctly even if it takes longer and costs more to develop initially. In the long run, carefully crafted software will have a lower total cost because of the reduced maintenance cost. Here's an important point to remember:

software
maintenance

Helpful Reminder

Well-designed and -constructed software is easy to maintain.

In this book, we will focus on the design, coding, and testing phases. We will present a requirements specification in the form of a problem statement for the sample programs we will develop in this book. We present the first sample program developed by following the design, coding, and testing phases in Chapter 2. We will come back to the discussion of software engineering and the software life cycle throughout the book and provide more details.

Quick
CHECK

1. Name the stages of the software life cycle.
2. How does the quality of design affect the software maintenance cost?
3. What is debugging?

Summary

- The style of programming we teach in this book is called object-oriented programming.
- An object is an instance of a class. Many instances can be created from a single class.
- There are class and instance methods. We can send messages to objects and classes if they possess matching methods.
- There are class and instance data values. Data values are also called data members.
- Inheritance is a powerful mechanism to model two or more entities that are different but share common features.
- The sequence of software development stages from conception to operation is called the software life cycle.
- Five major phases of the software life cycle are analysis, design, coding, testing, and operation.
- Software engineering is the application of a systematic and disciplined approach to the development, testing, and maintenance of a program.

Key Concepts

object-oriented programming
class
object
message
instance and class method
instance and class data value
variable
constant
inheritance

superclass (ancestor, base class)
subclass (descendant, derived class)
software life cycle
software engineering
requirements analysis
design
coding
testing
operation

Exercises

1. Graphically represent a Vehicle class and three Vehicle objects named car1, car2, and car3.

2. Graphically represent a Person class with the following components:

   - Instance variables name, age, and gender.
   - Instance methods setName, getName, and getAge.
   - Class method getAverageAge.

3. Design a CD class where a CD object represents a single music CD. What kinds of information (artist, genre, total playing time, etc.) do you want to know about a CD? Among the information in which you are interested, which are instance variables? Are there any class variables or class constants?

4. Suppose the Vehicle class in Exercise 1 is used in a program that keeps track of vehicle registration for the Department of Motor Vehicles. What kinds of instance variables would you define for such Vehicle objects? Can you think of any useful class variables for the Vehicle class?

5. Suppose the following formulas are used to compute the annual vehicle registration fee for the vehicle registration program of Exercise 4:

   - For cars, the annual fee is 2 percent of the value of the car.
   - For trucks, the annual fee is 5 percent of the loading capacity (in pounds) of the truck.

   Define two new classes Car and Truck as subclasses of Vehicle.
   Hint: Associate class and instance variables common to both Car and Truck to Vehicle.

6. Consider a student registration program used by the registrar's office. The program keeps track of students who are registered for a given semester. For each student registered, the program maintains the student's name, address, and phone number; the number of classes in which the student is enrolled; and the student's total credit hours. The program also keeps track of the total number of registered students. Define instance and class variables of a Student class that is suitable for this program.

7. Suppose the minimum number and maximum number of courses for which a student can register are different depending on whether the student is a graduate, undergraduate, or work/study student. Redo Exercise 6 by defining classes for different types of students. Relate the classes, using inheritance.

8. Imagine you are given a task of designing an airline reservation system that keeps track of flights for a commuter airline. List the classes you think would be necessary for designing such a system. Describe the data values and methods you would associate with each class you identify. *Note:* For this exercise and Exercises 9 through 12, we are not expecting you to design the system in complete detail. The objective of these exercises is to give you a

taste of thinking about a program at a very high level. Try to identify about a half dozen or so classes, and for each class, describe several methods and data members.

9. Repeat Exercise 8, designing a university course scheduling system. The system keeps track of classes offered in a given quarter, the number of sections offered, and the number of students enrolled in each section.

10. Repeat Exercise 8, designing the state Department of Motor Vehicles registration system. The system keeps track of all licensed vehicles and drivers. How would you design objects representing different types of vehicles (e.g., motorcycles and trucks) and drivers (e.g., class A for commercial licenses and class B for towing vehicles)?

11. Repeat Exercise 8, designing a sales tracking system for a fast-food restaurant. The system keeps track of all menu items offered by the restaurant and the number of daily sales per menu item.

12. When you write a term paper, you have to consult many references: books, journal articles, newspaper articles, and so forth. Repeat Exercise 8, designing a bibliography organizer that keeps track of all references you used in writing a term paper.

13. Consider the inheritance hierarchy given in Figure 1.12. List the features common to all classes and the features unique to individual classes. Propose a new inheritance hierarchy based on the types of accounts your bank offers.

14. Consider a program that maintains an address book. Design an inheritance hierarchy for the classes such as Person, ProfessionalContact, Friend, and Student that can be used in implementing such a program.

15. Do you think the design phase is more important than the coding phase? Why or why not?

16. How does the quality of design affect the total cost of developing and maintaining software?

2 Getting Started with Java

Objectives

After you have read and studied this chapter, you should be able to

- Identify the basic components of Java programs.

- Write simple Java programs.

- Describe the difference between object declaration and object creation.

- Describe the process of creating and running Java programs.

- Use the **Date, SimpleDateFormat, String,** and **JOptionPane** classes from the standard Java packages.

- Develop Java programs, using the incremental development approach.

e will describe the basic structure of simple Java programs in this chapter. We will also describe the steps you follow to run Java programs. We expect you to actually run these sample programs to verify that your computer (either your own or the one at the school's computer center) is set up properly to run the sample programs presented in the book. It is important to verify this now. Otherwise, if you encounter a problem later, you won't be able to determine whether the problem is the result of a bad program or a bad setup. Please check Appendix A for information on how to run the textbook's sample programs.

We will develop a sample application program in Section 2.4 following the design, coding, and testing phases of the software life cycle. We stress here again that our objective in this book is to teach object-oriented programming and how to apply object-oriented thinking in program development. The Java language is merely a means to implement a design into an executable program. We chose Java for this book because Java is a much easier language than other object-oriented programming languages to translate a design into an actual code. Beginning students often get lost in the language details and forget the main objective of learning the development process, but the use of Java should minimize this problem.

2.1 | The First Java Program

pixel

Our first Java application program displays a window on the screen, as shown in Figure 2.1. The size of the window is set to 300 pixels wide and 200 pixels high. A *pixel* is a shorthand for *picture element,* and it is the standard unit of measurement for the screen resolution. A common resolution for a 17-in screen, for example, is 1024 pixels wide and 768 pixels high. The title of the window is set to My First Java Program.

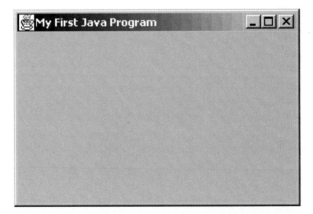

Figure 2.1 Result of running the **Ch2Sample1** program. The window size is 300 by 200 pixels and has the title **My First Java Program**.

Although this program is very simple, it still illustrates the fundamental structure of an object-oriented program, which is

Helpful Reminder

An object-oriented program uses objects.

It may sound too obvious, but let's begin our study of object-oriented programming with this obvious notion. Here's the program code:

```java
/*

    Chapter 2 Sample Program: Displaying a Window

    File: Ch2Sample1.java

*/

import javax.swing.*;

class Ch2Sample1 {

    public static void main( String[] args ) {

        JFrame    myWindow;

        myWindow = new JFrame();

        myWindow.setSize(300, 200);
        myWindow.setTitle("My First Java Program");
        myWindow.setVisible(true);
    }
}
```

Take my Advice

This will not concern the majority of you, but if you are using a Java development tool that does not let you stop a running program easily, then insert the statement

```java
myWindow.setDefaultCloseOperation(JFrame.EXIT_ON_CLOSE);
```

after

```java
myWindow.setVisible(true);
```

so the program terminates automatically when the frame window is closed.

This program declares one class called Ch2Sample1, and the class includes one method called main. From this main method, the Ch2Sample1 class creates and uses a JFrame object named myWindow by sending the three messages setSize, setTitle, and setVisible to the object. The JFrame class is one of many classes that come with the Java system. An instance of this JFrame class is used to represent a single window on the computer screen. To differentiate the classes that programmers define, including ourselves, and the predefined classes that come with the Java system, we will call the first *programmer-defined classes* and the latter *Java standard classes,* or simply, *standard classes*. We also use the term *system classes* to refer to the standard classes.

Expressing this program visually results in the diagram shown in Figure 2.2. In this diagram, we draw individual messages, but doing so would easily clutter a diagram when we have more than a handful of messages. Instead of drawing messages individually, we can draw one arrow to represent a *dependency relationship*. For this program, we say the Ch2Sample1 class is *dependent* on the services provided by a JFrame object, because the Ch2Sample1 class sends messages to the MyWindow object. We draw a dotted arrow from Ch2Sample1 to myWindow to indicate the dependency relationship, as shown in Figure 2.3.

We begin the explanation of the program from the following core five lines of code:

```
JFrame      myWindow;

myWindow = new JFrame();

myWindow.setSize(300, 200);
myWindow.setTitle("My First Java Program");
myWindow.setVisible(true);
```

margin notes:
- programmer-defined classes
- standard classes
- dependency relationship

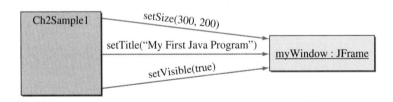

Figure 2.2 The program diagram for the **Ch2Sample1** program.

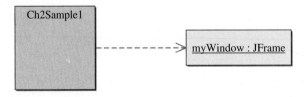

Figure 2.3 The program diagram for the **Ch2Sample1** program that shows the dependency relationship.

We will explain the rest of the program in Section 2.2. These five lines of code represent the crux of the program, namely, an object-oriented program that uses objects. The rule to remember in using objects is as follows:

Helpful Reminder

To use an object in a program, first we declare and create an object, and then we send messages to it.

In the remainder of this section, we will describe how to declare an object, create an object, and use an object by sending messages to the object.

Object Declaration

Every object we use in a program must be declared. An object declaration designates the name of an object and the class to which the object belongs. Its syntax is

object
declaration
syntax

```
<class name>  <object names>  ;
```

where <object names> is a sequence of object names separated by commas and <class name> is the name of a class to which these objects belong. Here's how the general syntax is matched to the object declaration of the program:

Class Name
The class must be
defined beforehand.

Object Names
One object is
declared here.

```
          JFrame          myWindow;
```

Here are more examples:

```
Account    checking;
Customer   john, jack, jill;
```

The first declaration declares an Account object named checking, and the second declaration declares three Customer objects.

To declare an object as an instance of some class, the class must be defined already. First we will study how to use objects from system classes. Later in the book, we will show you how to define your own classes, from which you can create instances.

When we declare an object, we must give it a name. Any valid identifier that is not reserved for other uses can be used as an object name. A Java *identifier* is a sequence of letters, digits, underscores (_), and dollar signs ($) with the first one being

identifier

a letter. We use an identifier to name a class, object, method, and others. The following words are all valid identifiers:

```
MyFirstApplication
FunTime
ComputeArea
DEFAULT_VALUE
```

Upper- and lowercase letters are distinguished, so the following four identifiers are distinct:

```
myWindow          mywindow
MYwindow          MYWINDOW
```

No spaces are allowed in an identifier, and therefore, the three lines

```
Sample Program
My First Application
Program FunTime
```

are all invalid identifiers.

Since upper- and lowercase letters are distinguished, you can use robot as the name for an object of the class Robot. We name objects in this manner whenever possible in this book so we can easily tell to which class the object belongs. We follow the Java *naming convention* of using an uppercase letter for the first letter of the class names and a lowercase letter for the first letter of the object names in this book. It is important to follow the standard naming convention so others who read your program can easily distinguish the purposes of identifiers. Programs that follow the standard naming convention are easier to read than those that do not. And remember that software maintenance is easier with easy-to-understand programs.

When an identifier consists of multiple words, the Java naming convention dictates the first letter from every word, except the first word, will be capitalized, for example, myMainWindow, not mymainwindow.

naming
convention

Design Guidelines

Follow the standard naming convention in writing your Java programs to make them easier to read.

Table 2.2 in the Summary section summarizes the naming convention.

Object Creation

No objects are actually created by the declaration. An object declaration simply declares the name (identifier) that we use to refer to an object. For example, the declaration

```
JFrame      myWindow;
```

designates that the name myWindow is used to refer to a JFrame object, but the actual JFrame object is not yet created. We create an object by invoking the new operation. The syntax for new is

object creation
syntax

```
<object name> = new <class name> ( <arguments> ) ;
```

where <object name> is the name of a declared object, <class name> is the name of the class to which the object belongs, and <arguments> is a sequence of values passed to the new operation. Let's match the syntax to the actual statement in the sample program:

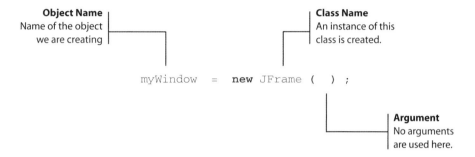

Figure 2.4 shows the distinction between object declaration and creation. Figure 2.5 shows the relationship between the UML-based program diagram and the state-of-memory diagram. The state-of-memory diagram borrows the notation from UML for consistency, but it is not a true UML diagram because it uses symbols and notations not found in UML.

Now, consider the following object declaration and two statements of object creation:

```
Customer  customer;
customer = new Customer( );
customer = new Customer( );
```

What do you think will happen? An error? No. It is permissible to use the same name to refer to different objects of the same class at different times. Figure 2.6

Take my Advice

Instead of writing statements for object declaration and creation separately, we can combine them into one statement. We can write, for example,

```
Student john = new Student();
```

instead of

```
Student john;
john = new Student();
```

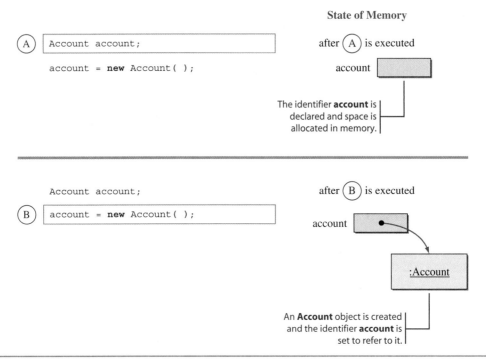

Figure 2.4 Distinction between object declaration and object creation.

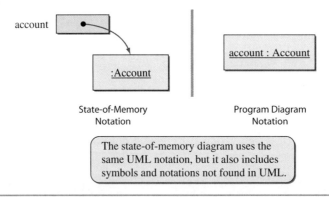

Figure 2.5 Relationship between the state-of-memory diagram and the program diagram notation.

shows the state-of-memory diagram after the second new is executed. Since there is no reference to the first Customer object anymore, it will eventually be erased and returned to the system. Remember that when an object is created, a certain amount of memory space is allocated for storing this object. If this allocated but unused space is not returned to the system for other uses, the space gets wasted. This

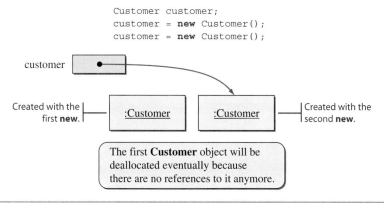

```
Customer customer;
customer = new Customer();
customer = new Customer();
```

customer

Created with the first **new**.   :Customer   :Customer   Created with the second **new**.

The first **Customer** object will be deallocated eventually because there are no references to it anymore.

Figure 2.6 The state after two **new** commands are executed.

returning of space to the system is called *deallocation,* and the mechanism to deallocate unused space is called *garbage collection*.

garbage collection

Message Sending

After the object is created, we can start sending messages to it. The syntax for sending a message to an object is

message-sending syntax

```
<object name> . <method name> ( <arguments> ) ;
```

where <object name> is an object name, <method name> is the name of a method of the object, and <arguments> is a sequence of values passed to the method. In the sample program, we send the setVisible message with the argument true to the mainWindow object to make it appear on the screen. Once again, let's match the components in the general syntax to the actual statement:

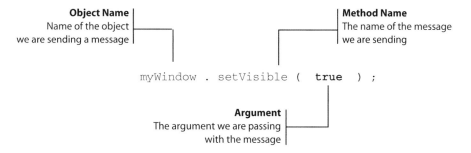

Object Name
Name of the object
we are sending a message

Method Name
The name of the message
we are sending

myWindow . setVisible (**true**) ;

Argument
The argument we are passing
with the message

Figure 2.7 shows the correspondence between message sending as represented in the program diagram and in the Java statement. Because the object that receives a message must possess a corresponding method, we often substitute the expression "sending a message" with "calling a method." We will use these expressions interchangeably.

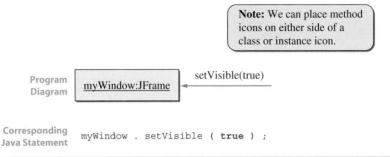

Figure 2.7 Correspondence between message sending as represented in the program diagram and in the actual Java statement.

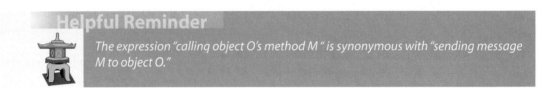

Helpful Reminder

The expression "calling object O's method M" is synonymous with "sending message M to object O."

Notice the argument for the setVisible message does not include double quotes as did the one for the setTitle message in the example shown on page 34. The argument true is one of the two possible logical values (the other is false) used in Java programs. We will study more about the use of logical values later in the book, starting from Chapter 5. For now, it suffices to remember that there are two logical values—true and false—used for certain specific purposes.

Passing true in the setVisible message makes the receiving object appear on the screen. Passing false makes the object disappear from the screen. So, for example, if we write

```
myWindow.setVisible( true );
myWindow.setVisible( false );
myWindow.setVisible( true );
```

then myWindow will appear once, disappear, and then appear on the screen again. (*Note:* Because the computer will execute these statements so quickly, you may not notice any difference from the original program. See Exercise 22 on page 82.)

reserved word

The word true (and false) is called a *reserved word*. It is an identifier that is used for a specific purpose and cannot be used for any other purpose such as for the name of an object.

Quick **CHECK** √

1. Which of the following are invalid identifiers?

  a. one
  b. my Window
  c. 1234

    d. `DecafeLattePlease`
    e. `hello`
    f. `JAVA`
    g. `hello, there`
    h. `acct122`

2. What's wrong with the following code?

```
JFrame myWindow();
myWindow.setVisible(true);
```

3. Is there anything wrong with the following declarations?

```
mainWindow            MainWindow;
Account, Customer     account, customer;
```

4. Which of the following statements is valid?

    a. `myFirstWindow.setVisible( "true" );`
    b. `myFirstWindow.setVisible( true );`

2.2 | Program Components

Now that we have covered the crux of the first sample program, let's examine the rest of the program. The first sample application program Ch2Sample1 is composed of three parts: comment, import statement, and class declaration. These three parts are included universally in Java programs.

Helpful Reminder

*A Java program is composed of comments, **import** statements, and class declarations.*

    You can write a Java program that includes only a single class declaration, but that is not a norm. In any nontrivial program, you will see these three components. We will explain the three components and their subparts in this section.

Comments

In addition to the instructions for computers to follow, programs contain comments in which we state the purpose of the program, explain the meaning of code, and provide any other descriptions to help programmers understand the program. Here's the comment in the sample Ch2Sample1 program:

```
/*
    Chapter 2 Sample Program: Displaying a Window

    File: Ch2Sample1.java

*/

import javax.swing.*;

class Ch2Sample1 {

    public static void main( String[] args ) {

        JFrame     myWindow;

        myWindow = new JFrame();

        myWindow.setSize(300, 200);
        myWindow.setTitle("My First Java Program");
        myWindow.setVisible(true);
    }
}
```

Comment

comment markers

A comment is any sequence of text that begins with the marker /* and terminates with another marker */. The beginning and ending *comment markers* are matched in pairs; that is, every beginning marker must have a matching ending marker. A beginning marker is matched with the next ending marker that appears. Any beginning markers that appear between the beginning marker and its matching ending marker are treated as part of the comment. In other words, you cannot put a comment inside another comment. The examples in Figure 2.8 illustrate how the matching is done.

single-line comment marker

Another marker for a comment is double slashes //. This marker is used for a *single-line comment marker*. Any text between the double-slash marker and the end of a line is a comment. The following example shows the difference between multi-line and single-line comments:

```
/*
    This is a comment with
    three lines of
    text.
*/

// This is a comment
// This is another comment
// This is a third comment
```

javadoc comment

The third type of comment is called a *javadoc comment*. It is a specialized comment that can appear before the class declaration and other program elements

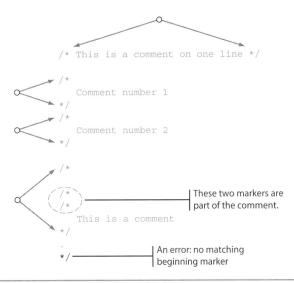

Figure 2.8 How the beginning and ending comment markers are matched.

yet to be described in the book. We will explain more about javadoc comments in Chapter 4.

Comments are intended for the programmers only and are ignored by the computer. Therefore, comments are really not necessary in making a program executable, but they are an important aspect of documenting the program. It is not enough to write a program that executes correctly. We need to document the program, and commenting the program is an important part of program documentation. Other parts of program documentation include program diagrams, programmers' work logs, design documents, and user manuals. If you can write a program once and use it forever without ever modifying it, then writing a program with no comments may be tolerable. However, in the real world, using programs without ever making any changes almost never happens. For example, you may decide to add new features and capabilities or modify the way the user interacts with the program. Even if you don't improve the program, you still have to modify the program when you detect some errors in it. Also, for commercial programs, those who change the programs are most often not the ones who developed them. When the time comes for a programmer to modify his own or someone else's program, the programmer must first understand the program, and program documentation is an indispensable aid to understanding the program.

header
comment

typical header
comment for a
beginning
programming
class

There are several different uses of comments. The first is the header comment. At the beginning of a program, we place a comment to describe the program. We characterize such a comment as a *header comment*. We also may include header comments at the beginning of methods to describe their purposes. Depending on the length and complexity of programs, the description may range from short and simple to long and very detailed. A typical header comment for a beginning programming class may look something like this:

```
/*
 * Program:         TextEditor
 *
 * Author:          Decafe Latte
 *                  decafe@latte.com
 *
 * Written:         May 1, 2003
 *
 * Course:          Comp Sci 101
 *                  Spring 2003
 *                  Program Assignment No. 7
 *
 * Compiler:        JDK 1.4
 * Platform:        Windows 2000
 *
 * Description:
 *   This is a simple text editor. The editor allows the user
 *   to save text to a file and read text from a file. The
 *   editor displays text using Courier font only and does not
 *   allow formatting (e.g., bold, italic, etc.). The editor
 *   supports standard editing functions Cut, Copy, and
 *   Paste, but does not support Undo. For more details,
 *   please refer to the TxEditReadme file.
 */
```

Note: The use of the asterisks is in the style of javadoc, but this is not a javadoc comment.

For your own programs, you should write header comments following the guideline provided by your instructor. For listing the sample programs in the book, we will include only the program name and a short description in the header comment, mainly for reference purposes. The header comment in the actual programs, available from our website, includes additional information. The header comment is written in the javadoc format.

Another use of comments is to explain code whose purpose may not be obvious. Your aim is always to write easily understandable, self-explanatory program code. But at times this is not possible, and you should attach comment to code that is not so easy to understand. There also are times when the original code may not work as intended, and as a temporary measure, you modify the code slightly so the program will continue to work. You should clearly mark such modification with a comment, so you remember what you have done. If you did not put in an appropriate comment and later read your code without remembering about the modification, you would have no idea why you wrote such code. If you cannot understand your own code, imagine the frustration of other programmers (or your T.A. or instructor) trying to understand your modified code.

Yet another use of comments is to identify or summarize a block of code. Suppose a program is divided into three major parts: getting input values from the user, performing computation using those values, and displaying the computation results. You can place comments at the top of each part to delineate the three major parts clearly.

Remember that adding comments to a poorly designed program will not make it a better program. Your foremost goal is to develop a well-designed program that runs efficiently and is easy to understand. Commenting a program is only a means toward that goal, not a goal itself. In fact, excessive use of comments makes it harder to follow and understand a program.

Design Guidelines

Always aim for self-explanatory code. Do not attempt to make poorly written code easier to read by comments. Good comments are not a substitute for good code. Bad code is bad, no matter how well your comments are written.

Take *my* **Advice**

Comment markers are useful in disabling a portion of a program. Let's say you find a portion that may be causing the program to crash, and you want to try out different code for the problem portion. Instead of replacing the whole problem portion with new code, you can leave the questionable code in the program by converting it into a "comment" with comment markers. You can remove the comment markers if you need this code later.

Import Statement

We develop object-oriented programs by using predefined classes, both system- and programmer-defined, whenever possible and defining our own classes when no suitable predefined classes are available. In Java, classes are grouped into *packages,* and the Java system comes with numerous packages. We also can logically group our own classes into a package so they can be reused conveniently by other programs.

package

To use a class from a package, we refer to the class in our program by using the following format:

```
<package name> . <class name>
```

For example, to use the Resident class in the dorm package, we refer to it as

```
dorm.Resident
```

dot notation

which we read as "dorm dot Resident." This notation is called *dot notation*.

A package can include subpackages, forming a hierarchy of packages. In referring to a class in a deeply nested package, we use multiple dots. For example, we write

```
javax.swing.JFrame
```

fully qualified name

to refer to the class JFrame in the javax.swing package; that is, the swing package is inside the javax package. Dot notation with the names of all packages to which a class belongs is called the class's *fully qualified name*. Using the fully qualified name of a class is frequently too cumbersome, especially when we have to refer to the same class many times in a program. We can use the import statement to avoid this problem. Here's the original Ch2Sample1 program that uses the import statement:

```
/*

    Chapter 2 Sample Program: Displaying a Window

    File: Ch2Sample1.java
*/
import javax.swing.*;

class Ch2Sample1 {

    public static void main( String[] args ) {

        JFrame    myWindow;

        myWindow = new JFrame();

        myWindow.setSize(300, 200);
        myWindow.setTitle("My First Java Program");
        myWindow.setVisible(true);
    }

}
```

Import Statement
The import statement allows the program to refer to classes defined in the designated package without using the fully qualified class name.

And here's the same Ch2Sample1 program without the import statement:

```
/*

    Chapter 2 Sample Program: Displaying a Window

    File: Ch2Sample1.java
*/
                                              No import statement
class Ch2Sample1 {

    public static void main( String[] args ) {

        javax.swing.JFrame      myWindow;
                                                      Fully qualified names
        myWindow = new javax.swing.JFrame ();

        myWindow.setSize(300, 200);
        myWindow.setTitle("My First Java Program");
        myWindow.setVisible(true);
    }

}
```

Instead of using the expression javax.swing.JFrame to refer to the class, we can refer to it simply as

```
JFrame
```

by including the import statement

```
import javax.swing.JFrame;
```

at the beginning of the program. Notice that the import statement is terminated by a semicolon. If we need to import more than one class from the same package, then instead of using an import statement for every class, we can import them all by using asterisk notation:

```
import <package name> . * ;
```

For example, if we state

```
import javax.swing.*;
```

then we are importing all classes from the javax.swing package. We use this asterisk notation in our sample program, even when we use only one of the many classes available in the javax.swing package. We could have used

```
import javax.swing.JFrame;
```

but it is more conventional to use asterisk notation. Notice that the package names are all in lowercase letters. This is another standard Java naming convention. Chapter 4 includes more discussion on packages.

You Might Want to Know

When we say "import a package," it sounds as if we are copying all those classes into our programs. That is not the case. Importing a package is only a shorthand notation for referencing classes. The only effect of importing a package is the elimination of the requirement to use the fully qualified name. No classes are physically copied into our programs.

Class Declaration

A Java program is composed of one or more classes; some are predefined classes, while others are defined by us. In the first sample program, there are two classes— JFrame and Ch2Sample1. The JFrame class is one of the standard classes, and the Ch2Sample1 class is the class we define ourselves. To define a new class, we must *declare* it in the program. The syntax for declaring the class is

```
class <class name> {

    <class member declarations>

}
```

where <class name> is the name of the class and <class member declarations> is a sequence of class member declarations. The word class is a reserved word used to mark the beginning of a class declaration. A class member is either a data value or a method. We can use any valid identifier that is not reserved to name the class. Here's the class declaration in the sample Ch2Sample1 program:

```
/*

    Chapter 2 Sample Program: Displaying a Window

    File: Ch2Sample1.java

*/

import javax.swing.*;
```

```
class Ch2Sample1 {

    public static void main( String[] args ) {

        JFrame    myWindow;

        myWindow = new JFrame();

        myWindow.setSize(300, 200);
        myWindow.setTitle("My First Java Program");
        myWindow.setVisible(true);

    }

}
```

Class Declaration
Every program
must include at
least one class.

main class

One of the classes in a program must be designated as the *main class*. The main class of the sample program is Ch2Sample1. Exactly how you designate a class as the main class of the program depends on which Java program development tool you use. We will use the name of a main class to refer to a whole application. For example, we say the Ch2Sample1 *class* when we refer to the class itself and say the Ch2Sample1 *application* when we refer to the whole application.

If we designate a class as the main class, then we must define a method called main, because when a Java program is executed, the main method of a main class is executed first. To define a method, we must declare it in a class.

Method Declaration

The syntax for method declaration is

```
<modifiers> <return type> <method name> ( <parameters> ) {

    <method body>

}
```

where <modifiers> is a sequence of terms designating different kinds of methods, <return type> is the type of data value returned by a method, <method name> is the name of a method, <parameters> is a sequence of values passed to a method, and <method body> is a sequence of instructions. Here's the method declaration for the main method:

```
/*

    Chapter 2 Sample Program: Displaying a Window

    File: Ch2Sample1.java
*/
```

```
import javax.swing.*;

class Ch2Sample1 {

    public static void main( String[] args ) {

        JFrame    myWindow;

        myWindow = new JFrame();

        myWindow.setSize(300, 200);
        myWindow.setTitle("My First Java Program");
        myWindow.setVisible(true);
    }
}
```

Method Declaration
This declaration declares the **main** method.

Let's match these components to the actual method declaration of the sample program:

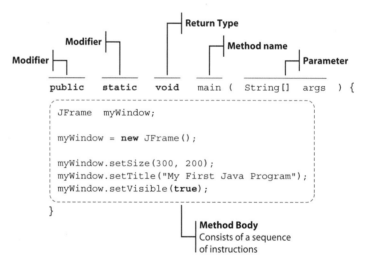

We will not explain the meanings of modifiers, return types, and parameters here. We will explain them in detail gradually as we progress through the book. For now, we ask you to follow a program template that we will present next.

A Program Template for Simple Java Applications

The diagram in Figure 2.9 shows a program template for simple Java applications. You can follow this program template to write very simple Java applications. The structure of the sample program Ch2Sample1 follows this template.

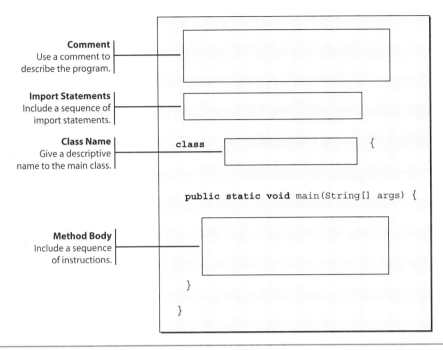

Figure 2.9 A program template for simple Java applications.

More Samples (Optional)

To reinforce the core concept of OOP and review the program structure for simple Java applications, we will provide two more sample programs. These two sample applications use the classes from the programmer-defined package called javabook. Details on how to use the javabook classes can be found in Appendix A.

The following Java application allows you to draw a picture by dragging the mouse (i.e., moving the mouse while holding down the left mouse button). You can erase the drawing by clicking the right mouse button. (Note to Mac users: Please click the mouse button when the text refers to the left mouse button and command-click the mouse button when the text refers to the right mouse button.) You can also erase the drawing by minimizing the window and opening it again.

```
/*
    Chapter 2 Sample Program: Freehand Drawing

    File: Ch2FunTime.java
```

```
    The program will allow you to draw a picture by
    dragging a mouse (move the mouse while holding the left mouse
    button down; hold the button on Mac). To erase the picture and
    start over, click the right mouse button (command-click on Mac).
*/

import javabook.*;          See Appendix A to learn
                            how to use this package.

class Ch2FunTime {

    public static void main (String[ ] args) {
        SketchPad    doodleBoard;
        doodleBoard = new SketchPad( );
        doodleBoard.setVisible( true );
    }
}
```

When the program is executed, the window shown in Figure 2.10 appears on the screen. Figure 2.11 is the same window after a picture is drawn on it. The program consists of two classes: FunTime and SketchPad. The FunTime class is defined in the above program. The SketchPad class is predefined in the javabook package. The program diagram for FunTime is shown in Figure 2.12.

Let's look at another sample program. This program will run a poor person's web browser. To run this program, make sure your computer is connected to the Internet. Figure 2.13 shows the web browser displaying a web page.

Figure 2.10 The window that appears on the screen when the program starts running.

```
/*

   Chapter 2 Sample Program: Poor Person's Web Browser

   File: Ch2MyWebBrowser.java

   The program will open a poor person's web browser.
*/

import javabook.*;          See Appendix A to learn
                            how to use this package.

class Ch2MyWebBrowser {

    public static void main(String[ ] args) {
        MiniBrowser    browser;
        browser = new MiniBrowser();
        browser.setVisible( true );
    }
}
```

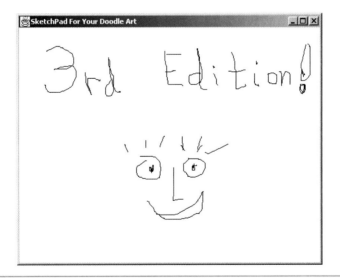

Figure 2.11 The same window after a picture is drawn.

The web browser is very rudimentary, but it nonetheless shows the power of objects. Notice the strong resemblance between the three sample programs. They are almost identical. We want to illustrate that a completely different program can be created readily by using different objects.

Incidentally, both SketchPad and MiniBrowser classes are subclasses of JFrame; that is, they are defined by using inheritance. They extend the inherited

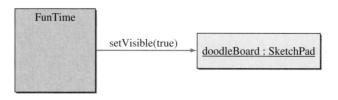

Figure 2.12 The program diagram for the **FunTime** program.

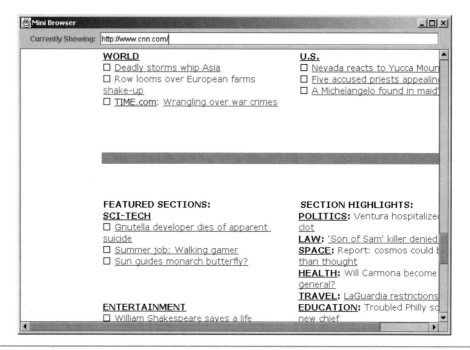

Figure 2.13 A **MiniBrowser** object displaying a sample web page.

functionality of a frame window by adding the capability of freehand drawing and displaying of web contents, respectively.

Quick
CHECK

1. Name three components of a Java program.
2. The main class of the program must have which method.
3. Locate three program components in the Ch2FunTime program.
4. Compare Ch2FunTime and Ch2Sample1 and list the similarities and differences.
5. Draw a program diagram for Ch2MyWebBrowser.

2.3 | Edit-Compile-Run Cycle

We will walk through the steps involved in executing the first sample program. What we outline here are the overall steps common to any Java development tool you use. You need to get detailed instructions on how to use your chosen development tool to actually run programs. The steps we present in this section should serve as a guideline for more detailed instructions specific to your program development tool. Additional information on how to run Java programs can be found in Appendix A.

Step 1

source file

Type in the program, using an editor, and save the program to a file. Use the name of the main class and the suffix .java for the filename. This file, in which the program is in a human-readable form, is called a *source file*.

Ch2Sample1.java

```
/*
    Chapter 2 Sample Program: Displaying a Window

    File: Ch2Sample1.java
*/

import javax.swing.*;

class Ch2Sample1 {

    public static void main( String[] args ) {

        JFrame    myWindow;

        myWindow = new JFrame();

        myWindow.setSize(300, 200);
        myWindow.setTitle("My First Java Program");
        myWindow.setVisible(true);
    }
}
```

Editor

(source file)

Step 2

project file

bytecode

Compile the source file. Many compilers require you to create a *project file* and then place the source file in the project file in order to compile the source file. When the compilation is successful, the compiled version of the source file is created. This compiled version is called *bytecode,* and the file that contains bytecode is called a

bytecode file

bytecode file. The name of the compiler-generated bytecode file will have the suffix .class while its prefix is the same as the one for the source file.

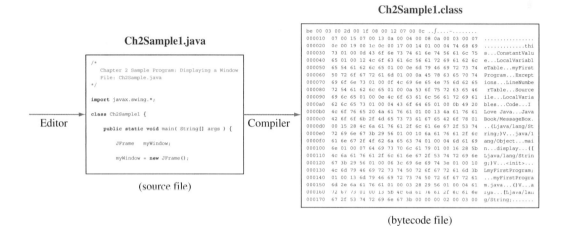

Ch2Sample1.class

Ch2Sample1.java

```
/*
    Chapter 2 Sample Program: Displaying a Window
    File: Ch2Sample.java
*/

import javax.swing.*;

class Ch2Sample1 {

    public static void main( String[] args ) {

        JFrame   myWindow;

        myWindow = new JFrame();
```

Editor   Compiler

(source file)   (bytecode file)

When any error occurs in a program, an error message will be displayed. If the sample program contains no errors in syntax, then instead of an error message, you will get nothing or a message stating something like "Compiled successfully." To see what kind of error messages are displayed, try compiling the following program. We purposely introduced three errors. Can you find them? Make sure to compile the correct **Ch2Sample1** again before proceeding to the next step.

```
import javax.swing.*;

class Ch2Sample1 {

    public static void main( String[] args ) {

        myWindow = new JFrame();

        myWindow.setSize( );
        myWindow.setTitle("My First Java Program");
        myWindow.setVisible(true)
    }
}
```

compilation error

Errors detected by the compiler are called *compilation errors*. Compilation errors are actually the easiest type of errors to correct. Most compilation errors are due to the violation of syntax rules.

Step 3

Execute the bytecode file. A Java interpreter will go through the bytecode file and execute the instructions in it. If your program is error-free, a window will appear on the screen.

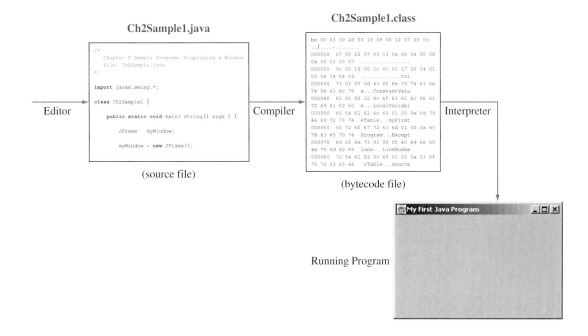

Ch2Sample1.java

```
/*
    Chapter 2 Sample Program: Displaying a Window
    File: Ch2Sample.java
*/

import javax.swing.*;

class Ch2Sample1 {

    public static void main( String[] args ) {

        JFrame  myWindow;

        myWindow = new JFrame();
```

(source file)

Editor → Compiler → Interpreter

Ch2Sample1.class

```
be 00 03 00 2d 00 1f 08 00 12 07 00 0c
..f....-........
000010  07 00 15 07 00 13 0a 00 04 00 08
0a 00 03 00 07  ..............
000020  0c 00 19 00 1c 0c 00 17 00 14 01
00 04 74 68 69  .............thi
000030  73 01 00 0d 43 6f 6e 73 74 61 6e
74 56 61 6c 75  s...ConstantValu
000040  65 01 00 12 4c 6f 63 61 6c 56 61
72 69 61 62 6c  e...LocalVariabl
000050  65 54 61 62 6c 65 01 00 0e 6d 79
46 69 72 73 74  eTable...myFirst
000060  50 72 6f 67 72 61 6d 01 00 0a 45
78 63 65 70 74  Program...Except
000070  69 6f 6e 73 01 00 0f 4c 69 6e 65
4e 75 6d 62 65  ions...LineNumbe
000080  72 54 61 62 6c 65 01 00 0a 53 6f
75 72 63 65 46  rTable...Source
```

(bytecode file)

Running Program

If an error occurs while running the program, the interpreter will catch it and stop its execution. Errors detected by the interpreter are called *execution errors*. If you did not see the expected results, go back to the previous steps and verify that your program is entered correctly. If you still do not see the expected results, then most likely your development environment is not set up correctly. Please refer to other sources of information for further help.

execution error

You Might Want to Know

Unlike machine-language instructions, or machine code, Java bytecode is not tied to any particular operating system or CPU. All we need to run the same Java programs on different operating systems is the Java interpreters for the desired operating systems. Currently, there are Java interpreters for Windows, Mac, Unix, and other operating systems. A Java interpreter is also called a Java Virtual Machine (JVM) because it is like a virtual machine that executes bytecode, whereas a CPU is a real machine that executes machine code.

2.4 | Sample Java Standard Classes

Eventually, you must learn how to define your own classes, the classes you will reuse in writing programs. But before you can become adept at defining your own classes, you must learn how to use existing classes. In this section, we will introduce four standard classes. Sample code using these classes helps us reinforce the core object-oriented programming (OOP) concepts introduced in Chapter 1 with the actual Java statements. Four standard classes we introduce here are JOptionPane, String, Date, and SimpleDateFormat. It is not our objective here to explain these classes fully. Rather, our objective is to get you started in writing practical Java programs with a minimal explanation of some of the useful standard classes. We will introduce additional capabilities of these classes as we progress through the textbook. Although we will scratch only the surface of these classes in this section, what we provide here should serve as a foundation for you to delve more deeply into these classes. For a more detailed description, please consult the documentation for the standard classes. The documentation for the standard classes is commonly called Java API documentation, where API stands for *application programming interface*.

Helpful Reminder

To become a good object-oriented programmer, you must first learn how to use predefined classes.

Take my Advice

Please do not get alarmed with the number of standard classes we introduce here. Although we cover four standard classes at once, we limit ourselves to the most basic operations, so we won't overwhelm you with too much information. Their documentation can be located online at
http://java.sun.com/j2se/1.4/docs/api/index.html.

2.4.1 JOptionPane **for Output**

When a program computes a result, we need a way to display this result to the user of the program. One of the easiest ways to do this in Java is to use the JOptionPane class. For example, when we execute the statement

```
JOptionPane.showMessageDialog(null, "I Love Java");
```

the dialog shown in Figure 2.14 appears on the center of the screen.

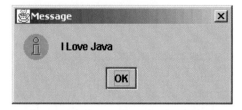

Figure 2.14 A simple "message" dialog created by the **showMessageDialog** method of the **JOptionPane** class.

In a Graphical User Interface (GUI) environment, there are basically two types of windows: a *general-purpose frame* and a *special-purpose dialog*. In Java, we use a JFrame object for a frame window and a JDialog object for a dialog. The first argument to the showMessageDialog method is a frame object that controls this dialog, and the second argument is the text to display. In the example statement, we pass null, a reserved word, meaning there is no frame object. If we pass null as the first argument, the dialog appears on the center of the screen. If we pass a frame object, then the dialog is positioned at the center of the frame. Run the Ch2ShowMessageDialog class and confirm this behavior.

null

```
/*

    Chapter 2 Sample Program: Shows a Message Dialog

    File: Ch2ShowMessageDialog.java

*/

import javax.swing.*;

class Ch2ShowMessageDialog {

    public static void main( String[] args ) {

        JFrame jFrame;

        jFrame = new JFrame( );
        jFrame.setSize(400,300);
        jFrame.setVisible(true);

        JOptionPane.showMessageDialog(jFrame, "How are you?");

        JOptionPane.showMessageDialog(null, "Good Bye");

    }
}
```

Notice that we are not creating an instance of the JDialog class directly by ourselves. However, when we call the showMessageDialog method, the JOptionPane class is actually creating an instance of JDialog internally. Notice that showMessageDialog is a class method, and therefore, we are not creating a JOptionPane object. If we needed a more complex dialog, then we would create an instance of JDialog. But for a simple display of a text, calling the showMessageDialog class method of JOptionPane would suffice.

We can indeed create an instance of **JDialog** for a dialog window, but we are not showing that here because being able to create a **JDialog** instance correctly requires the understanding of more materials than we can reasonably cover in Chapter 2. When the **showMessageDialog** method is called, the **JOptionPane** class is in fact creating a **JDialog** instance internally.

*The **showMessageDialog** method of **JOptionPane** is a class method. As such, there's no need to create an instance of **JOptionPane**.*

If we want to display multiple lines of text, we can use a special character sequence \n to separate the lines, as in

```
JOptionPane.showMessageDialog(null, "one\ntwo\nthree");
```

which will result in the dialog shown in Figure 2.15.

1. Write Java statements to display a message dialog with the text I Love Java.
2. Write statements to display the following shopping list on a message dialog:

```
Shopping List:
        Apple
        Banana
        Lowfat Milk
```

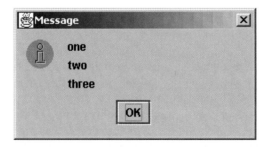

Figure 2.15 A dialog with multiple lines of text.

2.4.2 String

The textual values we passed to the showMessageDialog method or the constructor of the JFrame class are instances of the String class. A sequence of characters separated by double quotes is String constants. As String is a class, we can create an instance and give a name. For example,

```
String name;

name = new String("Jon Java");
```

will result in a situation as follows:

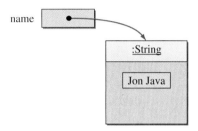

Unlike in other classes, the explicit use of new to create an instance is optional for the String class. We can create a new String object, for example, in this way:

```
String name;

name = "Decafe Latte";
```

substring

There are close to 50 methods defined in the String class. We will introduce three of them here: substring, length, and indexOf. We can extract a *substring* from a given string by specifying the beginning and ending positions. For example,

```
String text;

text = "Espresso";

JOptionPane.showMessageDialog(null, text.substring(2, 7));
```

will display the dialog shown in Figure 2.16.

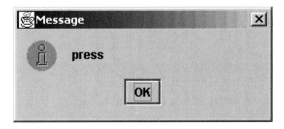

Figure 2.16 A dialog showing the substring of "Espresso" from index position 2 to 6. The index position of the first character in a string is 0.

method
composition

Notice the use of *method composition* in the last statement where the result of a method call is used as an argument in another method call. In the statement

```
JOptionPane.showMessageDialog(null, text.substring(2,7));
```

the result of method call

```
text.substring(2,7)
```

is passed as an argument when calling the **showMessageDialog** method. The sample statement is equivalent to

```
String tempStr;

tempStr = text.substring(2,7);
JOptionPane.showMessageDialog(null, tempStr);
```

Individual characters in a **String** object are indexed from 0, as illustrated in Figure 2.17. The first argument of the substring method specifies the position of the first character, and the second argument specifies the value that is 1 more than the position of the last character. Figure 2.18 shows how the substring method works.

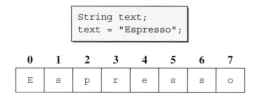

Figure 2.17 Individual characters in a string are numbered from 0.

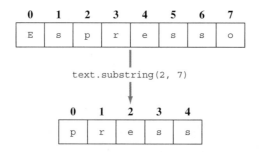

Figure 2.18 The effect of the **substring** method is shown. Notice that a new string is created, and the original string remains intact.

Here are some more examples:

```
text.substring( 6, 8 )  ⟶  "so"

text.substring( 0, 8 )  ⟶  "Espresso"

text.substring( 1, 5 )  ⟶  "spre"
```

An error will result if you pass invalid arguments, such as negative values, the second argument larger than the number of characters in a string, or the first argument larger than the second argument.

length

We can find out the number of characters in a String object by using the length method. For example, if the name **text** refers to a string **Espresso**, then

```
text.length()
```

will return the value **8**, because there are eight characters in the string. Here are some more examples:

```
text1 = "";        //empty string
text2 = "Hello";
text3 = "Java";

text1.length( )  ⟶  0

text2.length( )  ⟶  5

text3.length( )  ⟶  4
```

indexOf

To locate the index position of a substring within another string, we use the *indexOf* method. For example, if the name **text** refers to a string **I Love Java**, then

```
text.indexOf("Love")
```

will return the value **2**, the index position of the first character of the designated string **Love**. If the searched substring is not located in the string, then −1 is returned. Notice that the search is done in a case-sensitive manner. Thus,

```
text.indexOf("java")
```

will return −1. If there is more than one occurrence of the same substring, the index position of the first character of the first matching substring is returned. Here are some more examples:

```
                  3    7              21
                  |    |              |
                  |    |              |
text = "I Love Java and Java loves me.";

text.indexOf("J")          ⟶    7

text.indexOf("love")       ⟶    21

text.indexOf("ove")        ⟶    3

text.indexOf("ME")         ⟶    -1
```

string concatenation

Beyond the three methods we cover here and the remaining methods of the String class, we have one very useful string operation in Java called *string concatenation*. We can create a new string from two strings by concatenating the two strings. We use the plus symbol (+) for string concatenation. Here are the examples:

```
                 text1 = "Jon";
                 text2 = "Java";

text1 + text2              ⟶        "JonJava"

text1 + " " + text2        ⟶        "Jon Java"

"How are you, " + text1 + "?"

                           ⟶        "How are you, Jon?"
```

The sample class Ch2StringProcessing divides the given full name into the first and last names and displays the number of letters in the last name.

```
/*

    Chapter 2 Sample Program: Simple String Processing

    File: Ch2StringProcessing.java

*/
```

```java
import javax.swing.*;

class Ch2StringProcessing {

    public static void main( String[] args ) {

        String fullName, firstName, lastName, space;

        fullName = new String("Decafe Latte");
        space    = new String(" ");

        firstName = fullName.substring(0, fullName.indexOf(space));
        lastName = fullName.substring(fullName.indexOf(space) + 1,
                                       fullName.length());

        JOptionPane.showMessageDialog(null, "Full Name: " + fullName);

        JOptionPane.showMessageDialog(null, "First: " + firstName);

        JOptionPane.showMessageDialog(null, "Last: " + lastName);

        JOptionPane.showMessageDialog(null, "You last name has " +
                                           lastName.length( )    +
                                           " characters.");

    }
}
```

Quick
CHECK

1. What will be the value of **mystery** when the following code is executed?

```java
String text, mystery;

text    = "mocha chai latte";
mystery = text.substring(1,5);
```

2. What will be displayed on the message dialog when the following code is executed?

```java
String text = "I, Claudius";

JOptionPane.showMessageDialog( null,
                               text.indexOf("I") );
```

3. What will be displayed on the message dialog when the following code is executed?

```java
String text = "Augustus";

JOptionPane.showMessageDialog(null, text.length());
```

4. What will be the value of **text3** when the following code is executed?

```
String text1 = "a" + "b";
String text2 = "c";

String text3 = text1 + text2 + text1;
```

2.4.3   Date **and** SimpleDateFormat

The Date class is used to represent a time instance to a millisecond (one thousandth of a second) precision. This class is in the java.util package. When a new Date object is created, it is set to the time it is created (the current time is determined by reading the time maintained by the operating system on your machine). The Date class includes the toString method that converts its internal format to a string representation, which we can use to display the time. For example, executing the code

```
Date today;

today = new Date( );
JOptionPane.showMessageDialog(null, today.toString());
```

will display the current time in format

```
Sat Apr 20 15:05:18 PDT 2002
```

Notice that the current time, when converted to a string format, includes the date information also. Internally, the time is kept as an elapsed time in milliseconds since the standard base time is known as the epoch, which is January 1, 1970, 00:00:00 GMT (Greenwich mean time).

You **Might Want** to **Know**

Why is the class called **Date** when its purpose is to keep track of time? The reason is historical. In the older versions of Java, prior to JDK 1.1, the **Date** class was indeed used to manipulate the year, month, and day components of the current time. However, the way they are implemented was not amenable to internationalization. With the newer versions of Java, we use the **GregorianCalendar** class for date manipulation. The **GregorianCalendar** class is explained in Chapter 3.

If we do not like the default format, say, we want to display only the month and year or only the hours and minutes in the AM/PM designation, we can use the SimpleDateFormat class. This class is in the java.text package. For example, if we want to display the month, day, and year in the MM/dd/yy shorthand format, such as 07/04/03, we write

```
Date              today;
SimpleDateFormat  sdf;
```

```
today = new Date( );
sdf   = new SimpleDateFormat("MM/dd/yy");

JOptionPane.showMessageDialog(null, sdf.format(today));
```

If today is April 20, 2003, the code will display the date as

```
04/20/03
```

Notice the format designation is done by passing the formatting string when a new SimpleDateFormat object is created. The letters in the formatting string are case-sensitive. The formatting string in this example must be MM/dd/yy, and the letters d and y must be in lowercase. By increasing the number of formatting letters, we can change the length of the information, say, 2003 instead of 03. In case of the month, we change it from the number to a name. For example, when we change sdf to

```
sdf = new SimpleDateFormat("MMMM dd, yyyy");
```

the dialog will display

```
April 20, 2003
```

If we want to display which day of the week today is, we can use the letter E as in

```
Date             today;
SimpleDateFormat sdf;

today = new Date( );
sdf   = new SimpleDateFormat("EEEE");

JOptionPane.showMessageDialog(null, "Today is " +
                                    sdf.format(today));
```

Table 2.1 lists the common letters used in the formatting for SimpleDate-Format. For more details, please consult the Java API documentation.

Take my Advice

Table 2.1 is provided solely for the purpose of quick reference when you start using the class in real programs. Nobody expects you to remember all those symbols. What is important here is for you to grasp the key OOP concepts and the fundamental way in which objects and classes are used, not memorizing minute details that nobody remembers.

If you do not pass any string when creating a new SimpleDataFormat object, the default formatting is used. The sample Ch2DateDisplay class displays today's date, using the default and programmer-designated format.

Table 2.1 Some common formatting symbols for *SimpleDateFormat* and their meaning. Please check the Java API documentation for full details.

Symbol	Meaning	Value	Sample
y	Year	Number	yyyy → 2002
M	Month in year	Text or number	MM → 10 MMM → Oct MMMM → October
d	Day in month	Number	dd → 20
D	Day in year	Number	DDD → 289
h	Hour in am/pm	Number	hh → 09
H	Hour in day (0–23)	Number	HH → 17
a	AM/PM marker	Text	a → AM
m	Minutes in hour	Number	mm → 35
s	Seconds in minute	Number	ss → 54
S	Millisecond	Number	mmm → 897
E	Day in week	Text	E → Sat EEEE → Saturday

```
/*
    Chapter 2 Sample Program: Displays Formatted Date Information

    File: Ch2DateDisplay.java

*/

import javax.swing.*;
import java.util.*;   //for Date
import java.text.*;   //for SimpleDateFormat

class Ch2DateDisplay {

    public static void main( String[] args ) {

        Date              today;

        SimpleDateFormat simpleDF1,
                         simpleDF2;

        today    = new Date();

        simpleDF1 = new SimpleDateFormat( );
        simpleDF2 = new SimpleDateFormat("EEEE MMMM dd, yyyy");
```

```
//Default short format display
JOptionPane.showMessageDialog(null, "Today is " +
                                    simpleDF1.format(today) );

//Programmer-designated long format display
JOptionPane.showMessageDialog(null, "Today is " +
                                    simpleDF2.format(today) );
    }
}
```

Quick **CHECK**

1. Write a code fragment to display today's date in the 07-04-2002 format.
2. What will be displayed on the message dialog when the following code is executed if today is July 4, 1776?

```
Date            today;
SimpleDateFormat  sdf;

today = new Date( );
sdf   = new SimpleDateFormat("MMM dd, yyyy");

JOptionPane.showMessageDialog(null, "Today is " +
                              sdf.format(today));
```

2.4.4 JOptionPane **for Input**

So far we used the class method showMessageDialog of the JOptionPane class to display a string. We can use the class to get an input string, too. For example, when we execute

```
JOptionPane.showInputDialog(null, "Enter text:");
```

the dialog shown in Figure 2.19 appears on the screen. To assign the name input to an input string, we write

```
String  input;

input = JOptionPane.showInputDialog(null, "Enter text:");
```

Using the showInputDialog method, we can upgrade the Ch2StringProcessing class by replacing the statement

```
fullName = new String("Decafe Latte");
```

with

```
fullName = JOptionPane.showInputDialog(null,
                              "Your full name:");
```

Figure 2.19 An input dialog that appears as a result of calling the **showInputDialog** class method of the **JOptionPane** class with "What is your name?" as the method's second argument.

With the original class, the program processes only the fixed string Decafe Latte. By including the input statement, the upgraded class Ch2StringProcessing2 is now capable of processing any string entered by the user. (We won't list the upgraded class because it is the same as the original except for the statement for input.)

Here's another sample. The Ch2Greetings class prompts the user for his or her name and replies with a greeting.

```
/*
    Chapter 2 Sample Program: Reads a String Input

    File: Ch2Greetings.java
*/

import javax.swing.*;

class Ch2Greetings {

    public static void main( String[] args ) {

        String name;

        name = JOptionPane.showInputDialog(null, "What is your name?");

        JOptionPane.showMessageDialog(null, "Nice to meet you, "
                                            + name + ".");

    }
}
```

In both Ch2Greetings and Ch2StringProcessing2, we assume that the end user will type in something and then click the OK button or press the Enter (Return) key. In other words, we assume a valid input. But what would happen if the end user clicked the Cancel button or entered nothing and clicked the OK button? When the

Cancel button is clicked, regardless of whether any characters are entered, a null is returned. When nothing is entered and the OK button is clicked, an empty string is returned. Try it with Ch2Greetings and confirm this behavior. When you enter invalid input for Ch2StringProcessing2, the program will crash (i.e., the program terminates with an error message). Can you guess why?

Until we learn the selection control structure in Chapter 5, we continue to assume valid input values for our sample code.

Quick
CHECK

1. Using JOptionPane input dialog, write a statement to input the user's middle initial.
2. Using JOptionPane input dialog, write a statement to input the name of the user's dormitory.

Printing the Initials

Now that we have acquired a basic understanding of Java application programs, let's write a new application. We will go through the design, coding, and testing phases of the software life cycle to illustrate the development process. Since the program we develop here is very simple, we can write it without really going through the phases. However, it is extremely important for you to get into a habit of developing a program by following the software life cycle stages. Small programs can be developed in a haphazard manner, but not large programs. We will teach you the development process with small programs first, so you will be ready to use it to create large programs later.

We will develop this program by using an incremental development technique, which will develop the program in small incremental steps. We start out with a bare-bones program and gradually build up the program by adding more and more code to it. At each incremental step, we design, code, and test the program before moving on to the next step. This methodical development of a program allows us to focus our attention on a single task at each step, and this reduces the chance of introducing errors into the program.

Problem Statement

We start our development with a problem statement. The problem statement for our sample programs will be short, ranging from a sentence to a paragraph, but the problem statement for complex and advanced applications may contain many pages. Here's the problem statement for this sample development exercise:

> *Write an application that asks for the user's first, middle, and last names and replies with their initials.*

2.5   Sample Development—*continued*

Overall Plan

Our first task is to map out the overall plan for development. We will identify classes necessary for the program and the steps we will follow to implement the program. We begin with the outline of program logic. For a simple program such as this one, it is kind of obvious; but to practice the incremental development, let's put down the outline of program flow explicitly. We can express the program flow as having three tasks:

program tasks

1. Get the user's first, middle, and last names.

2. Extract the initials to formulate the monogram.

3. Output the monogram.

Having identified the three major tasks of the program, we will now identify the classes we can use to implement the three tasks. First, we need an object to handle the input. At this point, we have only learned about the **JOptionPane** class, so we will use it here. Second, we need an object to display the result. Again, we will use the **JOptionPane** class, as it is the only one we know at this point for displaying a string value. For the string manipulation, we will use the **String** class. Finally, we will use these classes from the main class, which we will call **Ch2Monogram.** Let's summarize these in a design document:

program classes

Design Document: Ch2Monogram	
Class	**Purpose**
Ch2Monogram	The main class of the program.
JOptionPane	The showInputDialog method is used for getting the full name, and the showMessageDialog is used for displaying the resulting monogram.
String	The class is used for string manipulation, extracting initials from the first, middle, and last names.

The program diagram of **Ch2Monogram** is shown in Figure 2.20. Keep in mind that this is only a preliminary design. Although we are not going to see any changes made to this design document because this sample application is very simple, changes to the design document are expected as the programs we develop become larger and more complex. The preliminary document is really a working document that we will modify and expand as we progress through the development steps.

Before we can actually start our development, we must sketch the steps we will follow to develop the program. There is more than one possible sequence of steps to develop a program, and the number of possible sequences will increase as

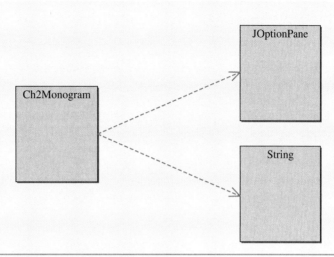

Figure 2.20 The program diagram for **Ch2Monogram**.

the program becomes more complex. For this program, we will develop the program in two steps:

develop-
ment steps

1. Start with the program template and add code to get input.

2. Add code to compute and display the monogram.

Step 1 Development: Getting Input

step 1
design

The problem states that the program is to input the user's name and display its initials. It does not specify how, so in the design stage, we will decide how to do this. Since, at this point, we know only one way to input data, that is, using the **showInputDialog** class method of **JOptionPane,** we will use it here. But in which form shall we input three pieces of data? There are two possible design alternatives.

alternative
design 1

In the first design, we will input them separately:

```
String firstName, middleName, lastName;

firstName  = JOptionPane.showInputDialog(null,
                                    "First Name:");

middleName = JOptionPane.showInputDialog(null,
                                    "Middle Name:");

lastName   = JOptionPane.showInputDialog(null,
                                    "Last Name:");
```

alternative
design 2

In the second design, we will input them together:

```
String fullName;

fullName = JOptionPane.showInputDialog(null,
                                    "Full Name:");
```

Which design is better? There is never "the correct answer" to the design problems. We have to select the one from the possible alternatives that satisfies the different criteria most effectively in a given situation. The criteria may include the user's needs and preferences, faster performance, development costs, time contraints, and other factors. For example, in one situation, we may decide to forgo some great user interface features so the development can be completed under budget.

In this sample development, we will consider the alternative designs from the overall quality of the program's user interface. In other words, we want to make our program as user-friendly as possible. We want our users to have a pleasant experience using our program. The program should not be cumbersome to use, or else the users will get very frustrated in using the program. Which design would give the better user experience? In the first approach, the user enters the information separately with three dialogs, while in the second approach, the user enters the information together with one dialog. We choose the second approach because it allows quicker data entry, and in general, it is more natural to treat the name as a single entity rather than as three separate entitites. If we were to enter the name, address, and phone number, then we would use three dialogs as they are three separate entities. In this situation, we consider the first, middle, and last names as part of a single entity.

Notice that the decision to enter the full name by using one dialog makes our task as the programmer slightly more difficult because we need to extract the first, middle, and last names from a single string. In the first approach, as we get the first, middle, and last names separately, there's no such need. So, if we consider strictly the ease of development, the first approach is better. It is important to remember, however, that we are developing the program for the sake of the users, not for ourselves.

Helpful Reminder

We develop programs for the sake of users, not for ourselves. Ease of use has higher priority than ease of development.

step 1 code

echo
printing

Let's implement the second design alternative. In the code, notice the use of the **showMessageDialog** method to display the entered string. One important objective of this step is to verify that the input values are read in correctly by the program. This method of printing out the values just entered is called *echo printing*. Here's the code:

```
/*
    Chapter 2 Sample Program: Displays the Monogram

    File: Step1/Ch2Monogram.java

*/
```

```
import javax.swing.*;

class Ch2Monogram {

    public static void main( String[] args ) {

        String name;

        name = JOptionPane.showInputDialog(null,
                    "Enter your full name (first, middle, last):");
        JOptionPane.showMessageDialog(null, name);
    }
}
```

step 1 test

After the program is written, we test the program to verify that the program runs as intended. The step 1 program may seem so trivial and not so useful, but it does serve a very useful purpose. Successful execution of this program verifies that the program setup is okay, the necessary packages are imported, and the objects are declared correctly. Since this program is very simple, there's not much testing strategy we can employ other than simply running it. For subsequent sample programs, however, the testing strategy will be more involved. After the step 1 program is compiled and executed correctly, we move on to step 2.

Step 2 Development: Computing and Displaying the Monogram

step 2 design

The next task is to extract initials from the input string. First, because of our limited knowledge of programming at this point, we will assume the input is correct. That is, the input string contains first, middle, and last names, and they are separated by single blank spaces. Second, there are many possible solutions, but we will solve this problem by using only the methods covered in this chapter. Reviewing the string methods we covered in this chapter and the **Ch2Sample3** class, we know that a sequence of **indexOf** and **substring** methods can divide a string (full name) into two substrings (first and last names). How can we adapt this technique to now divide a string (full name) into three substrings (first, middle, and last names)? Aha! We apply the sequence one more time, as shown in Figure 2.21.

Once we divide the input name into first, middle, and last names, extracting the initials is a fairly straightforward application of the **indexOf** method. We can extract the first letter of a string as

```
str.substring(0, 1)
```

And the monogram can be formulated by concatenating three initials as

```
first.substring(0, 1)
  + middle.substring(0, 1)
    + last.substring(0, 1)
```

2.5   Sample Development—*continued*

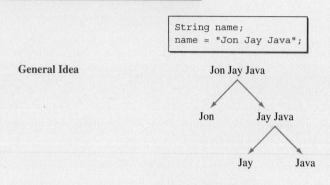

```
String name;
name = "Jon Jay Java";
```

General Idea

Jon Jay Java

Jon   Jay Java

Jay   Java

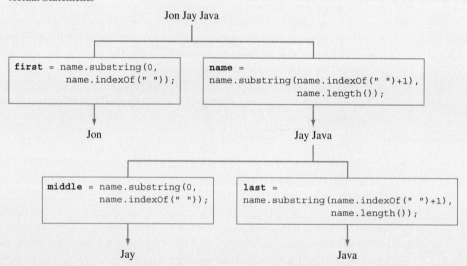

Actual Statements

Jon Jay Java

```
first = name.substring(0,
        name.indexOf(" "));
```

```
name =
name.substring(name.indexOf(" ")+1,
                name.length());
```

Jon

Jay Java

```
middle = name.substring(0,
         name.indexOf(" "));
```

```
last =
name.substring(name.indexOf(" ")+1,
                name.length());
```

Jay

Java

Figure 2.21 Apply the two sequences of **indexOf** and **substring** methods to extract three substrings from a given string.

step 2 code   Here's our step 2 code:

```
/*

    Chapter 2 Sample Program: Displays the Monogram

    File: Step2/Ch2MonogramStep2.java

*/
```

```
import javax.swing.*;

class Ch2Monogram {

    public static void main( String[] args ) {

        String   name, first, middle, last,
                 space, monogram;
        space = " ";

        //Input the full name
        name = JOptionPane.showInputDialog(null,
                        "Enter your full name (first, middle, last):");

        //Extract first, middle, and last names
        first  = name.substring(0, name.indexOf(space));
        name   = name.substring(name.indexOf(space)+1, name.length());

        middle = name.substring(0, name.indexOf(space));
        last   = name.substring(name.indexOf(space)+1, name.length());

        //Compute the monogram
        monogram = first.substring(0, 1)
                      + middle.substring(0, 1)
                          + last.substring(0, 1);

        //Output the result
        JOptionPane.showMessageDialog(null, "Your monogram is "
                                                    + monogram);

    }
}
```

step 2 test

To verify the computation is working correctly, we run the program multiple times and enter different names. Remember that we are assuming there is no error in input; that is, first, middle, and last names are separated by single blank spaces. Since there are two subtasks involved in this step, it is important to test them separately. To verify that the input string is divided into three substrings correctly, we place the following temporary test output statements.

```
JOptionPane.showMessageDialog(null, "First:"  + first);
JOptionPane.showMessageDialog(null, "Middle:" + middle);
JOptionPane.showMessageDialog(null, "Last:"   + last);
```

These statements are not shown in the step 2 program listing, but they are included in the actual sample code.

S u m m a r y

- The three basic components of a Java program are comments, import statements, and class declarations.
- A Java program must have one class designated as the main class. The designated main class must have the main method.
- An object must be declared and created before we can use it.
- To command an object or a class to perform a task, we send a message to it. We use the expression "calling a method" synonymously with "sending a message."
- A single name can be used to refer to different objects (of the same class) at different times. An object with no reference will be returned to a system.
- We follow the edit-compile-run cycle to execute programs.
- A source file is compiled into a bytecode file by a Java compiler.
- A Java interpreter (also called a Java Virtual Machine) executes the bytecode.
- The standard classes introduced in this chapter are

```
JFrame            SimpleDateFormat
JOptionPane       String
Date
```

- Table 2.2 lists the Java naming convention.

Table 2.2 Standard naming convention for Java.

Category	Convention	Example

Class	Use an uppercase letter for the first letter of the class names. If the name consists of multiple words, the first letter of every word is capitalized.	`Customer`
		`MainWindow`
		`MyInputHandler`

Instance	Use a lowercase letter for the first letter of the object names. If the name consists of multiple words, the first letter of every word (except the first word) is capitalized.	`customer`
		`inputHandler`
		`myFirstApplication`

Constant	(*Note:* Sample use of a constant will appear in Chapter 4. We include it here for completeness and easy reference later.) Use all uppercase letters. If the constant consists of multiple words, the underscore characters are used to separate the words.	`DEFAULT_RATE`
		`DEG_TO_RAD`
		`CANCEL`

Package	Use all lowercase letters.	`java`
		`game`
		`finance`

Key Concepts

frame window	comments
dialog window	packages
program diagram	class declaration
identifier	method declaration
standard naming convention	edit-compile-run cycle
new operator	source file
garbage collection	bytecode file
dot notation	standard classes

Exercises

1. Identify all errors in the following program (color highlighting is disabled):

```
/*

    Program Exercise1

    Attempting to display a frame window

//
import swing.JFrame;

class Exercise 1 {
    public void Main() {
        JFrame frame;
        frame.setVisible(TRUE)
    }
}
```

2. Identify all errors in the following program (color highlighting is disabled):

```
//

    Program Exercise2

    Attempting to display a frame of size 300 by 200 pixels

//

import    Javax.Swing.*;

class two {

    public static void main method() {
        myFrame JFrame;
        myFrame = new JFrame();
        myFrame.setSize(300, 200);
        myFrame.setVisible();
    }
}
```

3. Identify all the errors in the following program (color highlighting is disabled):

```
/ *

   Program Exercise3

   Attempting to display the number of characters
   in a given input.
* /

class three {
   public static void main( ) {
      String input;
      input = JOptionPane("input:");

      JOptionPane.showMessageDialog(null, "Input has " +
                input.length() + " characters");
   }
}
```

4. Describe the purpose of comments. Name the types of comments available. Can you include comment markers inside a comment?

5. What is the purpose of the import statement? Does a Java program always have to include an import statement?

6. Show the syntax for importing one class and all classes in a package.

7. Describe the class that must be included in any Java application.

8. What is a reserved word? List all the Java reserved words mentioned in this chapter.

9. Which of the following are invalid Java identifiers?

a. R2D2
b. Whatchamacallit
c. HowAboutThis?
d. Java
e. GoodChoice
f. 12345

g. 3CPO
h. This is okay.
i. thisIsReallyOkay
j. DEFAULT_AMT
k. Bad-Choice
l. A12345

10. Describe the steps you take to run a Java application and the tools you use in each step. What are source files and bytecode files? What different types of errors are detected at each step?

11. Describe the difference between object declaration and object creation. Use a state-of-memory diagram to illustrate the difference.

12. Show a state-of-memory diagram after each of these statements is executed:

```
JFrame       window1;
Resident     res1, res2;

window1    = new JFrame();
res1       = new Resident( );
res2       = new Resident( );
```

13. Show a state-of-memory diagram after each of these statements is executed:

```
Person      person1, person2;

person1     = new Person();
person2     = new Person();
person2     = new Person();
```

14. Which of these identifiers violate the naming convention for class names?

    a. r2D2
    b. whatchamacallit
    c. Java
    d. GoodName

    e. CPO
    f. ThisIsReallyOkay
    g. java
    h. badName

15. Which of these identifiers violate the naming convention for object names?

    a. R2D2
    b. isthisokay?
    c. Java
    d. goodName

    e. 3CPO
    f. ThisIsReallyOkay
    g. java
    h. anotherbadone

16. For each of these expressions, determine its result. Assume the value of text is a string Java Programming.

```
String text = "Java Programming";
```

    a. `text.substring(0, 4)`
    b. `text.length( )`
    c. `text.substring(8, 12)`
    d. `text.substring(0, 1) + text.substring(7, 9)`
    e. `text.substring(5,6)`
                `+ text.substring(text.length()-3,`
                            `text.length())`

17. Write a Java application that displays today's date in this format: Sunday November 10, 2002.

18. Write a Java application that displays a frame window 300 pixels wide and 200 pixels high with the title My First Frame. Place the frame so that its top, left corner is at a position 50 pixels from the top of the screen and 100 pixels from the left of the screen. To position a window at a specified location, you use the setLocation method, as in

```
//assume mainWindow is declared and created
frame.setLocation( 50, 50 );
```

    Through experimentation, determine how the two arguments in the setLocation method affect the positioning of the window.

19. Write a Java application that displays the two messages I Can Design and And I Can Program, using two separate dialogs.

20. Write a Java application that displays the two messages I Can Design and And I Can Program, using one dialog but in two separate lines.

21. Write a Java application that displays a very long message. Try a message that is wider than the display of your computer screen, and see what happens.

22. Because today's computers are very fast, you will probably not notice any discernible difference on the screen between the code

```
JFrame myWindow;
myWindow = new JFrame( );
myWindow.setVisible( true );
```

and

```
JFrame myWindow;
myWindow = new JFrame( );
myWindow.setVisible( true  );
myWindow.setVisible( false );
myWindow.setVisible( true  );
```

One way to see the disappearance and reappearance of the window is to put a delay between the successive setVisible messages. To put a delay, you can use a Clock object from the javabook package. Here's a simple usage of the Clock class:

```
import javabook.*;
...
Clock myClock;
myClock = new Clock( );

//put statement X here

myClock.pause( 2 );

//put statement Y here
```

Delay
The computer will pause for 2 seconds before executing statement Y.

The unit for the argument you pass in the pause message is seconds. If you want a 0.5-s delay, for example, then you pass 0.5 as an argument. Using the Clock class, write a program that makes a JFrame object appear, disappear, and appear again. The window remains visible for 5 s when it appears for the first time, and once it disappears, it won't reappear for 3 s.

23. At the author's website, you will find a Java package called galapagos. The galapagos package includes a Turtle class that is modeled after Seymour Papert's logo. This Turtle has a pen, and when you move the Turtle, its pen will trace the movement. So by moving a Turtle object, you can draw many different kinds of geometric shapes. For example, this program commands a Turtle to draw a square:

```
import galapagos.*;

class Square {
   public static void main( String[] arg ) {
      Turtle turtle;
```

```
turtle = new Turtle( );

turtle.move( 50 ); //move 50 pixels
turtle.turn( 90 ); //turn 90 deg counterclockwise

turtle.move( 50 );
turtle.turn( 90 );

turtle.move( 50 );
turtle.turn( 90 );

turtle.move( 50 );
    }
  }
```

Write a program to draw a triangle. Read the documentation and see if you can find a way to draw the square in a different color and line thickness.

24. Write a program to draw a star, using a Turtle from Exercise 23.

25. Write a program to draw a big letter J, using a Turtle from Exercise 23.

26. Using a Turtle from Exercise 23, write a Java application that displays the text Hello as illustrated here:

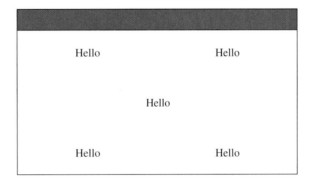

27. Using a Turtle from Exercise 23 and employing the incremental development steps, build a Java application that draws a house.

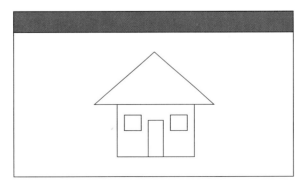

28. Add the moon and a tree to the house you drew in Exercise 27.

29. Follow the incremental development methodology explained in this chapter to implement a program for the following problem statement. You must clearly write down the program tasks, create a design document with class descriptions, and draw the program diagram. Identify the development steps. State any assumptions you must make about the input. Articulate any design alternatives and justify your selection. Be sure to perform adequate testing at the end of each development step.

    Problem Statement: Write an application that asks the user for his or her birth date and replies with the day of the week on which he or she was born.

    We learned in this chapter that we can create a Date object for today's date by writing

    ```
    import java.util.*;
    ...
    Date today = new Date();
    ```

    To create a Date object for a date other than today, we can use the Date class from the java.sql package. (A more general and flexible way to deal with a date by using the GregorianCalendar class is introduced in Chapter 3.) Notice that there are two distinct classes with the same name Date, but from different packages—one from java.util and another from java.sql. To distinguish the two, we will use the fully qualified names. To create a new java.util.Date object, we can call the class method valueOf of the java.sql.Date class with the string representation of a date. The string representation must be in the format yyyy-MM-dd. For example, to create a java.util.Date object for July 4, 1776, we write

    ```
    java.util.Date bdate = java.sql.Date.valueOf("1776-07-04");
    ```

    Notice that valueOf is a class method of the Date class in the java.sql package. Calling it with a correct argument will return a java.util.Date object for the specified date.

30. Repeat Exercise 29 for this problem statement:

    Problem Statement: Write an application that asks the user for her or his full name in the format

    first middle last

    and replies with the name in the format

    last , first middle-initial.

    where the last name is followed by comma and the middle initial is followed by period.

    For example, if the input is

    ```
    Decafe Chai Latte
    ```

    then the output is

    ```
    Latte, Decafe C.
    ```

3 Numerical Data

Objectives

After you have read and studied this chapter, you should be able to

- Select proper types for numerical data.

- Write arithmetic expressions in Java.

- Evaluate arithmetic expressions, following the precedence rules.

- Describe how the memory allocation works for objects and primitive data values.

- Write mathematical expressions, using methods in the **Math** class.

- Use the **GregorianCalendar** class in manipulating date information such as year, month, and day.

- Use the **DecimalFormat** class to format numerical data.

- Convert input string values to numerical data.

- Input data by using **System.in** and output data by using **System.out.**

- Apply the incremental development technique in writing programs.

- (Optional) Describe how the integers and real numbers are represented in memory.

W hen we review the Ch2Monogram sample program, we can visualize three tasks: input, computation, and output. We view computer programs as getting input, performing computation on the input data, and outputting the results of the computations. The type of computation we performed in Chapter 2 is string processing. In this chapter, we will study another type of computation, the one that deals with numerical data. Consider, for example, a metric converter program that accepts measurements in U.S. units (input), converts the measurements (computation), and displays their metric equivalents (output). The three tasks are not limited to numerical or string values, though. An input could be a mouse movement. A drawing program may accept mouse dragging (input), remember the points of mouse positions (computation), and draw lines connecting the points (output). Selecting a menu item is yet another form of input. For beginners, however, it is easiest to start writing programs that accept numerical or string values as input and display the result of computation as output.

We will introduce more standard classes to reinforce the object-oriented style of programming. The Math class includes methods we can use to express mathematical formulas. The DecimalFormat class includes a method to format numerical data so we can display the data in a desired precision. The GregorianCalendar class includes methods to manipulate the date. In Chapter 2, we performed input and output using JOptionPane. We will describe another way of doing input and output using System.in and System.out.

Finally, we will continue to employ the incremental development technique introduced in Chapter 2 in developing the sample application, a loan calculator program. As the sample program gets more complex, well-planned development steps will smooth the development effort.

3.1 | Variables

Suppose we want to compute the sum and difference of two numbers. Let's call the two numbers x and y. In mathematics, we say

```
x + y
```

and

```
x - y
```

To compute the sum and the difference of x and y in a program, we must first declare what kind of data will be assigned to them. After we assign values to them, we can compute their sum and difference.

Let's say x and y are integers. To declare that the type of data assigned to them is an integer, we write

```
int    x, y;
```

variable

When this declaration is made, memory locations to store data values for x and y are allocated. These memory locations are called *variables,* and x and y are the names we associate with the memory locations. Any valid identifier can be used as a variable name. After the declaration is made, we can assign only integers to x and y. We cannot, for example, assign real numbers to them.

Helpful Reminder

A variable has three properties: a memory location to store the value, the type of data stored in the memory location, and the name used to refer to the memory location.

Although we must say "x and y are variable names" to be precise, we will use abbreviated forms "x and y are variables" or "x and y are integer variables" whenever appropriate.

The general syntax for declaring variables is

variable
declaration
syntax

```
<data type>      <variables> ;
```

where <variables> is a sequence of identifiers separated by commas. Every variable we use in a program must be declared. We may have as many declarations as we wish. For example, we can declare x and y separately as

```
int    x;
int    y;
```

However, we cannot declare the same variable more than once; therefore, the second declaration below is invalid because y is declared twice:

```
int    x, y, z;
int    y;
```

six numerical
data types

There are *six numerical data types* in Java: byte, short, int, long, float, and double. The data types byte, short, int, and long are for integers; and the data types float and double are for real numbers. The data type names byte, short, and others are all reserved words. The difference among these six numerical data types is in the range of values they can represent, as shown in Table 3.1.

higher
precision

A data type with a larger range of values is said to have a *higher precision.* For example, the data type double has a higher precision than the data type float. The tradeoff for higher precision is memory space—to store a number with higher precision, you need more space. A variable of type short requires 2 bytes and a variable of type int requires 4 bytes, for example. If your program does not use many integers, then whether you declare them as short or int is really not that critical. The difference in memory usage is very small and not a deciding factor in the program

Table 3.1 **Java numerical data types and their precisions.**

Data Type	Content	Default Value[†]	Minimum Value	Maximum Value
byte	Integer	0	−128	127
short	Integer	0	−32768	32767
int	Integer	0	−2147483648	2147483647
long	Integer	0	−9223372036854775808	9223372036854775807
float	Real	0.0	−3.40282347E+38[‡]	3.40282347E+38
double	Real	0.0	−1.79769313486231570E+308	1.79769313486231570E+308

[†] No default value is assigned to a local variable. A local variable is explained on page 171 Section 4.4.
[‡] The character E indicates a number is expressed in scientific notation. This notation is explained on page 99.

design. The storage difference becomes significant only when your program uses thousands of integers. Therefore, we will almost always use the data type int for integers. We use long when we need to process very large integers that are outside the range of values int can represent. For real numbers, it is more common to use double. Although it requires more memory space than float, we prefer double because of its higher precision in representing real numbers. We will describe how the numbers are stored in memory in Section 3.10.

You Might Want to Know

Application programs we develop in this book are intended for computers with a large amount of memory (such as desktops or laptops), so the storage space is not normally a major concern because we have more than enough. However, when we develop applications for embedded or specialized devices with a very limited amount of memory, such as PDAs, cellular phones, mobile robots for Mars exploration, and others, reducing the memory usage becomes a major concern.

Here is an example of declaring variables of different data types:

```
int      i, j, k;
float    numberOne, numberTwo;
long     bigInteger;
double   bigNumber;
```

At the time a variable is declared, it also can be initialized. For example, we may initialize the integer variables count and height to 10 and 34 as in

```
int count = 10, height = 34;
```

As we mentioned in Chapter 2, you can declare and create an object just as you can initialize variables at the time you declare them. For example, the declaration

```
Date today = new Date();
```

is equivalent to

```
Date today;
today = new Date();
```

assignment statement

We assign a value to a variable by using an *assignment statement*. To assign the value 234 to the variable named firstNumber, for example, we write

```
firstNumber = 234;
```

Be careful not to confuse mathematical equality and assignment. For example, the following are not valid Java code:

```
4 + 5 = x;
x + y = y + x;
```

The syntax for the assignment statement is

assignment statement syntax

```
<variable> = <expression> ;
```

where <expression> is an arithmetic expression, and the value of <expression> is assigned to the <variable>. The following are sample assignment statements:

```
sum      = firstNumber + secondNumber;
solution = x * x - 2 * x + 1;
average  = (x + y + z) / 3.0;
```

We will present a detailed discussion of arithmetic expressions in Section 3.2. One key point we need to remember about variables is

Helpful Reminder

Before using a variable, first we must declare and assign a value to it.

The diagram in Figure 3.1 illustrates the effect of variable declaration and assignment. Notice the similarity with this and memory allocation for object declaration and creation, illustrated in Figure 2.4 on page 38. Figure 3.2 compares the two. What we have been calling object names are really variables. The only difference

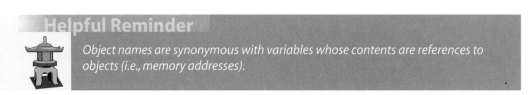

State of Memory

after Ⓐ is executed

```
int firstNumber, secondNumber;
```
```
firstNumber  = 234;
secondNumber = 87;
```

firstNumber

secondNumber

The variables **firstNumber** and **secondNumber** are declared and set in memory.

```
int firstNumber, secondNumber;
```
```
firstNumber  = 234;
secondNumber = 87;
```

after Ⓑ is executed

firstNumber   234

secondNumber   87

Values are assigned to the variables **firstNumber** and **secondNumber**.

Figure 3.1 A diagram showing how two memory locations (variables) with names **firstNumber** and **secondNumber** are declared, and values are assigned to them.

between a variable for numbers and a variable for objects is the contents in the memory locations. For numbers, a variable contains the numerical value itself; and for objects, a variable contains an address where the object is stored. We use an arrow in the diagram to indicate that the content is an address, not the value itself.

Helpful Reminder

Object names are synonymous with variables whose contents are references to objects (i.e., memory addresses).

Figure 3.3 contrasts the effect of assigning the content of one variable to another variable for numerical data values and for objects. Because the content of a variable for objects is an address, assigning the content of a variable to another makes two variables that refer to the same object. Assignment does not create a new object. Without executing the new command, no new object is created. We can view the situation, where two variables refer to the same object, as the object having two distinct names.

For numbers, the amount of memory space required is fixed. The values for data type int require 4 bytes, for example, and this won't change. However, with objects, the amount of memory space required is not constant. One instance of the Account class may require 120 bytes, while another instance of the same class may

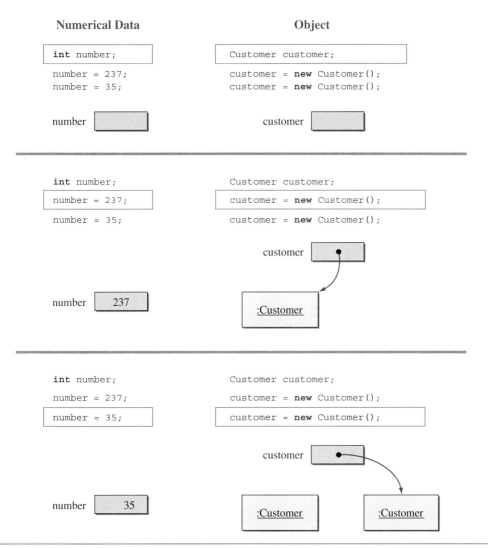

Figure 3.2 A difference between object declaration and numerical data declaration.

require 140 bytes. The difference in space usage for the account objects would occur if we had to keep track of checks written against the accounts. If one account has 15 checks written and the second account has 25 checks written, then we need more memory space for the second account than for the first account.

We use the new command to actually create an object. Remember that declaring an object only allocates the variable whose content will be an address. On the other hand, we don't "create" an integer because the space to store the value is already allocated at the time the integer variable is declared. Because the contents are addresses that refer to memory locations where the objects are actually stored, objects are called *reference data types*. In contrast, numerical data types are called *primitive data types*.

reference
versus
primitive data
types

Numerical Data   **Object**

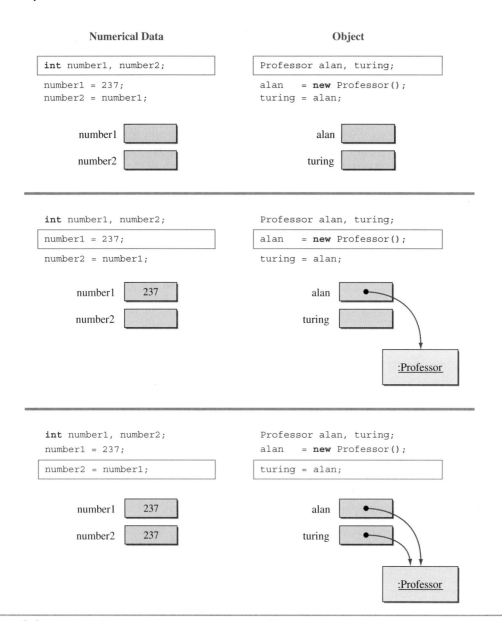

Figure 3.3 An effect of assigning the content of one variable to another.

Quick
CHECK

1. Why are the following declarations all invalid (color highlighting is disabled)?

```
int       a, b, a;
float     x, int;
float     w, int x;
bigNumber double;
```

2. Assuming the following declarations are executed in sequence, why are the second and third declarations invalid?

```
int        a, b;
int        a;
float      b;
```

3. Name six data types for numerical values.

4. Which of the following are valid assignment statements (assuming the variables are properly declared)?

```
x       =   12;
12      =   x;
y + y   =   x;
y       =   x + 12;
```

5. Draw the state-of-memory diagram for the following code:

```
Account latteAcct, espressoAcct;

latteAcct    = new Account();
espressoAcct = new Account();
latteAcct    = espressoAcct;
```

3.2 | Arithmetic Expressions

An expression involving numerical values such as

```
23 + 45
```

arithmetic
operator

is called an *arithmetic expression*, because it consists of arithmetic operators and operands. An *arithmetic operator*, such as + in the example, designates numerical computation. Table 3.2 summarizes the arithmetic operators available in Java.

Table 3.2 Arithmetic operators.

Operation	Java Operator	Example	Value (x = 10, y = 7, z = 2.5)
Addition	+	x + y	17
Subtraction	–	x – y	3
Multiplication	*	x * y	70
Division	/	x / y	1
		x / z	4.0
Modulo division (remainder)	%	x % y	3

integer division

Notice how the division operator works in Java. When both numbers are integers, the result is an integer quotient. That is, any fractional part is truncated. Division between two integers is called *integer division*. When either or both numbers are float or double, the result is a real number. Here are some division examples:

Division Operation	Result
23 / 5	4
23 / 5.0	4.6
25.0 / 5.0	5.0

The modulo operator returns the remainder of a division. Although real numbers can be used with the modulo operator, the most common use of the modulo operator involves only integers. Here are some examples:

Modulo Operation	Result
23 % 5	3
23 % 25	23
16 % 2	0

The expression 23 % 5 results in 3 because 23 divided by 5 is 4 with remainder 3. Notice that x % y = 0 when y divides x perfectly, for example, 16 % 2 = 0. Also notice that x % y = x when y is larger than x, for example, 23 % 25 = 23.

operand

An *operand* in arithmetic expressions can be a constant, a variable, a method call, or another arithmetic expression, possibly surrounded by parentheses. Let's look at examples. In the expression

```
x  +  4
```

binary operator

we have one addition operator and two operands—a variable x and a constant 4. The addition operator is called a *binary operator* because it operates on two operands. All other arithmetic operators except the minus are also binary. The minus and plus operators can be both binary and unary. A unary operator operates on one operand as in

```
-  x
```

In the expression

```
x  +  3  *  y
```

subexpression

the addition operator acts on operands x and 3 * y. The right operand for the addition operator is itself an expression. Often a nested expression is called a *subexpression*. The subexpression 3 * y has operands 3 and y. The following diagram illustrates this relationship:

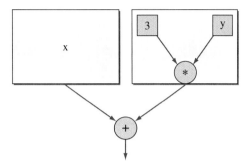

precedence rules

When two or more operators are present in an expression, we determine the order of evaluation by following the *precedence rules*. For example, multiplication has a higher precedence than addition. Therefore, in the expression x + 3 * y, the multiplication operation is evaluated first, and the addition operation is evaluated next. Table 3.3 summarizes the precedence rules for arithmetic operators.

Table 3.3 Precedence rules for arithmetic operators and parentheses.

Order	Group	Operator	Rule
High	Subexpression	( )	Subexpressions are evaluated first. If parentheses are nested, the innermost subexpression is evaluated first. If two or more pairs of parentheses are on the same level, then they are evaluated from left to right.
	Unary operator	-, +	Unary minuses and pluses are evaluated second.
	Multiplicative operator	*, /, %	Multiplicative operators are evaluated third. If two or more multiplicative operators are in an expression, then they are evaluated from left to right.
Low	Additive operator	+, -	Additive operators are evaluated last. If two or more additive operators are in an expression, then they are evaluated from left to right.

The following example illustrates the precedence rules applied to a complex arithmetic expression:

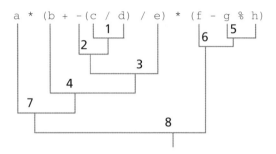

When an arithmetic expression consists of variables and constants of the same data type, then the result of the expression will be that data type also. For example, if the data type of a and b is int, then the result of the expression

        a * b + 23

is also an int. When the data types of variables and constants in an arithmetic expression are different data types, then a casting conversion will take place. A *casting conversion*, or *type casting*, is a process that converts a value of one data type to another data type. Two types of casting conversions in Java are *implicit* and *explicit*. An implicit conversion called *numeric promotion* is applied to the operands of an arithmetic operator. The promotion is based on the rules stated in Table 3.4. This conversion is called promotion because the operand is converted from a lower to a higher precision.

type casting

numeric
promotion

Table 3.4   **Rules for arithmetic promotion.**

Operator Type	Promotion Rule
Unary	1. If the operand is of type `byte` or `short`, then it is converted to `int`. 2. Otherwise, the operand remains the same type.
Binary	1. If either operand is of type `double`, then the other operand is converted to `double`. 2. Otherwise, if either operand is of type `float`, then the other operand is converted to `float`. 3. Otherwise, if either operand is of type `long`, then the other operand is converted to `long`. 4. Otherwise, both operands are converted to `int`.

Instead of relying on implicit conversion, we can use explicit conversion to convert an operand from one data type to another. Explicit conversion is applied to an operand by using a *type cast operator*. For example, to convert the int variable x in the expression

type cast operator

```
x / 3
```

to float so the result will not be truncated, we apply the type cast operator (float) as

```
(float) x / 3
```

The syntax is

type casting syntax

```
( <data type> ) <expression>
```

The type cast operator is a unary operator and has a precedence higher than any that of binary operator. You must use parentheses to type cast a subexpression; for example, the expression

```
a + (double) (x + y * z)
```

will result in the subexpression x + y * z type cast to double.

Assuming the variable x is an int, then the assignment statement

```
x = 2 * (14343 / 2344);
```

will assign the integer result of the expression to the variable x. However, if the data type of x is other than int, then an implicit conversion will occur so that the data type of the expression becomes the same as the data type of the variable. An *assignment conversion* is another implicit conversion that occurs when the variable and the value of an expression in an assignment statement are not of the same data type. An assignment conversion occurs only if the data type of the variable has a higher precision than the data type of the expression's value. For example,

assignment conversion

```
double number;
number = 25;
```

is valid, but

```
int number;
number = 234.56;
```

is not.

Take **my**

Advice

If we wish to assign a value to multiple variables, we can cascade the assignment operations as

```
x = y = 1;
```

which is equivalent to saying

```
y = 1;
x = 1;
```

The assignment symbol = is actually an operator, and its precedence order is lower than that of any other operators. Assignment operators are evaluated right to left.

Quick
CHECK
√

1. Evaluate the following expressions:

    a. `3 + 5 / 7`
    b. `3 * 3 + 3 % 2`
    c. `3 + 2 / 5 + -2 * 4`
    d. `2 * (1 + -(3/4) / 2) * (2 - 6 % 3)`

2. What is the data type of the result of the following expressions?

    a. `(3 + 5) / 7`
    b. `(3 + 5) / (float) 7`
    c. `(float) ( (3 + 5) / 7 )`

3. Which of the following expressions is equivalent to $-b(c + 34)/(2a)$?

    a. `-b * (c + 34) /  2 * a`
    b. `-b * (c + 34) / (2 * a)`
    c. `-b *  c + 34  / (2 * a)`

3.3 | Constants

While a program is running, different values may be assigned to a variable at different times (thus the name *variable,* since the values it contains can *vary*), but in some cases we do not want this to happen. In other words, we want to "lock" the assigned value so that no changes can take place. If we want a value to remain fixed, then we use a *constant.* A constant is declared in a manner similar to a variable but with the additional reserved word final. A constant must be assigned a value at the time of its declaration. Here's an example declaring four constants:

constant

```
final double  PI = 3.14159;
final short   FARADAY_CONSTANT = 23060; // unit is cal/volt
final double  CM_PER_INCH = 2.54;
final int     MONTHS_IN_YEAR = 12;
```

We follow the standard Java convention to name a constant, using only capital letters and underscores. Judicious use of constants makes programs more readable. You will be seeing many uses of constants later in the book, beginning with the sample program in this chapter.

named constant

The constant PI is called a *named constant* or *symbolic constant*. We refer to symbolic constants with identifiers such as PI and FARADAY_CONSTANT. The second type of constant is called a *literal constant,* and we refer to it by using an actual value. For example, the following statements contain three literal constants:

literal constant

```
final double    PI    = 3.14159 ;
double area;
area = 2 * PI * 345.79 ;
```

Literal constants

When we use the literal constant 2, the data type of the constant is set to int by default. Then how can we specify a literal constant of type long?[1] We append the constant with an l (a lowercase letter L) or L as in

```
2L * PI * 345.79
```

How about the literal constant 345.79? Since the literal constant contains a decimal point, its data type can only be float or double. But which one? The answer is double. If a literal constant contains a decimal point, then it is of type double by default. To designate a literal constant of type float, we must append the letter f or F. For example,

```
2 * PI * 345.79F
```

To represent a double literal constant, we may optionally append a d or D. So, the following two constants are equivalent:

```
2 * PI * 345.79      is equivalent to    2 * PI * 345.79D
```

We also can express float and double literal constants in scientific notation as

$$\text{Number} \times 10^{\text{exponent}}$$

which in Java is expressed as

exponential notation in Java

```
<number> E <exponent>
```

---

[1] In most cases, it is not significant to distinguish the two because of automatic type conversion; see Section 3.2.

Take
my
Advice

Since a numerical constant such as 345.79 represents a **double** value, these statements

```
float number;
number = 345.79;
```

for example, would result in a compilation error. The data types do not match, and the variable (**float**) has lower precision than that of the constant (**double**). To correct this error, we have to write the assignment statement as

```
number = 345.79f;
```

or

```
number = (float) 345.79;
```

This is one of the common errors that people make in writing Java programs, especially those with prior programming experience.

where <number> is a literal constant that may or may not contain a decimal point and <exponent> is a signed or an unsigned integer. Lowercase e may be substituted for the exponent symbol E. The whole expression may be suffixed by f, F, d, or D. The <number> itself cannot be suffixed with symbols f, F, d, or D. Here are some examples:

```
12.40e+209
23E33
29.0098e-102
234e+5D
4.45e2
```

Here are some additional examples of constant declarations:

```
final double SPEED_OF_LIGHT = 3.0E+10D; // unit is cm/sec
final short  MAX_WGT_ALLOWED = 400;
```

3.4 | Getting Numerical Input Values

In Chapter 2, we introduced the use of the showInputDialog method to get the string input. So it is natural for us to consider writing the following statements to get a numerical input value:

```
int age;
age = JOptionPane.showInputDialog(null, "Enter Age:");
```

type mismatch

This code will not work because of *type mismatch*. Notice that an assignment such as

```
String num = 14;
```

or

```
int num = "14";
```

is invalid because of type mismatch. We cannot assign a value of incompatible type to a variable of another type. Incompatible types mean the values of one type are represented differently in computer memory than the values of the other type. The literal constant "14", for example, is a String object and represented in computer memory differently from the integer constant 14. This difference in representation makes the assignments such as those just shown invalid.

The showInputDialog method returns a String object, and therefore, we cannot assign it directly to a variable of numerical data type. To input a numerical value, we have to first input a String object and then convert it to a numerical representation. We call such operation a *type conversion*.

type conversion

wrapper classes

Integer

To perform the necessary type conversion in Java, we use different utility classes called *wrapper classes*. The name *wrapper* derives from the fact that these classes surround, or wrap, a primitive data with useful methods. Type conversion is one of several methods provided by these wrapper classes. To convert a string data to an integer data, we use the parseInt class method of the Integer class. For example, to convert a string "14" to an int value 14, we write

```
int num = Integer.parseInt("14");
```

To input an integer value, say, age, we can write the code as

```
String str
   = JOptionPane.showInputDialog(null, "Enter age:");

int age = Integer.parseInt(str);
```

If the user enters a string that cannot be converted to an int, for example, 12.34 or abc123, an error will result. Table 3.5 lists common wrapper classes and their corresponding conversion method.

Let's write a short program that inputs the radius of a circle and computes the circle's area and circumference. Here's the program:

```
/*

   Chapter 3 Sample Program: Compute Area and Circumference

   File: Ch3Circle.java

*/
```

```
import javax.swing.*;
import java.text.*;

class Ch3Circle {

    public static void main( String[] args ) {

        final  double PI = 3.14159;

        String radiusStr;
        double radius, area, circumference;

        radiusStr = JOptionPane.showInputDialog(null, "Enter radius:");

        radius = Double.parseDouble(radiusStr);

        //compute area and circumference
        area          = PI * radius * radius;
        circumference = 2.0 * PI * radius;

        JOptionPane.showMessageDialog(null,
                                "Given Radius: " + radius + "\n"
                           + "Area: " + area+ "\n"
                       + "Circumference: " + circumference);
    }
}
```

We are allowed to concatenate **String** and numerical data.

the + symbol means addition or concatenation

Notice the long expression we pass as the second argument for the showMessageDialog method. In Chapter 2, we use the plus symbol to concatenate strings. We can use the same symbol to concatenate strings and numerical data. Numerical data are automatically converted to string representation and then concatenated.

Table 3.5 Common wrapper classes and their conversion method.

Class	Method	Example
Integer	parseInt	Integer.parseInt("25") → 25 Integer.parseInt("25.3") → error
Long	parseLong	Long.parseLong("25") → 25L Long.parseLong("25.3") → error
Float	parseFloat	Float.parseFloat("25.3") → 25.3F Float.parseFloat("ab3") → error
Double	parseDouble	Double.parseDouble("25") → 25.0 Double.parseDouble("ab3") → error

operator
overloading

We learned in this chapter that the plus symbol is used for arithmetic addition also. When a symbol is used to represent more than one operation, this is called *operator overloading*. When the Java compiler encounters an overloaded operator, how does it know which operation the symbol represents? The Java compiler determines the meaning of a symbol by its context. If the left and the right operands of the plus symbol are numerical values, then the compiler will treat the symbol as addition. Otherwise, it will treat the symbol as concatenation. The plus symbol operator is evaluated from left to right, and the result of concatenation is a text, so the code

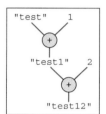

```java
int x = 1;
int y = 2;
String output = "test" + x + y ;
```

will result in output being set to

```
test12
```

while the statement

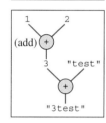

```java
String output = x + y + "test" ;
```

will result in output being set to

```
3test
```

To get the result of test3, we have to write the statement as

```java
String output = "test" + (x + y);
```

so the arithmetic addition is performed first.

Let's get back to the program. When we run the program and enter 2.35, the dialog shown in Figure 3.4 appears on the screen. Notice the precision of decimal places displayed for the results, especially the one for the circumference. We can

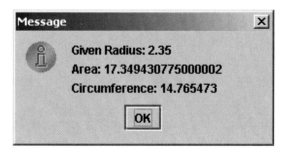

Figure 3.4 The dialog that appears when the input value 2.35 was entered into the **Ch3Circle** program.

DecimalFormat specify the number of decimal places to display by using the DecimalFormat class from the java.text package. The usage is similar to the one for the SimpleDate-Format class.

Although the full use of the DecimalFormat class can be fairly complicated, it is very straightforward if all we want is to limit the number of decimal places to be displayed. To limit the decimal places to three, we create a DecimalFormat object as

```
DecimalFormat df = new DecimalFormat("0.000");
```

and use it to format the number as

```
double num = 234.5698709;

JOptionPane.showMessageDialog("Num: " + df.format(num));
```

When we add an instance of the DecimalFormat class named df and change the output statement of the Ch3Circle class to

```
JOptionPane.showMessageDialog(null,
                    "GivenRadius: " + radius + "\n"
                    +"Area:. "+df.format(area)+"\n"
                    +"Circumference: "
                    + df.format(circumference));
```

the dialog shown in Figure 3.5 appears on the screen. The modified class is named Ch3Circle2.

Quick
CHECK

1. Write a code fragment to input the user's height in inches and assign the value to an int variable named height.

2. Write a code fragment to input the user's weight in pounds and display the weight in kilograms. 1 lb = 453.592 g.

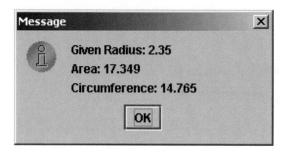

Figure 3.5 The result of formatting the output values by using a **DecimalFormat** object.

3.5 | Standard Output

The showMessageDialog method of the JOptionPane class can be used to output multiple lines of text by separating the lines with the special control characters \n. However, the use of showMessageDialog becomes cumbersome and inconvenient when we have to output many lines of text. The showMessageDialog method is intended for displaying short one-line messages, not for a general-purpose output mechanism.

standard output window

System.out

Among different approaches, we will introduce the simplest technique to display multiple lines of text in this section. When we execute the earlier sample programs, we see a window with black background—something similar to one shown in Figure 3.6 appears on the screen. This window is called the *standard output window*, and we can output multiple lines of text (we can output any numerical values by converting them to text) to this window via System.out. The actual appearance of this standard output window will differ depending on which Java development tool we use. Despite the difference in the actual appearance, its functionality of displaying multiple lines of text is the same among different Java tools.

Helpful Reminder

System.out refers to a precreated **PrintStream** object we use to output multiple lines of text to the standard output window. The actual appearance of the standard output window depends on which Java tool we use.

The System class includes a number of useful class data values. One of them is an instance of the PrintStream class named out. Since this is a class data value, we refer to it through the class name, as System.out, and this PrintStream object is tied

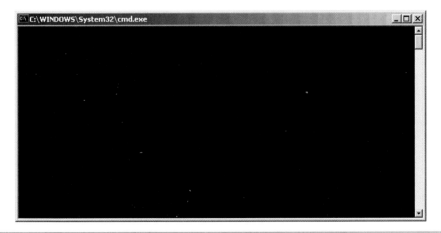

Figure 3.6   The standard output window for displaying multiple lines of text. We can output text to this window via the **System.out** object.

to the standard output window. Every text we send to System.out will appear on the standard output window. We call the technique to output data by using System.out the *standard output*.

standard output

We use the print method to output a value. For example, executing the code

```
System.out.print("Hello, Dr. Caffeine.");
```

will result in the standard output window shown in Figure 3.7.

The print method will continue printing from the end of the currently displayed output. Executing the following statements after the preceding print message will result in the standard output window shown in Figure 3.8.

```
int x, y;
x = 123;
y = x + x;
System.out.print(" x = ");
System.out.print( x );
System.out.print(" x + x = ");
System.out.print( y );
System.out.print(" THE END");
```

Notice that in the statement

```
System.out.print( x );
```

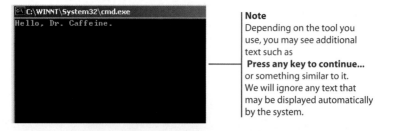

Note
Depending on the tool you use, you may see additional text such as
Press any key to continue...
or something similar to it. We will ignore any text that may be displayed automatically by the system.

Figure 3.7 Result of executing **System.out.print("Hello, Dr. Caffeine.").**

Figure 3.8 Result of sending five **print** messages to **System.out** of Figure 3.7.

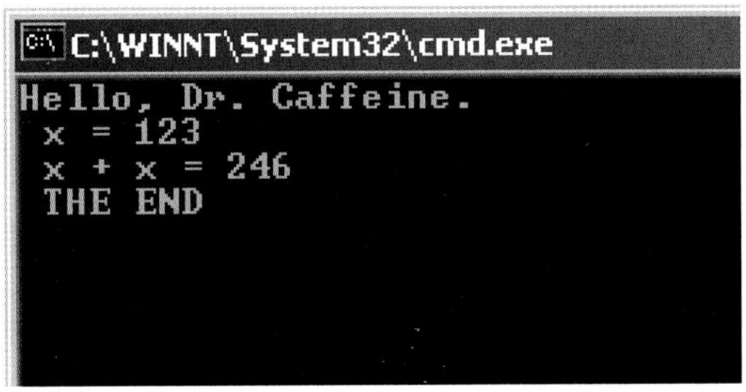

```
C:\WINNT\System32\cmd.exe
Hello, Dr. Caffeine.
 x = 123
 x + x = 246
 THE END
```

Figure 3.9 Result of mixing **print** with four **println** messages to **System.out.**

we are sending a numerical value as the parameter. But we stated earlier that we use the standard output window for displaying multiple lines of text, that is, string data. Actually, the statement

```
System.out.print( x );
```

is equivalent to

```
System.out.print( Integer.toString(x) );
```

because the print method will do the necessary type conversion if we pass numerical data. We can pass any primitive data value as the parameter to the print method.

We can print an argument and skip to the next line so that subsequent output will start on the next line by using println instead of print. The standard output window of Figure 3.9 will result if we use println instead of print in the preceding example; that is,

```
int x, y;
x = 123;
y = x + x;
System.out.println("Hello, Dr. Caffeine.");
System.out.print(" x = ");
System.out.println( x );
System.out.print(" x + x = ");
System.out.println( y );
System.out.println(" THE END");
```

Let's rewrite the Ch3Circle2 class by using the standard output for displaying the results. Here's the modified program:

```
/*
    Chapter 3 Sample Program:  Compute Area and Circumference
                               with formatting using standard
                               output
```

```
    File: Ch2Circle3.java
*/

import javax.swing.*;
import java.text.*;

class Ch3Circle3 {

    public static void main( String[] args )  {

        final double PI = 3.14159;

        String radiusStr;
        double radius, area, circumference;

        DecimalFormat df = new DecimalFormat("0.000");

        //Get input
        radiusStr = JOptionPane.showInputDialog(null, "Enter radius:");
        radius    = Double.parseDouble(radiusStr);

        //Compute area and circumference
        area          = PI * radius * radius;
        circumference = 2.0 * PI * radius;

        //Display the results
        System.out.println("");
        System.out.println("Given Radius: " + radius);
        System.out.println("Area: " + df.format(area));
        System.out.println("Circumference: " + df.format(circumference));
    }
}
```

The output statements can be written by using only one println method as

```
System.out.println("\nGiven Radius: " + radius + "\n"
                  + "Area: " + df.format(area)+ "\n"
                  + "Circumference: "
                  + df.format(circumference));
```

It was necessary to pass all information at once when using the showMessageDialog method, but for System.out, it is typical to use one println method for each line of output.

Quick
CHECK

1. Using the standard output, write a Java statement to display a message dialog with the text I Love Java.

2. Using the standard output, write statements to display the following shopping list:

```
Shopping List:
     Apple
     Banana
     Lowfat Milk
```

3.6 | Standard Input

As an alternative of using JOptionPane for a simple input routine, we will introduce an approach that works nicely with System.out. Some people may prefer this approach because of the tighter integration with System.out.

System.in

standard input

console input

Analogous to System.out for output, we have System.in for input. We call the technique to input data using System.in *standard input*. We also use the term *console input* to refer to standard input. Using System.in for input is slightly more complicated than using System.out for output. System.in is an instance of the InputStream class that provides only a facility to input 1 byte at a time with its read method. However, multiple bytes are required to represent a primitive data type or a string (e.g., 4 bytes is used to store an int value). So to input primitive data values or strings easily, we need an input facility to process multiple bytes as a single unit.

Scanner

The most common way of using System.in for input is to connect a Scanner object to the System.in object. A Scanner object will allow us to read primitive data types and strings. Let's start with an example to input an integer. First we create a new Scanner object (the Scanner class is located in the java.util package) by calling its class method create with System.in as an argument:

```
import java.util.*;
...
Scanner scanner;

scanner = Scanner.create(System.in);
```

factory method

Notice how a new Scanner object is created differently. We are not using the new operator. Rather, we are calling a class method that returns an instance of the Scanner class. Such an instance-creating method is called a *factory method*. (There are reasons for wanting to use a factory method over the regular new operator, but understanding these reasons requires the knowledge of advanced topics we have not yet studied.)

Once we have a Scanner object, then we call its nextInt method to input an int. Here's an example of reading a person's age:

```
int age;
System.out.print("Enter age: ");
age = scanner.nextInt();
```

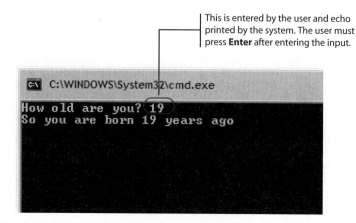

This is entered by the user and echo printed by the system. The user must press **Enter** after entering the input.

Figure 3.10 Sample interaction using **System.in** and **System.out**.

It is important to prompt the user by printing out an appropriate message such as Enter age: so the user knows the program is waiting for an input. The characters entered by the user are displayed in the standard output window as they are typed in, so the user can see what's been entered. Printing out the values just entered is called *echo printing*. The input line is not processed until the Enter (or Return) key is pressed, so we can erase the characters by pressing the Backspace key while entering the line. Figure 3.10 shows the standard output window when the following code is executed and the user enters the input 19:

echo printing

```
Scanner scanner = Scanner.create(System.in);

int age;

System.out.print("How old are you? ");
age = scanner.nextInt();

System.out.println("So you are born "
                        + age + " years ago");
```

You can enter more than one input value on a single line. The following code reads two integers:

```
Scanner scanner = Scanner.create(System.in);

int num1, num2;

System.out.print("Enter two integers: ");
num1 = scanner.nextInt(); //get the first int
num2 = scanner.nextInt(); //get the second int

System.out.println("num1 = " + num1 +
                        " and num2 = " + num2);
```

Figure 3.11 shows a sample run. The user must press the Enter key after the second input. Notice that one blank space separates the two input values. Any number of

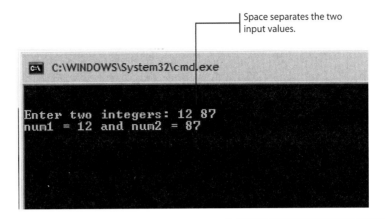

Figure 3.11 Entering two input values on a single line.

white space characters, such as spaces, tabs, and newlines, can be used to separate the input values.

To input other numerical primitive data types, we use the corresponding methods such as readDouble and readLong. The following code reads a double, an int, and another double:

```
Scanner scanner = Scanner.create(System.in);

int iNum1;
double dNum1, dNum2;

System.out.print("Enter double, int, double: ");

dNum1 = scanner.nextDouble();
iNum1 = scanner.nextInt();
dNum1 = scanner.nextDouble();
```

Table 3.6 lists six input methods to read numerical data types.

Table 3.6 Methods to input six numerical data types.

Method	Example
nextByte( )	byte b = scanner.nextByte( );
nextDouble( )	double d = scanner.nextDouble( );
nextFloat( )	float f = scanner.nextFloat( );
nextInt( )	int i = scanner.nextInt( );
nextLong( )	long l = scanner.nextLong( );
nextShort( )	short s = scanner.nextShort( );

Reading a string input is slightly more complicated than reading numerical data. To input a single word, we use the next method as follows:

```
Scanner scanner = Scanner.create(System.in);

String name;

System.out.print("Enter your first name: ");

name = scanner.next( );
```

If we need to read a whole line as a single input, then we must override the default delimiter (the white space) and set the line separator as the delimiter. For example, the following code will accept the whole line as a single string input:

```
Scanner scanner = Scanner.create(System.in);

String lineSeparator
          = System.getProperties("line.separator");

scanner.useDelimiter(lineSeparator);

String quote;

System.out.print("Enter your favorite quote: ");

quote = scanner.next( );

System.out.println("You entered: " + quote);
```

```
Enter your favorite quote: I think, therefore I am.
You entered: I think, therefore I am.
```
Values entered by the user are shown in blue.

If, however, we do not override the default delimiter and enter the same input, only the first word is read by the system because the white space is used as the delimiter:

```
Scanner scanner = Scanner.create(System.in);

String quote;

System.out.print("Enter your favorite quote: ");

quote = scanner.next( );

System.out.println("You entered: " + quote);
```

```
Enter your favorite quote: I think, therefore I am.
You entered: I
```
Values entered by the user are shown in blue.

We override the default delimiter by calling the useDelimiter method and pass the appropriate argument. Since each computer platform could use a different sequence of control characters as the line separator, we use System.getProperties to retrieve the sequence that is specific to the platform which our program is running. For the Windows platform, we can call the useDelimiter method as

```
scanner.useDelimiter("\r\n");
```

But such code may not work on other platforms. To make the code general enough to work on all platforms, we use System.getProperties.

If you have more than one input with a mixture of string and primitive data, then the recommended approach is to set the line separator as the delimiter and input one value per input line.

Helpful Reminder

To input a mixture of strings and primitive data, set the line separator as the delimiter and input one value per input line.

Let's finish this section with a sample program. We will rewrite the Ch3Circle3 class by using the standard input. Here's the program:

```
/*
    Chapter 3 Sample Program: Compute Area and Circumference
                              with formatting using standard
                              input and output

    File: Ch2Circle4.java
*/

import java.util.*;
import java.text.*;

class Ch3Circle4 {

    public static void main( String[] args ) {

        final double PI = 3.14159;

        double radius, area, circumference;
        Scanner scanner;

        DecimalFormat df = new DecimalFormat("0.000");

        scanner = Scanner.create(System.in);

        //Get input
        System.out.print("Enter radius: ");

        radius = scanner.nextDouble();

        //Compute area and circumference
        area          = PI * radius * radius;
        circumference = 2.0 * PI * radius;

        //Display the results
        System.out.println("");
```

```
System.out.println("Given Radius: " + radius);
System.out.println("Area: " + df.format(area));
System.out.println("Circumference: " + df.format(circumference));
    }
}
```

Quick
CHECK

1. Using the standard input, write a code fragment to input the user's height in inches and assign the value to an int variable named height.

2. Write a code fragment that sets the line separator as the input delimiter.

3. Using the standard input and output, write a code fragment to input weight in pounds and display the weight in kilograms. 1 lb = 453.592 g.

3.7 | The Math Class

Using only the arithmetic operators to express numerical computations is very limiting. Many computations require the use of mathematical functions. For example, to express the mathematical formula

$$\frac{1}{2} \sin \left(x - \frac{\pi}{\sqrt{y}} \right)$$

we need the trigonometric sine and square root functions. The Math class in the java.lang package contains class methods for commonly used mathematical functions. Table 3.7 is a partial list of class methods available in the Math class. The class also has two class constants PI and E for π and the natural number e, respectively. Using the Math class constant and methods, we can express the preceding formula as

```
(1.0 /2.0) * Math.sin( x - Math.PI / Math.sqrt(y) )
```

Notice how the class methods and class constants are referred to in the expression. The syntax is

```
<class name> . <method name> ( <arguments> )
```

or

```
<class name> . <class constant>
```

Let's conclude this section with a sample program. Today is the final meet of the women's rowing team against the arch rival university before the upcoming Division I NCAA championship. The cheerleaders of the rival team hoisted their school flag on the other shore of the river to boost their morale. Not to be outdone, we want to hoist our school flag, too. To bring the Goddess of Victory to our side, we want our pole to be taller than theirs. Since they won't let us, we can't find the height of their pole by actually measuring it. We can, however, determine the height

Table 3.7 Math **class methods for commonly used mathematical functions.**

Class Method	Argument Type	Result Type	Description	Example
abs(a)	int	int	Returns the absolute int value of a.	abs(10) → 10 abs(−5) → 5
	long	long	Returns the absolute long value of a.	
	float	float	Returns the absolute float value of a.	
	double	double	Returns the absolute double value of a.	
acos(a)†	double	double	Returns the arccosine of a.	acos(−1) → 3.14159
asin(a)†	double	double	Returns the arcsine of a.	asin(1) → 1.57079
atan(a)†	double	double	Returns the arctangent of a.	atan(1) → 0.785398
ceil(a)	double	double	Returns the smallest whole number greater than or equal to a.	ceil(5.6) → 6.0 ceil(5.0) → 5.0 ceil(−5.6) → −5.0
cos(a)†	double	double	Returns the trigonometric cosine of a.	cos(π/2) → 0.0
exp(a)	double	double	Returns the natural number *e* (2.718 . . .) raised to the power of a.	exp(2) → 7.389056099
floor(a)	double	double	Returns the largest whole number less than or equal to a.	floor(5.6) → 5.0 floor(5.0) → 5.0 floor(−5.6) → −6.0
log(a)	double	double	Returns the natural logarithm (base *e*) of a.	log(2.7183) → 1.0
max(a, b)	int	int	Returns the larger of a and b.	max(10, 20) → 20
	long	long	Same as above.	
	float	float	Same as above.	
min(a, b)	int	int	Returns the smaller of a and b.	min(10, 20) → 10
	long	long	Same as above.	
	float	float	Same as above.	

Table 3.7 Math class methods for commonly used mathematical functions. *(Continued)*

Class Method	Argument Type	Result Type	Description	Example
pow(a, b)	double	double	Returns the number a raised to the power of b.	pow(2.0, 3.0) → 8.0
random( )	<none>	double	Generates a random number greater than or equal to 0.0 and less than 1.0	Examples given in Chapter 5
round(a)	float	int	Returns the int value of a rounded to the nearest whole number.	round(5.6) → 6 round(5.4) → 5 round(−5.6) → −6
	double	long	Returns the float value of a rounded to the nearest whole number.	
sin(a)†	double	double	Returns the trigonometric sine of a.	sin(π/2) → 1.0
sqrt(a)	double	double	Returns the square root of a.	sqrt(9.0) → 3.0
tan(a)†	double	double	Returns the trigono- metric tangent of a.	tan(π/4) → 1.0
toDegrees	double	double	Converts the given angle in radians to degrees	toDegrees(π/4) → 45.0
toRadians	double	double	Reverse of toDegrees	toRadians(90.0) → 1.5707963

†All trigonometric functions are computed in radians.

without actually measuring it if we know the distance *b* to their flag pole. We can use the tangent of angle to determine the pole's height *h* as follows:

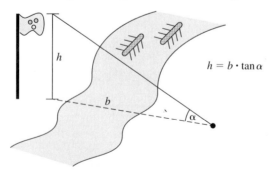

$$h = b \cdot \tan \alpha$$

Unfortunately, there's no means for us to go across the river to find out the distance *b*. After a moment of deep meditation, it hit us that there's no need to go across the river. We can determine the pole's height by measuring angles from two points on this side of the river bank, as shown below:

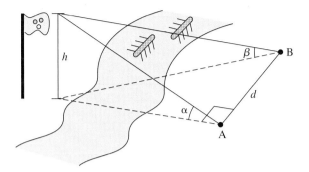

And the equation to compute the height *h* is

$$h = \frac{d \sin \alpha \sin \beta}{\sqrt{\sin(\alpha + \beta)\sin(\alpha - \beta)}}$$

Once we have this equation, all that's left is to put together a Java program. Here's the program:

```
/*
    Chapter 3 Sample Program: Estimate the Pole Height
    File: Ch3PoleHeight.java
*/
import java.text.*;
import java.util.*;

class Ch3PoleHeight {

    public static void main( String[] args ) {

        double height;          //height of the pole
        double distance;        //distance between points A and B
        double alpha;           //angle measured at point A
        double beta;            //angle measured at point B
        double alphaRad;        //angle alpha in radians
        double betaRad;         //angle beta in radians

        Scanner scanner = Scanner.create(System.in);
        scanner.useDelimeter(System.getProperties("line.separator"));

        //Get three input values
        System.out.print("Angle alpha (in degrees):");
        alpha = scanner.nextDouble();

        System.out.print("Angle beta (in degree):");
        beta  = scanner.nextDouble();

        System.out.print("Distance between points A and B (ft):");
        distance   = scanner.nextDouble();
```

```
//compute the height of the tower
alphaRad = Math.toRadians(alpha);
betaRad  = Math.toRadians(beta);

height = ( distance * Math.sin(alphaRad) * Math.sin(betaRad) )
                /
              Math.sqrt( Math.sin(alphaRad + betaRad) *
                        Math.sin(alphaRad - betaRad) );

DecimalFormat df = new DecimalFormat("0.000");

System.out.println("Estimating the height of the statue"
      + "\n\n"
      + "Angle at point A (deg): "        + df.format(alpha)   + "\n"
      + "Angle at point B (deg): "        + df.format(beta)    + "\n"
      + "Distance between A and B (ft): " + df.format(distance)+ "\n"
      + "Estimated height (ft): "      + df.format(height));
      }
}
```

Quick **CHECK**

1. What's wrong with the following?

    a. `y = (1/2) * Math.sqrt( X );`
    b. `y = sqrt(38.0);`
    c. `y = Math.exp(2, 3);`
    d. `y = math.sqrt( b*b - 4*a*c) / ( 2 * a );`

2. If another programmer writes the following statements, do you suspect any misunderstanding on the part of this programmer? What will be the value of y?

    a. `y = Math.sin( 360 ) ;`
    b. `y = Math.cos( 45 );`

3.8 | The GregorianCalendar **Class**

In Chapter 2, we introduced the java.util.Date class to represent a specific instant in time. Notice that we are using here the more concise expression "the java.util.Date class" to refer to a class from a specific package instead of the longer expression "the Date class from the java.util package." This shorter version is our preferred way of notation when we need or want to identify the package to which the class belongs.

Helpful Reminder

*When we need to identify the specific package to which a class belongs, we will commonly use the concise expression with the full path name, such as **java.util.Date**, instead of writing "the **Date** class from the **java.util** package."*

Gregorian-
Calendar

In addition to this class, we have a very useful class named java.util.Gregorian-Calendar in manipulating calendar information such as year, month, and day. We can create a new GregorianCalendar object that represents today as

```
GregorianCalendar today = new GregorianCalendar( );
```

or a specific day, say, July 4, 1776, by passing year, month, and day as the parameters as

The value of 6
means July.

```
GregorianCalendar independenceDay =
        new GregorianCalendar(1776, 6, 4);
```

No, the value of 6 as the second parameter is not an error. The first month of a year, January, is represented by 0, the second month by 1, and so forth. To avoid confusion, we can use constants defined for months in the superclass Calendar (GregorianCalendar is a subclass of Calendar). Instead of remembering that the value 6 represents July, we can use the defined constant Calendar.JULY as

```
GregorianCalendar independenceDay =
        new GregorianCalendar(1776, Calendar.JULY, 4);
```

Table 3.8 explains the use of some of the more common constants defined in the Calendar class.

When the date and time are November 11, 2002, 6:13 p.m. and we run the Ch3TestCalendar program, we will see the result shown in Figure 3.12.

Table 3.8 Constants defined in the Calendar class for retrieved different pieces of calendar/time information.

Constant	Description
YEAR	The year portion of the calendar date
MONTH	The month portion of the calendar date
DATE	The day of the month
DAY_OF_MONTH	Same as DATE
DAY_OF_YEAR	The day number within the year
DAY_OF_MONTH	The day number within the month
DAY_OF_WEEK	The day of the week (Sun — 1, Mon — 2, etc.)
WEEK_OF_YEAR	The week number within the year
WEEK_OF_MONTH	The week number within the month
AM_PM	The indicator for AM or PM (AM — 0 and PM — 1)
HOUR	The hour in 12-hour notation
HOUR_OF_DAY	The hour in 24-hour notation
MINUTE	The minute within the hour

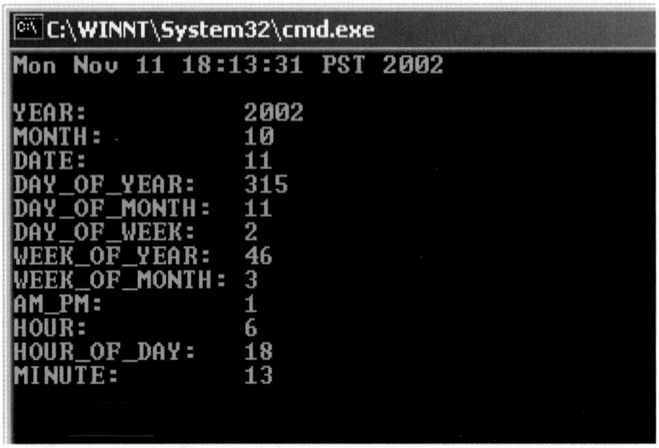

Figure 3.12 Result of running the **Ch3TestCalendar** program at November 11, 2002, 6:13 p.m.

```
/*
    Chapter 3 Sample Program: Display Calendar Info
    File: Ch3TestCalendar.java
*/

import java.util.*;

class Ch3TestCalendar {

    public static void main( String[] args ) {

        GregorianCalendar cal = new GregorianCalendar();

        System.out.println(cal.getTime());
        System.out.println("");

        System.out.println("YEAR:          " + cal.get(Calendar.YEAR));
        System.out.println("MONTH:         " + cal.get(Calendar.MONTH));
        System.out.println("DATE:          " + cal.get(Calendar.DATE));

        System.out.println("DAY_OF_YEAR:   "
                                  + cal.get(Calendar.DAY_OF_YEAR));
        System.out.println("DAY_OF_MONTH:  "
                                  + cal.get(Calendar.DAY_OF_MONTH));
        System.out.println("DAY_OF_WEEK:   "
                                  + cal.get(Calendar.DAY_OF_WEEK));

        System.out.println("WEEK_OF_YEAR:  "
                                  + cal.get(Calendar.WEEK_OF_YEAR));
        System.out.println("WEEK_OF_MONTH: "
                                  + cal.get(Calendar.WEEK_OF_MONTH));

        System.out.println("AM_PM:         " + cal.get(Calendar.AM_PM));
        System.out.println("HOUR:          " + cal.get(Calendar.HOUR));
```

```
        System.out.println("HOUR_OF_DAY:    "
                                + cal.get(Calendar.HOUR_OF_DAY));
        System.out.println("MINUTE:         " + cal.get(Calendar.MINUTE));
    }
}
```

getTime

Notice that the first line in the output shows the full date and time information. The full date and time information can be accessed by calling the calendar object's getTime method. This method returns the same information as a Date object.

Notice also that we get only the numerical values when we retrieve the day of the week or month information. We can spell out the information by using the SimpleDateFormat class. Since the constructor of the SimpleDateFormat class accepts only the Date object, first we need to convert a GregorianCalendar object to an equivalent Date object by calling its getTime method. For example, here's how we can display the day of the week on which our Declaration of Independence was signed in Philadelphia:

```
/*
    Chapter 3 Sample Program: Day of the week the Declaration of
                            Independence was adopted

    File: Ch3IndependenceDay.java

*/

import java.util.*;
import java.text.*;
import javax.swing.*;

class Ch3IndependenceDay {

    public static void main( String[] args ) {

        GregorianCalendar independenceDay
            = new GregorianCalendar(1776, Calendar.JULY, 4);

        SimpleDateFormat sdf = new SimpleDateFormat("EEEE");

        JOptionPane.showMessageDialog(null, "It was signed on "
                        + sdf.format(independenceDay.getTime()));
    }
}
```

Let's finish the section with a sample program that extends the Ch3IndependenceDay program. We will allow the user to enter the year, month, and day, and we will reply with the day of the week of the given date (our birthday, grandparent's wedding day, and so on). We will use the standard input and output for this program.

Here's the program:

```java
/*
    Chapter 3 Sample Program: Find the Day of Week of a Given Date
    File: Ch3FindDayOfWeek.java
*/

import java.util.*;
import java.text.*;

class Ch3FindDayOfWeek {

    public static void main( String[] args ) {

        String  inputStr;
        int     year, month, day;

        GregorianCalendar cal;
        SimpleDateFormat  sdf;

        Scanner scanner = Scanner.create(System.in);
        scanner.useDelimiter(System.getProperty("line.separator"));

        System.out.print("Year (yyyy): ");
        year     = scanner.nextInt();

        System.out.print("Month (1-12): ");
        month    = scanner.nextInt();

        System.out.print("Day (1-31): ");
        day      = scanner.nextInt();

        cal = new GregorianCalendar(year, month-1, day);
        sdf = new SimpleDateFormat("EEEE");

        System.out.println("");
        System.out.println("Day of Week: " + sdf.format(cal.getTime()));
    }
}
```

Notice that we are allowing the user to enter the month as an integer between 1 and 12, so we need to subtract 1 from the entered data in creating a new
GregorianCalendar object.

You Might Want to Know   The Gregorian calendar system was adopted by England and its colonies, including the colonial United States, in 1752. So the technique shown here works only after this adoption. For a fascinating story about calendars, visit **http://webexhibits.org/calendars/year-countries.html**

Running **Ch3IndpendenceDay** will tell you that our venerable document was signed on Thursday. History textbooks will say something like "the document was formally adopted July 4, 1776, on a bright, but cool Philadelphia day" but never the day of the week. Well, now you know. See how useful Java is? By the way, the document was adopted by the Second Continental Congress on July 4, but the actual signing did not place until August 2 (it was Friday—what a great reason for a TGIF party) after the approval of all 13 colonies. For more stories behind the Declaration of Independence, visit
http://www.archives.gov/exhibit_hall/charters_of_freedom/declaration/declaration.html
or
http://www.ushistory.org/declaration/

3.9 Sample Development

Loan Calculator

In this section, we will develop a simple loan calculator program. We will develop this program by using an incremental development technique, which will develop the program in small incremental steps. We start out with a bare-bones program and gradually build up the program by adding more and more code to it. At each incremental step, we design, code, and test the program before moving on to the next step. This methodical development of a program allows us to focus our attention on a single task at each step, and this reduces the chance of introducing errors into the program.

Problem Statement

The next time you buy a new TV or a stereo, watch out for those "0% down, 0% interest until next July" deals. Read the fine print, and you'll notice that if you don't make the full payment by the end of a certain date, a hefty interest will start accruing. You may be better off to get an ordinary loan from the beginning with a cheaper interest rate. What matters most is the total payment (loan amount plus total interest) you'll have to make. To compare different loan deals, let's develop a loan calculator. Here's the problem statement:

> *Write a loan calculator program that computes both monthly and total payments for a given loan amount, annual interest rate, and loan period.*

Overall Plan

Our first task is to map out the overall plan for development. We will identify classes necessary for the program and the steps we will follow to implement the program. We begin with the outline of program logic. For a simple program such as this one, it is kind of obvious; but to practice the incremental development, let's put down the outline of program flow explicitly. We can express the program flow as having three tasks:

program tasks

1. Get three input values: **loanAmount, interestRate,** and **loanPeriod.**

2. Compute the monthly and total payments.

3. Output the results.

Having identified the three major tasks of the program, we will now identify the classes we can use to implement the three tasks. First, we need an object to handle the input of three values. Second, we need an object to display the monthly and total payments. For output, we can use either **JOptionPane** or **System.out.** Since we plan to output multiple lines of text, we will use **System.out.** For input, we can use either **JOption-Pane** or **System.in.** If we use **System.in** with **System.out,** then we cannot avoid mixing the echo printing from the input routines with the computation results. We would like to have a clean slate for displaying nicely formatted input values and computation results, so we will choose **JOptionPane** for input. Finally, we need to consider how we are going to compute the monthly and total payments. There are no objects in standard packages that will do the computation, so we have to write our own code.

The formula for computing the monthly payment can be found in any mathematics book that covers geometric sequences. It is

$$\text{Monthly payment} = \frac{L \times R}{1 - [1/(1 + R)]^N}$$

where L is the loan amount, R is the monthly interest rate, and N is the number of payments. The monthly rate R is expressed in a fractional value, for example, 0.01 for 1 percent monthly rate. Once the monthly payment is derived, the total payment can be determined by multiplying the monthly payment by the number of months the payment is made. Since the formula includes exponentiation, we will have to use the **pow** method of the **Math** class.

Let's summarize what we have decided so far in a design document:

program classes

Design Document: `LoanCalculator`	
Class	**Purpose**
`LoanCalculator`	The main class of the program.
`JOptionPane`	The `showInputDialog` of the `JOptionPane` class is used to get three input values: loan amount, annual interest rate, and loan period.
`PrintStream` `(System.out)`	`System.out` is used to display the input values and two computed results: monthly payment and total payment.

Design Document: LoanCalculator *(Continued)*	
Class	**Purpose**
Math	The pow method is used to evaluate exponentiation in the formula for computing the monthly payment. This class is from java.lang. *Note:* You don't have to import java.lang. The classes in java.lang are available to a program without importing.

The program diagram based on the classes listed in the design document is shown in Figure 3.13. Keep in mind that this is only a preliminary design. The preliminary document is really a working document that we will modify and expand as we progress through the development steps.

Before we can actually start our development, we must sketch the steps we will follow to implement the program. There is more than one possible sequence of steps to implement a program, and the number of possible sequences will increase as the program becomes more complex. For this program, we will implement the program in four steps:

develop-
ment steps

1. Start with code to accept three input values.

2. Add code to output the results.

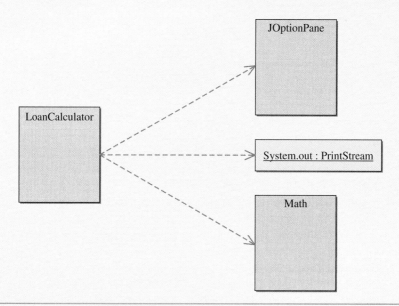

Figure 3.13 The object diagram for the program **LoanCalculator.**

3. Add code to compute the monthly and total payments.

4. Update or modify code and tie up any loose ends.

Notice how the first three steps are ordered. Other orders are possible to develop this program. So why did we choose this particular order? The main reason is our desire to defer the most difficult task until the end. It's possible, but if we implement the computation part in the second incremental step, then we need to code some temporary output routines to verify that the computation is done correctly. However, if we implement the real output routines before implementing the computation routines, then there is no need for us to worry about temporary output routines. As for Step 1 and Step 2, their relative order does not matter much. We simply chose to implement the input routine before the output routine because input comes before output in the program.

Step 1 Development: Input Three Data Values

step 1
design

The next task is to determine how we will accept the input values. We will use the **JOptionPane** class we learned in this chapter. We will call the **showInputDialog** method three times to accept three input values: loan amount, annual interest rate, and loan period. The problem statement does not specify the exact format of input, so we will decide that now. Based on how people normally refer to loans, the input values will be accepted in the following format:

Input	Format	Data Type
Loan amount	In dollars and cents (e.g., 15000.00)	double
Annual interest rate	In percent (e.g., 12.5)	double
Loan period	In years (e.g., 30)	int

Be aware that we need to convert the annual interest rate to the monthly interest rate and the input value loan period to the number of monthly payments, to use the given formula. In this case, the conversion is very simple, but even if the conversion routines were more complicated, we must do the conversion. It is not acceptable to ask users to enter an input value that is unnatural to them. For example, people do not think of interest rates in fractional values such as 0.07. They think of interest in terms of percentages such as 7 percent. Computer programs work for humans, not the other way round. Programs we develop should not support an interface that is difficult and awkward for humans to use.

When the user inputs an invalid value, for example, an input string value that cannot be converted to a numerical value or that converts to a negative number, the program should respond accordingly, such as by printing an error message. We do not possess enough skills to implement such a robust program yet, so we will make the following assumptions: (1) The input values are nonnegative numbers, and (2) the loan period is a whole number.

One important objective of this step is to verify that the input values are read in correctly by the program. To verify this, we will use **System.out** to print out the values accepted by **JOptionPane.** Remember that characters entered by the user via **System.in** are echo-printed in the standard output window. What we are doing here is another form of echo-printing in which our program displays the values entered by the user. Since we are going to use **System.out** in the final program, we will use it for echo printing in this step.

step 1 code

Here's our Step 1 program:

```
/*
    Chapter 3 Sample Development: Loan Calculator   (Step 1)

    File: Step1/Ch3LoanCalculator.java

    Step 1: Input Data Values
*/

import javax.swing.*;

class Ch3LoanCalculator {

    public static void main (String[] args) {
        double  loanAmount,
                annualInterestRate;

        int     loanPeriod;

        String  inputStr;

        //get input values
        inputStr            = JOptionPane.showInputDialog(null,
                                 "Loan Amount (Dollars+Cents):");
        loanAmount          = Double.parseDouble(inputStr);

        inputStr            = JOptionPane.showInputDialog(null,
                                 "Annual Interest Rate (e.g., 9.5):");
        annualInterestRate  = Double.parseDouble(inputStr);

        inputStr            = JOptionPane.showInputDialog(null,
                                  "Loan Period - # of years:");
        loanPeriod          = Integer.parseInt(inputStr);

        //echo print the input values
        System.out.println("Loan Amount:          $" + loanAmount);
        System.out.println("Annual Interest Rate:  "
                                     + annualInterestRate + "%");
        System.out.println("Loan Period (years):  " + loanPeriod);
    }
}
```

3.9   Sample Development—*continued*

step 1 test

To verify the input routine is working correctly, we run the program multiple times and enter different sets of data. We make sure the values are displayed in the standard output window as entered.

Step 2 Development: Output Values

step 2 design

The second step is to add code to display the output values. We will use the standard output window for displaying output values. We need to display the result in a layout that is meaningful and easy to read. Just displaying numbers such as the following is totally unacceptable.

```
132.151.15858.1
```

We must label the output values so the user can tell what the numbers represent. In addition, we must display the input values with the computed result so it will not be meaningless. Which of the two shown in Figure 3.14 do you think is more meaningful? The output format of this program will be

```
For
Loan Amount:              $ <amount>
Annual Interest Rate:     <annual interest rate> %
Loan Period (years):      <year>

Monthly payment is $ <monthly payment>
   TOTAL payment is $ <total payment>
```

with **<amount>, <annual interest rate>,** and others replaced by the actual figures.

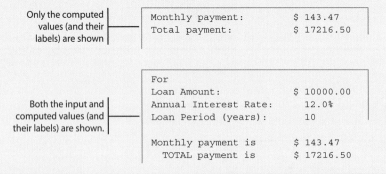

Only the computed values (and their labels) are shown
```
Monthly payment:          $ 143.47
Total payment:            $ 17216.50
```

Both the input and computed values (and their labels) are shown.
```
For
Loan Amount:              $ 10000.00
Annual Interest Rate:     12.0%
Loan Period (years):      10

Monthly payment is        $ 143.47
   TOTAL payment is       $ 17216.50
```

Figure 3.14 Two different display formats: One with input values displayed, and the other with only the computed values displayed.

Since the computations for the monthly and the total payments are not yet implemented, we will use the following dummy assignment statements:

```
monthlyPayment = 135.15;
totalPayment   = 15858.10;
```

We will replace these statements with the real ones in the next step.

step 2 code

Here's our Step 2 program with the newly added portion surrounded by a rectangle and white background:

```
/*
    Chapter 3 Sample Development: Loan Calculator  (Step 2)

    File: Step2/Ch3LoanCalculator.java

    Step 2: Display the Result
*/

import javax.swing.*;

class Ch3LoanCalculator {

    public static void main (String[] args){
        double  loanAmount,
                annualInterestRate;

        double  monthlyPayment,
                totalPayment;

        int     loanPeriod;

        String  inputStr;

        //get input values
        inputStr            = JOptionPane.showInputDialog(null,
                                  "Loan Amount (Dollars+Cents):");
        loanAmount          = Double.parseDouble(inputStr);

        inputStr            = JOptionPane.showInputDialog(null,
                                  "Annual Interest Rate (e.g., 9.5):");
        annualInterestRate  = Double.parseDouble(inputStr);

        inputStr            = JOptionPane.showInputDialog(null,
                                  "Loan Period - # of years:");
        loanPeriod          = Integer.parseInt(inputStr);

        //compute the monthly and total payments
        monthlyPayment = 132.15;
        totalPayment   = 15858.10;
```

```
                  //display the result
                  System.out.println("Loan Amount:              $" + loanAmount);
                  System.out.println("Annual Interest Rate:  "
                                                       + annualInterestRate + "%");
                  System.out.println("Loan Period (years):   " + loanPeriod);

                  System.out.println("\n"); //skip two lines
                  System.out.println("Monthly payment is $ "    + monthlyPayment);
                  System.out.println("  TOTAL payment is $ "    + totalPayment);
        }
    }
```

step 2 test

To verify the output routine is working correctly, we run the program and verify the layout. Most likely, we have to run the program several times to fine-tune the arguments for the **printLine** methods until we get the layout that looks clean and nice on the screen.

Step 3 Development: Compute Loan Amount

step 3
design

We are now ready to complete the program by implementing the formula derived in the design phase. The formula requires the monthly interest rate and the number of monthly payments. The input values to the program, however, are the annual interest rate and the loan period in years. So we need to convert the annual interest rate to a monthly interest rate and the loan period to the number of monthly payments. The two input values are converted as

```
monthlyInterestRate = annualInterestRate / 100.0 / MONTHS_IN_YEAR;

numberOfPayments    = loanPeriod * MONTHS_IN_YEAR;
```

where **MONTHS_IN_YEAR** is a symbolic constant with value **12.** Notice that we need to divide the input annual interest rate by 100 first because the formula for loan computation requires that the interest rate be a fractional value, for example, 0.01, but the input annual interest rate is entered as a percentage point, for example, 12.0. Please read Exercise 23 on page 146 for information on how the monthly interest rate is derived from a given annual interest rate.

The formula for computing the monthly and total payments can be expressed as

```
monthlyPayment = (loanAmount * monthlyInterestRate)
                      /
```

```
                              (1 - Math.pow( 1 /(1 + monthlyInterestRate),
                                             numberOfPayments) );

          totalPayment = monthlyPayment * numberOfPayments;
```

step 3 code   Let's put in the necessary code for the computations and complete the program. Here's our program:

```java
/*
    Chapter 3 Sample Development: Loan Calculator  (Step 3)

    File: Step3/Ch3LoanCalculator.java

    Step 3: Compute the monthly and total payments
*/

import javax.swing.*;

class Ch3LoanCalculator {

    public static void main (String[] args) {

        final int MONTHS_IN_YEAR = 12;

        double  loanAmount,
                annualInterestRate;

        double  monthlyPayment,
                totalPayment;

        double  monthlyInterestRate;

        int     loanPeriod;

        int     numberOfPayments;

        String  inputStr;

        //get input values
        inputStr        = JOptionPane.showInputDialog(null,
                             "Loan Amount (Dollars+Cents):");
        loanAmount      = Double.parseDouble(inputStr);

        inputStr        = JOptionPane.showInputDialog(null,
                             "Annual Interest Rate (e.g., 9.5):");
        annualInterestRate = Double.parseDouble(inputStr);

        inputStr        = JOptionPane.showInputDialog(null,
                             "Loan Period - # of years:");
        loanPeriod      = Integer.parseInt(inputStr);
```

```
//compute the monthly and total payments
monthlyInterestRate = annualInterestRate / MONTHS_IN_YEAR / 100;
numberOfPayments    = loanPeriod * MONTHS_IN_YEAR;

monthlyPayment = (loanAmount * monthlyInterestRate) /
                 (1 - Math.pow(1/(1 + monthlyInterestRate),
                                    numberOfPayments ) );

totalPayment   = monthlyPayment * numberOfPayments;
//display the result
System.out.println("Loan Amount:            $" + loanAmount);
System.out.println("Annual Interest Rate:   "
                                  + annualInterestRate + "%");
System.out.println("Loan Period (years):    " + loanPeriod);

System.out.println("\n"); //skip two lines
System.out.println("Monthly payment is   $ " + monthlyPayment);
System.out.println("  TOTAL payment is   $ " + totalPayment);
    }
}
```

step 3 test

After the program is coded, we need to run the program through a number of tests. Since we made the assumption that the input values must be valid, we will test the program only for valid input values. If we don't make that assumption, then we need to test that the program will respond correctly when invalid values are entered. We will perform such testing beginning in Chapter 5. To check that this program produces correct results, we can run the program with the following input values. The right two columns show the correct results. Try other input values as well.

	Input		Output (shown up to three decimal places only)	
Loan Amount	Annual Interest Rate	Loan Period (Years)	Monthly Payment	Total Payment
10000	10	10	132.151	15858.088
15000	7	15	134.824	24268.363
10000	12	10	143.471	17216.514
0	10	5	0.000	0.000
30	8.5	50	0.216	129.373

Step 4 Development: Finishing Up

step 4
design

We finalize the program in the last step by making any necessary modifications or additions. We will make two additions to the program. The first is necessary while the second is optional but desirable. The first addition is the inclusion of a program description. One of the necessary features of any nontrivial program is the description of what the program does for the user. We will print out a description at the beginning of the program to **System.out.** The second addition is the formatting of the output values. We will format the monthly and total payments to two decimal places, using a **DecimalFormat** object.

step 4 code

Here is our final program:

```java
/*
    Chapter 3 Sample Development: Loan Calculator   (Step 4)

    File: Step4/Ch3LoanCalculator.java

    Step 4: Finalize the program

*/

import javax.swing.*;

import java.text.*;

class Ch3LoanCalculator {

    public static void main (String[] args) {

        final int MONTHS_IN_YEAR = 12;

        double  loanAmount,
                annualInterestRate;

        double  monthlyPayment,
                totalPayment;

        double  monthlyInterestRate;

        int     loanPeriod;

        int     numberOfPayments;

        String  inputStr;

    DecimalFormat df = new DecimalFormat("0.00");
```

3.9 **Sample Development**—*continued*

```
//describe the program
System.out.println("This program computes the monthly and total");
System.out.println("payments for a given loan amount, annual ");
System.out.println("interest rate, and loan period.");
System.out.println("Loan amount in dollars and cents,
                                           e.g., 12345.50");
System.out.println("Annual interest rate in percentage e.g., 12.75");
System.out.println("Loan period in number of years, e.g., 15");
System.out.println("\n"); //skip two lines
```

```
//get input values
inputStr          = JOptionPane.showInputDialog(null,
                         "Loan Amount (Dollars+Cents):");
loanAmount        = Double.parseDouble(inputStr);

inputStr          = JOptionPane.showInputDialog(null,
                         "Annual Interest Rate (e.g., 9.5):");
annualInterestRate = Double.parseDouble(inputStr);

inputStr          = JOptionPane.showInputDialog(null,
                         "Loan Period - # of years:");
loanPeriod        = Integer.parseInt(inputStr);

//compute the monthly and total payments
monthlyInterestRate = annualInterestRate / MONTHS_IN_YEAR / 100;
numberOfPayments    = loanPeriod * MONTHS_IN_YEAR;

monthlyPayment = (loanAmount * monthlyInterestRate) /
                   (1 - Math.pow(1/(1 + monthlyInterestRate),
                                      numberOfPayments ) );

totalPayment   =  monthlyPayment * numberOfPayments;

//display the result
System.out.println("Loan Amount:           $" + loanAmount);
System.out.println("Annual Interest Rate:  "
                              + annualInterestRate + "%");
System.out.println("Loan Period (years):   " + loanPeriod);

System.out.println("\n"); //skip two lines
```

```
System.out.println("Monthly payment is    $ "
                              + df.format(monthlyPayment));
System.out.println("  TOTAL payment is    $ "
                              + df.format(totalPayment));
```

```
    }
}
```

step 4 test

We repeat the test runs from Step 3 and confirm the modified program still runs correctly. Since we have not made any substantial additions or modifications, we fully expect the program to work correctly. However, it is very easy to introduce errors in coding so even if we think the changes are trivial, we should never skip the testing after even a slight modification.

Helpful Reminder

Always test after making any additions or modifications to a program, no matter how trivial you think the changes are.

3.10 | Numerical Representation (Optional)

twos
complement

In this section we explain how integers and real numbers are stored in memory. Although computer manufacturers have used various formats for storing numerical values, today's standard is to use the *twos complement* format for storing integers and the *floating-point* format for real numbers. We describe these formats in this section.

An integer can occupy 1, 2, 4, or 8 bytes depending on which data type (i.e., byte, short, int, or long) is declared. To make the examples easy to follow, we will use 1 byte (= 8 bits) to explain twos complement form. The same principle applies to 2, 4, and 8 bytes. (They just utilize more bits.)

The following table shows the first five and the last four of the 256 positive binary numbers using 8 bits. The right column lists their decimal equivalents.

8-Bit Binary Number	Decimal Equivalent
00000000	0
00000001	1
00000010	2
00000011	3
00000100	4
. . .	
11111100	252
11111101	253
11111110	254
11111111	255

sign bit

Using 8 bits, we can represent positive integers from 0 to 255. Now let's see the possible range of negative and positive numbers that we can represent, using 8 bits. We can designate the leftmost bit as a *sign bit*: 0 means positive and 1 means negative. Using this scheme, we can represent integers from -127 to $+127$ as shown in the following table:

8-Bit Binary Number (with a Sign Bit)	Decimal Equivalent
0 0000000	+0
0 0000001	+1
0 0000010	+2
...	
0 1111111	+127
1 0000000	−0
1 0000001	−1
...	
1 1111110	−126
1 1111111	−127

Notice that zero has two distinct representations ($+0 = 00000000$ and $-0 = 10000000$), which adds complexity in hardware design. Twos complement format avoids this problem of duplicate representations for zero. In twos complement format all positive numbers have zero in their leftmost bit. The representation of a negative number is derived by first inverting all the bits (changing 1s to 0s and 0s to 1s) in the representation of the positive number and then adding 1. The following diagram illustrates the process:

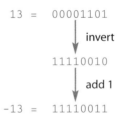

```
13  =   00001101
              |  invert
              ▼
        11110010
              |  add 1
              ▼
-13  =   11110011
```

The following table shows the decimal equivalents of 8-bit binary numbers by using twos complement representation. Notice that zero has only one representation.

8-Bit Binary Number (Twos Complement)	Decimal Equivalent
00000000	+0
00000001	+1
00000010	+2
...	
01111111	+127
10000000	−128
10000001	−127
...	
11111110	−2
11111111	−1

Now let's see how real numbers are stored in memory in floating-point format. We will present only the basic ideas of storing real numbers in computer memory here. We will omit the precise details of the Institute of Electronics and Electrical Engineers (IEEE) Standard 754 that Java uses to store real numbers.

Real numbers are represented in the computer by using scientific notation. In base-10 scientific notation, a real number is expressed as

$$A \times 10^N$$

where A is a real number and N is an integral exponent. For example, the mass of a hydrogen atom (in grams) is expressed in decimal scientific notation as 1.67339×10^{-24}, which is equal to 0.00000000000000000000000167339.

We use base-2 scientific notation to store real numbers in computer memory. Base-2 scientific notation represents a real number as

$$A \times 2^N$$

The float and double data types use 32 and 64 bits, respectively, with the number A and exponent N stored as

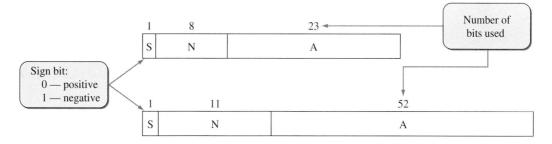

The value A is a *normalized fraction*, where the fraction begins with a binary point, followed by a 1 bit, and the rest of the fraction. (*Note:* A decimal number has a decimal point; a binary number has a binary point.) The following numbers are sample normalized and unnormalized binary fractions:

normalized fraction

Normalized	Unnormalized
1.1010100	1.100111
1.100011	.0000000001
1.101110011	.0001010110

Since a normalized number always start with a 1, this bit does not actually have to be stored. The following diagram illustrates how the A value is stored.

excess format

The sign bit S indicates the sign of a number, so A is stored in memory as an unsigned number. The integral exponent N can be negative or positive. Instead of using twos complement for storing N, we use a format called *excess format*. The 8-bit exponent uses the excess-127 format, and the 11-bit exponent uses the excess-1023 format. We will explain the excess-127 format here. The excess-1023 works similarly. With the excess-127 format, the actual exponent is computed as

$$N - 127$$

Therefore, the number 127 represents an exponent of zero. Numbers less than 127 represent negative exponents, and numbers greater than 127 represent positive exponents. The following diagram illustrates that the number 125 in the exponent field represents $2^{125-127} = 2^{-2}$.

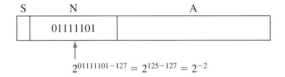

Summary

- A variable is a memory location in which to store a value.
- A variable has a name and a data type.
- A variable must be declared before we can assign a value to it.
- There are six numerical data types in Java: byte, short, int, long, float, and double.
- Object names are synonymous with variables whose contents are memory addresses.
- Numerical data types are called primitive data types, and objects are called reference data types.
- Precedence rules determine the order of evaluating arithemetic expressions.
- Symbolic constants hold values just as variables do, but we cannot change their values.
- The standard classes introduced in this chapter are

Math	InputStream
GregorianCalendar	InputStreamReader
DecimalFormat	BufferedReader
PrintStream	IOException
Integer, Double, etc.	

- We use methods from the wrapper classes Integer, Double, and others to convert an input string to a numerical value.

- System.out is used to output multiple lines of text to the standard output window.

- System.in is used to input a stream of bytes. We associate a BufferedReader object to System.in (with an intermediate InputStreamReader) to input one line of text at at time.

- The Math class contains many class methods for mathematical functions.

- The GregorianCalendar class is used in the manipulation of calendar information.

- The DecimalFormat class is used to format the numerical data.

- (Optional) Twos complement format is used for storing integers, and floating-pointing format is used for storing real numbers.

Key Concepts

variables	constants
primitive data types	string-to-number conversion
reference data types	standard output
arithmetic expression	standard input
arithmetic operators	thrown exceptions
precedence rules	echo printing
type casting	twos complement (optional)
implicit and explicit casting	floating point (optional)
assignment conversion	

Exercises

1. Suppose we have the following declarations:

```
int i = 3, j = 4, k = 5;
float x = 34.5f, y = 12.25f;
```

Determine the value for each of the following expressions, or explain why it is not a valid expression.

a. `(x + 1.5) / (250.0 * (i/j))`   f. `Math.exp(3, 2)`
b. `x + 1.5 / 250.0 * i / j`   g. `y % x`
c. `-x * -y * (i + j) / k`   h. `Math.pow(3, 2)`
d. `(i / 5) * y`   i. `(int)y % k`
e. `Math.min(i, Math.min(j,k))`   j. `i / 5 * y`

2. Suppose we have the following declarations:

```
int m, n, i = 3, j = 4, k = 5;
float v, w, x = 34.5f, y = 12.25f;
```

Determine the value assigned to the variable in each of the following assignment statements, or explain why it is not a valid assignment.

a. `w = Math.pow(3,Math.pow(i,j));`

b. `v = x / i;`

c. `w = Math.ceil(y) % k;`

d. `n = (int) x / y * i / 2;`

e. `x = Math.sqrt(i*i - 4*j*k);`

f. `m = n + i * j;`

g. `n = k /(j * i) * x + y;`

h. `i = i + 1;`

i. `w = float(x + i);`

j. `x = x / i / y / j;`

3. Suppose we have the following declarations:

```
int    i, j;
float  x, y;
double u, v;
```

Which of the following assignments are valid?

a. `i = x;`

b. `x = u + y;`

c. `x = 23.4 + j * y;`

d. `v = (int) x;`

e. `y = j / i * x;`

4. Write Java expressions to compute each of the following:

a. The square root of $B^2 + 4AC$ (A and C are distinct variables)

b. The square root of $X + 4Y^3$

c. The cube root of the product of X and Y

d. The area πR^2 of a circle

5. Determine the output of the following program without running it:

```
class TestOutputBox {
    public static void main (String[] args) {

        System.out.println("One");
        System.out.print("Two");
        System.out.print("\n");

        System.out.print("Three");
        System.out.println("Four");
        System.out.print("\n");

        System.out.print("Five");
        System.out.println("Six");
    }

}
```

6. Determine the output of the following code:

```
int x, y;
x = 1;
y = 2;
System.out.println("The output is " + x + y );
System.out.println("The output is " + (x + y) );
```

7. Write an application that displays the following pattern in the standard output window:

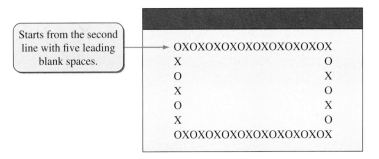

Note: The output window is not drawn to scale.

8. Write an application to convert centimeters (input) to feet and inches (output). Use JOptionPane for input and output. 1 inch = 2.54 centimeters.

9. Write an application that inputs temperature in degrees Celsius and prints out the temperature in degrees Fahrenheit. Use System.in for input and System.out for output. The formula to convert degrees Celsius to the equivalent degrees Fahrenheit is

$$\text{Fahrenheit} = 1.8 \times \text{Celsius} + 32$$

10. Write an application that accepts a person's weight and displays the number of calories the person needs in one day. A person needs 19 calories per pound of body weight, so the formula expressed in Java is

```
calories = bodyWeight * 19;
```

Use JOptionPane for input and output. (*Note:* We are not distinguishing between genders.)

11. A quantity known as the *body mass index* (BMI) is used to calculate the risk of weight-related health problems. BMI is computed by the formula

$$\text{BMI} = \frac{w}{\left(\dfrac{h}{100.0}\right)^2}$$

where w is weight in kilograms and h is height in centimeters. A BMI of about 20 to 25 is considered "normal." Write an application that accepts weight and height (both integers) and outputs the BMI. Use System.in for input and System.out for output.

12. Your weight is actually the amount of gravitational attraction exerted on you by the earth. Since the moon's gravity is only one-sixth of the earth's gravity, on the moon you would weigh only one-sixth of what you weigh on earth. Write an application that inputs the user's earth weight and outputs her or his weight on Mercury, Venus, Jupiter, and Saturn. Use your preferred choice for input and output. Use the values in this table.

Planet	Multiply the Earth Weight by
Mercury	0.4
Venus	0.9
Jupiter	2.5
Saturn	1.1

13. When you say you are 18 years old, you are really saying that the earth has circled the sun 18 times. Since other planets take fewer or more days than earth to travel around the sun, your age would be different on other planets. You can compute how old you are on other planets by the formula

$$y = \frac{x \times 365}{d}$$

where x is the age on the earth, y is the age on planet Y, and d is the number of earth days the planet Y takes to travel around the sun. Write an application that inputs the user's earth age and print outs his or her age on Mercury, Venus, Jupiter, and Saturn. Use your preferred choice for input and output. The values for d are listed in the table.

Planet	d = Approximate Number of Earth Days for This Planet to Travel Around the Sun
Mercury	88
Venus	225
Jupiter	4380
Saturn	10767

14. Write an application to solve quadratic equations of the form

$$Ax^2 + Bx + C = 0$$

where the coefficients A, B, and C are real numbers. The two real number solutions are derived by the formula

$$x = \frac{-B \pm \sqrt{B^2 - 4AC}}{2A}$$

For this exercise, you may assume that $A \neq 0$ and the relationship

$$B^2 \geq 4AC$$

holds, so there will be real number solutions for x. Use the standard input and output.

15. Write an application that determines the number of days in a given semester. Input to the program is the year, month, and day information of the first and the last days of a semester. *Hint:* Create GregorianCalendar objects for the start and end dates of a semester and manipulate their DAY_OF_YEAR data.

16. Modify the Ch3FindDayOfWeek program by accepting the date information as a single string instead of accepting the year, month, and day information separately. The input string must be in the MM/dd/yyyy format. For example, July 4, 1776, is entered as 07/04/1776. There will be exactly two digits for the month and day and four digits for the year.

17. Write an application that accepts the unit weight of a bag of coffee in pounds and the number of bags sold and displays the total price of the sale, computed as

```
totalPrice        = unitWeight * numberOfUnits * 5.99;
totalPriceWithTax = totalPrice + totalPrice * 0.0725;
```

where **5.99** is the cost per pound and **0.0725** is the sales tax. Display the result in the following manner:

```
Number of bags sold:   32
   Weight per bag:   5 lb
   Price per pound:   $5.99
       Sales tax:   7.25%

      Total price: $ 1027.884
```

Use JOptionPane for input and System.out for output. Draw the program diagram.

18. If you invest P dollars at R percent interest rate compounded annually, in N years, your investment will grow to

$$\frac{P[1-(R/100)^{N+1}]}{1-R/100}$$

dollars. Write an application that accepts P, R, and N and computes the amount of money earned after N years. Use JOptionPane for input and output.

19. Leonardo Fibonacci of Pisa was one of the greatest mathematicians of the Middle Ages. He is perhaps most famous for the Fibonacci sequence that can be applied to many diverse problems. One amusing application of the

Fibonacci sequence is in finding the growth rate of rabbits. Suppose a pair of rabbits matures in 2 months and is capable of reproducing another pair every month after maturity. If every new pair has the same capability, how many pairs will there be after 1 year? (We assume here that no pairs die.) The table below shows the sequence for the first 7 months. Notice that at the end of the second month, the first pair matures and bears its first offspring in the third month, making the total two pairs.

Month No.	Number of Pairs
1	1
2	1
3	2
4	3
5	5
6	8
7	13

The Nth Fibonacci number in the sequence can be evaluated with the formula

$$F_N = \frac{1}{\sqrt{5}}\left[\left(\frac{1+\sqrt{5}}{2}\right)^N - \left(\frac{1-\sqrt{5}}{2}\right)^N\right]$$

Write an application that accepts N and displays F_N. Note that the result of computation using the Math class is double. You need to display it as an integer. Use JOptionPane for input and output.

20. According to Newton's universal law of gravitation, the force F between two bodies with masses M_1 and M_2 is computed as

$$F = k\left(\frac{M_1 M_2}{d^2}\right)$$

where d is the distance between the two bodies and k is a positive real number called the *gravitational constant*. The gravitational constant k is approximately equal to 6.67E-8 dyn · cm²/g². Write an application that accepts the mass for two bodies in grams and the distance between the two bodies in centimeters, and compute the force F. Use the standard input and output, and format the output appropriately. For your information, the force between the earth and the moon is 1.984E25 dyn. The mass of the earth is 5.983E27 g, the mass of the moon is 7.347E25 g, and the distance between the two is 3.844E10 cm.

21. Dr. Caffeine's Law of Program Readability states that the degree of program readability R (whose unit is *mocha*) is determined as

$$R = k \cdot \frac{CT^2}{V^3}$$

where k is Ms. Latte's constant, C is the number of lines in the program that contain comments, T is the time spent (in minutes) by the programmer developing the program, and V is the number of lines in the program that contain nondescriptive variable names. Write an application to compute the program readability R. Use your preferred choice for input and output. Ms. Latte's constant is 2.5E2 mocha lines^2/min^2. (*Note:* This is just for fun. Develop your own law, using various functions from the Math class.)

22. If the population of a country grows according to the formula

$$y = ce^{kx}$$

where y is the population after x years from the reference year, then we can determine the population of a country for a given year from two census figures. For example, given that a country with a population of 1,000,000 in 1970 grows to 2,000,000 by 1990, we can predict the country's population in the year 2000. Here's how we do the computation. Letting x be the number of years after 1970, we obtain the constant c as 1,000,000 because

$$1,000,000 = ce^{k0} = c$$

Then we determine the value of k as

$$y = 1,000,000e^{kx}$$

$$\frac{2,000,000}{1,000,000} = e^{20k}$$

$$k = \frac{1}{20} \ln \frac{2,000,000}{1,000,000} \approx 0.03466$$

Finally we can predict the population in the year 2000 by substituting 0.03466 for k and 30 for x (2000 − 1970 = 30). Thus, we predict

$$y = 1,000,000e^{0.03466(30)} \approx 2,828,651$$

as the population of the country for the year 2000. Write an application that accepts five input values—year A, population in year A, year B, population in year B, and year C—and predict the population for year C. Use any technique for input and output.

23. In Section 3.9, we use the formula

$$MR = \frac{AR}{12}$$

to derive the monthly interest rate from a given annual interest rate, where MR is the monthly interest rate and AR is the annual interest rate (expressed in a fractional value such as 0.083). This annual interest rate AR is called the *stated annual interest rate* to distinguish it from the *effective annual interest rate*, which is the true cost of a loan. If the stated annual interest rate is 9 percent, for example, then the effective annual interest rate is actually 9.38 percent. Naturally, the rate that the financial institutions advertise more prominently is the stated interest rate. The loan calculator program in

Section 3.9 treats the annual interest rate that the user enters as the stated annual interest rate. If the input is the effective annual interest rate, then we compute the monthly rate as

$$MR = (1 + EAR)^{1/12} - 1$$

where EAR is the effective annual interest rate. The difference between the stated and effective annual interest rates is negligible only when the loan amount is small or the loan period is short. Modify the loan calculator program so that the interest rate that the user enters is treated as the effective annual interest rate. Run the original and modified loan calculator programs, and compare the differences in the monthly and total payments. Use the loan amount of 1, 10, and 50 million dollars with the loan period of 10, 20, and 30 years and the annual interest rates of 0.07, 0.10, and 0.18, respectively. Try other combinations also.

Visit several websites that provide a loan calculator for computing a monthly mortgage payment (one such site is the financial page at www.cnn.com). Compare your results to the values computed by the websites you visited. Determine whether the websites treat the input annual interest rate as stated or effective.

Development Exercises

For the following exercises, use the incremental development methodology to implement the program. For each exercise, identify the program tasks, create a design document with class descriptions, and draw the program diagram. Map out the development steps at the start. State any assumptions you must make about the input. Present any design alternatives and justify your selection. Be sure to perform adequate testing at the end of each development step.

24. Develop an application that reads a purchase price and an amount tendered and then displays the change in dollars, quarters, dimes, nickels, and pennies. Two input values are entered in cents, for example, 3480 for $34.80 and 70 for $0.70. Use any appropriate technique for input and output. Display the output in the following format:

```
 Purchase Price: $ 34.80
Amount Tendered: $ 40.00

 Your change is: $ 5.20

                    5 one-dollar bill(s)
                    0 quarter(s)
                    2 dime(s)
                    0 nickel(s)
                    0 penn(y/ies)

Thank you for your business. Come back soon.
```

Notice the input values are to be entered in cents (int data type), but the echo-printed values must be displayed with decimal points (float data type).

25. MyJava Coffee Outlet runs a catalog business. It sells only one type of coffee beans, harvested exclusively in the remote area of Irian Jaya. The company sells the coffee in 2-lb bags only, and the price of a single 2-lb bag is $5.50. When a customer places an order, the company ships the order in boxes. The boxes come in three sizes: the large box holds twenty 2-lb bags, the medium 10 bags, and the small 5 bags. The cost of a large box is $2.00; a medium box, $1.00; and a small box, $0.50. The order is shipped using the least number of boxes with the cheapest cost. For example, the order of 25 bags will be shipped in two boxes, one large and one small. Develop an application that computes the total cost of an order. Use any appropriate technique for input and output. Display the output in the following format:

```
Number of Bags Ordered: 52 - $ 286.00

Boxes Used:
            2 Large  - $4.00
            1 Medium - $1.00
            1 Small  - $0.50

Your total cost is: $ 291.50
```

26. Repeat exercise 25, but this time, accept the date when the order is placed and display the expected date of arrival. The expected date of arrival is two weeks (14 days) from the date of order. The order date is entered as a single string in the *MM/dd/yyyy* format. For example, November 1, 2002 is entered as 11/01/2002. There will be exactly two digits for the month and day and four digits for the year. Display the output in the following format:

```
Number of Bags Ordered: 52 - $ 286.00

Boxes Used:
            2 Large  - $4.00
            1 Medium - $1.00
            1 Small  - $0.50

Your total cost is: $ 291.50

Date of Order:              November 1, 2002
Expected Date of Arrival:   November 15, 2002
```

27. Using a Turtle object from the galapagos package (see exercise 23 on page 82), draw three rectangles. Use JOptionPane to accept the width and the length of

the smallest rectangle from the user. The middle and the largest rectangles are 40 and 80 percent larger than the smallest rectangle. The galapagos package and its documentation are available at www.drcaffeine.com.

28. Develop a program that draws a bar chart using a Turtle object (see exercise 23 on page 82). Input five int values and draw the vertical bars that represent the entered values in the following manner:

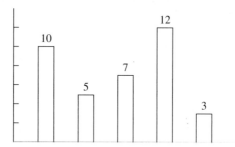

Your Turtle must draw everything shown in the diagram, including the axes and numbers. Use any suitable approach for input.

4 Defining Your Own Classes

Objectives

After you have read and studied this chapter, you should be able to

- Define an instantiable class with multiple methods and constructors.

- Differentiate the local and instance variables.

- Define and use value-returning methods.

- Distinguish private and public methods.

- Distinguish private and public data members.

- Describe how the arguments are passed to the parameters in method definitions.

- Describe how the result is returned from a method.

- Define a reusable class for handling input routines.

- Define an instantiable main class.

The sample application programs we have written so far included only one class, the main class of the program. And the main class contained only one method, the main method. From this main method, we used only objects from the standard packages such as javax.swing and java.util. For very small programs, this arrangement may be acceptable. But for large programs, it is not. We cannot develop large application programs in a similar manner for two reasons:

1. Placing all programming code for a large application in a single method main makes the method very huge and impossible to manage.

2. Predefined classes alone cannot satisfy all our programming needs in writing a large application.

Even for the simple LoanCalculator program in Chapter 3 the size of its main method is approaching the limit that can be considered acceptable. We don't write a program whose main method is 10 pages long. A large program that is properly built will include many classes—some are predefined and others are defined by us—and each of these classes will include many methods.

Learning how to define your own classes is the first step toward mastering the skills necessary in building large programs. In this chapter we will learn how to define *instantiable classes* and different types of methods included in the instantiable classes. A class is instantiable if we can create instances of the class. The DecimalFormat, GregorianCalendar, and String classes are all instantiable classes while the Math class is not.

instantiable class

Take my *Advice*

Many new concepts will be introduced in this chapter because we want to give you a full and complete picture. Instead of scattering the related topics throughout the book, we present all the core topics of defining a class in this chapter, so you will be able to find the necessary materials in one place. We do not expect you to remember or memorize every rule we present here completely before moving on to the following chapters. You will develop deeper and better understanding and appreciation of the materials we teach here as you study the rest of the book and develop your own programs. When you study this chapter, focus on the key ideas by going over the sample programs carefully. Follow the pattern, a style of programming, presented in them when writing your own programs. When you encounter a problem in your program whose cause you cannot easily discern, this chapter is one of the first places you want to revisit, to check the rules presented in the chapter.

4.1 | Defining Instantiable Classes

Suppose we want to write a program that converts Japanese yen to U.S. dollars and vice versa. What kinds of objects are necessary? Well, we can do a simple input and output with JOptionPane. But what about the conversion process? Is there any class in the standard Java packages that does currency conversion? No. There is a possibility that such class is already defined by others and made available to us free of charge or with a nominal fee. If that's the case, then we prefer to use the class already defined (and tested). However, it is unrealistic of us to expect to be able to find predefined classes for all our computing needs every time. The simple fact in object-oriented programming is that we cannot avoid developing our own instantiable classes in implementing nontrivial programs.

As an illustration for defining instantiable classes, we will define a class called CurrencyConverter. Through this example, we will provide you the basics of defining instantiable classes. We will cover only the very basics in this section. We will provide in the remainder of the chapter a more detailed explanation of the basic features introduced here.

When we design our own class, we start with the specification for the class. We must decide how we want to interact with the class and its instances. We must decide what kinds of instance and class methods the class should support. We will design the class so that we can use it in a way that is natural and logical. Let's start with one possible design. After we design the class, we will discuss an alternative way to design the class.

How should a CurrencyConverter object behave? What would be a natural and logical way for us to interact with it? Since we want the object to be able to do the conversion between a foreign currency and the U.S. dollar, let's define two methods, one for converting U.S. dollars to the equivalent amount in the foreign currency and the other for the reverse transaction. Let's call these methods fromDollar and toDollar. To convert $200 U.S. to Japanese yen, for example, we will have to write something like this:

```
CurrencyConverter    yenConverter;
double               amountInYen, amountInDollar;

yenConverter = new CurrencyConverter();
...
amountInYen  = yenConverter.fromDollar( 200 );
                                              //from dollar
                                              //to yen
```

And to convert ¥15,000 to U.S. dollars, we will write

```
amountInDollar = yenConverter.toDollar( 15000 );
                                       //from yen to dollar
```

Since the exchange rate fluctuates, we need a method, say, setExchangeRate, to set the exchange rate before doing the conversion. Assuming the exchange rate is

¥118.65 for $1.00 U.S., we will do the conversion as

```
CurrencyConverter   yenConverter;
double              amountInYen, amountInDollar;

yenConverter      = new CurrencyConverter();
yenConverter.setExchangeRate(118.65);

amountInYen       = yenConverter.fromDollar( 200 );
amountInDollar    = yenConverter.toDollar( 15000 );
```

Once the class is defined, we can easily create additional CurrencyConverter objects for other currencies. For example, if we want to convert U.S. dollars into euro and Japanese yen, then we can do the following:

```
CurrencyConverter   yenConverter, euroConverter;
double              amountInYen, amountInEuro;

yenConverter      = new CurrencyConverter();
yenConverter.setExchangeRate(118.65);

euroConverter     = new CurrencyConverter( );
euroConverter.setExchangeRate(0.926);

amountInYen       = yenConverter.fromDollar( 200 );
amountInEuro      = euroConverter.fromDollar( 200 );
```

Because any currency can be converted to a dollar equivalent and vice versa, we can do the conversion between two currencies other than the U.S. dollar, for example, between Japanese yen and euro. For example, to convert ¥10,000 to the equivalent euro, we convert first the yen to dollars and then the dollars to euro, as in

```
amountInDollar= yenConverter.toDollar( 10000 );
amountInEuro  = euroConverter.fromDollar(amountInDollar);
```

Being able to do a conversion easily between any two currencies is a direct benefit of defining a separate class for currency conversion.

A CurrencyConverter object has three methods: setExchangeRate, toDollar, and fromDollar. Its class diagram (at this point) is

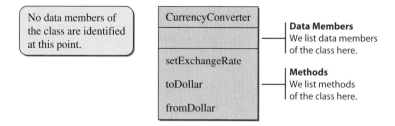

Alternative Design for CurrencyConverter

We gave one possible design for the CurrencyConverter class. Is there any alternative design? The way the class is implemented, we must create a new instance of each foreign currency for which we want to do a conversion. Another possibility is to design the class so that one instance of the class can handle conversions for more than one foreign currency. We won't get into any more details here because we do not yet have the necessary programming skills to implement this alternative design.

Suppose we know how to implement the alternative design of Currency-Converter. Which design alternative is better? When we design a class, we must always consider alternative designs to select the one most appropriate for a given program. Whether one design is better than the other depends on how the class is used in programs. Unlike in the engineering disciplines, we do not have a formula to measure the effectiveness of a software. Instead of mathematical formulas, we have design guidelines we can follow in designing classes. One such guideline is to keep the class simple. Whenever appropriate in the remainder of the book, we will mention the design alternatives for the classes used in the sample programs and discuss their pros and cons.

The CurrencyConverter **Class**

data members

Let's implement the class, using the first design. Figure 4.1 is a template for defining a class. In this class, we need to define three methods—setExchangeRate, toDollar, and fromDollar—and any data values used by these methods. We call the data values for the class *data members,* which include class and instance variables and constants. We will first identify the data members of the class and then define the three methods. We will explain the rules for defining the data members and methods along the way.

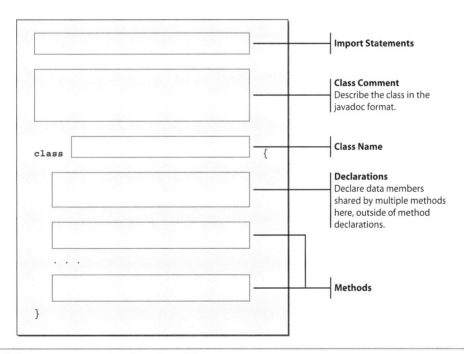

Figure 4.1 A program template for a class definition.

What kind of data members does a CurrencyConverter object need in order for the object to carry out the conversion task? To do the conversion, the object must keep track of the exchange rate. This exchange rate is used by the two methods toDollar and fromDollar. What will be the data type for the exchange rate? The data type int is not acceptable because we expect the rate will include decimal places. So the data type should be either float or double, but which? Since the magnitude of the number is small, float seems adequate. However, to maintain the higher accuracy for conversion where the exchange rate may include more than five or six decimal places, we will use the data type double for the exchange rate.

You Might Want to Know

There were times when computer memory was very expensive. In those days, the main memory size was something like 64K (*note:* 128 Mb memory, which is common for today's desktop PC, is 2000 times larger than 64K memory), so the memory was a precious commodity. To run a program in such an environment, we used data type **float** to save space, unless data type **double** was really necessary. In today's computing environment, with an abundance of memory, there isn't much to gain by using **float** instead of **double**. For example, representing 25 real numbers as **float** requires 100 bytes while doing the same using **double** requires 200 bytes. Saving of 100 bytes is insignificant and negligible today. Using **double** is more of a standard in Java, and in this book, **double** will be a preferred data type for representing real numbers.

Here's the partial class declaration with the variable exchangeRate declared as data type double:

```
/**
 * This class is used to do the currency conversion
 * between a foreign currency and the U.S. dollar.
 *
 * @author Dr. Caffeine
 */
class CurrencyConverter {

    /**
     * how much $1.00 U.S. is worth in the foreign currency
     */
    private double exchangeRate;

    //method declarations come here

}
```

Notice that we are using here the javadoc style comment introduced in Chapter 2 to describe the class and its one data member, exchangeRate. Starting from this chapter, we will gradually introduce the elements of javadoc comments. The javadoc comments begin with the marker /** and end with the marker */. The asterisks on the lines between the first and the last markers have no significance; they are there to provide a visual aid to highlight the comments in the program. It is an accepted standard to use the asterisks in this manner for the javadoc comments.

javadoc tags

Inside the javadoc comments, we can use a number of *javadoc tags,* special markers that begin with the @ mark. In this example, we see one javadoc tag @author, which we use to list the authors of the class. We will introduce other javadoc tags later in the chapter.

@author tag

For more information on javadoc, please visit
http://java.sun.com/j2se/javadoc/writingdoccomments/index.html

www

instance variable

The variable exchangeRate is declared within the class declaration, but outside of any method of the class. The variable exchangeRate is an *instance variable,* which is equivalent to the term *instance data value* we used in Chapter 1. Every object of the class will have its own copy of an instance variable. Figure 4.2 shows that three CurrencyConverter objects have their own copy of exchangeRate.

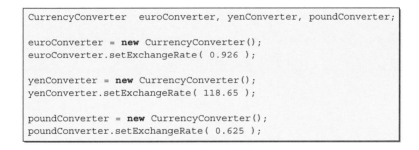

```
CurrencyConverter  euroConverter, yenConverter, poundConverter;

euroConverter = new CurrencyConverter();
euroConverter.setExchangeRate( 0.926 );

yenConverter = new CurrencyConverter();
yenConverter.setExchangeRate( 118.65 );

poundConverter = new CurrencyConverter();
poundConverter.setExchangeRate( 0.625 );
```

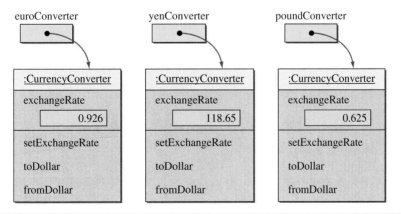

Figure 4.2 Every object of a class has its own copy of instance variables. **CurrencyConverter** objects have their own copy of the **exchangeRate** instance variable.

Notice the use of the reserved word private in declaring exchangeRate. This modifier is called a *visibility modifier,* and it specifies the visibility, or accessibility, of the data members and methods. Another visibility modifier is public. The full explanation of the visibility modifier will require a whole section, so we will defer its discussion until Section 4.3. For now, it suffices to know that the data type for exchangeRate is double.

Now let's study how the methods are defined. We will start with the setExchangeRate method. Its purpose is to set the instance variable exchangeRate to the value passed to the method. The method is declared as

```
public void setExchangeRate( double rate ) {

    exchangeRate = rate;
}
```

The syntax for defining a method, as given in Chapter 2, is

```
<modifiers> <return type> <method name> ( <parameters> ) {

    <statements>
}
```

Take my Advice

Is it really important to use javadoc comments? It's true that we have to learn a few extra items to use javadoc comments, but the benefits warrant a little extra effort. First, by using javadoc comments, we can easily produce the standard online documentation. Even if we don't have an immediate need to produce an online documentation, we can use javadoc comments because they are really not that different from other styles of commenting, and their use gives us an option to produce an online documentation later. Second, since javadoc is a standard, other programmers will have an easier time reading your code with javadoc comments than reading code with a nonstandard style of comments.

The following diagram shows how the components in the general syntax correspond to the actual elements in the exchangeRate method:

```
        Return Type ⊢               ⊢ Method Name
   Modifier ⊢                                     ⊢ Parameter
      ___        ___      _____      _____
     public    void    setExchangeRate    ( double rate ) {
        ┌──────────────────────────────┐
        ⌐ exchangeRate = rate;          ⌐─⊢ Statements
        └──────────────────────────────┘
     }
```

Since the method returns no value, it is declared as void. Notice that the method has no static modifier. If the method declaration includes the static modifier, then it is a class method. If the method declaration does not include the static modifier, then it is an instance method.

Helpful Reminder

Instance methods are declared without the **static** *modifier. Class methods are declared with the* **static** *modifier.*

We must declare the setExchangeRate method as an instance method because class methods cannot access instance variables, but this method needs to access the instance variable exchangeRate. Class methods can access only the class variables and constants, while the instance methods can access them in addition to the instance variables.

Helpful Reminder

Class methods can access class variables and constants but not instance variables. Instance methods can access all types of data members.

When we define an instantiable class, we are in essence defining how the instances of the class will behave. So it makes sense that the methods we define for the class are instance methods. There are times when a class method is useful and necessary, but for the most part, when we define an instantiable class, we will define the instance methods almost exclusively. We will describe the use of class methods for the instantiable classes later in the book.

The visibility modifier public designates the setExchangeRate method as accessible from outside methods. If two methods belong to different classes, then they are *outside methods* relative to each other. If this method is declared private, then we will not be able to call the method from outside, as in

outside
method

```
class TestProgram {

    public static void main (String[] args) {

        CurrencyConverter yenConverter;
        yenConverter = new CurrencyConverter();

        yenConverter.setExchangeRate( 118.65 );
        ...
    }
}
```

This call is valid if the
method is declared **public**
and invalid if the method
is declared **private**.

Since all three methods are intended to be called from the outside methods, the three methods are all declared public.

As a part of class documentation, we include a *method header comment* to every method to describe the method. A typical method header comment in javadoc looks something like this:

method header comment

```
/**
  * Converts a given amount in dollars into
  * an equivalent amount in a foreign currency.
  *
  * @param dollar the amount in dollars to be converted
  *
  * @return amount in foreign currency
  */
```

In the method header comment, we record the method's purpose, a list of parameters passed to the method, and the value returned from the method. For the list of parameters, we attach a short description of each parameter in addition to the parameter's name. Each parameter is marked by the @param javadoc *tag*. Its syntax is

@param tag

```
@param <parameter name> <description>
```

The <description> portion can go beyond one line. If the method returns a value, then we add the @return javadoc *tag*. Its syntax is

@return tag

```
@return <description>
```

To save space, we will show the javadoc method comments only in the final listing of the class.

Now let's move on to the second method. The toDollar method accepts an amount in a foreign currency and returns the equivalent amount in U.S. dollars. The amount in the foreign currency, which is a double value, is passed to the method as an argument, so the corresponding parameter is declared as double. Since the method returns a double value, we must declare its return type as double. The method is therefore declared as

```
public double toDollar( double foreignMoney ) {

    //method body comes here
}
```

value-returning method

We call a method that returns a value a *value-returning method,* or *non*-void *method.* A value-returning method must include a return statement of the format

return statement syntax

```
return <expression> ;
```

The void method may optionally include a return statement. When it does, then the statement must not have the <expression> portion, only the reserved word return, as in

```
return;
```

We will be seeing examples of using a return statement with the void methods after the selection control structure (Chapter 5) is covered.

We can convert a given value foreignMoney to the equivalent dollar amount by the expression

```
foreignMoney / exchangeRate
```

so the complete method is defined as

```
public double toDollar( double foreignMoney ) {

    return (foreignMoney / exchangeRate) ;
}
```

We use the parentheses in the return statement to delineate the expression part of the statement clearly.

The method to convert a given amount in dollars to the equivalent amount in a foreign currency is similarly defined as

```
public double fromDollar( double dollar ) {

    return (dollar * exchangeRate) ;
}
```

We are now ready to provide the complete listing of the CurrencyConverter class. In listing the data members and methods of a class, we will use this convention:

class-listing convention

```
class <class name> {
    // data members

    // public methods

    // private methods
}
```

We list first the data members, then the public methods in alphabetical order, and finally the private methods in alphabetical order. For the public and private method groups, we will include a block comment that provides a quick reference to the methods in the group. For example, we will include this comment for the public method group of the CurrencyConverter class:

```
//--------------------------------------------------------------------------------
//  Public Methods:
//
//      double   fromDollar         ( double )
//      void     setExchangeRate    (        )
//      double   toDollar           ( double )
//
//--------------------------------------------------------------------------------
```

Such a list in the source code, of course, is not needed by the javadoc generator to produce similar indexes to methods and data members when creating online documentation from the source code. However, we still include such quick reference lists of methods in the source code so that programmers reading the program will have a handy reference to the list of methods without referring to any online documentation. Notice that we don't use the javadoc style for a quick reference list because javadoc comments are used only for describing the class and its data members and methods.

Helpful Reminder

The Java compiler does not care how we order the methods and data members in the class declaration. We adopt the listing convention to make the class declaration easier for us to follow.

Here's the class declaration:

```
/**
 * This class is used to do the currency conversion
 * between a foreign currency and the U.S. dollar.
 *
 * @author Dr. Caffeine
 */

class CurrencyConverter {

//------------------------------------------------------------------------------------
//      Data Members
//------------------------------------------------------------------------------------
```

```java
    /**
     * how much $1.00 U.S. is worth in the foreign currency
     */
    private double exchangeRate;
//-------------------------------------------------------------------------------------------
//      Public Methods:
//
//          double    fromDollar          (   double      )
//          void      setExchangeRate     (   double      )
//          double    toDollar            (   double      )
//
//-------------------------------------------------------------------------------------------
    /**
     * Converts a given amount in dollars into
     * an equivalent amount in a foreign currency.
     *
     * @param dollar the amount in dollars to be converted
     *
     * @return amount in foreign currency
     */
    public double fromDollar( double dollar ) {

        return (dollar * exchangeRate) ;
    }

    /**
     * Sets the exchange rate to the value passed
     * to this method.
     *
     * @param rate the exchange rate
     *
     */
    public void setExchangeRate( double rate ) {

        exchangeRate = rate;
    }

    /**
     * Converts a given amount in a foreign currency into
     * an equivalent dollar amount.
     *
     * @param  foreignMoney the amount in dollars to be converted
     *
     * @return amount in dollar
     */
    public double toDollar( double foreignMoney ) {

        return (foreignMoney / exchangeRate) ;
    }
}
```

Quick
CHECK

1. The following is invalid. Why?

```
public void myMethod( int one ) {

    return (one + one) ;
}
```

2. Which of the following methods are class methods?

```
public  static void   one( ) { ... }
private        int    two( ) { ... }
private static int    three( ) { ... }
public         float  four( ) { ... }
```

3. Define a Student class. A Student has name. There are two methods, one called identify that returns the student's name and another called assign that assigns the student's name.

4.2 | Instantiable Classes and Constructors

When we design a class, we try to make the class as robust as we can. We do not want the class to be so fragile that a simple misstep by the programmer will cause the class to stop working properly. Consider the following sequence of statements that use a CurrencyConverter object to convert $200 to the equivalent in yen:

```
CurrencyConverter   yenConverter;
double              amountInYen;

yenConverter    = new CurrencyConverter();
amountInYen     = yenConverter.fromDollar( 200 );
```

Does the code work? No, it does not, because the method setExchangeRate is not called to set the exchange rate. The programmer must call the setExchangeRate method before calling the fromDollar method to perform the currency conversion correctly.

The way the class is currently defined, the correct value for exchangeRate is not set when an instance of the CurrencyConverter class is created. This means that we must rely on the programmer to call the setExchangeRate method before calling the fromDollar method. But relying solely on the programmers to use the class correctly is not a good approach. When we design a class, we must define the class as robust as it can be, so the class will not "break" easily under the programmer's misuse of the class. One possible solution is to define a special method called a *constructor* so that an instance of the CurrencyConverter class cannot be created without setting the value for exchangeRate.

constructor

A *constructor* is a special method that is executed when the new operation is executed, that is, when a new instance of the class is created. The name of a constructor must be the same as the name of the class. For the CurrencyConverter class, we can define its constructor as

```
public CurrencyConverter( double rate ) {

    exchangeRate = rate;
}
```

To call this constructor, we create a new CurrencyConverter object, as in

```
CurrencyConverter  moneyChanger;
moneyChanger = new CurrencyConverter( 130.45 );
```

The syntax of a constructor is

```
public <class name> ( <parameters> ) {

    <statements>
}
```

where <class name> is the name of the class to which this constructor belongs. The following diagram shows how the components in the general syntax correspond to the actual elements in the constructor of the CurrencyConverter class:

Notice that a constructor does not have a return type. The modifier of a constructor does not have to be public, but non-public constructors are rarely used, so we will not discuss non-public constructors.

If no constructor is defined for a class, then the Java compiler will include a default constructor. Since we did not define any constructor for the Currency-Converter class before, the default constructor

```
public CurrencyConverter() {

}
```

was added to the class by the compiler. A default constructor has no parameters. Once we define our own constructor, no default constructor is added. This means that once the constructor

```
public CurrencyConverter( double  rate ) {

    exchangeRate = rate;
}
```

is defined, we will not be allowed to create a CurrencyConverter object such as

```
CurrencyConverter   moneyChanger;
moneyChanger   =   new CurrencyConverter( );
```

because no matching constructor is defined for the class. However, it is possible to define multiple constructors for a class, so the programmer can create a new instance of the class in different ways. For example, if we want the programmers to create a new instance either as

```
moneyChanger = new CurrencyConverter( );
```

or as

```
moneyChanger = new CurrencyConverter( 142.00 );
```

we simply define two constructors for the class.

There will be no problems defining multiple constructors as long as the constructors defined for a class have either

1. A different number of parameters.
2. Different data types for the parameters if the number of parameters is the same.

For example, the three constructors

```
public ClassA( int X ) {

   . . .

}

public ClassA(       ) { //different number of parameters

   . . .

}

public ClassA( double X ) { //same number of parameters as
                            //the first one, but a different
   . . .                    //data type

}
```

are valid, but the two constructors

```
public ClassB( int X , double Y ) {

   . . .

}

public ClassB( int A, double B  )  {
                   //invalid: same number and same data types

   . . .

}
```

are not. Notice that parameter names are irrelevant in deciding whether the constructor is valid. Only the number of parameters and their data types are relevant.

The purpose of the constructor is to initialize an object to a valid state. For example, when the CurrencyConverter class has the default constructor only, then a newly created CurrencyConverter object is not in a valid state since the object does not have a valid exchange rate at the time of its creation. Whenever an object is created, we must ensure that it is created in a valid state by properly initializing all instance variables in a constructor. We can guarantee this by always defining a constructor to a class and initializing instance variables in the constructor's method body.

Design Guidelines

Always define a constructor and initialize instance variables fully in the constructor so an object will be created in a valid state.

Remember that even after we add constructors to the CurrencyConverter class, the setExchangeRate method is still necessary for the class because we want the programmer to be able to change the exchange rate to different rates after the object is created.

this

If we define multiple constructors, it is cleaner to make one constructor call another by using the reserved word this. For example, suppose we have two constructors for the CurrencyConverter class, one with no parameter and the other with one parameter. Since we do not want to leave a newly created object in an invalid state, we will set the exchange rate to some default value, say, 1.00. Here's one way to define the two constructors:

```
public CurrencyConverter() {

    exchangeRate = DEFAULT_RATE;
}

public CurrencyConverter( double  rate ) {

    exchangeRate = rate;
}
```

where DEFAULT_RATE is a class constant defined as

```
private static final double DEFAULT_RATE = 1.00;
```

Instead of writing this way, we can make the default constructor call the second constructor in the following manner, using the reserved word this:

```
public CurrencyConverter() {

    this(DEFAULT_RATE);
}
```

The statement calls the constructor that accepts one **int** parameter.

When a constructor calls another constructor using the reserved word this, it is recommended that the statement be the only statement in the constructor, as in the example. If there are multiple statements, then the statement that calls another constructor via this must be the first statement.

Quick
CHECK

1. Which of the following constructors are invalid?

   ```
   public int ClassA( int one ) {

       . . .
   }

   public ClassB( int one, int two ) {

       . . .
   }

   void ClassC( ) {

       . . .
   }
   ```

2. Are there any conflicts in the following three constructors for ClassX to be valid?

   ```
   public ClassX( int X ) {

       . . .
   }

   public ClassX( float X ) {

       . . .
   }

   public ClassX( int Y ) {

       . . .
   }
   ```

3. Define a Student class. A Student has name. There are two methods, one called identify that returns the student's name and another called assign that assigns the student's name. Define two constructors, one with no argument and the other with the name as its argument.

4.3 | Information Hiding and Visibility Modifiers

We introduced the notion of a visibility modifer in Section 4.1. The modifiers public and private designate the accessibility of data members and methods. Although valid in Java, we do not recommend to programmers, especially beginners, to leave out the visibility modifier in declaring data members and methods. From the object-oriented design standpoint, we recommend that you always designate the data members and methods as private or public. We will explain how to use these modifiers in this section. But before we get into the details, we will discuss the object-oriented design philosophy behind these modifiers.

When we design an instantiable class, we are designing the behavior of its instances. For example, the core behavior of a CurrencyConverter object is represented by its two conversion methods toDollar and fromDollar. Consider a mobile robot as another example. What kind of behavior do we expect from a mobile robot? Behavior such as moving forward, turning, stopping, and changing speed comes to mind easily. When we define a class, say, MobileRobot, we would include public methods such as move, turn, stop, and changeSpeed. These methods are declared public so the programmers who use a MobileRobot object can call these methods from their programs. We call these programmers *client programmers* and their programs *client programs*.

client programmers

Now let's assume that the move method accepts an integer argument as a distance to travel in meters. Suppose this mobile robot has three wheels with a motor attached to each of the left and right rear wheels. The robot has no steering mechanism, so the turning is done by rotating the left and right rear wheels at different speeds. For example, by rotating the left wheel faster than the right wheel, the robot will make a gradual right turn. To move forward, the robot must send the same amount of power to the two motors. While the motors are rotating, the robot must constantly monitor the distance traveled and stop the motors when the designated distance is traveled.

The MobileRobot class would include methods such as rotate to rotate the motor and readDistance to read the distance traveled. These methods are declared private because they are internal details that need to be hidden from the client programmers. From our perspective as a client programmer, all we care is that the mobile robot exhibits the behavior of moving the desired distance when we call its move method. We do not care what's going on inside. This is called *information hiding*. It is not our concern how many motors the robot has or what type of mechanism is employed to move the robot. We say the mobile robot *encapsulates* the internal workings.

information hiding

encapsulate

This encapsulation mechanism allows easier modification of program code. For example, suppose the motion mechanism of a mobile robot is modified to a single motor and rack-and-pinion steering. Both wheels are now connected to a single axle, and the motor turns this axle (via gears). The internal mechanism has changed, but this will not affect the client programs. Calling the move method still exhibits the same behavior.

To implement its methods (both public and private), the MobileRobot class will necessarily include many data members, such as current speed, current direction, and power levels of the motors. These data members are internal details of the class because it is not a concern of the client programmers to know which and how many of them are defined in the class. As such, data members are declared as private.

In summary, behavior of the instances is determined by public methods, while the internal details that must be hidden from the client programmers are implemented by private methods and private data members.

Moving a mobile robot forward in reality is actually a far more difficult task than described in the text. First, applying the same power to the two motors does not guarantee the straight movement, due to the difference in the motor characteristics and the floor condition. Second, the robot needs to carry out some form of obstacle avoidance, using a device such as a sonar or infrared sensor because we normally do not want a robot to crash into a wall. Third, stopping is not achieved by abruptly shutting off the power to the motors. This will make the stopping too sudden. We want to gradually reduce the power level so the robot comes to a smooth stop. And there are other complexities involved in actually moving a physical robot. If you are interested in writing Java programs to control a Lego Mindstorms robot, a fun website to start your exploration is **www.lejos.org**.

Design Guidelines

Public methods of a class determine the behavior of its instances. Internal details are implemented by private methods and private data members.

Now let's go through a concrete example to see what would happen if something that should be an internal detail were declared public. To illustrate why declaring data members public is considered a bad design, let's modify the Currency-Converter class. In the modified class, a fee is automatically charged and deducted from the converted amount. Let's say the rate of charge is 5 percent of the exchange rate. We add the second instance variable feeRate to store this fee rate. We will declare feeRate as public to illustrate the point. The fee rate is based on the exchange rate, so we will set it inside the setExchangeRate method as

```
public void setExchangeRate( double rate ) {

    exchangeRate = rate;
    feeRate = rate * FEE_PERCENTAGE;
}
```

◀ This is a class constant whose value is set to 0.05

The conversion routines are now defined as

```
public double toDollar( double foreignMoney ) {

    return foreignMoney / (exchangeRate + feeRate);
}

public double fromDollar( double dollar ) {

    return dollar * (exchangeRate - feeRate) ;
}
```

Because the instance variable feeRate is public, we cannot prevent client programmers from writing code such as

```
CurrencyConverter    yenConverter;
yenConverter =  new CurrencyConverter( );
yenConverter.setExchangeRate( 118.65 );

yenConverter.feeRate = 0.0;
...
```

thereby breaking the CurrencyConverter class. The problem is the result of not hiding the internal detail. The fact the feeRate is used in computing the fee is the internal detail. If the instance variable feeRate is properly hidden by declaring it private, then client programmers using the CurrencyConverter class cannot modify its value directly. They can modify the value only through the setExchangeRate method. So by declaring the data members private, we can maintain the integrity of the class and enforce the rule, because the values of the data members are changed only via the public methods we provide. The client programmers cannot access or modify the data member values through the back door.

Design Guidelines

Declaring the data members private *ensures the integrity of the class.*

The only data members we may want to declare as public are the class constants. First, a constant is "read only" by its nature, so it won't have a negative impact if we declare it as public. Second, a constant is a clean way to make certain characteristics of the instances known to the client programmers. For example, if there's a maximum possible top speed of the MobileRobot class (i.e., no instances of MobileRobot can go any faster than this speed), we can make this information available to the client programmers as a class constant by declaring the class as

```
class MobileRobot {

   public static final double TOP_SPEED = 8.25; //meter/sec

   ...
}
```

A client program can access this information as

```
MobileRobot fido = new MobileRobot();
MobileRobot aibo = new MobileRobot();
...
System.out.println("The top speed of both aibo & fido is "
                      + MobileRobot.TOP_SPEED);
```

Notice that the public class data members are accessed by the syntax

```
<class name> . <class data members>
```

The use of public class constants is quite common in Java, and we will be seeing many examples of it in the later sample programs.

Here are some useful guidelines for you to follow.

Design Guidelines

Guidelines in determining the visibility of data members and methods:

1. *Declare the class and instance variables* **private**.

2. *Declare the class and instance methods* **private** *if they are used only by the other methods in the same class.*

3. *Declare the class constants* **public** *if you want to make their values directly readable by the client programs. If the class constants are used for internal purposes only, then declare them* **private**.

To distinguish the private and public components of a class in the program diagram, we use the plus symbol $(+)$ for public and the minus symbol $(-)$ for private. Using these symbols, the diagram for the CurrencyConverter class becomes

CurrencyConverter
− exchangeRate
+ setExchangeRate
+ toDollar
+ fromDollar

Quick **CHECK**

1. If the data member feeRate is private, is the following statement valid?

```
CurrencyConverter converter
        = new CurrencyConverter();
double amount = converter.feeRate;
```

2. Suppose you wrote down important information such as your bank account number, student registration ID, and so forth, on a single sheet of paper. Will this sheet be declared private, and kept in your desk drawer, or public, and placed next to the dorm's public telephone?

4.4 | Local Variables, Return Values, and Parameter Passing

We will provide more detailed coverage of methods in this section. Specifically, we will discuss how local variables are declared, how arguments are passed to a method, and how values are returned from a method. In this section, we limit our discussion to primitive data types. How objects are passed to and returned from methods is described in Section 4.6.

local variable

A variable declared within the method declaration is called a *local variable*. Local variables are used for temporary purposes, such as storing intermediate results of a computation. For example, we can rewrite the method

```
public double fromDollar( double dollar ) {

    return dollar * (exchangeRate - feeRate);
}
```

using local variables, as in

These are local variables

```
public double fromDollar( double dollar ) {

    double amount, fee;

    fee    = exchangeRate - feeRate;
    amount = dollar * fee;

    return amount;
}
```

While the data members of a class are accessible from all instance methods of the class, local variables and parameters are accessible only from the method in which they are declared, and they are available only while the method is being executed. Memory space for local variables and parameters is allocated at the beginning of the method and erased upon exiting from the method. Figure 4.3 shows how memory space is allocated and deallocated for the two local variables and the one parameter when the modified fromDollar method is executed.

Helpful Reminder

Local variables and parameters are erased when the execution of a method is completed.

The next topic is the mapping of arguments to the corresponding parameters. In the example shown in Figure 4.3, the constant argument 200 was passed to the parameter of the fromDollar method. The passed value was used in the method and erased upon exiting from the method. In this example the argument was a constant. What would happen if the argument were a variable and the value of the corresponding parameter were changed during the method execution? Let's study how the values are passed between the argument and the corresponding parameter.

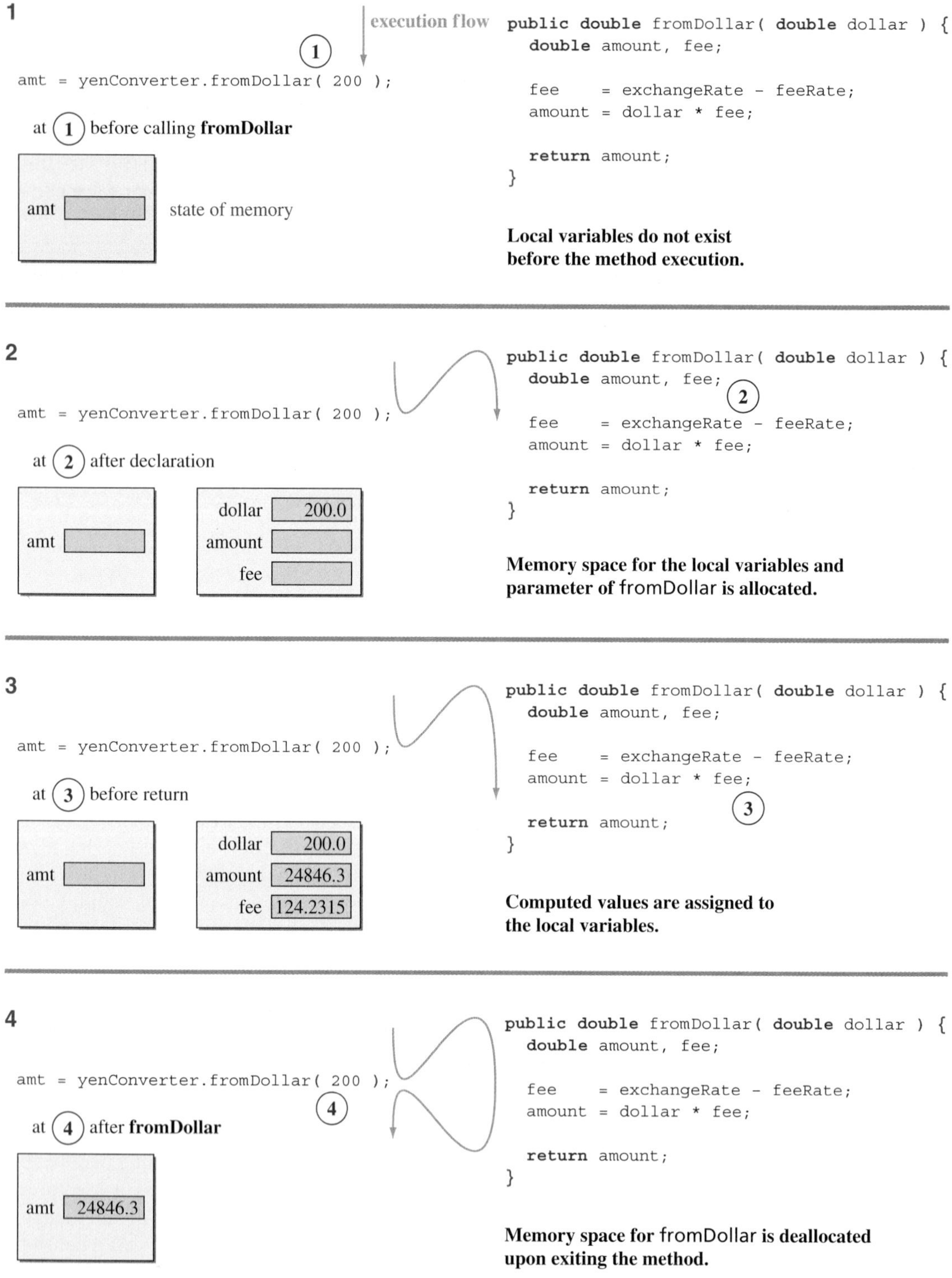

1

execution flow

```
public double fromDollar( double dollar ) {
    double amount, fee;

    fee     = exchangeRate - feeRate;
    amount  = dollar * fee;

    return amount;
}
```

①

```
amt = yenConverter.fromDollar( 200 );
```

at ① before calling **fromDollar**

amt	

state of memory

**Local variables do not exist
before the method execution.**

2

```
public double fromDollar( double dollar ) {
    double amount, fee;
                                            ②
    fee     = exchangeRate - feeRate;
    amount  = dollar * fee;

    return amount;
}
```

```
amt = yenConverter.fromDollar( 200 );
```

at ② after declaration

amt	

dollar	200.0
amount	
fee	

**Memory space for the local variables and
parameter of fromDollar is allocated.**

3

```
public double fromDollar( double dollar ) {
    double amount, fee;

    fee     = exchangeRate - feeRate;
    amount  = dollar * fee;
                                            ③
    return amount;
}
```

```
amt = yenConverter.fromDollar( 200 );
```

at ③ before return

amt	

dollar	200.0
amount	24846.3
fee	124.2315

**Computed values are assigned to
the local variables.**

4

```
public double fromDollar( double dollar ) {
    double amount, fee;

    fee     = exchangeRate - feeRate;
    amount  = dollar * fee;

    return amount;
}
```

```
amt = yenConverter.fromDollar( 200 );
```

④

at ④ after **fromDollar**

amt	24846.3

**Memory space for fromDollar is deallocated
upon exiting the method.**

Figure 4.3 How memory space for local variables and parameters is allocated and deallocated. Data
members **exchangeRate** and **feeRate** are not shown.

When a method is called, the value of the argument is passed to the matching parameter, and separate memory space is allocated to store this value. This way of passing the value of arguments is called a *pass-by-value*, or *call-by-value*, *scheme*. Since separate memory space is allocated for each parameter during the execution of the method, the parameter is local to the method, and, therefore, changes made to the parameter will not affect the value of the corresponding argument.

pass-by-value

Consider the following myMethod method of the Tester class. The method does not do anything meaningful. We use it here to illustrate how the pass-by-value scheme works.

```
class Tester {

    public void myMethod(int one, double two ) {

        one = 25;
        two = 35.4;

    }
}
```

What will be the output from the following code?

```
Tester tester;
int    x, y;

tester = new Tester();
x = 10;
y = 20;

tester.myMethod( x, y );

System.out.println( x + "    " + y );
```

The output will be

```
10      20
```

because with the pass-by-value scheme, the values of arguments are passed to the parameters, but changes made to the parameters are not passed back to the arguments. Figure 4.4 shows how the pass-by-value scheme works.

Notice that the arguments are matched against the parameters in the left-to-right order; that is, the value of the leftmost argument is passed to the leftmost parameter, the value of the second-leftmost argument is passed to the second-leftmost parameter, and so forth. The number of arguments in the method call must match the number of parameters in the method definition. For example, the following calls to myMethod of the Tester class are all invalid because the numbers of arguments and parameters do not match.

```
tester.myMethod( 12 );
tester.myMethod( x, y, 24.5);
```

1

```
x = 10;
y = 20;          (1)
tester.myMethod( x, y );
```

execution flow ↓

```
public void myMethod( int one, double two ) {

    one = 25;
    two = 35.4;
}
```

at (1) before calling **myMethod**

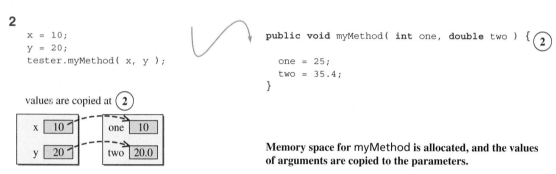

state of memory

**Local variables do not exist
before the method execution.**

2

```
x = 10;
y = 20;
tester.myMethod( x, y );
```

```
public void myMethod( int one, double two ) { (2)

    one = 25;
    two = 35.4;
}
```

values are copied at (2)

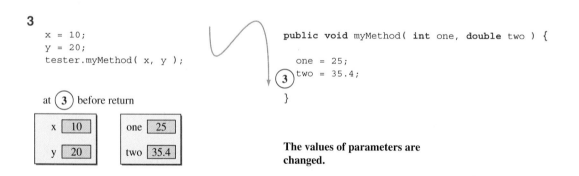

**Memory space for myMethod is allocated, and the values
of arguments are copied to the parameters.**

3

```
x = 10;
y = 20;
tester.myMethod( x, y );
```

```
public void myMethod( int one, double two ) {

    one = 25;
(3) two = 35.4;
}
```

at (3) before return

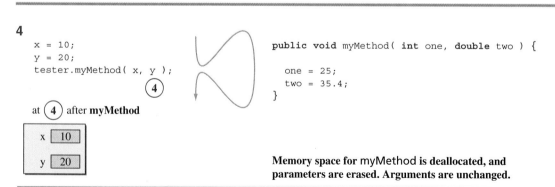

**The values of parameters are
changed.**

4

```
x = 10;
y = 20;
tester.myMethod( x, y );
        (4)
```

```
public void myMethod( int one, double two ) {

    one = 25;
    two = 35.4;
}
```

at (4) after **myMethod**

```
x  10
y  20
```

**Memory space for myMethod is deallocated, and
parameters are erased. Arguments are unchanged.**

Figure 4.4 How memory space for the parameters is allocated and deallocated.

Since we are assigning the value of an argument to the matching parameter, the data type of an argument must be assignment-compatible with the data type of the matching parameter. For example, we can pass an integer argument to a **float** parameter, but not vice versa. In the following, the first call is valid, but the second one is invalid:

```
tester.myMethod( 12, 25 );
tester.myMethod( 23.0, 34.5 );
```

The name of the parameter and the argument can be the same. Keep in mind, however, that the values of arguments are still passed to a method by the pass-by-value scheme; that is, local copies are made whether the argument and the parameter share the same name or not.

Helpful Reminder

The key points to remember about arguments and parameters are

1. *Arguments are passed to a method using the pass-by-value scheme.*
2. *Arguments are matched to the parameters from left to right. The data type of an argument must be assignment-compatible with the data type of the matching parameter.*
3. *The number of arguments in the method call must match the number of parameters in the method definition.*
4. *Parameters and arguments do not have to have the same name.*
5. *Local copies, which are distinct from arguments, are created even if the parameters and arguments share the same name.*
6. *Parameters are input to a method, and they are local to the method. Changes made to the parameters will not affect the value of corresponding arguments.*

Finally, let's study how values are returned from methods. Consider the following toDollar method:

The data type of the value returned from a method must be assignment-compatible with the declared return type of the method.

```
public   double toDollar( double foreignMoney ) {

    return   foreignMoney / (exchangeRate + feeRate) ;

}
```

Because a value is returned from the method, we can place the call to the method anywhere an expression can appear. For example, the following statement is valid:

```
double totalAmount;

totalAmount = yenConverter.toDollar( 100 )
                    + yenConverter.toDollar( 50 ) ;
```

Similarly, we can pass the returned value as an argument to another method call, such as

```
double yenAmount;

yenAmount
  = yenConverter.fromDollar( euroConverter.toDollar(100) );
```

method composition

to convert 100 euros to the equivalent yen. Passing a value returned from one method as an argument to another method is called *method composition*. *Note:* Fees are charged twice here because there are two conversions. See Exercise 17 on page 229.

In the program diagram, we denote the parameters and return types in the following manner:

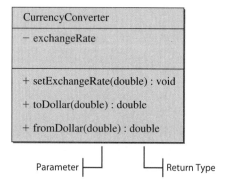

Notice that we list only the data type for the parameters, and the return type is listed at the end following the colon. We can use the same notation of a colon followed by the data type to record the data type of the data members, as in

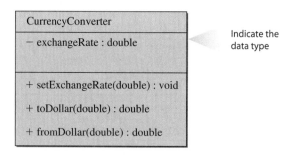

Differentiating Data Members from Local Variables and Parameters

In the examples so far, we used different identifiers for local variables, parameters, and data members, so there wasn't any confusion. However, it is valid (although not recommended for the most part) to use the same identifier for a data member and a local variable or for a data member and a parameter. A local variable and a parameter can never share the same identifier because they are both declared locally.

Consider the following class declaration:

```
class MusicCD {

    private String    artist;
    private String    title;
    private String    id;

    public MusicCD(String name1, String name2) {

        artist = name1;
        title  = name2;
        id     = artist.substring(0,2) + "-" +
                 title.substring(0,9);

    }
    ...
}
```

The constructor has two **String** parameters, one for the artist and the other for the title. An ID for a **MusicCD** object is set to be the first three letters of the artist followed by a hyphen and the first 10 letters of the title.

Now, consider what happens if we include (say, inadvertently) a local declaration for the identifier id as

Local declaration for **id**

This **id** is now a local variable

```
public MusicCD(String name1, String name2) {
    String id;

    artist = name1;
    title  = name2;
    id     = artist.substring(0,2) + "-" +
             title.substring(0,9);

}
```

Because there is a matching local declaration for id, the identifier refers to the local variable, not to the third data member anymore. When an identifier is encountered in a method, the following rules are applied to determine the association:

Helpful Reminder

Rules for associating an identifier to a local variable, a parameter, and a data member:

1. *If there's a matching local variable declaration or a parameter, then the identifier refers to the local variable or the parameter.*
2. *Otherwise, if there's a matching data member declaration, then the identifier refers to the data member.*
3. *Otherwise, it is an error because there's no matching declaration.*

Why does the Java compiler not catch such an error? When would anyone want to use the same identifier for both the data member and the local variable or parameter? Yes, in general, we strongly recommend to always use an identifier different from any data member in declaring a local variable. But there is a situation where we may want to use the same identifier for a parameter and a data member. In the MusicCD constructor, we declared the parameters name1 and name2 to avoid a naming conflict. It would actually be more meaningful to use the conflicting identifiers artist and title. To do so, we can rewrite the method as

```
public MusicCD(String artist, String title) {

    this.artist = artist;
    this.title  = title;
    id      = artist.substring(0,2) + "-" +
                title.substring(0,9);

}
```

This refers to the data member → `this.artist` = `artist;`

This refers to the parameter ← `artist;`

Following the stated rules, the identifier artist refers to the parameter. To refer to the data member artist from within this constructor, we prefix the identifier artist with the reserved word this, using dot notation, as this.artist. We can read the expression as "this object's data member artist." In the modified constructor, we did not use the reserved word this to refer to the data member id because it was not necessary. Its use is optional, so we could have used it to make three assignment statements look consistent. The reserved word this can be used to refer to a data member regardless of the existence of a naming conflict.

Helpful Reminder

*Optionally, dot notation with the reserved **this** can be used to refer to an object's data member from the object's methods and constructors.*

In general, following the common practice, we will not use dot notation (with the reserved word this) to refer to an object's data members from the object's methods unless it is necessary.

We can also avoid the naming conflict and still use a meaningful name for a parameter by prefixing an article to the parameter. For example, we could use the identifiers anArtist and aTitle instead of name1 and name2. This naming will not conflict with the data members, so the use of the reserved word this is not necessary in the constructor. As long as you use meaningful identifiers, which technique you adopt to avoid naming conflict is more of a personal preference.

Quick **CHECK**

1. Identify the local variables, parameters, and data members in the following method myMethod:

```
class Question1 {
    private int one;
    private int four;

    public void myMethod( int one ) {
        double two   = 2;
        int    three = 3;
        return one + two * four;
    }
}
```

2. What is the problem with the following method?

```
public  void problem( ) {
    int one = 1;
    return one + 45;
}
```

3. Identify the private methods from the following diagram:

```
┌─────────────────────────────────┐
│ MyClass                         │
├─────────────────────────────────┤
│  − mydata : double              │
│                                 │
├─────────────────────────────────┤
│  + methodOne(double) : void     │
│                                 │
│  − methodTwo(double) : double   │
│                                 │
│  − methodThree(double) : double │
└─────────────────────────────────┘
```

4. Complete the following constructor :

```
class Test {
    private double score;

    public Test(double score) {
        //assign the value of parameter to
        //the data member
    }
}
```

4.5 | Accessors, Mutators, and Overloaded Methods

In this section, we will create another instantiable class as a way to review what we have learned so far and to introduce new concepts. In the United States, the units we use in measuring weights are pounds (lb) and ounces (oz) while in other parts of the world, the metric system [i.e., gram (g)] is used. We will define a class named Weight that can express weight in either system. In defining this class, we will learn how to define multiple methods with the same name and the types of methods for assigning and reading the properties of objects.

Let's study the Weight class from the client programmer's perspective. What kind of behavior do we expect from a Weight object? Since a Weight object can represent itself in grams or in pounds and ounces, we want methods to set the weight in either units. We use double to express weight in grams and int to express it in pounds and ounces. Here are the three set methods:

```
public void setGram(double gram)
public void setPound(int lb)
public void setOunce(int oz)
```

mutator

A set method is called a *mutator* because it changes a property of an object. Ordinarily, a single property of an object, such as the current speed of a mobile robot, is maintained by a single data member; but there are other possibilities, such as a single property maintained by using multiple data members. Again, how a property of an object is represented inside the object is an internal detail and does not concern the client programmers.

accessor

When we define a set of mutator methods, it is common practice to provide a complementary set of accessor methods. An *accessor* is a method that returns a property of an object. We will define the following complementary accessors for the Weight class:

```
public double getGram( )
public int    getPound( )
public int    getOunce( )
```

Notice the setPound and getPound methods affect only the pound portion of a weight. For example, if the weight is 3 lb 4 oz, then calling the getPound method will return 3 and calling the setPound method with an argument 5 will change the weight to 5 lb 4 oz. The effect of setOunce and getOunce is analogous to the effect of setPound and getPound.

In addition to the mutators and accessors, we would like to have a method to change the weight. We will define two methods for this behavior: one will accept the amount to change in grams, and the other will accept the amount to change in pounds and ounces. To add, we pass positive arguments, and to subtract, we pass negative arguments. The two methods are both named adjust.

```
public void adjust(double gram)
public void adjust(int lb, int oz)
```

There is no problem naming multiple methods with the same name as long as the same rules for defining multiple constructors, as described on page 164, are obeyed. We can define multiple methods with the same name if

1. They have a different number of parameters.
2. The parameters are of different data types when they have the same number of parameters.

overloaded
methods

The methods with the same name are called *overloaded methods*.

Finally, we will define three constructors for the class. The default constructor with no argument will initialize the weight to 0.0. The second constructor accepts the initial weight in pounds and ounces. And the last constructor accepts the initial weight in grams.

```
public Weight( )
public Weight(int lb, int oz)
public Weight(double gram)
```

Now we are ready to begin our implementation. The first decision we must make is how to store the weight inside a Weight object. There are two viable possibilities. The first is to use a single data member and store the weight in grams. The second is to use two data members, one for storing the pound portion and the other for storing the ounce portion of the weight. We will adopt the first approach here. It is left as an exercise to implement the class by using the second approach.

Because the weight is maintained in grams internally, we must perform unit conversion to implement the mutators and accessors involving pounds and ounces. The conversion factors are stored as private class constants in the class. Here's the class skeleton with data members:

```
class Weight {

    /** 1 oz = 28.349523125 */
    private static final double OZ_TO_GRAM = 28.349523125;

    /** 1 lb = 453.59237 grams */
    private static final double LB_TO_GRAM = 453.59237;

    /** 1 lb = 16 oz */
    private static final double LB_TO_OZ   = 16.0;

    /** the weight in grams */
    private double gram;

    . . .

}
```

The getGram and setGram methods are straightforward because we have the data member gram.

```
public double getGram( ) {
    return gram;
}
```

```
public void setGram(double amount) {
    gram = amount;
}
```

The other accessors and mutators require careful thinking because of the necessary conversions. To get the pound portion of the weight, we must first convert the gram data member to the equivalent pound with fractional values and then truncate the decimals. For example, 498 g is equivalent to 1.098 lb (rounded to three decimal places). Truncating it will result in 1. The method is implemented as

```
public int getPound( ) {
    return (int) Math.floor(gram/LB_TO_GRAM);
}
```

The companion getOunce is slightly more difficult. In converting 498 g to the equivalent pounds, we get 1.098 lb. The fractional value 0.098 is the value we need to convert to ounces in the getOunce method. We can get this fractional value by the expression

```
fractionalValue = gram/LB_TO_GRAM
                    - Math.floor(gram/LB_TO_GRAM);
```

Then we return it, after converting it to an ounce equivalent, rounded to a nearest integer, as

```
return (int) Math.round(fractionalValue * LB_TO_OZ);
```

We round the value because, for example, we want to return 9 if the value before rounding is 8.7 oz. The method is implemented as

A method calling another method belonging to the same object.

```
public int getOunce( ) {

    double decimalPound   = gram/LB_TO_GRAM;
    double fractionalValue = decimalPound - getPound();

    return (int) Math.round(fractionalValue * LB_TO_OZ);
}
```

Notice the call to the getPound method within the getOunce method. Instead of duplicating the same code (which should be avoided whenever possible), the getOunce method calls the getPound method to compute the pound portion of the weight. Because the duplication is only one statement, the need to eliminate the duplication may not be obvious, but imagine a method with 10 lines of statements. It is far better to define a method and call this method from multiple places than to duplicate the same 10 lines of code at multiple places. Duplication of code makes the modification of code tedious and error-prone.

Up until now, whenever we called a method of some object, we used dot notation, such as yenConverter.setExchangeRate(1.77). Just as we can call a method of another object, it is possible to call a method from a method of the same object. In this case, as illustrated in the getOunce method, the use of dot notation is optional.

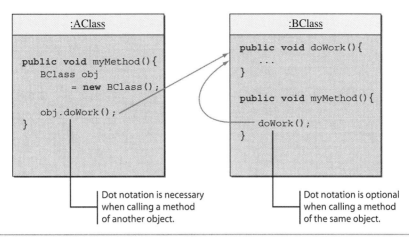

Figure 4.5 The difference between calling a method belonging to the same object and calling a method belonging to a different object.

Figure 4.5 illustrates the difference between calling another method of the same object and calling a method of a different object.

The fact of dot notation being optional means we can use it if we want to. To use dotation notation in calling a method from a method that belongs to the same object, we use the reserved word this. The getOunce method can be written as

```
public int getOunce( ) {

    double decimalPound = gram/LB_TO_GRAM;
    double decimalOunce = decimalPound - this.getPound();

    return (int) Math.round(decimalOunce * LB_TO_OZ);
}
```

Use the reserved this to refer to the same object.

Some programmers prefer to use the reserved word this so dot notation is applied consistently throughout the code, but it is more common to omit the reserved this when calling a method from another method belonging to the same object.

Helpful Reminder

Dot notation is optional when you call a method from another method if the two methods belong to the same object. If dot notation is used, then we must use the reserved **this** *to refer to the same object.*

We will implement the setPound and setOunce methods, using the getPound and getOunce methods just defined. Remember that these two mutators change only the pound and ounce portions of the weight, respectively. To change the pound portion of the weight, first we get the ounce portion of the current weight. Then we add the new value for the pound portion to this extracted ounce value and convert it to a gram equivalent. Finally the result is assigned back to data member gram. Putting this idea in code, we have

```
public void setPound(int lb) {

    int oz = getOunce();

    double wgt = convertToGram(lb,oz);

    setGram(wgt);
}
```

The setOunce method is similarly defined as

```
public void setOunce(int oz) {

    int lb = getPound();

    double wgt = convertToGram(lb,oz);

    setGram(wgt);
}
```

The convertToGram is a private method (because it is for internal use only) defined as

```
private double convertToGram(int lb, int oz) {
    return lb * LB_TO_GRAM + oz * OZ_TO_GRAM;
}
```

The first adjust method is defined as

```
public void adjust( double amount ) {

    double currentwgt = getGram();

    setGram(currentwgt + amount);
}
```

And the second adjust method can be implemented as

```
public void adjust(int lb, int oz) {

    double amount    = convertToGram(lb,oz);
    double currentwgt = getGram();

    setGram(currentwgt + amount);
}
```

but we will implement it more succinctly as

```
public void adjust(int lb, int oz) {

    adjust(convertToGram(lb,oz));
}
```

Finally the three constructors are defined as

```
public Weight( ) {
    setGram(DEFAULT_WEIGHT);
}

public Weight(int lb, int oz) {
    double wgt = convertToGram(lb,oz);
    setGram(wgt);
}

public Weight(double wgtInGram) {
    setGram(wgtInGram);
}
```

Notice how all three methods call the setGram method to initialize the weight. The first constructor can be written as

```
public Weight( ) {
    this(DEFAULT_WEIGHT);
}
```

 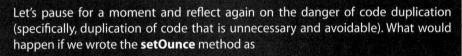

Let's pause for a moment and reflect again on the danger of code duplication (specifically, duplication of code that is unnecessary and avoidable). What would happen if we wrote the **setOunce** method as

```
public void setOunce(int oz) {
    int    lb  = (int) Math.floor(gram/LB_TO_GRAM);

    double wgt = lb * LB_TO_GRAM + oz * OZ_TO_GRAM;

    setGram(wgt);
}
```

and other methods in a similar manner? We would end up repeating the same formula throughout the class. If we need to change the formula (e.g., to correct an error, to improve it, etc.), then we have to locate all occurrences of the duplicated code. But such a task is very tedious and error-prone. It is so easy to miss one or two occurrences, which could result in code that works for some cases but not for other cases. So avoid any excessive duplication of code whenever possible.

However, the second constructor cannot be written as

```
public Weight(int lb, int oz) {
    double wgt = convertToGram(lb,oz);
    this(wgt);
}
```

Bad Version

because the call to this, if used in the constructor, must be the first statement. The constructor can be written as

```
public Weight(int lb, int oz) {
    this(convertToGram(lb,oz));
}
```

Watch out
To make this statement valid, **convertToGram** must be a class method.

provided that the private method convertToGram is declared as a class method (i.e., with the static modifier). If a constructor includes a call to this, an instance is created after the call to this is complete. The convertToGram method is called before calling this because the result of convertToGram is an argument to this. So at the point convertToGram is called, no instance of this class is created yet, and therefore, we are not allowed to call an instance method of the Weight class. Here are the rules for calling a constructor from another constructor of the same class by using the reserved word this:

Helpful Reminder

*The rules for using **this** to call a constructor from another constructor of the same class are that*

1. *The **this** statement must be the first statement in the constructor.*
2. *An argument in the **this** statement cannot make a call to an instance method of the same class.*

Here's the complete definition of the class (we do not show the javadoc comments to conserve space):

```
/*

    Chapter 4 Sample Class: The Weight class

    File: Weight.java

*/
```

```java
class Weight {

    private static final double DEFAULT_WGT = 0.0;
    private static final double OZ_TO_GRAM = 28.349523125;
    private static final double LB_TO_GRAM = 453.59237;
    private static final double LB_TO_OZ   = 16.0;

    private double gram;

    public Weight( ) {
        setGram(DEFAULT_WGT);
    }

    public Weight(int lb, int oz) {
        double wgt = convertToGram(lb,oz);
        setGram(wgt);
    }

    public Weight(double wgtInGram) {
        setGram(wgtInGram);
    }

    public void adjust( double amount ) {

        double currentwgt = getGram();

        setGram(currentwgt + amount);
    }

    public void adjust( int lb, int oz ) {
        adjust(convertToGram(lb,oz));
    }

    public double getGram(  ) {
        return gram;
    }

    public int getPound(  ) {
        return  (int) Math.floor(gram/LB_TO_GRAM);
    }

    public int getOunce( ) {

        double decimalPound    = gram/LB_TO_GRAM;
        double fractionalValue = decimalPound - getPound();

        return (int) Math.round(fractionalValue * LB_TO_OZ);
    }

    public void setGram(double amount) {
        gram = amount;
    }
```

```
    public void setPound(int lb) {

        int oz = getOunce();

        double wgt = convertToGram(lb,oz);

        setGram(wgt);
    }

    public void setOunce(int oz ) {

        int lb = getPound();

        double wgt = convertToGram(lb,oz);

        setGram(wgt);
    }

    private double convertToGram(int lb, int oz) {
        return lb * LB_TO_GRAM + oz * OZ_TO_GRAM;
    }
}
```

Let's write a test main class to confirm the expected behavior of a Weight object. Here's a short test class:

```
class Ch4TestWeight {

    public static void main( String[] args ) {

        Weight wgt;

        wgt = new Weight(1034.989);          Try other constructors with
                                             different argument values.

        System.out.println("Lb: "    + wgt.getPound());
        System.out.println("Oz: "    + wgt.getOunce());
        System.out.println("Gram: "  + wgt.getGram());
        System.out.println("");

        wgt.setPound(4);
        wgt.setOunce(9);

        System.out.println("Lb: "    + wgt.getPound());
        System.out.println("Oz: "    + wgt.getOunce());
        System.out.println("Gram: "  + wgt.getGram());
        System.out.println("");

        wgt.adjust(453.59237);   //add 1 lb
```

```
        System.out.println("Lb: "   + wgt.getPound());
        System.out.println("Oz: "   + wgt.getOunce());
        System.out.println("Gram: " + wgt.getGram());
        System.out.println("");
    }
}
```

It is important to test other constructors and methods with different values for arguments as well as different combinations of calling the accessors and mutators.

Quick **CHECK**

1. Rewrite the following class, using the optional this wherever it is allowed.

```
class One {
    private int var1;
    private int var2;

    public m1( ) {
        var1 = 20;
        m2(var1);
    }

    public m2(int x) {
        var2 = x * 2;
    }
}
```

2. Why is it not considered a good programming practice to write the setPound method as here?

```
public void setPound(int lb) {

    int oz = (int) (gram/LB_TO_GRAM
                    - Math.floor(gram/LB_TO_GRAM));

    weight = lb * LB_TO_GRAM + oz * OZ_TO_GRAM;
}
```

4.6 | Passing and Returning Objects

In Section 4.4, we explained how the values are passed to a method and the result is returned from a method. We will go through the same topics again here, but this time we will use objects instead of primitive data types. The same parameter-passing mechanism is used, so there's no new concept to learn here. The only difference between passing the primitive data type and the reference data type is that the value we are passing is either the actual data or the reference (address) to an object.

The Kennel and Pet Classes

To illustrate how objects are passed to the methods and returned from them, we will define two classes—Kennel and Pet—in this section. There are numerous online games in which the players interact with virtual pets with the objective of keeping them happy and healthy. The Pet class models a virtual online pet, and the Kennel class simulates a kennel where the pets can board. These classes are necessarily kept simple so the key concepts we want to cover can be illustrated effectively. Besides, our knowledge of OOP and Java is still not mature enough to develop more advanced and realistic classes (after all, there are many more chapters to study).

Our virtual pet has a name (String) and weight (Weight). A pet can sleep, eat, walk, and run. These activities will result in weight loss or gain. We define a number of class constants to set the amount of increase or decrease in weight in grams for each activity:

```java
private static final double BASE_WGT_CHANGE = 25.0; //grams

private static final double EAT_WGT_CHANGE
                            =  3.5 * BASE_WGT_CHANGE;

private static final double WALK_WGT_CHANGE
                            = -1.5 * BASE_WGT_CHANGE;

private static final double RUN_WGT_CHANGE
                            = -2.5 * BASE_WGT_CHANGE;

private static final double SLEEP_WGT_CHANGE
                            = 0.5 * BASE_WGT_CHANGE;
```

The data member weight, a Weight object, is used to keep the pet's weight. By using this data member, the eat method is implemented as

```java
public void eat( ) {
   weight.adjust(EAT_WGT_CHANGE);
}
```

The other methods—sleep, walk, and run—are defined in a similar manner.

We include two constructors for the class. The no-argument default constructor uses default values for the name and weight. The second constructor accepts the name and weight as arguments and initilizes the pet with the passed values.

We provide accessors (getName and getWeight) for both properties but only a mutator for the name of a pet (setName). We do not have a mutator for the weight because we do not want any client program to change it directly. We want the weight of a pet to be changed only through the activities such as eating and walking. The class actually includes the setWeight method, but the method is declared private, so no client programs can use it. The private setWeight method is strictly for internal use.

Here's the complete listing:

```java
/*
    Chapter 4 Sample Class: The Pet class for a virtual online pet

    File: Pet.java

*/
class Pet {

    private static final String DEFAULT_NAME = "unnamed";
    private static final double DEFAULT_WGT  = 500.0; //grams

    private static final double BASE_WGT_CHANGE  = 25.0; //grams
    private static final double EAT_WGT_CHANGE   =  3.5 * BASE_WGT_CHANGE;
    private static final double WALK_WGT_CHANGE  = -1.5 * BASE_WGT_CHANGE;
    private static final double RUN_WGT_CHANGE   = -2.5 * BASE_WGT_CHANGE;
    private static final double SLEEP_WGT_CHANGE =  0.5 * BASE_WGT_CHANGE;

    private String name;
    private Weight weight;

    public Pet( ) {
        this(DEFAULT_NAME, new Weight(DEFAULT_WGT));
    }

    public Pet(String aName, Weight wgt) {
        setName(aName);
        setWeight(wgt);
    }

    public void eat( ) {

        weight.adjust(EAT_WGT_CHANGE);
    }

    public String getName(  ) {
        return name;
    }

    public Weight getWeight(  ) {
        return  weight;
    }

    public void setName(String aName) {
        name = aName;
    }
```

```
    public void run( ) {
        weight.adjust(RUN_WGT_CHANGE);
    }

    public void sleep( ) {
        weight.adjust(SLEEP_WGT_CHANGE);
    }

    public void walk( ) {
        weight.adjust(WALK_WGT_CHANGE);
    }

    private void setWeight(Weight wgt) {
        weight = wgt;
    }
}
```

A Kennel object has a name and the corresponding setName and getName methods. In addition to these two methods, there's one public method named board. The method accepts a Pet as an argument and makes this Pet go through the routine of sleeping, eating, walking, and running. There's no rule to the routine, so we arbitrarily select one sequence: sleep, eat, walk, eat, run, and sleep.

Here's the complete class:

```
/*
    Chapter 4 Sample Class: The Kennel class for nurturing virtual pets

    File: Kennel.java
*/

class Kennel {

    private static final String DEFAULT_NAME = "No Name Store";

    private String name;

    public Kennel( ) {
        this(DEFAULT_NAME);
    }

    public Kennel(String aName) {
        setName(aName);
    }
```

```
    public void board(Pet pet) {
        pet.sleep();
        pet.eat();
        pet.walk();
        pet.eat();
        pet.run();
        pet.sleep();
    }

    public String getName(  ) {
        return name;
    }

    public void setName(String aName) {
        name = aName;
    }
}
```

Finally, here's a short test program to check the behavior of the Kennel and Pet classes:

```
/*
    Chapter 4 Sample Program: Testing the Kennel and Pet Classes

    File: Ch4TestKennel.java
*/

import java.io.*;

class Ch4TestKennel {

    public static void main( String[] args ) throws IOException {

        BufferedReader bufReader;

        Kennel  kennel;
        Pet     latte;
        Weight  wgt;
        double  grams;
        String  name;

        bufReader = new BufferedReader(
                new InputStreamReader( System.in ) );

        kennel = new Kennel("Happy Pets Kennel");
```

```
        System.out.print("Pet Name:");
        name = bufReader.readLine();

        System.out.print("Pet Weight (in grams): ");
        grams = Double.parseDouble(bufReader.readLine());

        latte = new Pet(name, new Weight(grams)); //grams

        wgt = latte.getWeight();
        System.out.println("Before Boarding: ");
        System.out.println("     Weight of " + latte.getName() +
                      " was " + wgt.getPound() + "lbs. " +
                           wgt.getOunce() + "oz.");
        System.out.println("");

        kennel.board(latte);

        wgt = latte.getWeight();
        System.out.println("After Boarding: ");
        System.out.println("     Weight of " + latte.getName() +
                      " is " + wgt.getPound() + "lbs. " +
                           wgt.getOunce() + "oz.");
    }
}
```

Take my Advice

It is not necessary to create an object for every variable we use. Many novice programmers often make this mistake. For example, in **Ch4TestKennel**, we wrote

```
        Weight wgt;
        ...
        wgt = pet.getWeight();
```

We didn't write

```
        Weight wgt;
        ...
        wgt = new Weight(); //not necessary
        wgt = pet.getWeight();
```

because it is not necessary. The **getWeight** method returns a **Weight** object, and in the main method, all we want is a name we can use to refer to this returned **Weight** object. Don't forget that the object name (variable) and the actual object instance are two separate things.

Passing an Object to a Method

Figures 4.6 and 4.7 show how an object is passed to a method. We use the method call

```
kennel.board(latte);
```

as an illustration. The same pass-by-value scheme is used for passing objects to a method. However, when a variable is an object name, then the value of the variable is a reference to an object (i.e., an address where the object is stored in memory). So the effect of passing this value (reference) is to have two variables (object names) referring to the same object, as illustrated in the figures. An object itself is not part of the memory space allocated for the called method, so the object does not get deallocated when the method terminates. An object does not get deallocated as long as there is a reference to it (in this particular example, latte is still referring to the object). As described in Chapter 2, the system will deallocate orphan objects (objects with no references) automatically in the process known as *garbage collection*.

Helpful Reminder

When we "pass an object to a method," we are actually passing the address, or reference, of an object to the method.

Returning an Object from a Method

Now let's study how an object is returned from a method. To illustrate this concept, we will define a new method called vanityWeight to the Pet class. Because our virtual pets always want to look bigger, the vanityWeight method returns the weight that is 1.5 times the true weight. Here's the method:

Belongs to
the **Pet** class

```
public Weight vanityWeight( ) {
    Weight vanityWgt = new Weight();

    double wgt = weight.getGram();

    vanityWgt.setGram(1.5*wgt); //add 50% of wgt

    return vanityWgt;
}
```

Figures 4.8 and 4.9 illustrate the concept.

Helpful Reminder

When we "return an object from a method," we are actually returning the address, or reference, of an object to the caller.

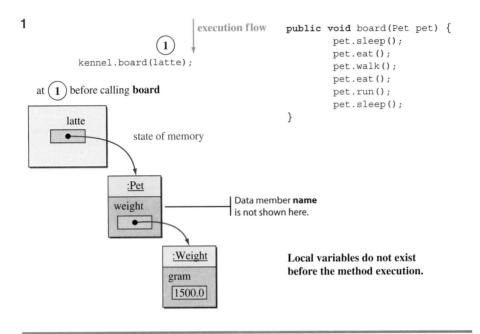

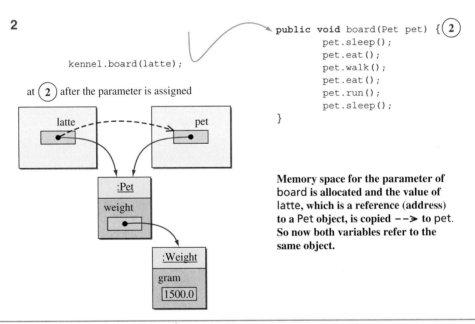

Figure 4.6 How an object is passed to a method. The value of the object name (variable), which is a reference to an object, is passed to a method.

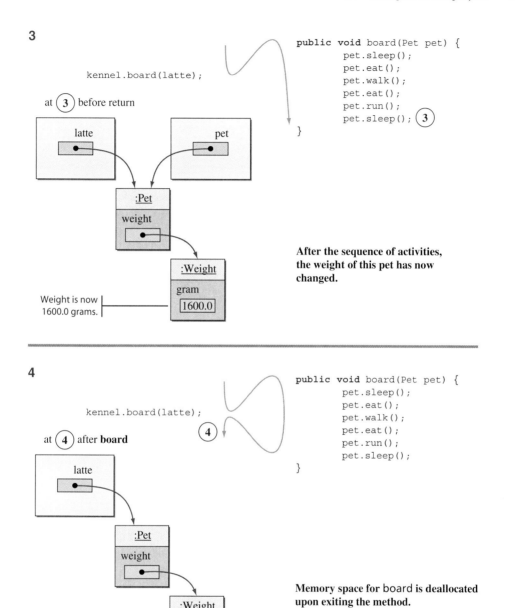

Figure 4.7 Continuation of Figure 4.6.

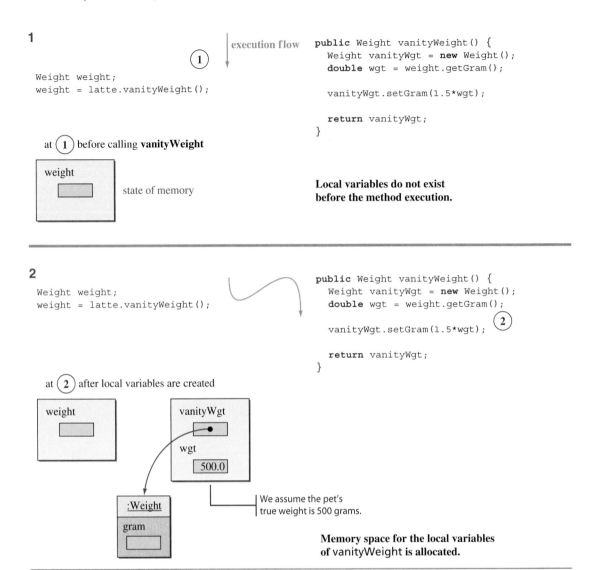

1

```
                              execution flow    public Weight vanityWeight() {
                        ①                           Weight vanityWgt = new Weight();
                                                    double wgt = weight.getGram();
Weight weight;
weight = latte.vanityWeight();                      vanityWgt.setGram(1.5*wgt);

                                                    return vanityWgt;
                                                }
```

at ① before calling **vanityWeight**

weight

state of memory

**Local variables do not exist
before the method execution.**

2

```
Weight weight;                                  public Weight vanityWeight() {
weight = latte.vanityWeight();                      Weight vanityWgt = new Weight();
                                                    double wgt = weight.getGram();
                                                                                  ②
                                                    vanityWgt.setGram(1.5*wgt);

                                                    return vanityWgt;
                                                }
```

at ② after local variables are created

weight

vanityWgt

wgt

500.0

:Weight

gram

We assume the pet's
true weight is 500 grams.

**Memory space for the local variables
of vanityWeight is allocated.**

Figure 4.8 How an object is returned from a method.

3

```
Weight weight;
weight = latte.vanityWeight();
```

```
public Weight vanityWeight() {
    Weight vanityWgt = new Weight();
    double wgt = weight.getGram();

    vanityWgt.setGram(1.5*wgt);

    return vanityWgt;       ③
}
```

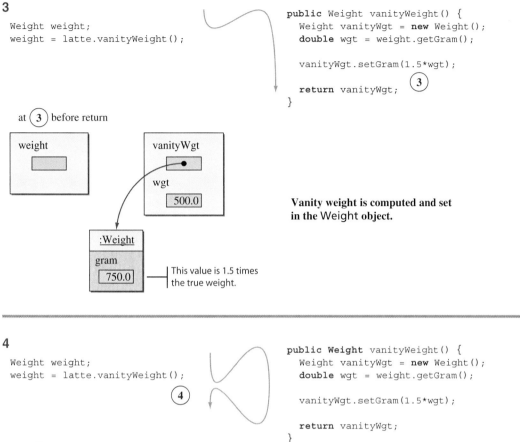

at ③ before return

Vanity weight is computed and set
in the Weight object.

This value is 1.5 times
the true weight.

4

```
Weight weight;
weight = latte.vanityWeight();
```

```
public Weight vanityWeight() {
    Weight vanityWgt = new Weight();
    double wgt = weight.getGram();

    vanityWgt.setGram(1.5*wgt);

    return vanityWgt;
}
```

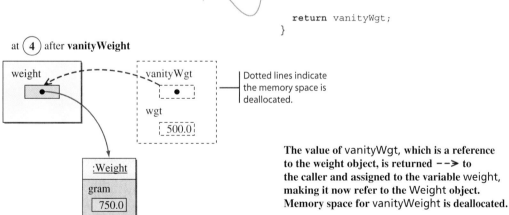

at ④ after **vanityWeight**

Dotted lines indicate
the memory space is
deallocated.

The value of vanityWgt, which is a reference
to the weight object, is returned - -> to
the caller and assigned to the variable weight,
making it now refer to the Weight object.
Memory space for vanityWeight is deallocated.

Figure 4.9   Continuation of Figure 4.8.

You Might Want to Know

Pass-by-value (also known as call-by-value) is the *only* parameter-passing mechanism Java supports. Because we are passing references when objects are passed to methods, many people with background in other programming languages use the term *pass-by-reference* (or *call-by-reference*) when referring to the passing of objects to methods. This is *wrong*. Pass-by-reference means an address (or reference) of a variable is passed, whereas pass-by-value means the content of a variable is passed (and copied into a parameter). In Java, the content of a variable is either a value of primitive data type or a reference to an object (this is the source of confusion). But it doesn't matter what the content of a variable is; as long as the content of a variable is passed and copied into a parameter, it is call-by-value. If a programming language supports the pass-by-reference mechanism, then it is possible, for example, to swap the values of two arguments in a single method call. No such thing is possible in Java.

4.7 | Modularizing the Input Routine Functionality

When we review the sample programs from Chapter 2 and 3, we see the common pattern was applied repeatedly to the input routines. This is the pattern we saw:

```
String      inputStr;
int         age;
double      score;

inputStr    = JOptionPane.showInputDialog(null,"Age:");
age         = Integer.parseInt(inputStr);

inputStr    = JOptionPane.showInputDialog(null,"Score:");
score       = Double.parseDouble(inputStr);
```

To get a numerical data, we need to convert a String object returned by the show-InputDialog method to a numerical value. Wouldn't it be nice if we could reuse an object that handles these details for us? For example, consider this:

```
InputHandler input = new InputHandler();

int    age   = input.getInteger("Age:");

double score = input.getDouble("Score:");
```

When we see a common task is repeated over and over, it's time for us to think objects. Instead of going back to the source files and cutting and pasting the common code—the lowest and most error-prone form of code reuse—we should capture the common task into a class and use an instance of this class when we need to carry out the common task. What we need here is a class that encapsulates the functionality of getting primitive data values as input.

We will define an instantiable class named InputHandler in this section. Although the InputHandler class is practical and useful, compared to the low-level cut-and-paste maneuver, it is still limited in capabilites and would not be as robust and reliable as we would like it to be. This is so because we will have to define the class using only the language features we have covered so far. We will be able to improve this class later as we learn more topics.

What would be the capability of the InputHandler class? We would like to use its instance to input String and primitive numerical data values, so let's define these public methods:

```
public double getDouble    (  )
public float  getFloat     (  )
public int    getInteger   (  )
public long   getLong      (  )
public String getString    (  )
```

These methods accept no parameters and use the default prompt of the form

```
Enter XXX
```

where XXX is replaced by the data type, such as long or double. In addition to a default prompt, we would like to allow the client programmer to customize the prompt. So we will define these methods also:

```
public double getDouble    ( String prompt )
public float  getFloat     ( String prompt )
public int    getInteger   ( String prompt )
public long   getLong      ( String prompt )
public String getString    ( String prompt )
```

Notice these are overloaded methods (more than one method sharing the same name).

We will show the portion of the class that corresponds to handling the integer input. The other portions follow the same pattern. Please view the actual source file for the complete class definition. Here's how the integer-handling portion of the class is defined:

```
class InputHandler {

    private static final String INT_DEFAULT_PROMPT
            = "Enter integer:";

    public int getInteger( ) {
        return getInteger(INT_DEFAULT_PROMPT);
    }

    public int getInteger(String prompt) {
        String inStr;

        inStr = JOptionPane.showInputDialog(null, prompt);

        return Integer.parseInt(inStr);
    }

}
```

This returns the value returned by the second method

Notice that the first method simply calls the second method and returns the value returned by the second method. This is a very common style of coding for overloaded methods (instead of duplicating the same code).

Instead of defining the **InputHandler** class as an instantiable class, we can define it as a noninstantiable class, much like the system's **Math** class, because we would most likely never need more than one instance of the **InputHandler** class at any one time. We chose not to do this because learning how to define instantiable classes is far more basic and important to master for beginners. Moreover, even if it is most desirable to define a class as a noninstantiable class, defining it as an instantiable class instead is not a serious shortcoming. In other words, for beginners, learning how to define instantiable classes is an absolute must, but learning how to define noninstantiable classes is not.

As mentioned already, we have not yet mastered all the necessary skills, so the InputHandler class is not as robust as we would like it to be. Specifically, when the user enters invalid data that cannot be converted to an integer value (entering a letter, for example), an error will result, and the program will stop. A better implementation would display an error message and give another chance to the user to enter an input value. We will describe the techniques necessary to increase the robustness of the InputHandler class in later chapters.

We have more robust classes than the **InputHandler** class presented here. These classes, for example, trap error conditions and provide added functionalities for handling input and output routines. The two classes called **InputBox** and **OutputBox** are available in the author-provided **javabook** package (along with other useful classes). Use of these **javabook** classes is strictly optional, but you might consider using them for added convenience and functionality. Information on how to use these classes can be found at **www.drcaffeine.com.**

1. Using the InputHandler class, write a code fragment to input the user's age.
2. What is wrong with this code?

```
InputHandler in = new InputHandler();
int roomNumber = in.getString("Your room #:");
```

4.8 | (Optional) Organizing Classes into a Package

The source file for the InputHandler class we defined in Section 4.7 is placed in the Ch4 sample program folder. If a client program that uses the InputHandler class is also placed in the same Ch4 folder, we can refer to the InputHandler class within the client program as

```
class MyClient {

    public static void main(String[] arg) {

        InputHandler inputHandler;

        inputHandler = new InputHandler();
        . . .
    }
}
```

But what if we want to use the InputHandler class from client programs outside of the Ch4 folder? It's easy; we place the InputHandler class into a package. We learned how to use system-defined classes such JOptionPane, Math, and others by importing system packages such as javax.swing. We can place our classes into a package also, not into the system packages, but to our own programmer-defined packages.

Let's name the package in which to place the InputHandler class simpleio. It is a Java convention to name the package with all lowercase letters. Once this package is set up correctly, we can use the classes in the package by importing them, just as we have been doing with the system packages:

```
import simpleio.*;

class MyClient {
    . . .
}
```

To set up the programmer-defined packages for general reuse, not just by the client programs in the same folder, we have to perform these tasks:

1. Include the statement

```
package simpleio;
```

   as the first statement of the source file for the InputHandler class.

2. The class declaration must include the visibility modifier public, as in

```
public class InputHandler {
    . . .
}
```

3. Create a folder named simpleio, the same name as the package name. In Java, the package must have a one-to-one correspondence with the folder.

4. Place the modified InputHandler class into the simpleio folder and compile it.

5. Modify the CLASSPATH environment variable to include the folder that contains the simpleio package (i.e., folder). See below.

Step 5 is the most troublesome step for those new to Java. Since the exact steps to change the CLASSPATH environment variable are different for each platform (Windows, Unix, Mac) and tool (BlueJ, TextPad, JBuilder, etc.), we will describe only the general idea for the Windows platform here. Please consult Appendix A or your instructor for more details on this step. Suppose we have a folder named JavaPrograms under the C: drive, and the simpleio package (folder) is placed inside this JavaPrograms folder. Then to use the classes in the simpleio package, the CLASSPATH environment should make a reference to the JavaPrograms folder, not to the package simpleio itself:

```
set classpath=.;c:\JavaPrograms
```

The period after the equals symbol refers to the current folder (the folder where the client program we are trying to execute is located). Without this reference to the current folder, the client program will not recognize other classes in the same folder.

Helpful Reminder

To make the programmer-defined packages accessible to all client programs, the CLASSPATH environment variable must be set up correctly. For details, please check Appendix A or our website at www.drcaffeine.com.

4.9 Sample Development

Defining and Using Instantiable Classes

In Chapter 3, we wrote a loan calculator program that computes the monthly and total payments for a given loan amount, loan period, and interest rate. We wrote the program using the simplified program structure where we had one main class with one method (**main**). We will implement the program again, but this time we will use instantiable classes called **Loan** and **LoanCalculator.** The problem statement is given in Section 3.9 on page 123. We will go through the incremental development process to derive the program. During the development we will also introduce the syntax for calling a method from another method that belongs to the same class.

Problem Statement

The problem statement is the same as before in Chapter 3. We will repeat the statement to refresh your memory:

Write a loan calculator program that computes both monthly and total payments for a given loan amount, annual interest rate, and loan period.

Overall Plan

The tasks we identified in Chapter 3 for the program are still the same.

program
tasks

1. Get three input values: **loanAmount, interestRate,** and **loanPeriod.**

2. Compute the monthly and total payments.

3. Output the results.

The main difference in this implementation lies in the use of instantiable classes. Instead of building the program using only the main class and performing all the tasks in one big **main** method, we will define two instantiable classes **Loan** and **Loan-Calculator.** An instance of the **LoanCalculator** class acts as a top-level agent that manages all other objects in the program, such as **Loan** and **JOptionPane.** The **Loan** class captures the logic of loan calculation. A single instance of the **Loan** class represents a loan; so if the program deals with five loans, for example, then five **Loan** objects are created in the program. The sole purpose of the main class in this program is to create a **LoanCalculator** object and give it a control to carry out the loan calculation.

Notice that although both **LoanCalculator** and **Loan** are instantiable classes, the roles they play in the program are quite different. The **Loan** class is a generic class that provides a service (e.g., loan computation and currency conversion) and is intended to be reused by different programs. The **LoanCalculator** class, on the other hand, is a class designed specifically for this program, so the class is not intended for reuse by other programs. It is important to recognize this distinction because the ways in which we design the reusable and nonreusable classes are quite different. We call the class that provides some type of service a *service provider* and the class that manages other classes and objects in a program a *controller.* In general, a service provider is designed as a reusable class, while a controller is designed as a non-reusable class.

service
provider

controller

What would be the development steps for this program? If we have multiple classes to implement, we can develop the program in either a top-down or bottom-up manner. With the *top-down development*, we develop in a kind of outside-in fashion. We develop the top-level controller class first. But to test its functionalities fully, we need the service objects it uses. In a top-down development, we use temporary dummy service objects that return a fake value from their methods. After we verify that the controller class is working correctly, we then complete the service class with the real methods. The top-down development for this program will implement the **LoanCalculator** class first with the dummy **Loan** class and then the real **Loan** class.

top-down
develop-
ment

bottom-up develop-ment

With the *bottom-up development*, we develop in the reverse inside-out fash-ion; that is, we develop the service classes first. To test the service classes, we write a temporary dummy main class. After the service classes are done, we will complete the top-level class that uses these service classes. The bottom-up development for this program will implement the **Loan** class fully and then the **LoanCalculator** class. For both approaches, the classes are developed incrementally as usual.

For this sample development, we will adopt the top-down development. We will leave the bottom-up development for this program as an exercise. For some sample applications in later chapters, we will adopt the bottom-up development. We will im-plement this program in five steps:

develop-ment steps

1. Start with the main class and a skeleton of the **LoanCalculator** class. The skeleton **LoanCalculator** class will include only an object/variable declaration and a constructor to create objects. Define a temporary placeholder **Loan** class.

2. Implement the input routine to accept three input values.

3. Implement the output routine to display the results.

4. Implement the computation routine to compute the monthly and total payments.

5. Finalize the program, implementing any remaining temporary methods and adding necessary methods as appropriate.

Step 1 Development: Program Skeleton

step 1 design

Since the **LoanCalculator** object is the top-level agent of the program that manages other objects, we need a method to create these objects. We will do this in the constructor. We will define separate methods for input, computation, and output to organize the class more logically. A class with a set of single-task methods is more manageable and easier to understand than a class with one method that performs all three tasks of input, computation, and output. We will call the methods **getInput, computePayment,** and **displayOutput.** We will also include one method called **describeProgram** that describes the purpose of the program to the user.

alternative design 1

We need the main class for the program, and we need to define its **main** method. In this **main** method, we have to create an instance of the **LoanCalculator** class. How should the **main** method interact with the **LoanCalculator** object? One possibility is to call the methods **getInput, computePayment,** and so forth individually, as in

```
public static void main ( String[ ] args ) {

    LoanCalculator loanCalculator;
    loanCalculator = new LoanCalculator( );

    loanCalculator.describeProgram();
    loanCalculator.getInput();
```

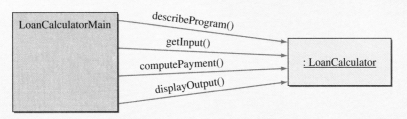

Figure 4.10 The program diagram for design alternative 1.

```
loanCalculator.computePayment();
loanCalculator.displayOutput();
}
```

The methods are all **public** methods and are called individually from the **main** method. The program diagram for this design is shown in Figure 4.10.

Notice that these four methods must be called in the correct sequence. For example, the program will not work if the **main** method calls **displayOutput** before calling **computePayment.** Except for the **describeProgram** method, these methods are not independent of one another. They must be called in the right sequence. The reason we divide the class into several methods is to make the class understandable for those who will implement and maintain the class.

One of our goals in developing programs is to design them so that they are easy to understand, which is critical in program maintenance. Program maintenance includes correcting errors undetected during development, making minor adjustments, and performing other tasks related to the upkeep of the program. Those who maintain programs are not normally the people who developed them, and maintenance personnel must understand the programs they maintain. A class with a number of cleanly written, short methods is more understandable than a class with one gigantic method even if it is cleanly written. Even if the developers themselves perform maintenance, the same argument applies.

alternative design 2

We should provide a lot simpler interface to the user of the **LoanCalculator** class. Since an instance of the class is the top-level agent, much like a general contractor, we will provide one method the programmer can call to initiate the whole task. We will name the method **start.** All other methods will be **private** and called from the **start** method. The program diagram for this design is shown in Figure 4.11. We will adopt this design for our implementation.

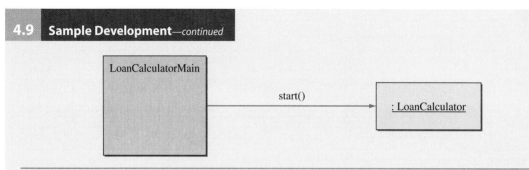

Figure 4.11 The program diagram for alternative design 2.

Let's summarize alternative design 2 for the **LoanCalculator** class:

Design Document: The `LoanCalculator` Class		
Method	**Visibility**	**Purpose**
`start`	`public`	Starts the loan calculation by calling the other private methods.
`computePayment`	`private`	Given three parameters—loan amount, loan period, and interest rate—it computes monthly and total payments. The actual computation is done by a `Loan` object.
`describeProgram`	`private`	Displays a short description of the program in `System.out`.
`displayOutput`	`private`	Displays the result—monthly and total payments—in `System.out`.
`getInput`	`private`	Uses `JOptionPane` to get three input values—loan amount, loan period, and interest rate.

There are three classes we have to define for the program: **LoanCalculatorMain, LoanCalculator,** and **Loan.** The main class is now called **LoanCalculatorMain.** Its **main** method will declare and create an instance of **LoanCalculator** and send a message **start** to it, to carry out the loan computation. So the method body of the **main** method will look like this:

```
LoanCalculator  loanCalculator;
loanCalculator = new LoanCalculator();
loanCalculator.start();
```

This is all we have to design for the main class because the real workhorse of this program is a **LoanCalculator** object. For the **LoanCalculator** class, we will begin with the skeleton and develop it incrementally. The purpose of the skeleton **LoanCalculator** class is to declare and create all the necessary data members. At this step, we only know of one object that will be used by **LoanCalculator**, namely, a **Loan** object. The declaration part of the **LoanCalculator** class will be

```
class LoanCalculator {

    private Loan loan;

    ...
}
```

At this point, the constructor for the **LoanCalculator** class is very simple. The only data member is a **Loan** object, so we will create it in the constructor as

```
public LoanCalculator( ) {
    loan = new Loan( );
}
```

For this constructor to work properly, we need the definition for the **Loan** class. We begin with the minimalist skeleton code for the **Loan** class:

```
class Loan {

    public Loan( ) {

    }
}
```

Since the **main** method calls the **start** method of **LoanCalculator,** we need to implement this method before we can compile the program. The **start** method will call the other private methods. It is written as

```
public void start ( ) {
    describeProgram();
    getInput();                    No dot notation is
    computePayment();              used here.
    displayOutput();
}
```

We will define the four private methods with only a temporary output statement inside their method body to verify that the methods are called correctly. A method that has no "real" statements inside the method body is called a *stub*. The four methods are defined as

stub

```
private void describeProgram() {

    System.out.println("inside describeProgram"); //TEMP
}
```

```java
    private void getInput() {

        System.out.println("inside getInput");        //TEMP
    }

    private void computePayment() {

        System.out.println("inside computePayment");   //TEMP
    }

    private void displayOutput() {

        System.out.println("inside displayOutput");    //TEMP
    }
```

Notice the comment marker **//TEMP** after the output statements. It is our convention to attach this comment marker so we can easily and quickly locate temporary statements. We use **System.out** for temporary output.

step 1 code

Let's put our design in an actual code. The class declaration for the main class is

```java
/**
 * Chapter 4 Sample Development: Loan Calculation (Step 1)
 *
 * File: Step1/LoanCalculatorMain.java
 */
class LoanCalculatorMain {

    public static void main (String[] args) {

        LoanCalculator loanCalculator;
        loanCalculator = new LoanCalculator( );
        loanCalculator.start();
    }
}
```

The skeleton **LoanCalculator** class is defined as

```java
/**
 * Chapter 4 Sample Development: Loan Calculation (Step 1)
 *
 * File: Step1/LoanCalculator.java
 *
 */
```

```
class LoanCalculator {

    private Loan loan;

    public LoanCalculator()

        loan = new Loan();
    }
```

> We will often remove comments for the sake of brevity. The actual source file will include full javadoc comments.

```
    /**
     * Top-level method that calls other private methods
     * to compute the monthly and total loan payments
     */
    public void start() {

        describeProgram();    //tell what the program does
        getInput();           //get three input values
        computePayment();     //compute the monthly payment and total
        displayOutput();      //display the results
    }

    /**
     * Computes the monthly and total loan payments.
     */
    private void computePayment() {

        System.out.println("inside computePayment");    //TEMP
    }

    /**
     * Provides a brief explanation of the program to the user.
     */
    private void describeProgram() {

        System.out.println("inside describeProgram");    //TEMP
    }

    /**
     * Displays the input values and monthly and total payments.
     */
    private void displayOutput() {

        System.out.println("inside displayOutput");    //TEMP
    }

    /**
     * Gets three input values-loan amount, interest rate, and
     * loan period-using an InputBox object
     */
```

```
    private void getInput() {

        System.out.println("inside getInput");    //TEMP
    }
}
```

And finally the skeleton **Loan** class is defined as

```
/**
 * Chapter 4 Sample Development: Loan Calculation (Step 1)
 *
 * File: Step1/Loan.java
 *
 */
class Loan {
    public Loan( ) {

    }
}
```

step 1 test

We run the step 1 program and verify that the following text appears in the standard output window:

```
inside describeProgram
inside getInput
inside computePayment
inside displayOutput
```

After the step 1 program is compiled and executed correctly, we move on to step 2.

Step 2 Development: Accept Input Values

step 2 design

In the second step of coding, we implement the **getInput** method. We will reuse the input routine we derived in Chapter 3. When we receive three input values, we must pass these values to the **Loan** object **loan.** We will add three data members to keep track of the three input values and one constant to aid the conversion:

```
class Loan {

    private static final int MONTHS_IN_YEAR;
    private double loanAmount;
```

```
private double monthlyInterestRate;
private int    numberOfPayments;

...
```
}

Notice that the annual interest rate and loan period expressed in years are the input, but we are keeping monthly interest rate and the number of monthly payments for the loan period to make them more compatible to the loan calculation formula we are using. We need to define three set methods (mutators) for interest rate, loan period, and loan amount. A set method for the number of payments, for example, can be defined as

```
public void setPeriod(int periodInYear) {
    numberOfPayments = periodInYear * MONTHS_IN_YEAR;
}
```

We define a complementary set of accessor methods. The **getPeriod** method, for example, is defined as

```
public int getPeriod( ) {
    return (numberOfPayments / MONTHS_IN_YEAR);
}
```

Notice that the value returned by an accessor may or may not be the data member. It is possible that the value returned is derived from the data member, as was the case with the **getLoanPeriod** method.

We mentioned in Section 4.2 the importance of a constructor's initializing an object properly. Now that we have associated data members to the **Loan** class, let's define two constructors in the manner analogous to the constructors for the **Currency-Converter** class:

```
private static double DEFAULT_AMOUNT = 1000.00;
private static double DEFAULT_RATE   =   10.00;
private static int    DEFAULT_PERIOD =   10   ;

public Loan( ) {
    this(DEFAULT_AMOUNT, DEFAULT_RATE, DEFAULT_PERIOD);
}

public Loan(double amount, double rate, int period) {

    setAmount(amount);
    setRate  (rate  );
    setPeriod(period);
}
```

Having this updated **Loan** class, we are now ready to tackle the **getInput** method of the **LoanCalculator** class. We perform the input routine as we did in the sample program from Chapter 3:

```
inputStr    = JOptionPane.showInputDialog(null,
                 "Loan Amount (Dollars+Cents):");
```

```
loanAmount     = Double.parseDouble(inputStr);

inputStr       = JOptionPane.showInputDialog(null,
                      "Annual Interest Rate (e.g., 9.5):");
annualInterestRate = Double.parseDouble(inputStr);

inputStr       = JOptionPane.showInputDialog(null,
                      "Loan Period - # of years:");
loanPeriod     = Integer.parseInt(inputStr);
```

Then we can call the mutators of the **Loan** class to assign values:

```
loan.setAmount(loanAmount          );
loan.setRate  (annualInterestRate);
loan.setPeriod(loanPeriod          );
```

Another possibility here is to create a new **Loan** object, using the second constructor. Instead of calling three mutators, we write

```
loan = new Loan(loanAmount,
                annualInterestRate,
                loanPeriod);
```

Finally, we include test output statements to verify that the values are read in and assigned to **loan** correctly:

```
System.out.println("Loan Amount: $"
                       + loan.getAmount());
System.out.println("Annual Interest Rate:"
                       + loan.getRate() + "%");
System.out.println("Loan Period (years):"
                       + loan.getPeriod());
```

step 2 code

From this point on, to maintain a focus on the changes we are making, we will show only the portion where we made modifications or additions. Unchanged portions are represented by three dots (. . .). Please refer to the actual source file for the viewing of complete source code. Here's the step 2 **LoanCalculator** class:

```
// LoanCalculator (Step 2 - Accept Input Values)

import javax.swing.*;

/**
 * Chapter 4 Sample Development: Loan Calculation (Step 2)
 *
 * File: Step2/LoanCalculator.java
 */
```

```java
class LoanCalculator {
    ...

    private void getInput() {

        double  loanAmount, annualInterestRate;

        int     loanPeriod;

        String  inputStr;

        inputStr           = JOptionPane.showInputDialog(null,
                                   "Loan Amount (Dollars+Cents):");
        loanAmount         = Double.parseDouble(inputStr);

        inputStr           = JOptionPane.showInputDialog(null,
                                   "Annual Interest Rate (e.g., 9.5):");
        annualInterestRate = Double.parseDouble(inputStr);

        inputStr           = JOptionPane.showInputDialog(null,
                                   "Loan Period - # of years:");
        loanPeriod         = Integer.parseInt(inputStr);

        //assign input values to the loan object
        loan.setAmount(loanAmount         );
        loan.setRate  (annualInterestRate);
        loan.setPeriod(loanPeriod         );

        //TEMP
        System.out.println("Loan Amount: $" + loan.getAmount());
        System.out.println("Annual Interest Rate:"
                           + loan.getRate() + "%");

        System.out.println("Loan Period (years):" + loan.getPeriod());
        //TEMP
    }
    ...
}
```

The step 2 **Loan** class is as follows:

```java
/**
 * Chapter 4 Sample Development: Loan Calculation (Step 2)
 *
 * File: Step2/Loan.java
 */
class Loan {
```

4.9   Sample Development—*continued*

```
//-----------------------------------
//     Data Members
//-----------------------------------

    private static double DEFAULT_AMOUNT = 1000.00;
    private static double DEFAULT_RATE   =   10.00;
    private static int    DEFAULT_PERIOD =   10   ;

    private final int   MONTHS_IN_YEAR = 12;

    private double      loanAmount;

    private double      monthlyInterestRate;

    private int         numberOfPayments;

//-----------------------------------
//     Constructors
//-----------------------------------

    public Loan( ) {
        this(DEFAULT_AMOUNT, DEFAULT_RATE, DEFAULT_PERIOD);
    }

    public Loan(double amount, double rate, int period) {
        setAmount(amount);
        setRate  (rate  );
        setPeriod(period);
    }

//-----------------------------------------------
//     Public Methods:
//
//         double  getAmount   (            )
//         double  getPeriod   (            )
//         int     getRate     (            )
//
//         void    setAmount   ( double     )
//         void    setPeriod   ( int        )
//         void    setRate     ( double     )
//
//-----------------------------------------------

    public double getAmount( ) {
        return loanAmount;
    }
```

```
public int getPeriod( ) {
    return numberOfPayments / MONTHS_IN_YEAR;
}

public double getRate( ) {
    return monthlyInterestRate * MONTHS_IN_YEAR;
}

public void setAmount(double amount) {
    loanAmount = amount;
}

public void setRate(double annualRate) {
    monthlyInterestRate = annualRate / 100.0 / MONTHS_IN_YEAR;
}

public void setPeriod(int periodInYears) {
    numberOfPayments = periodInYears * MONTHS_IN_YEAR;
}
}
```

step 2 test

As before, to verify the input routine is working correctly, we run the program multiple times. For each run, we enter a different set of data to verify that the values entered are displayed correctly.

Step 3 Development: Output Values

step 3 design

In the third step of development, we implement the **displayOutput** method. We will reuse the design of the output layout from Chapter 3. The actual task of computing the monthly and total payments is now delegated to the **Loan** class, so we will add two methods—**getMonthlyPayment** and **getTotalPayment**—to the **Loan** class. The focus in step 3 is on the layout for output, so we will define a temporary dummy code for these two methods in this manner:

```
public double getMonthlyPayment( ) {
    return 132.15; //TEMP
}

public double getTotalPayment( ) {
    return 15858.10;  //TEMP
}
```

To display the monthly and total payments, we add the following code in the **displayOutput** method:

```
private void displayOutput( ) {

    //echo print the input values here
```

```
            System.out.println("Monthly payment is $ "  +
                               loan.getMonthlyPayment() );
            System.out.println("  TOTAL payment is $ "  +
                               loan.getTotalPayment() );
    }
```

Notice that the **computePayment** method is no longer needed in the **Loan-Calculator** class. This makes sense because in Chapter 3, this class was the one responsible for computing the monthly and total loan payments, but now the **Loan** class is the one responsible for this task. The **LoanCalculator** class no longer handles the actual computation, so the method is removed from the class.

step 3 code   Here are the modified **LoanCalculator** and **Loan** classes:

```java
// LoanCalculator (Step 3 - Display Output Values)

import javax.swing.*;

/**
 * Chapter 4 Sample Development: Loan Calculation (Step 3)
 *
 * File: Step3/LoanCalculator.java
 */
class LoanCalculator {
    ...
    // computePayment method is removed from the source file

    private void displayOutput() {

        System.out.println("Loan Amount: $" + loan.getAmount());
        System.out.println("Annual Interest Rate:"
                            + loan.getRate() + "%");
        System.out.println("Loan Period (years): " + loan.getPeriod());

        System.out.println("Monthly payment is $ " +
                                        loan.getMonthlyPayment());

        System.out.println("  TOTAL payment is $ " +
                                        loan.getTotalPayment());

    }

    private void getInput() {

        //same code but the temporary echo print statements
        //are removed

    }
}
```

```
// Loan Class (Step 3)
/**
 * Chapter 4 Sample Development: Loan Calculation (Step 3)
 *
 * File: Step3/Loan.java
 */
class Loan {
    ...

    public double getMonthlyPayment( ) {
        return 132.15; //TEMP
    }

    public double getTotalPayment( ) {
        return 15858.10; //TEMP
    }

    ...
}
```

step 3 test

To verify the output routine is working correctly, we run the program multiple times and verify that the layout looks okay for different values. It is common for a programmer to run the program several times before the layout looks clean on the screen.

Step 4 Development: Compute Loan Amount

step 4 design

In the fourth step of development, we replace the temporary **getMonthlyPayment** and **getTotalPayment** methods with the final version. The changes are made only to the **Loan** class. The other two classes remain the same.

In the Chapter 3 **LoanCalculator** class, one method—**computePayment**—computed both monthly and total payments. In the method, we computed the monthly payment first and multiplied by the number of payments to the monthly payment to derive the total payment. We now have to divide the method into two methods. Suppose we define the required two methods in the following manner:

```
private double monthlyPayment;

public double getMonthlyPayment ( ) {
    monthlyPayment = ...;
    return monthlyPayment;
}

public double getTotalPayment ( ) {
    return monthlyPayment * numberOfPayments;
}
```

Bad Version

The idea is to use the value of the data member **monthlyPayment** set by the **getMonthlyPayment** method in computing the total payment. This setup is problematic because the **getTotalPayment** method will not work correctly unless **getMonthlyPayment** is called first. It is considered a very poor design, and generally unacceptable, to require the client programmer to call a collection of methods in a certain order. We must define the two methods so they can be called in any order, not necessarily in the order of **getMonthlyPayment** and **getTotalPayment**. The correct way here is to call **getMonthlyPayment** from the **getTotalPayment** method:

```
private double getTotalPayment( ) {
    double totalPayment;

    totalPayment = getMonthlyPayment() * numberOfPayments;

    return totalPayment;
}
```

With this approach the data member **monthlyPayment** is not necessary.

step 4 code Here's the updated **Loan** class:

```
// Loan Class (Step 4)

/**
 * Chapter 4 Sample Development: Loan Calculation (Step 4)
 *
 * File: Step4/Loan.java
 *
 */
class Loan {
    ...

  public double getMonthlyPayment( ) {
      double monthlyPayment;

      monthlyPayment = (loanAmount * monthlyInterestRate)
                     /
                        (1 - Math.pow(1/(1 + monthlyInterestRate),
                                      numberOfPayments ) ) );
      return monthlyPayment;
  }

  public double getTotalPayment( ) {
      double totalPayment;
```

```
        totalPayment = getMonthlyPayment( ) * numberOfPayments;

        return totalPayment;
    }
    ...
}
```

After the method is added to the class, we need to run the program through a number of test data. As in Chapter 3, we made the assumption that the input values must be valid, so we will only test the program for valid input values. For sample test data, we repeat the table from Chapter 3. The right two columns show the correct results. Remember that these three values are only suggestions, not a complete list of test data. You must try other input values as well.

Input			Output (shown up to three decimal places only)	
Loan Amount	Annual Interest Rate	Loan Period (Years)	Monthly Payment	Total Payment
10000	10	10	132.151	15858.088
15000	7	15	134.824	24268.363
10000	12	10	143.471	17216.514
0	10	5	0.000	0.000
30	8.5	50	0.216	129.373

Step 5 Development: Finalize

Now in the last step of development, we finalize the class declaration by completing the **describeProgram** method, the only method still undefined. We may give a very long description or a very terse one. An ideal program will let the user decide. We do not know how to write such code yet, so we will display a short description of the program, using **System.out.** We choose not to use **JOptionPane** here because the dialog opened by its **showMessageDialog** method must be closed before proceeding with the program. An output on **System.out,** on the other hand, will remain on the screen while the program is running. We prefer this mode of display so the description is always available to the user.

Another improvement is the display of monetary values in two decimal places. We can format the display to two decimal places by using the **DecimalFormat** class as explained in Chapter 3.

4.9 **Sample Development**—*continued*

step 5 code

Here are the two modified methods:

```
private void describeProgram() {
    System.out.println
            ("This program computes the monthly and total");
    System.out.println
            ("payments for a given loan amount, annual ");
    System.out.println
            ("interest rate, and loan period (# of years).");
    System.out.println("\n");
}

private void displayOutput () {

    DecimalFormat df = new DecimalFormat("0.00");

    System.out.println("Loan Amount: $" + loan.getAmount());
    System.out.println("Annual Interest Rate:" +
                                    loan.getRate() + "%");
    System.out.println("Loan Period (years): " +
                                        loan.getPeriod());

    System.out.println("Monthly payment is $ " +
                        df.format(loan.getMonthlyPayment()));

    System.out.println(" TOTAL payment is $ " +
                        df.format(loan.getTotalPayment()));

}
```

step 5 test

You may feel that there's not much testing we can do in this step. After all, we add only a single method that carries out a simple output routine. However, many things can go wrong between step 4 and step 5. You may have deleted some lines of code inadvertently. You may have deleted a necessary file by mistake. Anything could happen. The point is to test after every step of development to make sure everything is in order.

4.10 | Making an Instantiable Class the Main Class

In this section, we will show you a simple way to make any instantiable class also the main class of a program. Instead of defining a separate main class, as we have done so far in this chapter, it is possible to define the main method to an instantiable class so the class becomes the main class of a program also. There are a number of advantages in doing this. First, we have one less class to manage if we don't have to define a separate main class. This advantage may not seem substantial. However, when we write numerous classes (e.g., writing solutions to the chapter exercises), writing a separate main class for all those classes so they become executable becomes tedious. Second, when we develop instantiable and reusable classes for other programmers, we often want to include a simple example on how to use the classes. Instead of providing a separate sample main class, it is more convenient to add the main method to the instantiable classes.

We will illustrate the procedure using the LoanCalculatorMain and LoanCalculator classes from Section 4.9. We can eliminate the LoanCalculatorMain class by making the LoanCalculator class the main class. What we have to do is quite simple. We just copy the main method of LoanCalculatorMain and paste it to the LoanCalculator class. Here's the instantiable main class LoanCalculator:

```
//Instantiable Main Class
class LoanCalculator {

    //exactly the same code as before comes here

    public static void main (String[] args) {
        LoanCalculator loanCalculator;
        loanCalculator = new LoanCalculator( );
        loanCalculator.start();
    }
}
```

Remember that the new LoanCalculator class having the main method does not prohibit us from defining a separate main class. All Java requires us to do is to include the main method to the classes we designate as the main class of the program. So it is possible (although not likely) that every class in the program has the main method, and we can select one of them to be the main class when we execute the program.

Summary

- An *instantiable class* is a class in which we can create instances.
- An instantiable class will include data members and methods.
- Data members of a class refer to the instance and class variables and constants of the class.
- An object's properties are maintained by a set of data members.
- Class methods can access only the class variables and class constants.
- Instance methods can access all types of data members of the class.
- Public methods define the behavior of an object.
- Private methods and data members (except certain class constants) are considered internal details of the class.
- Components (data members and methods) of a class with the visibility modifier private cannot be accessed by the client programs.

- Components of a class with the visibility modifier public can be accessed by the client programs.

- A method may or may not return a value. One that does not return a value is called a void method.

- A *constructor* is a special method that is executed when a new object is created. Its purpose is to initialize the object into a valid state.

- An instantiable class may (and commonly does) have multiple constructors.

- Memory space for local variables and parameters is allocated when a method is called and deallocated when the method terminates.

- Arguments are passed to the methods using the call-by-value scheme where the value of an argument is passed. The value is the actual data in the case of primitive data type and a reference to an object in the case of reference data type.

- A public method that changes a property of an object is called a *mutator*.

- A public method that retrieves a property of an object is called an *accessor*.

- Methods with the same name are called *overloaded methods*.

- Dot notation is optional when you call a method from another method of the same object. If dot notation is used, then the reserved word this must be used.

- Dot notation is optional when you refer to a data member of an object from a method of the same object. If dot notation is used, then the reserved word this must be used.

- An instantiable class can be set as the main class of a program by adding the main method to it. In the main method, an instance of this class is created.

- (Optional section) Programmer-defined classes can be grouped into a programmer-defined package.

Key Concepts

instantiable class	reserved word this
data members	local variables
visibility modifiers	parameter passing
void methods	call-by-value
value-returning methods	accessors
constructors	mutators
information hiding	overloaded methods
encapsulation	instantiable main class
object behavior	programmer-defined
object properties	packages (optional)

1. Consider the following instantiable class.

```
class QuestionOne {
    public    final int A = 345;
    public    int        b;
    private   float      c;

    private void methodOne( int a) {
        b = a;
    }

    public float methodTwo( ) {
        return 23;
    }
}
```

Identify invalid statements in the following main class. For each invalid statement, state why it is invalid.

```
class Q1Main {
    public static void main( String[] args ) {
        QuestionOne q1;
        q1 = new QuestionOne( );

        q1.A = 12;   needs to be a
        q1.b = 12;
        q1.c = 12;

        q1.methodOne( 12 );
        q1.methodOne( );
        System.out.println( q1.methodTwo( 12 ) );
        q1.c = q1.methodTwo( );
    }
}
```

2. What will be the output from the following code?

```
class Q2Main {
    public static void main( String[] args ) {
        QuestionTwo q2;
        q2 = new QuestionTwo( );
        q2.init();

        q2.increment();
        q2.increment();

        System.out.println( q2.getCount() );
    }
}

class QuestionTwo {
    private   int   count;
```

```
        public void init( ) {
            count = 1;
        }

        public void increment( ) {
            count = count + 1;
        }

        public int getCount( ) {
            return count;
        }
    }
```

3. What will be the output from the following code? Q3Main and QuestionThree classes are the slightly modified version of Q2Main and QuestionTwo.

```
class Q3Main {
    public static void main( String[] args ) {
        QuestionThree q3;
        q3 = new QuestionThree( );
        q3.init();

        q3.count = q3.increment() + q3.increment();

        System.out.println( q3.increment() );
    }
}

class QuestionThree {
    public   int   count;

    public void init( ) {
        count = 1;
    }

    public int increment( ) {
        count = count + 1;
        return count;
    }
}
```

4. Determine the output of the following program.

```
/*
   Program Question4
*/

class Question4 {
    private int x, y, z;

    public void start ( ) {
```

```java
        int  x, y;
        setup();

        x = y = 10;
        modify(x, y);

        printout();
    }

    private void setup( ) {

        x = 100;
        y = 200;
        z = 300;
    }

    private void modify( int x, int y) {

        z = x + y;
        x = z;
        y = 2 * z;
    }

    private void printout( ) {

        System.out.println("x = " + x);
        System.out.println("y = " + y);
        System.out.println("z = " + z);
    }
}

/* Main Class */
class Q4Main {

    public static void main( String[ ] args ) {

        Question4 q4;
        q4 = new Question4( );
        q4.start( );
    }
}
```

5. Improve the following program Question5 by converting the class to two classes: the main Q5Main class and the instantiable Question5 class. Avoid duplicating the same code for computing the circumference of two circles. Define a private method in Question5 that accepts the radius of a circle as its parameter and returns the circumference of the circle.

```
/*
   Program Question5
*/
class Question5 {

   public static void main (String[ ] args ) {

      InputHandler input = new InputHandler(); //see Section 4.7
      double        radius ;
      double        circumference;

      int           smallRadius, largeRadius;
      double        smallCircum, largeCircum;

      //compute circumference of a smaller circle
      smallRadius = input.getDouble("Radius of smaller circle:");
      radius = smallRadius;
      smallCircum = 2 * Math.PI * radius;

      //compute circumference of a larger circle
      largeRadius = input.getDouble("Radius of larger circle:");
      radius = largeRadius;
      largeCircum = 2 * Math.PI * radius;

      //Display the difference
      System.out.println("Difference in circumference of two circles");
      System.out.println("Circumference of smaller circle: " + smallCircum);
      System.out.println("\n");
      System.out.println("Circumference of larger circle: " + largeCircum);
      System.out.println(("\n");
      System.out.println("Difference: " + (largeCircum - smallCircum));
   }
}
```

6. Is there any problem with the following class? Is the passing of an arugment to the private methods appropriate? Are the data members apppropriate? Explain.

```
/*
   Problem Question6
*/
class MyText {

   private String word;
   private String temp;
   private int    idx;
```

```
public String firstLetter( ) {
    idx = 0;
    return getLetter(word);
}

public String lastLetter( ) {
    idx = word.length() - 1;
    return getLetter(word);
}

private String getLetter(String str) {
    temp = str.substring(idx, idx+1);
    return temp;
}
}
```

7. Modify the Weight class from Section 4.5 by using two data members, one for tracking the pound portion of the weight and the other for the ounce portion of the weight, instead of keeping track of the weight in grams.

8. Write a Distance class that can express distance in both meters and feet and inches. Model this class after the Weight class from Section 4.5. 1 ft = 0.3048 m.

9. Write an Area class that can express an area in square meters and square yards. Model this class after the Weight class from Section 4.5. $1 \text{ m}^2 = 1.1960 \text{ yd}^2$.

10. Using the Distance class from Exercise 8, write an application that inputs distance between two cities in kilometers and displays the distance in miles. 1 mi = 1.6093 km. Do not modify the given Distance class.

11. In doing Exercise 10, if you were allowed to modify the Distance class, would you modify it? You have to realize that you cannot keep on modifying the service class for every possible need of client programs. How would you define the Distance class so it can serve a large number of client programs without having too many methods?

12. Modify the Kennel class from Section 4.6. Add three different types of boarding: superdelight, enhanced, and regular. The regular boarding is implemented by the original board method. The enhanced boarding has twice as many eating activities as the regular boarding. The superdelight boarding has 3 times as many eating activities as the regular boarding. You may do the activities in any order you wish. Write a test main class to let three different pets with the same initial weight go through three boarding options: the first goes through regular, the second goes through enhanced, and the third goes through superdelight. Display their pre- and postboarding weights.

13. Write a program that displays the recommended weight in kilograms, given the user's age and height in centimeters. The formula for calculating the recommended weight is

    ```
    recommendedWeight = (height - 100 + age % 10) * 0.90
    ```

    Define a service class named Height and include an appropriate method for getting a recommended weight of a designated height.

14. Write a program that computes the total ticket sales of a concert. There are three types of seatings: A, B, and C. The program accepts the number of tickets sold and the price of a ticket for each of the three types of seats. The total sales are computed as

    ```
    totalSales = numberOfA_Seats * pricePerA_Seat +
                 numberOfB_Seats * pricePerB_Seat +
                 numberOfC_Seats * pricePerC_Seat;
    ```

    Write this program, using only one class, the main class of the program.

15. Redo Exercise 14 by using a Seat class. An instance of the Seat class keeps track of the ticket price for a given type of seat (A, B, or C).

16. Write a program that computes the area of a circular region (the shaded area in the diagram) given the radius of the inner and the outer circles, r_i and r_o, respectively.

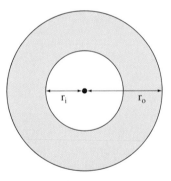

We compute the area of the circular region by subtracting the area of the inner circle from the area of the outer circle. Define an instantiable Circle class that has methods to compute the area and circumference. You set the circle's radius with the setRadius method or via a constructor.

17. In Section 4.3, we modified the conversion methods of the Currency-Converter class to include the fee deduction. With the modified methods, the sequence of calls such as

    ```
    yenAmount
        = yenConverter.fromDollar( markConverter.toDollar(100) );
    ```

    will result in charging the fee twice. Modify the class to eliminate this double-charging problem.

18. Write an instantiable WeightConverter class. Model this class after the CurrencyConverter class. An instance of this class is created by passing the gravity of an object relative to the earth's gravity (see Exercise 12 on page 141). For example, the moon's gravity is approximately 0.167 of the earth's gravity, so we create a WeightConverter instance for the moon as

```
WeightConverter moonWeight;
moonWeight = new WeightConverter( 0.167 );
```

To compute how much you weigh on the moon, you pass your weight on earth to the convert method as

```
yourMoonWeight = moonWeight.convert( 160 );
```

Use this class and redo Exercise 12 on page 141.

Development Exercises

For these exercises, use the incremental development methodology to implement the program. For each exercise, identify the program tasks, create a design document with class descriptions, and draw the program diagram. Map out the development steps at the start. Present any design alternatives and justify your selection. Be sure to perform adequate testing at the end of each development step.

19. Redo Exercise 26 on page 147, but this time, define and use instantiable classes.

20. Write a program that accepts the unit weight of a bag of coffee in pounds and the number of bags sold and displays the total price of the sale, computed as

```
totalPrice      = bagWeight * numberOfBags * pricePerLb;
totalPriceWithTax = totalPrice + totalPrice * taxrate;
```

Display the result in the following manner:

```
Number of bags sold: 32
     Weight per bag: 5 lb
   Price per pound: $5.99
         Sales tax: 7.25%

      Total price: $ 1027.88
```

> **Format to two decimal places.**

Define and use an instantiable CoffeeBag class. Include class constants for the price per pound and tax rate with the values $5.99 per pound and 7.25 percent, respectively.

21. In the Turtle exercises from earlier chapters, we dealt with only one Turtle (e.g., see Exercise 23 on page 82). It is possible, however, to let multiple turtles draw on a single drawing window. To associate multiple turtles to a single drawing, we create an instance of TurtleDrawingWindow and add turtles to it, as in

```
TurtleDrawingWindow canvas = new TurtleDrawingWindow( );
Turtle winky, pinky, tinky;

//create turtles;
//pass Turtle.NO_DEFAULT_WINDOW as an argument so
//no default drawing window is attached to a turtle.
winky = new Turtle(Turtle.NO_DEFAULT_WINDOW);
pinky = new Turtle(Turtle.NO_DEFAULT_WINDOW);
tinky = new Turtle(Turtle.NO_DEFAULT_WINDOW);

//now add turtles to the drawing window
canvas.add( winky );
canvas.add( pinky );
canvas.add( tinky );
```

Ordinarily, when you start sending messages such as turn and move to a Turtle, it will begin moving immediately. When you have only one Turtle, this is fine. However, if you have multiple turtles and want them to start moving at the same time, you have to pause them, give instructions, and then command them to start moving. Here's the basic idea:

```
winky.pause( );
pinky.pause( );
tinky.pause( );

//give instructions to turtles here,
//e.g., pinky.move(50); etc.

//now let the turtles start moving
winky.start( );
pinky.start( );
tinky.start( );
```

Using these Turtle objects, draw these three triangles:

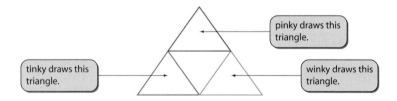

Use a different pen color for each triangle. Run the same program without pausing and describe what happens.

5 Selection Statements

Objectives

After you have read and studied this chapter, you should be able to

- Implement selection control in a program by using **if** statements.

- Implement selection control in a program by using **switch** statements.

- Write boolean expressions with relational and boolean operators.

- Evaluate given boolean expressions correctly.

- Nest an **if** statement inside another **if** statement's then or else part correctly.

- Describe how objects are compared.

- Choose the appropriate selection control statement for a given task.

Introduction

ecisions, decisions, decisions. From the moment we are awake until the time we go to sleep, we are making decisions. Should I eat cereal or toast? What should I wear to school today? Should I eat at the cafeteria today? And so forth. We make many of these decisions by evaluating some criteria. If the number of students in line for registration seems long, then come back tomorrow for another try. If today is Monday, Wednesday, or Friday, then eat lunch at the cafeteria.

Computer programs are no different. Any practical computer program contains many statements that make decisions. Often a course of action is determined by evaluating some kind of a test (e.g., is the input value negative?). Statements in programs are executed in sequence, which is called *sequential execution* or *sequential control flow*. However, we can add decision-making statements to a program to alter this control flow. For example, we can add a statement that causes a portion of a program to be skipped if an input value is greater than 100. The statement that alters the control flow is called a *control statement*. In this chapter we describe some important control statements, called *selection statements*. In Chapter 6 we will describe other control statements, called *repetition statements*.

sequential
execution

control
statement

5.1 | The if Statement

Suppose we wish to enter a student's test score and print out the message You did not pass if the score is less than 70 and You did pass if the score is 70 or higher. Here's how we express this logic in Java:

A reusable input
handling class
from Chapter 4

```
InputHandler input = new InputHandler();

int testScore = input.getInteger("Enter test score:");

if (testScore < 70)
```

This statement is
executed if **testScore**
is less than 70.

```
    JOptionPane.showMessageDialog("You did not pass");

else
```

This statement is
executed if **testScore**
is 70 or higher.

```
    JOptionPane.showMessageDialog("You did pass");
```

We use an if statement to specify which block of code to execute, where a block of code may contain zero or more statements. Which block is executed depends on the result of evaluating a test condition called a *boolean expression*. The if statement in the program follows this general format:

boolean
expression

if statement
syntax

```
if ( <boolean expression> )
    <then block>

else
    <else block>
```

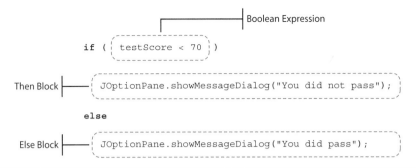

Figure 5.1 Mapping of the sample **if** statement to the general format.

Figure 5.1 illustrates the correspondence between the if statement we wrote and the general format.

The <boolean expression> is a conditional expression that is evaluated to either true or false. For example, the following three expressions are all conditional:

```
testScore < 80
testScore * 2 > 350
30 < w / (h * h)
```

relational operators

The six *relational operators* we can use in conditional expressions are as follow:

Symbol	Meaning
<	less than
<=	less than or equal to
==	equal to
!=	not equal to
>	greater than
>=	greater than or equal to

Here are some more examples:

```
a * a <= c    //true if a * a is less than or equal to c
x + y != z    //true if x + y is not equal to z
a == b        //true if a is equal to b
```

If the boolean expression evaluates to true, then the statements in the <then block> are executed. Otherwise, the statements in the <else block> are executed. We will cover more complex boolean expressions in Section 5.2. Notice that we can reverse the relational operator and switch the then and else blocks to derive the equivalent code, for example,

```
if (testScore >= 70)
    JOptionPane.showMessageDialog("You did pass");

else
    JOptionPane.showMessageDialog("You did not pass");
```

Notice that the reverse of < is >=, not >.

The if statement is called a *selection* or *branching statement* because it selects (or branches to) one of the alternative blocks for execution. In our example, either

selection or
branching
statement

```
JOptionPane.showMessageDialog("You did not pass");
```

or

```
JOptionPane.showMessageDialog("You did pass");
```

is executed depending on the value of the boolean expression. We can illustrate a branching path of execution with the diagram shown in Figure 5.2.

In the preceding if statement, both blocks contain only one statement. The then or else block can contain more than one statement. The general format for both the <then block> and the <else block> is either a

```
<single statement>
```

or a

```
<compound statement>
```

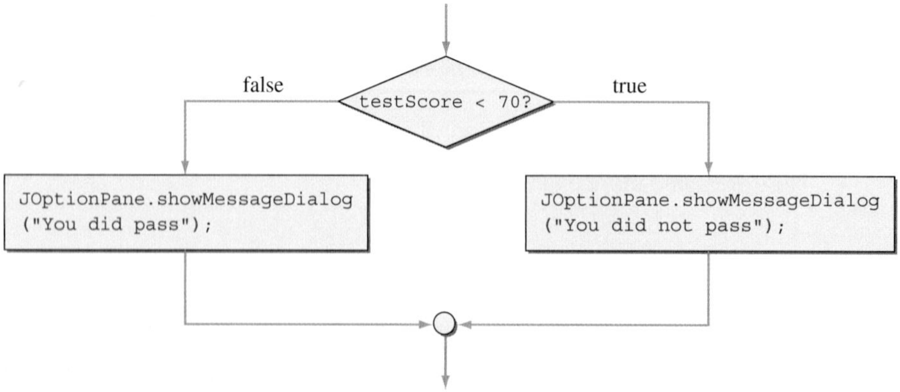

Figure 5.2 The diagram showing the control flow of the sample **if** statement.

where <single statement> is a Java statement and <compound statement> is a sequence of Java statements surrounded by braces, as shown below with $n \geq 0$ statements:

```
{
    <statement 1>
    <statement 2>
    ...
    <statement n>
}
```

If multiple statements are needed in the <then block> or the <else block>, they must be surrounded by braces { and }. For example, suppose we want to print out additional messages for each case. Let's say we also want to print Keep up the good work when the student passes and print Try harder next time when the student fails. Here's how:

Compound statements

```
if (testScore < 70)
{
    JOptionPane.showMessageDialog("You did not pass");
    JOptionPane.showMessageDialog("Try harder next time");
}
else
{
    JOptionPane.showMessageDialog("You did pass");
    JOptionPane.showMessageDialog("Keep up the good work");
}
```

The braces are necessary to delineate the statements inside the block. Without the braces, the compiler will not be able to tell whether a statement is a part of the block or the statement that follows the if statement.

Notice the absence of semicolons after the right braces. A semicolon is not necessary immediately after a right brace. A compound statement may contain zero or more statements, so it is perfectly valid for a compound statement to include only one statement. Indeed, we can write the sample if statement as

```
if (testScore < 70)
{
    JOptionPane.showMessageDialog("You did not pass");
}
else
{
    JOptionPane.showMessageDialog("You did pass");
}
```

Although not required, many programmers prefer to use the syntax for the compound statement even if the then or else block includes only one statement. In this textbook, we will use the syntax for the compound statement regardless of the number of statements inside the then and else blocks. Following this policy is beneficial for a number of reasons. One is the ease of adding temporary output statements inside the blocks. Frequently, we want to include a temporary output statement to verify that the boolean expression is written correctly. Suppose we add output statements such as

```
if (testScore < 70)
{
    System.out.println("inside then: " + testScore);
    JOptionPane.showMessageDialog("You did not pass");
}
else
{
    System.out.println("inside else: " + testScore);
    JOptionPane.showMessageDialog("You did pass");
}
```

If we always use the syntax for the compound statement, we just add and delete the temporary output statements. However, if we use the syntax of the single statement, then we have to remember to add the braces when we want to include a temporary output statement. Another reason for using the compound statement syntax exclusively is to avoid the dangling-else problem. We will discuss this problem in Section 5.3.

The placement of left and right braces does not matter to the compiler. The compiler will not complain if you write the earlier if statement as

```
if (testScore < 70)
{ JOptionPane.showMessageDialog("You did not pass");
  JOptionPane.showMessageDialog("Try harder next time");}
else
{
    JOptionPane.showMessageDialog("You did pass");
    JOptionPane.showMessageDialog("Keep up the good work");}
```

However, to keep your code readable and easy to follow, you should format your if statements by using one of the two most common styles:

Style 1
```
if ( <boolean expression> ) {
    ...
} else {
    ...
}
```

Style 2
```
if ( <boolean expression> )
{
    ...
}
else
{
    ...
}
```

In this book, we will use style 1, mainly because this style adheres to the code conventions for the Java programming language. If you prefer style 2, then go ahead and use it. Whichever style you choose, be consistent, because a consistent look and feel is very important to make your code readable.

www

The document that provides the details of code conventions for Java can be found at **http://java.sun.com/docs/codeconv/html/CodeConventions.doc.html** This document describes the Java language coding standards dictated in the Java Language Specification. It is important to follow the code conventions as closely as possible in order to increase the readability of the software.

There is a third style in which we place the reserved word else on a new line as

Style 3

```
if ( <boolean expression> ) {
    . . .
}
else {
    . . .
}
```

Many programmers prefer this variation of style 3 because the reserved word else aligns with the matching if. However, if we nitpick, style 3 goes against the logic behind the recommended style 1 format, which is to begin a new statement at one position with a reserved word. The reserved word else is a part of the if statement, not a begining of a new statement. Thus style 1 places the reserved word else to the right of the matching if.

Again, the actual format is not that important. Consistent use of the same format is. So, whichever style you use, use it consistently. To promote consistency among all programmers, we recommend everybody to adopt the code conventions. Even though the recommended format may look peculiar at first, with some repeated use, the format becomes natural in no time.

Let's summarize the key points to remember:

Helpful Reminder

Rules for writing the then and else blocks:

1. *Left and right braces are necessary to surround the statements if the then or else block contains multiple statements.*
2. *Braces are not necessary if the then or else block contains only one statement.*
3. *A semicolon is not necessary after a right brace.*

Now let's study a second version of the if statement. Suppose we want to print out the message You are an honor student if the test score is 95 or above and print out nothing otherwise. For this type of testing, we use the second version of the if statement, whose general format is

```
if ( <boolean expression> )
    <then block>
```

The second version contains only the <then block>. Using this version and the compound statement syntax, we express the selection control as

```
if (testScore >= 95)   {
   JOptionPane.showMessageDialog("You are an honor student");
}
```

Figure 5.3 illustrates the control flow for this if statement. To distinguish the two, we call the first version *if–then–else* and the second version *if–then*.

Notice that the if–then statement is not necessary, because we can write any if–then statement using if–then–else by including no statement in the else block. For instance, the sample if–then statement can be written as

```
if (testScore >= 95) {

   JOptionPane.showMessageDialog("You are an honor student");

} else { }
```

In this book, we use if–then statements whenever appropriate.

Let's conclude this section with a sample class. We will define a class called Ch5Circle that is capable of computing the circumference and area of a circle, given its radius. We will include a check in this class so the methods such as getArea and getCircumference return the constant INVALID_DIMENSION when the dimension of

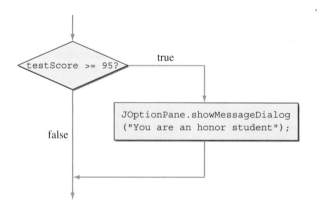

Figure 5.3 The diagram showing the control flow of the second version of the **if** statement.

the radius is invalid. Here's the Ch5Circle class (javadoc comments are removed for the sake of brevity):

```
/*
    Chapter 5 The Circle class

    File: Ch5Circle.java
*/

class Ch5Circle {

    public static final int INVALID_DIMENSION = -1;

    private double radius;

    public Ch5Circle( ) {

        this(INVALID_DIMENSION);
    }

    public Ch5Circle(double r) {
        setRadius(r);
    }

    public double getArea( ) {

        double result = INVALID_DIMENSION;

        if (isRadiusValid())   {

            result = Math.PI * radius * radius;
        }

        return result;
    }

    public double getCircumference( ) {

        double result = INVALID_DIMENSION;

        if (isRadiusValid()) {

            result = 2.0 * Math.PI * radius;
        }

        return result;
    }

    public double getDiameter( ) {

        double diameter = INVALID_DIMENSION;
```

As the number of methods gets larger, we will use this marker to quickly locate the program components. Shaded icon is used for a private element.

Data members

Constructors

getArea

getCircumference

getDiameter

```
        if (isRadiusValid()) {

            diameter = 2.0 * radius;
        }

        return diameter;
    }

    public double getRadius( ) {
        return radius;
    }

    public void setDiameter(double d) {

        if (d > 0) {
            setRadius(d/2.0);
        } else {
            setRadius(INVALID_DIMENSION);
        }
    }

    public void setRadius(double r) {

        if (r > 0) {
            radius = r;
        } else {
            radius = INVALID_DIMENSION;
        }
    }

    private boolean isRadiusValid( ) {

        return radius != INVALID_DIMENSION;
    }
}
```

> getRadius

> setDiameter

> setRadius

> isRadiusValid

Here's a short main class to test the functionality of the Ch5Circle class:

```
/*
    Chapter 5 Sample Program: Computing Circle Dimensions

    File: Ch5Sample1.java
*/
import javax.swing.*;

class Ch5Sample1 {
```

```
public static void main( String[] args ) {

    double      radius, circumference, area;

    Ch5Circle circle;

    radius = Double.parseDouble(
                JOptionPane.showInputDialog(null, "Enter radius:"));

    circle = new Ch5Circle(radius);

    circumference = circle.getCircumference();

    area          = circle.getArea();

    System.out.println("Input radius:  " + radius);
    System.out.println("Circumference: " + circumference);
    System.out.println("Area:          " + area);

    }
}
```

Notice that the program will display -1.0 when the input radius is invalid. We can improve the display by adding an if test in the main program, as in

```
System.out.print("Circumference: ");
if (circumference == Ch5Circle.INVALID_DIMENSION) {
   System.out.println("Cannot compute. Input invalid");
} else {
   System.out.println(circumference);
}
```

Another possible improvement in the main program is to check the input value first, for instance,

```
radius = ... ;
if (radius > 0) {
   //do the computation as the sample main method
} else {
   //print out the error message
}
```

Even when a client programmer does not include appropriate tests in the program, we must define an instantiable and reusable class in a robust manner so it will not crash or produce erroneous results. For the Ch5Circle class, we add a test so the data member radius is set to either a valid data value or a specially designated value (INVALID_DIMENSION) for any invalid data. By designing the class in this manner, we protect the class from a possible misuse (e.g., attempting to assign a negative radius) and producing meaningless results such as -5.88. We always strive for a reliable and robust reusable class that will withstand the abuse and misuse of client programmers.

Quick
CHECK

1. Identify the invalid if statements.

a. `if ( a < b ) then`
   `    x = y;`
   `else`
   `    x = z;`

b. `if ( a < b )`
   `    else x = y;`

c. `if ( a < b )`
   `    x = y;`
   `    else {`
   `    x = z;`
   `    };`

d. `if ( a < b ) {`
   `    x = y; } else`
   `    x = z;`

2. Express the following if–then statements by using if–then–else.

a. `if ( a < b ) x = y;`
b. `if ( a < b ) { }`
c. `if ( a < b )    x = y;`
   `if ( a >= b ) x = z;`

5.2 | Boolean Expressions and Variables

In addition to the arithmetic operators introduced in Chapter 3 and relational operators introduced in Section 5.1, boolean expressions can contain conditional and
boolean operators. A *boolean operator,* also called a *logical operator,* takes boolean
values as its operands and returns a boolean value. Three boolean operators are
AND, OR, and NOT. In Java, symbols &&, ‖, and ! represent the AND, OR, and
NOT operators, respectively. Table 5.1 explains how these operators work.

boolean
operator

 The AND operation results in true only if both P and Q are true. The OR operation results in true if either P or Q is true. The NOT operation is true if A is false
and false if P is true. Combining boolean operators with relational and arithmetic
operators, we can come up with long boolean expressions such as

```
(x + 150) == y || x < y && !(y < z && z < x)
(x < y) && (a == b || a == c)
a != 0 && b != 0 && (a + b < 10)
```

P	Q	P && Q	P ‖ Q	!P
false	false	false	false	true
false	true	false	true	true
true	false	false	true	false
true	true	true	true	false

Table 5.1 Boolean operators and their meanings.

In Section 5.1 we stated that we can reverse the relational operator and switch the then and else blocks to derive the equivalent code. For example,

```java
if (age < 0) {
    System.out.println("Invalid age is entered");
} else {
    System.out.println("Valid age is entered");
}
```

is equivalent to

```java
if ( !(age < 0) ) {
    System.out.println("Valid age is entered");
} else {
    System.out.println("Invalid age is entered");
}
```

which can be written more naturally as

```java
if (age >= 0) {
    System.out.println("Valid age is entered");
} else {
    System.out.println("Invalid age is entered");
}
```

Reversing the relational operator means negating the boolean expression. In other words, !(age < 0) is equivalent to (age >= 0). Now, consider the following if–else statement:

```java
if (temperature >= 65 && distanceToDestination < 2) {
    System.out.println("Let's walk");
} else {
    System.out.println("Let's drive");
}
```

If the temperature is greater than or equal to 65 degrees and the distance to the destination is less than 2 miles, we will walk. Otherwise (it's too cold or too far away), we will drive. How do we reverse the if–else statement? We can rewrite the statement by negating the boolean expression and switching the then and else blocks as

```java
if ( !(temperature >= 65 && distanceToDestination < 2) ) {
    System.out.println("Let's drive");
} else {
    System.out.println("Let's walk");
}
```

or more directly and naturally as

```java
if (temperature < 65 || distanceToDestination >= 2) {
    System.out.println("Let's drive");
```

```
    } else {
        System.out.println("Let's walk");
    }
```

The expression

```
!(temperature >= 65 && distanceToDestination < 2)
```

is equivalent to

```
!(temperature >= 65) || !(distanceToDestination < 2)
```

which, in turn, is equivalent to

```
(temperature < 65 || distanceToDestination >= 2)
```

The logical equivalence is derived by applying *DeMorgan's law:*

Rule 1:   `!(P && Q)` ⟺ `!P || !Q`

Rule 2:   `!(P || Q)` ⟺ `!P && !Q`

This symbol means equivalence

Table 5.2 shows their equivalence.
Now consider the following expression:

```
x / y > z || y == 0
```

What will be the result if y is equal to 0? Easy, the result is true, many of you might say. Actually a runtime error called *arithmetic exception* will result, because the expression

arithmetic exception

```
x / y
```

divide-by-zero error

causes a problem known as a *divide-by-zero error*. Remember that you cannot divide a number by zero.

Table 5.2 The truth table illustrating DeMorgan's law.

P	Q	!(P && Q)	!P || !Q	!(P || Q)	!P && !Q
false	false	true	true	true	true
false	true	true	true	false	false
true	false	true	true	false	false
true	true	false	false	false	false

However, if we reverse the order to

```
y == 0 || x / y > z
```

short-circuit
evaluation

then no arithmetic exception will occur because the test x / y > z will not be evaluated. For the OR operator ||, if the left operand is evaluated to true, then the right operand will not be evaluated, because the whole expression is true, whether the value of the right operand is true or false. We call such evaluation method a *short-circuit evaluation*. For the AND operator &&, the right operand need not be evaluated if the left operand is evaluated to false, because the result will then be false whether the value of the right operand is true or false.

Just as the operator precedence rules are necessary to evaluate arithmetic expressions unambiguously, they are required for evaluating boolean expressions. Table 5.3 expands Table 3.3 by including all operators introduced so far.

Table 5.3 Operator precedence rules. Groups are listed in descending order of precedence. An operator with a higher precedence will be evaluated first. If two operators have the same precedence, then the associativity rule is applied.

Group	Operator	Precedence	Associativity
subexpression	( )	9 (If parentheses are nested, then innermost subexpression is evaluated first.)	Left to right
unary operators	– !	8	Right to left
multiplicative operators	* / %	7	Left to right
additive operators	+ –	6	Left to right
relational operators	< <= > >=	5	Left to right
equality operators	== !=	4	Left to right
boolean AND	&&	3	Left to right
boolean OR	||	2	Left to right
assignment	=	1	Right to left

Take my
Advice

We introduced the logical AND and OR operations using the symbols && and ||. In Java, there are single ampersand and single vertical bar operations. For example, if we write an **if** statement as

```
if ( 70 <= x & x < 90 )
```

it will compile and run. Unlike the double ampersand, the single ampersand will not do a short-circuit evaluation. It will evaluate both left and right operands. The single vertical bar works in an analogous manner. So, which one should we use? Use double ampersand for AND and double vertical bar for OR. We will most likely never encounter a situation where we cannot use the double ampersand or the double vertical bar.

In mathematics, we specify the range of values for a variable as

```
80 ≤ x < 90
```

In Java, to test that the value for x is within the specified lower and upper bounds, we express it in Java as

```
80 <= x && x < 90
```

You cannot specify it as

```
80 <= x < 90        ◄        Wrong
```

which is a syntax error because the relational operators (<, <=, etc.) are binary operators whose operands must be numerical values. Notice that the result of the subexpression

```
80 <= x
```

is a boolean value, which cannot be compared to the numerical value **90**. Their data types are not compatible.

The result of a boolean expression is either **true** or **false**, which are the two values of data type **boolean**. As is the case with other data types, a value of a data type can be assigned to a variable of the same data type. In other words, we can declare a variable of data type **boolean** and assign a boolean value to it. Here are examples:

```
boolean pass, done;

pass = 70 < x;
done = true;
```

boolean flag

One possible usage of boolean variables is to keep track of the program settings or user preferences. A variable (of any data type, not just **boolean**) used for this purpose is called a *flag*. Suppose we want to allow the user to display either short or long messages. Many people, when using a new program, prefer to see long messages such as Enter a person's age and press the Enter key to continue. But once they are familiar with the program, many users prefer to see short messages such as Enter age. We can use a flag to remember the user's preference. We can set the flag longMessageFormat at the beginning of the program to true or false depending on the user's choice. Once this flag is set, we can refer to the flag at different points in the program as

```
if (longMessageFormat) {

    //display the message in long format

} else {

    //display the message in short format

}
```

Notice the value of a boolean variable is true or false, so even though it is valid, we write a boolean expression not as

```
if (isRaining == true) {
    JOptionPane.showMessageDialog(null, "Store is open");
} else {
    JOptionPane.showMessageDialog(null, "Store is closed");
}
```

but more succinctly as

```
if (isRaining) {
    JOptionPane.showMessageDialog(null, "Store is open");
} else {
    JOptionPane.showMessageDialog(null, "Store is closed");
}
```

Another point we have to be careful with in using boolean variables is the choice of identifier. Instead of using a boolean variable such as motionStatus, it is more meaningful and descriptive to use the variable isMoving. For example, the statement

```
if (isMoving) {
    //the mobile robot is moving
} else {
    //the mobile robot is not moving
}
```

is much clearer than the statement

```
if (motionStatus) {
    //the mobile robot is moving
} else {
    //the mobile robot is not moving
}
```

We again conclude the section with a sample class. We will define a class called Ch5Triangle that is capable of computing the perimeter and area of a triangle, given its three sides a, b, and c, as shown. Notice that side b is the base of the triangle.

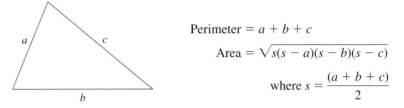

$$\text{Perimeter} = a + b + c$$

$$\text{Area} = \sqrt{s(s - a)(s - b)(s - c)}$$

$$\text{where } s = \frac{(a + b + c)}{2}$$

The design of this class is identical to the one for the Ch5Circle class from Section 5.1. The key difference is the use of a boolean condition in the private isValid method. We use this method to check the validity of three sides. If any one of them is invalid, the methods getArea and getPerimeter will return the constant INVALID_DIMENSION. Here's the Ch5Triangle class:

```
/*
    Chapter 5 The Triangle class

    File: Ch5Triangle.java

*/

class Ch5Triangle {

    public static final int INVALID_DIMENSION = -1;          Data members

    private double a;
    private double b;
    private double c;
                                                             Constructors
    public Ch5Triangle( ) {

        this(INVALID_DIMENSION, INVALID_DIMENSION, INVALID_DIMENSION);
    }

    public Ch5Triangle(double a, double b, double c) {
        setSideA(a);
        setSideB(b);
        setSideC(c);
    }

    public double getArea( ) {                                getArea

        double result = INVALID_DIMENSION;

        double s = (a + b + c) / 2.0;
```

```
    if (isValid()) {

        result = Math.sqrt(s * (s-a) * (s-b) * (s-c));
    }

    return result;
}

public double getBase( ) {
    return getSideB();
}

public double getHeight( ) {

    double result = INVALID_DIMENSION;

    if (isValid()) {

        result = (2.0/b) * getArea();
    }

    return result;
}

public double getPerimeter( ) {

    double result = INVALID_DIMENSION;

    if (isValid()) {

        result = a + b + c;
    }

    return result;
}

public double getSideA( ) {
    return a;
}

public double getSideB( ) {
    return b;
}

public double getSideC( ) {
    return c;
}

public void setBase(double value) {
    setSideB(value);
}

public void setSideA(double value) {

    if (value <= 0) {
```

getBase

getHeight

getPerimeter

getSideA

getSideB

getSideC

setBase

setSideA

```
            a = INVALID_DIMENSION;
        } else {
            a = value;
        }
    }

    public void setSideB(double value) {

        if (value <= 0) {
            b = INVALID_DIMENSION;
        } else {
            b = value;
        }
    }

    public void setSideC(double value) {

        if (value <= 0) {
            c = INVALID_DIMENSION;
        } else {
            c = value;
        }
    }

    private boolean isValid( ) {

        if (a != INVALID_DIMENSION &&
            b != INVALID_DIMENSION &&
            c != INVALID_DIMENSION &&
            a + c > b && a + b > c && b + c > a ) {
            return true;

        } else {
            return false;
        }
    }

}
```

setSideB

setSideC

isValid

And here's a simple test main class that illustrates the use of the Ch5Triangle class:

```
/*

    Chapter 5 Sample Program: Computing Triangle Dimensions

    File: Ch5Sample2.java

*/
```

```
import java.util.*;

class Ch5Sample2 {

    public static void main( String[] args ) {

        Ch5Triangle    triangle;
        double         a, b, c, area, perimeter;

        Scanner scanner = Scanner.create(System.in);
        scanner.useDelimiter(System.getProperty("line.separator"));

        System.out.print("Enter Side 1:");
        a = scanner.nextDouble();

        System.out.print("Enter Side 2 (base):");
        b = scanner.nextDouble();

        System.out.print("Enter Side 3:");
        c = scanner.nextDouble();

        triangle = new Ch5Triangle(a, b, c);

        perimeter = triangle.getPerimeter();

        area      = triangle.getArea();

        System.out.println("Three sides a, b, c:   " +
                                      a + "   " + b + "   " + c);
        System.out.println("Perimeter: " + perimeter);
        System.out.println("Area:        " + area);
    }
}
```

Take my Advice

One very common error in writing programs is to mix up the assignment and equality operators. We frequently make the mistake of writing

```
        if (x = 5) ...
```

when we actually wanted to say

```
        if (x == 5) ...
```

Quick **CHECK** √

1. Evaluate the following boolean expressions. Assume x, y, and z have some numerical values.

   a. `4 < 5 || 6 == 6`
   b. `2 < 4 && (false || 5 <= 4)`
   c. `x <= y && !(z != z) || x > y`
   d. `x < y || z < y && y <= z`

2. Identify errors in the following boolean expressions and assignments.

   a. `boolean done;`
      `done = x = y;`
   b. `2 < 4 && (3 < 5) + 1 == 3`
   c. `boolean quit;`
      `quit = true;`
      `quit == ( 34 == 20 ) && quit;`

5.3 | Nested-if Statements

nested-**if** statement

The then and else blocks of an if statement can contain any statement including another if statement. An if statement that contains another if statement in either its then or else block is called a *nested-if statement*. Let's look at an example. In the earlier example, we printed out the message You did pass or You did not pass depending on the test score. Let's modify the code to print out three possible messages. If the test score is lower than 70, then we print You did not pass, as before. If the test score is 70 or higher, then we will check the student's age. If the age is less than 10, we will print You did a great job. Otherwise, we will print You did pass, as before. Figure 5.4 is a diagram showing the logic of this nested test. The code is written as follows:

```java
if (testScore >= 70) {
    if (studentAge < 10) {
        System.out.println("You did a great job");
    } else {
        System.out.println("You did pass");//test score >= 70
    }                                      //and age >= 10
} else { //test score < 70

    System.out.println("You did not pass");
}
```

Since the then clause of the outer if contains another if statement, the outer if is called a nested-if statement. It is possible to write if tests in different ways to achieve the same result. For example, the preceding code can also be expressed as

```java
if (testScore >= 70 && studentAge < 10) {

    System.out.println("You did a great job");
} else {
    //either testScore < 70 OR studentAge >= 10
```

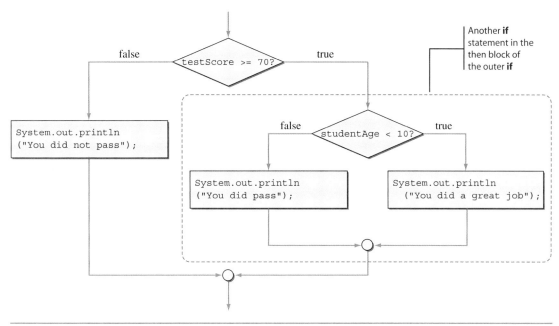

Figure 5.4 A diagram showing the control flow of the example nested-**if** statement.

```
if (testScore >= 70) {
    System.out.println("You did pass");
} else {
    System.out.println("You did not pass");
}
}
```

Several other variations can also achieve the same result. As a general rule, we strive to select the one that is most readable (i.e., most easily understood) and most efficient. Often no one variation stands out, and the one you choose depends on your preferred style of programming.

Here's an example in which one variation is clearly a better choice. Suppose we input three integers and determine how many of them are negative. Here's the first variation. To show the structure more clearly, we purposely do not use the braces in the then and else blocks.

> In this and the following examples, we purposely do not use the braces so we can provide a better illustration of the topics we are presenting.

```
if (num1 < 0)
    if (num2 < 0)
        if (num3 < 0)
            negativeCount = 3; //all three are negative
        else
            negativeCount = 2; //num1 and num2 are negative
    else
        if (num3 < 0)
            negativeCount = 2; //num1 and num3 are negative
```

```
            else
                negativeCount = 1; //num1 is negative
        else
            if (num2 < 0)
                if (num3 < 0)
                    negativeCount = 2; //num2 and num3 are negative
                else
                    negativeCount = 1; //num2 is negative
            else
                if (num3 < 0)
                    negativeCount = 1; //num3 is negative
            else
                negativeCount = 0; //no negative numbers
```

It certainly did the job. But elegantly? Here's the second variation:

```
negativeCount = 0;

if (num1 < 0)
        negativeCount++;
if (num2 < 0)
        negativeCount++;
if (num3 < 0)
        negativeCount++;
```

The statement

```
negativeCount++;
```

increments the variable by 1 and, therefore, is equivalent to

```
negativeCount = negativeCount + 1;
```

increment and
decrement
operators

The double plus operator (++) is called the *increment operator*, and the double minus operator (--) is the *decrement operator* (which decrements the variable by 1).

Which version should we use? The second variation is the only reasonable way to go. The first variation is not a viable option because it is very inefficient and very difficult to read. We apply the nested-if structure if we have to test conditions in some required order. In this example these three tests are independent of one another, so they can be executed in any order. In other words, it doesn't matter whether we test num1 first or last.

Notice that we indent the then and else blocks to show the nested structure clearly. Indentation is used as a visual guide for the readers. It makes no difference to a Java compiler. For example, we make our intent clear by writing the statement as

```
if (x < y)
    if (z != w)
        a = b + 1;
    else
        a = c + 1;
else
    a = b * c;
```

It takes some practice before you can write well-formed **if** statements. Here are some rules to help you write the **if** statements.

Rule 1:   Minimize the number of nestings.
Rule 2:   Avoid complex boolean expressions. Make them as simple as possible. Don't include many ANDs and ORs.
Rule 3:   Eliminate any unnecessary comparisons.
Rule 4:   Don't be satisfied with the first correct statement. Always look for improvement.
Rule 5:   Read your code again. Can you follow the statement easily? If not, try to improve it.

But to the Java compiler, it does not matter if we write the same code as

```
if (x < y)if (z != w)a = b + 1;else a = c + 1; else a = b * c;
```

Although indentation is not required to run the program, using proper indentation is an important aspect of good programming style. Since the goal is to make your code readable, not to follow any one style of indentation, you are free to choose your own style. We recommend style 1 shown on page 238.

The next example shows a style of indentation accepted as standard for a nested-if statement in which nesting occurs only in the else clause. Let's look at an example. Instead of determining whether a student passes or not, we will now display a letter grade based on the following formula:

Test Score	Grade
90 ≤ score	A
80 ≤ score < 90	B
70 ≤ score < 80	C
60 ≤ score < 70	D
score < 60	F

The statement can be written as

```
if (score >= 90)
    System.out.println("Your grade is A");
else
    if (score >= 80)
        System.out.println("Your grade is B");
    else
        if (score >= 70)
            System.out.println("Your grade is C");
```

```
      else
         if (score >= 60)
             System.out.println("Your grade is D");
         else
             System.out.println("Your grade is F");
```

However, the standard way to indent the statement is

```
if (score >= 90)
    System.out.println("Your grade is A");

else if (score >= 80)
    System.out.println("Your grade is B");

else if (score >= 70)
    System.out.println("Your grade is C");

else if (score >= 60)
    System.out.println("Your grade is D");

else
    System.out.println("Your grade is F");
```

We mentioned that indentation is meant for human eyes only. For example, we can clearly see the intent of a programmer just by looking at the indentation when we read

```
if (x < y)
    if (x < z)
        System.out.println("Hello");
else
    System.out.println("Good bye");
```

Indentation style A

A Java compiler, however, will interpret the above as

```
if (x < y)
    if (x < z)
        System.out.println("Hello");
    else
        System.out.println("Good bye");
```

Indentation style B

dangling else problem

This example has a *dangling else problem*. The Java compiler matches an else with the previous unmatched if, so the compiler will interpret the statement by matching the else with the inner if (if (x < z)), whether you use indentation style A or B. If you want to express the logic of indentation style A, you have to express it as

```
if (x < y) {
    if (x < z)
        System.out.println("Hello");
} else
    System.out.println("Good bye");
```

This dangling else problem is another reason why we recommend that beginners use the syntax for <compound statement> in the then and else blocks. In other words, always use the braces in the then and else blocks.

Let's design a reusable class to illustrate the use of nested-if statements. This time we define a class called Ch5LetterGrader that will help us assign letter grades and find the average, minimum, and maximum grades. When we create an instance with the default constructor, we will be using the default grading scale of

A: $90 \leq \text{score} \leq 100$
B: $80 \leq \text{score} < 90$
C: $70 \leq \text{score} < 80$
D: $60 \leq \text{score} < 70$
F: $0 \leq \text{score} < 60$

If we want to change the grading scale to something different, we pass the boundaries when we create an instance. For example, to change the scale to

A: $88 \leq \text{score} \leq 105$
B: $75 \leq \text{score} < 88$
C: $62 \leq \text{score} < 75$
D: $40 \leq \text{score} < 62$
F: $0 \leq \text{score} < 40$

we create the instance as

```
Ch5LetterGrader grader =
    new Ch5LetterGrader(100, 88, 75, 62, 40);
```

With the current implementation, we cannot change the lowest possible grade of 0. Once the object is created, we easily get the letter grade, for example, as

```
String lettergrade = grader.getLetterGrade(87);
```

To get the statistics on grade distribution, we must enter the test scores by calling the enter method for each test score:

```
grader.enter(89);
grader.enter(76);
grader.enter(94);
. . .
```

Any invalid test score is ignored by the enter method. (*Note:* We will learn a better way to enter multiple test scores at once, instead of writing one statement per score, in Chapter 6.)

After all the scores are entered, we can get some statistics as

```
double avg = grader.getAverage();
double max = grader.getMaxScore();
double min = grader.getMinScore();

int numAs = grader.getGradeCount(grader.A_LEVEL);
```

If the statistical method is called before any scores are entered, the constant value INVALID_DATA will be returned.

Here is the sample main class followed by the Ch5LetterGrader class.

```
/*
    Chapter 5 Sample Program: Grade Distribution

    File: Ch5Sample3.java
*/

import javax.swing.*;

class Ch5Sample3 {

    public static void main( String[] args ) {

        Ch5LetterGrader grader
            = new Ch5LetterGrader(105, 92, 85, 72, 50);

        grader.enter(75);
        grader.enter(83);
        grader.enter(98);
        grader.enter(93);
        grader.enter(72);

        System.out.println("Max score " + grader.getMaxScore());
        System.out.println("Min score " + grader.getMinScore());
        System.out.println("Avg score " + grader.getAverage());

        System.out.println("Grade Distribution: \nA B C D F");
        System.out.print   (grader.getGradeCount(grader.A_LEVEL) + " ");
        System.out.print   (grader.getGradeCount(grader.B_LEVEL) + " ");
        System.out.print   (grader.getGradeCount(grader.C_LEVEL) + " ");
        System.out.print   (grader.getGradeCount(grader.D_LEVEL) + " ");
        System.out.println(grader.getGradeCount(grader.F_LEVEL) + "\n");

        System.out.println("Score of " + 92 + " is equivalent to "
                            + grader.getLetterGrade(92));
    }
}
```

```
/*
    Chapter 5 The LetterGrader class

    File: Ch5LetterGrader.java
*/
```

```
class Ch5LetterGrader {

    public static final int INVALID_DATA = -1;

    public static final String UNKNOWN_GRADE = "U";

    public static final int A_LEVEL = 1;
    public static final int B_LEVEL = 2;
    public static final int C_LEVEL = 3;
    public static final int D_LEVEL = 4;
    public static final int F_LEVEL = 5;

    private static final double DEFAULT_POSSIBLE_MAX = 100;
    private static final double DEFAULT_A_CUTOFF = 90;
    private static final double DEFAULT_B_CUTOFF = 80;
    private static final double DEFAULT_C_CUTOFF = 70;
    private static final double DEFAULT_D_CUTOFF = 60;

    private int numberOfAs, numberOfBs, numberOfCs,
                numberOfDs, numberOfFs;

    private double cutoffA, cutoffB, cutoffC,
                   cutoffD, cutoffF;

    private double sum;
    private int    count;
    private double maxScore;
    private double minScore;
    private double possibleMax;

    public Ch5LetterGrader( ) {
        this(DEFAULT_POSSIBLE_MAX,
            DEFAULT_A_CUTOFF, DEFAULT_B_CUTOFF,
            DEFAULT_C_CUTOFF, DEFAULT_D_CUTOFF);
    }

    public Ch5LetterGrader(double max,
                           double minA, double minB,
                           double minC, double minD) {

        possibleMax = max;
        cutoffA     = minA;
        cutoffB     = minB;
        cutoffC     = minC;
        cutoffD     = minD;

        minScore = Double.MAX_VALUE; //set these so they will be changed
        maxScore = Double.MIN_VALUE; //when the first score is entered

        numberOfAs = 0;
        numberOfBs = 0;
        numberOfCs = 0;
```

Data members

Constructors

```
            numberOfDs = 0;
            numberOfFs = 0;

            count      = 0;
            sum        = 0;
      }

      public void enter(double score) {

            if (score < 0 || score > possibleMax ) {
                return;     //invalid data, so
                            //return from the method immediately
                            //without doing anything

            }

            if (score > maxScore) {

                maxScore = score;
            }

            if (score < minScore) { //don't use 'else if' here because
                                    //we want the first entered score
                                    //to be both min and max.
                minScore = score;
            }

            distribute(score);

            count++;
            sum += score;
      }

      public double getAverage( ) {

            double result = INVALID_DATA;

            if (count > 0) {
                result = sum / count;
            }

            return result;
      }

      public int getGradeCount(int gradeLevel ) {

            int count = INVALID_DATA;

            if (gradeLevel == A_LEVEL) {
                count = numberOfAs;

            } else if (gradeLevel == B_LEVEL) {
                count = numberOfBs;
```

```java
    } else if (gradeLevel == C_LEVEL) {
        count = numberOfCs;

    } else if (gradeLevel == D_LEVEL) {
        count = numberOfDs;

    } else if (gradeLevel == F_LEVEL) {
        count = numberOfFs;
    }

    return count;
}

public String getLetterGrade(double score) {

    String letterGrade = UNKNOWN_GRADE;

    if (0 <= score && score < cutoffD) {

        letterGrade = "F";

    } else if (score < cutoffC) {

        letterGrade = "D";

    } else if (score < cutoffB) {

        letterGrade = "C";

    } else if (score < cutoffA) {

        letterGrade = "B";

    } else if (score <= possibleMax) {

        letterGrade = "A";
    }

    return letterGrade;
}

public double getMinScore( ) {

    double result = INVALID_DATA;

    if (minScore != Double.MAX_VALUE) {

        result = minScore;
    }

    return result;
}

public double getMaxScore( ) {

    double result = INVALID_DATA;
```

getLetterGrade

getMinScore

getMaxScore

```
        if (maxScore != Double.MIN_VALUE) {

            result = maxScore;
        }

        return result;
    }

    private void distribute(double score) {

        if (0 <= score && score < cutoffD) {

            numberOfFs++;

        } else if (score < cutoffC) {

            numberOfDs++;

        } else if (score < cutoffB) {

            numberOfCs++;

        } else if (score < cutoffA) {

            numberOfBs++;

        } else if (score <= possibleMax) {

            numberOfAs++;
        }
    }
}
```

distribute

Quick
CHECK
√

1. Rewrite the following nested-if statements without using any nesting.

```
a. if ( a < c )
      if ( b < c )
         x = y;
      else
         x = z;
      else
         x = z;
b. if ( a == b )
      x = y;
   else
      if ( a > b )
         x = y;
      else
         x = z;
```

```
c. if ( a < b )
       if ( a >= b )
           x = z;
       else
           x = y;
   else
       x = z;
```

2. Format the following if statements with indentation.

```
a. if ( a < b  ) if ( c > d ) x = y;
   else x = z;
b. if ( a < b ) { if ( c > d ) x = y; }
   else x = z;
c. if ( a < b ) x = y; if ( a < c ) x = z;
   else if ( c < d ) z = y;
```

5.4 | Comparing Objects

When we are dealing with primitive data types, we have only one way to compare them. With objects (reference data type), we have two ways to compare them. We will discuss the ways the objects can be compared in this section. First, let's review how we can compare primitive data types. What would be the output of the following code?

```
int num1, num2;

num1 = 15;
num2 = 15;

if (num1 == num2) {
    System.out.println("They are equal");
} else {
    System.out.println("They are not equal");
}
```

Because the two variables hold the same value, the output is

```
They are equal
```

Now, consider the following code that attempts to compare two Weight objects (the Weight class is defined in Chapter 4):

```
Weight wgt1, wgt2;

wgt1 = new Weight(2450.0);
wgt2 = new Weight(2450.0);

if (wgt1 == wgt2) {
    System.out.println("They are equal");
```

```
    } else {
        System.out.println("They are not equal");
    }
```

What would be an output? The answer is

```
They are not equal
```

The two objects are constructed with the same value of 2450 g, but the result of comparison came back that they were not equal. Why?

When two variables are compared, we are comparing their contents. In the case of primitive data types, the content is the actual value. In the case of reference data types, the content is the address where the object is stored. Since there are two distinct Weight objects, stored at different addresses, the contents of wgt1 and wgt2 are different, and therefore, the equality testing results in false. If we change the code to

```
Weight wgt1, wgt2;

wgt1 = new Weight(2450.0);       No new object is created here. The content
wgt2 = wgt1;                     (address) of wgt1 is copied to wgt2, making
                                 them both point to the same object.

if (wgt1 == wgt2) {
    System.out.println("They are equal");
} else {
    System.out.println("They are not equal");
}
```

then the output would be

```
They are equal
```

because now we have one Weight object and both variables wgt1 and wgt2 point to this object. This means the contents of wgt1 and wgt2 are the same because they refer to the same address. Figure 5.5 shows the distinction.

What shall we do if we want to check whether two distinct Weight objects represent the same weight? One way is to access their weights in grams and compare them as

```
if (wgt1.getGram() == wgt2.getGram()) {
    . . .
```

A better approach is to define comparison methods for the class. Let's modify the Weight class from Chapter 4 by adding two methods for comparing two weights. We will call the new class Ch5Weight. The first method checks if two objects have the same weight. Here's the equals method:

```
class Ch5Weight {
    . . .
```

Case A: Two variables referring to two different objects.

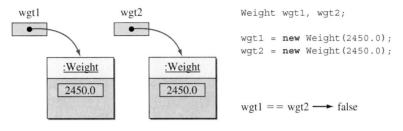

Case B: Two variables referring to the same object.

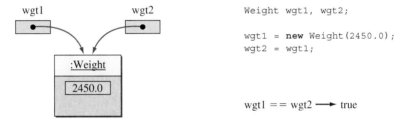

Figure 5.5 How the equality == testing works with the objects.

```
public boolean equals(Ch5Weight wgt) {
                                    The use of this is
    boolean result;                optional here.

    double thisGram  = this.getGram();
    double otherGram = wgt.getGram();

    if (thisGram == otherGram) {
        result = true;
    } else {
        result = false;
    }

    return result;
}
...
}
```

This **if** statement can be written succinctly as

result
  = thisGram == otherGram:

The equals method is called in the following manner:

```
Ch5Weight wgt1, wgt2;
wgt1 = new Ch5Weight();
wgt2 = new Ch5Weight();
...
if (wgt1.equals(wgt2)) {
    ...
```

Because both wgt1 and wgt2 are Ch5Weight objects, it makes no difference when we write the if statement as

```
if (wgt2.equals(wgt1)) {
    ...
```

Instead of just returning true or false, we add the second method that returns a numerical value. Here's the compareTo method:

```
class Ch5Weight {
    public static final int SMALLER = -1;
    public static final int EQUAL   =  0;
    public static final int LARGER  = +1;
    ...
    public int compareTo(Ch5Weight wgt) {
        int    status;

        double thisGram  = this.getGram();
        double otherGram = wgt.getGram();

        if (thisGram < otherGram) {
            status = SMALLER;

        } else if (thisGram == otherGram) {
            status = EQUAL;

        } else { //thisGram > otherGram
            status = LARGER;
        }

        return status;
    }
    ...
}
```

The compareTo method is used in the following manner:

```
Ch5Weight wgt1, wgt2;
wgt1 = new Ch5Weight();
wgt2 = new Ch5Weight();
...
int result = wgt1.compareTo(wgt2);

if (result == Ch5Weight.SMALLER) {
    System.out.println("wgt1 is less than wgt2");
} else if (result == Ch5Weight.EQUAL) {
    System.out.println("wgt1 is equal to wgt2");
} else {
    System.out.println("wgt1 is greater than wgt2");
}
```

Many standard classes already define the comparison methods such as equals. The String class, for example, includes the equals and equalsIgnoreCase comparison methods. The equals method returns true if two String objects have the exact same sequence of characters. The equalsIgnoreCase method does the same as the equals method, but the comparison is done in a case-insensitive manner. Here are examples:

```
String str1 = "java";
String str2 = "JaVa";
```

str1.equals(str2)   ⟶   **false**

str1.equalsIgnoreCase(str2)   ⟶   **true**

We will discuss string comparisons in greater detail in Chapter 9.

Quick
CHECK

1. Determine the output of the following code.

```
Ch5Weight wgt1 = new Ch5Weight(1234.56);
Ch5Weight wgt2 = new Ch5Weight(1234.56);

boolean result1 = wgt1 == wgt2;
boolean result2 = wgt.equals(wgt2);

System.out.println(result1);
System.out.println(result2);
```

2. Determine the output of the following code.

```
String str1 = new String("latte");
String str2 = new String("LATTE");

boolean result1 = str1 == str2;
boolean result2 = str1.equals(str2);

System.out.println(result1);
System.out.println(result2);
```

5.5 | The switch **Statement**

Another Java statement that implements a selection control flow is the switch statement. Suppose we want to direct the students to the designated location for them to register for classes. The location where they register is determined by their grade level. The user enters 1 for freshman, 2 for sophomore, 3 for junior, and 4 for senior. Using the switch statement, we can write the code as

```
int gradeLevel;

gradeLevel = Integer.parseInt(
                 JOptionPane.showInputDialog
                    ("Grade (Frosh-1,Soph-2,...):" ));

switch (gradeLevel) {

   case 1: System.out.println("Go to the Gymnasium");
          break;

   case 2: System.out.println("Go to the Science Auditorium");
          break;

   case 3: System.out.println("Go to Halligan Hall Rm 104");
          break;

   case 4: System.out.println("Go to Root Hall Rm 101");
          break;
}
```

The syntax for the switch statement is

switch statement syntax

```
switch ( <arithmetic expression> ) {

   <case label 1> : <case body 1>
   ...
   <case label n> : <case body n>
}
```

Figure 5.6 illustrates the correspondence between the switch statement we wrote and the general format.

The <case label i> has the form

default reserved word

```
case <constant>    or    default
```

and <case body i> is a sequence of zero or more statements. Notice that <case body i> is not surrounded by left and right braces. The <constant> can be either a named or literal constant.

The data type of <arithmetic expression> must be char, byte, short, or int. (*Note:* We will cover the data type char in Chapter 8.) The value of <arithmetic expression> is compared against the constant value i of <case label i>. If there is a matching case, then its case body is executed. If there is no matching case, then the execution continues to the statement that follows the switch statement. No two cases are allowed to have the same value for <constant>, and the cases can be listed in any order.

Notice that each case in the sample switch statement is terminated with the break statement. The break statement causes execution to continue from the statement

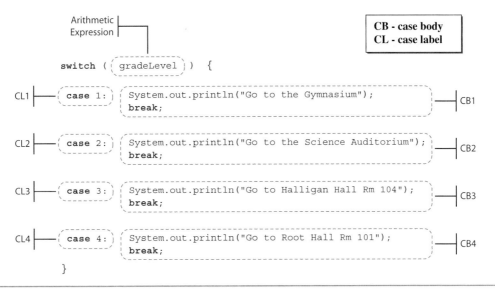

Figure 5.6 Mapping of the sample **switch** statement to the general format.

following this switch statement, skipping the remaining portion of the switch statement. The following example illustrates how the break statement works:

```
//Assume necessary declaration and object creation are done

int selection = 1;

switch (selection) {
    case 0: System.out.println(0);
    case 1: System.out.println(1);
    case 2: System.out.println(2);
    case 3: System.out.println(3);
}
```

When this code is executed, the following output is produced

```
1
2
3
```

because after the statement in case 1 is executed, statements in the remaining cases will be executed also. To execute statements in one and only one case, we need to include the break statement at the end of each case, as we have done in the first example. Figure 5.7 shows the effect of the break statement.

The break statement is not necessary in the last case, but for consistency we place it in every case. Also, by doing so we don't have to remember to include the break statement in the last case when we add more cases to the end of the switch statement.

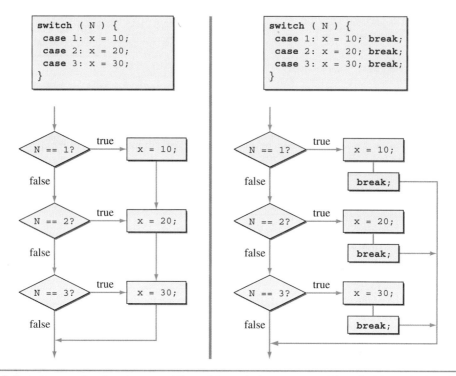

Figure 5.7 A diagram showing the control flow of the **switch** statement with and without the **break** statements.

Individual cases do not have to include a statement, so we can write something like

```
int ranking;
ranking = Integer.parseInt(
            JOptionPane.showInputDialog(null, "Input:"));

switch (ranking) {
    case 10:
    case  9:
    case  8: System.out.println("Master");
            break;

    case  7:
    case  6: System.out.println("Journeyman");
            break;

    case  5:
    case  4: System.out.println("Apprentice");
            break;
}
```

The code will print Master if the value of ranking is 10, 9, or 8; Journeyman if the value of ranking is either 7 or 6; or Apprentice if the value of ranking is either 5 or 4.

We may include a default case that will always be executed if there is no matching case. For example, we can add a default case to print out an error message if any invalid value for ranking is entered.

```
switch (ranking) {

    case 10:
    case  9:
    case  8: System.out.println("Master");
             break;

    case  7:
    case  6: System.out.println("Journeyman");
             break;

    case  5:
    case  4: System.out.println("Apprentice");
             break;

    default: System.out.println("Error: Invalid Data");
             break;
}
```

There can be at most one default case. Since the execution continues to the next statement if there is no matching case (and no default case is specified), it is safer to always include a default case. By placing some kind of output statement in the default case, we can detect an unexpected switch value. Such style of programming is characterized as *defensive programming*. Although the default case does not have to be placed as the last case, we recommend you do so, in order to make the switch statement more readable.

defensive programming

As the last example in this section, let's rewrite the getLetterGrade method of the Ch5LetterGrader class from Section 5.4. The method can be written succinctly by using the switch statement.

```
public int getGradeCount(int gradeLevel ) {

    int count = INVALID_DATA;

    switch (gradeLevel) {

        case A_LEVEL: count = numberOfAs; break;

        case B_LEVEL: count = numberOfBs; break;

        case C_LEVEL: count = numberOfCs; break;

        case D_LEVEL: count = numberOfDs; break;

        case F_LEVEL: count = numberOfFs; break;

    }

    return count;
}
```

Quick
CHECK

1. What's wrong with the following switch statement?

```
switch ( N ) {
    case  0:
    case  1:  x = 11;
              break;
    default:  System.out.println("Switch Error");
              break;
    case  2:  x = 22;
              break;
    case  1:  x = 33;
              break;
}
```

2. What's wrong with the following switch statement?

```
switch ( ranking ) {
    case  >4.55:  pay = pay * 0.20;
                  break;

    case  =4.55:  pay = pay * 0.15;
                  break;

    default:      pay = pay * 0.05;
                  break;
}
```

5.6 | Drawing Graphics

We will introduce four standard classes related to drawing geometric shapes on a window. These four standard classes will be used in the sample development section. We'll describe their core features here. More details can be found in the online Java API documentation.

java.awt.Graphics

java.awt.
Graphics

We can draw geometric shapes on a frame window by calling appropriate methods of the Graphics object. For example, if g is a Graphics object, then we can write

```
g.drawRect(50, 50, 100, 30);
```

to display a rectangle 100 pixels wide and 30 pixels high at the specified position (50, 50). The position is determined as illustrated in Figure 5.8. The complete program is shown on the next page. The top left corner, just below the window title bar, is position (0, 0), and the x value increases from left to right and the y value increases from top to bottom. Notice that the direction of which the y value increases is opposite of the normal two-dimensional graph.

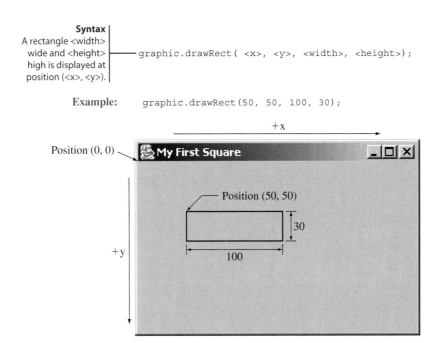

Syntax

A rectangle <width> wide and <height> high is displayed at position (<x>, <y>). ——— `graphic.drawRect( <x>, <y>, <width>, <height>);`

Example: `graphic.drawRect(50, 50, 100, 30);`

Figure 5.8 The diagram illustrates how the position of rectangle is determined by the **drawRect** method.

The area of a frame which we can draw is called the frame's *content pane*. The content pane excludes the area of a frame such as the border, scroll bars, the title bar, the menu bar, and others. To draw on the content pane of a frame window, first we must get the content pane's Graphics object. Then we call this Graphics method to draw geometric shapes. Here's a sample code:

```
/*
    Chapter 5 Sample Program: Draw a square on a frame
                             window's content pane

    File: Ch5SampleGraphics.java
*/
import javax.swing.*; //for JFrame
import java.awt.*; //for Graphics and Container

class Ch5SampleGraphics {

    public static void main( String[] args ) {

        JFrame     win;
        Container contentPane;
        Graphics  g;
```

```
win = new JFrame("My First Square");
win.setSize(300, 200);
win.setLocation(100,100);
win.setVisible(true);

contentPane = win.getContentPane();
g = contentPane.getGraphics();
g.drawRect(50,50,100,30);
    }
}
```

win must be visible on the screen before you can get its content pane's **Graphics** object

Here are the key points to remember in drawing geometric shapes on the content pane of a frame window.

Helpful Reminder

To draw geometric shapes on the content pane of a frame window, remember that

1. *The content pane is declared as a* **Container,** *for example,*

```
Container contentPane;
```

2. *The frame window must be visible on the screen before we can get the content pane's* **Graphics** *object.*

www

If there is a window that covers the area in which the drawing takes place or the drawing window is minimized and restored to its normal size, the drawn shape (or portion of it, in the case of the overlapping windows) gets erased. The **DrawingBoard** class used in the sample development section eliminates this problem. For information on the technique to avoid the disappearance of drawn shape, please check our website at **www.drcaffeine.com**

Table 5.4 lists some of the available graphic drawing methods.

Notice the distinction between the draw and fill methods. The draw method will draw the boundary only while the fill method fills the designated area with the currently selected color. Figure 5.9 illustrates the difference.

java.awt.Color

java.awt.Color

To designate the color for drawing, we will use the Color class from the standard java.awt package. A Color object uses a coloring scheme called an *RGB scheme,*

Table 5.4   A partial list of drawing methods defined for the `Graphics` class.

Method	Meaning
`drawLine(x1,y1,x2,y2)`	Draws a line between (x1,y1) and (x2,y2).
`drawRect(x,y,w,h)`	Draws a rectangle with width w and height h at (x,y).
`drawRoundRect(x,y,w,h,aw,ah)`	Draws a rounded-corner rectangle with width w and height h at (x,y). Parameters aw and ah determine the angle for the rounded corners.
`drawOval(x,y,w,h)`	Draws an oval with width w and height h at (x,y).
`drawString("text",x,y)`	Draws the string `text` at (x,y).
`fillRect(x,y,w,h)`	Same as the `drawRect` method but fills the region with the currently set color.

Table 5.4 A partial list of drawing methods defined for the Graphics class. *(Continued)*	
Method	**Meaning**
fillRoundRect(x,y,w,h,aw,ah)	Same as the drawRoundRect method but fills the region with the currently set color.
fillOval(x,y,w,h)	Same as the drawOval method but fills the region with the currently set color.

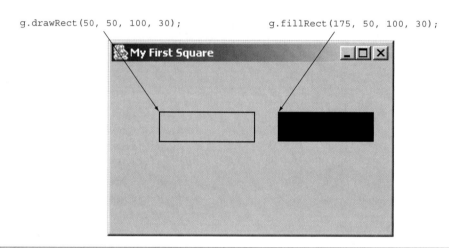

```
g.drawRect(50, 50, 100, 30);                    g.fillRect(175, 50, 100, 30);
```

Figure 5.9 The diagram illustrates the distinction between the **draw** and **fill** methods. We assume the currently selected color is black (default).

which specifies a color by combining three values, ranging from 0 to 255, for red, green, and blue. For example, the color black is expressed by setting red, green, and blue to zero, and the color white by setting all three values to 255. We create, for example, a Color object for the pink color by executing

```
Color pinkColor;
pinkColor = new Color(255,175,175);
```

Instead of dealing with the three numerical values, we can use the public class constants defined in the Color class. The class constants for common colors are

```
Color.black      Color.magenta
Color.blue       Color.orange
Color.cyan       Color.pink
Color.darkGray   Color.red
Color.gray       Color.white
Color.green      Color.yellow
Color.lightGray
```

Since J2SDK1.4, constants in all uppercase letters, such as Color.BLUE, are allowed.

Each of the above is a Color object with its RGB values correctly set up. We will pass a Color object as an argument to the setColor method of the Graphics class to change the color. To draw a blue rectangle, for example, we write

```
//Assume g is set correctly
g.setColor(Color.blue);
g.drawRect(50, 50, 100, 30);
```

We can also change the background color of a content pane by using the setBackground method of Container, as in

```
contentPane.setBackground(Color.white);
```

Running the following program will result in a frame shown in Figure 5.10.

```
/*
    Chapter 5 Sample Program: Draw one blue square and
                             one filled red square on white
                             background content pane

    File: Ch5SampleGraphics2.java
*/

import javax.swing.*;
import java.awt.*;

class Ch5SampleGraphics2 {
    public static void main( String[] args ) {

        JFrame    win;
        Container contentPane;
        Graphics  g;

        win = new JFrame("Colored Squares");
        win.setSize(300, 200);
        win.setLocation(100,100);
        win.setVisible(true);

        contentPane = win.getContentPane();
        contentPane.setBackground(Color.white);

        g = contentPane.getGraphics();
        g.setColor(Color.blue);
        g.drawRect(50,50,100,30);

        g.setColor(Color.red);
        g.fillRect(175,50,100,30);
    }
}
```

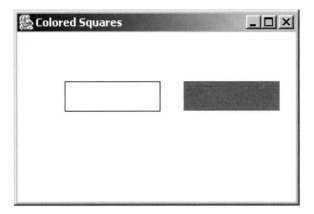

Figure 5.10 A frame with a white background content pane and two colored squares.

java.awt.Point

A Point object is used to represent a point in two-dimensional space. It contains x and y values, and we can access these values via its public data member x and y. Here's an example to assign a position (10, 20):

```
Point pt = new Point();
pt.x = 10;
pt.y = 20;
```

It is also possible to set the position at the creation time as

```
Point pt = new Point(10, 20);
```

java.awt.Dimension

bounding
rectangle

In manipulating shapes, such as moving them around a frame's content pane, the concept of the bounding rectangle becomes important. A *bounding rectangle* is a rectangle that completely surrounds the shape. Figure 5.11 shows some examples of bounding rectangles.

Just as the (x, y) values are stored as a single Point object, we can store the width and height of a bounding rectangle as a single Dimension object. The Dimension class has the two public data members width and height to maintain the width and height of a bounding rectangle. Here's an example to create a 40 pixels by 70 pixels high bounding rectangle:

```
Dimension dim = new Dimension();
dim.width  = 40;
dim.height = 70;
```

It is also possible to set the values at the creation time as

```
Dimension dim = new Dimension(40, 70);
```

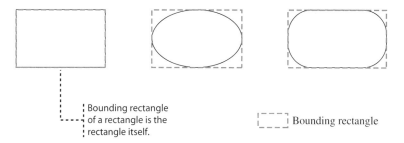

Figure 5.11 Bounding rectangles of various shapes.

Drawing Shapes

When a certain time passes without any activity on a computer, a screensaver becomes active and draws different types of geometric patterns or textual messages. In this section we will develop an application that simulates a screensaver. We will learn a development skill very commonly used in object-oriented programming. Whether we develop alone or as a project team member, we often find ourselves writing a class that needs to behave in a specific way so that it works correctly with other classes. The other classes may come from standard Java packages or could be developed by the other team members.

In this particular case, we use the **DrawingBoard** class provided to us. This class takes care of programming aspects we have not yet mastered, such as moving multiple geometric shapes in a smooth motion across the screen. But it is not an issue whether we can develop this class by ourselves, because no matter how good we become as programmers, we rarely develop an application completely on our own.

We already used many predefined classes from the Java standard libraries, but the way we will use the predefined class here is different. When we developed programs before, the classes we wrote called the methods of predefined classes. Our main method creating a **GregorianCalendar** object and calling its methods is one example. Here, for us to use a predefined class, we must define another class that provides necessary services to this predefined class. Figure 5.12 differentiates the two types of predefined classes. The first type does not place any restriction other than calling the methods correctly, while the second type requires us to implement helper classes in a specific manner.

In this particular case, the predefined class **DrawingBoard** will require another class named **DrawableShape** that will assume the responsibility of drawing individual geometric shapes. So, to use the **DrawingBoard** class in our program, we must implement the class named **DrawableShape.** And we must implement the **DrawableShape** class in a specific way. The use of the **DrawingBoard** class dictates that we define a set of fixed methods in the **DrawableShape** class. We can add more, but at

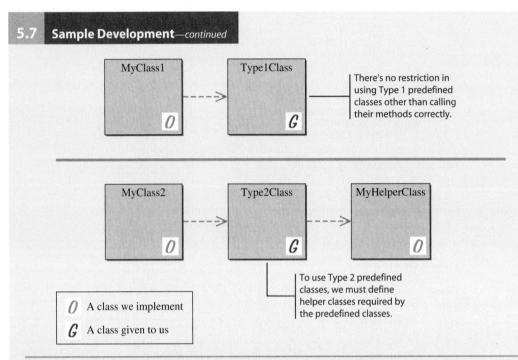

Figure 5.12 Two types of predefined classes. The first type does not require us to do anything more than use the predefined classes by calling their methods. The second type requires us to define helper classes for the predefined classes we want to use.

the minimum we must provide the specified set of fixed methods because the **DrawingBoard** class will need to call these methods. The methods are "fixed" in the method prototype—method name, the number of parameters and their types, and return type—but the method body can be defined in any way we like. This is how the flexibility is achieved. For example, the **DrawableShape** class we define must include a method named **draw** with the dictated prototype. But it's up to us to decide what we put in the method body. So we can choose, for example, to implement the method to draw a circle, rectangle, or any other geometric shape of our choosing.

As always, we will develop this program by following incremental development steps. The incremental development steps we will take here are slightly different in character from those we have seen so far. In the previous incremental developments, we knew all the ingredients, so to speak. Here we have to include a step to explore the **DrawingBoard** class. We will find out shortly that to use the **DrawingBoard** class, we will have to deal with some Java standard classes we have not yet seen. Pedagogically, a textbook may try to explain beforehand everything that is necessary to undertand the sample programs, but no textbook can explain everything. When we develop programs, there will always be a time when we encounter some unknown classes. We need to learn how to deal with such situations in our development steps.

Problem Statement

Write an application that simulates a screensaver by drawing various geometric shapes in different colors. The user has an option of choosing a type (ellipse or rectangle), color, and movement (stationary, smooth, or random).

Overall Plan

We will begin with our overall plan for the development. Let's begin with the outline of program logic. We first let the user select the shape, its movement, and its color and then start drawing. We express the program flow as having four tasks:

program tasks

1. Get the shape the user wants to draw.

2. Get the color of the chosen shape.

3. Get the type of movement the user wants to use.

4. Start the drawing.

Let's look at each task and determine an object that will be responsible for handling the task. For the first three tasks, we can use our old friend **JOptionPane.** We will get into the details of exactly how we allow the users to input those values in the later incremental steps. For the last task of actually drawing the selected shape, we need to define our own class. The task is too specific to the program, and there is no suitable object in the standard packages that does the job. As discussed earlier, we will use a given predefined class **DrawingBoard** and define the required helper class **DrawableShape.**

We will define a top-level control object that manages all these objects. We will call this class **Ch5DrawShape.** As explained in Section 4.10, we will make this control object as the instantiable main class. Here's our working design document:

program classes

Design Document: Ch5DrawShape	
Class	**Purpose**
Ch5DrawShape	The top-level control object that manages other objects in the program. This is an instantiable main class, as explained in Section 4.10.
DrawingBoard	The given predefined class that handles the movement of DrawableShape objects.
DrawableShape	The class for handling the drawing of individual shapes.
JOptionPane	The standard class for handling input routines.

Figure 5.13 is the program diagram for this program.

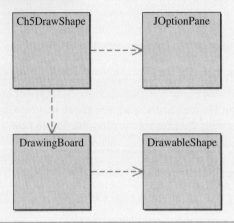

Figure 5.13 The program diagram for the **Ch5DrawShape** program.

We will implement this program in six major steps:

develop-
ment steps

1. Start with a program skeleton. Explore the **DrawingBoard** class.

2. Define an experimental **DrawableShape** class that draws a dummy shape.

3. Add code to allow the user to select a shape. Extend the **DrawableShape** and other classes as necessary.

4. Add code to allow the user to specify the color. Extend the **DrawableShape** and other classes as necessary.

5. Add code to allow the user to specify the motion type. Extend the **DrawableShape** and other classes as necessary.

6. Finalize the code by tying up loose ends.

Our first task is to find out about the given class. We could have designed the input routines first, but without knowing much about the given class, it would be difficult to design suitable input routines. When we use an unknown class, it is most appropriate to find out more about this class before planning any input or output routines. Just as the development steps are incremental, our exploration of the given class will be incremental. Instead of trying to find out everything about the class at once, we begin with the basic features and skeleton code. As we learn more about the given class incrementally, we extend our code correspondingly.

Step 1 Development: Program Skeleton

step 1
design

We begin the development with the skeleton instantiable main class. The main purpose in step 1 is to use the **DrawingBoard** class in the simplest manner to establish the launch pad for the development. To do so, we must first learn a bit about the

DrawingBoard class. Here's a brief description of the **DrawingBoard** class. In a real-world situation, we would be finding out about the given class by reading its accompanying documentation or some other external sources. The documentation may come in form of online javadoc documents or reference manuals.

DrawingBoard
An instance of this class will support the drawing of `DrawableShape` objects. Shapes can be drawn at fixed stationary positions, at random positions, or in a smooth motion at the specified speed. The actual drawing of the individual shapes is done inside the `DrawableShape` class. The client programmer decides which shape to draw.
public void addShape(DrawableShape shape)   Adds shape to this `DrawingBoard` object. You can add unlimited number of `DrawableShape` objects.
public void setBackground(java.awt.Color color)   Sets the background color of this `DrawingBoard` object to the designated color. The default background color is black.
public void setDelayTime(**double** delay)   Sets the delay time between drawings to `delay` seconds. The smaller the delay time, the faster the shapes move. If the movement type is other than `SMOOTH`, then setting the delay time has no visual effect.
public void setMovement(**int** type)   Sets the movement type to `type`. Class constants for three types of motion are: `STATIONARY`—draw shapes at fixed positions, `RANDOM`— draw shapes at random positions, and `SMOOTH`—draw shapes in a smooth motion.
public void setVisible(**boolean** state)   Makes this `DrawingBoard` object appear on or disappear from the screen if `state` is `true` or `false`, respectively. To simulate the screensaver, setting it visible will cause a maximized window to appear on the screen.
public void start(   )   Starts the drawing. If the window is not visible yet, it will be made visible before the drawing begins.

Among the defined methods, we see the **setVisible** method is the one to make it appear on the screen. All other methods pertain to adding **DrawableShape** objects and setting the properties of a **DrawingBoard** object. We will explain the standard **java.awt.Color** class when we use the **setBackground** method in the later step. In this step, we will keep the code very simple by only making it appear on the screen. We will deal with other methods in the later steps.

5.7   Sample Development—*continued*

Our working design document for the **Ch5DrawShape** class is as follows:

Design Document: The Ch5DrawShape **Class**		
Method	**Visibility**	**Purpose**
<constructor>	public	Creates a DrawingBoard object.
main	public	This is the main method of the class.
start	public	Starts the program by opening a DrawingBoard object.

step 1 code

Since this is a skeleton code, it is very basic. All we have is a standard structure of instantiable main class. Here's the code:

```java
/**
 * Chapter 5 Sample Development: Drawing Shapes (Step 1)
 *
 * The instantiable main class of the program.
 */

class Ch5DrawShape {

    private DrawingBoard canvas;

    public Ch5DrawShape( ) {

        canvas = new DrawingBoard( );
    }

    public void start( ) {

        canvas.setVisible(true);
    }

    public static void main( String[] args ) {

        Ch5DrawShape screensaver = new Ch5DrawShape( );

        screensaver.start();
    }
}
```

step 1 test

The purpose of step 1 testing is to verify that a **DrawingBoard** object appears correctly on the screen. Since this is our first encounter with the **DrawingBoard** class, it is likely that we are not reading its documentation correctly. We need to verify this in this step. When a maximized window with the black background appears on the screen, we know the main class was executed properly. After we verify the correct execution of the step 1 program, we will proceed to implement additional methods of **Ch5DrawShape** and gradually build up the required **DrawableShape** class.

Step 2 Development: Draw a Shape

step 2
design

In the second development step, we will implement a preliminary **DrawableShape** class and make some shapes appear on a **DrawingBoard** window. To draw shapes, we need to add them to a **DrawingBoard** window. And to do so, we need to define the **DrawableShape** class with the specified set of methods. Here are the required methods and a brief description on what to accomplish in them:

Required Methods of DrawableShape

public void draw(java.awt.Graphics)
  Draw a geometric shape on the java.awt.Graphics. The Drawing-Board window calls the draw method of DrawableShape objects added to it.

public java.awt.Point getCenterPoint( )
  Return the center point of this shape.

public java.awt.Dimension getDimension( )
  Return the bounding rectangle of this shape as a Dimension.

public void setCenterPoint(java.awt.Point)
  Set the center point of this shape. The DrawingBoard window calls the setCenterPoint method of DrawableShape objects to update their positions in the SMOOTH movement type.

At this stage, the main task is for us to confirm our understanding of the requirements in implementing the **DrawableShape** class. Once we get this confirmation, we can get into the details of a full-blown **DrawableShape** class.

To keep the preliminary class simple, we will draw three filled circles of a fixed size and color. The **DrawableShape** class will include a single data member **center-Point** to keep track of the shape's center point. If we fix the radius of the circles to 100 pixels, that is, the bounding rectangle is 200 pixels by 200 pixels, and color to blue, then the **draw** method can be written as

```
public void draw(Graphics g) {

    g.setColor(Color.blue);
    g.fillOval(centerPoint.x-100, centerPoint.y-100,
            200, 200);
}
```

Since the size is fixed, we simply return a new **Dimension** object for the **getDimension** method:

```
public Dimension getDimension( ) {

    return new Dimension(200, 200);
}
```

For the **setCenterPoint** and **getCenterPoint** methods, we assign the passed parameter to the data member **centerPoint** and return the current value of the data member **centerPoint,** respectively.

We are now ready to modify the **Ch5DrawShape** class to draw three filled circles. We will implement this by modifying the start method. First we need to create three **DrawableShape** objects and add them to the **DrawingBoard** object **canvas:**

```
DrawableShape shape1 = new DrawableShape();
DrawableShape shape2 = new DrawableShape();
DrawableShape shape3 = new DrawableShape();

shape1.setCenterPoint(new Point(250,300));
shape2.setCenterPoint(new Point(500,300));
shape3.setCenterPoint(new Point(750,300));

canvas.addShape(shape1);
canvas.addShape(shape2);
canvas.addShape(shape3);
```

Then we set the motion type to **SMOOTH** movement, make the window appear on the screen, and start the drawing:

```
canvas.setMovement(DrawingBoard.SMOOTH);
canvas.setVisible(true);
canvas.start();
```

step 2 code   Here's the code for the preliminary **DrawableShape** class:

```
import java.awt.*;

/**
 * Step 2: Add a preliminary DrawableShape class
 *
 * A class whose instances know how to draw themselves.
 *
 * @author Dr Caffeine
 */
```

```
class DrawableShape {

    private Point   centerPoint;

    public DrawableShape( ) {

        centerPoint = null;
    }

    public void draw(Graphics g) {

        g.setColor(Color.blue);
        g.fillOval(centerPoint.x-100, centerPoint.y-100, 200, 200);
    }

    public Point getCenterPoint( ) {

        return centerPoint;
    }

    public Dimension getDimension( ) {

        return new Dimension(200, 200);
    }

    public void setCenterPoint(Point point) {

        centerPoint = point;
    }
}
```

Data members

Constructors

draw

getCenterPoint

getDimension

setCenterPoint

The **Ch5DrawShape** class now has the modified **start** method as designed (the rest of the class remains the same):

```
import java.awt.*;

/**
 * Chapter 5 Sample Development: Start drawing shapes (Step 2)
 *
 * The instantiable main class of the program.
 */

class Ch5DrawShape {

    . . .
```

```
public void start( ) {

    DrawableShape shape1 = new DrawableShape();
    DrawableShape shape2 = new DrawableShape();
    DrawableShape shape3 = new DrawableShape();

    shape1.setCenterPoint(new Point(250,300));
    shape2.setCenterPoint(new Point(500,300));
    shape3.setCenterPoint(new Point(750,300));

    canvas.addShape(shape1);
    canvas.addShape(shape2);
    canvas.addShape(shape3);

    canvas.setMovement(DrawingBoard.SMOOTH);

    canvas.setVisible(true);
    canvas.start();
}

    . . .

}
```

> start

step 2 test

Now we run the program and verify the three bouncing circles moving around. To test other options of the **DrawingBoard** class, we will try the other methods with different parameters:

Method	Test Parameter
setMovement	Try both `DrawingBoard.STATIONARY` and `DrawingBoard.RANDOM`.
setDelayTime	Try values ranging from 0.1 to 3.0.
setBackground	Try several different `Color` constants such as `Color.white`, `Color.red`, and `Color.green`.

We insert these testing statements before the statement

```
canvas.setVisible(true);
```

in the **start** method.

Another testing option we should try is the drawing of different geometric shapes. We can replace the drawing statement inside the **draw** method from

```
g.fillOval(centerPoint.x-100, centerPoint.y-100,
           200, 200);
```

to

```
g.fillRect(centerPoint.x-100, centerPoint.y-100,
        200, 200);
```

or

```
g.fillRoundRect(centerPoint.x-100, centerPoint.y-100,
        200, 200, 50, 50);
```

to draw a filled rectangle or a filled rounded rectangle, respectively.

Step 3 Development: Allow the User to Select a Shape

step 3
design

Now that we know how to interact with the **DrawingBoard** class, we can proceed to develop the user interface portion of the program. There are three categories in which the user can select an option: shape, color, and motion. We will work on the shape selection here and on the color and motion selection in the next two steps. Once we are done with this step, the next two steps are fairly straightforward because the idea is essentially the same.

Let's allow the user to select one of the three shapes—ellipse, rectangle, and rounded rectangle—the shapes we know how to draw at this point. We can add more fancy shapes later. In what ways should we allow the user to input the shape? There are two possible alternatives: The first would ask the user to enter the text and spell out the shape, and the second would ask the user to enter a number that corresponds to the shape, (e.g., 1 for ellipse, 2 for rectangle, 3 for rounded rectangle). Which is the better alternative?

design alternative 1

We anticipate at least two problems with the first input style. When we need to get a user's name, for example, there's no good alternative to asking the user to enter his or her name. But when we want the user to select one of the few available choices, it is cumbersome and too much of a burden for the user. Moreover, it is prone to mistyping.

design alternative 2

To allow the user to make a selection quickly and easily, we can let the user select one of the available choices by entering a corresponding number. Among the techniques we have learned so far, this technique would be the most appropriate. Using the **JOptionPane,** we will list the choices with numbers 1, 2, and 3 and get the user's selection as

```
String str = JOptionPane.showInputDialog(null,
                "Selection: Enter the Shape number\n" +
                "   1 - Ellipse \n" +
                "   2 - Rectangle \n" +
                "   3 - Rounded Rectangle \n" );

int selection = Integer.parseInt(str);
```

For getting the dimension of the shape, we use **JOptionPane** again to accept the width and height values from the user. The values cannot be negative, for sure, but we also want to restrict the values to a certain range. We do not want the shape to be too small or too large. Let's set the minimum to 100 pixels and the maximum to 500 pixels. If the user enters a value outside the acceptable range, we will set the value to 100. The input routine for the width can be written as

```
String str = JOptionPane.showInputDialog(null,
                  "Enter the width of the shape\n" +
                  "    between 100 and 500 inclusive");

int width = Integer.parseInt(str);

if (width < 100 || width > 500) {
    width = 100;
}
```

The input routine for the height will work in the same manner.

For getting the *x* and *y* values of the shape's center point, we follow the pattern of getting the width and height values. We will set the acceptable range for the *x* value to 200 and 800, inclusive, and the *y* value to 100 and 600, inclusive.

Our next task is to modify the **DrawableShape** class so it will be able to draw three different geometric shapes. First we will add a new constructor that accepts the three input values:

```
public DrawableShape(int sType, Dimension sDim,
                     Point sCenter) {

    type        = sType;
    dimension   = sDim;
    centerPoint = sCenter;
}
```

The variables **type, dimension,** and **centerPoint** are data members for keeping track of necessary information. We modify the default constructor to

```
public DrawableShape( ) {

    this(ELLIPSE, DEFAULT_DIMENSION, DEFAULT_CENTER_PT);
}
```

with the data member constants defined as

```
public static final int ELLIPSE           = 0;
public static final int RECTANGLE         = 1;
public static final int ROUNDED_RECTANGLE = 2;

private static final Dimension DEFAULT_DIMENSION
                            = new Dimension(200, 200);

private static final Point DEFAULT_CENTER_PT
                            = new Point(350, 350);
```

In the previous step, the draw method drew a fixed-size circle. We need to modify it to draw three different geometric shapes based on the value of the data member **type.** We can modify the method to

```
public void draw(Graphics g) {

    g.setColor(Color.blue);

    drawShape(g);

}
```

with the private method **drawShape** defined as

```
private void drawShape(Graphics g) {

    switch (type) {

        case ELLIPSE:
                //code to draw a filled oval comes here
                break;

        case RECTANGLE:
                //code to draw a filled rectangle comes here
                break;

        case ROUNDED_RECTANGLE:
                //code to draw a filled rounded rectangle
                //comes here
                break;

    }

}
```

step 3 code

Here's the modified main class **Ch5DrawShape:**

```
import java.awt.*;
import javax.swing.*;

/**
 * Chapter 5 Sample Development: Handle User Input for Shape Type (Step 3)
 *
 * The instantiable main class of the program.
 */

class Ch5DrawShape {

    . . .

    public void start( ) {

        DrawableShape shape1 = getShape();
```

start

```
        canvas.addShape(shape1);

        canvas.setMovement(DrawingBoard.SMOOTH);

        canvas.setVisible(true);
        canvas.start();

    }

    private DrawableShape getShape( ) {                    getShape

        int type = inputShapeType();

        Dimension dim = inputDimension();

        Point centerPt = inputCenterPoint();

        DrawableShape shape = new DrawableShape(type, dim, centerPt);

        return shape;
    }

    private int inputShapeType( ) {                    inputShape Type

        String str = JOptionPane.showInputDialog(null,
                        "Selection: Enter the Shape number\n" +
                        "   1 - Ellipse \n" +
                        "   2 - Rectangle \n" +
                        "   3 - Rounded Rectangle \n" );

        int selection = Integer.parseInt(str);

        int type;
        switch (selection) {

            case 1:   type = DrawableShape.ELLIPSE;
                      break;

            case 2:   type = DrawableShape.RECTANGLE;
                      break;

            case 3:   type = DrawableShape.ROUNDED_RECTANGLE;
                      break;

            default:  type = DrawableShape.ELLIPSE;
                      break;
        }

        return type;
    }
```

```java
    private Dimension inputDimension( ) {

        String str = JOptionPane.showInputDialog(null,
                          "Enter the width of the shape\n" +
                          "    between 100 and 500 inclusive");

        int width = Integer.parseInt(str);

        if (width < 100 || width > 500) {
            width = 100;
        }

        str = JOptionPane.showInputDialog(null,
                          "Enter the height of the shape\n" +
                          "    between 100 and 500 inclusive");

        int height = Integer.parseInt(str);

        if (height < 100 || height > 500) {
            height = 100;
        }

        return new Dimension(width, height);
    }

    private Point inputCenterPoint( ) {

        String str = JOptionPane.showInputDialog(null,
                          "Enter the x value of the center point\n" +
                          "    between 200 and 800 inclusive");

        int x = Integer.parseInt(str);

        if (x < 200 || x > 800) {
            x = 200;
        }

        str = JOptionPane.showInputDialog(null,
                          "Enter the y value of the center point\n" +
                          "    between 100 and 500 inclusive");

        int y = Integer.parseInt(str);

        if (y < 100 || y > 500) {
            y = 100;
        }

        return new Point(x, y);
    }
    . . .
}
```

inputDimension

inputCenterPoint

The **DrawableShape** class is now modified to

```
import java.awt.*;

/**
 * Step 3: Draw different shapes
 *
 * A class whose instances know how to draw themselves.
 *
 */
class DrawableShape {                                    Data members

    public static final int ELLIPSE = 0;

    public static final int RECTANGLE = 1;

    public static final int ROUNDED_RECTANGLE = 2;

    private static final Dimension DEFAULT_DIMENSION
                                        = new Dimension(200, 200);

    private static final Point DEFAULT_CENTER_PT = new Point(350, 350);

    private Point      centerPoint;

    private Dimension dimension;

    private int        type;

    public DrawableShape( ) {                            Constructors

        this(ELLIPSE, DEFAULT_DIMENSION, DEFAULT_CENTER_PT);
    }

    public DrawableShape(int sType, Dimension sDim, Point sCenter) {

        type       = sType;
        dimension  = sDim;
        centerPoint = sCenter;
    }

    public void draw(Graphics g) {                       draw

        g.setColor(Color.blue);
```

```
        drawShape(g);
    }

    . . .

    public void setType(int shapeType) {                    setType

        type = shapeType;
    }

    private void drawShape(Graphics g) {                    drawShape
        switch (type) {
            case ELLIPSE:
                    g.fillOval(centerPoint.x - dimension.width/2,
                                centerPoint.y - dimension.height/2,
                                dimension.width,
                                dimension.height);
                    break;

            case RECTANGLE:
                    g.fillRect(centerPoint.x - dimension.width/2,
                                centerPoint.y - dimension.height/2,
                                dimension.width,
                                dimension.height);
                    break;

            case ROUNDED_RECTANGLE:
                    g.fillRoundRect(centerPoint.x - dimension.width/2,
                                    centerPoint.y - dimension.height/2,
                                    dimension.width,
                                    dimension.height,
                                    (int) (dimension.width * 0.3),
                                    (int) (dimension.height * 0.3));
                    break;
        }
    }

}
```

Notice how we add code for handling the case when an invalid number is entered in the **inputShapeType** method. We use the **default** case to set the shape type to **ELLIPSE** if an invalid value is entered. In addition to handling the invalid entries, it is critical for us to make sure that all valid entries are handled correctly. For example, we cannot leave the type undefined or assigned to a wrong value when one of the valid data is entered.

Helpful Reminder

When we write a selection control statement, we must make sure that all possible cases are handled correctly.

Also notice that we did not write the **inputShapeType** method as

```java
private int inputShapeType( ) {

    String str = JOptionPane.showInputDialog(null,
                "Selection: Enter the Shape number\n" +
                "   0 - Ellipse \n" +
                "   1 - Rectangle \n" +
                "   2 - Rounded Rectangle \n" );

    int selection = Integer.parseInt(str);

    if (selection < 0 || selection > 2) {
       selection = 1;
    }

    return selection;
}
```

Bad Version

This bad version is based on the fact that the value 0 is used for the constant **DrawableShape.ELLIPSE,** 1 for the constant **DrawableShape.RECTANGLE,** and 2 for the constant **DrawableShape.ROUNDED_RECTANGLE**. What would happen if, for whatever reasons, these values were changed in the **DrawableShape** class? We must update this version of **inputShapeType** accordingly. A situation in which a change in one class forces changes in another class is not a reliable and robust way to implement classes. First, keeping track of required changes is a very heavy burden to the programmers and prone to not making all the required changes. Second, the actual process of updating the source file is often tedious and also prone to errors. This bad version of **inputShapeType** is too heavily reliant on the internal details (knowing which values are used for the constants) of the **DrawableShape** class. In other words, the **Ch5DrawShape** class is too tightly coupled with the **Drawable-Shape** class. We want to keep the relationships between the classes as loosely coupled as possible.

Design Guidelines

In designing classes, we aim for loosely coupled relationships among classes.

Here's another bad version of **inputShapeType:**

```
private int inputShapeType( ) {

    String str = JOptionPane.showInputDialog(null,
                    "Selection: Enter the Shape number\n" +
                    DrawableShape.ELLIPSE +
                            " - Ellipse \n" +
                    DrawableShape.RECTANGLE +
                            " - Rectangle \n" +
                    DrawableShape.ROUNDED_RECTANGLE +
                            " - Rounded Rectangle \n" );

    int selection = Integer.parseInt(str);

    if (selection < DrawableShape.ELLIPSE ||
       selection > DrawableShape.ROUNDED_RECTANGLE) {
       selection = DrawableShape.ELLIPSE;
    }

    return selection;
}
```

The first problem is that the values assigned to the constants may not be consecutive, so it's possible to end with an awkward display such as

```
Selection: Enter the Shape number
20 - Ellipse
4 - Rectangle
1 - Rounded Rectangle
```

More important than the clumsy display is how fragile the code is. The code will work only if the values for the constants are set in such a way that **DrawableShape.ELLIPSE** is the minimum and **DrawableShape.ROUNDED_RECTANGLE** is the maximum. If this property is not maintained, then the **if** statement inside the method will fail to work correctly.

step 3 test
    Now we run the program multiple times, trying various shape types, dimensions, and center points. After we verify that everything is working as expected, we proceed to the next step.

Step 4 Development: Allow the User to Select a Color

step 4 design
In the fourth development step, we add a routine that allows the user to specify the color of the selected shape. We will adopt the same input style for accepting the shape in step 3. We will list five different color choices and let the the user select one by entering the corresponding number. We will use a default color when an invalid number is entered. Analogous to the shape selection routine, we will add a method named **inputColor** to the **Ch5DrawShape** class. The structure of this method is identical to that of the **getShape** method, except the return type is **Color.** Using this

method, we can set the color of the shape in the **start** method as

```
public void start( ) {

    DrawableShape shape1 = getShape();

    shape1.setColor(inputColor());

        . . .

}
```

We make a small extension to the **DrawableShape** class by adding a data member to keep track of the selected color and a method to set the color. Here's the modified **Ch5DrawShape** class:

step 4 code

```
import java.awt.*;
import javax.swing.*;

/**
 * Chapter 5 Sample Development: Color selection (Step 4)
 *
 * The instantiable main class of the program.
 */

class Ch5DrawShape {

    . . .

    public void start( ) {

        DrawableShape shape1 = getShape();

        shape1.setColor(inputColor());

        canvas.addShape(shape1);

        canvas.setMovement(DrawingBoard.SMOOTH);

        canvas.setVisible(true);
        canvas.start();

    }

    private Color inputColor( ) {

        String str = JOptionPane.showInputDialog(null,
                    "Selection: Enter the Color number\n" +
                    "    1 - Red \n" +
                    "    2 - Green \n" +
```

start

inputColor

```
                         "    3 - Blue \n" +
                         "    4 - Yellow \n" +
                         "    5 - Magenta \n" );

        int selection = Integer.parseInt(str);

        Color color;
        switch (selection) {

            case 1:   color = Color.red;
                      break;

            case 2:   color = Color.green;
                      break;

            case 3:   color = Color.blue;
                      break;

            case 4:   color = Color.yellow;
                      break;

            case 5:   color = Color.magenta;
                      break;

            default: color = Color.red;
                      break;
        }

        return color;
    }
    . . .
}
```

The **DrawableShape** class is now modified to

```
import java.awt.*;

/**
 * Step 4: Adds the color choice
 *
 * A class whose instances know how to draw themselves.
 *
 */
```

```
class DrawableShape {

    . . .

    private static final Color DEFAULT_COLOR = Color.blue;

    . . .                                                    Data members

    private Color      fillColor;

    . . .

    public DrawableShape(int sType, Dimension sDim, Point sCenter) {

        type        = sType;
        dimension   = sDim;                                  Constructors
        centerPoint = sCenter;

        fillColor   = DEFAULT_COLOR;
    }

    public void draw(Graphics g) {                           draw

        g.setColor(fillColor);

        drawShape(g);

    }

    . . .

    public void setColor(Color color) {                      setColor

        fillColor = color;

    }

    . . .

}
```

step 4 test

Now we run the program several times, each time selecting a different color, and verify that the shape is drawn in the chosen color. After we verify the program, we move on to the next step.

Step 5 Development: Allow the User to Select a Motion Type

step 5
design

In the fifth development step, we add a routine that allows the user to select the motion type. We give three choices to the user: stationary, random, or smooth. The same design we used in steps 3 and 4 is applicable here, so we will adopt it for the motion type selection also. Since we adopt the same design, we can ease into the coding phase.

step 5 code   Here's the modified main class **Ch5DrawShape:**

```java
import java.awt.*;
import javax.swing.*;

/**
 * Chapter 5 Sample Development: Color selection (Step 5)
 *
 * The instantiable main class of the program.
 */
class Ch5DrawShape {
    . . .

    public void start( ) {

        DrawableShape shape1 = getShape();

        shape1.setColor(inputColor());

        canvas.addShape(shape1);

        canvas.setMovement(inputMotionType());

        canvas.setVisible(true);
        canvas.start();

    }

    . . .

    private int inputMotionType( ) {

        String str = JOptionPane.showInputDialog(null,
                        "Selection: Enter the Motion number\n" +
                        "   1 - Stationary (no movement) \n" +
                        "   2 - Random Movement\n" +
                        "   3 - Smooth Movement \n"  );

        int selection = Integer.parseInt(str);

        int type;
        switch (selection) {

            case 1:  type = DrawingBoard.STATIONARY;
                     break;
```

start

inputMotionType

```
        case 2:   type = DrawingBoard.RANDOM;
                  break;

        case 3:   type = DrawingBoard.SMOOTH;
                  break;

        default:  type = DrawingBoard.SMOOTH;
                  break;
      }

      return type;
    }
      . . .
  }
```

No changes are required for the **DrawableShape** class, as the **DrawingBoard** class is the one responsible for the shape movement.

step 5 test

Now we run the program multiple times and test all three motion types. From what we have done, we can't imagine the code we have already written in the earlier steps to cause any problems, but if we are not careful, a slight change in one step could cause the code developed from the earlier steps to stop working correctly (e.g., erroneously reusing data members in newly written methods). So we should continue to test all aspects of the program diligently. After we are satisfied with the program, we proceed to the final step.

Step 6 Development: Finalize

program review

We will perform a critical *program review*, looking for any unfinished method, inconsistency or error in the methods, unclear or missing comments, and so forth. We should also not forget to improve the program for cleaner code and better readability. Another activity we can pursue in the final step is to look for extensions.

interesting extensions

There are several *interesting extensions* we can make to the program. First is the morphing of an object. In the current implementation, once the shape is selected, it will not change. It would be more fun to see the shape changes, for example, the width and height of the shape's dimension could be set to vary while the shape is drawn. Another interesting variation is to make a circle morph into a rectangle and morph back into a circle. Second is the drawing of multiple shapes. Third is the variation in color while the shape is drawn. Fourth is the drawing of a text (we "draw" a text on the **Graphics** context just as we draw geometric shapes). You can make the text scroll across the screen from right to left by setting the motion type of **DrawingBoard** to **STATIONARY** and updating the center point value within our **DrawableShape** class. Some of these extensions are given as chapter exercises.

S u m m a r y

- A selection control statement is used to alter the sequential flow of control.

- The if and switch statements are two types of selection control.

- A boolean expression contains conditional and boolean operators and evaluates to true or false.

- Three boolean operators in Java are AND (&&), OR (||), and NOT (!).

- DeMorgan's laws state that !(P &&Q) and !P || !Q are equivalent and that !(P || Q) and !P && !Q are equivalent.

- Logical operators && and || are evaluated by using the short-circuit evaluation technique.

- A boolean flag is useful in keeping track of program settings.

- An if statement can be a part of the then or else block of another if statement to formulate nested-if statements.

- Careful attention to details is important to avoid illogically constructed nested-if statements.

- When the equality symbol == is used in comparing the variables of reference data type, we are comparing the addresses.

- The switch statement is useful when expressing a selection control based on equality testing between data of type char, byte, short, or int.

- The break statement causes the control to break out of the surrounding switch statement (*note:* also from other control statements introduced in Chapter 6).

- The standard classes introduced in this chapter are

    > java.awt.Graphics
    > java.awt.Color
    > java.awt.Point
    > java.awt.Dimension

- The java.awt.Graphics is used to draw geometric shapes.

- The java.awt.Color is used to set the color of various GUI components.

- The java.awt.Point is used to represent a point in two-dimensional space.

- The java.awt.Dimension is used to represent a bounding rectangle of geometric shapes and other GUI components.

K e y   C o n c e p t s

selection control	nested-if statements
if statements	switch statements
boolean operators and expressions	break statements
precedence rules for boolean expressions	graphics
	content pane of a frame

1. Indent the following if statements properly.

   a. `if (a == b) if (c == d) a = 1; else b = 1; else c = 1;`
   b. `if (a == b) a = 1; if (c == d) b = 1; else c = 1;`
   c. `if (a == b) {if (c == d) a = 1; b = 2; } else b = 1;`
   d. `if (a == b) {`
      `if (c == d) a = 1; b = 2; }`
      `else {b = 1; if (a == d) d = 3;}`
      `else c = 1;`

2. Which two of the following three if statements are equivalent?

   a. `if (a == b)`
      `if (c == d) a = 1;`
      `else b = 1;`
   b. `if (a == b) {`
      `if (c == d) a = 1; }`
      `else b = 1;`
   c. `if (a == b)`
      `if (c == d) a = 1;`
      `else b = 1;`

3. Evaluate the following boolean expressions. For each of the following expressions, assume x is **10**, y is **20**, and z is **30**. Indicate which of the following boolean expressions are always true and which are always false, regardless of the values for x, y, or z.

   a. `x < 10 || x > 10`
   b. `x > y && y > x`
   c. `(x < y + z) && (x + 10 <= 20)`
   d. `z - y == x && Math.abs(y - z) == x`
   e. `x < 10 && x > 10`
   f. `x > y || y > x`
   g. `!(x < y + z) || !(x + 10 <= 20)`
   h. `!(x == y) && (x != y) && (x < y || y < x)`

4. Express the following switch statement, using nested-if statements.

```
switch (grade) {
   case 10:
   case  9:  a = 1;
             b = 2;
             break;

   case  8:  a = 3;
             b = 4;
             break;

   default:  a = 5;
             break;
}
```

5. Write an if statement to find the smallest of three given integers without using the min method of the Math class.

6. Draw control flow diagrams for the following two switch statements.

```
switch (choice) {
   case 1: a = 0;
           break;

   case 2: b = 1;
           break;

   case 3: c = 2;
           break;

   default: d = 3;
            break;
}
```

```
switch (choice) {
   case 1: a = 0;

   case 2: b = 1;

   case 3: c = 2;

   default: d = 3;
}
```

7. Write an if statement that prints out a message based on the following rules:

If the Total Points Are	Message to Print
≥ 100	You won a free cup of coffee.
≥ 200	You won a free cup of coffee and a regular-size doughnut.
≥ 300	You won a free cup of coffee and a regular-size doughnut and a 12-oz orange juice.
≥ 400	You won a free cup of coffee and a regular-size doughnut and a 12-oz orange juice and a combo breakfast.
≥ 500	You won a free cup of coffee and a regular-size doughnut and a 12-oz orange juice and a combo breakfast and a reserved table for one week.

8. Rewrite the following if statement, using a switch statement:

```
int selection = Integer.parseInt(
                    JOptionPane.showInputDialog(null,
                        "Enter selection:"));

if (selection == 0)
    System.out.println("You selected Magenta");

else if (selection == 1)
    System.out.println("You selected Cyan");

else if (selection == 2)
    System.out.println("You selected Red");
```

```
     else if (selection == 3)
        System.out.println("You selected Blue");

     else if (selection == 4)
        System.out.println("You selected Green");
     else
        System.out.println("Invalid selection");
```

9. At the end of movie credits you see the year that movies are produced in Roman numerals, for example, MCMXCVII for 1997. To help the production staff determine the correct Roman numeral for the production year, write an application that reads a year and displays the year in Roman numerals.

Roman Numeral	Number
I	1
V	5
X	10
L	50
C	100
D	500
M	1000

Remember that certain numbers are expressed by using a "subtraction," for example, IV for 4, CD for 400, and so forth.

10. Write a program that replies either Leap Year or Not a Leap Year when given a year. It is a leap year if the year is divisible by 4 but not by 100 (for example, 1796 is a leap year because it is divisible by 4 but not by 100). A year that is divisible by both 4 and 100 is a leap year if it is also divisible by 400 (for example, 2000 is a leap year, but 1800 is not).

11. A million is 10^6 and a billion is 10^9. Write an application that reads a power of 10 (6, 9, 12, etc.) and displays how big the number is (Million, Billion, etc.). Display an appropriate message for the input value that has no corresponding word. The table below shows the correspondence between the power and the word for that number.

Power of 10	Number
6	Million
9	Billion
12	Trillion
15	Quadrillion
18	Quintillion
21	Sextillion
30	Nonillion
100	Googol

12. Write a program RecommendedWeightWithTest by extending the RecommendedWeight (see Exercise 13 on page 229). The extended program

will include the following test:

```
if (the height is between 140cm and 230cm)

    compute the recommended weight

else

    display an error message
```

13. Extend the RecommendedWeightWithTest program in Exercise 12 by allowing the user to enter his or her weight and printing out the message You should exercise more if the weight is more than 10 pounds over the recommended weight and You need more nourishment if the weight is more than 20 pounds under the recommended weight.

14. Employees at MyJava Lo-Fat Burgers earn the basic hourly wage of $7.25. They will receive time-and-a-half of their basic rate for overtime hours. In addition, they will receive a commission on the sales they generate while tending the counter. The commission is based on this formula:

Sales Volume	Commission
$1.00–$99.99	5% of total sales
$100.00–$299.99	10% of total sales
≥ $300.00	15% of total sales

Write an application that inputs the number of hours worked and the total sales and computes the wage.

15. Using the DrawingBoard class, write a screensaver that displays a scrolling text message. The text message moves across the window, starting from the right edge toward the left edge. Set the motion type to stationary, so the DrawingBoard does not adjust the position. You have to adjust the text's position inside your DrawableShape.

16. Using the DrawingBoard class, write a screensaver that displays three morphing objects. The objects are initially circles, but gradually morph into rectangles and morph back to circles. Hint: Use the drawRoundRect or fillRoundRect method. Adjust the values for the arc width and height when calling the method.

Development Exercises

For the following exercises, use the incremental development methodology to implement the program. For each exercise, identify the program tasks, create a design document with class descriptions, and draw the program diagram. Map out the development steps at the start. Present any design alternatives and justify your selection. Be sure to perform adequate testing at the end of each development step.

17. MyJava Coffee Outlet (see Exercise 25 from Chapter 3) decided to give discounts to volume buyers. The discount is based on this table:

Order Volume	Discount
≥ 25 bags	5% of total price
≥ 50 bags	10% of total price
≥ 100 bags	15% of total price
≥ 150 bags	20% of total price
≥ 200 bags	25% of total price
≥ 300 bags	30% of total price

Each bag of beans costs $5.50. Write an application that accepts the number of bags ordered and prints out the total cost of the order in the following style.

```
Number of Bags Ordered: 173 - $ 951.50

            Discount:
                      20% - $ 190.30

    Your total charge is: $ 761.20
```

18. Combine Exercises 4.17 and 3.25 to compute the total charge including discount and shipping costs. The output should look like this:

```
Number of Bags Ordered: 43 - $ 236.50

            Discount:
                      5% - $ 11.83

          Boxes Used:
                      1 Large - $3.00
                      2 Medium - $2.00

    Your total charge is: $ 229.67
```

Note: The discount applies to the cost of beans only.

19. You are hired by Expressimo Delivery Service to develop an application that computes the delivery charge. The company allows two types of packaging—letter and box—and three types of service—Next Day Priority, Next Day Standard, and Two-Day. The following table shows the formula for computing the charge:

Package Type	Next Day Priority	Next Day Standard	Two-Day
Letter	$12.00, up to 8 oz	$10.50, up to 8 oz	Not available
Box	$15.75 for the first pound. Add $1.25 for each additional pound over the first pound.	$13.75 for the first pound. Add $1.00 for each additional pound over the first pound.	$7.00 for the first pound. Add $0.50 for each additional pound over the first pound.

The program will input three values from the user: the type of package, the type of service, and the weight of the package.

20. Ms. Latte's Mopeds 'R Us rents mopeds at Monterey Beach boardwalk. To promote business during the slow weekdays, the store gives a huge discount. The rental charges are as follows:

Moped Type	Weekday Rental	Weekend Rental
50cc Mopette	$15.00 for the first 3 hours, $2.50 per hour after the first 3 hours	$30.00 for the first 3 hours, $7.50 per hour after the first 3 hours
250cc Mohawk	$25.00 for the first 3 hours, $3.50 per hour after the first 3 hours	$35.00 for the first 3 hours, $8.50 per hour after the first 3 hours

Write a program that computes the rental charge, given the type of moped, when it is rented (either weekday or weekend), and the number of hours rented.

21. Write an application program that teaches children how to read a clock. Use JOptionPane to enter the hour and minute. Accept only numbers between 0 and 12 for hour and between 0 and 59 for minute. Print out an appropriate error message for an invalid input value. Draw a clock that looks something like this:

To draw a clock hand, you use the drawLine method of the Graphics class. The endpoints of the line are determined as

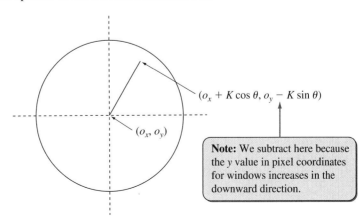

$(o_x + K \cos \theta, o_y - K \sin \theta)$

(o_x, o_y)

Note: We subtract here because the y value in pixel coordinates for windows increases in the downward direction.

The value for constant K determines the length of the clock hand. Make the K larger for the minute hand than for the hour hand. The angle θ is expressed in radians. The angle θ_{min} of the minute hand is computed as

$$(90 - \text{Minute} \times 6.0) \frac{\pi}{180}$$

and the angle θ_{hr} of the hour hand is computed as

$$\left(90 - \left(\text{Hour} + \frac{\text{Minute}}{60.0}\right) \times 30.0\right) \frac{\pi}{180}$$

where Hour and Minute are input values. The values 6.0 and 30.0 designate the degrees for 1 minute and 1 hour (i.e., the minute hand moves 6 degrees in 1 minute and the hour hand moves 30.0 degrees in 1 hour). The factor $\pi/180$ converts a degree to the radian equivalent.

You can draw the clock on the content pane of a frame window by getting the content pane's Graphic object, as described in the chapter. Here's a sample code:

```
import javax.swing.*;
import java.awt.*; //for Graphics
...
JFrame    win;
Container contentPane;
Graphics  g;
...
win = new JFrame();
win.setSize(300, 300);
win.setLocation(100,100);
win.setVisible(true);
...
contentPane = win.getContentPane();
g = contentPane.getGraphics();
g.drawOval(50,50,200,200);
```

22. Extend the application in Exercise 21 by drawing a more realistic, better-looking clock. For example,

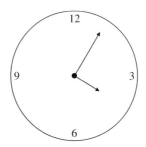

23. After starting a successful coffee beans outlet business, MyJava Coffee Outlet is now venturing into the fast-food business. The first thing the management decides is to eliminate the drive-through intercom. MyJava Lo-Fat Burgers is the only fast-food establishment in town that provides a computer screen and mouse for its drive-through customers. You are hired as a freelance computer consultant. Write a program that lists items for three menu categories: entree, side dish, and drink. The following table lists the items available for each entry and their prices. Choose appropriate methods for input and output.

Entree		Side Dish		Drink	
Tofu Burger	$3.49	Rice Cracker	$0.79	Cafe Mocha	$1.99
Cajun Chicken	$4.59	No-Salt Fries	$0.69	Cafe Latte	$1.99
Buffalo Wings	$3.99	Zucchini	$1.09	Espresso	$2.49
Rainbow Fillet	$2.99	Brown Rice	$0.59	Oolong Tea	$0.99

6 Repetition Statements

After you have read and studied this chapter, you should be able to

- Implement repetition control in a program by using **while** statements.

- Implement repetition control in a program by using **do–while** statements.

- Implement a generic loop-and-a-half repetition control statement.

- Implement repetition control in a program by using **for** statements.

- Nest a loop repetition statement inside another repetition statement.

- Choose the appropriate repetition control statement for a given task.

- Prompt the user for a yes/no reply by using the **showConfirmDialog** method from the **JOptionPane** class.

- (Optional) Write simple recursive methods.

Introduction

he selection statements we covered in Chapter 5 alter the control flow of a program. In this chapter we will cover another group of control statements, called repetition statements. *Repetition statements* control a block of code to be executed for a fixed number of times or until a certain condition is met. We will describe Java's three repetition statements: while, do–while, and for. In addition to the repetition statements, we will introduce the third useful method of the JOptionPane class, called showConfirmDialog. The confirmation dialog is often used in conjunction with a repetition statement. For example, we can set up a repetition statement to keep playing a game while the user replies yes to a confirmation dialog. Finally, in an optional section at the end of the chapter, we will describe recursive methods. A

recursive method is a method that calls itself. Instead of using a repetition statement, a recursive method can be used to program the repetition control flow.

6.1 | The while **Statement**

Suppose we want to compute the sum of the first 100 positive integers $1, 2, \ldots, 100$. Here's how we compute the sum, using a while statement:

```
int sum = 0, number = 1;

while (number <= 100) {
    sum    =  sum + number;
    number = number + 1;
}
```

Let's analyze the while statement. The statement follows the general format

```
while ( <boolean expression> )

    <statement>
```

where <statement> is either a <single statement> or a <compound statement>. The <statement> of the sample while statement is a <compound statement> and therefore has the left and right braces. Repetition statements are also called *loop statements,* and we characterize the <statement> as the *loop body*. Figure 6.1 shows how

this while statement corresponds to the general format. As long as the <boolean expression> is true, the loop body is executed. Figure 6.2 is a diagram showing the control flow of the sample code.

Let's modify the loop so this time we keep on adding the numbers 1, 2, 3, and so forth until the sum becomes more than 1,000,000. Here's how we write the while statement:

```
int sum = 0, number = 1;

while ( sum <= 1000000 ) {
```

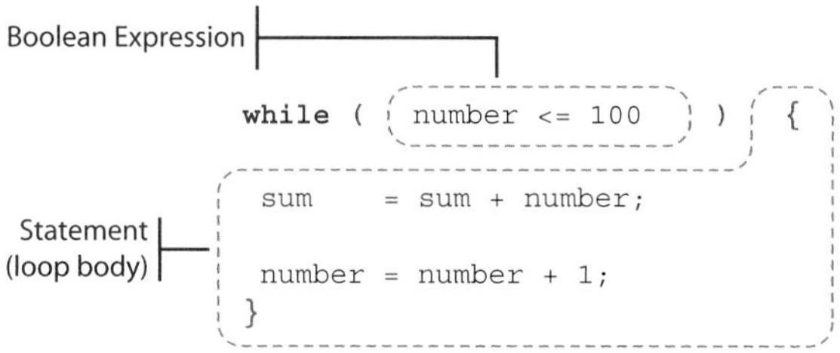

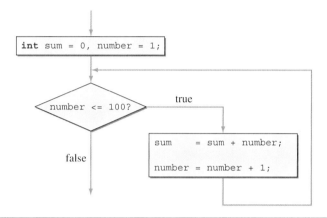

Figure 6.1 Correspondence of the example **while** statement to the general format.

```
int sum = 0, number = 1;

number <= 100?          true

    false       sum     = sum + number;

                number = number + 1;
```

Figure 6.2 A diagram showing the control flow of a **while** statement.

```
        sum    =   sum + number;
        number = number + 1;
    }
```

Notice how the <boolean expression> is modified, and it is the only part of the while statement that is modified.

Let's try another example. This time, we compute the product of the first 20 odd integers. (*Note:* The ith odd integer is 2 * i − 1. For example, the fourth odd integer is 2 * 4 − 1 = 7.)

```
int product = 1, number = 1, count = 20, lastNumber;

lastNumber = 2 * count - 1;

while (number <= lastNumber) {
    product = product * number;
    number  = number + 2;
}
```

count-controlled loop

The first and the third sample while statements are called *count-controlled loops* because the loop body is executed for a fixed number of times (as if we were counting).

Now let's study how the repetition control in the program will improve the user interface of the program. In earlier sample programs, we assumed the input data were valid. The programs we have written may produce wrong results or simply stop running if the user enters an invalid value. Assuming that the input values are valid makes the writing of programs easier because we do not have to write code to handle the invalid values. Although it is easier for us to write such programs, it would be an inferior interface from the user's standpoint. Requiring the user to make no mistake in entering input values is too restrictive and not user-friendly. We need to develop programs that are more user-friendly. Imagine you successfully entered 19 values, but on the 20th input value, you mistyped. A user-hostile program would stop, and you would have to run the program again. A more user-friendly program would allow you to reenter a correct 20th value.

All we could have done by using a selection statement was either to print out an error message or set a default value if the user enters an invalid value. In the inputShapeType method of the Chapter 5 sample development, for example, if the user enters any invalid value, we set the shape type to ellipse. Instead of quitting the program after displaying an error message or continuing the program with a default value, it would be better in general to allow the user to reenter the value until the correct value is entered. We need a repetition control to achieve this.

Let's look at an example. Suppose we want to input a person's age, and the value must be between 0 and 130. We know the age cannot be negative, so the age input must be greater than or equal to 0. We set the upper bound to 130 to take into account the possibility of some long-living human beings in a remote hamlet in Timbuktu. Let's say we will let the user enter the age until the valid age is entered. We can code this repetition control by using a while statement:

```
String inputStr;
int    age;

inputStr = JOptionPane.showInputDialog(null,
                     "Your Age (between 0 and 130):");
age      = Integer.parseInt(inputStr);

while (age < 0 || age > 130) {
   JOptionPane.showMessageDialog(null,
      "An invalid age was entered. Please try again.");

   inputStr = JOptionPane.showInputDialog(null,
                        "Your Age (between 0 and 130):");
   age      = Integer.parseInt(inputStr);
}
```

Notice that we included the statements

```
inputStr = JOptionPane.showInputDialog(null,
                     "Your Age (between 0 and 130):");
age      = Integer.parseInt(inputStr);
```

to input the age *before* the while statement. Without this input statement, the variable age will not have a value when the boolean expression is evaluated for the very

priming read first time. This reading of a value before the testing is done is called a *priming read*. We will discuss this issue of priming read in greater detail in Section 6.4.

As the second example, let's modify the inputShapeType method from Section 5.6. To refresh our memory, here's the original code:

```java
private int inputShapeType( ) {

    String str = JOptionPane.showInputDialog(null,
                    "Selection: Enter the Shape number\n" +
                    "   1 - Ellipse \n" +
                    "   2 - Rectangle \n" +
                    "   3 - Rounded Rectangle \n" );

    int selection = Integer.parseInt(str);

    int type;
    switch (selection) {

        case 1:  type = DrawableShape.ELLIPSE;
                 break;

        case 2:  type = DrawableShape.RECTANGLE;
                 break;

        case 3:  type = DrawableShape.ROUNDED_RECTANGLE;
                 break;

        default: type = DrawableShape.ELLIPSE;
                 break;
    }

    return type;
}
```

To allow the user to reenter the value until the valid entry is made, we can modify the method to this:

```java
private int inputShapeType( ) {

    int selection = getSelection();
```
getSelection is defined after this method.
```java
    int type;
    switch (selection) {

        case 1:  type = DrawableShape.ELLIPSE;
                 break;

        case 2:  type = DrawableShape.RECTANGLE;
                 break;

        case 3:  type = DrawableShape.ROUNDED_RECTANGLE;
                 break;
```
This default case should never happen if **getSelection** is implemented correctly. We put this here to catch any internal coding error.
```java
        default: JOptionPane.showMessageDialog(null,
                    "Internal Error: Proceed with Default");
```

```
                           type = DrawableShape.ELLIPSE;
                           break;
        }

        return type;
    }

    private int getSelection( ) {

        String str = JOptionPane.showInputDialog(null,
                        "Selection: Enter the Shape number\n" +
                        "   1 - Ellipse \n" +
                        "   2 - Rectangle \n" +
                        "   3 - Rounded Rectangle \n" );

        int selection = Integer.parseInt(str);

        while (selection < 1 || selection > 3) {

            JOptionPane.showMessageDialog(null,
                                    "Invalid Entry");

            str = JOptionPane.showInputDialog(null,
                        "Selection: Enter the Shape number\n" +
                        "   1 - Ellipse \n" +
                        "   2 - Rectangle \n" +
                        "   3 - Rounded Rectangle \n" );

            selection = Integer.parseInt(str);
        }

        return selection;
    }
```

The next example keeps reading in integers and computes their running sum until a negative number is entered.

```
    int sum = 0, number;

    //priming read
    number = Integer.parseInt(
                JOptionPane.showInputDialog(null,
                                    "Enter integer"));
    while (number >= 0) {
        sum = sum + number;

        number = Integer.parseInt(
                JOptionPane.showInputDialog(null,
                                    "Enter integer"));
    }
```

sentinel-controlled loop

The previous two sample statements are called sentinel-controlled loops. With a *sentinel-controlled loop*, the loop body is executed repeatedly until any one of the designated values, called a *sentinel*, is encountered. The sentinel for this example is any negative number, and the sentinel for the one before is any valid age between 0 and 130.

Let's conclude this section with a short sample program. It is a well-known fact that students in college do not get enough sleep, some studying hard while others are enjoying life too much. Which dorm we live in also makes a huge difference, so why don't we develop a program that determines the average sleeping time of the residents in a given dorm? This information can be made available on the housing office website so the students can make an informed decision on which dorm to choose for the next academic year.

We will define an instantiable main class. Using JOptionPane, we will input the dorm name first. Then we loop and input the length of sleep of the residents until the input value of zero is entered. When the input is done, the average sleep time is displayed. We assume the input values are valid. Here's the program listing:

```java
/*
    Chapter 6 Sample Program: Sleep Statistics for Dorm Residents

    File: Ch6SleepStatistics.java

*/

import javax.swing.*;
import java.text.*;

class Ch6SleepStatistics {

    public static void main (String[] args) {
        Ch6SleepStatistics prog = new Ch6SleepStatistics( );
        prog.start();
    }

    public void start( ) {

        double sleepHour, sum = 0;
        int    cnt = 0;

        //enter the dorm name
        String dorm = JOptionPane.showInputDialog(null,"Dorm name:");

        //Loop: get hours of sleep for each resident
        //      until 0 is entered.
        sleepHour = getDouble("Enter sleep hours (0 - to stop:)");

        while (sleepHour != 0) {

            sum += sleepHour;
            cnt++;

            sleepHour = getDouble("Enter sleep hours (0 - to stop:");
        }
```

main

start

```
        if (cnt == 0) {

            JOptionPane.showMessageDialog(null,"No Data Entered");

        } else {

            DecimalFormat df = new DecimalFormat("0.00");
            JOptionPane.showMessageDialog(null,
                        "Average sleep time for   " +
                        dorm + " is  \n\n          " +
                        df.format(sum/cnt) + " hours.");

        }
    }

    private double getDouble(String message) {
        double result;

        String str = JOptionPane.showInputDialog(null, message);

        result = Double.parseDouble(str);

        return result;
    }

}
```

getDouble

6.2 | Pitfalls in Writing Repetition Statements

No matter what you do with the while statement (and other repetition statements), make sure that the loop will eventually terminate. Watch out for an *infinite loop* such as this one:

infinite loop

```
int product = 0;

while (product < 500000) {
    product = product * 5;
}
```

Do you know why this is an infinite loop? The variable product is multiplied by 5 in the loop body, so the value for product should eventually become larger than 500000, right? Wrong. The variable product is initialized to 0, so product remains 0. The boolean expression product < 500000 will never be false, and, therefore, this while statement is an infinite loop. You have to make sure the loop body contains a statement that eventually makes the boolean expression false.

Here's another example of an infinite loop.

```
int count = 1;

while (count != 10) {
   count = count + 2;
}
```

Since the variable count is initialized to 1 and the increment is 2, count will never be equal to 10. *Note:* In theory, this while statement is an infinite loop, but in programming languages other than Java, this loop will eventually terminate because of an overflow error. An *overflow error* will occur if you attempt to assign a value larger than the maximum value the variable can hold. When an overflow error occurs, the execution of the program is terminated in almost all programming languages. With Java, however, an overflow will not cause program termination. When an overflow occurs in Java, a value that represents infinity (IEEE 754 infinity, to be precise) is assigned to a variable and no abnormal termination of a program will happen. Also, in Java an overflow occurs only with float and double variables; no overflow will happen with int variables. When you try to assign a value larger than the maximum possible integer that an int variable can hold, the value "wraps around" and becomes a negative value.

overflow error

Whether the loop terminates or not because of an overflow error, the logic of the loop is still an infinite loop, and we must watch out for it. When you write a loop, you must make sure that the boolean expression of the loop will eventually become false.

Another pitfall lies in using real numbers for testing and increment. Consider the following two loops:

imprecise loop counter

```
//Loop 1
double count = 0.0;

while (count != 1.0)
   count = count + 0.333333333333333;
                        //there are fifteen 3s

//Loop 2
double count = 0.0;

while (count != 1.0)
   count = count + 0.3333333333333333;
                        //there are sixteen 3s
```

The second while terminates correctly, but the first while is an infinite loop. Why the difference? Because only an approximation of real numbers can be stored in a computer. We know in mathematics that

$$\frac{1}{3} + \frac{1}{3} + \frac{1}{3}$$

is equal to 1. However, in a computer, an expression such as

```
1.0/3.0 + 1.0/3.0 + 1.0/3.0
```

may or may not get evaluated to 1.0, depending on how precise the approximation is. In general, we should avoid using real numbers as counter variables because of this imprecision.

off-by-one error

Another thing to watch out for in writing a loop is the so-called *off-by-one error*. Suppose we want to execute the loop body 10 times. Does this code work?

```
count = 1;
while (count < 10 ) {
    ...
    count++;
}
```

No, the loop body is executed 9 times. How about this code?

```
count = 0;
while (count <= 10 ) {
    ...
    count++;
}
```

No, this time the loop body is executed 11 times. The correct while loop is

```
count = 0;
while (count < 10 ) {
    ...
    count++;
}
```

or

```
count = 1;
while (count <= 10 ) {
    ...
    count++;
}
```

Yes, we can write the desired loop as

```
count = 1;
while (count != 10 ) {
    ...
    count++;
}
```

but this condition for stopping the count-controlled loop is dangerous. We already mentioned the potential trap of an infinite loop. In summary,

Helpful Reminder

Watch out for the off-by-one error (OBOE).

You Might Want to Know

To show you just how common the off-by-one error occurs in everyday life, consider the following two questions. When you want to put a fence post every 10 ft, how many posts do you need for a 100-ft fence? If it takes 0.5 second for an elevator to rise one floor, how long does it take to reach the fourth floor from the first floor? The answers that come immediately are 10 posts and 2 seconds, respectively. But after a little more thought, we realize the correct answers are 11 posts (we need the final post at the end) and 1.5 seconds (there are three floors to rise to reach the fourth floor from the first floor).

And here are the points for you to remember in writing a loop.

Helpful Reminder

The checklist for the repetition control:

1. *Make sure the loop body contains a statement that will eventually cause the loop to terminate.*
2. *Make sure the loop repeats exactly the correct number of times.*
3. *If you want to execute the loop body N times, then initialize the counter to 0 and use the test condition counter < N or initialize the counter to 1 and use the test condition counter <= N.*

The loop body in the sample repetition statements included statements such as

```
sum = sum + number;
```

shorthand assignment operator

This assignment statement can be expressed succinctly without repeating the same variable sum by using the *shorthand assignment operator* **+=**:

```
sum += number;
```

Table 6.1 lists shorthand assignment operators available in Java.

Table 6.1 Shorthand assignment operators.

Operator	Usage	Meaning
+=	a += b;	a = a + b;
-=	a -= b;	a = a - b;
*=	a *= b;	a = a * b;
/=	a /= b;	a = a / b;
%=	a %= b;	a = a % b;

These shorthand assignment operators have precedence lower than that of any other arithmetic operators, so, for example, the statement

```
sum *= a + b;
```

is equivalent to

```
sum = sum * (a + b);
```

We will be using shorthand assignment operators from now on.

Quick **CHECK**

1. Which of the following is an infinite loop?

   a.
   ```
   int sum = 0, i = 0;
   while ( i >= 0 ) {
       sum += i;
       i++;
   }
   ```
   b.
   ```
   int sum = 0, i = 100;
   while ( i != 0 ) {
       sum += i;
       i--;
   }
   ```

2. For each of the following loop statements, determine the value of sum after the loop is executed.

   a.
   ```
   int count = 0, sum = 0;
   while ( count < 10 ) {
       sum += count;
       count++;
   }
   ```
   b.
   ```
   int count = 1, sum = 0;
   while ( count <= 30 ) {
       sum    += count;
       count += 3;
   }
   ```

```
c. int count = 0, sum = 0;
   while ( count < 20 ) {
       sum    += 3*count;
       count += 2;
   }
```

6.3 | The do–while **Statement**

pretest loop

The while statement is characterized as a *pretest loop* because the test is done before execution of the loop body. Because it is a pretest loop, the loop body may not be executed at all. The do–while statement is a repetition statement that is characterized as a *posttest loop*. With a posttest loop statement, the loop body is executed at least once.

posttest loop

The general format for the do–while statement is

do–while
syntax

```
do

    <statement>

while ( <boolean expression> ) ;
```

The <statement> is executed until the <boolean expression> becomes false. Remember that <statement> is either a <single statement> or a <compound statement>. We will adopt the same policy for the if statement; that is, we will use the syntax of <compound statement> even if there is only one statement in the loop body. In other words, we will use the left and right braces even if the loop body contains only one statement.

Let's look at a few examples. We begin with the second example from Section 6.1, which adds the whole numbers 1, 2, 3, . . . until the sum becomes larger than 1,000,000. Here's the equivalent code in a do–while statement:

```
int sum = 0, number = 1;
do {

    sum += number;
    number++;

} while ( sum <= 1000000 );
```

Figure 6.3 shows how this do–while statement corresponds to the general format, and Figure 6.4 is a diagram showing the control flow of this do–while statement.

Let's rewrite the routine that inputs a person's age, using the do–while statement. Here's our first attempt:

```
do {

    age = Integer.parseInt(
            JOptionPane.showInputDialog(null,
                    "Your Age (between 0 and 130):"));

} while (age < 0 || age > 130);
```

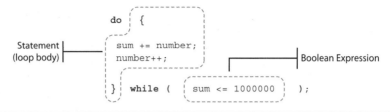

Figure 6.3 Correspondence of the example **do–while** statement to the general format.

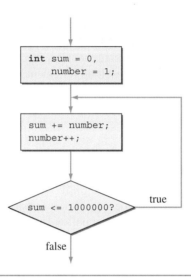

Figure 6.4 A diagram showing the control flow of the **do–while** statement.

It works, but unlike the version using the while statement, the code does not display an error message. The user could be puzzled as to why the input is not accepted. Suppose the user tries to enter 130 but actually enters 139 unintentionally. Without an error message to inform the user that the input was invalid, he or she may wonder why the program is asking again for input. A program should not be confusing to the user. We must strive for a program with a user-friendly interface.

To display an error message, we rewrite the do–while statement as

```
do {

    age = Integer.parseInt(
            JOptionPane.showInputDialog(null,
                    "Your Age (between 0 and 130):"));

    if (age < 0 || age > 130) {
        JOptionPane.showMessageDialog(null,
                "An invalid age was entered. " +
                "Please try again." );
    }

} while (age < 0 || age > 130);
```

This code is not as good as the version using the while statement. Do you know why? This do–while statement includes an if statement inside its loop body. Since the loop body is executed repeatedly, it is important not to include any extraneous statements. The if statement is repeating the same boolean expression of the do–while. Duplicating the testing conditions tends to make the loop statement harder to understand. For this example, we can avoid the extra test inside the loop body and implement the control flow a little more clearly by using a while statement. In general, the while statement is more frequently used than the do–while statement. However, the while statement is not universally better than the do–while statement. It depends on a given task, and our job as programmers is to use the most appropriate one. We choose the repetition statement that implements the control flow clearly, so the code is easy to understand.

When you have multiple conditions to stop the loop and if you need to execute different responses to each of the multiple conditions, then the use of boolean variables often clarifies the meaning of the loop statement. Consider this example. Suppose we need to compute the sum of odd integers entered by the user. We will stop the loop when the sentinel value 0 is entered, an even integer is entered, or the sum becomes larger than 1000. Without using any boolean variables, we can write this loop as

boolean variable and loop

```
sum = 0;
do {
    num = Integer.parseInt(
                JOptionPane.showInputDialog(null,
                                "Enter integer:"));

    if (num == 0) {   //sentinel
        System.out.print("Sum = " + sum);

    } else if (num % 2 == 0)     //invalid data
        System.out.print("Error: even number was entered");

    } else {
        sum += num;
        if (sum > 1000) { //pass the threshold
            System.out.print("Sum became larger than 1000");
        }
    }

} while ( !(num % 2 == 0 || num == 0 || sum > 1000) );
```

The ending condition is tricky. We need to stop the loop if any one of the three conditions num % 2 == 0, num == 0, or sum > 1000 is true. So we repeat the loop when none of the three conditions are true, which is expressed as

```
!(num % 2 == 0 || num == 0 || sum > 1000)
```

We can also state the condition as

```
do {

    . . .

} while( num % 2 != 0 && num != 0 && sum <= 1000 );
```

> **Note:**
> !(a || b) is equal to (!a && !b)

which means "repeat the loop while num is odd and num is not 0 and sum is less than or equal to 1000." Regardless of the method used, the test conditions are duplicated inside the loop body and in the boolean expression.

Now, by using a boolean variable, the loop becomes

```
boolean repeat = true;

sum = 0;
do {
    num = Integer.parseInt(
                JOptionPane.showInputDialog(null,

                                    "Enter integer:"));

    if (num == 0)  {  //sentinel
        System.out.print("Sum = " + sum);
        repeat = false;

    } else if (num % 2 == 0)  {  //in valid data
        System.out.print("Error: even number was entered");
        repeat = false;

    } else {
        sum += num;
        if (sum > 1000) { //pass the threshold
            System.out.print("Sum became larger than 1000");
            repeat = false;
        }
    }
} while ( repeat );
```

Note: **continue** is a reserved word in Java, while **repeat** is not.

Set the variable to **false** so the loop terminates.

This loop eliminates duplicate tests. The use of boolean variables is helpful in making loop statements readable, especially when the loop has multiple stop conditions.

Quick CHECK

1. Write a do–while loop to compute the sum of the first 30 positive odd integers.
2. Rewrite the following while loops as do–while loops.

   a. ```
      int count = 0, sum = 0;
      while (count < 10) {
          sum += count;
          count++;
      }
      ```

   b. ```
      int count = 1, sum = 0;
      while ( count <= 30 ) {
          sum    += count;
          count += 3;
      }
      ```

6.4 | Loop-and-a-Half Repetition Control

When we compare the while and do–while repetition control, we realize the key difference is the position of the testing relative to the loop body. The while loop tests the terminating condition before the loop body, but the do–while loop tests the terminating condition after the loop body. What happens when we want to test the terminating condition right in the middle of the loop body? Such repetition control can be characterized as a *loop-and-a-half repetition control* because only the top half of the loop body is executed for the last repetition. Do we ever need such a looping statement?

loop-and-a-half repetition control

Consider the following while loop with the priming read:

```
String name;

name = JOptionPane.showInputDialog(null, "Your name:");

while (name.length() == 0) {

    JOptionPane.showMessageDialog(null, "Invalid entry. " +
                "You must enter at least one character.");

    name = JOptionPane.showInputDialog(null, "Your name:");
}
```

Because the while loop tests the terminating condition at the beginning, we must place some statements before the loop to ensure the condition can be evaluated. The same statements are repeated inside the loop so that the terminating condition can be evaluated correctly after each repetition. This duplication of the statements can become tedious depending on what is to be duplicated. We can avoid the duplication of code with the loop-and-a-half structure. Java does not support any special reserved word for the loop-and-a-half repetition control. Rather, we implement it by using the while, if, and break reserved words. Here's how we express the sample priming read while loop in a loop-and-a-half format:

```
String name;

while (true) {
    name = JOptionPane.showInputDialog(null, "Your name:");

    if (name.length() > 0) break;

    JOptionPane.showMessageDialog(null,"Invalid entry. " +
                "You must enter at least one character.");
}
```

*If the test evaluates to **true**, then jump out of the loop.*

We have seen the use of the break statement in Chapter 5. Execution of the break statement causes the control to jump out of the switch statement. We can in fact use the break statement with any control statement. In this example, the break statement causes the control to jump out of the while statement. Since it is executed when the if

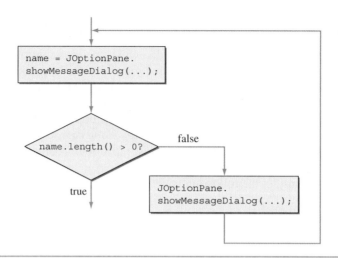

Figure 6.5 A diagram showing the control flow of a loop-and-a-half statement.

test is true, that is, the String variable name contains at least one character. If the test fails, the next statement is executed and the control loops back to the top of the while loop. Expressing this control flow in a flowchart results in the one shown in Figure 6.5.

There are two concerns when we use the loop-and-a-half control. The first is the danger of an infinite loop. Notice the boolean expression of the while statement is simply true, which, of course, will always evaluate to true. So, if we forget to include an if statement to break out of the loop, it will end up in an infinite loop. The second concern is the complexity of multiple exit points. It is possible to write a loop-and-a-half statement with multiple break statements, something like

```
while (true) {
    ...
    if (<condition 1>) break;
    ...
    if (<condition 2>) break;
    ...
    if (<condition 3>) break;
    ...
}
```

It may get tricky to write a correct control loop with multiple exit points. One of the frequently cited software engineering practices for reliable code is to enforce the *one-entry one-exit control* flow. In other words, there is one entry point to the loop and one exit point from the loop. With the standard while and do–while with no break statements inside the loop, we have this one-entry one-exit control flow. A loop-and-a-half control with multiple break statements, however, violates it.

If we watch out for these two points, a loop-and-a-half control can be quite handy and can make the code more readable. Here are the things to remember in using the loop-and-a-half control.

one-entry
one-exit
control

Helpful Reminder

The checklist for the loop-and-a-half control:

1. *To avoid an infinite loop, make sure the loop body contains at least one* **if** *statement that breaks out of the loop.*

2. *To keep the control simple and easy to read, avoid using multiple* **if** *statements that break out of the loop.*

3. *Make sure the loop is short to keep the control logic as self-evident as possible. (Notice this applies to all loop statements, but more so for a loop-and-a-half.)*

In this textbook, we will be using loop-and-a-half statements whenever appropriate, that is, whenever its use makes the code more readable and clearer. Before we conclude this section, here's another loop-and-a-half statement. The loop evaluates the average score, and it terminates when the input is a negative number.

```
int    cnt = 0;
double score, sum = 0.0;

while (true) {

    score = Double.parseDouble(
              JOptionPane.showInputDialog(null,
                                       "Enter score"));

    if (score < 0) break;

    sum += score;
    cnt++;
}

if (cnt > 0) {
    avg = sum / cnt;
} else {
    //error: no input
}
```

Quick **CHECK**

1. Translate the following while loop to a loop-and-a-half format.

```
int sum = 0, num = 1;
while (num <= 50) {
    sum += num;
    num++;
}
```

2. Translate the following do–while loop to a loop-and-a-half format.

```
int sum = 0, num = 1;
do {
    sum += num;
    num++;
} while (sum <= 5000);
```

6.5 | Confirmation Dialog

So far we have used two methods from the JOptionPane class—showMessage-
Dialog and showInputDialog. We will introduce the third method in this section.
Often we need to write a loop statement that continues the repetition as long as
the user wants to. We can use a confirmation dialog that prompts the user whether
to continue the repetition or not. Let's begin with a simple example. Executing
the code

```
JOptionPane.showConfirmDialog(null,
            /*prompt*/              "Play Another Game?",
            /*dialog title*/    "Confirmation",
            /*button options*/  JOptionPane.YES_NO_OPTION);
```

**showConfirm-
Dialog**

will result in the window shown in Figure 6.6. The showConfirmDialog method
returns a value corresponding to the button clicked by the user. We can check the
returned value against the defined constants in the JOptionPane class. If the user
clicks the Yes button, the method returns JOptionPane.YES_OPTION. If the user
clicks the No button, the method returns JOptionPane.NO_OPTION.

Here's how we use the confirmation dialog in writing a loop statement:

```
boolean keepPlaying = true;

int     selection;

while (keepPlaying) {

    //code to play one game comes here

    selection = JOptionPane.showConfirmDialog(null,
                "Play Another Game?",
                "Confirmation",
                JOptionPane.YES_NO_OPTION);

    keepPlaying = (selection == JOptionPane.YES_OPTION);
}
```

This simple use of the showConfirmDialog should suffice for the majority of
the situations we encounter, but there are other options with the showConfirmDialog
method. For more details, please consult the Java API documentation.

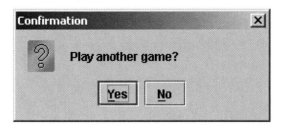

Figure 6.6 A confirmation dialog created by using the **showConfirmDialog** method of the **JOptionPane** class.

Quick
CHECK

1. What will be the title of the dialog if the following code is executed?

```
JOptionPane.showConfirmDialog(null,
            "hello",
            "world",
            JOptionPane.YES_NO_OPTION);
```

2. Write a code to prompt the user with the message "Are you a minor?" and display "Go to Theater 3" using a message dialog if the user clicks the Yes button. If the user clicks the No button, then display "Go to Theater 8" instead.

6.6 | The for Statement

The for statement is the third repetition control statement and is especially suitable for count-controlled loops. Let's begin with an example. The following code computes the sum of the first 100 positive integers:

```
int i, sum = 0;
for (i = 1; i <= 100; i++) {
    sum += i; //equivalent to sum = sum + i;
}
```

The general format of the for statement is

```
for ( <initialization>; <boolean expression>; <increment>  )

    <statement>
```

control variable

Figure 6.7 shows the correspondence of the sample code above to the general format. The diagram in Figure 6.8 shows how this statement is executed. The variable i in the statement is called a *control variable,* and it keeps track of the number of repetitions. In the sample code, the control variable i is first initialized to 1, and immediately the boolean expression is evaluated. If the evaluation results in true, the loop body is executed. Otherwise, the execution of the for statement is terminated, and the control flows to the statement following this for statement. Every time the loop body is executed, the increment operator (i++) is executed and then the boolean expression is evaluated.

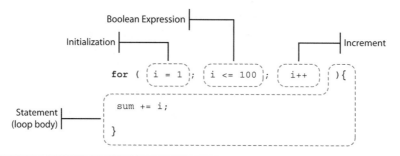

Figure 6.7 Correspondence of the example **for** statement to the general format.

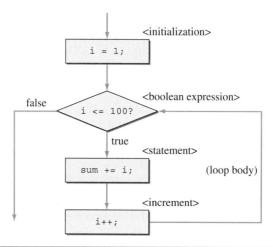

Figure 6.8 A diagram showing the control flow of the example **for** statement.

The <initialization> component also can include a declaration of the control variable. We can do something like this

```
for (int i = 1; i <= 100; i++)
```

instead of

```
int i;
for (i = 0; i < 10; i++)
```

The control variable may be initialized to any value, although it is almost always 0 or 1.

The <increment> expression in the example increments the control variable by 1. We can increment it with values other than 1, including negative values, for example,

```
for (int i = 0; i < 100; i += 5) //i = 0, 5, 10, ... , 95
for (int j = 2; j < 40; j *= 2)//j = 2, 4, 8, 16, 32
for (int k = 100; k > 0; k--) //k = 100, 99, 98, 97, ..., 1
```

Notice that the control variable appears in all three components: <initialization>, <conditional expression>, and <increment>. A control variable does not have to appear in all three components, but this is the most common style. Many other variations are allowed for these three components, but for novices, it is safer to use this style exclusively.

Let's look at an example from physics. When an object is dropped from height H, the position P of the object at time t can be determined by the formula

$$P = -16t^2 + H$$

For example, if a watermelon is dropped from the roof of a 256-ft-high dormitory, it will drop like this:

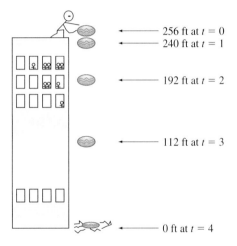

We can use a **for** statement to compute the position P at time t. We will input the initial height and compute the position every second. We repeat this computation until the watermelon touches the ground. The time the watermelon touches the ground is derived by solving for t when $P = 0$.

$$0 = -16t^2 + H$$

$$t = \sqrt{\frac{H}{16}}$$

```
/*
    Chapter 6 Sample Program: Dropping a Watermelon

    File: Ch6DroppingWaterMelon.java

*/
import java.util.*;
```

```
class Ch6DroppingWaterMelon {

    public static void main( String[] args ) {

        double   initialHeight,
                 position,
                 touchTime;

        Scanner scanner = new Scanner(System.in);
        scanner.useDelimiter(System.getProperty("line.separator"));

        System.out.print("Initial Height:");
        initialHeight  = scanner.nextDouble();

        touchTime      = Math.sqrt(initialHeight / 16.0);
        touchTime      = Math.round(touchTime * 10000.0) / 10000.0;
                        //convert to four decimal places

        System.out.println("\n\n   Time t       Position at Time t \n");

        for (int time = 0; time < touchTime;  time++) {
            position = -16.0 * time*time + initialHeight;
            System.out.print("    " + time);
            System.out.println("             " + position);
        }

        //print the last second
        System.out.println("   " + touchTime + "        0.00");
    }
}
```

Running the program with the input value 500.0 for the initial height will result in the window shown in Figure 6.9.

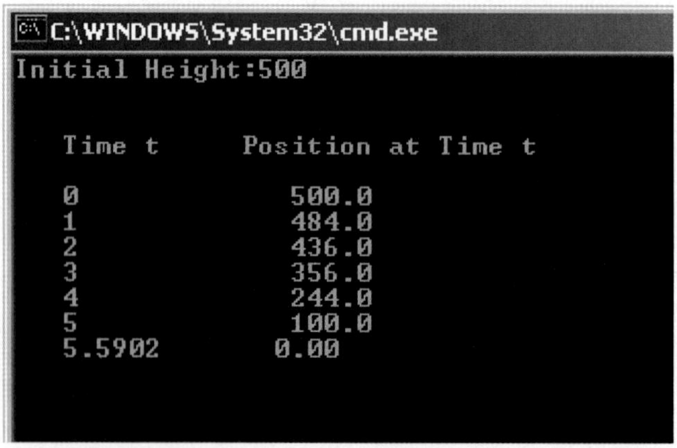

Figure 6.9 The positions of a watermelon dropped from a height of 500 ft.

Take my Advice

The format for the **for** loop presented in this section is the most basic version. The Java language allows more complex **for** statements. For instance, the **<initialization>** and **<increment>** parts of the **for** statement are not limited to a single statement. They can contain zero or more statements. The following two statements, for example, are both valid.

```
int val, i, j;
for (i = 0, j = 100, val = 0;   //init
        i < 100 && j > 50;          //bool exp
      i++, j--) {                   //increment
   val += i - j;
}

System.out.println("val = " + val);

int sum, cnt, n;
for (sum = 0, cnt = 0;        //init
        cnt < 10;                 //bool expr
                                  //increment

     n = Integer.parseInt(
                   JOptionPane.showInputDialog(null,
                              "Enter number:")),
     sum += n,
     cnt++ ) {
}
```

Do you ever need to write such intricate **for** statements? Most likely, no. The two sample statements can be written more clearly and logically in other ways. We strongly recommend that you stick to the basic, and most logical, form of the **for** statement.

Take my Advice

We have introduced three forms of repetition statements—**while, do–while,** and **for.** They are equivalent in their expressive power. In other words, a loop written in one form of repetition statement can be written by using the other two forms of repetition statement. Although they are equivalent, in many cases, one form would express the repetition control in a more natural and direct manner. It is your responsibility as a programmer to implement the repetition control using the most appropriate form.

Quick **CHECK**

1. Write a for loop to compute

   a. The sum of 1, 2, . . . , 100
   b. The sum of 2, 4, . . . , 500
   c. The product of 5, 10, . . . , 50

2. Rewrite these while loops as for statements.

a. ```
int count = 0, sum = 0;
while (count < 10) {
    sum += count;
    count++;
}
```

b. ```
int count = 1, sum = 0;
while ( count <= 30 ) {
    sum    += count;
    count += 3;
}
```

6.7 | Nested-for **Statements**

In many processing tasks, we need to place a for statement inside another for statement. In this section, we will introduce a simple nested-for statement. We will be seeing more examples of nested-for statements later in the book, especially in Chapter 10 on array processing.

Suppose we want to display a quick reference table for clerks at the Rugs-R-Us carpet store. The table in Figure 6.10 lists the prices of carpets ranging in size from 11 × 5 ft to 20 × 25 ft (using System.out for output). The width of a carpet ranges from 11 to 20 ft with an increment of 1 ft. The length of a carpet ranges from 5 to 25 ft with an increment of 5 ft. The unit price of a carpet is $19 per square foot.

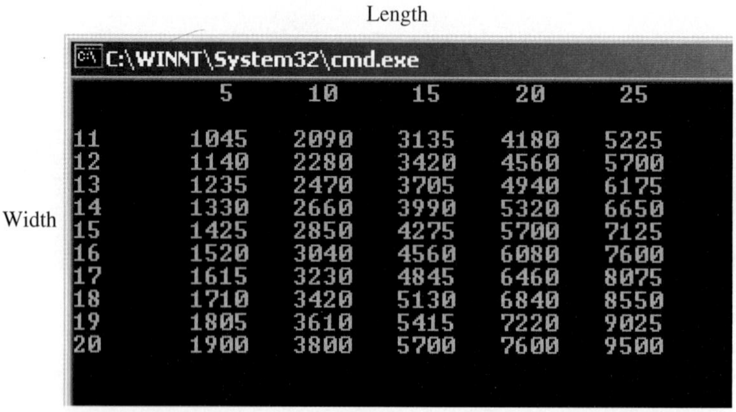

Length

C:\WINNT\System32\cmd.exe

Width	5	10	15	20	25
11	1045	2090	3135	4180	5225
12	1140	2280	3420	4560	5700
13	1235	2470	3705	4940	6175
14	1330	2660	3990	5320	6650
15	1425	2850	4275	5700	7125
16	1520	3040	4560	6080	7600
17	1615	3230	4845	6460	8075
18	1710	3420	5130	6840	8550
19	1805	3610	5415	7220	9025
20	1900	3800	5700	7600	9500

Figure 6.10 The price table for carpets ranging in size from 11 × 5 ft to 20 × 25 ft whose unit price is $19 per square foot.

We use a nested-for statement to print out the table. Let's concentrate first on printing out prices. We'll worry about printing out length and width values later. The following nested-for statement will print out the prices:

```
int              price;

for (int width = 11; width <= 20; width++) {

    for (int length = 5; length <= 25; length += 5) {

        price = width * length * 19; //$19 per sq ft.
        System.out.print("   " + price);
    }

    //finished one row; now move on to the next row
    System.out.println("");
}
```

The outer for statement is set to range from the first row (width = 11) to the last row (width = 20). For each repetition of the outer for, the inner for statement is executed, which ranges from the first column (length = 5) to the fifth column (length = 25). The loop body of the inner for computes the price of a single carpet size and prints out this price. So the complete execution of the inner for, which causes its loop body to be executed 5 times, completes the output of one row. The following is the sequence of values for the two control variables.

width	length	
11		
	5	
	10	
	15	
	20	
	25	Completes the printing of the first row.
12		
	5	
	10	
	15	
	20	
	25	Completes the printing of the second row.
13		
	5	
	10	

Now let's add the code to print out the row and column index values for width and length.

```
int               price;
```

```
System.out.print("          5    10    15    20    25");
```

```
System.out.print("\n\n");
```

```
for (int width = 11; width <= 20; width++) {
```

```
    System.out.print(width + "     ");
```

```
    for (int length = 5; length <= 25; length += 5) {
        price = width * length * 19; //$19 per sq ft.
        System.out.print("    " + price);
    }

    //finished one row; now move on to the next row
    System.out.print("\n");
}
```

Added statements

The next improvement is to include the labels Width and Length in the output. This enhancement is left as Exercise 19 at the end of the chapter. Also, in the example, literal constants are used for the carpet sizes and the increment value on length (11, 20, 5, 25, and 5), but in a real program, named constants should be used.

Quick **CHECK**

1. What will be the value of sum after the following nested-for loops are executed?

   a.
   ```
   int sum = 0;
   for (int i = 0; i < 5; i++) {
       sum = sum + i;
       for (int j = 0; j < 5; j++) {
           sum = sum + j;
       }
   }
   ```

   b.
   ```
   int sum = 0;
   for (int i = 0; i < 5; i++) {
       sum = sum + i;
       for (int j = i; j < 5; j++) {
           sum = sum + j;
       }
   }
   ```

2. What is wrong with the following nested-for loop?

   ```
   int sum = 0;
   for (int i = 0; i < 5; i++) {
       sum = sum + i;
       for (int i = 5; i > 0; i--) {
           sum = sum + j;
       }
   }
   ```

6.8 | Formatting Output

In the table shown in Figure 6.10, the values are aligned very nicely. We purposely selected the unit price and the ranges of width and length so that the table output would look good. Notice that the output values are all four-digit numbers. Realistically, we cannot expect output values to be so uniform. Let's change the unit price to $15 and the range of widths to 5 through 14 ft and see what happens. The result is shown in Figure 6.11, which is not as neat as the previous output. What we need is a way to format the output so the values are printed out with the proper alignment.

In the code, we used the fixed number of spaces between the values, and it worked because the output values have the same number of digits. To align the values with a varying number of digits, we must vary the number of spaces in front of the values, as shown in Figure 6.12.

The basic idea of formatted output is to allocate the same amount of space for the output values and align the values within the allocated space. We call the space occupied by an output value the *field* and the number of characters allocated to a field its *field width*. In Figure 6.12, the field width is 6.

field

We have already used two formatting classes—DecimalFormat and Simple-DateFormat—introduced in Chapters 2 and 3. The most recent version of Java

```
 C:\WINDOWS\System32\cmd.exe
            5        10        15        20        25
5         375       750      1125      1500      1875
6         450       900      1350      1800      2250
7         525      1050      1575      2100      2625
8         600      1200      1800      2400      3000
9         675      1350      2025      2700      3375
10        750      1500      2250      3000      3750
11        825      1650      2475      3300      4125
12        900      1800      2700      3600      4500
13        975      1950      2925      3900      4875
14       1050      2100      3150      4200      5250
```

Figure 6.11 The price table for carpets with $15 per square foot and width ranging from 5 through 14 ft.

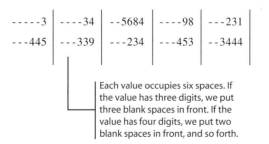

| - - - - -3 | - - - -34 | - -5684 | - - - -98 | - - -231 |
| - - -445 | - - -339 | - - -234 | - - -453 | - -3444 |

Each value occupies six spaces. If the value has three digits, we put three blank spaces in front. If the value has four digits, we put two blank spaces in front, and so forth.

Figure 6.12 How to place a varying number of spaces to align the output values. Hyphen is used here to indicate the blank space.

SDK 1.5 includes a new general-purpose formatting class called Formatter that includes the functionalities of DecimalFormat and SimpleDateFormat. For its power, using the Formatter class is slightly more complicated than using the DecimalFormat and SimpleDateFormat classes.

To format output using Formatter, we first create its instance by passing the destination of the output as an argument. Suppose we want to send the formatted output to System.out; we create a Formatter object as

```
Formatter formatter = new Formatter(System.out);
```

Then we call its **format** method to output the formatted values. For example, to output an integer with the field width of 6, we write

```
int num = 467;
formatter.format("%6d", num);
```

control string

The string %6d is called a *control string* that directs how the formatting will take place. The value **6** specifies the field width, and the control character **d** indicates the output value is a decimal integer.

The general syntax for the format method is as follows:

```
format(<control string>, <expr1>, <expr2>, ...)
```

The first argument is the control string, and it is followed by zero or more expressions. The control string may include the actual output string in addition to control values. For example, the statement

```
int num1, num2, num3;

num1 = 34;
num2 = 9;
num3 = num1 + num2;

formatter.format("%3d + %3d = %5d", num1, num2, num3);
```

will output

```
34 +  9 =   43
```

Figure 6.13 shows how the control values are matched left to right against the arguments. Figure 6.13 also illustrates how the noncontrol values (such as + and = symbols) are output to the destination.

We can change the default left-to-right argument matching by including the argument index in the control string. The arguments can be indexed as **1$, 2$,** and so forth. For example, the output of

```
formatter.format("%3$3d is the sum of %2$3d and %1$3d",
                  num1, num2, num3);
```

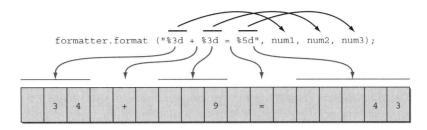

```
formatter.format ("%3d + %3d = %5d", num1, num2, num3);
```

| | 3 | 4 | | + | | | 9 | | = | | | 4 | 3 |

Figure 6.13 The control values are matched left to right.

will be

```
43 is the sum of  9 and  34
```

To format real numbers, we include the number of decimal places along with the field width in the following format:

```
%<field width> . <decimal places> f
```

The control letter **f** designates for formatting a floating point number. Here's an example to format **345.9867** by using a field of width 15 and two decimal places:

```
formatter.format("%15.3f", 345.9867);
```

To format a string, we use the control letter **s**. Here's an example:

```
String name = "John";

formatter.format("Hello, %s. Nice to meet you.", name);
```

The output will be

```
Hello, John. Nice to meet you.
```

We can also use the **format** method to format the date information. We use the control letter **t** for formatting an instance of **GregorianCalendar** or **Date**. The control letter **t** must be followed by another control letter that designates the formatting of the components of the date information such as month, day, or year. For example, if we write

```
GregorianCalendar day = new GregorianCalendar(1776, 6, 4);

formatter.format("%1$tB %1$te, %1$tY", day);
```

the output will be

```
July 4, 1776
```

The date control letter B designates the full month name, e designates the day in two digits, and Y designates the year in with four digits. For other data control letters, please consult the documentation. Notice that there is only one output argument, and it is referred to as **1$** three times in the control string.

The use of the Formatter class gives us the greatest control over the formatting, but for common output formatting, we can do it by using the **format** method of System.out or the String class instead. (In this section, we only present a subset of common formatting.) For example, the code

```
System.out.format("%5s is %3d years old", "Bill", 20);
```

is equivalent to

```
Formatter formatter = new Formatter(System.out);
formatter.format("%5s is %3d years old", "Bill", 20);
```

(Note: For those who are familiar with C or C++, there's a method named printf defined for System.out that works exactly the same as the format method. However, Java's printf is similar but not identical to the one in C or C++.)

The format method of the String class is useful in creating a formatted string when the destination is not the standard output, such as JOptionPane in the following example:

```
String outputStr
    = String.format("%3d + %3d = %5d", num1, num2, num3);

JOptionPane.showMessageDialog(null, outputStr);
```

Notice that the format method of the String class is a class method.

We close the section with a program that produces the carpet price table with a proper alignment for the range of values used in producing the table in Figure 6.11. Running this program will produce the table shown in Figure 6.14.

C:\WINDOWS\System32\cmd.exe				
5	10	15	20	25
5	375	750	1125	1500	1875
6	450	900	1350	1800	2250
7	525	1050	1575	2100	2625
8	600	1200	1800	2400	3000
9	675	1350	2025	2700	3375
10	750	1500	2250	3000	3750
11	825	1650	2475	3300	4125
12	900	1800	2700	3600	4500
13	975	1950	2925	3900	4875
14	1050	2100	3150	4200	5250

Figure 6.14 Carpet price table of Figure 6.11 with proper alignment.

```
/*
    Chapter 6 Sample Program: Sample formatting statements

    File: Ch6CarpetPriceTableWithFormat.java

*/

class Ch6CarpetPriceTableWithFormat {

    public static void main (String[] args) {

        int     price;

        //print out the column labels
        System.out.print("   "); //put three blank spaces first

        for (int colLabel = 5; colLabel <=25; colLabel += 5) {
            System.out.format("%8d", colLabel);
        }

        System.out.println("");
        System.out.println("");

        //print out rows of prices
        for (int width = 5; width <= 14; width++) {

            System.out.format("%3d", width);

            for (int length = 5; length <= 25; length += 5) {
                price = width * length * 15;

                System.out.format("%8d", price);
            }

            //finished one row; now move on to the next row
            System.out.println("");
        }

        System.out.println("");
        System.out.println("");
    }
}
```

1. Determine the output of the following code:

```
System.out.format("%3d + %3d = %3d", 1, 2, 3);
System.out.format("%tY", new Date());
System.out.format("%2$s,%1$s, "John", "Smith");
```

2. What's wrong with the following code?

```
Formatter f = new Formatter( );
f.format("%8.3f", 232.563);
```

6.9 | Loan Tables

The LoanCalculator program computed the monthly and total payments for a given loan amount, annual interest rate, and loan period. To see the monthly payment for the same loan amount and loan period but with a different interest rate, we would need to repeat the calculation, entering the three values again. To illustrate the use of the concepts introduced in this chapter, let's design a program that generates a loan table (similar to the carpet price table) for a given loan amount so we can compare different monthly payments easily and quickly. The columns of the table are the loan periods in number of years (5, 10, 15, 20, 25, 30), and the rows are interest rates ranging from 6 percent to 10 percent in increments of 0.25.

In this section, we will provide a discussion of the relevant methods only. Let's begin with a design of the topmost start method of the top-level controller class. The start method can be expressed as

```
tell the user what the program does;

prompt the user "Do you want to generate a loan table?";
while (the user says YES) {

    input the loan amount;
    generate the loan table;

    prompt the user "Do you want another loan table?";
}
```

pseudocode

The start method is expressed in pseudocode. A *pseudocode* is an informal language we often use to express an algorithm. Pseudocode is useful in expressing an algorithm without being tied down to the rigid syntactic rules of a programming language. We can express a simple algorithm in the actual programming language statements, but for a more complex algorithm, especially those involving nonsequential control flow logic, pseudocode is very helpful in expressing the algorithm concisely and clearly. Whenever appropriate, we will be using pseudocode to express more complex algorithms in the remainder of the book.

Translating the pseudocode into Java code will result in

```
public void start ( ) {
    int response;
    describeProgram();

    response = prompt("Generate a loan table?");

        while (response == JOptionPane.YES_OPTION) {
```

```
            loanAmount = getLoanAmount();    //get input
            generateLoanTable(loanAmount);   //generate table

            response = prompt("Generate another loan table?");
        }
    }

    private int prompt(String question) {

        int reply;

        reply = JOptionPane.showConfirmDialog(null,
                            question,
                            "Confirmation",
                            JOptionPane.YES_NO_OPTION);
        return reply;
    }
```

Notice how the actual start method is almost as easy to read as the pseudocode. By using objects and well-designed (sub)methods, we can express methods that are as easy to read as pseudocode.

The describeProgram method tells the user what the program does if the user requests it. The getLoanAmount method gets the loan amount from the user. The method will allow the user to enter the loan amount between 100.0 and 500,000.0. The generateLoanTable method generates the loan table, which we will explain in detail next.

We use a nested loop to generate the table. Both the inner and outer loops are count-controlled loops. The loop for columns (years) will range from 5 to 30 with an increment of 5, and the loop for rows (rates) will range from 6.0 to 10.0 with an increment of 0.25. So the nested loop can be written as follows:

```
private static final int MIN_LOAN_PERIOD   =  5;
private static final int MAX_LOAN_PERIOD   = 30;
private static final int LOAN_PERIOD_INCR  =  5;

private static final double BEGIN_RATE =  6.0;
private static final double END_RATE   = 10.0;
private static final double RATE_INCR  =  0.25;
...

for (double rate = BEGIN_RATE; rate <= END_RATE;
                                rate += RATE_INCR){

    for (int year = BEGIN_YEAR; year <= END_YEAR;
                                year += YEAR_INCR){

    ...

        //compute and display the monthly loan payment
        //for a given year and rate
    }
}
```

Notice the outer loop is using **double** as the loop counter, something we discouraged in Section 6.2. In this particular case, with the increment value of 0.25, there will be no problem. If we increment with the value of, say, 0.33, the loop may not repeat the exact number of times we expect. It is left as an exercise to remove any chance of imprecision.

To compute the monthly loan payment, we simply reuse the Loan class we defined in Chapter 4 as

```
double amount = ... ;
double rate   = ... ;
int    period = ... ;

Loan   loan   = new Loan( );

double monthyPayment
          = loan.getMonthlyPayment(amount, rate, period);
```

This is the power of object-oriented programming. Because a single well-defined task of loan computation and nothing else is coded in the Loan class, we are able to reuse it here easily. What would happen had we not designed the Loan class? It was certainly possible for us to complete the Chapter 4 sample development program with one service class that handles everything: input, output, and computation tasks. The chance of reusing such a class, however, is very low. Just as we do not expect to buy a textbook that teaches all five subjects of single-variable calculus, introduction to economics, organic chemistry, introduction to programming, and Western civilization, we do not want a service class that is overloaded with many different types of tasks. We do not want one class that does everything. Rather, we want many classes, with each class doing one task effectively and efficiently. This will allow us to mix and match the classes easily.

Finally, the output values can be formatted by using the technique introduced in Section 6.8. The overall design is now complete. It is left as an exercise to implement the loan table calculation program.

6.10 | Random Number Generation

In many computer applications, especially in simulation and games, we need to generate random numbers. For example, to simulate a roll of dice, we can generate an integer between 1 and 6. In this section, we will explain how to generate random numbers by using the random method of the Math class.

pseudorandom number generator

The method **random** is called a *pseudorandom number generator* and returns a number (type double) that is greater than or equal to 0.0 but less than 1.0, that is, $0.0 \leq X < 1.0$. The generated number is called a *pseudorandom number* because the number is not truly random. When we call this method repeatedly, eventually the numbers generated will repeat. Therefore, theoretically the generated numbers are not random; but for all practical purposes, they are random enough.

The random numbers we want to generate for most applications are integers. For example, to simulate a draw of a card, we need to generate an integer between

1 and 4 for the suit and an integer between 1 and 13 for the number. Since the number returned from the random method ranges from 0.0 up to but not including 1.0, we need to perform some form of conversion so the converted number will fall in our desired range. Let's assume the range of integer values we want is [min, max]. If X is a number returned by random, then we can convert it into a number Y such that Y is in the range [min, max], that is, min $\leq Y \leq$ max by applying the formula

$$Y = \lfloor X \times (\text{max} - \text{min} + 1)\rfloor + \text{min}$$

For many applications, the value for min is 1, so the formula is simplified to

$$Y = \lfloor X \times \text{max}\rfloor + 1$$

Expressing the general formula in Java will result in the following statement:

```
//assume correct values are assigned to 'max' and 'min'
int randomNumber
        = (int) (Math.floor(Math.random() * (max-min+1))
                + min);
```

Notice that we have to type cast the result of Math.floor to int because the data type of the result is double.

Let's write a program that generates N random numbers between 1 and 4 to simulate the suit of a drawn card. The value for N is an input to the program. We keep four counters, one for each suit, and increment the matching counter after a random number is generated. At the end of the generation, we print out the ratio count/N. This ratio approaches $1/4 = 0.25$ as the value for N gets larger. Since we want to test a large value for N, we declare it as long. When the value for N is long, we need each counter to be able to store a large value also, so we consequently declare them as long too.

When the value for N is small, the program will return the result almost instantaneously. However, as the value for N gets larger, the amount of time it takes to generate N random numbers increases dramatically. It is helpful to find out how long it takes to generate N numbers. We can time the execution by using the Date class from the java.util package. Before we get into the loop to generate N random numbers, we record the start time by creating a Date object. After the loop is completed, we record the end time by creating a second Date object. Calling the getTime method of the Date class returns the number of milliseconds (1 ms = $1/1000$ s) since January 1, 1970, 00:00:00 Greenwich mean time. So by subtracting the start time from the end time, we can get the elapsed time in milliseconds. Here's the general idea:

```
Date startTime = new Date();

//the loop statement comes here

Date endTime = new Date();

long elapsedTimeInMilliseconds =
        endTime.getTime() - startTime.getTime();
```

Keep in mind that the value we get for the elapsed time is a rough estimate. For one thing, the values we get for the elapsed time differ dramatically according to the CPU on which we run the program and whether other programs are running at the same time. Also, the granularity is very coarse when timed from a high-level language such as Java. For example, it is not possible to distinguish between the program that runs in 5 ms and the program that runs in 6 ms. Although the value is a rough estimate, it still gives us useful information such as the rate of increase in execution time as we increase the value for *N*.

Here's the program:

```java
/*
    Chapter 6 Sample Program: Test the random number generator

    File: Ch6TestRandomGenerator.java

*/

import javax.swing.*;
import java.util.*;

class Ch6TestRandomGenerator {

    private static final int CLUB    = 1;          Data members
    private static final int SPADE   = 2;
    private static final int HEART   = 3;
    private static final int DIAMOND = 4;

    public static void main( String[] args ) {

        Ch6TestRandomGenerator tester = new Ch6TestRandomGenerator();

        tester.start();
    }

    public void start( ) {                          start

        long N;

        while (keepTesting()) {

            N = getSize();

            generate(N);
        }
    }

    private long getSize( ) {                       getSize

        String inputStr;
        long    size;
```

```
    while (true) {
        inputStr = JOptionPane.showInputDialog(null, "Enter size:");

        size = Long.parseLong(inputStr);

        if (size > 0) break; //input okay so exit

        JOptionPane.showMessageDialog(null, "Input must be positive");
    }

    return size;
}

private void generate(long size) {
```

generate

```
    Date startTime, endTime;
    int suit;
    long clubCnt, spadeCnt, heartCnt, diamondCnt;

    clubCnt = spadeCnt = heartCnt = diamondCnt = 0;

    startTime = new Date();

    for (int i = 0; i < size; i++) {

        suit = getRandom(CLUB, DIAMOND);

        switch (suit) {
            case CLUB:      clubCnt++;
                            break;

            case SPADE:     spadeCnt++;
                            break;

            case HEART:     heartCnt++;
                            break;

            case DIAMOND: diamondCnt++;
                            break;

            default: //default case should never happen
                JOptionPane.showMessageDialog(null,"Internal Error");
                System.exit(0); //terminate the program
        }
    }

    endTime = new Date();

    System.out.println("N is " + size + "\n");
    System.out.println("Club:    " + clubCnt    + "       "
                                    + (double)clubCnt/size);
    System.out.println("Spade:   " + spadeCnt   + "       "
                                    + (double)spadeCnt/size);
```

```
        System.out.println("Heart:    " + heartCnt   + "      "
                                       + (double)heartCnt/size);
        System.out.println("Diamond: " + diamondCnt + "     "
                                       + (double)diamondCnt/size);

        double elapsedTimeInSec = (double) (endTime.getTime()
                                    - startTime.getTime())/1000.0;
        System.out.println("Elapsed time (sec): " + elapsedTimeInSec );

        System.out.println("\n");
    }

    private int getRandom(int min, int max) {

        int randomNumber
                = (int) (Math.floor(Math.random() * (max-min+1)) + min);

        return randomNumber;
    }

    private boolean keepTesting( ) {

        boolean result;

        int response = JOptionPane.showConfirmDialog(null,
                    /*prompt*/              "Perform Test?",
                    /*dialog title*/        "Random Number Generator",
                    /*button options*/      JOptionPane.YES_NO_OPTION);

        if (response == JOptionPane.YES_OPTION) {
            result = true;
        } else {
            result = false;
        }

        return result;
    }
}
```

getRandom

keepTesting

Here's one set of results we get after running the program.

```
N is 100

Club:    28      0.28
Spade:   23      0.23
Heart:   30      0.3
Diamond: 19      0.19
Elapsed time (sec): 0.0
```

It doesn't mean it took no time. It means the time it took was so minute, we weren't able to detect it by the technique we used.

```
N is 1000

Club:     258     0.258
Spade:    249     0.249
Heart:    255     0.255
Diamond: 238      0.238
Elapsed time (sec): 0.02
```

1 million

```
N is 1000000

Club:     249883     0.249883
Spade:    250617     0.250617
Heart:    249860     0.24986
Diamond: 249640      0.24964
Elapsed time (sec): 0.571
```

100 million

```
N is 100000000

Club:     24996841     0.24996841
Spade:    25001743     0.25001743
Heart:    25002041     0.25002041
Diamond: 24999375      0.24999375
Elapsed time (sec): 52.425
```

1 billion

```
N is 1000000000

Club:     249978595     0.249978595
Spade:    250000685     0.250000685
Heart:    250017704     0.250017704
Diamond: 250003016      0.250003016
Elapsed time (sec): 525.115
```

Helpful Reminder

To estimate the running time of a loop statement:

1. *Record the start time by creating a* **Date** *object, say,* **startTime**, *before the loop statement.*

2. *Record the end time by creating another* **Date** *object, say,* **endTime**, *after the loop statement.*

3. *Elapsed time (in milliseconds) is computed as*

```
elapsedTime = endTime.getTime()
                  - startTime.getTime();
```

Quick **CHECK**

1. Write a Java statement to generate a random number between 20 and 50.

2. Based on the outputs from the sample execution of the Ch6TestRandom-Generator program, give your estimate of the running time when the input *N* is 10 billion.

6.11   **Sample Program**

Hi-Lo Game

In this section we will develop a program that plays a Hi-Lo game. This program illustrates the use of repetition control, the random number generator, and the testing strategy. The objective of the game is to guess a secret number between 1 and 100. The program will respond with HI if the guess is higher than the secret number and LO if the guess is lower than the secret number. The maximum number of guesses allowed is six. If we allow up to seven, one can always guess the secret number. Do you know why?

Problem Statement

Write an application that will play Hi-Lo games with the user. The objective of the game is for the user to guess the computer-generated secret number in the least number of tries. The secret number is an integer between 1 and 100, inclusive. When the user makes a guess, the program replies with HI or LO depending on whether the guess is higher or lower than the secret number. The maximum number of tries allowed for each game is six. The user can play as many games as she wants.

Overall Plan

We will begin with our overall plan for the development. Let's identify the major tasks of the program. The first task is to generate a secret number every time the game is played, and the second task is to play the game itself. We also need to add a loop to repeat these two tasks every time the user wants to play the Hi-Lo game. We can express this program logic in pseudocode as

program
tasks

```
do {

    Task 1: generate a secret number;

    Task 2: play one game;

} while ( the user wants to play );
```

Let's look at the two tasks and determine objects that will be responsible for handling the tasks. For the first task, we will use the **random** method of the **Math** class. We will examine this method in detail later to determine whether it is the one we can use in the program. If this method does not meet our needs, then we will explore further and most likely will have to derive our own random number generator.

For the second task of playing the game itself, we need an object to accept the user's guess and another object to respond to the user with a **HI** or **LO.** For input, we will use the **showInputDialog** method of **JOptionPane.** For output, we will use the **showMessageDialog** of **JOptionPane.** If we want the game to be slightly easier, we could use the **System.out** or **javabook.OutputBox** and display the history of guesses along with the hints:

```
GUESS           HINT
  50             LO
  60             HI
  55             LO
```

We opt to use the **showMessageDialog** so the game player has to keep track in her mind of the guesses she made and the hints. At the end of one game, we use the message dialog again to display either **You guessed it in <N> tries** or **You lost. Secret number was <X>** with **<N>** or **<X>** replaced with the actual value. We also need a way for the user to tell the program whether to play another game. We will use the **show-ConfirmDialog** method of **JOptionPane** for this purpose.

Finally, we will define a top-level control object that manages all other objects. We will call this class **Ch6HiLo.** This will be our instantiable main class. Here's our working design document:

program
classes

Design Document: HiLo	
Class	**Purpose**
Ch6HiLo	The top-level control object that manages other objects in the program. This is the instantiable main class.
JOptionPane	This class is for handling the input, message, and confirmation dialogs.

Figure 6.15 is the program diagram for this program. A keen observer may have noticed that the **Ch6HiLo** class is handling both types of tasks: handling of user interface with the help from **JOptionPane** and controlling the logic of game playing. We will revisit this design in Chapter 7 and provide an alternative. The one-class design we adopt here may not be an ideal design, but is acceptable for a simplistic game such as this one. The design also provides us a meaningful comparison when we present an alternative design in Chapter 7.

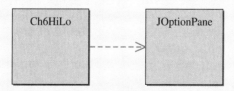

Figure 6.15 The program diagram for the **HiLo** program.

6.11 **Sample Program**—*continued*

development steps

We will implement this program by using these four major steps:

1. Start with a skeleton **Ch6HiLo** class.

2. Add code to the **Ch6HiLo** class to play a game using a dummy secret number.

3. Add code to the **Ch6HiLo** class to generate a random number.

4. Finalize the code by removing temporary statements and tying up loose ends.

Step 1 Development: Program Skeleton

step 1 design

The structure of the **HiLoMain** class is the same as that of other main classes. All we need is to declare, create, and start a **HiLo** object. Instead of forcing the user to play at least one game, we will implement the program so the user has the option of not playing a game at all. In pseudocode we can express this logic as

```
describe the game rules;
prompt the user to play a game or not;
while ( answer is yes ) {
    generate the secret number;
    play one game;
    prompt the user to play another game or not;
}
```

Notice that we use a **while** loop here, so the user can quit the program without playing a game. If we use a **do–while** loop instead, then the user must play at least one game before stopping the program. We opt to use the **while** loop because the user may not want to play the game at all after reading the game rules.

We use a private method **describeRules** to display the game rules. To prompt the user to play a game or not, we will use the **showConfirmDialog** method of **JOptionPane**; and to generate a secret number, we define another private method called **generateSecretNumber**. Last, we define a third private method **playGame** to play one game. We declare these three methods **private** because these methods are for internal use. As always, we will use the constructor to perform necessary object creation and initialization.

Our working design document for the **HiLo** class is as follows:

Design Document: The Ch6HiLo Class		
Method	**Visibility**	**Purpose**
`<constructor>`	`public`	Creates and initializes the objects used by a `HiLo` object.
`start`	`public`	Starts the Hi-Lo game playing. The user has an option of playing a game or not.

Design Document: The Ch6HiLo Class *(Continued)*		
Method	**Visibility**	**Purpose**
describeRules	private	Displays the game rules in System.out.
generateSecretNumber	private	Generates a secret number for the next Hi-Lo game.
playGame	private	Plays one Hi-Lo game.
prompt	private	Prompts the user for a yes/no reply using the showConfirmDialog of JOptionPane.

step 1 code

For the skeleton program, we include temporary output statements in the private methods to verify that they are called correctly in the right order. Here's the skeleton **Ch6HiLo** class:

```java
import javax.swing.*;

/**
 * Chapter 6 Sample Development: HiLo Game (Step 1)
 *
 * The instantiable main class of the program.
 */
class Ch6HiLo {

    public Ch6HiLo( ) {

    }

    //Main Method
    public static void main (String[] args) {
        Ch6HiLo hiLo = new Ch6HiLo( );
        hiLo.start();
    }

    public void start ( ) {

        int answer;

        describeRules();

        answer = prompt("Do you want to play a Hi-Lo game?");

        while (answer == JOptionPane.YES_OPTION) {
            generateSecretNumber( );
```

Constructors

main

start

6.11   Sample Program—*continued*

```
            playGame();
            answer = prompt("Do you want to play another Hi-Lo game?");
        }
    }

    private void describeRules( ) {                           describeRules
        System.out.println("Inside describeRules"); //TEMP
    }
                                                          generateSecretNumber
    private void generateSecretNumber( ) {
        System.out.println("Inside generateSecretNumber");    //TEMP
    }
                                                              playGame
    private void playGame( ) {
        System.out.println("Inside playGame");    //TEMP
    }


    private int prompt(String question) {
                                                               prompt
        int reply;

        reply = JOptionPane.showConfirmDialog(null,
                    question,
                    "Confirmation",
                    JOptionPane.YES_NO_OPTION);
        return reply;

    }
}
```

step 1 test

We execute the skeleton **Ch6HiLo** class to verify that the classes are coded correctly. To verify the correct execution of step 1, we attempt to play the game

1. Zero times.

2. One time.

3. One or more times.

For the first run, we select **No** to the prompt **Do you want to play a Hi-Lo game?** and we make sure the program stops without playing a game. For the second run, we select **Yes** to the first prompt and verify that the messages **Inside generateSecretNumber** and **Inside playGame** are shown in the standard output window. We select **No** to the prompt **Do you want to play another Hi-Lo game?** and make sure the program stops. For the third run, we make sure we can play more than one game. After we verify that all the scenarios work correctly, we proceed to the next step.

Step 2 Development: Play a Game with a Dummy Secret Number

step 2
design

In the second development step, we add a routine that plays a Hi-Lo game. We decided in the overall planning step that we will use the **showInputDialog** method to accept the user guess and the **showMessageDialog** method to display a hint. Let's begin with the control flow of the **playGame** method.

There are two cases to end a Hi-Lo game: Either the user guesses the number in less than six tries or uses up all six tries without guessing the number. So we need a counter to keep track of the number of guesses made. Let's call this counter **guessCount**. We stop the game when **guessCount** becomes larger than six or the user's guess is equal to the secret number. At the end of the game, we output an appropriate message. Expressing this in pseudocode, we have

```
//Method: playGame

set guessCount to 0;

do {
    get next guess;

    increment guessCount;

    if (guess < secretNumber) {
        print the hint LO;
    } else if (guess > secretNumber) {
        print the hint HI;
    }

} while (guessCount < number of guesses allowed &&
        guess != secretNumber );

if (guess   == secretNumber) {

    print the winning message;
} else {
    print the losing message;
}
```

All variables used in this method will be local except **secretNumber,** which will be an instance variable. The value for **secretNumber** is set inside the **generateSecret-Number** method.

To support a better user interface, we will include an input error handling that allows the user to enter only values between 1 and 100. We will do this input-error-checking routine in a new private method **getNextGuess** because we do want to keep the **playGame** method clean and simple. If we included the code for input error handling directly inside the **playGame** method, the method would become too cluttered and lose the overall clarity of what the method is doing. Pseudocode for the

getNextGuess method is

```
//Method: getNextGuess

while ( true ) {
   get input value;

   if (valid input) return input value;

   print error message;
}
```

The working design document of the class now includes this new **private** method:

Design Document: The Ch6HiLo Class		
Method	**Visibility**	**Purpose**
. . .	. . .	. . .
getNextGuess	private	Returns the next guess from the user. Only accepts a guess between 1 and 100. Prints an appropriate error message when an invalid guess is entered.

step 2 code

In the step 2 coding, we need to implement three methods. In addition to the **playGame** and **getNextGuess** methods, we need to define a temporary **generate-SecretNumber** method so we can test the **playGame** method. The temporary **generateSecretNumber** method assigns a dummy secret number to the instance variable **secretNumber.** The temporary method is coded as

```
private void generateSecretNumber( ) {
   secretNumber = 45;        //TEMP
}
```

Any number will do; we simply picked the number **45.** Knowing that the secret number is **45**, we will be able to test whether the **playGame** method is implemented correctly or not.

We implement the **playGame** method as

```
private void playGame( ) {
   int guessCount = 0;
   int guess;

   do {

      //get the next guess
      guess = getNextGuess();          getNextGuess is a
                                       new private method.
      guessCount++;
```

```
               //check the guess
               if (guess < secretNumber) {
                  JOptionPane.showMessageDialog(null,
                                              "Your guess is LO");

               } else if (guess > secretNumber) {
                  JOptionPane.showMessageDialog(null,
                                              "Your guess is HI");
               }
            } while ( guessCount < MAX_GUESS_ALLOWED &&
                      guess != secretNumber );

            //output appropriate message
            if ( guess == secretNumber ) {
               JOptionPane.showMessageDialog(null,
                            "You guessed it in "
                            + guessCount  + " tries.");
            } else {
               JOptionPane.showMessageDialog(null,
                            "You lost. Secret No. was "
                            + secretNumber);
            }
         }
```

Repeat the loop if the number of tries is not used up and the correct guess is not made.

This class constant is set to 6.

The **getNextGuess** method will accept an integer between **1** and **100**. The method uses a **while** loop to accomplish this:

```
      private int getNextGuess( ) {
         String inputStr;
         int    input;

         while (true) {
            inputStr = JOptionPane.showInputDialog(null,
                                           "Next Guess");
            input    = Integer.parseInt(inputStr);

            if (LOWER_BOUND <= input && input <= UPPER_BOUND) {
               return input;
            }

            //invalid input; print error message
            JOptionPane.showMessageDialog(null,
                                       "Invalid Input: " +
                                       "Must be between " +
                                       LOWER_BOUND + "and " +
                                       UPPER_BOUND);
         }
      }
```

The necessary constant and instance variable are declared in the data member section of the **HiLo** class as

```
//-----------------------------------
// Data Members
//-----------------------------------
private final int   MAX_GUESS_ALLOWED   = 6;
private final int   LOWER_BOUND         = 1;
private final int   UPPER_BOUND         = 100;

private int         secretNumber;
```

step 2 test

We need to test two methods in this step. To verify the **getNextGuess** method, we input both invalid and valid guesses. Notice that we place a temporary output statement in the method to verify the input value. We verify the method by running the following tests:

1. Enter a number less than 1.

2. Enter a number greater 100.

3. Enter a number between 2 and 99.

4. Enter 1.

5. Enter 100.

test cases

The first two *test cases* are called *error cases*, the third is called the *normal case*, and the last two are called *end cases*. One of the common errors that beginners make is to create a loop statement that does not process the end cases correctly. When our code handles all three types of cases correctly, we will proceed to test the **playGame** method.

To verify the **playGame** method, we need to perform a more elaborate testing. Knowing that the dummy secret number is **45**, we verify the **playGame** method by running the following tests:

1. Enter a number less than 45 and check that the correct hint **LO** is displayed.

2. Enter a number greater than 45 and check that the correct hint **HI** is displayed.

3. Enter the correct guess and check that the game terminates after displaying the appropriate message.

4. Enter six wrong guesses and check that the game terminates after displaying the appropriate message.

When all four tests are successfully completed, we proceed to the next step.

Step 3 Development: Generate a Random Number

step 3 design

In the third development step, we add a routine that generates a random number between 1 and 100. As explained in Section 6.10, we can use the method **random** from the **Math** package. Since the range is between 1 and 100, we can simplify the formula as

$$secretNumber = \lfloor X \times 100 \rfloor + 1$$

where $0.0 \leq X < 1.0$.

step 3 code

The **generateSecretNumber** method is defined as

```
private void generateSecretNumber( ) {
    double X = Math.random();

    secretNumber = (int) Math.floor( X * 100 ) + 1;

    System.out.println("Secret Number: " + secretNumber);
                                                    // TEMP
}
```

The method includes a temporary statement to output the secret number so we can stop the game anytime we want by entering the correct guess.

step 3 test

To verify that the method generates correct random numbers, we will write a separate test program. If we don't use such a test program and instead include the method immediately in the **Ch6HiLo** class, we have to play the game, say, 100 times to verify that the first 100 generated numbers are valid. The test program generates **N** random numbers and stops whenever an invalid number is generated. We will set **N** to **1000**. Here's the test program:

TestRan-
dom class
for testing

```
class TestRandom {
    public static void main (String[] args) {

        int    N = 1000, count = 0, number;
        double X;

        do {

            count++;

            X       = Math.random();
            number = (int) Math.floor( X * 100 ) + 1;

        } while ( count < N &&
                    1 <= number && number <= 100 );

        if ( number < 1 || number > 100 ) {
            System.out.println("Error: " + number);
        } else {
            System.out.println("Okay");
        }
    }
}
```

Keep in mind that successfully generating 1000 valid random numbers does not guarantee that the 1001st number is also valid. We did not make any formal mathematical proof that the routine for the random number generator works correctly. What we are doing here is making an assumption that no user wants to play more than 1000 Hi-Lo games in one session, which we believe is a practical assumption. After the **TestRandom** class is executed correctly, we make the necessary changes to the **Ch6HiLo** class and run it. When we verify that the program runs as expected, we proceed to the final step.

Step 4 Development: Finalize

program review

We finalize the program in the last step. We will perform a critical review of the program, looking for any unfinished method, inconsistency, error in the methods, unclear or missing comments, and so forth. We should also not forget to keep an eye on any improvement we can make to the existing code.

We still have a temporary code inside the **describeRules** method, so we will complete the method by adding code to describe the game rules. This method is left as an exercise. Use **showConfirmDialog** and display the game rules only if the user wants to see them.

There are still temporary output statements that we used for verification purposes. We can either delete them from the program or comment them out. We will leave them in the program by commenting them out so that when the time comes for us to modify, debug, or update the program, we do not have to reenter them.

6.12 (Optional) Recursive Methods

In addition to the three repetition control statements we introduced in this chapter, there is a fourth way to control the repetition flow of a program by using recursive methods. A *recursive method* is a method that contains a statement (or statements) that makes a call to itself. We will explain recursive methods briefly in this section. Realistic examples of recursive methods will be given in Chapter 15.

So far, we have seen only methods that call other methods, something like this:

```
methodOne(...) {
   ...
   methodTwo(...); //methodOne called methodTwo
   ...
}

methodTwo(...) {
   ...
}
```

A recursive method calls itself, and it looks something like this:

```
methodOne(...) {
   ...
   methodOne(...); //calls the method itself
   ...
}
```

At first glance, it seems as if a recursive call will never end since the call is made to the same method. Indeed, if you do not follow the rules, you could end up with infinite recursive calls. In this section we will explain how to write recursive methods correctly.

Suppose we want to compute the factorial of *N*. The *factorial* of *N* is the product of the first *N* positive integers, denoted mathematically as

```
N! = N * (N-1) * (N-2) * ... * 2 * 1
```

We will write a recursive method to compute the factorial of *N*. Mathematically, we can define the factorial of *N* recursively as

$$
\text{factorial}(N) = \begin{cases} 1 & \textbf{if } N = 1 \\ N * \text{factorial}(N-1) & \text{otherwise} \end{cases}
$$

The definition states that if N is 1, then the function factorial(N) has the value 1. Otherwise, the function factorial(N) is the product of N and factorial(N−1). For example, the function factorial(4) is evaluated as

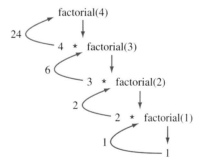

The recursive factorial method parallels the preceding mathematical definition. The method is defined as

```
public int factorial(int N) {

   if (N == 1)              Test to stop or continue


      return 1;            End case: recursion stops
```

```
        else
```
                                    Recursive case:
                                    recursion continues with
                                    another recursive call.

```
        return N * factorial (N-1);
    }
```

The diagram in Figure 6.16 illustrates the sequence of calls for the recursive factorial method. Recursive methods will contain three necessary components.

Helpful Reminder

The three necessary components in a recursive method are

1. *A test to stop or continue the recursion.*

2. *An end case that terminates the recursion.*

3. *A recursive call(s) that continue(s) the recursion.*

To ensure that the recursion will stop eventually, we must pass arguments different from the incoming parameters. In the factorial method, the incoming parameter was N, while the argument passed in the recursive call was N−1. This difference of 1 between the incoming parameter and the argument will eventually make the argument in a recursive call be 1, and the recursion will stop.

Let's implement two more mathematical functions, using recursion. The next method computes the sum of the first N positive integers 1, 2, . . . , N. Notice how this method includes the three necessary components of a recursive method.

```
public int sum ( int N ) {

    if (N == 1)
        return 1;
    else
        return N + sum( N-1 );
}
```

The last method computes the exponentiation A^N, where A is a real number and N is a positive integer. This time, we have to pass two arguments: A and N. The value of A will not change in the calls, but the value of N is decremented after each recursive call.

```
public double exponent ( double A, int N ) {

    if (N == 1)
        return A;

    else
        return A * exponent( A, N-1 );
}
```

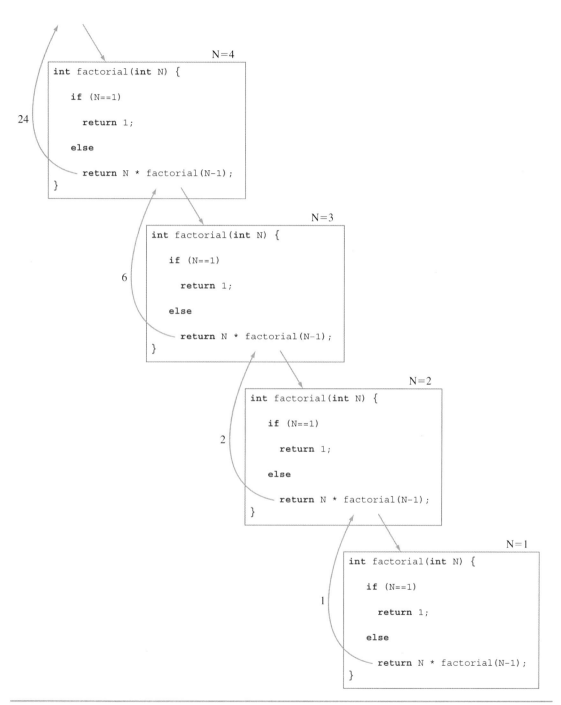

Figure 6.16 The sequence of calls for the recursive **factorial** method.

So far we used only mathematical functions to illustrate recursive methods, but recursion is not limited to mathematical functions. Let's look at one example. We know the length method of the String class returns the number characters in a given string. Let's write a recursive method that does the same thing. Here's how we think recursively. The total number of characters in a string is 1 plus the number of characters in the substring from the second position to the end of the string. If the string has no characters, then the length is zero. Puting this idea into an actual method, we have

```java
public int length(String str) {

    if (str.equals("")) { //str has no characters
        return 0;

    } else {

        return 1 + length(str.substring(1));
    }
}
```

Index of the second position is 1.

We will present more examples of recursive methods that implement nonnumerical operations in Chapter 15.

We used factorial, sum, exponentiation, and length as examples to introduce some of the basic concepts of recursion, but we should never actually write these methods using recursion. The methods can be written more efficiently with an iterative (i.e., nonrecursive) manner by using a simple for loop. In practice, we use recursion if certain conditions are met.

Helpful Reminder

Use recursion if

1. *A recursive solution is natural and easy to understand.*
2. *A recursive solution does not result in excessive duplicate computation.*
3. *The equivalent iterative solution is too complex.*

S u m m a r y

- A repetition control statement is used to repeatedly execute a block of code until a certain condition is met.
- Three repetition control statements are while, do–while, and for.
- The count-controlled loop executes the loop body for a fixed number of times.

- The sentinel-controlled loop executes the loop body until any one of the designted values called a *sentinel* is encountered.

- Count-controlled loops can be implemented most naturally with the for statements.

- Sentinel-controlled loops can be implemented most naturally with the while or do–while statements.

- The while statement is called a *pretest loop,* and the do–while statement is called a *posttest loop.* The for statement is also a pretest loop.

- Reading a value before the loop statement is called a *priming read.*

- Off-by-1 error and infinite loops are two common mistakes in writing a loop control.

- The loop-and-a-half repetition control is the most general way of writing a loop. The break statement is used within the loop body to exit the loop when a certain condition is met.

- The showConfirmationDialog method of the JOptionPane class is used to display a confirmation dialog.

- The nested-for statement is used very often because it is ideally suited to process tabular data.

- The random method of the Math class is used to generate a pseudorandom number.

Key Concepts

repetition control	nested-for statements
while statements	random number generation
do–while statements	confirmation dialog
for statements	a loop-and-a-half control
off-by-one error	count-controlled loops
infinite loop	sentinel-controlled loops
priming read	pretest and posttest loops

Exercises

1. Identify all the errors in the following repetition statements. Some errors are syntactical while others are logical (e.g., infinite loops).

   a.
   ```
   for (int i = 10; i > 0; i++) {
       x = y;
       a = b;
   }
   ```

b.
```
sum = 0;
do {
    num = Integer.parseInt(
                JOptionPane.showInputDialog(null,
                                    "Enter value:"));
    sum += num;
} until (sum > 10000);
```

c.
```
while (x < 1 && x > 10) {
    a = b;
}
```

d.
```
while (a == b) ;
{
    a = b;
    x = y;
}
```

e.
```
for (int i = 1.0; i <= 2.0; i += 0.1) {
    x = y;
    a = b;
}
```

2. Write for, do–while, and while statements to compute the following sums and products.

a. $1 + 2 + 3 + \cdots + 100$

b. $5 + 10 + 15 + \cdots + 50$

c. $1 + 3 + 7 + 15 + 31 + \cdots + (2^{20} - 1)$

d. $1 + \dfrac{1}{2} + \dfrac{1}{3} + \dfrac{1}{4} + \cdots + \dfrac{1}{15}$

e. $1 \times 2 \times 3 \times \cdots \times 20$

f. $1 \times 2 \times 4 \times 8 \times \cdots \times 2^{20}$

3. What will be the value of sum after each of the following nested loops is executed?

a.
```
sum = 0;
for (int i = 0; i <= 10; i++)
    for (int j = 0; j <= 10; j++)
        sum += i ;
```

b.
```
sum = 0;
j = 0;
do {
    j++;
    for (int i = 5; i > j; i--)
        sum = sum + (i+j);
} while (j < 11);
```

```
c. sum = 0;
   i = 0;
   while (i < 5) {
       j = 5;
       while (i != j) {
           sum += j;
           j--;
       }
       i++;
   }
```

```
d. sum = 0;
   for (int i = 0; i <= 10; i++)
       for (int j = 10; j > 2*i; j--)
           sum = sum + (j - i);
```

4. Determine the output from the following code without actually executing it.

```
System.out.format("%4d", 234);
System.out.format("%5d", 234);

System.out.format("%s", "\n");

System.out.format("$%6.2f", 23.456);
System.out.format("%s", "\n");

System.out.format("%1$3d+%1$3d=%2$5d", 5, (5+5));
```

5. Rewrite the following nested-for statements, using nested do–while and while statements.

```
a. sum = 0;
   number = 0;
   for (int i = 0; i <= 10; i++)
       for (int j = 10; j >= i; j--) {
           number++;
           sum = sum + (j - i);
       }
```

```
b. product = 1;
   number = 0;
   for (int i = 1; i < 5; i++)
       for (int j = 1; j < 5; j++) {
           number++;
           product *= number;
       }
```

6. You can compute sin x and cos x, using the following power series:

$$\sin x = x - \frac{x^3}{3!} + \frac{x^5}{5!} - \frac{x^7}{7!} + \cdots$$

$$\cos x = 1 - \frac{x^2}{2!} + \frac{x^4}{4!} - \frac{x^6}{6!} + \cdots$$

Write a program that evaluates sin x and cos x, using the power series. Use the double data type and increase the number of terms in the series until the overflow occurs. You can check if the overflow occurs by comparing the value against Double.POSITIVE_INFINITY. Compare the results you obtained to the values returned by the sin and cos methods of the Math class.

7. Write an application to print out the numbers 10 through 49 in the following manner:

```
10 11 12 13 14 15 16 17 18 19
20 21 22 23 24 25 26 27 28 29
30 31 32 33 34 35 36 37 38 39
40 41 42 43 44 45 46 47 48 49
```

How would you do it? Here is an example of poorly written code:

```
for (int i = 10; i < 50; i++) {
    switch (i) {
        case 19:
        case 29:
        case 39: System.out.println(" " + i); //move to the
                 break;                        //next line
        default: System.out.print(" " + i);
    }
}
```

This code is not good because it works only for printing 10 through 49. Try to develop the code so that it can be extended easily to handle any range of values. You can do this coding in two ways: with a nested-for statement or with modulo arithmetic. (If you divide a number by 10 and the remainder is 9, then the number is 9, 19, 29, or 39, and so forth.)

8. A *prime number* is an integer greater than 1 and divisible only by itself and 1. The first seven prime numbers are 2, 3, 5, 7, 11, 13, and 17. Write a method that returns true if its parameter is a prime number.

9. There are 25 primes between 2 and 100, and there are 1229 primes between 2 and 10,000. Write a program that inputs a positive integer $N > 2$ and displays the number of primes between 2 and N (inclusive). Use the timing technique explained in Section 6.10 to show the amount of time it took to compute the result.

10. Instead of actually computing the number of primes between 2 and N, we can get an estimate by using the *prime number theorem,* which states that

$$\text{prime}(N) \approx \left\lfloor \frac{N}{\ln(N)} \right\rfloor$$

where prime(N) is the number of primes between 2 and N (inclusive). The function ln is the natural logarithm. Extend the program for Exercise 9 by printing the estimate along with the actual number. You should notice the pattern that the estimate approaches the actual number as the value of N gets larger.

11. A *perfect number* is a positive integer that is equal to the sum of its proper divisors. A proper divisor is a positive integer other than the number itself that divides the number evenly (i.e., no remainder). For example, 6 is a perfect number because the sum of its proper divisors—1, 2, and 3—is equal to 6. Eight is not a perfect number because $1 + 2 + 4 \neq 8$. Write an application that accepts a positive integer and determines whether the number is perfect. Also, display all proper divisors of the number. Try a number between 20 and 30 and another number between 490 and 500.

12. Write an application that lists all perfect numbers between 6 and N, an upper limit entered by the user. After verifying the program with a small number for N, gradually increase the value for N and see how long the program takes to generate the perfect numbers. Since there are only a few perfect numbers, you might want to display the numbers that are not perfect so you can easily tell that the program is still running.

13. Write a program that displays all integers between *low* and *high* that are the sum of the cube of their digits. In other words, find all numbers xyz such that $xyz = x^3 + y^3 + z^3$, for example, $153 = 1^3 + 5^3 + 3^3$. Try 100 for *low* and 1000 for *high*.

14. Write a method that returns the number of digits in an integer argument; for example, 23,498 has five digits.

15. Your freelance work with MyJava Lo-Fat Burgers was a success (see Exercise 22 of Chapter 5). The management loved your new drive-through ordering system because the customer had to order an item from each of the three menu categories. As part of a public relations campaign, however, management decided to allow a customer to skip a menu category. Modify the program to handle this option. Before listing items from each category, use a confirmation dialog to ask the customer whether he or she wants to order an item from that category.

16. Extend the program in Exercise 15 so that customers can order more than one item from each menu category. For example, the customer can buy two orders of Tofu Burgers and three orders of Buffalo Wings from the Entree menu category.

17. Complete the loan table application discussed in Section 6.9.

18. Implement the describeRules method of the HiLo class from Section 6.10. Use a confirmation dialog to ask the user whether to display the game rules.

19. The price table for carpet we printed out in Section 6.7 contains index values for width and length, but not labels to identify them. Write an application to generate this table:

```
C:\WINDOWS\System32\cmd.exe
                              LENGTH
                  5        10        15        20        25
          11    1045      2090      3135      4180      5225
          12    1140      2280      3420      4560      5700
          13    1235      2470      3705      4940      6175
          14    1330      2660      3990      5320      6650
WIDTH     15    1425      2850      4275      5700      7125
          16    1520      3040      4560      6080      7600
          17    1615      3230      4845      6460      8075
          18    1710      3420      5130      6840      8550
          19    1805      3610      5415      7220      9025
          20    1900      3800      5700      7600      9500
```

20. Extend the HiLo class to allow the user to designate the lower and upper bounds of the secret number. In the original HiLo class, the bounds are set to 1 and 100, respectively.

21. A formula to compute the Nth Fibonacci number was given in Exercise 19 in Chapter 3. The formula is useful in finding a number in the sequence, but a more efficient way to output a series of numbers in the sequence is to use the recurrence relation $F_N = F_{N-1} + F_{N-2}$, with the first two numbers in the sequence F_1 and F_2 both defined as 1. Using this recurrence relation, we can compute the first 10 Fibonacci numbers as follows:

```
F1  = 1
F2  = 1
F3  = F2 + F1 =  1 +  1 =  2
F4  = F3 + F2 =  2 +  1 =  3
F5  = F4 + F3 =  3 +  2 =  5
F6  = F5 + F4 =  5 +  3 =  8
F7  = F6 + F5 =  8 +  5 = 13
F8  = F7 + F6 = 13 +  8 = 21
F9  = F8 + F7 = 21 + 13 = 34
F10 = F9 + F8 = 34 + 21 = 55
```

Write an application that accepts N, $N \geq 1$, from the user and displays the first N numbers in the Fibonacci sequence.

22. Modify the application of Exercise 21 to generate and display all the numbers in the sequence until a number becomes larger than the value maxNumber entered by the user.

23. Improve the LoanCalculator class from Chapter 4 to accept only the valid input values for loan amount, interest rate, and loan period. The original LoanCalculator class assumed the input values were valid. For the exercise, let the loan amount between $100.00 and $1,000,000.00, the interest rate between 5 and 20 percent, and the loan period between 1 year and 30 years be valid.

24. Extend Exercise 20 in Chapter 5 by drawing a more realistic clock. Instead of drawing a clock like

draw a circle at 5-minute intervals as

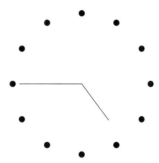

Use a for loop to draw 12 circles.

25. In the formatting examples from the chapter, we always provided a fixed control string, such as

```
System.out.format("%4d", 23);
```

It is possible, however, to dynamically create the control string, such as

```
int i = 4;
System.out.format("%" + i + "d", 23);
```

Using this idea of dynamically creating a control string, write a code fragment that outputs 50 X's, using a separate line for each X. An X on a single line is preceded by two more leading spaces than the X on the previous line. The following figure shows the output for the first five lines.

26. The sample loan table program from Section 6.9 implements the outer loop using double as the loop counter. Rewrite the loop using int as the loop counter.

27. (Optional) Write a recursive method to reverse a given string. For example, if the argument to the method is Java, then the method returns avaJ. *Note:* This is strictly for exercise. You should not write the real method recursively.

28. (Optional) Write a recursive method to compute the sum of the first N positive odd integers. *Note:* This is strictly for exercise. You should not write the real method recursively.

Development Exercises

For the following exercises, use the incremental development methodology to implement the program. For each exercise, identify the program tasks, create a design document with class descriptions, and draw the program diagram. Map out the development steps at the start. Present any design alternatives and justify your selection. Be sure to perform adequate testing at the end of each development step.

29. Write an application that draws nested N squares, where N is an input to the program. The smallest square is 10 pixels wide, and the width of each successive square increases by 10 pixels. The following pattern shows seven squares whose sides are 10, 20, 30, . . . , and 70 pixels wide.

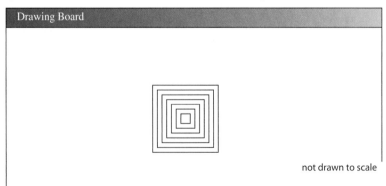

not drawn to scale

30. The monthly payments for a given loan are divided into amounts that apply to the principal and to the interest. For example, if you make a monthly payment of $500, only a portion of the $500 goes to the principal, and the remainder is the interest payment. The monthly interest is computed by

multiplying the monthly interest rate by the unpaid balance. The monthly payment minus the monthly interest is the amount applied to the principal. The following table is the sample loan payment schedule for a one-year loan of $5000 with a 12 percent annual interest rate.

Payment No.	Interest	Principal	Unpaid Balance	Total Interest to Date
1	50.00	394.24	4605.76	50.00
2	46.06	398.19	4207.57	96.06
3	42.08	402.17	3805.40	138.13
4	38.05	406.19	3399.21	176.19
5	33.99	410.25	2988.96	210.18
6	29.89	414.35	2574.61	240.07
7	25.75	418.50	2156.11	265.82
8	21.56	422.68	1733.42	287.38
9	17.33	426.91	1306.51	304.71
10	13.07	431.18	875.34	317.78
11	8.75	435.49	439.85	326.53
12	4.40	435.45	0.00	330.93

Write an application that accepts a loan amount, annual interest rate, and loan period (in number of years) and displays a table with five columns: payment number, the interest and principal paid for that month, the remaining balance after the payment, and the total interest paid to date. *Note:* The last payment is generally different from the monthly payment, and your application should print out the correct amount for the last payment. Align the output values neatly.

31. Instead of dropping a watermelon from a building, let's shoot it from a cannon and compute its projectile. The (x, y) coordinates of a watermelon at time t are

$$x = V \cos(\alpha)\, t$$

$$y = V \sin(\alpha)\, t - \frac{gt^2}{2}$$

where g is the acceleration of gravity, V is the initial velocity, and α is the initial angle. The acceleration of gravity on earth is 9.8 m/s^2.

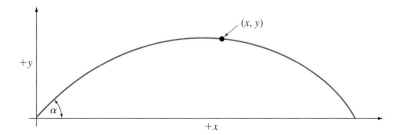

Write an application that inputs an initial velocity V (m/s) and an initial angle alpha (in degrees) and computes the projectile of a watermelon cannon ball. The program should repeat the computation until the user wants to quit. The program outputs the (x, y) coordinate value for every second, that is, t = 0, 1, 2, and so forth. The program stops the output when the y value becomes zero or less. To use the cos and sin methods of the Math class, don't forget that you have to convert the input angle given in degrees to radians. You can convert a degree to the equivalent radians by using

$$\text{Radian} = \frac{\text{degree} \times \pi}{180}$$

or calling the toRadians method of the Math class. *Note:* Air resistance is not considered in the formula. Also, we assumed the watermelon will not get smashed at firing.

32. Write an application that simulates a slot machine. The player starts out with *M* coins. The value for *M* is an input to the program, and you charge 25 cents per coin. For each play, the player can bet 1 to 4 coins. If the player enters 0 as the number of coins to bet, then the program stops playing. At the end of the game, the program displays the number of coins left and how much the player won or lost in the dollar amount. There are three slots on the machine, and each slot will display one of the three possible pieces: BELL, GRAPE, and CHERRY. When certain combinations appear on the slots, the machine will pay the player. The payoff combinations are as follow:

No.	Combination			Payoff (Times the Betting Amount)
1	BELL	BELL	BELL	10
2	GRAPES	GRAPES	GRAPES	7
3	CHERRY	CHERRY	CHERRY	5
4	CHERRY	CHERRY	-----------	3
5	CHERRY	-----------	CHERRY	3
6	-----------	CHERRY	CHERRY	3
7	CHERRY	-----------	-----------	1
8	-----------	CHERRY	-----------	1
9	-----------	-----------	CHERRY	1

The symbol ----------- means any piece. If the player bets 4 coins and gets combination 5, for example, the machine pays the player 12 coins.

7 Event-Driven Programming and Basic GUI Objects

After you have read and studied this chapter, you should be able to

- Define a subclass of the **JFrame** class, using inheritance.

- Write graphical user interface (GUI) application programs using **JButton, JLabel, ImageIcon, JTextField,** and **JTextArea** objects from the **javax.swing** package.

- Write GUI application programs with menus, using **menu** objects from the **javax.swing** package.

- Write event-driven programs, using Java's delegation-based event model.

I n t r o d u c t i o n

he sample programs we have written so far used standard classes such as JOption-Pane, PrintStream (System.out is an instance of PrintStream), and others for handling user interface. These standard classes are convenient and adequate for a basic program that does not require any elaborate user interface. For example, when we need to input a single integer value, calling the showInputDialog method of JOptionPane once to read that input is appropriate and effective. However, when we need to input, say, ten values for a Student object (e.g., name, age, address, phone number, GPA), then calling the showInputDialog method ten times is not adequate. It is very cumbersome to go through ten input dialogs and enter a value one at a time. Also, there is no simple and elegant way to allow the user to reenter any one of the values after all ten input values are entered. So, instead of using ten input dialogs, it is a much better user interface to employ a single customized input dialog that allows the user to enter all ten values. We will learn how to build such a customized user interface in this chapter.

Take *my* *Advice*

When we write a program for our own use, then we may choose to tolerate ten input dialogs to enter ten values. When we write a program for others, however, an effective user interface becomes of paramount importance. Next to the program correctness, the user interface of a program is often the most important criterion for the users to select one program over another, so it is critical for the success of the program to include the user interface that is logical, easy to use, and visually appealing.

graphical user interface

The type of user interface we cover in this chapter is called a *graphical user interface* (GUI). In contrast, the user interface that uses System.in and System.out exclusively is called *non-GUI*, or *console user interface*. In Java, GUI-based programs are implemented by using the classes from the standard javax.swing and java.awt packages. We will refer to them collectively as *GUI classes*. When we need to differentiate them, we will refer to the classes from javax.swing as *Swing classes* and those from java.awt as *AWT classes*. Some of the GUI objects from the javax.swing package are shown in Figure 7.1.

Swing and AWT classes

Before Java 2 SDK 1.2, we only had AWT classes to build GUI-based programs. Many of the AWT classes are now superseded by their counterpart Swing classes (e.g., AWT Button class is superseded by Swing JButton class). AWT classes are still available, but it is generally preferable to use Swing classes. There are two main advantages in using the Swing classes over the AWT classes.

First, the Swing classes provide greater compatibility across different operating systems. The Swing classes are implemented fully in Java, and they behave the

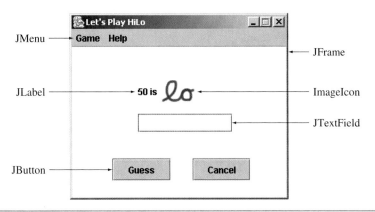

Figure 7.1 Various GUI objects from the **javax.swing** package.

same on different operating systems. The AWT classes, on the other hand, are implemented by using the native GUI objects. For example, an AWT Button is implemented by using the Windows button object for the Windows operating system, the Macintosh button object for the Mac operating system, and so forth. Because the behaviors of underlying platform-specific GUI objects are not necessarily identical, an application that uses AWT classes may not behave the same on the different operating systems. To characterize the difference in implementation, the Swing classes are called *lightweight classes* and the AWT classes *heavyweight classes*.

Second, the Swing classes support many new functionalities not supported by the AWT counterparts. For example, we can easily display an image inside a button in addition to a text by using a Swing JButton, but only text can be displayed inside a button with an AWT Button.

In this book we will use the Swing classes exclusively. We only use the AWT classes when there are no counterpart Swing classes. One thing we must be careful of in using them is not to mix the counterparts in the same program because of their differences in implementation. For example, we should not mix Swing buttons and AWT buttons or Swing menus and AWT menus. If an AWT class has no counterpart Swing class, for example, the AWT Graphics class, then using it with other Swing classes poses no problem.

Helpful Reminder

*The Swing classes are called lightweight classes and the AWT classes heavyweight classes. As a general rule, because they are implemented differently, it is best not to mix the counterparts (e.g., Swing **JButton** and AWT **Button**) in the same program.*

event-driven
programming

To build an effective graphical user interface (GUI) using objects from the javax.swing and java.awt packages, we must learn a new style of program control called *event-driven programming*. An *event* occurs when the user interacts with a GUI object. For example, when you move the cursor, click on a button, or select a menu choice, an event occurs. In event-driven programs, we program objects to respond to these events by defining event-handling methods. In this chapter we will learn the fundamentals of event-driven programming. Almost all modern GUI-based application software is event-driven, so it is very important to learn this programming style well.

Since the main objective for this chapter is to teach the fundamentals of GUI and event-driven programming and not to provide an exhaustive coverage of the Swing classes, we will cover only those that are essential to understanding event-driven programming. More Swing classes and additional topics for advanced GUI will be covered later in (optional) Chapter 14.

The chapter's other objective is the reiteration of practicing the single-task object design, the design philosophy that leads to a high degree of reusability. Designing an object that implements a single well-designed task becomes critical when we start building customized user interfaces. If we are not careful, it is easy to fall into the trap of creating an object that does both the user interface and the logical aspect of the program. For example, it is possible to design improperly a single class whose instance would handle both the customized user interface and the logic of playing the HiLo game. A proper design will result in two classes, one for handling the user interface and another for handling the logic of playing the game. This division of labor achieves a higher degree of reusability. Why? Because we can easily mix and match the classes that provide different styles of user interface with the classes that handle the game-playing logic. Suppose a single class implements both tasks. Then, for example, we won't be able to use only the game-playing portion of this class, and we have to use the user interface this class provides, whether we like it or not. We will explore the design philosophy of single-task classes in this chapter.

Design Guidelines

Design a class that implements a single well-defined task. Do not overburden the class with multiple tasks.

7.1 | Creating a Subclass of JFrame

In Chapter 1, we described the concept of inheritance, a feature we use to define a more specialized class from an existing class. We call the existing class the *superclass* and the specialized class the *subclass*. We say the subclass *inherits,* or *extends,* the superclass. Because inheritance is an integral part of creating customized user interface classes, we will briefly introduce the inheritance mechanism of Java in this section. Only the basics are covered here, and we limit the discussion to creating subclasses of the standard classes. Additional, more in-depth discussion of inheritance is presented in Chapter 13.

Although we have not used inheritance directly, most of the standard classes we have been using so far are subclasses of other standard classes, which in turn are themselves subclasses of yet other standard classes, forming an inheritance hierarchy. We can see the inheritance hierarchy of a standard class when we view its API documentation. For example, Figure 7.2 shows the inheritance hierarchy of JOptionPane. Each successive subclass inherits everything from its superclass and either adds new features or replaces the inherited ones. In Figure 7.2, we see that javax.swing.JOptionPane is a subclass of javax.swing.JComponent, which in turn is a subclass of java.awt.Container, and so forth.

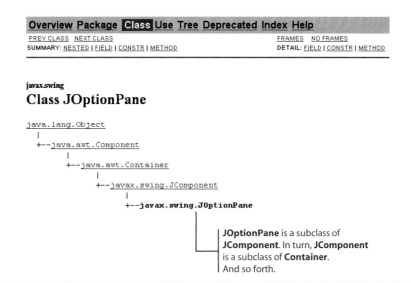

Figure 7.2 The inheritance hierarchy of **JOptionPane** as shown in the API documentation.

To create a customized user interface, we often define a subclass of the JFrame class. The JFrame class contains the most rudimentary functionalities to support features found in any frame window, such as minimizing the window, moving the window, and resizing the window. In writing practical programs, we normally do not create an instance of the JFrame class because a JFrame object is not capable of doing anything meaningful. For example, if we want to use a frame window for a word processor, we need a frame window capable of allowing the user to enter, cut, and paste text; change font; print text; and so forth. To design such a frame window, we would define a subclass of the JFrame class and add methods and data members to implement the needed functionalities.

Let's define a very simple subclass of JFrame to illustrate how the inheritance mechanism works in Java. First, consider the following program that displays a default JFrame object on the screen:

```
/*
    Chapter 7 Sample Program: Displays a default JFrame window

    File: Ch7DefaultJFrame.java
*/

import javax.swing.*;

class Ch7DefaultJFrame {

    public static void main( String[] args ) {

        JFrame defaultJFrame;

        defaultJFrame = new JFrame();

        defaultJFrame.setVisible(true);
    }
}
```

When this program is executed, a default JFrame object, shown in Figure 7.3, appears on the screen. Since no methods (other than setVisible) to set the properties of the JFrame object (such as its title, location, and size) are called, a very small default JFrame object appears at the top left corner of the screen.

We'll define a subclass of the JFrame class and add some default characteristics. To define a subclass of another class, we declare the subclass with the reserved

You may not notice this frame window on the screen at first because it is so small. Look carefully at the top left corner of the screen.

Figure 7.3 A default **JFrame** window appears at the top left corner of the screen.

extends

word **extends**. So, to define a class named Ch7JFrameSubclass1 as a subclass of JFrame, we declare the subclass as

```
class Ch7JFrameSubclass1 extends JFrame {
    . . .
}
```

Helpful Reminder

*To define **X** as a subclass of **Y**, we declare the subclass **X** with the reserved word* **extends** *as*

```
class X extends Y { ... }
```

For the Ch7JFrameSubclass1 class, we will add the following default characteristics:

- The title is set to My First Subclass.
- The program terminates when the close box is clicked.[1]
- The size of the frame is set to 300 pixels wide and 200 pixels high.
- The frame is positioned at screen coordinate (150, 250).

The effect of these properties is illustrated in Figure 7.4.

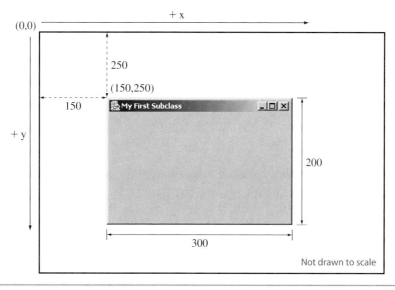

Figure 7.4 How an instance of **Ch7JFrameSubclass1** will appear on the screen.

---

[1]If we don't add this functionality, the window will close, but the program does not terminate. In a normal environment, we can still terminate the program by closing the command window, the one with the black background on the Windows platform.

All these properties are set inside the default constructor. To set the frame's title, we pass the title to the setTitle method. To set the frame's size, we pass its width and height to the setSize method. To position the frame's top left corner to the coordinate (x, y), we pass the values x and y to the setLocation method. Finally, to terminate the program when the frame is closed, we call the setDefaultCloseOperation with the class constant EXIT_ON_CLOSE as an argument. The Ch7JFrameSubclass1 class is declared as follows:

```
/*
    Chapter 7 Sample Program: A simple subclass of JFrame

    File: Ch7JFrameSubclass1.java
*/

import javax.swing.*;

class Ch7JFrameSubclass1 extends JFrame {

    private static final int FRAME_WIDTH    = 300;
    private static final int FRAME_HEIGHT   = 200;
    private static final int FRAME_X_ORIGIN = 150;
    private static final int FRAME_Y_ORIGIN = 250;

    public Ch7JFrameSubclass1( ) {

        //set the frame default properties
        setTitle      ( "My First Subclass" );
        setSize       ( FRAME_WIDTH, FRAME_HEIGHT );
        setLocation   ( FRAME_X_ORIGIN, FRAME_Y_ORIGIN );

        //register 'Exit upon closing' as a default close operation
        setDefaultCloseOperation( EXIT_ON_CLOSE );
    }
}
```

Calls the inherited methods.

Notice the methods such as setTitle, setSize, and others are all defined in the JFrame and its ancestor classes (ancestors are the superclasses in the inheritance hierarchy). Every method of a superclass is inherited by its subclass. Because the subclass-superclass relationships are formed into an inheritance hierarchy, a subclass inherits all methods defined in its ancestor classes. And we can call an inherited method from the method of a subclass in the manner identical to calling a method defined in the subclass, that is, without using dot notation or by using dot notation with the reserved word this.

Helpful Reminder

Inherited methods are called from the method of a subclass without using dot notation or by using dot notation with the reserved word **this.**

Here's the main class to test the Ch7JFrameSubclass1 class:

```
/*
    Chapter 7 Sample Program: Displays a default Ch7JFrameSubclass window

    File: Ch7TestJFrameSubclass.java
*/

class Ch7TestJFrameSubclass {

    public static void main( String[] args ) {

        Ch7JFrameSubclass1 myFrame;

        myFrame = new Ch7JFrameSubclass1();

        myFrame.setVisible(true);
    }
}
```

When it is executed, an instance of Ch7JFrameSubclass1 appears on the screen, as illustrated in Figure 7.4. Notice this main class is identical to Ch7DefaultJFrame except for the creation of a Ch7JFrameSubclass1 instance instead of a JFrame instance. Also notice that there's no need to import the javax.swing package because the main class does not make any direct reference to the classes in this package.

Since we did not set the background color for Ch7JFrameSubclass1, the default gray was used as the frame's background color. Let's define another subclass named Ch7JFrameSubclass2 that has a white background color instead. We will define this class as an instantiable main class so we don't have to define a separate main class. To make the background appear in white, we need to access the content pane of a frame. A frame's *content pane* designates the area of the frame that excludes the title and menu bars and the border. It is the area we can use to display the content (text, image, etc.). We access the content pane of a frame by calling the frame's getContentPane method. And to change the background color to white, we call the content pane's setBackground method. We carry out these

content pane

operations in the private changeBkColor method of Ch7JFrameSubclass2. Here's the class definition:

```
/*
    Chapter 7 Sample Program: A simple subclass of JFrame
                              that changes the background
                              color to white.

    File: Ch7JFrameSubclass2.java
*/

import javax.swing.*;
import java.awt.*;

class Ch7JFrameSubclass2 extends JFrame {

    private static final int FRAME_WIDTH    = 300;
    private static final int FRAME_HEIGHT   = 200;
    private static final int FRAME_X_ORIGIN = 150;
    private static final int FRAME_Y_ORIGIN = 250;

    public static void main(String[] args) {
        Ch7JFrameSubclass2 frame = new Ch7JFrameSubclass2();
        frame.setVisible(true);
    }

    public Ch7JFrameSubclass2( ) {

        //set the frame default properties
        setTitle      ( "White Background JFrame Subclass" );
        setSize       ( FRAME_WIDTH, FRAME_HEIGHT );
        setLocation   ( FRAME_X_ORIGIN, FRAME_Y_ORIGIN );

        //register 'Exit upon closing' as a default close operation
        setDefaultCloseOperation( EXIT_ON_CLOSE );

        changeBkColor( );
    }

    private void changeBkColor() {
        Container contentPane = getContentPane();
        contentPane.setBackground(Color.white);
    }
}
```

Running the program will result in the frame shown in Figure 7.5 appearing on the screen. Notice that we declare the variable contentPane in the changeBkColor method as Container. We do *not* have a class named ContentPane. By declaring the

Figure 7.5 An instance of **Ch7JFrameSubclass2** that has white background.

variable contentPane as Container, we can make it refer to any instance of the Container class or the descendant classes of Container. This makes our code more general because we are not tying the variable contentPane to any one specific class. By default, the getContentPane method of JFrame in fact returns the descendant class of Container called JPanel. We will describe the JPanel class in Chapter 14.

7.2 | Placing Buttons on the Content Pane of a Frame

In this section and Section 7.3, we will develop a sample frame window, a subclass of JFrame, that illustrates the fundamentals of GUI programming. The sample frame window has two buttons, labeled CANCEL and OK. When you click the CANCEL button, the window's title is changed to You clicked CANCEL. Likewise, when you click the OK button, the window's title is changed to You clicked OK. Figure 7.6 shows the window when it is first opened and after the CANCEL button is clicked.

We will develop the sample program in two steps. In this section, we will define a JFrame subclass called Ch7JButtonFrame to show how the two buttons labeled OK and CANCEL are placed on the frame. In Section 7.3, we will implement another subclass called Ch7JButtonEvents to show how the frame title is changed when the buttons are clicked.

Window title changes
when the CANCEL button
is clicked.

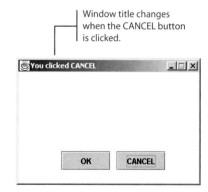

Figure 7.6 A sample window when it is first opened and after the **CANCEL** button is clicked.

pushbutton

The type of button we use here is called a *pushbutton*. Since we discuss the pushbuttons only in this chapter, we will simply call them buttons. To use a button in a program, we create an instance of the javax.swing.JButton class. We will create two buttons and place them on the frame's content pane in the constructor. Let's name the two buttons cancelButton and okButton.

layout manager

There are two general approaches to placing buttons (and other types of GUI objects) on a frame's content pane—one that uses a layout manager and another that does not. The *layout manager* for a container is an object that controls the placement of the GUI objects. For example, the simplest layout manager, called FlowLayout, places GUI objects in the top-to-bottom, left-to-right order. If we do not use any layout manager, then we place GUI objects by explicitly specifying their position

absolute positioning

and size on the content pane. We call this approach *absolute positioning*. Although layout managers are very useful in practical applications, understanding them is not essential in learning event-driven programming, so we will use absolute positioning for the sample programs in this chapter to keep things simple. We will discuss various layout managers in Chapter 14.

To use absolute positioning, we set the layout manager of a frame's content pane to none by passing null to the setLayout method:

```
contentPane.setLayout(null);
```

After the layout manager is set to null, we place two buttons at the position and in the size we want by calling the button's setBounds method, as in

```
okButton.setBounds( 75, 125, 80, 30 );
```

where the first two arguments specify the position of the button and the last two arguments specify the width and height of the button. Finally, to make a button appear on the frame, we need to add it to the content pane by calling the add method. For example, to add okButton, we call

```
contentPane.add(okButton);
```

Figure 7.7 illustrates the process.

Here's the complete listing of the Ch7JButtonFrame class:

```
/*
    Chapter 7 Sample Program: Displays a frame with two buttons

    File: Ch7JButtonFrame.java
*/

import javax.swing.*;
import java.awt.*;
import java.awt.event.*;
```

```java
class Ch7JButtonFrame extends JFrame {

    private static final int FRAME_WIDTH    = 300;
    private static final int FRAME_HEIGHT   = 200;
    private static final int FRAME_X_ORIGIN = 150;
    private static final int FRAME_Y_ORIGIN = 250;

    private static final int BUTTON_WIDTH  = 80;
    private static final int BUTTON_HEIGHT = 30;

    private JButton cancelButton;
    private JButton okButton;

    public static void main(String[] args) {
        Ch7JButtonFrame frame = new Ch7JButtonFrame();
        frame.setVisible(true);
    }

    public Ch7JButtonFrame() {

        Container contentPane = getContentPane( );

        //set the frame properties
        setSize      ( FRAME_WIDTH, FRAME_HEIGHT );
        setResizable ( false );
        setTitle     ( "Program Ch7JButtonFrame" );
        setLocation  ( FRAME_X_ORIGIN, FRAME_Y_ORIGIN );

        //set the content pane properties
        contentPane.setLayout( null );
        contentPane.setBackground( Color.white );

        //create and place two buttons on the frame's content pane
        okButton = new JButton("OK");
        okButton.setBounds(70, 125, BUTTON_WIDTH, BUTTON_HEIGHT);
        contentPane.add(okButton);

        cancelButton = new JButton("CANCEL");
        cancelButton.setBounds(160, 125, BUTTON_WIDTH, BUTTON_HEIGHT);
        contentPane.add(cancelButton);

        //register 'Exit upon closing' as a default close operation
        setDefaultCloseOperation( EXIT_ON_CLOSE );

    }
}
```

When we run the program, we see two buttons appear on the frame. We can click the buttons, but nothing happens, of course, because the code to handle the button clicks has not yet been added to the class. We'll add the required code in Section 7.3.

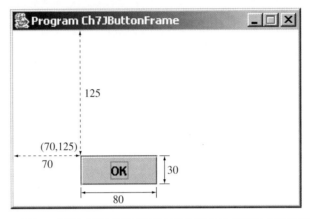

```
Container contentPane = getContentPane();
JButton    okButton    = new JButton("OK");

contentPane.setLayout(null);
okButton.setBounds(70, 125, 80, 30);

contentPane.add(okButton);
```

Figure 7.7 The process of creating a button and placing it on a frame.

Quick
CHECK

1. What is the purpose of a layout manager?
2. Using the **setBounds** method, position a button **50** pixels wide and **30** pixels high at the location (**125, 85**).
3. To use absolute positioning, how must we set the content pane's layout manager?

7.3 | Handling Button Events

In this section, we will explain the mechanism of processing the button clicks. An action such as clicking a button is called an *event,* and the mechanism to process the events is called *event handling*. The event-handling model of Java is based on the concept known as the *delegation-based event model*. With this model, event handling is implemented by two types of objects: event source objects and event listener objects.

A GUI object, such as a button, where the event occurs is called an *event source object,* or simply the *event source*. We say an event source *generates* events. So, for example, when the user clicks on a button, the corresponding JButton object will generate an action event. When an event is generated, the system notifies the relevant event listener objects. An *event listener object,* or simply, an *event listener,* is an object that includes a method that gets executed in response to the generated events. It is possible for a single object to be both an event source and an event listener.

event

delegation-based event model

event source

event listener

action event

Among the many different types of events, the most common one is called an *action event*. For example, when a button is clicked or a menu item is selected, an event source will generate an action event. For the generated events to be processed, we must associate, or register, event listeners to the event sources. If the event sources have no registered listeners, then generated events are simply ignored (this is what happened in the Ch7JButtonFrame program). For each type of event, we have a corresponding listener. For example, we have action listeners for action events, window listeners for window events, mouse listeners for mouse events, and so forth. (Event types other than action events are discussed later in this chapter and in Chapter 14.) If we wish to process the action events generated by a button, then we must associate an action listener to the button.

An object that can be registered as an action listener must be an instance of a class that is declared specifically for the purpose. We call such class an *action listener class*. For this sample program, let's name the action listener class Button-Handler. We will describe how to define the ButtonHandler class shortly. But first, we will show the step to register an instance of ButtonHandler as the action listener of the two action event sources—okButton and cancelButton—of the sample frame window.

An action listener is associated to an action event source by calling the event source's addActionListener method with this action listener as its argument. For example, to register an instance of ButtonHandler as an action listener of okButton and cancelButton, we can execute the following code:

```
ButtonHandler handler  = new ButtonHandler( );
    okButton.addActionListener(handler);
cancelButton.addActionListener(handler);
```

Notice that we are associating a single ButtonHandler object as an action listener of both buttons, because, although we can, it is not necessary to associate two separate listeners, one for the OK button and another for the CANCEL button. A single listener can be associated to multiple event sources. Likewise, although not frequently used, multiple listeners can be associated to a single event source.

Helpful Reminder

A single listener can be associated to multiple event sources, and multiple listeners can be associated to a single event source.

When an event source generates an event, the system checks for matching registered listeners (e.g., for action events the system looks for registered action listeners, for window events the system looks for registered window listeners, and so forth). If there is no matching listener, the event is ignored. If there is a matching listener, the system notifies the listener by calling the listener's corresponding method.

In case of action events, this method is actionPerformed. To ensure that the programmer includes the necessary actionPerformed method in action listener class, the class must be defined in a specific way. The ButtonHandler class, for example, must be defined in the following way:

```
import java.awt.event.*;
```

ActionListener is defined in this package.

```
class ButtonHandler implements ActionListener {
    . . .
}
```

We say the ButtonHandler class *implements* the ActionListener interface. ActionListener is not a class, but an interface. Like a class, an *interface* is a reference data type; but unlike a class, an interface includes only constants and abstract methods. An *abstract method* has only the method header (or, more formally, the *method prototype*); that is, it has no method body. The java.awt.event.ActionListener, for instance, is defined as

interface

abstract
method

```
interface ActionListener {
    public void actionPerformed(ActionEvent evt);
}
```

There's no method body, only the method header.

To differentiate the user interface and the reference data type interface, we will also use the term *Java interface* to refer to the latter. A class that implements a Java interface must provide the method body to all the abstract methods defined in the interface. For example, the ActionListener interface includes one abstract method named actionPerformed, so any class that implements this interface must provide the method body for the actionPerformed method. By requiring an object we pass as an argument to the addActionListener method to be an instance of a class that implements the ActionListener interface, the system ensures that this object will include the necessary actionPerformed method.

The ButtonHandler class is defined as

```
class ButtonHandler implements ActionListener {

    //data members and constructors come here

    public void actionPerformed(ActionEvent evt) {

        //event handling statements come here
    }
}
```

An argument to the actionPerformed method is an ActionEvent object that represents an action event, and the ActionEvent class includes methods to access the properties of a generated event.

We want to change the title of a frame to You clicked OK or You clicked CANCEL depending on which button is clicked. This is done inside the actionPerformed method. The general idea of the method is this:

```
public void actionPerformed(ActionEvent evt) {

    String buttonText
            = get the text of the event source;

    JFrame frame
            = the frame that contains this event source;

    frame.setTitle("You clicked " + buttonText);
}
```

The first statement retrieves the text of the event source (the text of the okButton is the string OK and the text of the cancelButton is the string CANCEL). We can do this in two ways. The first way is to use the getActionCommand method of the action event object evt. Using this method we can retrieve the text of the clicked button as

```
String buttonText = evt.getActionCommand();
```

The second way is to use the getSource method of the action event object evt. Using this method, we can retrieve the text of the clicked button as

> Notice the type casting to an
> appropriate class is necessary.

```
JButton clickedButton = (JButton) evt.getSource();
String  buttonText    = clickedButton.getText();
```

Notice the type casting of an object returned by the getSource method to JButton. The object returned by the getSource method can be an instance of any class, so we need to type cast the returned object to a proper class in order to use the desired method.

Now, to find the frame that contains the event source, we proceed in two steps. First, we get the root pane to which this event source belongs. Second, we get the frame that contains this root pane. Here's the necessary sequence of statements to access the frame that contains the event source:

```
JRootPane rootPane = clickedButton.getRootPane( );
Frame     frame    = (JFrame) rootPane.getParent();
```

> Type casting is necessary
> here, too.

A frame window contains nested layers of panes (the content pane where we place GUI objects is one). The topmost pane is called the *root pane* (an instance of JRootPane). We can access the root pane of a frame by calling the GUI object's getRootPane method. From the root pane, we can access the frame object by calling the root pane's getParent method. Because a root pane can be contained by different types of containers (frames, dialogs, etc.), we need to type cast the returned object to JFrame in this example.

Here's the complete ButtonHandler class:

```
/*
    Chapter 7 Sample Program: Event listener for button click events

    File: ButtonHandler.java
*/

import javax.swing.*;
import java.awt.*;
import java.awt.event.*;

class ButtonHandler implements ActionListener {

    public ButtonHandler() {

    }

    public void actionPerformed(ActionEvent event) {

        JButton clickedButton = (JButton) event.getSource();

        JRootPane rootPane = clickedButton.getRootPane( );
        Frame     frame    = (JFrame) rootPane.getParent();

        String  buttonText = clickedButton.getText();

        frame.setTitle("You clicked " + buttonText);
    }
}
```

And here's the complete Ch7JButtonEvents class (notice that this class is essentially the same as the Ch7JButtonFrame class except for the portion that deals with the registration of a ButtonHandler to two event sources):

```
/*
    Chapter 7 Sample Program: Displays a frame with two buttons
                              and associate an instance of
                              ButtonHandler to the two buttons

    File: Ch7JButtonEvents.java
*/

import javax.swing.*;
import java.awt.*;
```

```java
class Ch7JButtonEvents extends JFrame {

    private static final int FRAME_WIDTH    = 300;
    private static final int FRAME_HEIGHT   = 200;
    private static final int FRAME_X_ORIGIN = 150;
    private static final int FRAME_Y_ORIGIN = 250;

    private static final int BUTTON_WIDTH  = 80;
    private static final int BUTTON_HEIGHT = 30;

    private JButton cancelButton;
    private JButton okButton;

    public static void main(String[] args) {
        Ch7JButtonEvents frame = new Ch7JButtonEvents();
        frame.setVisible(true);
    }

    public Ch7JButtonEvents() {

        Container contentPane = getContentPane( );

        //set the frame properties
        setSize      ( FRAME_WIDTH, FRAME_HEIGHT );
        setResizable ( false );
        setTitle     ( "Program Ch7JButtonFrame" );
        setLocation  ( FRAME_X_ORIGIN, FRAME_Y_ORIGIN );

        //set the content pane properties
        contentPane.setLayout( null );
        contentPane.setBackground( Color.white );

        //create and place two buttons on the frame's content pane
        okButton = new JButton("OK");
        okButton.setBounds(70, 125, BUTTON_WIDTH, BUTTON_HEIGHT);
        contentPane.add(okButton);

        cancelButton = new JButton("CANCEL");
        cancelButton.setBounds(160, 125, BUTTON_WIDTH, BUTTON_HEIGHT);
        contentPane.add(cancelButton);

        //registering a ButtonHandler as an action listener of the
        //two buttons
        ButtonHandler handler = new ButtonHandler();
        cancelButton.addActionListener(handler);
        okButton.addActionListener(handler);

        //register 'Exit upon closing' as a default close operation
        setDefaultCloseOperation( EXIT_ON_CLOSE );
    }
}
```

Making a Frame the Event Listener

Instead of creating a separate event listener class such as ButtonHandler, it is actually more common to let a frame be the event listener of the GUI objects that it contains. We stated earlier that any class can implement the ActionListener interface. We can declare a subclass of JFrame that implements the ActionListener interface. As an illustration of this technique, let's define a subclass of JFrame called Ch7JButtonFrameHandler. This class combines the functionalities of the Ch7JButtonEvents and ButtonHandler classes.

Here's the class:

```java
/*
    Chapter 7 Sample Program: Displays a frame with two buttons
                             and handles the button events

    File: Ch7JButtonFrameHandler.java
*/

import javax.swing.*;
import java.awt.*;
import java.awt.event.*;

class Ch7JButtonFrameHandler extends JFrame implements ActionListener {

    private static final int FRAME_WIDTH    = 300;
    private static final int FRAME_HEIGHT   = 200;
    private static final int FRAME_X_ORIGIN = 150;
    private static final int FRAME_Y_ORIGIN = 250;

    private static final int BUTTON_WIDTH  = 80;
    private static final int BUTTON_HEIGHT = 30;

    private JButton cancelButton;
    private JButton okButton;

    public static void main(String[] args) {
        Ch7JButtonFrameHandler frame = new Ch7JButtonFrameHandler();
        frame.setVisible(true);
    }

    public Ch7JButtonFrameHandler() {

        Container contentPane = getContentPane( );

        //set the frame properties
        setSize        ( FRAME_WIDTH, FRAME_HEIGHT );
        setResizable   ( false );
        setTitle       ( "Program Ch7JButtonFrameHandler" );
        setLocation    ( FRAME_X_ORIGIN, FRAME_Y_ORIGIN );
```

```
        //set the content pane properties
        contentPane.setLayout( null );
        contentPane.setBackground( Color.white );

        //create and place two buttons on the frame's content pane
        okButton = new JButton("OK");
        okButton.setBounds(70, 125, BUTTON_WIDTH, BUTTON_HEIGHT);
        contentPane.add(okButton);

        cancelButton = new JButton("CANCEL");
        cancelButton.setBounds(160, 125, BUTTON_WIDTH, BUTTON_HEIGHT);
        contentPane.add(cancelButton);

        //register this frame as an action listener of the two buttons
        cancelButton.addActionListener(this);
        okButton.addActionListener(this);

        //register 'Exit upon closing' as a default close operation
        setDefaultCloseOperation( EXIT_ON_CLOSE );

    }

    public void actionPerformed(ActionEvent event) {
        JButton clickedButton = (JButton) event.getSource();

        String  buttonText = clickedButton.getText();

        setTitle("You clicked " + buttonText);
    }
}
```

Calls the **setTitle** method of this frame object.

Notice how we call the addActionListener method of cancelButton and okButton. This frame object is the action event listener, so we pass it as an argument to the method as

```
        cancelButton.addActionListener(this);
            okButton.addActionListener(this);
```

Likewise, because the actionPerformed method now belongs to this frame class itself, we can call other methods of the frame class from the actionPerformed method without dot notation. So the statement to change the title is simply

```
        setTitle("You clicked " + buttonText);
```

Quick **CHECK**

1. Which object generates events? Which object processes events?
2. A class that implements the **ActionListener** interface must implement which method?
3. What does the **getActionCommand** method of the **ActionEvent** class return?

7.4 | JLabel, JTextField, **and** JTextArea **Classes**

In this section we will introduce three Swing GUI classes—JLabel, JTextField, and JTextArea—that deal with text. The first two deal with a single line of text. A TextField object allows the user to enter a single line of text, while a JLabel object is for displaying uneditable text. A JTextArea object allows the user to enter multiple lines of text. It can also be used for displaying multiple lines of uneditable text.

Like a JButton object, an instance of JTextField generates an action event. A TextField object generates an action event when the user presses the ENTER key while the object is active (it is active when you see the vertical blinking line in it). JLabel, on the other hand, does not generate any event. A JTextArea object also generates events, specifically the types of events called *text events* and *document events*. Handling of these events is more involved than handling action events, so to keep the discussion manageable, we won't be processing the JTextArea events.

We will describe the JTextField class first. We set a JTextFiled object's size and position and register its action listener in the same way as we did for the JButton class. To illustrate its use, we will modify the Ch7JButtonFrameHandler by adding a single JTextField object. We will call the new class Ch7TextFrame1. The effect of clicking the buttons CANCEL and OK is the same as before. If the user presses the ENTER key while the JTextField object is active, then we will change the title to whatever text is entered in this JTextField object. In the data declaration part, we add

```
JTextField inputLine;
```

and in the constructor we create a JTextField object and register the frame as its action listener:

```
public Ch7TextFrame1 {
    . . .
    inputLine = new JTextField( );
    inputLine.setBounds(90, 50, 130, 25);
    contentPane.add( inputLine );

    inputLine.addActionListener( this );
    . . .
}
```

Now we need to modify the actionPerformed method to handle both the button click events and the ENTER key events. We have three event sources (two buttons and one text field), so the first thing we must do in the actionPerformed method is to determine the source. We will use the instanceof operator to determine the class to which the event source belongs. Here's the general idea:

instanceof

```
if ( event.getSource() instanceof JButton ) {
    //event source is either cancelButton
    //or okButton
    . . .
} else { //event source must be inputLine
    . . .
}
```

We use the getText method of JTextField to retrieve the text that the user has entered. The complete method is written as

```
public void actionPerformed(ActionEvent event) {

    if (event.getSource() instanceof JButton) {
        JButton clickedButton = (JButton) event.getSource();

        String  buttonText = clickedButton.getText();

        setTitle("You clicked " + buttonText);

    } else { //the event source is inputLine
        setTitle("You entered '" +
                            inputLine.getText() + "'");
    }
}
```

Notice that we can—but did not—write the else part as

```
JTextField textField = (JTextField) event.getSource();
setTitle("You entered '" + textField.getText() + "'");
```

because we know that the event source is inputLine in the else part. So we wrote it more succinctly as

```
setTitle("You entered '" + inputLine.getText() + "'");
```

Another approach to event handling is to associate a ButtonHandler (defined in Section 7.3) to the two button event sources and a TextHandler (need to add this new class) to the text field event source. This approach is left as an exercise.

Here's the complete Ch7TextFrame1 class:

```
/*
    Chapter 7 Sample Program: Displays a frame with two buttons,
                        and one text field

    File: Ch7TextFrame1.java
*/

import javax.swing.*;
import java.awt.*;
import java.awt.event.*;

class Ch7TextFrame1 extends JFrame implements ActionListener {

    private static final int FRAME_WIDTH    = 300;
    private static final int FRAME_HEIGHT   = 200;
```

```java
private static final int FRAME_X_ORIGIN = 150;
private static final int FRAME_Y_ORIGIN = 250;

private static final int BUTTON_WIDTH  = 80;
private static final int BUTTON_HEIGHT = 30;

private JButton cancelButton;
private JButton okButton;

private JTextField inputLine;

public static void main(String[] args) {
    Ch7TextFrame1 frame = new Ch7TextFrame1();
    frame.setVisible(true);
}

public Ch7TextFrame1() {
    Container contentPane;

    //set the frame properties
    setSize      (FRAME_WIDTH, FRAME_HEIGHT);
    setResizable (false);
    setTitle     ("Program Ch7SecondJFrame");
    setLocation  (FRAME_X_ORIGIN, FRAME_Y_ORIGIN);

    contentPane = getContentPane( );
    contentPane.setLayout( null );
    contentPane.setBackground( Color.white );

    //create and place two buttons on the frame
    okButton = new JButton("OK");
    okButton.setBounds(70, 125, BUTTON_WIDTH, BUTTON_HEIGHT);
    contentPane.add(okButton);

    cancelButton = new JButton("CANCEL");
    cancelButton.setBounds(160, 125, BUTTON_WIDTH, BUTTON_HEIGHT);
    contentPane.add(cancelButton);

    //register this frame as an action listener of the two buttons
    cancelButton.addActionListener(this);
    okButton.addActionListener(this);

    inputLine = new JTextField();
    inputLine.setBounds(90, 50, 130, 25);
    contentPane.add(inputLine);

    inputLine.addActionListener(this);

    //register 'Exit upon closing' as a default close operation
    setDefaultCloseOperation( EXIT_ON_CLOSE );
}
```

Adding the **inputLine** text field.

```
public void actionPerformed(ActionEvent event) {

    if (event.getSource() instanceof JButton) {
        JButton clickedButton = (JButton) event.getSource();

        String  buttonText = clickedButton.getText();

        setTitle("You clicked " + buttonText);

    } else { //the event source is inputLine
        setTitle("You entered '" + inputLine.getText() + "'");
    }
}
}
```

Now, let's add a JLabel object to the frame. In the Ch7TextFrame1 class, we have one text field without any indication what this text field is for. A JLabel object is useful in displaying a label that explains the purpose of the text field. Let's modify the Ch7TextFrame1 class by placing the label Please enter your name above the inputLine text field. We will call the modified class Ch7TextFrame2. We add the data member declaration

```
private JLabel prompt;
```

and create the object and position it in the constructor as

```
public Ch7TextFrame2 {
    . . .
    prompt = new JLabel( );
    prompt.setText("Please enter your name");
    prompt.setBounds(85, 20, 150, 25);
    contentPane.add(prompt);
    . . .
}
```

We can also set the text at the time of object creation as

```
prompt = new JLabel("Please enter your name");
```

ImageIcon

The JLabel class is not limited to the display of text. We can also use it to display an image. To display an image, we pass an **ImageIcon** object when we create a JLabel object instead of a string. To create this ImageIcon object, we must specify the filename of an image. In the Chapter 7 sample program folder, we put one image file named cat.gif. Notice that the program we are running, Ch7TextFrame2, and the image file are placed in the same directory. We can place the image file anywhere we want, but the way we write the code here requires the image file to be placed in

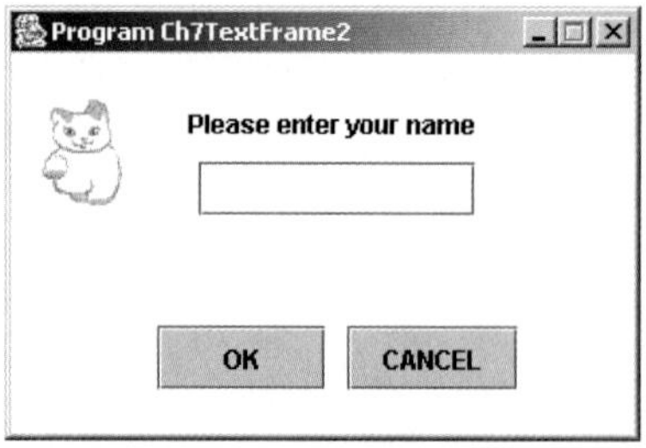

Figure 7.8 The **Ch7TextFrame2** window with one text **JLabel,** one image **JLabel,** one **JTextField,** and two **JButton** objects.

the same directory. We keep it this way to keep the code simple. We add the data member declaration

```
private JLabel image;
```

and then create it in the constructor as

```
public Ch7TextFrame2 {
    . . .
    image = new JLabel(new ImageIcon("cat.gif"));
    image.setBounds(10, 20, 50, 50);
    contentPane.add( image );
    . . .
}
```

Figure 7.8 shows the frame that appears on the screen when the program is executed. As the sample code shows, it is a simple matter to replace the image. All we have to do is to put the image we want in the right directory and refer to this image file correctly when creating a new ImageIcon object. When we use a different image, we have to be careful, however, to adjust the width and height values in the setBounds method so the values will be large enough to display the complete image.

Here's the Ch7TextFrame2 class (only the portion that is different from Ch7TextFrame1 is listed here):

```
/*
    Chapter 7 Sample Program: Displays a frame with two buttons,
                        one text field and one label

    File: Ch7TextFrame2.java
*/

import javax.swing.*;
import java.awt.*;
import java.awt.event.*;
```

```java
class Ch7TextFrame2 extends JFrame implements ActionListener {

    ...

    private JLabel prompt;
    private JLabel image;
    public static void main(String[] args) {
        Ch7TextFrame2 frame = new Ch7TextFrame2();
        frame.setVisible(true);
    }

    public Ch7TextFrame2() {
        ...

        prompt = new JLabel( );
        prompt.setText("Please enter your name");
        prompt.setBounds(85, 20, 150, 25);
        contentPane.add( prompt );

        image = new JLabel( new ImageIcon( "cat.gif" ) );
        image.setBounds(10, 20, 50, 50);
        contentPane.add(image);

        ...

    }

    ...

}
```

Now let's create the third example by using a JTextArea object. We will call the sample class Ch7TextFrame3. In this sample program, we will add two buttons labeled ADD and CLEAR, one text field, and one text area to a frame. When a text is entered in the text field and the ENTER (RETURN) key is pressed or the ADD button is clicked, the entered text is added to the list shown in the text area. Figure 7.9 shows the state of this frame after six words are entered.

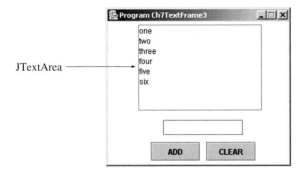

Figure 7.9 The state of a **Ch7TextFrame3** window after six words are entered.

We declare a JTextArea object textArea in the data member section as

```
private JTextArea textArea;
```

and add the statements to create it inside the constructor as

```
textArea = new JTextArea();
textArea.setBounds(50, 5, 200, 135);
textArea.setBorder(
            BorderFactory.createLineBorder(Color.red));
textArea.setEditable(false);
contentPane.add(textArea);
```

By default, unlike the single-line JTextField, the rectangle that indicates the boundary of a JTextArea object is not displayed on the frame. We need to create the border for a JTextArea object explicitly. The easiest way to do so is to call one of the class methods of the BorderFactory class. In the example, we called the createLineBorder method with a Color object as its argument. We passed Color.red so the red rectangle is displayed, as shown in Figure 7.9. The createLineBorder method returns a properly created Border object, and we pass this Border object to the setBorder method of the text area object. There are other interesting borders you might want to try. Table 7.1 lists other border types and the methods to create them. The API documentation of the BorderFactory class records more options and variations.

Table 7.1   **Border-creating methods of the** `javax.swing.BorderFactory` **class. The listed methods are all class methods.**

Some Class Methods of `javax.swing.BorderFactory`

`public static Border createEtchedBorder`
`        (java.awt.Color lineColor, java.awt.Color shadowColor)`
Creates an etched border with `lineColor` as line color and `shadowColor` as shadow color.

`public static Border createLoweredBevelBorder( )` Creates a border with a lowered beveled edge with a bright shade of the GUI object's current background color for line and dark shading for shadow. This border is effective when you change the background color of the GUI object.
`public static Border createRaisedBevelBorder( )` Creates a border with a raised beveled edge with a bright shade of the GUI object's current background color for line and dark shading for shadow. This border is effective when you change the background color of the GUI object.
`public static Border createTitledBorder(String title )` Creates a default (etched) border with `title` displayed at the left corner of the border.

In the sample frame, we do not want the user to edit the text displayed in the text area, so we disable editing by the statement

```
textArea.setEditable(false);
```

To add a text to the text area, we use the append method. Notice that we cannot use the setText method of JTextArea here because it will replace the old content with the new text. What we want here is to add new text to the current content. Also, since we need to add new text on a separate line, we need to output the new-line control character \n. Here's the basic idea for adding new text to the text area object textArea:

```
String enteredText = inputLine.getText();

textArea.append(enteredText + "\n");
```

Because the actual sequence of characters to separate lines is dependent on the operating systems, if we want to maintain consistent behavior across all operating systems, it is best to not use a fixed character such as \n. Instead, we should call the getProperty method of the System class, passing the string line.separator as an argument, to get the actual sequence of characters used by the operating system on which the program is being executed. We can define a class constant as

```
private static final String NEWLINE
                = System.getProperty("line.separator");
```

and use it in the program as

```
textArea.append(enteredText + NEWLINE);
```

Here's the Ch7TextFrame3 class:

```
/*
    Chapter 7 Sample Program: Displays a frame with two buttons,
                              one text field, and one text area

    File: Ch7TextFrame3.java
*/

import javax.swing.*;
import java.awt.*;
import java.awt.event.*;

class Ch7TextFrame3 extends JFrame implements ActionListener {

    private static final int FRAME_WIDTH    = 300;
    private static final int FRAME_HEIGHT   = 250;
    private static final int FRAME_X_ORIGIN = 150;
    private static final int FRAME_Y_ORIGIN = 250;
```

```java
private static final int BUTTON_WIDTH  = 80;
private static final int BUTTON_HEIGHT = 30;

private static final String EMPTY_STRING = "";
private static final String NEWLINE
                        = System.getProperty("line.separator");

private JButton    clearButton;
private JButton    addButton;
private JTextField inputLine;
private JTextArea  textArea;

public static void main(String[] args) {
    Ch7TextFrame3 frame = new Ch7TextFrame3();
    frame.setVisible(true);
}

public Ch7TextFrame3() {
    Container contentPane;

    //set the frame properties
    setSize      (FRAME_WIDTH, FRAME_HEIGHT);
    setResizable (false);
    setTitle     ("Program Ch7TextFrame3");
    setLocation  (FRAME_X_ORIGIN, FRAME_Y_ORIGIN);

    contentPane = getContentPane( );
    contentPane.setLayout( null );
    contentPane.setBackground( Color.white );

    //create and place two buttons on the frame
    addButton = new JButton("ADD");
    addButton.setBounds(70, 190, BUTTON_WIDTH, BUTTON_HEIGHT);
    contentPane.add(addButton);

    clearButton = new JButton("CLEAR");
    clearButton.setBounds(160, 190, BUTTON_WIDTH, BUTTON_HEIGHT);
    contentPane.add(clearButton);

    //register this frame as an action listener of the two buttons
    clearButton.addActionListener(this);
    addButton.addActionListener(this);

    inputLine = new JTextField();
    inputLine.setBounds(90, 155, 130, 25);
    contentPane.add(inputLine);

    inputLine.addActionListener(this);

    textArea = new JTextArea();
    textArea.setBounds(50, 5, 200, 135);
    textArea.setBorder(BorderFactory.createLineBorder(Color.red));
    textArea.setEditable(false);
    contentPane.add(textArea);
```

```
        //register 'Exit upon closing' as a default close operation
        setDefaultCloseOperation( EXIT_ON_CLOSE );
    }

    public void actionPerformed(ActionEvent event) {

        if (event.getSource() instanceof JButton) {
            JButton clickedButton = (JButton) event.getSource();

            if (clickedButton == addButton) {
                addText(inputLine.getText());
            } else {
                clearText( );
            }

        } else { //the event source is inputLine
            addText(inputLine.getText());
        }
    }

    private void addText(String newline) {
        textArea.append(newline + NEWLINE);
        inputLine.setText("");
    }

    private void clearText( ) {
        textArea.setText(EMPTY_STRING);
        inputLine.setText(EMPTY_STRING);
    }
}
```

Using a JScrollPane **to Add Scroll Bars Automatically**

When we run the Ch7TextFrame3 class and add more lines than the maximum number of lines the text area can display at once, what happens? Suppose the text area can display, say, 10 lines of text at once. Then we cannot see any text entered after the first 10 lines. Also, when we enter a line longer than the width of the text area, what happens? Likewise, any text that goes beyond the right boundary cannot be viewed. The easiest way to handle the situation is to wrap the text area with an instance of **javax.swing.JScrollPane** that adds the vertical and horizontal scroll bars when necessary.

JScrollPane

In the original Ch7TextFrame3 class, this is what we did to create and set the JTextArea object:

```
        textArea = new JTextArea();
        textArea.setBounds(50, 5, 200, 135);
        textArea.setBorder(
                    BorderFactory.createLineBorder(Color.red));
        textArea.setEditable(false);
        contentPane.add(textArea);
```

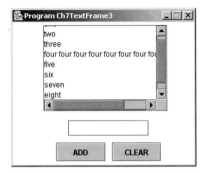

Figure 7.10 A sample **Ch7TextFrame3** window when the **JScrollPane** GUI object is used.

To add scroll bars that will appear automatically when needed, we replace the code with the following:

The scroll pane "wraps around" the text area.

```
textArea = new JTextArea();
textArea.setEditable(false);
JScrollPane scrollText= new JScrollPane(textArea);
scrollText.setBounds(50, 5, 200, 135);
scrollText.setBorder(
            BorderFactory.createLineBorder(Color.red));
contentPane.add(scrollText);
```

Notice that the properties, such as the border and bounds, of the JScrollPane object are set, no longer the properties of the JTextArea. Figure 7.10 shows a sample Ch7TextFrame3 object when the JScrollPane class is used.

Quick
CHECK

1. What is the purpose of the instanceof operator?
2. What user action will result in a JTextField object generating an action event?
3. Does a JLabel object generate an event?
4. What is the difference between textArea.setText("Hello") and textArea.append("Hello")?

7.5 | Menus

Practical programs with a graphical user interface will almost always support menus. In this section we will describe how to display menus and process menu events by using JMenu, JMenuItem, and JMenuBar from the javax.swing package. Figure 7.1 shows these objects. JMenuBar is a bar where the menus are placed. JMenu is a single menu in the JMenuBar. In Figure 7.1, we have two JMenu objects: File and Edit. JMenuItem is an individual menu choice in the JMenu. When a menu selection is made (e.g., selection of the item Cut under the Edit menu), a menu action event occurs. We process the menu selections by registering an action listener to menu items. Although it is more common to register one action listener to all menu items, we could register a different listener to individual menu items.

Let's write a sample code to illustrate the display of menus and the processing of menu item selections. We will create two menus, File and Edit, with the following menu items:

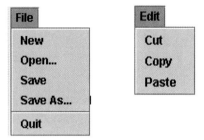

If the menu item Quit is selected, then we terminate the program. When a menu item other than Quit is selected, we print a message that identifies the selected menu item, for example,

```
Menu item 'New' is selected
```

Figure 7.11 shows a Ch7JMenuFrame when it is first opened and after the menu choice Save is selected.

One possible sequence of steps to create and add menus is this:

1. Create a JMenuBar object and attach it to a frame.
2. Create a JMenu object.
3. Create JMenuItem objects and add them to the JMenu object.
4. Attach the JMenu object to the JMenuBar object.

We will create two JMenu objects: fileMenu and editMenu. We create a fileMenu object as

```
fileMenu = new JMenu( "File" );
```

When the frame first
appears on the screen.

After the menu item
Save is selected.

Figure 7.11 **Ch7JMenuFrame** window when it is first opened and after the menu item **Save** is selected.

The argument to the JMenu constructor is the name of the menu. After the menu is created, we add a menu item to it. A menu item is the event source of menu selection, so we need to register an action listener to every menu item we add to the menu. In this sample code, we will let a Ch7JMenuFrame object be the action listener of all menu items. To create and add a menu item New to fileMenu, we execute

```
item = new JMenuItem("New");          //New
item.addActionListener( this );
fileMenu.add( item );
```

We repeat this sequence for all other menu items. Menu items are placed from the top in the order they are added to the menu. We can also include a horizontal line as a separator between menu items by calling the menu's addSeparator method

```
fileMenu.addSeparator();
```

After the menus and their menu items are created, we attach them to a menu bar. In the constructor, we create a JMenuBar object, attach it to the frame by calling the frame's setMenuBar method, and add these two JMenu objects to the menu bar.

```
JMenuBar menuBar = new JMenuBar();
setMenuBar(menuBar);                   //attach it to the frame
menuBar.add(fileMenu);
menuBar.add(editMenu);
```

To display which menu item was selected, we use a JLabel object response. We add response to the frame by

```
response = new JLabel("Hello, this is your menu tester.");
response.setBounds(100, 100, 250, 50);
contentPane.add(response);
```

When a menu item is selected, the registered action listener's actionPerformed method is called. The actionPerformed method of the Ch7JMenuFrame is defined as follows: If an event source is a menu item, the getActionCommand method of ActionEvent returns the menu's text. We test if the returned text is Quit. If it is, we terminate the program. Otherwise, we set the text of response to indicate which menu item was selected. Here's the method body of actionPerformed:

```
String       menuName;

menuName = event.getActionCommand();

if ( menuName.equals("Quit") ) {
   System.exit(0);

} else {
   response.setText("Menu item '" + menuName +
                    "' is selected");

}
```

Here's the complete Ch7JMenuFrame program:

```
/*
    Chapter 7 Sample Program: Displays a frame with two menus

    File: Ch7JMenuFrame.java
*/

import javax.swing.*;
import java.awt.*;
import java.awt.event.*;

class Ch7JMenuFrame extends JFrame implements ActionListener {

    private static final int FRAME_WIDTH    = 300;
    private static final int FRAME_HEIGHT   = 250;
    private static final int FRAME_X_ORIGIN = 150;
    private static final int FRAME_Y_ORIGIN = 250;

    private JLabel   response;
    private JMenu    fileMenu;
    private JMenu    editMenu;

//------------------------------
//      Main method
//------------------------------
    public static void main(String[] args) {
        Ch7JMenuFrame frame = new Ch7JMenuFrame();
        frame.setVisible(true);
    }

    public Ch7JMenuFrame(){
        Container contentPane;

        //set the frame properties
        setTitle      ("Ch7JMenuFrame: Testing Swing Menus");
        setSize       (FRAME_WIDTH, FRAME_HEIGHT);
        setResizable (false);
        setLocation  (FRAME_X_ORIGIN, FRAME_Y_ORIGIN);

        contentPane = getContentPane( );
        contentPane.setLayout(null);
        contentPane.setBackground( Color.white );

        //create two menus and their menu items
        createFileMenu();
        createEditMenu();

        //and add them to the menubar
        JMenuBar menuBar = new JMenuBar();
```

```
        setJMenuBar(menuBar);
        menuBar.add(fileMenu);
        menuBar.add(editMenu);

        //create and position response label
        response = new JLabel("Hello, this is your menu tester." );
        response.setBounds(50, 50, 250, 50);
        contentPane.add(response);

        setDefaultCloseOperation(EXIT_ON_CLOSE);
    }

    public void actionPerformed(ActionEvent event) {
        String  menuName;

        menuName = event.getActionCommand();

        if (menuName.equals("Quit")) {
            System.exit(0);

        } else {
            response.setText("Menu Item '" + menuName + "' is selected.");
        }
    }

    private void createFileMenu( ) {
        JMenuItem    item;

        fileMenu = new JMenu("File");

        item = new JMenuItem("New");        //New
        item.addActionListener( this );
        fileMenu.add( item );

        item = new JMenuItem("Open...");    //Open...
        item.addActionListener( this );
        fileMenu.add( item );

        item = new JMenuItem("Save");       //Save
        item.addActionListener( this );
        fileMenu.add( item );

        item = new JMenuItem("Save As..."); //Save As...
        item.addActionListener( this );
        fileMenu.add( item );

        fileMenu.addSeparator();            //add a horizontal separator line

        item = new JMenuItem("Quit");       //Quit
        item.addActionListener( this );
        fileMenu.add( item );
    }

    private void createEditMenu( ) {
        JMenuItem    item;
```

```
editMenu = new JMenu("Edit");

item = new JMenuItem("Cut");         //Cut
item.addActionListener( this );
editMenu.add( item );

item = new JMenuItem("Copy");        //Copy
item.addActionListener( this );
editMenu.add( item );

item = new JMenuItem("Paste");       //Paste
item.addActionListener( this );
editMenu.add( item );
    }
}
```

Take my
Advice

If the size of text for the response label is too small, then we can make it bigger by including the following statement in the constructor:

```
response.setFont( new Font("Helvetica", /*font name*/
                           Font.BOLD,    /*font style*/
                           16 ) );       /*font size*/
```

Quick
CHECK

1. To which object do we register an action listener—JMenu, JMenuItem, or JMenuBar?
2. How do we get the text of a selected menu item in the **actionPerformed** method?
3. How do we place a horizontal bar between two menu items?

7.6 Sample Development

HiLo Game with GUI

In Chapter 6, we developed a program that plays the Hi-Lo game. We will reimplement the program by adding a customized graphical user interface. Instead of using a generic **JOptionPane** for the user interface, we will implement a customized **JFrame** for playing the HiLo game. With the inclusion of the customized frame, we must redesign the control logic of playing the game. The control we used for the Chapter 6

7.6 **Sample Development**—*continued*

program-
driven
control

event-
driven
control

HiLo program can be described as program-driven. With the *program-driven control*, the control logic is explicitly written inside the program. If we look at the **playGame** method of the **Ch6HiLo** class, we see the repetition control (the **do–while** statement) that implements the logic of playing one HiLo game. We will reimplement the program, using the event-driven control. With the *event-driven control*, our code will implement the event listeners and include methods that will be executed in response to the events. There will be no explicit repetition control (such as **while, do–while,** or **for**) inside our program.

Problem Statement

Reimplement the HiLo program with a graphical user interface and event-driven control logic.

Overall Plan

We implemented the complete HiLo program in just one class in Chapter 6. Using one class to implement the whole program is acceptable only for a very small program or as an illustration of key concepts while we are learning programming. For any real program, we will need multiple classes with each class implementing a single well-defined task. We mentioned the importance of this design philosophy at the beginning of this chapter. We will now implement the HiLo program using multiple classes, with each class handling one specific task.

What are the major tasks for this program? The first major task is the user interface. We need some form of user interface to interact with the player. The second major task is the playing of the game. We need a logic object to generate secret numbers, determine whether the guess is low or high, and declare the win or loss. We'll define a class for each task. The first class handles the graphical user interface and the second class the logic of playing one HiLo game. In addition to these two classes, we expect to use the **JOptionPane** class for message and confirmation dialogs, so we'll include it in our working design document. We'll begin our development with these classes.

Here's our working design document:

program
classes

Design Document: `HiLo`

Class	Purpose
`Ch7HiLoFrame`	This class supports the GUI of the program. This is the instantiable main class.
`Ch7HiLo`	This class handles the logic of playing the HiLo game. An instance of this class works under the control of GUI.
`JOptionPane`	This service class is for handling the message and confirmation dialogs.

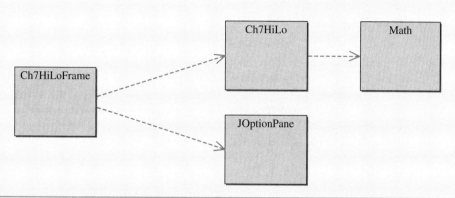

Figure 7.12 The working program diagram for the HiLo program. The **JOptionPane** class and an instance of the **Ch7HiLo** class provide the necessary service in support of the GUI object **Ch7HiLoFrame.**

The working program diagram is shown in Figure 7.12.

We will implement the program in four steps:

development steps

1. Start with a skeleton frame class **Ch7HiLoFrame** with menus.

2. Design and implement the visual layout of GUI objects on the frame.

3. Design and implement the game-playing logic class **Ch7HiLo**. Make necessary modifications to the other classes.

4. Finalize the code and make improvements wherever appropriate.

Step 1 Development: Skeleton Frame Class

step 1 design

We will establish the foundation for the whole development in step 1. We begin with the core object that controls other objects and classes in the program. For a GUI-based program, it is very common to provide menu choices and let the top-level frame handle the menu selections. Menu items are action event sources, and we'll make the frame event handler for menu selections. The class definition would look as follows:

```
class Ch7HiLoFrame extends JFrame
                        implements ActionListener {
    . . .
}
```

What menu choices should we provide? We will begin with a few basic ones and consider adding more menu choices later. Let's include two menus: **Game** and **Help.** Under the **Game** menu, we will put two menu items: **New** to begin a new game and **Quit** to exit the program. Under the **Help** menu, we will put two menu items also: **Game Rules** to present the game rules and **About** . . . to display brief information about the program. We will define a temporary **actionPerformed** method to terminate the program when the menu item Quit is selected and to display the label of the selected item on **System.out** when other menu items are selected.

step 1 code

The step 1 **Ch7HiLoFrame** class can be modeled after the **Ch7JMenuFrame** class because they are identical in structure. One minor difference between the two lies in how the private methods for creating menus are implemented. Instead of referring to the data members as in the **Ch7JMenuFrame** class, the menu-creating private methods in **Ch7HiLoFrame** return a **JMenu** object. Here's the complete listing of the class:

```java
/*
    Chapter 7 Sample Development: HiLo Game

    File: Step1/Ch7HiLoFrame.java

*/

import javax.swing.*;
import java.awt.*;
import java.awt.event.*;

class Ch7HiLoFrame extends JFrame implements ActionListener {

    private static final int FRAME_WIDTH    = 300;
    private static final int FRAME_HEIGHT   = 250;
    private static final int FRAME_X_ORIGIN = 150;
    private static final int FRAME_Y_ORIGIN = 250;

//------------------------
//      Main method
//------------------------
    public static void main(String[] args) {
        Ch7HiLoFrame frame = new Ch7HiLoFrame();
        frame.setVisible(true);
    }

    public Ch7HiLoFrame() {
        Container contentPane;

        //set the frame properties
        setTitle     ("Let's Play HiLo");
        setSize      (FRAME_WIDTH, FRAME_HEIGHT);
        setResizable (false);
        setLocation  (FRAME_X_ORIGIN, FRAME_Y_ORIGIN);
```

```
        contentPane = getContentPane( );
        contentPane.setBackground( Color.white );

        //and add them to the menubar
        JMenuBar menuBar = new JMenuBar();
        setJMenuBar(menuBar);
        menuBar.add(createGameMenu());
        menuBar.add(createHelpMenu());

        setDefaultCloseOperation(EXIT_ON_CLOSE);
    }

    public void actionPerformed(ActionEvent event) {
        String   menuName;

        menuName = event.getActionCommand();

        if (menuName.equals("Quit")) {
           System.exit(0);

        } else {
         System.out.println("Menu Item '" + menuName + "' is selected.");
        }
    }

    private JMenu createGameMenu( ) {
        JMenuItem    item;

        JMenu menu = new JMenu("Game");

        item = new JMenuItem("New");        //New
        item.addActionListener( this );
        menu.add( item );

        menu.addSeparator();            //add a horizontal separator line

        item = new JMenuItem("Quit");       //Quit
        item.addActionListener( this );
        menu.add( item );

        return menu;
    }

    private JMenu createHelpMenu( ) {
        JMenuItem    item;

        JMenu menu = new JMenu("Help");

        item = new JMenuItem("Game Rules");      //Game Rules
        item.addActionListener( this );
        menu.add( item );
```

7.6 **Sample Development**—*continued*

```
        menu.addSeparator();

        item = new JMenuItem("About...");       //About...
        item.addActionListener( this );
        menu.add( item );

        return menu;
    }
}
```

step 1 test

Testing the skeleton **Ch7HiLoMainControl** class is straightforward. We run the program and select all menu choices. We verify that all selections are handled in the expected manner before continuing. Figure 7.13 shows the state after three menu choices are selected.

Step 2 Development: Visual Layout of GUI Objects

step 2 design

After the skeleton frame with menus is done, we're ready to add some GUI objects to handle user interaction. Which GUI components shall we use? We need a text field to let the player enter the guess and a label to display the response. We will put in a couple of buttons: one to submit the guess and another to cancel the guess. We will lay out these GUI components as shown in Figure 7.14. Their names and the classes they belong to are identified in the figure.

Figure 7.13 Test running the step 1 program. The screen shot shows the state after three menu choices were selected.

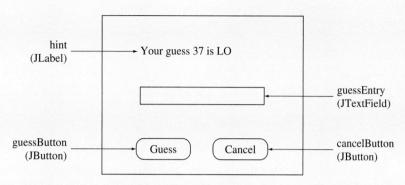

Figure 7.14 The layout of GUI objects on the HiLo frame.

We will make the frame also the action listener of two buttons and one text field. This complicates the **actionPerformed** method slightly because we must differentiate three types of event sources. We will define three private methods, one for each type of event source, and name them **processMenuAction, processTextField-Action,** and **processButtonAction.** The modified **actionPerformed** method is written as follows:

```
public void actionPerformed(ActionEvent event) {

    String command = event.getActionCommand();
    if (event.getSource() instanceof JMenuItem) {
        processMenuAction(command);

    } else if (event.getSource() instanceof JTextField) {
        processEnterAction(command);

    } else { //event source is a button
        processButtonAction(command);
    }
}
```

Notice the **getActionCommand** method returns the menu item name when the event source is **JMenuItem,** the content of the text field when the event source is **JTextField,** and the label of the button when the event source is **JButton.**

The **processMenuAction** method responds to menu selections. The method is defined as

```
private void processMenuAction(String menuName) {

    if (menuName.equals("Quit")) {

        System.exit(0);

    } else if (menuName.equals("New")) {

        newGame();
```

7.6 **Sample Development**—*continued*

```
    } else if (menuName.equals("Game Rules")) {

        describeGame();

    } else if (menuName.equals("About...")) {

        aboutProgram();
    }
}
```

The three methods **newGame, describeGame,** and **aboutProgram** are stubs with temporary code. We will work on them in the later development steps.

The **processEnterAction** method responds to the pressing of the **ENTER (RETURN)** key when the text field is active. When this action event occurs, we need to retrieve the content of the text field and check it against the secret number. Since the **getText** method of the text field returns a **String** object, we need to convert the content to an integer before checking the guess against the secret number. The actual checking will be done by the logic object **Ch7HiLo,** so here we only write the code to convert the content to an integer and display this number with a temporary message **You entered <value>,** where **<value>** is the actual value entered by the player. We will replace this message later with the real message such as **Your guess 45 is LO.** If the content of the text field is empty, that is, the **getText** method returns an empty **String,** then we will display an error message using **JOptionPane.** Here's the method:

```
private static final String BLANK = "";
...

private void processEnterAction(String entry) {

    if (entry.equals(BLANK)) {
        JOptionPane.showMessageDialog(this,
                    "Error: No guess was entered");

    } else {

        int input = Integer.parseInt(entry);
        hint.setText("You entered " + input);  //TEMP

        System.out.println("Guess: " + input); //TEMP
    }
}
```

We add this statement here so we can see all entered values in the standard output window

The **processButtonAction** method responds to the clicking of the two buttons. When the **Guess** button is clicked, we need to retrieve the content of the text field and check it against the secret number. This response is the same as the one for the action event of the text field, so we will call the **processEnterAction.** When the **Cancel** button is clicked, all we need to do is to clear the current content of the text field. Here's the method:

```java
private static final String GUESS = "Guess";
...

private void processButtonAction(String buttonText) {

    if (buttonText.equals(GUESS)) {

        processEnterAction(guessEntry.getText());

    } else {//cancel button

        processCancelAction( );
    }

}

private void processCancelAction( ) {
    guessEntry.setText(BLANK);
}
```

We have now completed the step 2 design.

step 2 code

Here's the step 2 **Ch7HiLoFrame** class (we use three dots ... for the parts that remain unchanged):

```java
/*
    Chapter 7 Sample Development: HiLo Game

    File: Step2/Ch7HiLoFrame.java

*/

import javax.swing.*;
import java.awt.*;
import java.awt.event.*;

class Ch7HiLoFrame extends JFrame implements ActionListener {

    ...

    private static final int BUTTON_WIDTH  = 80;
    private static final int BUTTON_HEIGHT = 30;

    private static final String GUESS = "Guess";
    private static final String CANCEL = "Cancel";
    private static final String BLANK = "";
```

7.6   Sample Development—*continued*

```java
    private JTextField guessEntry;
    private JLabel     hint;
    private JButton    cancelButton;
    private JButton    guessButton;

//----------------------------
//      Main method
//----------------------------
    public static void main(String[] args) {
        Ch7HiLoFrame frame = new Ch7HiLoFrame();
        frame.setVisible(true);
    }

    public Ch7HiLoFrame() {
        ...

        addComponents(contentPane);

        ...
    }

    public void actionPerformed(ActionEvent event) {

        String command = event.getActionCommand();

        if (event.getSource() instanceof JMenuItem) {
            processMenuAction(command);

        } else if (event.getSource() instanceof JTextField) {
            processEnterAction(command);

        } else { //event source is a button
            processButtonAction(command);
        }
    }

    private void addComponents(Container contentPane) {

        contentPane.setLayout(null);

        //create and place two buttons on the frame
        guessButton = new JButton(GUESS);
        guessButton.setBounds(55, 150, BUTTON_WIDTH, BUTTON_HEIGHT);
        contentPane.add(guessButton);

        cancelButton = new JButton(CANCEL);
        cancelButton.setBounds(165, 150, BUTTON_WIDTH, BUTTON_HEIGHT);
        contentPane.add(cancelButton);
```

```
        guessEntry = new JTextField();
        guessEntry.setBounds(90, 90, 130, 25);
        contentPane.add(guessEntry);

        hint = new JLabel( );
        hint.setText("Let's play HiLo");
        hint.setBounds(90, 45, 150, 25);
        contentPane.add(hint);

        //register this frame as an action listener of the event sources
        cancelButton.addActionListener(this);
        guessButton.addActionListener(this);
        guessEntry.addActionListener(this);
    }

    private JMenu createGameMenu( ) {
        ...
    }

    private JMenu createHelpMenu( ) {
        ...
    }

    private void processButtonAction(String buttonText) {

        if (buttonText.equals(GUESS)) {

            processEnterAction(guessEntry.getText());

        } else {//cancel button

            processCancelAction( );
        }
    }

    private void processCancelAction( ) {
        guessEntry.setText(BLANK);
    }

    private void processEnterAction(String entry) {

        if (entry.equals(BLANK)) {
            JOptionPane.showMessageDialog(this,
                        "Error: No guess was entered");

        } else {

            int input = Integer.parseInt(entry);
            hint.setText("You entered " + input);  //TEMP
```

```
                System.out.println("Guess: " + input); //TEMP
        }
    }

    private void processMenuAction(String menuName) {

        if (menuName.equals("Quit")) {

            System.exit(0);

        } else if (menuName.equals("New")) {

            newGame();

        } else if (menuName.equals("Game Rules")) {

            describeGame();

        } else if (menuName.equals("About...")) {

            aboutProgram();
        }
    }

    private void aboutProgram( ) {
      JOptionPane.showMessageDialog(this, "HiLo Program version 1.01");
                                                                //TEMP
    }

    private void describeGame( ) {
      JOptionPane.showMessageDialog(this, "Describe Game Rules"); //TEMP
    }

    private void newGame( ) {
        JOptionPane.showMessageDialog(this, "Starts a New Game"); //TEMP
    }
}
```

step 2 test   We run the **Ch7HiLoFrame** class and check the visual appearance. If the GUI components do not appear as we wished, we adjust the arguments for the **setBounds** methods until we get what we want. We then test the event-handling routines. We select all menu items, click both buttons, and press the **ENTER** key when the text field is active. We test the **ENTER** action with and without typing in the guess to verify that both cases are handled correctly. They all work fine except for one minor point. The value entered in the text field remains there, so the player has to erase the previous entry before entering the next guess. It would work better if the content of the text field were erased after each guess. To implement this behavior, we need to add a single statement to the **processEnterAction** method as follows:

```
private void processEnterAction(String entry) {

    if (entry.equals(BLANK)) {
        JOptionPane.showMessageDialog(this,
                    "Error: No guess was entered");

    } else {

        int input = Integer.parseInt(entry);

        guessEntry.setText(BLANK); //erase entry

        hint.setText("You entered " + input); //TEMP

        System.out.println("Guess: " + input); //TEMP
    }
}
```

Added statement → `guessEntry.setText(BLANK); //erase entry`

The final step 2 code reflects this change in the source file. Figure 7.15 shows the output displayed by the final step 2 program after we entered five guesses.

Step 3 Development: Add the Ch7HiLo Class

step 3 overall design

In step 3 of development, we add the class whose instance will handle the playing of one game of HiLo. What kind of service should a **Ch7HiLo** object provide to its client (in this program the client is a **Ch7HiLoFrame** object because it is the one that uses the service of a **Ch7HiLo** object)?

Figure 7.15 Sample output of the step 2 **Ch7HiLoFrame** program after five guesses are entered.

Every time there's a new guess, we want a **Ch7HiLo** to tell **Ch7HiLoFrame** whether the guess is low, high, or a match. Also, a **Ch7HiLo** must be able to detect when the maximum number of guesses allowed is made. Let's define a method called **nextGuess** to handle this request. To provide this service, the object must keep track of several pieces of information, such as the secret number, the minimum and maximum bounds for the guess, the number of guesses allowed, and the number of guesses made so far. Data members are used to keep track of this information, and the data are initialized in a constructor.

Last, we need a method to reset the data members of **Ch7HiLo.** When a **Ch7HiLo** object is created, the data members are initialized to play a game. To play another game after one game is over, these data members must be reset to their initial values. We will define a method called **newGame** to reset the data members. Notice that if we create a new instance of **Ch7HiLo** for each new game we play, then the **newGame** method is not necessary. However, it is more natural for a single **Ch7HiLo** object to be able to play multiple games.

The initial design document is as follows:

Design Document: The Ch7HiLo Class		
Method	**Visibility**	**Purpose**
<constructors>	public	Creates and initializes a Ch7HiLo object.
nextGuess	public	Checks the next guess and returns the result.
newGame	public	Resets a Ch7HiLo object for a new game.

We will complete step 3 in two substeps:

3.1 Start with the skeleton **Ch7HiLo** class. Define constructors and the **newGame** method to initialize an instance to a valid state ready to play a game. Define data members and modify the existing classes as necessary.

3.2 Implement the **nextGuess** method. Modify the existing classes as necessary.

Step 3.1 Development: Skeleton Ch7HiLo

step 3.1 design

Let's begin the design of the class with its constructors and data members. By using the default constructor, a **Ch7HiLo** object is created with default values for the low and high bounds of a guess and the number of guesses allowed. We define constants for these default values:

```
private static final int DEFAULT_LOW    =   1;
private static final int DEFAULT_HIGH    = 100;
```

Since the low and high bounds of a guess and the number of guesses allowed are different for each **HiLo** object, we need a data member for each of these values. Also, we have to keep track of number of guesses made and the secret number for each game. The data members are declared as

```
private int numberOfGuessesAllowed;
private int guessLowBound;
private int guessHighBound;

private int guessCount;
private int secretNumber;
```

We will use the technique of defining one constructor that initializes the object and having all other constructors directly or indirectly call this constructor. This constructor accepts three arguments: low bound, high bound, and number of guesses allowed. Is the following an acceptable way to define this?

```
public Ch7HiLo( int low, int high, int numberOfGuesses ) {
    guessLowBound = low;
    guessHighBound = high;
    numberOfGuessesAllowed = numberOfGuesses;
}
```

This allows no rooms for mistakes. We must aim to make the class as robust as possible. What would happen if the programmer got confused and switched the low and high bounds by mistake? What would happen if the programmer passed a nonpositive number as the third argument? When an invalid value is passed to the constructor, we will initialize the data members by using this rule:

```
if ( low > high ) {
    //switch the low and high
}

if ( numberOfGuesses <= 0 ) {
    //if the given numberOfGuesses is invalid
    //derive the value from the given low and high
    numberOfGuessesAllowed = maxGuess( low, high );
}

//assign arguments to data members
```

The private **maxGuess** method determines the number of guesses allowed based on the low and high bounds. The idea is to derive a formula to compute the maximum number of allowed guesses based on the valid range of a guess, so that we allow more guesses when a range is bigger and fewer guesses when a range is smaller. What kind of formula should it be?

If we always use the middle value of low and high bounds as the next guess, we can make a correct guess in at most N tries, where N is derived as

$$N = \lceil \log_2 (high - low + 1) \rceil$$

For example, if the low is **1** and high is **100**, then *N* is **7**. Our first guess is 50. If this guess is, say, low, then our next guess is 75. We continue in this manner, and the maximum number of times we need to guess the number is 7. Try it. The basic idea behind this formula is that we cannot divide 100 more than 7 times before the range of values where the secret number is located becomes empty.

Since the **Math** class does not support the logarithm to base 2, we need to convert the formula to the logarithm to base 10:

$$N = \lceil \log_2(\text{high} - \text{low} + 1) \rceil$$

$$= \left\lceil \frac{\log_{10}(\text{high} - \text{low} + 1)}{\log_{10}(2)} \right\rceil$$

Note:
$$\log_a b = \frac{\log_c b}{\log_c a}$$

Expressing the formula in a Java statement, we have

```
Math.ceil( Math.log( high - low + 1 ) / Math.log( 2 ) )
```

We will define two additional constructors. The second constructor accepts two arguments—low and high bounds—we call the three-argument constructor as

```
public Ch7HiLo(int low, int high) {
    this( low, high, maxGuess(low, high));
}
```

As noted in Chapter 4, in order for this call to work correctly, the **maxGuess** method must be a class method (i.e., with the **static** modifier). When the statement that calls another constructor via the reserved word **this** is complete, an instance of the class is created, and therefore, we can call instance methods after this statement without any problem. In this case, however, the call to **maxGuess** is made before an instance is created. Notice that the call to **maxGuess** must return before the call to the three-argument constructor can be made because the value returned by **maxGuess** is an argument we pass to the three-argument constructor. Since there is no instance when the call to **maxGuess** is made, the **maxGuess** method must be declared as a class method.

Helpful Reminder

*Before an instance of the class is created, we can only call class methods (methods with the **static** modifier).*

The last constructor is the default constructor with no argument. The default constructor will call the two-argument constructor as

```
this(DEFAULT_LOW, DEFAULT_HIGH);
```

When a new instance of **Ch7HiLo** is created, it must be in a valid state, ready to start playing a game. We decided that a single **Ch7HiLo** object can play multiple games, but we have not yet decided which parameters can be changed when playing a new game. For example, should we allow the values for the low and high bounds of guesses to be changed? For this development, we will not allow any changes to the game condition (maximum number of guesses allowed, low and high bound of guesses, etc.). Since there will be no changes to the game condition once a **Ch7HiLo** object is created, for each new game we only need to reset the guess counter **guessCount** to **0** and generate a new secret number. The **newGame** method will do this resetting, and the constructor will call the **newGame** method so the object is ready to play when it is first created.

step 3.1
code

Here's the step 3.1 **Ch7HiLo** class:

```
/*
    Chapter 7 Sample Development: HiLo Game (Step 3.1)

    File: Step3/Step3.1/Ch7HiLo.java
*/

import javax.swing.*;

class Ch7HiLo {

    private static final int DEFAULT_LOW   = 1;                  Data members
    private static final int DEFAULT_HIGH  = 100;

    private int    numberOfGuessesAllowed;
    private int    guessLowBound;
    private int    guessHighBound;
    private int    guessCount;
    private int    secretNumber;

    public Ch7HiLo( ) {                                          Constructors
        this(DEFAULT_LOW, DEFAULT_HIGH);
    }

    public Ch7HiLo(int low, int high) {
        this(low, high, maxGuess(low, high));
    }

    public Ch7HiLo(int low, int high, int numGuess) {
        if (low > high) {
            int temp = low;
            low = high;
            high = temp;
        }
```

7.6 **Sample Development**—*continued*

```
        if (numGuess <= 0) {
            numGuess = maxGuess(low, high);
        }

        guessLowBound  = low;
        guessHighBound = high;
        numberOfGuessesAllowed = numGuess;

        newGame();

        System.out.println("low bound:    " + guessLowBound);     //TEMP
        System.out.println("high bound:   " + guessHighBound);    //TEMP
        System.out.println("max guesses:  " + numberOfGuessesAllowed);
        System.out.println("secretNumber: " + secretNumber);      //TEMP
        System.out.println("    ");                               //TEMP
    }

    public void newGame () {                          [ newGame ]
        guessCount = 0;
        secretNumber = getRandomNumber( );

        System.out.println("Inside newGame. Secret number = "
                                            + secretNumber);
    }

    private int getRandomNumber() {                   [ getRandomNumber ]
        double x;
        int    number;

        x = Math.random();

        number = (int) Math.floor(x * (guessHighBound -
                          guessLowBound + 1)) +
                          guessLowBound;

        return number;
    }

    private static int maxGuess(int low, int high) {
        return (int) Math.ceil(Math.log(high - low + 1) / Math.log(2));
    }
}
```

Here's the modified **Ch7HiLoFrame** class. We add a new data member to refer to a **Ch7HiLo** object and modify the **newGame** method.

```
/*
    Chapter 7 Sample Development: HiLo Game

    File: Step3/Step3.1/Ch7HiLoFrame.java

*/

import javax.swing.*;
import java.awt.*;
import java.awt.event.*;

class Ch7HiLoFrame extends JFrame implements ActionListener {

    private Ch7HiLo     hiLo;

    public Ch7HiLoFrame() {
        . . .

        //create the game-playing logic object
        hiLo = new Ch7HiLo();
    }

    . . .

    private void newGame( ) {
        JOptionPane.showMessageDialog(this, "Starts a New Game"); //TEMP

        hiLo.newGame();
    }
}
```

step 3.1 test   We run the main class and verify that the expected messages are displayed from the temporary output statements. We select the **New** menu choice and verify the expected result. Figure 7.16 shows the output from a sample test run.

Notice that the main class creates an instance of **Ch7HiLo** by calling the default constructor only. To test the **Ch7HiLo** class further, we will perform unit testing, where we test the class individually. The following is a simple main class for unit testing the **Ch7HiLo** class:

```
class TestCh7HiLo {

    public static void main(String[] args) {

        Ch7HiLo hilo;

        hilo = new Ch7HiLo();
```

7.6   Sample Development—*continued*

```
    hilo = new Ch7HiLo(200, 300);

    hilo = new Ch7HiLo(1, 200, 5);

    hilo.newGame();
    hilo.newGame();
  }
}
```

The fact that we can unit-test the **Ch7HiLo** class shows the high degree of its modularity. It is an indication of poor design if a unit test cannot be performed with relative ease. Running this test main class results in an output similar to the one shown in Figure 7.17 (since we are using a random number generator, the actual values we see would be different for every run).

Step 3.2 Development: Implement the nextGuess Method

step 3.2
design

Our next task is to implement the logic of playing a game. The key methods in this step are the private **processNextGuess** method in **Ch7HiLoFrame** and the **nextGuess** method in **Ch7HiLo.** We will implement these two methods in this step. To see how the two methods fit in the whole program, let's study the sequence of calls from the point

Figure 7.16 An output from a test run of the step 3.1 **Ch7HiLoFrame** program. The output shows the state after the menu choice **New** is selected three times. Note that the program is ready to play the first game when it is created. We need to select the menu choice **New** from the second game.

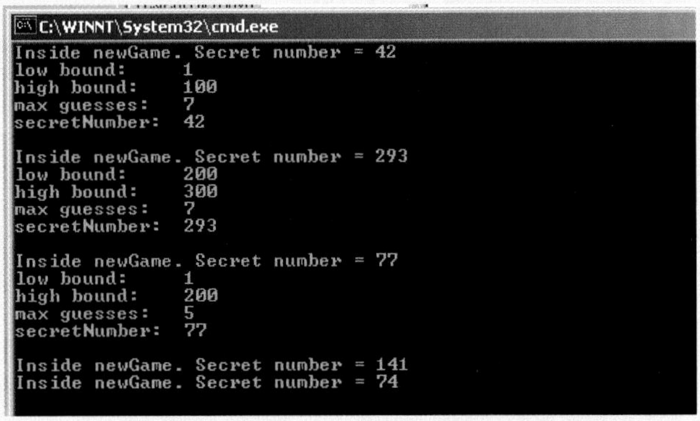

Figure 7.17 The output from a sample test run of **TestCh7HiLo.** Since a random number generator is used, the actual values will be different for each test run.

where the player enters a guess to the point where the response is displayed. Here's the sequence:

1. The end user enters a guess (a valid input value). This generates an action event that results in calling the frame's **processEnterAction** method.

2. The **processsEnterAction** method calls the private **processNextGuess** method (which belongs to the same class **Ch7HiLoFrame**).

3. This **processNextGuess** method calls the **nextGuess** method of **Ch7HiLo.** The value returned by the **nextGuess** method determines the message we display to the player, and whether the game is over or not.

In the **actionPerformed** method, we replace the statement

```
hint.setText("You entered " + input);
```

by

```
processNextGuess(input);
```

The **processNextGuess** method calls the **nextGuess** method of **Ch7HiLo,** passing the player's guess as its argument. The **nextGuess** method will reply with a result. What would be the possible result? We could easily think of at least three possible outcomes: the guess is low, the guess is high, and the guess is correct. What should be the data type for this result? One possibility is a **String.** The method can return **String** values such as **LO, HI,** and **BINGO.** Although the use of a **String** is a very general way of passing information back, it is also error-prone. It is very easy for the programmer to make a mistake and compare the string **HI** against **Hi,** for example. When the number of values to return from a method is only a handful or less, then using a simple integer is a better choice. By declaring public class constants for each of the possible return values, we can reduce programmer errors. We will declare the constants as

```
public static final int HI = 1;
public static final int LO = 2;
//and so forth
```

Will there be other possible outcomes returned by the **nextGuess** method? Since we have a **Ch7HiLo** object that keeps track of the number of guesses the user has made, the **nextGuess** method should return a fourth value—**GAMEOVER**—when the allowed number of guesses is made without guessing correctly. In addition, we will define a fifth value—**INVALID**—that is returned by **nextGuess** when the guess is outside the valid range of low (**guessLowBound**) and high (**guessHighBound**) bounds.

Here's how we will implement the **nextGuess** method:

```
public int nextGuess (int userGuess) {
    int status;

    guessCount++;

    if (userGuess == secretNumber) {

        status = BINGO;

    } else if (guessCount == numberOfGuessesAllowed) {

        status = GAMEOVER;

    } else if (!isValid(userGuess)) {

        status = INVALID;

    } else if (userGuess < secretNumber) {

        status = LO;

    } else {
        status = HI;
    }

    return status;
}

private boolean isValid(int guess) {
    boolean status;

    status = guessLowBound <= guess
            && guess <= guessHighBound;

    return status;
}
```

Given this **nextGuess** method, how can we define the **processNextGuess** method? Based on the value returned by **nextGuess,** the **processNextGuess** will display an appropriate message to the player. Here's the general idea:

```
switch (hilo.nextGuess(guess)) {

    case Ch7HiLo.LO:
            //the guess is low
            break;

    case Ch7HiLo.HI:
            //the guess is high
            break;

    case Ch7HiLo.GAMEOVER:
            //the player lost the game
            break;

    case Ch7HiLo.BINGO:
            //the player won the game
            break;

    case Ch7HiLo.INVALID:
            //the guess is invalid
            break;
}
```

When the guess is low or high, we can inform the player with a simple response such as

```
37 is LO
```

or

```
89 is HI
```

The response we display when a game is over or a guess is invalid, however, should be a little more informative, such as

```
You Lose! Secret number was 49.
```

or

```
INVALID. Valid guess must be in the range [10, 60].
```

To provide an informative display, we need to access information such as the secret number, the lower and upper bounds of the guesses, and the number of guesses made from a **Ch7HiLo** object. To make necessary information accessible, we will define a number of accessors (**getSecretNumber, getLowBound,** etc.) to the **Ch7HiLo** class.

step 3.2
code

Here's the final **Ch7HiLo** class:

```
/*
    Ch 7 Sample Program: HiLo

    File: Step3/Step3.2/Ch7HiLo.java
*/

class Ch7HiLo {
    public static final int INVALID  = -1;
    public static final int HI       = 1;
    public static final int LO       = 2;
    public static final int BINGO    = 3;
    public static final int GAMEOVER = 4;

    ...

    public int getHighBound( ) {
        return guessHighBound;
    }

    public int getLowBound( ) {
        return guessLowBound;
    }

    public int getMaxGuess( ) {
        return numberOfGuessesAllowed;
    }

    public int getSecretNumber( ) {
        return secretNumber;
    }

    public int nextGuess ( int userGuess ) {
        int status;

        guessCount++;

        if (userGuess == secretNumber) {

            status = BINGO;

        } else if (guessCount == numberOfGuessesAllowed) {

            status = GAMEOVER;

        } else if (!isValid(userGuess)) {

            status = INVALID;
```

Data members

getHighBound

getLowBound

getMaxGuess

getSecretNumber

nextGuess

```
        } else if (userGuess < secretNumber) {

            status = LO;

        } else {
            status = HI;
        }

        return status;
    }

    private boolean isValid(int guess) {
        boolean status;

        status = guessLowBound <= guess && guess <= guessHighBound;

        return status;
    }
    ...
}
```

isValid

And here's the step 3.2 **Ch7HiLoFrame** class:

```
/*
    Chapter 7 Sample Development: HiLo Game

    File: Step3/Step3.2/Ch7HiLoFrame.java
*/

import javax.swing.*;
import java.awt.*;
import java.awt.event.*;

class Ch7HiLoFrame extends JFrame implements ActionListener {

    ...

    private void processEnterAction(String entry) {

        if (entry.equals(BLANK)) {
            JOptionPane.showMessageDialog(this,
                        "Error: No guess was entered");

        } else {
```

processEnterAction

```
              int input = Integer.parseInt(entry);
              guessEntry.setText(BLANK);

              processNextGuess(input);

              System.out.println("Guess: " + input); //TEMP
          }
      }
      ...

  private void processNextGuess(int guess) {

      // System.out.println("next guess " + guess); //TEMP

      switch (hiLo.nextGuess(guess)) {

          case Ch7HiLo.LO:
                  hint.setText(guess + " is LO");
                  break;

          case Ch7HiLo.HI:
                  hint.setText(guess + " is HI");
                  break;

          case Ch7HiLo.GAMEOVER:
                  hint.setText("You Lost (secret="
                                      + hiLo.getSecretNumber() + ")");
                  break;

          case Ch7HiLo.BINGO:
                  hint.setText("BINGO! You Won");
                  break;

          case Ch7HiLo.INVALID:
                  hint.setText("INVALID. Valid range is [" +
                                      hiLo.getLowBound() + ", " +
                                      hiLo.getHighBound() + "]");
                  break;
      }
  }
  ...
}
```

processNextGuess

step 3.2 test   We run the **Ch7HiLoFrame** class and verify the expected behavior. We play many games and verify the correct responses from the program, especially the cases when the player loses or wins the game. We select the **New** menu choice and verify everything is reset properly for playing the next game.

The program works correctly for the most part, but there's a slight problem after a game is over. The current implementation allows the player to continue entering new guesses even after a game is over. The program will make a response, but such response is meaningless once the game is finished. What we need to do is to disable the input routine when a game is over and reactivate the routine when the player selects the **New** menu choice. How can we disable the input routine so the player cannot enter new guesses when a game is over? There are three possible ways to achieve this.

The first way is to remove the listeners from the event sources. For example, to remove the action event listener **this** from a **JButton** named **guessButton,** we write

```
guessButton.removeActionListener(this);
```

The second way is to disable the event sources by calling the **setEnabled** method with **false** as an argument. For example, to disable **guessButton,** we write

```
guessButton.setEnabled(false);
```

We call the same method with **true** as an argument to enable the button again. GUI objects are enabled by default when they are first created. Figure 7.18 is a **Ch7HiLoFrame** with the **Guess** button disabled.

The third way is to maintain a boolean data member, say, **active.** When a **Ch7HiLoFrame** object is created, we initialize **active** to **true.** When a certain condition occurs (such as a game is over), we set **active** to **false.** We set **active** back to **true** every time a new game is started. We can use the data member **active** in the **action-Performed** method.

```
public void actionPerformed(ActionEvent event) {

    String command = event.getActionCommand();

    if (event.getSource() instanceof JMenuItem) {
        processMenuAction(command);

    } else {

        if (!active) return;

        if (event.getSource() instanceof JTextField) {
            processEnterAction(command);

        } else { //event source is a button
            processButtonAction(command);
        }
    }
}
```

Exit from the method when **active** is **false**

Notice that we are not disabling the response to the menu events. We are only disabling the response to the text field and button events when **active** is **false.**

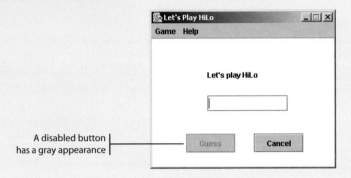

A disabled button
has a gray appearance

Figure 7.18 Ch7HiLoFrame with the disabled **Guess** button.

Any one of the three approaches will work, but in this case the third one is the best. If we want to enable or disable GUI objects individually, either the first or the second would work better. But here we want to disable or enable the response to the buttons and the text field as a group, so keeping a single data member to disable and enable them as a single unit is a preferred approach. Here's the final step 3.2 **Ch7HiLoFrame** class that includes the disabling and enabling of the input routine using a boolean data member **active:**

```
/*
    Chapter 7 Sample Development: HiLo Game

    File: Step3/Step3.2/Ch7HiLoFrame.java

*/

import javax.swing.*;
import java.awt.*;
import java.awt.event.*;

class Ch7HiLoFrame extends JFrame implements ActionListener {

    ...

    private boolean    active;                    Data members

    public Ch7HiLoFrame() {                        Constructors
        ...

        setActive(true);
    }
```

```java
public void actionPerformed(ActionEvent event) {

    if (!active) return;

    String command = event.getActionCommand();

    if (event.getSource() instanceof JMenuItem) {
        processMenuAction(command);

    } else if (event.getSource() instanceof JTextField) {
        processEnterAction(command);

    } else { //event source is a button
        processButtonAction(command);
    }
}

private void processNextGuess(int guess) {

    // System.out.println("next guess " + guess); //TEMP

    switch (hiLo.nextGuess(guess)) {

        case Ch7HiLo.LO:
                hint.setText(guess + " is LO");
                break;

        case Ch7HiLo.HI:
                hint.setText(guess + " is HI");
                break;

        case Ch7HiLo.GAMEOVER:
                hint.setText("You Lost (secret="
                                + hiLo.getSecretNumber() + ")");
                setActive(false);
                break;

        case Ch7HiLo.BINGO:
                hint.setText("BINGO! You Won");
                setActive(false);
                break;

        case Ch7HiLo.INVALID:
                hint.setText("INVALID. Valid range is [" +
                                hiLo.getLowBound() + ", " +
                                hiLo.getHighBound() + "]");
                break;
    }
}
```

actionPerformed

processNextGuess

7.6 **Sample Development**—*continued*

```
    private void setActive(boolean state) {
        active = state;
    }

    ...

    private void newGame( ) {
        JOptionPane.showMessageDialog(this, "Starts a New Game"); //TEMP
        hiLo.newGame();
        setActive(true);
        hint.setText(BLANK);
    }
}
```

setActive

newGame

Finally, as we did in the step 3.1 testing phase, we will test the **Ch7HiLo** class fully with a unit testing. The key operation we want to test here is, of course, the **nextGuess** method. Here's one possible class for unit-testing the **Ch7HiLo** class:

```
/**
 * A main class to unit test the Step 3.2 HiLo class.
 * Test the nextGuess method.
 */
class TestCh7HiLo {

    public static void main(String[] args) {

        Ch7HiLo hiLo;

        int low = 200;
        int high = 500;

        hiLo = new Ch7HiLo(low, high);

        int status;
        int guess = (low + high) / 2;

        do {
            status = hiLo.nextGuess(guess);

            switch (status) {
```

```
        case Ch7HiLo.LO:
            System.out.println("Guess: " + guess + "  status = LO");
            low = guess;
            break;

        case Ch7HiLo.HI:
            System.out.println("Guess: " + guess + "  status = HI");
            high = guess;
            break;

        case Ch7HiLo.GAMEOVER:
            System.out.println("Guess: " + guess + " status = GAMEOVER");
            break;

        case Ch7HiLo.BINGO:
            System.out.println("Guess: " + guess + "  status = BINGO");
            break;

        case Ch7HiLo.INVALID:
            System.out.println("Guess: " + guess + "  status = INVALID");
            break;
        }

        guess = (low + high) / 2;

    } while (status != Ch7HiLo.GAMEOVER && status != Ch7HiLo.BINGO);
    }
}
```

We will run this main class many times with different parameters for **low** and **high** to improve our level of confidence in the program's correctness.

Step 4 Development: Finalize

code
review

As always, we will perform a *code review* of the classes, looking for any unfinished methods. There are two unfinished methods in the **Ch7HiLoMainControl** class: **aboutProgram** and **describeGame.** Most commercial application software open a small window with a short description about the program when the user selects the menu choice **About.** The final **aboutProgram** method should open such a description window. Instead of using a customized format for the help system, more and more commercial application software programs are now using the standard HTML format. Among the many benefits, a major one is the capability of adding hyperlinks in the document. By placing a hyperlink to the company's website, users can easily get the most up-to-date information by following the hyperlink. Step 4 **Ch7HiLoFrame** uses a **MiniBrowser** object, introduced in Chapter 2, to display the game rules. The sample HTML file named **gamerules.html** is provided in the step 4 directory.

code
improve-
ment

Images, if used effectively, can spruce up the visual appearance of the user inter-face. This is called *code improvement*. Instead of allowing only plain text for hints, let's allow the addition of an image. We will define two **showResponse** methods:

```java
public void showResponse(String response) {

    hint.setText(response);
    hint.setIcon(null); //remove any leftover icon from
                        //the previous showResponse if any
}

public void showResponse(String response, ImageIcon image){
    hint.setText(response);
    hint.setIcon(image);
    hint.setHorizontalTextPosition(SwingConstants.LEFT);
                    //place text left of image
}
```

We provide two image files, **hi.gif** and **lo.gif,** in the step 4 directory. The **processNextGuess** method of the step 4 **Ch7HiLoFrame** class is modified so the the second version of **showResponse** is called when the guess is low or high. In case the guess is high, the call is

```java
showResponse(guess + " is", hiImg);
```

where **hiImg** is a new data member of type **ImageIcon** and created in the constructor as

```java
hiImg = new ImageIcon("hi.gif");
```

An analogous modification is made to handle the case when the guess is low. For all other cases, we still display text only, so the first version is called.

Here's the improved **Ch7HiLoFrame** class in its entirety (minus javadoc comments):

```java
/*
    Chapter 7 Sample Development: HiLo Game

    File: Step4/Ch7HiLoFrame.java
*/

import javax.swing.*;
import java.awt.*;
import java.awt.event.*;
```

```java
class Ch7HiLoFrame extends JFrame implements ActionListener {

    private static final int FRAME_WIDTH    = 300;
    private static final int FRAME_HEIGHT   = 250;
    private static final int FRAME_X_ORIGIN = 150;
    private static final int FRAME_Y_ORIGIN = 250;

    private static final int BUTTON_WIDTH  = 80;
    private static final int BUTTON_HEIGHT = 30;

    private static final String GUESS = "Guess";
    private static final String CANCEL = "Cancel";
    private static final String BLANK = "";

    private JTextField guessEntry;
    private JLabel     hint;
    private JButton    cancelButton;
    private JButton    guessButton;

    private Ch7HiLo    hiLo;

    private boolean    active;

    private ImageIcon    hiImg;
    private ImageIcon    loImg;

//---------------------------------
//      Main method
//---------------------------------
    public static void main(String[] args) {
        Ch7HiLoFrame frame = new Ch7HiLoFrame();
        frame.setVisible(true);
    }

    public Ch7HiLoFrame() {
        Container contentPane;

        //set the frame properties
        setTitle      ("Let's Play HiLo");
        setSize       (FRAME_WIDTH, FRAME_HEIGHT);
        setResizable (false);
        setLocation  (FRAME_X_ORIGIN, FRAME_Y_ORIGIN);

        contentPane = getContentPane( );
        contentPane.setBackground( Color.white );
        addComponents(contentPane);

        //and add them to the menubar
        JMenuBar menuBar = new JMenuBar();
```

Data members

Constructors

```
        setJMenuBar(menuBar);
        menuBar.add(createGameMenu());
        menuBar.add(createHelpMenu());

        setDefaultCloseOperation(EXIT_ON_CLOSE);

        //create the game-playing logic object
        hiLo = new Ch7HiLo();

        setActive(true);

        //set the image icons for response
        hiImg = new ImageIcon("hi.gif");
        loImg = new ImageIcon("lo.gif");
    }

    public void actionPerformed(ActionEvent event) {
```
> **actionPerformed**
```
        String command = event.getActionCommand();

        if (event.getSource() instanceof JMenuItem) {
            processMenuAction(command);

        } else {

            if (!active) return;

            if (event.getSource() instanceof JTextField) {
                processEnterAction(command);

            } else { //event source is a button
                processButtonAction(command);
            }
        }
    }

    private void addComponents(Container contentPane) {
```
> **addComponents**
```
        contentPane.setLayout(null);

        //create and place two buttons on the frame
        guessButton = new JButton(GUESS);
        guessButton.setBounds(55, 150, BUTTON_WIDTH, BUTTON_HEIGHT);
        contentPane.add(guessButton);

        cancelButton = new JButton(CANCEL);
        cancelButton.setBounds(165, 150, BUTTON_WIDTH, BUTTON_HEIGHT);
        contentPane.add(cancelButton);
```

```
        guessEntry = new JTextField();
        guessEntry.setBounds(90, 90, 130, 25);
        contentPane.add(guessEntry);

        hint = new JLabel( );
        hint.setText("Let's play HiLo");
        hint.setBounds(90, 45, 150, 30);
        contentPane.add(hint);

       //register this frame as an action listener of the event sources
        cancelButton.addActionListener(this);
        guessButton.addActionListener(this);
        guessEntry.addActionListener(this);
    }

    private JMenu createGameMenu( ) {
        JMenuItem    item;

        JMenu menu = new JMenu("Game");

        item = new JMenuItem("New");          //New
        item.addActionListener( this );
        menu.add( item );

        menu.addSeparator();          //add a horizontal separator line

        item = new JMenuItem("Quit");        //Quit
        item.addActionListener( this );
        menu.add( item );

        return menu;
    }

    private JMenu createHelpMenu( ) {
        JMenuItem    item;

        JMenu menu = new JMenu("Help");

        item = new JMenuItem("Game Rules");       //Game_Rules
        item.addActionListener( this );
        menu.add( item );

        menu.addSeparator();

        item = new JMenuItem("About...");    //About...
        item.addActionListener( this );
        menu.add( item );

        return menu;
    }
```

createGameMenu

createHelpMenu

7.6 **Sample Development**—*continued*

```java
    private void processButtonAction(String buttonText) {

        if (buttonText.equals(GUESS)) {

            processEnterAction(guessEntry.getText());

        } else {//cancel button

            processCancelAction( );
        }
    }

    private void processCancelAction( ) {
        guessEntry.setText(BLANK);
    }

    private void processEnterAction(String entry) {

        if (entry.equals(BLANK)) {
            JOptionPane.showMessageDialog(this,
                        "Error: No guess was entered");

        } else {

            int input = Integer.parseInt(entry);
            guessEntry.setText(BLANK);

            processNextGuess(input);
        }
    }

    private void processMenuAction(String menuName) {

        if (menuName.equals("Quit")) {

            System.exit(0);

        } else if (menuName.equals("New")) {

            newGame();

        } else if (menuName.equals("Game Rules")) {

            describeGame();

        } else if (menuName.equals("About...")) {

            aboutProgram();
        }
    }
```

processButtonAction

processCancelAction

processEnterAction

processMenuAction

```
private void processNextGuess(int guess) {

    switch (hiLo.nextGuess(guess)) {

        case Ch7HiLo.LO:
                showResponse(guess + " is", loImg);
                break;

        case Ch7HiLo.HI:
                showResponse(guess + " is", hiImg);
                break;

        case Ch7HiLo.GAMEOVER:
                showResponse("You Lost (secret="
                                + hiLo.getSecretNumber() + ")");
                setActive(false);
                break;

        case Ch7HiLo.BINGO:
                showResponse("BINGO! You Won");
                setActive(false);
                break;

        case Ch7HiLo.INVALID:
                showResponse("INVALID. Valid range is [" +
                                hiLo.getLowBound() + ", " +
                                hiLo.getHighBound() + "]");
                break;
    }
}
```

processNextGuess

```
private void setActive(boolean state) {
    active = state;
}
```

setActive

```
private void aboutProgram( ) {
   JOptionPane.showMessageDialog(this, "HiLo Program version 1.01");
                                                      //TEMP
}
```

aboutProgram

```
private void describeGame( ) {
   //!!!!!!!!!!!!!!!!!!!!!!!!!!
   // WARNING: You must change the file path to reflect your
   //          directory organization!!!
   //!!!!!!!!!!!!!!!!!!!!!!!!!!

   MiniBrowser browser = new MiniBrowser(
                "file://N:/Programs/CS1ThirdEdSamplePrograms" +
                        "/Chapter7/Step4/gamerules.html");
```

describeProgram

```
      browser.setVisible(true);
   }

   private void newGame( ) {
      JOptionPane.showMessageDialog(this, "Starts a New Game"); //TEMP
      hiLo.newGame();
      setActive(true);
      hint.setText(BLANK);
   }

   public void showResponse(String response) {

      hint.setText(response);
      hint.setIcon(null); //remove any leftover icon
                          //from the showResponse

   }

   public void showResponse(String response, ImageIcon image) {
      hint.setText(response);
      hint.setIcon(image);
      hint.setHorizontalTextPosition(SwingConstants.LEFT);
                       //place text left of image
   }
}
```

> newGame

> showResponse

Summary

- The type of user interface covered in this chapter is called a *graphical user interface* (GUI).
- GUI objects in the javax.swing package are collectively called *Swing classes*.
- To program the customized user interface effectively, we must learn a new style of programming control called *event-driven programming*.
- The GUI and related classes and interfaces introduced in this chapter are

JFrame	Container
JButton	ImageIcon
ActionListener	BorderFactory
ActionEvent	JScrollPane
JLabel	JMenuBar
JTextField	JMenu
JTextArea	JMenuItem

- We often define a subclass of JFrame as the top-level main window of a program.

- A subclass is defined by using inheritance.

- GUI objects such as buttons and text fields are placed on the content pane of a frame window.

- The layout manager determines the placement of the GUI objects.

- GUI objects can be placed on the content pane without using any layout manager. Such placement is called *absolute positioning*.

- Event handling is divided into event sources and event listeners. Event sources generate events, and event listeners include a method that gets executed in response to the generated events.

- The most common event type is called an *action event*.

- We can find out the class to which an object belongs by using the instanceof operator.

- We use an instance of JButton to represent a pushbutton on a frame. JButton objects generate action events.

- GUI objects dealing with text are JLabel, JTextfield, and JTextArea. JTextField objects generate action events.

- A JLabel object can include an image of type ImageIcon.

- A Java interface is a reference data type that includes only constants and abstract methods.

- A frame has one JMenuBar object. A single JMenuBar can have many JMenu objects with many JMenuItem objects associated to a single JMenu object.

- JMenuItem objects generate action events.

Key Concepts

graphical user interface

Swing classes

inheritance

content pane

null layout manager

absolute positioning

events

event-driven programming

event sources

event listeners

Java interface

instanceof operator

buttons

menus

Exercises

1. Define a subclass of JFrame and name it Ch7Q1Frame. Set the subclass so its instances will be 400 pixels wide and 450 pixels high and will have a blue background. The program terminates when the Close box is clicked.

2. Define a JFrame subclass that has four vertically aligned buttons. The labels for the four buttons are Senior, Junior, Sophomore, and Freshman. This is one possible layout:

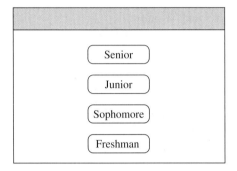

When a button is clicked, display a message that identifies which button is clicked, using JOptionPane.

3. In the Ch7TextFrame1 class, event handling was done with this class. Modify the class so the button events are handled by a ButtonHandler and the text events are handled by a TextHandler. You can use the ButtonHandler class defined in the chapter, but you need to define your own TextHandler class.

4. Modify the Ch7HiLoFrame class so the user has the option of quitting the game. Add a button Give Up to the frame. When the user clicks on this button, display the secret number and the number of guesses the user has made. Then reset the frame for a new game.

5. Write a MyMenuFrame class with these menu choices.

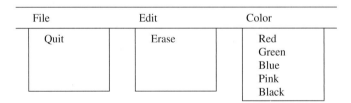

When the user selects Quit, stop the program. When the user selects one of the colors, change the background of the frame (i.e., change the background color of the frame's content pane) to the selected color. When the user selects Erase, reset the background color to white.

6. Extend the Ch7HiLoFrame class to include a list of guesses made by the player. Use a JTextArea object to list the history of guesses. This is one possible layout.

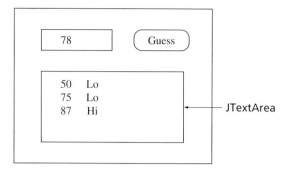

7. Using the same frame layout created in Exercise 6, write a program that displays *N* prime numbers, where *N* is a value entered in the text field. A *prime number* is an integer greater than 1 and divisible only by itself and 1.

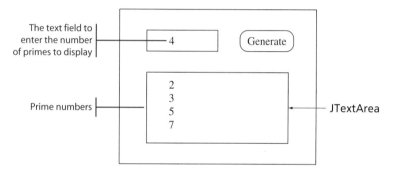

8. Define an OutputBox class as a subclass of JFrame. The OutputBox class provides the functionality of System.out (PrintStream) by supporting these methods:

```
public void println(String line)
public void print(String text)
```

The OutputBox class contains one JTextArea object. Do not use absolute positioning. Use the default layout and add a JScrollPane that wraps the JTextArea object to the content pane.

9. Redo Exercise 19 on page 376 but this time use the OutputBox class created in Exercise 8 for output.

10. A slugging percentage of a baseball player is computed by dividing the total bases of all hits by the total times at bat (single = 1 base, double = 2 bases, triple = 3 bases, and home run = 4 bases). Write an application that computes the slugging percentage. Create a customized frame and use JTextField objects to accept five input values: number of singles, number of doubles, number of triples, number of home runs, and number of times at bat. When the user clicks the Compute button, display the slugging percentage, using JLabel.

11. Write a program that draws a selected geometric shape in random color and at a random location. The menu choices for the program are

```
Shape
    Circle
    Rectangle
    Square
```

12. Write a graphical user interface for the slot machine program in Exercise 32 on page 380. Use three JLabel objects for displaying bells, grapes, and cherries. Add a button that simulates the motion of pulling down the handle.

13. Add images to the Exercise 12 solution. Create three gif files, one each for the bell, grape, and cherry. Use JLabel objects with ImageIcon to display these images on the frame.

Development Exercises

For Exercises 14 through 19, use the incremental development methodology to implement the program. For each exercise, identify the program tasks, create a design document with class descriptions, and draw the program diagram. Map out the development steps at the start. Present any design alternatives and justify your selection. Be sure to perform adequate testing at the end of each development step.

14. Write a TeachArithmeticFrame class that teaches children arithmetic. The frame uses a JLabel for a problem and a JTextField for the user answer. When the user presses the ENTER key (while the JTextField object is active) or clicks the OK button, display a message stating whether the user's answer is correct. When the Next button is clicked, display a new problem. The numbers are limited to two digits.

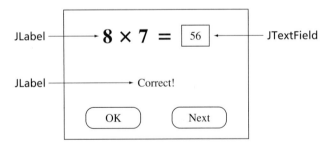

Consider using a larger font for the JLabel and JTextField text. You can change the color of text by calling the setForeground method, for example.

```
questionLbl.setForeground(Color.red);
```

Define a helper class that generates problems.

15. Extend the TeachArithmeticFrame class so that the numbers of correct and incorrect answers are kept. Display these two numbers somewhere on the frame. Add the third button labeled Reset. When this button is clicked, the counters for correct and incorrect answers are reset to zero.

16. Modify Exercise 16 in Chapter 6 by providing a customized graphical user interface.

17. Modify the mortgage table program of Exercise 30 in Chapter 6. Add this menu

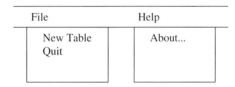

to the program. When the user selects the menu choice New Table, the program opens another frame in which the user can enter three input values. The input frame should look something like this:

Loan Amount:

Interest Rate:

Loan Period:

Cancel   Compute

If the user clicks on the Compute button and the three input values are valid, generate a mortgage table. Use the OutputBox class from Exercise 8 to display the mortgage table. If the input values are invalid, then print out an appropriate error message. Decide on the range of valid values for the loan amount, interest rate, and loan period. When the user selects the menu choice About . . . , describe the purpose of the program by using another frame. You should create only one input frame, but may decide to use more than one OutputBox frame so you can see multiple loan tables at once.

18. (Challenge) Write a class that implements a calculator with the layout similar to this:

The user enters a number, using digit buttons only. Some of the issues you need to consider:

- How to determine whether the user is entering a left operand or a right operand.
- How to handle the entering of multiple decimal points. A typical calculator accepts the first decimal point and ignores the rest. For example, if you press 1 . 4 . 3 . , the number entered is 1.43.
- When the display is 0 and the user enters 0, the display will not change. However, if the display is nonzero and the user enters 0, the 0 is appended to the number currently displayed.
- How to handle the operator precedence. For example, what will be the result if the user enters 4 + 3 × 2? Will it be 14 or 10? It is easier to treat all operators as having equal precedence and process them from left to right.

Study any real four-function calculator and try to implement a software calculator that simulates the real calculator as faithfully as possible, but feel free to make any reasonable changes.

19. Extend the calculator of Exercise 18 to allow the user to enter a number by using the keyboard. The class needs to implement the KeyListener interface and define the keyTyped method. You have to find information on KeyListener and KeyEvent from a Java API reference manual.

8 Exceptions and Assertions

Objectives

After you have read and studied this chapter, you should be able to

- Improve the reliability of code by incorporating exception-handling and assertion routines.

- Write methods that propagate exceptions.

- Implement the **try-catch** blocks for catching and handling the thrown exceptions.

- Write programmer-defined exception classes.

- Distinguish between the checked and unchecked, or runtime, exceptions.

- Use assertions in methods to increase the chance of detecting bugs during the development.

- Construct a program using the supervisor-subordinate design pattern.

hen someone says his or her program is reliable, what do we expect from the program? The majority of people would probably reply correctness as the most important criterion in determining the reliability of a program. When a program is claimed to be reliable, we certainly expect the program will produce correct results for all valid input. It is hardly a reliable program if it produces correct results only for some input values. As we all know by now, writing a correct program is easier said than done. If we are not diligent and careful enough, we can easily introduce bugs in our programs. And more often than not, we fail to eradicate them. A mechanism called an *assertion,* a new feature from Java 2 SDK 1.4, can be used to improve the likelihood of catching logical errors during the development. We will introduce assertions in this chapter and show how to use them effectively in our programs.

assertion

Program correctness guarantees the correct results for all valid input. But what happens when the input is invalid? Another important criterion of program reliability is the robustness, which measures how well the program runs under various conditions. If a program crashes too easily when a wrong type of argument is passed to a method or an invalid input value is entered, we cannot say the program is very reliable. A mechanism called *exception handling* can be used to improve the program's robustness. We briefly introduced the notion of exceptions and exception handling in Chapter 3 when we explained the console input using System.in. In this chapter, we will provide a full discussion of the exception-handling mechanism in Java.

exception handling

Last, as the programs we develop continue to grow in size and complexity, we need to introduce design patterns which will aid us in developing large programs. In Section 8.7, we will introduce a design pattern which we characterize as a *supervisor-subordinate pattern.* In this design pattern, we define a supervisor object that controls subordinate objects. Each subordinate is programmed to perform a single well-defined task, and by managing these subordinates the supervisor fulfills the program requirements. The supervisor and its subordinate "talk" to each other by calling each other's methods. To make such a two-way communication link possible, we need to establish mutual references between the supervisor and its subordinate. We will use this design pattern in developing the sample program in Section 8.8.

8.1 | Catching Exceptions

In Chapters 5 and 6 we presented two types of control flows: selection control and repetition control. Using these control structures, we alter the default sequential flow of control. We use a selection control to select and execute one block of code out of many choices, and we use a repetition control to execute a block of code repeatedly until certain conditions are met. The exception-handling mechanism can be viewed as another form of control structure. An *exception* represents an error condition that can occur during the normal course of program execution. When an exception occurs, the normal sequence of flow is terminated and the exception-handling routine is executed. When an exception occurs, we say an exception is *thrown.*

exception

When the matching exception-handling code is executed, we say the thrown exception is *caught*. By using exception-handling routines judiciously in our code, we can increase its robustness. In this section, we will show how the thrown exceptions can be caught and processed.

We have been dealing with exceptions all along. For example, consider this code:

```
String inputStr = JOptionPane.showInputDialog(null,"");
int    number  = Integer.parseInt(inputStr);
```

What would happen if we entered, say, abc123, an input value that cannot be converted to an int? We would get an error message such as

```
java.lang.NumberFormatException: abc123
    at java.lang.Integer.parseInt(Integer.java:405)
    at java.lang.Integer.parseInt(Integer.java:454)
    at Ch8Sample1.main(Ch8Sample1.java:20)
```

This error message indicates the system has caught an exception called Number-FormatException, an error that occurs when we try to convert a string that cannot be converted to a numerical value. Up until now, we have let the system handle the thrown exceptions. However, when we let the system handle the exceptions, a single thrown exception most likely will result in erroneous results or a program termination. Instead of depending on the system for exception handling, we can increase the program's reliability and robustness if we catch the exceptions ourselves by including error recovery routines in our program.

Let's begin with a short program to illustrate the exception-handling mechanism. We will define a service class that supports a method to input a person's age. This class is mainly for the illustrative purpose of introducing the exception-handling concept. We first define it without exception handling and then improve it gradually by adding exception-handling features. Because we will be defining many different versions of the class, we will name them AgeInputVer1, AgeInputVer2, and so forth. Here's the AgeInputVer1 class without exception handling:

```
/*
    Chapter 8 Sample Class: Class to input age

    File: AgeInputVer1.java
*/

import javax.swing.*;

class AgeInputVer1 {

    private static final String DEFAULT_MESSAGE = "Your age:";

    public AgeInputVer1( ) {

    }
```

```
    public int getAge() {

        return getAge(DEFAULT_MESSAGE);
    }

    public int getAge(String prompt) {

        String inputStr = JOptionPane.showInputDialog(null, prompt);
        int age = Integer.parseInt(inputStr);
        return age;
    }
}
```

Using this service class, we can write a program that gets a person's age and replies with the year in which the person was born. Notice the program takes into consideration whether the person already had a birthday this year. Here's the program:

```
/*
    Chapter 8 Sample Program: Input a person's age

    File: Ch8AgeInputMain.java

*/

import javax.swing.*;
import java.util.*;

class Ch8AgeInputMain {

    public static void main( String[] args ) {

        GregorianCalendar today;
        int                 age, thisYear, bornYr, answer;

        AgeInputVer1 input = new AgeInputVer1( );
        age   = input.getAge("How old are you?");

        today     = new GregorianCalendar( );
        thisYear = today.get(Calendar.YEAR);

        bornYr   = thisYear - age;

        answer = JOptionPane.showConfirmDialog(null,
                            "Already had your birthday this year?",
                            "",
                            JOptionPane.YES_NO_OPTION);
```

```
            if (answer == JOptionPane.NO_OPTION) {
                bornYr--;
            }

            JOptionPane.showMessageDialog(null, "You are born in " + bornYr);
        }
    }
```

The program works fine as long as valid input is entered. But what would happen if the user spelled out the age, say, nine instead of 9? A number format exception is thrown because the input value nine cannot be converted to an integer by using the parseInt method. With the current implementation, the system will handle the thrown exception by displaying the error message

```
java.lang.NumberFormatException: nine
    at java.lang.Integer.parseInt(Integer.java:405)
    at java.lang.Integer.parseInt(Integer.java:454)
    at AgeInput.getAge(AgeInput.java:46)
    at Ch8AgeInputMain.main(Ch8AgeInputMain.java:24)
```

and terminating the program. It would be a much better program if we could handle the thrown number format exception ourselves. Let's modify the getAge method so that it will loop until a valid input that can be converted to an integer is entered. To do this, we need to wrap the statements that can potentially throw an exception with the **try-catch** control statement. In this example, there's only one statement that can potentially throw an exception, namely,

try-catch

```
int age = Integer.parseInt(inputStr);
```

We put this statement inside the try block and the statements we want to be executed in response to the thrown exception in the matching catch block. If we just want to display an error message when the exception is thrown, then we can write the try-catch statement as follows:

```
inputStr = JOptionPane.showInputDialog(null, prompt);

try {

    int age = Integer.parseInt(inputStr);

} catch (NumberFormatException e) {

    JOptionPane.showMessageDialog(null, "'" + inputStr
                                        + "' is invalid\n"
                                        + "Please enter digits only");
}
```

A statement that
could throw an
exception

The type of exception
to be caught

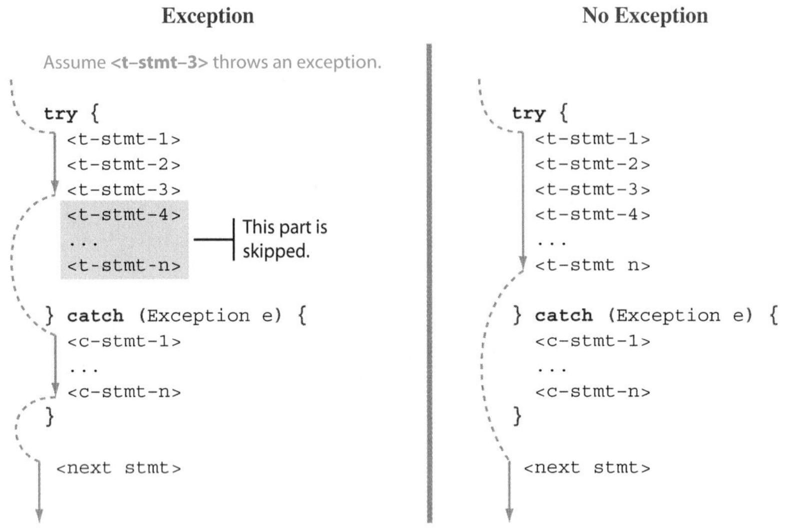

Figure 8.1 Two possible control flows of the **try-catch** statement with one **catch** block. Assume **\<t-stmt-3\>** throws an exception.

Statements in the try block are executed in sequence. When one of the statements throws an exception, then control is passed to the matching catch block and statements inside the catch block are executed. The execution next continues to the statement that follows this try-block statement, ignoring any remaining statements in the try block. If no statements in the try block throw an exception, then the catch block is ignored and execution continues with the statement that follows this try-catch statement. Figure 8.1 shows the two possible control flows: one when an exception is thrown and another when no exceptions are thrown.

In the sample code, we have only one statement in the try block. If the conversion does not throw an exception, then we want to exit from the method and return the integer. If there's an exception, we display an error message, using the showMessageDialog inside the catch block, and repeat the input routine. To accomplish this repetition, we will put the whole try-catch statement inside a loop:

```java
public int getAge (String prompt) {

    String inputStr;
    int     age;
    boolean keepGoing = true;

    while (keepGoing) {
        inputStr = JOptionPane.showInputDialog(null, prompt);
        try {
            age = Integer.parseInt(inputStr);
            keepGoing = false; //input okay so stop looping

        } catch (NumberFormatException e) {
```

This statement is executed only if no exception is thrown by **parseInt**.

```
            JOptionPane.showMessageDialog(null, "'" + inputStr
                                + "' is invalid\n"
                                + "Please enter digits only");
        }
    }

    return age;
}
```

Notice we can get rid of the boolean variable by rewriting the statement as

```
while (true) {
    inputStr = JOptionPane.showInputDialog(null, prompt);

    try {
        age = Integer.parseInt(inputStr);
        return age; //input okay so return the value & exit

    } catch (NumberFormatException e) {

        JOptionPane.showMessageDialog(null, "'" + inputStr
                            + "' is invalid\n"
                            + "Please enter digits only");
    }
}
```

The improved class with the exception-handling getAge method is named
AgeInputVer2.

There are many types of exceptions the system can throw, and we must specify which exception we are catching in the catch block's parameter list (there
can be exactly one exception in the list). In the sample code, we are catching
the number format exception, and the parameter e represents an instance of the
NumberFormatException class. In Java an exception is represented as an instance
of the Throwable class or its subclasses. The Throwable class has two subclasses—
Error and Exception. The Error class and its subclasses represent serious problems
that should not be caught by ordinary applications, while the Exception class and its
subclasses represent error conditions that should be caught. So for all practical
purposes, we are only interested in the Exception class and its subclasses in our
program. Later in the chapter we will learn how to define our own exception
classes. We will declare these programmer-defined exception classes as subclasses
of the Exception class.

There are two methods defined in the Throwable class that we can call to get
some information about the thrown exception: getMessage and printStackTrace. We
can call these methods inside the catch block as

```
try {
    age = Integer.parseInt(inputStr);
    return age; //input okay so return the value & exit
```

```
    } catch (NumberFormatException e) {
        System.out.println(e.getMessage());
        e.printStackTrace();
    }
```

With this modified code, if we enter **ten** as an input, then we will receive the following output:

getMessage

printStackTrace

```
ten
java.lang.NumberFormatException: ten
   at java.lang.Integer.parseInt(Integer.java:405)
   at java.lang.Integer.parseInt(Integer.java:454)
   at AgeInputImproved.getAge(AgeInputImproved.java:51)
   at Ch8AgeInputMain.main(Ch8AgeInputMain.java:26)
```

Notice that the result we see from the **printStackTrace** method is the one we saw when the system handled the thrown exception. The stack trace shows the sequence of calls made from the **main** method of the main class to the method that throws the exception.

Quick
CHECK
√

1. What is an output from the following code?

```
try {
    int num1 = Integer.parseInt("14");
    System.out.println("Okay 1");
    int num2 = Integer.parseInt("one");
    System.out.println("Okay 2");
} catch (NumberFormatException e) {
    System.out.println("Error");
}
```

2. What is wrong with the following code? It attempts to loop until the valid input is entered.

```
String inputStr;
int    num;

try {
    while (true) {
        inputStr = JOptionPane.showInputDialog(null,
                                         "Input:");
        num      = Integer.parseInt(inputStr);
    }
} catch (NumberFormatException e) {
    JOptionPane.showMessageDialog(null, "Error");
}
```

8.2 | Throwing Exceptions

Compared to the original AgeInputVer1 class, the AgeInputVer2 class is more robust because the program does not terminate abruptly when an invalid value is entered. However, the improved class is not robust enough yet. There is still room for improvements. For example, the current implementation accepts invalid negative integers. Since negative age is not possible, let's improve the code to take care of the invalid input of negative integers. Notice that a negative integer is an integer, so the parseInt method will not throw an exception. We will define the third class, AgeInputVer3, to throw (and catch) an exception when the invalid input of a negative integer is detected. Here's the while loop of the modified getAge method of the AgeInputVer3 class:

```
while (true) {
  inputStr = JOptionPane.showInputDialog(null, prompt);

  try {
    age = Integer.parseInt(inputStr);

    if (age < 0) {
      throw new Exception("Negative age is invalid");
    }

      return age; //input okay so return the value & exit

  } catch (NumberFormatException e) {

    JOptionPane.showMessageDialog(null, "'" + inputStr
              + "' is invalid\n"
              + "Please enter digits only");

  } catch (Exception e) {

    JOptionPane.showMessageDialog(null, "Error: "
              + e.getMessage());
  }
}
```

Throws an exception when **age** is a negative integer

The thrown exception is caught by this **catch** block.

An exception is thrown by using the throw statement. Its syntax is

```
throw <a throwable object>
```

where <a throwable object> is an instance of the Throwable class or its subclasses. As mentioned earlier, in common applications, it will be an instance of the Exception class or its subclasses. In the sample code, we threw an instance of the Exception class. This is only for illustration purposes. In real applications, we normally throw an instance of more specialized exception classes. When we create this instance, we can pass the string that describes the error. The thrown exception is caught by the corresponding catch block, and this error message is displayed.

Notice the multiple catch blocks in the sample code. When there are multiple catch blocks in a try-catch statement, they are checked in sequence, and because the exception classes form an inheritance hierarchy, it is important to check the more specialized exception classes before the more general exception classes. For example, if we reverse the order of the catch blocks to

```
try {
    ...
} catch (Exception e) {
    ...
} catch (NumberFormatExcepton e) {
    ...
}
```

then the second catch block will never be executed because any exception object that is an instance of Exception or its subclasses will match the first catch block. When an exception is thrown, a matching catch block is executed and all other catch blocks are ignored. This is similar to the switch statement with break at the end of each case block. The execution continues to the next statement that follows the try-catch statement. When no exception is thrown, all catch blocks are ignored and the execution continues to the next statement. Figure 8.2 illustrates the control flow of the try-catch statement with multiple catch blocks.

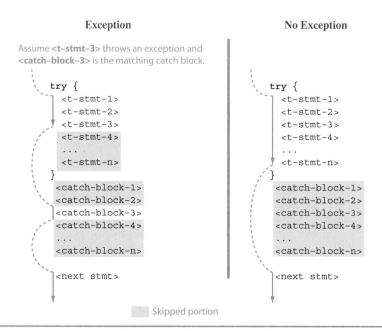

Figure 8.2 Two possible control flows of the **try-catch** statement with multiple **catch** blocks. Assume **<t-stmt-3>** throws an exception and **<catch-block-3>** is the matching **catch** block.

Helpful Reminder

*List the **catch** blocks in the order of specialized to more general exception classes. At most one **catch** block is executed, and all other **catch** blocks are ignored.*

We assume in Figure 8.2 that one of the catch blocks will match the thrown exception. It is possible that none of the catch blocks matches the thrown exception. If there is no matching catch block, then the system will search down the stack trace for a method with a matching catch block. If none is found, then the system will handle the thrown exception. We will explain this traversing of the stack trace in greater detail in Section 8.3.

If there is a block of code that needs to be executed regardless of whether an exception is thrown, then we use the reserved word finally. Consider this code.

```
inputStr = JOptionPane.showInputDialog(null, "");

try {
   number = Integer.parseInt(inputStr);

   if (num > 100) {
      throw new Exception("Out of bound");
   }

} catch (NumberFormatException e) {
   System.out.println("Cannot convert to int");

} catch (Exception e) {
   System.out.println("Error: " + e.getMessage());

} finally {
   System.out.println("DONE");
}
```

If there is no error in input, then no exception is thrown and the output will be

```
DONE
```

If there is an error in input, one of the two exceptions is thrown and the output will be

```
Cannot convert to int
DONE
```

or

```
Error: Out of bound
DONE
```

The example shows that the finally block is always executed. This feature is useful in a situation where we need to execute some cleanup code after the try-catch statement. For example, suppose we open a communication channel from our Java

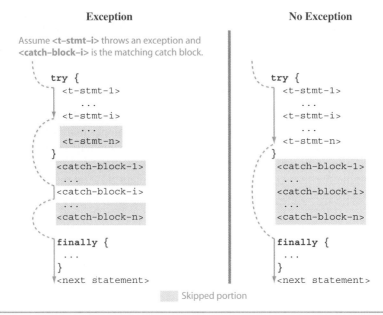

Figure 8.3 Two possible control flows of the **try-catch** statement with multiple **catch** blocks and the **finally** block. The **finally** block is always executed.

program to a remote web server to exchange data. If the data exchange is successfully completed in the try block, then we close the communication channel and finish the operation. If the data exchange is interrupted for some reason, an exception is thrown and the operation is aborted. In this case also, we need to close the communication channel, because leaving the channel open by one application blocks other applications from using it. Closing a channel is much like hanging up the phone. The code to close the communication channel should therefore be placed in the finally block. Figure 8.3 shows two possible control flows for the try-catch statement with the finally clause.

Note that even if there's a return statement inside the try block, the finally block is executed. When the return statement is encountered in the try block, statements in the finally block are executed before actually returning from the method.

Quick **CHECK** √

1. What's wrong with the following code? Identify all errors.

```
try {
    number = Integer.parseInt("123");

    if (num > 100) {
        catch new Exception("Out of bound");
    }
```

```
} catch {
    System.out.println("Cannot convert to int");
} finally (Exception e) {
    System.out.println("Always print");
}
```

2. Determine the output of the following code.

```
try {
    number = Integer.parseInt("a23");
    if (number < 0) {
        throw new Exception("No negative");
    }
} catch (NumberFormatException e) {
    System.out.println("Cannot convert to int");
} catch (Exception e) {
    System.out.println("Error: " + e.getMessage());
} finally {
    System.out.println("DONE");
}
```

3. Determine the output of the following code.

```
try {
    number = Integer.parseInt("-30");
    if (number < 0) {
        throw new Exception("No negative");
    }
} catch (Exception e) {
    System.out.println("Error: " + e.getMessage());
} catch (NumberFormatException e) {
    System.out.println("Cannot convert to int");
}
```

8.3 | Propagating Exceptions

In Section 8.2 we introduced the possibility of no catch block matching the thrown exception, but we did not explain exactly how does the system handle such a case. We stated only briefly that the system will search down the stack trace for a method with a matching catch block, and if no matching catch block is found, the system will handle the thrown exception. We will now describe this mechanism in detail.

To present a precise description, we start with some definitions. When a method may throw an exception, either directly by including a throw statement or exception thrower

exception catcher

exception propagator

indirectly by calling a method that throws an exception, we call the method an *exception thrower*. Every exception thrower must be one of the two types: catcher or propagator. An *exception catcher* is an exception thrower that includes a matching catch block for the thrown exception, while an *exception propagator* does not. For example, the getAge method of the AgeInputVer1 class is an exception propagator, while the getAge method of the AgeInputVer2 class is an exception catcher. Note that the designation of a method as being a catcher or propagator is based on a single exception. Suppose a method throws two exceptions. This method can be a catcher of the first exception and a propagator of the second exception.

Let's consider the sequence of method calls shown in Figure 8.4. Method A calls method B, method B in turn calls method C, and so forth. Notice the stack trace in the figure. Every time a method is executed, the method's name is placed on top of the stack. By the time method D is executed, we have A, B, C, and D in the stack. When an exception is thrown, the system searches down the stack from the top, looking for the first matching exception catcher. Method D throws an exception, but no matching catch block exists in the method, so method D is an exception propagator. The system then checks method C. This method is also an exception propagator. Finally, the system locates the matching catch block in method B, and therefore, method B is the catcher for the exception thrown by method D.

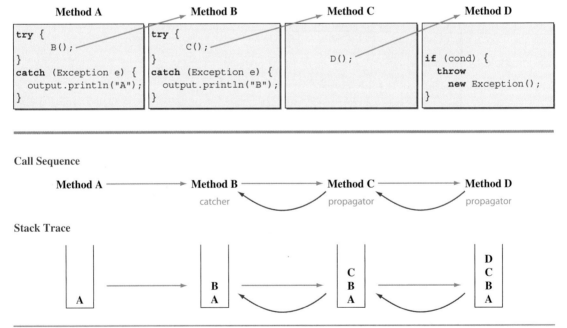

Figure 8.4 A sequence of method calls among the exception throwers. Method D throws an instance of **Exception.** The green arrows indicate the direction of calls. The red arrows show the reversing of call sequence, looking for a matching catcher. Method B is the catcher in this example. The call sequence is traced by using a stack. (*Note:* **output == System.out.**)

Method A also includes the matching catch block, but it will not be executed because the thrown exception is already caught by method B, and method B does not propagate this exception. Although the technique is not used often, an exception catcher can also be set to propagate the caught exception. For example, if we rewrite method B as

```
try {
    C();

} catch (Exception e) {
    ...         //do something here
    throw e;  //propagate the caught exception to the
              //method below this one in the trace stack
}
```

it is both a catcher and a propagator. With the modified method B, method A's matching catch block will get executed, because method B, in addition to handling the exception, throws the same exception, causing the system to look for a matching catcher down the stack.

We have one last detail to complete the description of the exception propagation mechanism. If a method is an exception propagator, we need to modify its header to declare the type of exceptions the method propagates. We use the reserved word throws for this declaration. Methods C and D in Figure 8.4 must have the following declaration (visibility modifier and return type are not relevant here):

```
void C( ) throws Exception {
    ...
}

void D( ) throws Exception {
    ...
}
```

Without the required throws Exception clause, the program will not compile. There is one exception (no pun intended) to this rule. For the exceptions of the type called *runtime exceptions,* the throws clause is optional. For example, the getAge method of AgeInputVer1 does not include the throws clause because NumberFormatException is a runtime exception. Its being optional means we can include it to explicitly state the fact if we want to. If we restate the declaration to

```
public int getAge(String prompt)

                    throws NumberFormatException {
    ...
}
```

the code will compile just fine. We will explain further about different types of exceptions in Section 8.4.

Now that the exception propagation mechanism is explained, let's study how we can apply it in designing useful service classes. Consider the AgeInputVer3 class. It disallows input of negative integers. When that happens, an exception is thrown. Instead of disallowing only negative integers, wouldn't it make more sense to restrict the valid input by specifying the lower and upper bounds? For example, we may want to restrict the input to an integer between 10 and 20 for one application and between 0 and 250 (e.g., entering the age of a building on the campus) for another application. To illustrate this concept, we will define the fourth class, AgeInputVer4, that allows the client programmers to specify the lower and upper bounds of acceptable input values.

The client specifies the lower and upper bounds at the time of object creation, for example,

```
AgeInputVer4 input = new AgeInputVer4(10, 20);
```

The default constructor will set the lower and upper bounds to 0 and 99, respectively. The lower and upper bounds are kept as data members lowerBound and upperBound, respectively, and they are initialized in the constructor.

How should the getAge respond when it detects the input is outside the range of the client-designated lower and upper bounds? Instead of catching it, we will propagate the thrown exception to the caller of this method. Our responsibility as a provider of the service class is to tell the client by throwing an exception when a condition set by the client is violated. We will let the client handle the thrown exception. The condition is set by the client, so it is more appropriate for this client to decide what to do in case of an exception. For the number format exception, the getAge method is still the catcher because this exception is thrown when a condition not dependent on any one specific client is violated. This exception is not a client-specific exception, but a generic exception suitably handled by the service class. So the modified getAge method is a propagator of an Exception (thrown when the bounds set by the client are violated) and a catcher of a NumberFormat-Exception (thrown when the input cannot be converted to an integer). Here's the method:

```
public int getAge(String prompt) throws Exception {

    String inputStr;
    int    age;                              Propagates an
                                             exception
    while (true) {
        inputStr
            = JOptionPane.showInputDialog(null, prompt);

        try {
            age = Integer.parseInt(inputStr);

            if (age < lowerBound || age > upperBound) {
                throw new Exception("Input out of bound");
            }

            return age;
```

```
                         } catch (NumberFormatException e) {

No catch block                JOptionPane.showMessageDialog(null, "'"
 for Exception                               + inputStr + "' is invalid\n"
                                             + "Please enter digits only");
                         }
                     }
                 }
```

The second getAge method that uses a default prompt calls this method, so we need to rewrite the second getAge method as

```
public int getAge() throws Exception {

    return getAge(DEFAULT_MESSAGE);
}
```

This call can throw an **Exception** so the method header must include the correct **throws** clause.

We have to specify the data members and the constructors to complete the AgeInputVer4 class. The data members are declared as

```
private static final int DEFAULT_LOWER_BOUND = 0;
private static final int DEFAULT_UPPER_BOUND = 99;

private int lowerBound;
private int upperBound;
```

What about the constructors? Are the following constructors acceptable?

```
public AgeInputVer4( ) {
    this(DEFAULT_LOWER_BOUND, DEFAULT_UPPER_BOUND);
}

public AgeInputVer4(int low, int high) {
    lowerBound = low;
    upperBound = high;
}
```

Yes, if we didn't know about exception handling. But now with the knowledge of exception handling, we can make the class more robust by ensuring that low is less than or equal to high. If this condition is not met, then we throw an exception. The

IllegalArgumentException class is precisely the class we can use for this situation. Here's the more robust constructor:

```java
public AgeInputVer4(int low, int high)
                    throws IllegalArgumentException {

    if (low > high) {
        throw new IllegalArgumentException(
                        "Low (" + low + ") was " +
                        "larger than high(" + high + ")");
    } else {
        lowerBound = low;
        upperBound = high;
    }
}
```

Now, what about the default constructor? Since the default constructor calls the other two-argument constructor, which can throw an exception, this constructor must handle the exception. One approach is to propagate the exception by declaring it as

```java
public AgeInputVer4( ) throws IllegalArgumentException {
    this(DEFAULT_LOWER_BOUND, DEFAULT_UPPER_BOUND);
}
```

This declaration is problematic, however, because when we use the throws clause, we are announcing that this method can potentially throw an exception. But this constructor will never throw an exception as long as the class is programmed correctly. The only time this constructor can be throwing an exception is when we set the value for DEFAULT_LOWER_BOUND or DEFAULT_UPPER_BOUND incorrectly. It is an internal error and must be corrected. Since this constructor should not throw an exception, we might be tempted to make this constructor an exception catcher as

```java
public AgeInputVer4( ) {
    try {
        this(DEFAULT_LOWER_BOUND, DEFAULT_UPPER_BOUND);
    } catch (IllegalArgumentException e) {
        //never happens, so do nothing
    }
}
```

Logically, this is what we want to accomplish. But syntactically, it is an error. Java requires the call to another constructor using the reserved word this to be the first statement. In the bad version, the try statement is the first statement. To correct this problem, we can define a private method setBounds as

```java
private void setBounds(int low, int high) {
    lowerBound = low;
    upperBound = high;
}
```

and write the two constructors as

```
public AgeInputVer4( ) {
    setBounds(DEFAULT_LOWER_BOUND, DEFAULT_UPPER_BOUND);
}

public AgeInputVer4(int low, int high)
                throws IllegalArgumentException {

    if (low > high) {
        throw new IllegalArgumentException(
                        "Low (" + low + ") was " +
                        "larger than high(" + high + ")");
    } else {
        setBounds(low, high);
    }
}
```

Here's the complete AgeInputVer4 class:

```
/*
    Chapter 8 Sample Class: Class to input age

    File: AgeInputVer4.java

*/

import javax.swing.*;

class AgeInputVer4 {

    private static final String DEFAULT_MESSAGE = "Your age:";
    private static final int DEFAULT_LOWER_BOUND = 0;
    private static final int DEFAULT_UPPER_BOUND = 99;

    private int lowerBound;
    private int upperBound;

    public AgeInputVer4( ) {
        setBounds(DEFAULT_LOWER_BOUND, DEFAULT_UPPER_BOUND);
    }

    public AgeInputVer4(int low, int high)
                throws IllegalArgumentException {

        if (low > high) {
            throw new IllegalArgumentException(
                "Low (" + low + ") was " +
                "larger than high(" + high + ")");
```

Data members

Constructors

```
        } else {
            setBounds(low, high);
        }
    }

    public int getAge() throws Exception {

        return getAge(DEFAULT_MESSAGE);

    }

    public int getAge(String prompt) throws Exception {

        String inputStr;
        int     age;

        while (true) {
            inputStr  = JOptionPane.showInputDialog(null, prompt);

            try {
                age = Integer.parseInt(inputStr);

                if (age < lowerBound || age > upperBound) {
                    throw new Exception("Input out of bound");
                }

                return age; //input okay so return the value & exit

            } catch (NumberFormatException e) {

                JOptionPane.showMessageDialog(null, "'" + inputStr
                                      + "' is invalid\n"
                                      + "Please enter digits only");

            }
        }
    }

    private void setBounds(int low, int high) {
        lowerBound = low;
        upperBound = high;
    }
}
```

getAge

setBounds

1. What's wrong with the following code?

```
    public void check(int num) {
        if (num < 0) {
            throw new Exception();
        }
    }
```

2. What is the difference between the reserved words **throw** and **throws**?

3. What's wrong with the following code?

```
public NumberFormatException getData( ) {
    try {
        String str = JOptionPane.showInputDialog(
                                null, "Input:");

        int num = Integer.parseInt(str);

        return num;
    }
}
```

8.4 | Types of Exceptions

We mentioned briefly in Section 8.1 that all types of thrown errors are instances of the Throwable class or its subclasses. Serious errors that signal abnormal conditions are represented by the instances of the Error class or its subclasses. Exceptional cases that common applications are expected to handle are represented by the instances of the Exception class or its subclasses. Figure 8.5 shows a very small portion of the inheritance hierarchy rooted in the Throwable class.

checked and unchecked exceptions

There are two types of exceptions: checked and unchecked. A *checked exception* is an exception that is checked at compile time. All other exceptions are *unchecked exceptions,* also called *runtime exceptions,* because they are unchecked at compile time and are detected only at runtime. Trying to divide a number by 0

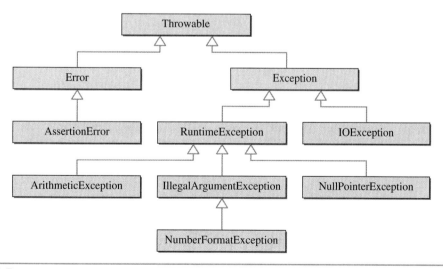

Figure 8.5 Some classes in the inheritance hierarchy from the **Throwable** class. There are over 60 classes in the hierarchy.

(ArithmeticException) and trying to convert a string with letters to an integer (NumberFormatException) are two examples of runtime exceptions.

   If a method is a propagator (a method that throws but does not catch an exception) of checked exceptions, then the method must have the throws clause. If a method is a propagator of runtime exceptions or errors (instances of Error or its subclasses), the throws clause is optional. When we call a method that can throw checked exceptions, then we must use the try-catch statement and place the call in the try block, or we must modify our method header to include the appropriate throws clause. When we call a method that can throw runtime exceptions or errors, then there's is no such requirement. We just make a call in our method. Figure 8.6 shows the valid callers of a method that throws checked exceptions, and Figure 8.7 shows the valid callers of a method that throws runtime, or unchecked, exceptions.

   Enforcing the requirement of explicitly handling runtime exceptions means, for all methods we write, that they must either have the throws clause in the header or have the try-catch statement in the body because almost every method we call from our methods can throw runtime exceptions. This is hardly an effective programming so we don't have to handle runtime exceptions explicitly in the program. For the errors of type Error and its subclasses, they indicate problems too serious for any ordinary application to handle, so we are not required to handle them explicitly. There's really nothing we can do even if we catch them, so we don't.

Helpful Reminder

*If a method throws a checked exception, the caller of this method must explicitly include the **try-catch** statement or the **throws** clause in the method header. If a method throws a runtime, or unchecked, exception, the use of the **try-catch** statement or the **throws** clause is optional.*

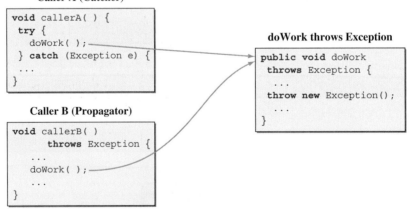

Figure 8.6 Callers of a method that can throw a checked exception must explicitly include the **try-catch** statement in the method body or the **throws** clause in the method header.

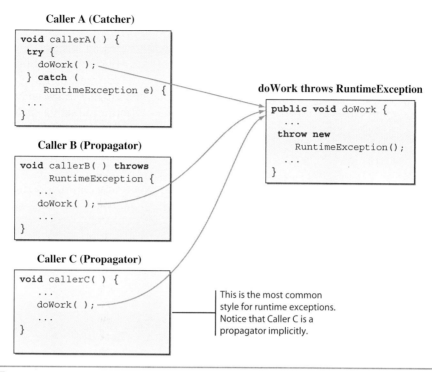

Figure 8.7 It is optional for the callers of a method that can throw runtime, or unchecked, exceptions to include the **try-catch** statement in the method body or the **throws** clause in the method header.

Quick
CHECK

1. Is this code wrong?

```
public void check(int num) {
    if (num < 0) {
        throw new IllegalArgumentException();
    }
}
```

2. What is the difference between the checked and unchecked exceptions?
3. Is this code wrong?

```
public void getData( ) {
    String str = JOptionPane.showInputDialog(
                            null, "Input:");

    if (str.equals("") {
        throw new IOException();
    }
}
```

8.5 | Programmer-Defined Exceptions

In the AgeInputVer4 class, the getAge methods throw an instance of the Exception class. The catch clause of the caller of the getAge method can use the getMessage method to retrieve the error message or use printStackTrace to display the sequence of method calls from the main method to the method that threw an exception. But there's no way for the client to get any other useful information such as the value actually entered by the user. Instead of using generic exception classes, we can define our own exception classes so we can attach useful information to the exception objects.

Let's define a class named AgeInputException as a subclass of the Exception class. To provide useful information to the client, we will define the class so the instances will carry three pieces of information: lower bound, upper bound, and the value entered by the user (in addition to the message inherited from the Exception class). We will define three public methods to access these data. Here's the class definition:

```
/*
    Chapter 8 Sample Class: Customized Exception Class

    File: AgeInputException.java
*/

class AgeInputException extends Exception {

    private static final String DEFAULT_MESSAGE = "Input out of bounds";

    private int lowerBound;
    private int upperBound;
    private int value;

    public AgeInputException(int low, int high, int input) {
        this(DEFAULT_MESSAGE, low, high, input);
    }

    public AgeInputException(String msg,
                             int low, int high, int input) {
        super(msg);

        if (low > high) {
            throw new IllegalArgumentException();
        }

        lowerBound = low;
        upperBound = high;
        value      = input;
    }
```

```
    public int lowerBound() {

        return lowerBound;
    }

    public int upperBound() {

        return  upperBound;
    }

    public int value() {
        return value;
    }
}
```

The new AgeInputVer5 class is essentially the same as the AgeInputVer4 class except the getAge method of the new class throws an AgeInputException. A sample main class that uses the AgeInputVer5 is as follows:

```
/*
    Chapter 8 Sample Program: Input a person's age

    File: Ch8TestAgeInputVer5.java
*/

import javax.swing.*;

class Ch8TestAgeInputVer5 {

    public static void main( String[] args ) {

        int    entrantAge;

        try {

            AgeInputVer5 input = new AgeInputVer5(25, 50);

            entrantAge   = input.getAge("Your Age:");

            //continue the processing
            JOptionPane.showMessageDialog(null, "Input Okay"); //TEMP

        } catch (AgeInputException e) {
            JOptionPane.showMessageDialog(null,
                "Error: " + e.value() + " is entered. It is " +
                "outside the valid range of [" + e.lowerBound() +
                ", " + e.upperBound() + "]");
        }
    }
}
```

e's methods are called to get info

Helpful Reminder

To provide useful information to the client programmers when an exception occurs, define a new exception class. Make this customized exception class a subclass of **Exception.**

Take my Advice

When we create a new customized exception class, we should define it as a checked exception, and the most logical choice for its superclass is the **Exception** class. We should not define the customized exception class as an unchecked exception. If we did, then the client programmers would have an option of omitting the **try-catch** statement or the **throws** clause in their code. This is not a good idea. The goal of defining a customized exception class is to ensure that the client programmers handle the thrown exceptions of the customized class explicitly in their code, to increase the robustness of the whole program.

Quick **CHECK**

1. When do we want to define a customized exception class?
2. Should a customized exception class be a checked or unchecked exception?

8.6 | Assertions

In this section we will describe a Java assertion and explain how to use it effectively in our programs. Let's begin with an example. Recall the CurrencyConverter class from Chapter 4. This class, as implemented in Chapter 4, works correctly as long as the data member exchangeRate is assigned a valid value. In other words, the value for exchangeRate must be set to positive for the conversion routines to work correctly. How can we ensure that this is the case? We can use the new assertion feature of Java as an aid.

Helpful Reminder

The new assertion feature is available only from Java 2 SDK 1.4. Be sure to use the right version when compiling and running the programs with assertions.

Inside the fromDollar and toDollar methods, where the conversion takes place, we can include the assert statement to verify that the value of exchangeRate is indeed positive. Here's how we can write the two methods with an assertion:

```
public double fromDollar(double dollar) {
    assert exchangeRate > 0.0;

    return (dollar * exchangeRate);
}

public double toDollar(double foreignMoney) {
    assert exchangeRate > 0.0;

    return (foreignMoney / exchangeRate);
}
```

The syntax for the assert statement is

```
assert <boolean expression> ;
```

where <boolean expression> represents the condition that must be true if the code is working correctly. When the statement is executed, the <boolean expression> is evaluated. If it results in true, then the normal execution of the program continues. Otherwise, an AssertionError (subclass of Error) is thrown. In this example, before we perform the currency conversion, we want to assert that exchangeRate is positive, so we write

```
assert exchangeRate > 0.0;
```

The syntax for the second form of the assert statement is

```
assert <boolean expression> : <expression> ;
```

where <expression> represents the value that is passed as an argument to the constructor of the AssertionError class. The value serves as the detailed message of a thrown error. For example, using the second form, we can rewrite the fromDollar method as

```
public double fromDollar(double dollar) {
    assert exchangeRate > 0.0 :
            "Exchange rate = " + exchangeRate +
            ".\nIt must be a positive value.";

    return (dollar * exchangeRate);
}
```

The reserved word assert is newly added to Java 2 SDK 1.4. Before this version, the word assert is a valid nonreserved identifier. To ensure compatibility with existing programs, when we compile the existing programs with the version 1.4 compiler, the word assert is treated as a regular identifier. To enable the assertion mechanism during the compilation, we must compile the source file using the -source 1.4

option. For example, to compile the CurrencyConverter class that includes the assert statements using version 1.4 or later compiler, we compile the source file as

```
javac -source 1.4 CurrencyConverter.java
```

The -source option can be omitted when version 1.5 compiler is used. To run the program with assertions enabled, we execute the program using the -ea option. If the main class that uses the new CurrencyConverter class is Ch8TestAssertMain, then we run the program, using the version 1.4 or later interpreter, as

```
java -ea Ch8TestAssertMain
```

If we do not provide the -ea option, then the program is executed without checking the assertions. When do we ever want to ignore the assertions we intentionally included in the program? Checking all assertions included in the program can be quite time consuming. By having an option of enabling or disabling the assertions, we can choose to enable the assertions while developing and testing the program and disable them once the program is fully developed and tested.

Helpful Reminder

To compile the source file that includes assertions, use

```
javac -source 1.4 <source file>
```

To run the program with assertions enabled, use

```
java -ea <main class>
```

When the assert statements are enabled, executing the Ch8TestAssertMain class that includes the statements

```
CurrencyConverter converter =
                    new CurrencyConverter(-120.00);

double yen = converter.fromDollar(234);
```

will result in this error message:

```
java.lang.AssertionError: Exchange rate = -120.0. It must be a
positive value.
   at CurrencyConverter.fromDollar(CurrencyConverter.java:69)
   at Ch8TestAssertMain.main(Ch8TestAssertMain.java:39)
```

With the assertion feature enabled, we were able to detect the existence of a bug somewhere in the program. But where? We have to search for the places where the instance variable exchangeRate is set. We notice that the value for exchange-Rate is set in two places: one in the constructor and another in the setExchangeRate method. In both places, we should modify the code so that only the valid positive integers are accepted. If an invalid value is passed as an argument, we shall reject it by throwing an exception. We can rewrite the constructor and the setExchangeRate method as

```
public CurrencyConverter(double rate)
                    throws IllegalArgumentException {
    check(rate);

    exchangeRate = rate;
}

public void setExchangeRate(double rate)
                    throws IllegalArgumentException {
    check(rate);

    exchangeRate = rate;
}

private void check(double rate) {
    if (rate <= 0.0) {
        throw new IllegalArgumentException(
                "Exchange rate must be positive");
    }
}
```

With this modification, the assertion rate > 0.0 will never fail. For a small class such as CurrencyConverter, the benefit of using assertions may not be obvious, but in designing and building classes that solve difficult and complex problems, effective use of assertions can be an indispensable aid. We will be seeing more examples of assertions (and exceptions, also) in the later sample code.

Notice that we are not writing

```
public CurrencyConverter(double rate) {
    assert rate > 0.0;

    exchangeRate = rate;
}

public void setExchangeRate(double rate) {
    assert rate > 0.0;

    exchangeRate = rate;
}
```

We should not use the assertion feature to ensure the validity of an argument. In principle, we use assertions to detect the internal programming errors, and we use exceptions to notify the client programmers of the misuse of our classes. The CurrencyConverter class is intended as a service class used by many different programs. It is the responsibility of the client programmers to pass valid arguments. If they don't, then we throw an exception to notify them of the misuse. Another problem is that we have an option of enabling or disabling assertions when we run the program. But the validity checking of the arguments should never be disabled. For the same reason, we should never use an assertion to check the validity of user input.

Helpful Reminder

Use assertions to detect internal errors. Use exceptions to notify the client programmers of the misuse of our class .

precondition
assertion

postcondition
assertion

control-flow
invariant

   The type of assertion we see in the CurrencyConverter constructor and the setExchangeRate method is called a *precondition assertion*. This assertion checks for a condition that must be true before executing a method. Opposite to the precondition assertion is a *postcondition assertion*, a checking of condition that must be true after a method is executed. The third type of assertion is called a *control-flow invariant*. Consider the following switch statement. It adds the appropriate fee to the tuition based on whether the student is a dorm resident or a commuter.

```
switch (residenceType) {

    case COMMUTER:        totalFee = tuition + parkingFee;
                          break;

    case DORM_RESIDENT:   totalFee = tuition + roomAndBoard;
                          break;
}
```

Now every student must be a dorm resident or a commuter, so if the variable residenceType has a value other than COMMUTER or DORM_RESIDENT, then there's a bug somewhere. To detect such a bug, we can rewrite the statement as

```
switch (residenceType) {

    case COMMUTER:        totalFee = tuition + parkingFee;
                          break;

    case DORM_RESIDENT:   totalFee = tuition + roomAndBoard;
                          break;

    default:              assert false:
                                "Value of residenceType " +
                                "is invalid. Value = " +
                                residenceType;
}
```

This statement documents the fact that the default case should never be executed when the program is running correctly. This is called a control-flow invariant because the control must flow invariably to one of the two cases. Alternatively, we can place an assertion before the switch statement as

```
assert (residenceType == COMMUTER ||
        residenceType == DORM_RESIDENT) :
        "Value of residenceType is invalid. Value = " +
        residenceType;

switch (residenceType) {

    case COMMUTER:      totalFee = tuition + parkingFee;
                        break;

    case DORM_RESIDENT: totalFee = tuition + roomAndBoard;
                        break;
}
```

Here's another use of an assertion. Consider the following actionPerformed method of the Ch7HiLoFrame class:

```
public void actionPerformed(ActionEvent event) {

    String command = event.getActionCommand();

    if (event.getSource() instanceof JMenuItem) {
       processMenuAction(command);

    } else if (event.getSource() instanceof JTextField) {
       processEnterAction(command);

    } else { //event source is a button
       processButtonAction(command);
    }
}
```

The method will work as long as the assumption that there are exactly three types of event sources—JMenuItem, JTextField, and JButton—is not violated. We can rewrite the if statement by replacing the comment with an assertion statement as

```
if (event.getSource() instanceof JMenuItem) {
   processMenuAction(command);

} else if (event.getSource() instanceof JTextField) {
   processEnterAction(command);

} else {
   assert event.getSource() instanceof JButton;
   processButtonAction(command);
}
```

If there is an internal error in which an event source is an object other than a menu item, a text field, or a button, then the assertion statement will detect it.

We will be seeing more examples of assertions in the later chapters.

Quick
CHECK

1. Why is this code wrong?

```java
public void doWork(int num) {
    assert num > 0;
    total += num;
}
```

2. Name three types of assertions.
3. Why is this code wrong?

```java
public void getData( ) {
    String str = JOptionPane.showInputDialog(
                                    null, "Input:");

    assert str.equals(""): "Input Error";
}
```

8.7 | Supervisor-Subordinate Design Pattern

If we review the structure of the sample programs we have developed, we will see the following pattern:

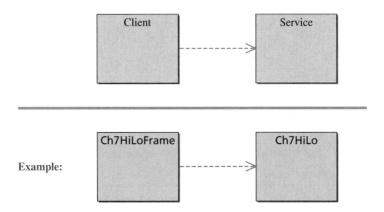

Example:

The client calls the method of a service object, and the service object carries out the requested operation or returns requested data to the client. As the program gets larger and more complex, we need to use different patterns of connecting objects. We will describe a design pattern that we call a *supervisor-subordinate* design pattern. In this design pattern, we have a supervisor object that controls a subordinate object. A subordinate object is created by its supervisor object, which is similar to a service object being created by the client object. However, unlike the client-service pattern where the method call is one-way (only the client calls the method of the service object), in this new pattern, a subordinate will also call the supervisor's method. The communication links will look as follows:

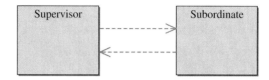

When do we need such a design pattern? Consider a control program for a mobile robot. Let's say we have an infrared sensor object whose task is to monitor the distance to the nearest obstacle and a motor object whose task is to manage the motor. A supervisor object, whose task is to navigate the mobile robot, controls these subordinates. The supervisor object may command the sensor object to send a warning message back when the distance becomes less than 2 cm. When the supervisor gets this distance warning notification, it commands the motor object to reduce the power gradually and get notified when the motor stops rotating. The motor object calls the supervisor when the motor stops rotating. In this hypothetical example, we see that the supervisor calls the methods of the subordinates to send commands, and the subordinates call the supervisor's methods to send notifications.

Consider another example. Suppose we have a customized user interface object. When the user finishes entering the data and clicks the OK button, the user interface object sends the notification to its supervisor. The supervisor then commands other objects in the program to process the entered data. We will see this example in Section 8.8.

To implement the supervisor-subordinate design pattern, we need to establish mutual references between the supervisor and the subordinate. Here's one way to achieve it:

```
class Supervisor {

    private Subordinate worker;

    public Supervisor( ) {
        ...
        worker = new Subordinate(this);
        ...
    }
    ...
}

class Subordinate {

    private Supervisor boss;

    public Subordinate(Supervisor boss) {
        ...
        this.boss = boss;
        ...
    }

    ...
}
```

> Don't use the identifier **super**, because it is a reserved word.

When a new supervisor object is created, the subordinate is created also, and the mutual references are established as follows:

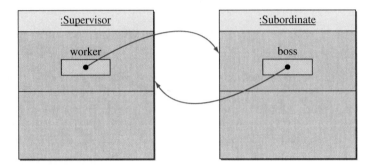

We will be using this design pattern in Section 8.8 and in many of the sample programs later in the book.

8.8 Sample Development

Keyless Entry System

We will develop a program that simulates a secure keyless entry system for a dormitory. Inside the entrance hall of a dorm, there is an entry system where the dorm residents must enter their name, room number, and password. Upon entry of valid data, the system will unlock the inner door that leads to the dorm's living quarters. To implement this program, two helper classes are provided. The **Door** class simulates unlocking of the inner door. The **Dorm** class manages resident information. An instance of the **Dorm** class is capable of adding and deleting resident information, reading and saving resident information from and to a file, and retrieving information if given the resident's name. We can verify the validity of the entered data by checking them against the information kept by a **Dorm** object.

We can turn our simulation program into a real one by replacing the **Door** class with a class that actually controls the door. Java provides a mechanism called Java Native Interface (JNI) which can be used to embed a link to a low-level device driver code, so calling the **open** method actually unlocks the door.

Problem Statement

Implement a sentry program that asks for three pieces of information: resident's name, room number, and a password. A password is any sequence of characters ranging in length from four to eight and is unique to an individual dorm resident. If everything matches, then the system unlocks and opens the door. We assume no two residents have the same name. Use the provided support classes **Door** *and* **Dorm.** *Sample resident data named* **samplelist.dat** *can be used for development.*

Overall Plan

To provide a complete system, we actually have to write two separate programs. The first one is the administrative module for adding, removing, and updating the resident information. The second is the user module that interacts with the residents. Figure 8.8 shows the program diagrams for the two modules.

In this section, we will implement the user module. The administrative module is left as an exercise. To begin our development effort, we must first find out the capabilities of the **Dorm** and **Door** classes. Also, for us to implement the class correctly, we need the specification of the **Resident** class.

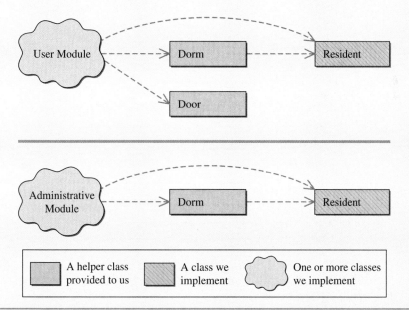

Figure 8.8 Program diagrams for the user and administrative modules. Notice the same **Dorm** and **Resident** classes are used in both programs. User and administrative modules will include one or more classes (at least one is programmer-defined).

Resident

The **Resident** class maintains information on individual dorm residents. We will be dealing with many instances of this class in the program. A password assigned to a resident must be a sequence of four to eight characters. For this class to work properly with the **Dorm** class, the class must include these public methods:

Public Methods of Resident
`public Resident( )` Default constructor that creates a `Resident` object with name = "unassigned", room = "000", and id = "@13&".

`public Resident(String name, String room, String password)`
                                    `throws IllegalArgumentException`
Creates a `Resident` object with the passed values.
`IllegalArgumentException` is thrown when the given password has less than four or more than eight characters.

`public void setName(String name)` Assigns the name.

`public void setPassword(String id)`
                                 `throws IllegalArgumentException`
Assigns the password. `IllegalArgumentException` is thrown when the given password has less than four or more than eight characters.

`public void setRoom(String room)` Assigns the room.
`public String getName( )` Returns the name.
`public String getPassWord( )` Returns the password.
`public String getRoom( )` Returns the room number.

One important restriction to the **Resident** class is the requirement for the class to implement the **Serializable** interface. Because the **Resident** objects are saved to a file, Java requires the class definition to include the phrase **implements Serializable** as

```
import java.io.*;

class Resident implements Serializable {

   . . .

}
```

Details on the significance of the clause **implements Serializable** will be given when we discuss the file input and output in Chapter 12.

Helpful Reminder

For any object we need to save to a file, its class definition must include the phrase **implements Serializable.**

Dorm

The **Dorm** class is a helper class provided to us. A **Dorm** object is capable of managing a list of **Resident** objects. It allows the client to add, delete, and retrieve **Resident** objects. In addition, it is capable of saving a list to a file or reading a list from a file. By having this file input and output features, our program can work with different lists of residents much as a word processor can work with different documents (files). The class definition is as follows:

Public Methods of Dorm
public Dorm( )   Default constructor that creates a Dorm object.
public Dorm(String filename)   Creates a Dorm object with the resident list read from the file with the name filename. Throws FileNotFoundException when the designated file cannot be found and IOException when the file cannot be read.
public void openFile(String filename)   Reads the resident list from the designated file. Throws FileNotFoundException when the designated file cannot be found and IOException when the file cannot be read.
public void saveFile(String filename)   Saves the resident list to the designated file. Throws IOException when the file cannot be saved.
public void add(Resident resident)   Adds the resident to the list. Throws IllegalArgumentException when a resident with the same name already exists in the list. We do not allow duplicate names. Every resident must have a unique name.
public void delete(String name)   Deletes the designated resident from the list. If no such resident is in the list, nothing happens.
public Resident getResident(String name)   Returns the Resident object with the given name. Returns null if no matching Resident is found.
public String getResidentList( )   Returns a list of residents as a String. A line separator is used after each resident. For each resident, the list contains his or her name, room number, and password.

Door

The **Door** class is another helper class. It simulates the opening of the door. In a real control program, a **Door** object can have an embedded low-level device driver code, so it really opens the door. The class definition is as follows:

Public Methods of Door

`public Door( )`
Default constructor that creates a new Door object.
`public void open()`
Opens the door. For this simulator class, it displays a simple message dialog.

overall design

Now let's study the overall design of the program. In addition to the given helper classes and the **Resident** class, what other classes should we define for this program? As the number of classes gets larger, we need to plan the classes carefully. For this program, we will define a supervisor class named **Ch8EntranceMonitor** whose instance will manage all other objects. We will define a user interface class called **InputFrame** that allows the user to enter his or her name, room number, and password. An **InputFrame** and a **Ch8EntranceMonitor** form a supervisor-subordinate relationship. When the **OK** button is clicked, the **InputFrame** object passes the entered data to the supervisor **Ch8EntranceMonitor.** The supervisor then

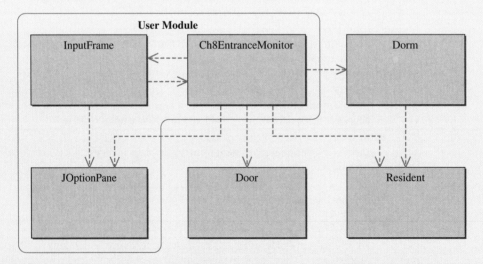

Figure 8.9 The program diagram for the **Ch8EntranceMonitor** program. There are three classes in the user module.

checks the validity of the input data with the help from a service **Dorm** object. If the **Dorm** object confirms the input data, then the supervisor instructs another service object, an instance of **Door,** to open the door. The following is our working design document, and Figure 8.9 shows the program diagram. Notice that we have to set up the mutual references between the **InputFrame** and **Ch8EntranceMonitor** objects because they will have to call each other's methods. We will describe how to set up such mutual references between the two classes in the step 2 development.

program
classes

Design Document: `Ch8EntranceMonitor`	
Class	**Purpose**
`Ch8EntranceMonitor`	The top-level control object manages other objects in the program. This is an instantiable main class.
`Door`	The given predefined class simulates the opening of a door.
`Dorm`	The given predefined class maintains a list of `Resident` objects.
`InputFrame`	The user interface class is for handling input routines. When the OK button is clicked, it calls its supervisor `Ch8EntranceMonitor`, passing the data entered by the user.
`JOptionPane`	This is the standard class for displaying messages.

We will implement the user module in three major steps:

development steps

1. Define the **Resident** class and explore the **Dorm** class. Start with a program skeleton to test the **Resident** class.

2. Define the user interface **InputFrame** class. Modify the top-level control class as necessary.

3. Finalize the code by making improvements and tying up loose ends.

Step 1 Development: Program Skeleton

step 1
design

Our first task is to find out about the given **Dorm** class. (The **Door** class is a very simple simulator class so there's not much to explore.) To be able to test-run the **Dorm** class, we must provide the **Resident** class, so this will be our first step. The purpose of the skeleton main class in this step is to verify the operations of the **Dorm** class.

The specification for the **Resident** class was given to us, so our task is to implement it according to the specification. No design work is necessary. When we can interact with an instance of the **Dorm** class correctly, it confirms that our implementation of the **Resident** class is working. To verify the key operations of the **Dorm** class, the top-level supervisor object **Ch8EntranceMonitor** will open a file and list the contents of the file.

step 1 code

Here's the **Resident** class:

```
/*
    Chapter 8 Sample Development: Keyless Entry System.

    File: Resident.java
*/

import java.io.*;

class Resident implements Serializable {

    private String  name;
    private String  room;
    private String  password;

    public Resident( ) {
        this("unassigned", "000", "@13&");
    }

    public Resident(String name, String room, String pwd)
                throws IllegalArgumentException {
        setName(name);
        setRoom(room);
        setPassword(pwd);
    }

    public String getName( ) {
        return name;
    }

    public String getPassword( ) {
        return password;
    }

    public String getRoom( ) {
        return room;
    }

    public void setName(String name) {
        this.name = name;
    }

    public void setPassword(String pwd) {
        int length = pwd.length();
```

Data members

Constructors

Accessors

Mutators

```
        if (length < 4 || length > 8) {
            throw new IllegalArgumentException();
        } else {
            this.password = pwd;
        }
    }

    public void setRoom(String room) {
        this.room = room;
    }
}
```

The skeleton instantiable main class is defined as follows:

```
/*
    Chapter 8 Sample Development: Keyless Entry System. (Step 1)

    File: Ch8EntranceMonitor.java
*/
import javax.swing.*;
import java.io.*;

class Ch8EntranceMonitor { //Step 1 Main Class

    private Dorm manager;

    public Ch8EntranceMonitor( ) {

        manager = new Dorm();
    }

    public static void main(String[] args) {

        Ch8EntranceMonitor sentry = new Ch8EntranceMonitor();
        sentry.start();
    }

    public void start( ) {

        openFile( );

        String roster = manager.getResidentList();

        System.out.println(roster);
    }
```

start

```
                                                              ┌──────────────┐
private void openFile( ) {                                    │   openFile   │
    String filename;                                          └──────────────┘

    while (true) { //loop until valid filename is entered
                   //or the dialog is canceled
        filename = JOptionPane.showInputDialog(null,"File to open:");

        if (filename == null) {//input dialog was canceled
            System.exit(0);
        }

        try {
            manager.openFile(filename);
            return;
        } catch (FileNotFoundException e) {
            JOptionPane.showMessageDialog(null,"No such file");
        } catch (IOException e) {
            JOptionPane.showMessageDialog(null,
                                        "Error in reading file");
        }
    }
}
```

step 1 test   The purpose of step 1 testing is to verify that the **Dorm** class is used correctly to open a file and get the contents of the file. To test it, we need a file that contains the resident information. A sample test file called **samplelist.dat** is provided for testing purposes. This file contains information on four residents. This file was created by executing the following program, which we can modify to create other test data files.

```
/*
    Chapter 8 Sample Development: Keyless Entry System.

    A simple class to create a dummy test data.

    File: SampleCreateResidentFile.java
*/
import javax.swing.*;
import java.io.*;

class SampleCreateResidentFile {
    public static void main(String[] args)throws IOException {
```

```
        Resident res;
        Dorm manager = new Dorm( );;

        res = new Resident("john", "1-101", "3457");
        manager.add(res);

        res = new Resident("java", "1-102", "4588");
        manager.add(res);

        res = new Resident("jill", "3-232", "8898");
        manager.add(res);

        res = new Resident("jack", "3-232", "8008");
        manager.add(res);

        String filename = JOptionPane.showInputDialog(null,
                                         "Save to which file:");

        manager.saveFile(filename);

        System.exit(0); //terminate the program
    }
}
```

Step 2 Development: Create the GUI

step 2
design

In the second development step, we will implement the user interface class **Input-Frame.** The **InputFrame** class and the **Ch8EntranceMonitor** class formulate the supervisor-subordinate relationship. Whenever the end user enters the information and clicks the **OK** button, **InputFrame** informs its supervisor **Ch8EntranceMonitor.** **Ch8EntranceMonitor** checks the entered information against the resident list and opens the door if the entered information is valid. These two objects will have mutual references, as shown in Figure 8.10.

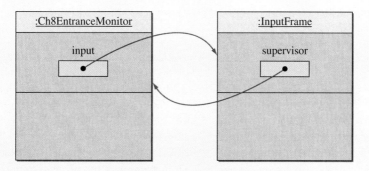

Figure 8.10 Mutual references between the two objects so they can "talk" to each other.

The constructor of **Ch8EntranceMonitor** is modified to

```
private Dorm       manager;
private Door       door;
private InputFrame input;
. . .
public Ch8EntranceMonitor( ) {
   manager = new Dorm();
   door    = new Door();
   input   = new InputFrame(this);
}
```

and the corresponding constructor of the **InputFrame** class will set a reference to its **Ch8EntranceMonitor** supervisor as

```
private Ch8EntranceMonitor supervisor;
. . .
public InputFrame(Ch8EntranceMonitor sup) {
   . . .
   supervisor = sup;
   . . .
}
```

The **InputFrame** class keeps three **JTextField** objects for entering name, room number, and password (and corresponding labels). There will be two buttons: **OK** and **Clear.** Here's our proposed layout:

Dorm Entrance Monitor

Name:

Room:

Pwd:

OK   Clear

When the **Clear** button is clicked, all text fields are cleared. When the **OK** button is clicked, we first check the text fields. If any one of them is empty, then we display an error message. If all text fields contains data, then we call the supervisor's **notify** method, passing the contents of the text fields.

The **notify** method of **Ch8EntranceMonitor** retrieves a **Resident** object from the **Dorm** object by passing the entered name. If the entered data match the data stored for the returned **Resident** object, then the door is unlocked. For any type of error, we display a single error message **Invalid Entry.** We do not want to give any meaningful error message here because we do not want to help a potential infiltrator by giving away any useful information. The basic idea of the **notify** method is as follows:

```
Resident res = manager.getResident(name);

if (res == null) {
    JOptionPane.showMessageDialog(null,"Invalid Entry");
} else if ( it is a match ) {
    door.open();
    input.clearEntries();
} else {
    JOptionPane.showMessageDialog(null, "Invalid Entry");
}
```

There's one last detail we have to consider for the **InputFrame** class. In an ordinary application, when the main frame of the program is closed, we terminate the program. We set this option by placing the statement

```
setDefaultCloseOperation(EXIT_ON_CLOSE);
```

inside the frame's constructor. In this application, we do not want to close the **InputFrame** window when the user clicks on the Close box. We want the frame to remain on the screen indefinitely. What we need to do is to ignore the clicking on the Close box. We can achieve this with

```
setDefaultCloseOperation(DO_NOTHING_ON_CLOSE);
```

For this simulation program, we terminate the program by closing the command prompt window or selecting an appropriate menu choice in the IDE. The real program may be terminated when the administrator enters a special code (see the chapter Exercise 7).

step 2 code   Here's the **InputFrame** class:

```
/*
    Chapter 8 Sample Development: Keyless Entry System

    File: InputFrame.java

*/

import javax.swing.*;
import java.awt.*;
import java.awt.event.*;
```

```
class InputFrame extends JFrame implements ActionListener {

    private static final int FRAME_WIDTH    = 300;        Data members
    private static final int FRAME_HEIGHT   = 200;
    private static final int FRAME_X_ORIGIN = 150;
    private static final int FRAME_Y_ORIGIN = 250;

    private static final String EMPTY = "";

    private JTextField nameTF;
    private JTextField roomTF;
    private JTextField pwdTF;

    private JButton okButton;
    private JButton clearButton;

    private Ch8EntranceMonitor supervisor;

    public InputFrame(Ch8EntranceMonitor sup) {           Constructor

        supervisor = sup;

        //set the frame properties
        setSize       ( FRAME_WIDTH, FRAME_HEIGHT );
        setResizable  ( false );
        setTitle      ( "Dorm Entrance Monitor" );
        setLocation   ( FRAME_X_ORIGIN, FRAME_Y_ORIGIN );

        addComponents( );

        okButton.addActionListener(this);
        clearButton.addActionListener(this);

        setDefaultCloseOperation(DO_NOTHING_ON_CLOSE);
    }
                                                          actionPerformed
    public void actionPerformed(ActionEvent event) {

        JButton clickedButton = (JButton) event.getSource();

        if (clickedButton == clearButton) {
            clearEntries();
        } else {

            if (isAllDataAvailable()) {

                supervisor.notify(getNameTF(), getRoomTF(), getPwdTF());
            } else {
```

```
            JOptionPane.showMessageDialog(null,
                                    "Not all data are entered");
        }
    }
}

public void clearEntries() {
    nameTF.setText(EMPTY);
    roomTF.setText(EMPTY);
     pwdTF.setText(EMPTY);
}

private void addComponents( ) {

    JLabel nameLbl, roomLbl, pwdLbl;

    Container contentPane = getContentPane();

    //set the content pane properties
    contentPane.setLayout( null );
    contentPane.setBackground( Color.white );

    //create GUI objects
    nameLbl = new JLabel("Name:");
    roomLbl = new JLabel("Room:");
    pwdLbl  = new JLabel(" Pwd:");

    nameTF = new JTextField( );
    roomTF = new JTextField( );
    pwdTF  = new JTextField( );

    okButton    = new JButton("OK");
    clearButton = new JButton("Clear");

    //set bounds
    nameLbl.setBounds(60, 20, 50, 25);
    roomLbl.setBounds(60, 55, 50, 25);
     pwdLbl.setBounds(60, 90, 50, 25);

    nameTF.setBounds(150, 20, 100, 25);
    roomTF.setBounds(150, 55, 100, 25);
     pwdTF.setBounds(150, 90, 100, 25);

       okButton.setBounds( 70, 130, 80, 30);
    clearButton.setBounds(160, 130, 80, 30);

    contentPane.add(nameLbl);
    contentPane.add(roomLbl);
    contentPane.add(pwdLbl);
```

clearEntries

addComponents

```
        contentPane.add(nameTF);
        contentPane.add(roomTF);
        contentPane.add(pwdTF);

        contentPane.add(okButton);
        contentPane.add(clearButton);
    }

    private boolean isAllDataAvailable( ) {

        if (!getNameTF().equals(EMPTY) &&
            !getRoomTF().equals(EMPTY) &&
            !getPwdTF().equals(EMPTY)) {

            return true;

        } else {

            return false;
        }
    }

    private String getNameTF( ) {

        return nameTF.getText();
    }

    private String getRoomTF( ) {
        return roomTF.getText();
    }

    private String getPwdTF( ) {
        return pwdTF.getText();
    }
}
```

isAllDataAvailable

Accessors

The main class is now modified to control an **InputFrame** object and to check entered information as the resident list maintained by a **Dorm** object. Here's the step 2 **Ch8EntranceMonitor** class:

```
/*

    Chapter 8 Sample Development: Keyless Entry System.

    File: Ch8EntranceMonitor.java

*/
```

```java
import javax.swing.*;
import java.io.*;
import java.awt.*;

class Ch8EntranceMonitor {

    private Dorm        manager;           // Data members

    private InputFrame input;

    private Door        door;

    public Ch8EntranceMonitor( ) {         // Constructor

        manager = new Dorm();
        input   = new InputFrame(this);
        door    = new Door();
    }

    public static void main(String[] args) {

        Ch8EntranceMonitor sentry = new Ch8EntranceMonitor();
        sentry.start();
    }

    public void start( ) {                 // start

        openFile( );

        String roster = manager.getResidentList(); //TEMP

        System.out.println(roster); //TEMP

        showInputFrame();
    }                                      // notify

    public void notify(String name, String room, String password) {

        System.out.println("Inside notify"); //TEMP

        Resident res = manager.getResident(name);

        if (res == null) {
            JOptionPane.showMessageDialog(input,"Invalid Entry");
        } else if (res.getName().equals(name) &&
                   res.getRoom().equals(room) &&
                   res.getPassword().equals(password)) {
            door.open();
            input.clearEntries();
```

```
        } else {
            JOptionPane.showMessageDialog(input, "Invalid Entry");
        }
    }

    private void openFile( ) {
        String filename;

        while (true) {
        filename = JOptionPane.showInputDialog(null,"File to open:");

            if (filename == null) {//input dialog was canceled
                System.exit(0);
            }

            try {
                manager.openFile(filename);
                return;
            } catch (FileNotFoundException e) {
                JOptionPane.showMessageDialog(null,"No such file");
            } catch (IOException e) {
                JOptionPane.showMessageDialog(null,
                                        "Error in reading file");

            }
        }
    }

    private void showInputFrame( ) {

        input   = new InputFrame(this);

        input.setTitle("Dorm Entrance Monitor");

        input.setVisible(true);
    }
}
```

openFile

showInputFrame

step 2 test

The purpose of step 2 testing is to verify the correct behavior of an **InputFrame** object and the **notify** method of **Ch8EntranceMonitor.** We need to test both successful and unsuccessful cases. We must verify that the door is in fact opened when valid information is entered. We must also verify that the error message is displayed when there's an error in input. We should test invalid cases such as entering a nonexistent name, correct name but wrong password, not entering all information, and so forth.

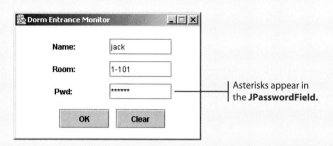

Figure 8.11 The **InputFrame** window with **JPasswordField** for password entry.

Step 3 Development: Improve and Finalize

One possible improvement is the use of **JPasswordField.** This is a subclass of **JTextField** that behaves exactly as **JTextField** except that the entered characters are not displayed. Instead an asterisk is shown for each character entered. This is perfect for the password entry. The step 3 **InputFrame** class includes this modification. See Figure 8.11. Notice the asterisks in the password field.

Another improvement is to allow the administrator to terminate the program by entering special code. See Exercise 7.

Summary

- Two techniques to improve program reliability are exception handling and assertion.
- Exception handling is another type of control flow.
- An exception represents an error condition, and when it occurs, we say an exception is thrown.
- A thrown exception must be handled by either catching it or propagating it to other methods.
- If the program does include code to handle the thrown exceptions, then the system will handle them.
- A single method can be both a catcher and a propagator of an exception.
- The standard classes described or used in this chapter are

Throwable	RuntimeException
Error	IllegalArgumentException
Exception	NumberFormatException
IOException	

- The assertion feature is new to Java 2 SDK 1.4. You must use this version of the compiler to use assertions in the program.

- The assertion feature is used to detect internal logic errors.

Key Concepts

exceptions	programmer-defined exceptions
try-catch	assertions
finally	precondition assertions
throws	postcondition assertions
throw	supervisor-subordinate design pattern
exception hierarchy	

Exercises

1. Determine the output of the following code when the input is (a) −1, (b) 0, and (c) 12XY.

```java
try {
    number = Integer.parseInt(
                    JOptionPane.showInputDialog(null,
                                                "input"));
    if (number != 0) {
        throw new Exception("Not Zero");
    }
} catch (NumberFormatException e) {
    System.out.println("Cannot convert to int");

} catch (Exception e) {
    System.out.println("Error: " + e.getMessage());
}
```

2. Determine the output of the following code when the input is (a) −1, (b) 0, and (c) 12XY. This is the same question as Exercise 1, but the code here has the finally clause.

```java
try {
    number = Integer.parseInt(
                    JOptionPane.showInputDialog(null,
                                                "input"));
    if (number != 0) {
        throw new Exception("Not Zero");
    }
} catch (NumberFormatException e) {
    System.out.println("Cannot convert to int");
```

```
} catch (Exception e) {
   System.out.println("Error: " + e.getMessage());

} finally {
   System.out.println("Finally Clause Executed");
}
```

3. Implement the improved version of InputHandler class from Chapter 4 by adding exception-handling routines. In the original version, when the user enters an input that cannot be converted to an integer, for example, the getInteger method will throw a runtime exception NumberFormatException. Modify all the get methods so they will repeat, asking the user until valid input is entered.

4. Modify the following code by adding the assert statement. The value of gender is either MALE or FEMALE if the program is running correctly.

```
switch (gender) {

    case MALE:      totalFee = tuition + parkingFee;
                    break;

    case FEMALE:    totalFee = tuition + roomAndBoard;
                    break;
}
```

5. Modify the following method by adding the assert statement. Assume the variable factor is a data member of the class.

```
public double compute(double value) {

    return (value * value) / factor;
}
```

6. Let the Professor class be the supervisor and the TeachingAssistant class the subordinate. There are two teaching assistants assigned to a professor. To simulate the grading done by teaching assistants, implement the TeachingAssistant class as a subclass of JFrame and include two text fields and one button. Two text fields are used to enter the student name and grade. When a grade of less than 50 is entered, the teaching assistant will notify the supervising professor. Each teaching assistant is given a unique name, and this name is passed to the professor when a notification is sent, in addition to the grade and the student name. The notified professor displays a warning message by using JOptionPane (this action simulates sending an e-mail to the students). Include all three pieces of information (teaching assistant name, student name, and grade) in the warning message.

7. The user module of the keyless entry system in Section 8.8 does not include any logic to terminate the program. Modify the program so it will terminate when the values Admin, X123, and $maTrix%TwO$ are entered for name, room, and password, respectively.

Development Exercises

For the following exercises, use the incremental development methodology to implement the program. For each exercise, identify the program tasks, create a design document with class descriptions, and draw the program diagram. Map out the development steps at the start. Present any design alternatives and justify your selection. Be sure to perform adequate testing at the end of each development step.

8. In the sample development, we developed the user module of the keyless entry system. For this exercise, implement the administrative module that allows the system administrator to add and delete Resident objects and modify information on existing Resident objects. The module will also allow the user to open a list from a file and save the list to a file. Is it proper to implement the administrative module by using one class? Wouldn't it be a better design if we used multiple classes with each class doing a single well-defined task?

9. Write an application that maintains the membership lists of five social clubs in a dormitory. The five social clubs are the Computer Science Club, Biology Club, Billiard Club, No Sleep Club, and Wine Tasting Club. Use the Dorm class to manage the membership lists. Members of the social clubs are Resident objects of the dorm. Use a separate file to store the membership list for each club. Your program should be able to include a menu item for each social club. When a club is selected, open a ClubFrame frame that will allow the user to add, delete, or modify members of the club. The program can have up to five ClubFrame frames opened at the same time. Make sure you do not open multiple instances of ClubFrame for the same club.

10. Implement the TeachArithmeticFrame program from Exercise 14 in Chapter 7 again. This time, include exception-handling routines and assertions as appropriate.

9 Characters and Strings

After you have read and studied this chapter, you should be able to

- Declare and manipulate data of the **char** type.

- Write string processing programs, using **String** and **StringBuffer** objects.

- Specify regular expressions for searching a pattern in a string.

- Differentiate the **String** and **StringBuffer** classes and use the correct class in solving a given task.

- Tell the difference between equality and equivalence testings for **String** objects.

Introduction

arly computers in the 1940s and 1950s were more like gigantic calculators because they were used primarily for numerical computation. However, as computers have evolved to possess more computational power, our use of computers is no longer limited to numerical computation. Today we use computers for processing information of diverse types. In fact, most application software today such as web browsers, word processors, database management systems, presentation software, and graphics design software is not intended specifically for number crunching. These programs still perform numerical computation, but their primary data are text, graphics, video, and other nonnumerical data. We have already seen examples of nonnumerical data processing. We introduced the String class and string processing in Chapter 2. A nonnumerical data type called boolean was used in Chapters 5 and 6. In this chapter, we will delve more deeply into the String class and present advanced string processing. We will also introduce the char data type for representing a single character and the StringBuffer class for an efficient operation on a certain type of string processing.

9.1 | Characters

char

In Java single characters are represented by using the data type **char**. Character constants are written as symbols enclosed in single quotes, for example, 'a', 'X', and '5'. Just as we use different formats to represent integers and real numbers using 0s and 1s in computer memory, we use special codes of 0s and 1s to represent single characters. For example, we may assign 1 to represent 'A' and 2 to represent 'B'. We can assign codes similarly to lowercase letters, punctuation marks, digits, and other special symbols. In the early days of computing, different computers used not only different coding schemes but also different character sets. For example, one computer could represent the symbol ¼, while other computers could not. Individualized coding schemes did not allow computers to share information. Documents created by using one scheme are complete gibberish if we try to read these documents by using another scheme. To avoid this problem, U.S. computer manufacturers devised several coding schemes. One of the coding schemes widely used today is *ASCII* (American Standard Code for Information Interchange). We pronounce ASCII "ăs kē." Table 9.1 shows the 128 standard ASCII codes.

ASCII

Adding the row and column indexes gives you the ASCII code for a given character. For example, the value 87 is the ASCII code for the character 'W'. Not all characters in the table are printable. ASCII codes 0 through 31 and 127 are nonprintable control characters. For example, ASCII code 7 is the bell (the computer beeps when you send this character to output), and code 9 is the tab.

When we use a word processor to create a document, the file that contains the document includes not only the contents but also the formatting information. Since each software company uses its own coding scheme for storing this information, we have to use the same word processor to open the document. Often it is even worse. We cannot open a document created by a newer version of the same word processor with an older version. If we just want to exchange the text of a document, then we can convert it to ASCII format. Any word processor can open and save ASCII file. If we would like to retain the formatting information also, we can convert the document using software such as Adobe Acrobat. This software converts a document (including text, formatting, images, etc.) created by different word processors to a format called PDF. Anybody with a free Acrobat Reader can open a PDF file. Many of the documents available from our website are in this PDF format.

To represent all 128 ASCII codes, we need 7 bits ranging from 000 0000 (0) to 111 1111 (127). Although 7 bits is enough, ASCII codes occupy 1 byte (8 bits) because the byte is the smallest unit of memory you can access. Computer manufacturers use the extra bit for other nonstandard symbols (e.g., lines and boxes). Using 8 bits, we can represent 256 symbols in total—128 standard ASCII codes and 128 nonstandard symbols.

Table 9.1   ASCII codes.

	0	1	2	3	4	5	6	7	8	9
0	nul	soh	stx	etx	eot	enq	ack	bel	bs	ht
10	lf	vt	ff	cr	so	si	dle	dc1	dc2	dc3
20	cd4	nak	syn	etb	can	em	sub	esc	fs	gs
30	rs	us	sp	!	"	#	$	%	&	'
40	(	)	*	+	,	-	.	/	0	1
50	2	3	4	5	6	7	8	9	:	;
60	<	=	>	?	@	A	B	C	D	E
70	F	G	H	I	J	K	L	M	N	O
80	P	Q	R	S	T	U	V	W	X	Y
90	Z	[	\	]	^	_	`	a	b	c
100	d	e	f	g	h	i	j	k	l	m
110	n	o	p	q	r	s	t	u	v	w
120	x	y	z	{	|	}	~	del		

The standard ASCII codes work just fine as long as we are dealing with the English language because all letters and punctuation marks used in English are included in the ASCII codes. We cannot say the same for other languages. For languages such as French and German, the additional 128 codes may be used to represent character symbols not available in standard ASCII. But what about different currency symbols? What about non-European languages? Chinese, Japanese, and Korean all use different coding schemes to represent their character sets. Eight bits is not enough to represent thousands of ideographs. If we try to read Japanese characters using ASCII, we will see only meaningless symbols.

To accommodate the character symbols of non-English languages, the Unicode Consortium established the *Unicode Worldwide Character Standard,* commonly known simply as *Unicode,* to support the interchange, processing, and display of the written texts of diverse languages. The standard currently contains 34,168 distinct characters, which cover the major languages of the Americas, Europe, the Middle East, Africa, India, Asia, and Pacifica. To accommodate such a large number of distinct character symbols, Unicode characters occupy 2 bytes. Unicode codes for the character set shown in Table 9.1 are the same as ASCII codes.

Unicode

Java, being a language for the Internet, uses the Unicode standard for representing char constants. Although Java uses the Unicode standard internally to store characters, to use foreign characters for input and output in our programs, the operating system and the development tool we use for Java programs must be capable of handling the foreign characters.

Characters are declared and used in a manner similar to data of other types. The declaration

```
char ch1, ch2 = 'X';
```

declares two char variables ch1 and ch2 with ch2 initialized to 'X'. We can display the ASCII code of a character by converting it to an integer. For example, we can execute

```
JOptionPane.showMessageDialog("ASCII code of character X is "
                            + (int)'X' );
```

Conversely, we can see a character by converting its ASCII code to the char data type, for example,

```
JOptionPane.showMessageDialog(
            "Character with ASCII code 88 is " + (char)88 );
```

Because the characters have numerical ASCII values, we can compare characters just as we compare integers and real numbers. For example, the comparison

```
'A' < 'c'
```

returns true because the ASCII value of 'A' is 65 while that of 'c' is 99.

1. Determine the output of the following statements:

```
a. System.out.println( (char) 65 );
b. System.out.println( (int) 'C' );
c. System.out.println( 'Y' );
d. if ( 'A' < '?' )
       System.out.println( 'A' );
   else
       System.out.println( '?' );
```

2. How many distinct characters can you represent by using 8 bits?

9.2 │ Strings

String

A *string* is a sequence of characters that is treated as a single value. Instances of the String class are used to represent strings in Java. Rudimentary string processing was already presented in Chapter 2, using methods such as substring, length, and indexOf. In this section we will learn more advanced string processing, using other methods of the String class.

To introduce additional methods of the String class, we will go through a number of common string-processing routines. The first is to process a string looking for a certain character or characters. Let's say we want to input a person's name and determine the number of vowels that the name contains. The basic idea is very simple:

```
for each character ch in the string {
    if (ch is a vowel) {
        increment the counter
    }
}
```

There are two details we need to know before being able to translate that into actual code. First, we need to know how to refer to an individual character in the string. Second, we need to know how to determine the size of the string, that is, the number of characters the string contains, so we can write the boolean expression to stop the loop correctly. We know from Chapter 2 that the second task is done by using the length method. For the first task, we use charAt.

charAt

We access individual characters of a string by calling the **charAt** method of the String object. For example, to display the individual characters of the string Sumatra one at a time, we can write

```
String name = "Sumatra";
int    size = name.length();

for (int i = 0; i < size; i++) {
    System.out.println(name.charAt(i));
}
```

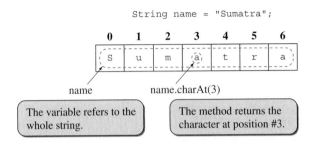

Figure 9.1 An indexed expression is used to refer to individual characters in a string.

Each character in a string has an index that we use to access the character. We use zero-based indexing; that is, the first character has index 0, the second character has index 1, the third character has index 2, and so forth. To refer to the first character of name, for example, we say

```
name.charAt(0)
```

Since the characters are indexed from 0 to size-1, we could express the preceding for loop as

```
for (int i = 0; i <= size - 1; i++)
```

However, we will use the first style almost exclusively to be consistent.

Figure 9.1 illustrates how the charAt method works. Notice that name refers to a String object, and we are calling its charAt method that returns a value of primitive data type char. Strictly speaking, we must say "name is a variable of type String whose value is a reference to an instance of String." However, when the value of a variable X is a reference to an instance of class Y, we usually say "X is an instance of Y" or "X is a Y object."

Helpful Reminder

*If the value of a variable **X** is a reference to an object of class **Y**, then we say "**X** is a **Y** object" or "**X** is an instance of **Y**."*

Since String is a class, we can create an instance of a class by using the new method. The statements we have been using so far, such as

```
String name1 = "Kona";

String name2;
name2 = "Espresso";
```

work as a shorthand for

```
String name1 = new String("Kona");

String name2;
name2 = new String("Espresso");
```

Be aware that this shorthand works for the String class only. Moreover, although the difference will not be critical in almost all situations, they are not exactly the same. We will discuss the subtle difference between the two in Section 9.5.

Here is the code for counting the number of vowels:

```
/*
    Chapter 9 Sample Program: Count the number of vowels
                              in a given string

    File: Ch9CountVowels.java
*/

import javax.swing.*;

class Ch9CountVowels {
    public static void main (String[] args) {
        String    name;

        int       numberOfCharacters,
                  vowelCount = 0;

        char      letter;

        name = JOptionPane.showInputDialog(null, "What is your name?");

        numberOfCharacters = name.length();

        for (int i = 0; i < numberOfCharacters; i++) {
            letter = name.charAt(i);
            if (   letter == 'a' || letter == 'A' ||
                   letter == 'e' || letter == 'E' ||
                   letter == 'i' || letter == 'I' ||
                   letter == 'o' || letter == 'O' ||
                   letter == 'u' || letter == 'U'      ) {
                vowelCount++;
            }
        }

        JOptionPane.showMessageDialog(null, name + ", your name has " +
                                      vowelCount + " vowels");
    }
}
```

We can shorten the boolean expression in the if statement by using the toUpperCase method of the String class. This method converts every character in a string to uppercase. Here's the rewritten code:

```java
/*
    Chapter 9 Sample Program: Count the number of vowels
                              in a given string using toUpperCase

    File: Ch9CountVowels2.java
*/

import javax.swing.*;

class Ch9CountVowels2 {

    public static void main (String[] args) {

        String      name, nameUpper;

        int         numberOfCharacters,
                    vowelCount = 0;

        char        letter;

        name = JOptionPane.showInputDialog(null, "What is your name?");

        numberOfCharacters = name.length();
        nameUpper = name.toUpperCase();

        for (int i = 0; i < numberOfCharacters; i++) {

            letter = nameUpper.charAt(i);

            if ( letter == 'A' ||
                 letter == 'E' ||
                 letter == 'I' ||
                 letter == 'O' ||
                 letter == 'U'      ) {

                vowelCount++;
            }
        }

        JOptionPane.showMessageDialog(null, name + ", your name has " +
                                    vowelCount + " vowels");

    }
}
```

toUpperCase

Notice that the original string name is unchanged. A new, converted string is returned from the **toUpperCase** method and assigned to the second String variable nameUpper.

Let's try another example. This time we read in a string and count how many words the string contains. For this example we consider a word as a sequence of characters separated, or delimited, by blank spaces. We treat punctuation marks and other symbols as part of a word. Expressing the task in pseudocode, we have the following:

```
read in a sentence;

while (there are more characters in the sentence) {

    look for the beginning of the next word;

    now look for the end of this word;

    increment the word counter;
}
```

We use a while loop here instead of do–while to handle the case when the input sentence contains no characters, that is, when it is an empty string. Let's implement the routine. Here's our first attempt:

```
//Attempt No. 1

static final char BLANK = ' ';

int index, wordCount, numberOfCharacters;
String sentence = JOptionPane.showInputDialog(null,
                                    "Enter a sentence:");

numberOfCharacters = sentence.length();
index       = 0;
wordCount = 0;

while (index < numberOfCharacters ) {

    //ignore blank spaces
    while (sentence.charAt(index) == BLANK) {
        index++;
    }


    //now locate the end of the word
    while (sentence.charAt(index) != BLANK) {
        index++;
    }

    //another word has been found, so increment the counter
    wordCount++;
}
```

Skip blank spaces until a character that is not a blank space is encountered. This is the beginning of a word.

Once the beginning of a word is detected, we skip nonblank characters until a blank space is encountered. This is the end of the word.

This implementation has a problem. The counter variable index is incremented inside the two inner while loops, and this index could become equal to numberOf-Characters, which is an error, because the position of the last character is numberOf-Characters – 1. We need to modify the two while loops so that index will not become larger than numberOfCharacters –1. Here's the modified code:

```
/*
    Chapter 9 Sample Program: Count the number of words
                              in a given string

    File: Ch9CountWords.java (ATTEMPT 2)
*/

import javax.swing.*;

class Ch9CountWords { //ATTEMPT 2

    private static final char BLANK = ' ';

    public static void main (String[] args) {

        int     index, wordCount, numberOfCharacters;

        String  sentence = JOptionPane.showInputDialog(null,
                                        "Enter a sentence:");

        numberOfCharacters  = sentence.length( );
        index               = 0;
        wordCount           = 0;

        while ( index < numberOfCharacters ) {

            //ignore blank spaces
            while (index < numberOfCharacters &&
                    sentence.charAt(index) == BLANK) {

                index++;
            }

            //now locate the end of the word
            while (index < numberOfCharacters &&
                    sentence.charAt(index) != BLANK) {

                index++;
            }

            //another word is found, so increment the counter
            wordCount++;

        }
```

```
            //display the result
            System.out.println( "Input sentence: " + sentence );
            System.out.println("\n");
            System.out.println( "    Word count: " + wordCount + " words" );

    }
}
```

Notice that the order of comparisons in the boolean expression

```
index < numberOfCharacters
        && sentence.charAt(index) == BLANK
```

is critical. If we switch the order to

```
sentence.charAt(index) == BLANK
        && index < numberOfCharacters
```

out-of-bound
exception

and if the last character in the string is a space, then an *out-of-bound exception* will occur because the value of index is a position that does not exist in the string sentence. By putting the expression correctly as

```
index < numberOfCharacters && sentence.charAt(index) != ' '
```

we will not get an out-of-bound exception because the boolean operator && is a short-circuit operator. If the relation index < numberOfCharacters is false, then the second half of the expression sentence.charAT(index) != BLANK will not get evaluated.

There is still a problem with the attempt 2 code. If the sentence ends with one or more blank spaces, then the value for wordCount will be one more than the actual number of words in the sentence. It is left as an exercise to correct this bug (see Exercise 15 at the end of the chapter).

Our third example counts the number of times the word Java occurs in the input. The repetition stops when the word STOP is read. Lowercase and uppercase letters are not distinguished when an input word is compared to Java, but the word STOP for terminating the loop must be in all uppercase letters. Here's the pseudocode:

```
javaCount = 0;

while (true) {
    read in next word;

    if (word is "STOP") {
        break;
    } else if (word is "Java" ignoring cases) {
        javaCount++;
    }
}
```

And here's the actual code. Pay close attention to how the strings are compared.

```
/*
    Chapter 9 Sample Program:

        Count the number of times the word 'java' occurs
        in input. Case-insensitive comparison is used here.
        The program terminates when the word STOP (case-sensitive)
        is entered.

    File: Ch9CountJava.java
*/

import javax.swing.*;

class Ch9CountJava {

    public static void main (String[] args) {

        int        javaCount = 0;

        String     word;

        while (true) {

            word = JOptionPane.showInputDialog(null, "Next word:");

            if ( word.equals("STOP") )    {
                break;

            } else if ( word.equalsIgnoreCase("Java") ) {
                javaCount++;
            }
        }

        System.out.println("'Java' count: " + javaCount );
    }
}
```

String comparison is done by two methods—**equals** and **equalsIgnoreCase**—whose meanings should be clear from the example. Another comparison method is **compareTo**. This method compares two **String** objects str1 and str2 as in

compareTo

```
str1.compareTo( str2 );
```

and returns 0 if they are equal, a negative integer if str1 is less than str2, and a positive integer if str1 is greater than str2. The comparison is based on the lexicographic order of Unicode. For example, caffeine is less than latte. Also, the string jaVa is less than the string java because the Unicode value of V is smaller than the Unicode value of v. (See the ASCII table, Table 9.1.)

Some of you may be wondering why we don't say

```
if ( word == "STOP" )
```

We can, in fact, use the equality comparison symbol == to compare two String objects, but the result is different from the result of the method equals. We will explain the difference in Section 9.5.

Let's try another example, using the substring method we introduced in Chapter 2. To refresh our memory, here's how the method works. If str is a String object, then the expression

```
str.substring ( beginIndex, endIndex )
```

returns a new string that is a substring of str from position beginIndex to endIndex – 1. The value of beginIndex must be between 0 and str.length() – 1, and the value of endIndex must be between 0 and str.length(). In addition, the value of beginIndex must be less than or equal to the value of endIndex. Passing invalid values for beginIndex or endIndex will result in a runtime error.

The following code creates a new string Javanist from Alpinist by using the substring method.

```
String oldWord = "Alpinist";
String newWord = "Java" + oldWord.substring(4,8);
```

In this example, we print out the words from a given sentence, using one line per word. For example, given an input sentence

```
I want to be a Java programmer
```

the code will print out

```
I
want
to
be
a
Java
programmer
```

This sample code is similar to the previous one that counts the number of words in a given sentence. Instead of just counting the words, we need to extract the word from the sentence and print it out. Here's how we write the code:

```
/*
    Chapter 9 Sample Program:

        Extract the words in a given sentence and
        print them using one line per word.

    File: Ch9ExtractWords.java
*/

import javax.swing.*;

class Ch9ExtractWords {

    private static final char BLANK = ' ';

    public static void main (String[] args) {

        int        index,      numberOfCharacters,
                   beginIdx, endIdx;

        String     word,
                   sentence = JOptionPane.showInputDialog(null, "Input:");

        numberOfCharacters = sentence.length();
        index = 0;

        while ( index < numberOfCharacters ) {

            //ignore leading blank spaces
            while (index < numberOfCharacters &&
                    sentence.charAt(index) == BLANK) {

                index++;
            }

            beginIdx = index;

            //now locate the end of the word
            while (index < numberOfCharacters &&
                    sentence.charAt(index) != BLANK) {

                index++;
            }

            endIdx = index;
```

```
      //System.out.println( beginIdx + "        " + endIdx );  //TEMP

   if (beginIdx != endIdx) {

      //another word is found, extract it from the
      //sentence and print it out

        word = sentence.substring( beginIdx, endIdx );

        System.out.println(word);
      }
   }
  }
 }
```

Notice the signficance of the test

```
      if (beginIdx != endIdx)
```

in the code. For what kinds of input sentences will the variables beginIdx and endIdx be equal? We'll leave this as an exercise (see Exercise 16 at the end of the chapter).

Quick
CHECK

1. Determine the output of the following code:

   a.
   ```
   String str = "Programming";
   for (int i = 0; i < 9; i+=2) {
      System.out.print( str.charAt( i ) );
   }
   ```

   b.
   ```
   String str = "World Wide Web";
   for (int i = 0; i < 10; i ++ ) }
      if ( str.charAt(i) == 'W') {
         System.out.println( 'M' );
      } else {
         System.out.print( str.charAt(i) );
      }
   }
   ```

2. Write a loop that prints out a string in reverse. If the string is Hello, then the code outputs olleH. Use System.out.

3. Assume two String objects str1 and str2 are initialized as follows:

   ```
   String str1 = "programming";
   String str2 = "language";
   ```

Determine the value of each of the following expressions if they are valid. If they are not valid, state the reason why.

a. `str1.compareTo( str2 )`
b. `str2.compareTo( str2 )`
c. `str2.substring( 1, 1 )`
d. `str2.substring( 0, 7 )`
e. `str2.charAt( 11 )`
f. `str1.length( ) + str2.length( )`

4. What is the difference between the two String methods equals and equalsIgnoreCase?

9.3 | Pattern Matching and Regular Expression

One sample code from Section 9.2 searched for the word Java in a given string. This sample code illustrated a very simplified version of a well-known problem called *pattern matching*. Word processor features such as finding a text and replacing a text with another text are two specialized cases of a pattern-matching problem. Because pattern matching is so common in many applications, from Java 2 SDK 1.4, two new classes—Pattern and Matcher—are added. The String class is also modifed to include several new methods that support pattern matching.

pattern matching

The matches Method

Let's begin with the matches method from the String class. In its simplest form, it looks very similar to the equals method. For example, given a string str, the two statements

```
str.equals("Hello");

str.matches("Hello");
```

both evaluate to true if str is the string Hello. However, they are not truly equivalent, because, unlike equals, the argument to the matches method can be a pattern, a feature that brings great flexibility and power to the matches method.

Suppose we assign a three-digit code to all incoming students. The first digit represents the major, and 5 stands for the computer science major. The second digit represents the home state: 1 is for in-state students, 2 is for out-of-state students, and 3 is for foreign students. And the third digit represents the residence of the student. On-campus dormitories are represented by digits from 1 through 7. Students living off campus are represented by digit 8. For example, the valid encodings for students majoring in computer science and living off campus are 518, 528, and 538. The valid three-digit code for computer science majors living in one of the on-campus dormitories can be expressed succinctly as

`5[123][1-7]`

and here's how we interpret the pattern:

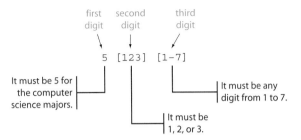

regular
expression

The pattern is called a *regular expression* that allows us to denote a large (often in-finite) set of words succinctly. The "word" is composed of any sequence of symbols and is not limited to alphabets. The brackets [ ] are used here to represent choices, so [123] means 1, 2, or 3. We can use the notation for alphabets also. For example, [aBc] means a, B, or c. Notice the notation is case-sensitive. The hyphen in the brackets shows the range, so [1-7] means any digit from 1 to 7. If we want to allow any lowercase letter, then the regular expression will be [a-z]. The hat symbol ^ is used for negation. For example, [^abc] means any character except a, b, or c. Notice that this expression does not restrict the character to lowercase letters; it can be any character including digits and symbols. To refer to all lowercase letters except a, b, or c, the correct expression is [a-z&&[^abc]]. The double ampersand represents an intersection. Here are more examples:

Expression	Description
[013]	A single digit 0, 1, or 3.
[0-9][0-9]	Any two-digit number from 00 to 99.
A[0-4]b[05]	A string that consists of four characters. The first character is A. The second character is 0, 1, 2, 3, or 4. The third character is b. And the last character is either 0 or 5.
[0-9&&[^4567]]	A single digit that is 0, 1, 2, 3, 8, or 9.
[a-z0-9]	A single character that is either a lowercase letter or a digit.

We can use repetition symbols * or + to designate a sequence of unbounded length. The symbol * means 0 or more times, and the symbol + means 1 or more times. Let's try an example using a repetition symbol. Remember the definition for a valid Java identifier? We define it as a seqence of alphanumeric characters, underscores, and dollar signs, with the first character being an alphabet. In regular expression, we can state this definition as

```
[a-zA-Z][a-zA-Z0-9_$]*
```

Let's write a short program that will input a word and determine whether it is a valid Java identifier. The program stops when the word entered is STOP. Here's the program:

```java
/*
    Chapter 9 Sample Program: Checks whether the input
            string is a valid identifier.

    File: Ch9MatchJavaIdentifier.java
*/

import javax.swing.*;

class Ch9MatchJavaIdentifier {

    private static final String STOP    = "STOP";
    private static final String VALID   = "Valid Java identifier";
    private static final String INVALID = "Not a valid Java identifier";

    private static final String VALID_IDENTIFIER_PATTERN
                    = "[a-zA-Z][a-zA-Z0-9_$]*";

    public static void main (String[] args) {

        String str, reply;

        while (true) {

            str = JOptionPane.showInputDialog(null, "Identifier:");

            if (str.equals(STOP)) break;

            if (str.matches(VALID_IDENTIFIER_PATTERN)) {
                reply = VALID;

            } else {
                reply = INVALID;
            }

            JOptionPane.showMessageDialog(null,
                                          str + ":\n" + reply);
        }
    }
}
```

It is also possible to designate a sequence of fixed length. For example, to specify four-digit numbers, we write [0-9]{4}. The number in the braces { and } denotes the number of repetitions. We can specify the minimum and maximum numbers of repetitions also. Here are the rules:

Expression	Description
X{N}	Repeat X exactly N times, where X is a regular expression for a single character.
X{N,}	Repeat X at least N times.
X{N,M}	Repeat X at least N but no more than M times.

Here's an example of using a sequence of fixed length. Suppose we want to determine whether the input string represents a valid phone number that follows the pattern of

```
xxx-xxx-xxxx
```

where x is a single digit from 0 through 9. The following is a program that inputs a string continually and replies whether the input string conforms to the pattern. The program terminates when a single digit 0 is entered. Structurally this program is identical to the **Ch9MatchJavaIdentifier** class. Here's the program:

```java
/*
    Chapter 9 Sample Program: Checks whether the input
            string conforms to the phone number
            pattern xxx-xxx-xxxx.

    File: Ch9MatchPhoneNumber.java
*/

import javax.swing.*;

class Ch9MatchPhoneNumber {

    private static final String STOP    = "0";
    private static final String VALID   = "Valid phone number";
    private static final String INVALID = "Not a valid phone number";

    private static final String VALID_PHONE_PATTERN
                = "[0-9]{3}-[0-9]{3}-[0-9]{4}";

    public static void main (String[] args) {

        String phoneStr, reply;

        while (true) {

            phoneStr = JOptionPane.showInputDialog(null, "Phone#:");

            if (phoneStr.equals(STOP)) break;
```

```
    if (phoneStr.matches(VALID_PHONE_PATTERN)) {
        reply = VALID;

    } else {
        reply = INVALID;
    }

    JOptionPane.showMessageDialog(null,
                                    phoneStr + ":\n" + reply);
        }
    }
}
```

Suppose, with the proliferation of cell phones, the number of digits used for a prefix increases from three to four in major cities. (In fact, Tokyo now uses a four-digit prefix. Phenomenal growth in the use of fax machines in both offices and homes caused the increase from three to four digits.) The valid format for phone numbers then becomes

xxx-xxx-xxxx   or   xxx-xxxx-xxxx

This change can be handled effortlessly by defining VALID_PHONE_PATTERN as

```
private static final String VALID_PHONE_PATTERN
    = "[0-9]{3}-[0-9]{3,4}-[0-9]{4}";
```

This is the power of regular expression and pattern-matching methods. All we need to do is to make one simple adjustment to the regular expression. No other changes are made to the program. Had we written the program without using the pattern-matching technique (i.e., written the program using repetition control to test the first to the last character individually), changing the code to handle both a three-digit and a four-digit prefix requires substantially greater effort.

The period symbol (.) is used to match any character except a line terminator such as \n or \r. (By using the Pattern class, we can make it match a line terminator also. We discuss more details on the Pattern class later.) We can use the period symbol with the zero-or-more-times notation * to check if a given string contains a sequence of characters we are looking for. For example, suppose a String object document holds the content of some document, and we want to check if the phrase "zen of objects" is in it. We can do it as

```
String document;

document = ...; //assign text to 'document'

if (document.matches(".*zen of objects.*")) {

    System.out.println("Found");
```

```
} else {

    System.out.println("Not found");

}
```

The brackets [and] are used for expressing a range of choices for a single character. If we need to express a range of choices for multiple characters, then we use the parentheses and the vertical bar. For example, if we search for the word *maximum* or *minimum,* we express the pattern as

```
(max|min)imum
```

Here are some more examples:

Expression	Description
[wb](ad|eed)	Matches wad, weed, bad, and beed.
(pro|anti)-OOP	Matches pro-OOP and anti-OOP.
(AZ|CA|CO)[0-9]{4}	Matches AZxxxx, CAxxxx, and COxxxx, where x is a single digit.

The replaceAll Method

The second method new to the Version 1.4 String class is the replaceAll method. Using this method, we can replace all occurrences of a substring that matches a given regular expression with a given replacement string. For example, here's how to replace all vowels in the string with the @ symbol:

```
String originalText, modifiedText;
originalText = ...; //assign string to 'originalText'

modifiedText = originalText.replaceAll("[aeiou]", "@");
```

Notice the original text is unchanged. The replaceAll method returns a modified text as a separate string. Here are more examples:

Expression	Description
str.replaceAll("OOP", "object-oriented programming")	Replace all occurrences of OOP with object-oriented programming.
str.replaceAll("[0-9]{3}-[0-9]{2}-[0-9]{4}", "xxx-xx-xxxx")	Replace all social security numbers with xxx-xx-xxxx.
str.replaceAll("o{2,}", "oo")	Replace all occurrences of a sequence that has two or more of letter o with oo.

If we want to match only the whole word, we have to use the \b symbol to designate the word boundary. Suppose we write

```
str.replaceAll("temp", "temporary");
```

expecting to replace all occurrences of the abbreviated word temp by temporary. We will get a surprising result. All occurrences of the sequence of characters temp will be replaced; so, for example, words such as attempt or tempting would be replaced by attemporaryt or temporaryting, respectively. To designate the sequence temp as a whole word, we place the word boundary symbol \b in the front and end of the sequence.

```
str.replaceAll("\\btemp\\b", "temporary");
```

Notice the use of two backslashes. The symbol we use in the regular expression is \b. However, we must write this regular expression in a String representation. And remember that the backslash symbol in a string represents a control character such as \n, \t, and \r. To specify the regular expression symbol with a backslash, we must use additional backslash, so the system will not interpret it as some kind of control character. The regular expression we want here is

```
\btemp\b
```

To put it in a string representation, we write

```
"\\btemp\\b"
```

Here are the common backslash symbols used in regular expressions:

Expression	String Representation	Description
\d	"\\d"	A single digit. Equivalent to [0-9].
\D	"\\D"	A single nondigit. Equivalent to [^0-9].
\s	"\\s"	A whitespace character, such as space, tab, new line, etc.
\S	"\\S"	A nonwhitespace character.
\w	"\\w"	A word character. Equivalent to [a-zA-Z_0-9].
\W	"\\W"	A nonword character.
\b	"\\b"	A word boundary (such as a white space and punctuation mark).
\B	"\\B"	A nonword boundary.

We also use the backslash if we want to search for a command character. For example, the plus symbol designates one or more repetitions. If we want to search for the plus symbol in the text, we use the backslash as \+ and to express it as a string, we write "\\+". Here's an example. To replace all occurrences of C and C++ (not necessarily a whole word) with Java, we write

```
str.replaceAll("(C|C\\+\\+)", "Java");
```

Quick
CHECK

1. Describe the string that the following regular expressions match.

   a. `a*b`
   b. `b[aiu]d`
   c. `[Oo]bject(s| )`

2. Write a regular expression for a state vehicle license number whose format is a single capital letter, followed by three digits and four lowercase letters.

3. Which of the following regular expressions are invalid?

   a. `(a-z)*+`
   b. `[a|ab]xyz`
   c. `abe-14`
   d. `[a-z&&^a^b]`
   e. `[//one]two`

9.4 | The Pattern and Matcher Classes

The matches and replaceAll methods of the String class are shorthand for using the Pattern and Matcher classes from the java.util.regex package. We will describe how to use these two classes for more efficient pattern matching.

The statement

```
str.matches(regex);
```

where str and regex are String objects is equivalent to

```
Pattern.matches(regex, str);
```

which in turn is equivalent to

```
Pattern pattern = Pattern.compile(regex);
Matcher matcher = pattern.matcher(str);
matcher.matches();
```

Similarly, the statement

```
str.replaceAll(regex, replacement);
```

where replacement is a replacement text is equivalent to

```
Pattern pattern = Pattern.compile(regex);
Matcher matcher = pattern.matcher(str);
matcher.replaceAll(replacement);
```

Explicit creation of **Pattern** and **Matcher** objects gives us more options and efficiency. We specify regular expressions as strings, but for the system to actually carry out the pattern-matching operation, the stated regular expression must first be converted to an internal format. This is done by the **compile** method of the **Pattern** class. When we use the **matches** method of the **String** or **Pattern** class, this conversion into the internal format is carried out every time the **matches** method is executed. So if we use the same pattern multiple times, then it is more efficient to convert just once, instead of repeating the same conversion, as was the case for the Ch9MatchJavaIdentifier and Ch9MatchPhoneNumber classes. The following is Ch9MatchJavaIdentifier2, a more efficient version of Ch9MatchJavaIdentifier:

```
/*
    Chapter 9 Sample Program: Checks whether the input
            string is a valid identifier. This version
            uses the Matcher and Pattern classes.

    File: Ch9MatchJavaIdentifier2.java
*/

import javax.swing.*;
import java.util.regex.*;

class Ch9MatchJavaIdentifier2 {

    private static final String STOP    = "STOP";
    private static final String VALID   = "Valid Java identifier";
    private static final String INVALID = "Not a valid Java identifier";

    private static final String VALID_IDENTIFIER_PATTERN
                    = "[a-zA-Z][a-zA-Z0-9_$]*";

    public static void main (String[] args) {

        String    str, reply;
        Matcher   matcher;
        Pattern   pattern
                        = Pattern.compile(VALID_IDENTIFIER_PATTERN);

        while (true) {

            str = JOptionPane.showInputDialog(null, "Identifier:");

            if (str.equals(STOP)) break;

            matcher = pattern.matcher(str);

            if (matcher.matches()) {
                reply = VALID;

            } else {
                reply = INVALID;
            }
```

```
                    JOptionPane.showMessageDialog(null, str + ":\n" + reply);
        }
    }
}
```

We have a number of options when the Pattern compiles into an internal format. For example, by default, the period symbol does not match the line terminator character. We can override this default by passing DOTALL as the second argument as

```
        Pattern pattern = Pattern.compile(regex, Pattern.DOTALL);
```

To enable case-insensitive matching, we pass the CASE_INSENSITIVE constant.

The find method is another powerful method of the Matcher class. This method searches for the next sequence in a string that matches the pattern. The method returns true if the patten is found. We can call the method repeatedly until it returns false to find all matches. Here's an example that counts the number of times the word java occurs in a given document. We will search for the word in a case-insensitive manner.

```
/*
    Chapter 9 Sample Program:

        Count the number of times the word 'java' occurs
        in input using pattern matching technique.
        The program terminates when the word STOP (case-sensitive)
        is entered.

    File: Ch9PMCountJava.java
*/

import javax.swing.*;
import java.util.regex.*;

class Ch9PMCountJava {

    public static void main (String[] args) {

        String    document;
        int       javaCount;

        Matcher   matcher;
        Pattern   pattern = Pattern.compile("java",
                                        Pattern.CASE_INSENSITIVE);

        document  = JOptionPane.showInputDialog(null, "Sentence:");

        javaCount = 0;
        matcher   = pattern.matcher(document);
```

```
            while (matcher.find()) {

                javaCount++;
            }

            JOptionPane.showMessageDialog(null,
                                          "The word 'java' occurred " +
                                javaCount + " times.");

        }
}
```

When a matcher finds a matching sequence of characters, we can query the location of the sequence by using the start and end methods. The start method returns the position in the string where the first character of the pattern is found, and the end method returns the value 1 more than the position in the string where the last character of the pattern is found. Here's the code that prints out the matching sequences and their locations in the string when searching for the word java in a case-insensitive manner.

```
/*
    Chapter 9 Sample Program:

            Displays the positions the word 'java' occurs
            in a given string using pattern matching technique.
            The program terminates when the word STOP (case-sensitive)
            is entered.

    File: Ch9PMCountJava2.java
*/

import javax.swing.*;
import java.util.regex.*;

class Ch9PMCountJava2 {

    public static void main (String[] args) {

        String    document;
        int       javaCount;

        Matcher   matcher;
        Pattern   pattern = Pattern.compile("java",
                                        Pattern.CASE_INSENSITIVE);

        document  = JOptionPane.showInputDialog(null, "Sentence:");

        javaCount = 0;
```

```
matcher   = pattern.matcher(document);

while (matcher.find()) {

    System.out.println(document.substring(matcher.start(),
                                            matcher.end())
                    + " found at position "
                    + matcher.start());
    }
  }
}
```

Quick
CHECK

1. Replace the following statements with the equivalent ones using the **Pattern** and **Matcher** classes:

   a. `str.replaceAll("1", "one");`
   b. `str.matches("alpha");`

2. Using the **find** method of the **Matcher** class, check if the given string document contains the whole word **Java**.

9.5 | Comparing Strings

We already discussed how objects are compared in Chapter 5. The same rule applies for the string, but we have to be careful for a certain situation because of the difference in the way a new **String** object is created. First, we will review how the objects are compared. The difference between

```
String word1, word2;
. . .

if ( word1 == word2 ) . . .
```

== versus
equals

and

```
if ( word1.equals(word2) ) . . .
```

is illustrated in Figure 9.2. The equality test **==** is **true** if the contents of variables are the same. For a primitive data type, the contents are values themselves; but for a reference data type, the contents are addresses. So for a reference data type, the equality test is **true** if both variables refer to the same object, because they both contain the same address. The equals method, on the other hand, is **true** if the **String** objects to which the two variables refer contain the same string value. To distinguish the two types of comparisons, we will use the term *equivalence test* for the equals method.

equivalence
test

Case A: Referring to the same object.

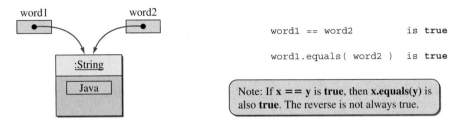

Case B: Referring to different objects having identical string values.

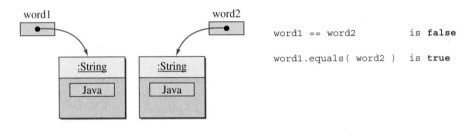

Case C: Referring to different objects having different string values.

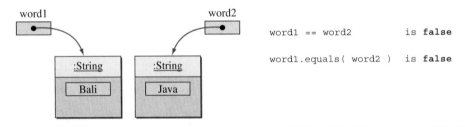

Figure 9.2 The difference between the equality test and the **equals** method.

As long as we create a new String object as

```
String str = new String("Java");
```

using the new operator, the rule for comparing objects applies to comparing strings. However, when the new operator is not used, for example,

```
String str = "Java";
```

we have to be careful. Figure 9.3 shows the difference in assigning a String object to a variable. If we do not use the new operator, then string data are treated as if they

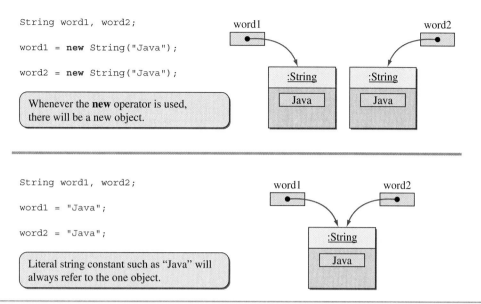

```
String word1, word2;

word1 = new String("Java");

word2 = new String("Java");
```

> Whenever the **new** operator is used, there will be a new object.

```
String word1, word2;

word1 = "Java";

word2 = "Java";
```

> Literal string constant such as "Java" will always refer to the one object.

Figure 9.3 Difference between using and not using the **new** operator for **String.**

are primitive data type. When we use the same literal String constants in a program, there will be exactly one String object.

Quick **CHECK**

1. Show the state of memory after the following statements are executed.

```
String str1, str2, str3;
str1 = "Jasmine";
str2 = "Oolong";
str3 = str2;
str2 = str1;
```

9.6 | StringBuffer

A String object is immutable, which means that once a String object is created, we cannot change it. In other words, we can read individual characters in a string, but we cannot add, delete, or modify characters of a String object. Remember that the methods of the String class, such as replaceAll and substring, do not modify the original string; they return a new string. Java adopts this immutability restriction to implement an efficient memory allocation scheme for managing String objects. The immutability is the reason why we can treat the string data much as a primitive data type.

Creating a new string from the old one will work for most cases, but sometimes manipulating the content of a string directly is more convenient. When we

string
manipulation

need to compose a long string from a number of words, for example, being able to manipulate the content of a string directly is much more convenient than creating a new copy of a string. *String manipulation* here means operations such as replacing a character, appending a string with another string, deleting a portion of a string, and so forth. If we need to manipulate the content of a string directly, we must use the StringBuffer class. For example, the code

```
StringBuffer word = new StringBuffer( "Java" );
word.setCharAt(0, 'D');
word.setCharAt(1, 'i');
```

will modify the string Java to Diva. No new string is created—the original string Java is modified. Also, you must use the new method to create a StringBuffer object.

StringBuffer

Let's look at some examples using **StringBuffer** objects. The first example reads a sentence and replaces all vowels in the sentence with the character X.

```
/*
    Chapter 9 Sample Program: Replace every vowel in a given sentence
                              with 'X' using StringBuffer.

    File: Ch9ReplaceVowelsWithX.java
*/

import javax.swing.*;

class Ch9ReplaceVowelsWithX {

    public static void main (String[] args) {

        StringBuffer    tempStringBuffer;
        String          inSentence;

        int             numberOfCharacters;
        char            letter;

        inSentence          = JOptionPane.showInputDialog(null,
                                                "Enter a sentence:");

        tempStringBuffer    = new StringBuffer(inSentence);

        numberOfCharacters = tempStringBuffer.length();

        for (int index = 0; index < numberOfCharacters; index++) {

            letter = tempStringBuffer.charAt(index);

            if ( letter == 'a' || letter == 'A' ||
                 letter == 'e' || letter == 'E' ||
                 letter == 'i' || letter == 'I' ||
                 letter == 'o' || letter == 'O' ||
                 letter == 'u' || letter == 'U'      ) {
```

```
            tempStringBuffer.setCharAt(index,'X');
        }
    }

    System.out.println( "Input:   " + inSentence + "\n");
    System.out.println( "Output: " + tempStringBuffer );
    }
}
```

Notice how the input routine is done. We are reading in a String object and converting it to a StringBuffer object, because we cannot simply assign a String object to a StringBuffer variable. For example, the following code is invalid:

```
StringBuffer strBuffer = JOptionPane.showInputDialog(null,
                                    "Enter a sentence:");
```

We are required to create a StringBuffer object from a String object as in

```
String       str   = "Hello";
StringBuffer strBuf = new StringBuffer( str );
```

Helpful Reminder

*We cannot input **StringBuffer** objects. We have to input **String** objects and convert them to **StringBuffer** objects.*

Our next example constructs a new sentence from input words that have an even number of letters. The program stops when the word STOP is read. Let's begin with the pseudocode:

```
set tempStringBuffer to empty string;

repeat = true;

while ( repeat ) {

    read in next word;

    if (word is "STOP") {

        repeat = false;

    } else if (word has even number of letters) {

        append word to tempStringBuffer;

    }
}
```

And here's the actual code:

```
/*
    Chapter 9 Sample Program: Constructs a new sentence from
                             input words that have an even number of letters.

    File: Ch9EvenLetterWords.java
*/

import javax.swing.*;

class Ch9EvenLetterWords {

    public static void main (String[] args) {

        boolean        repeat = true;
        String         word;

        StringBuffer tempStringBuffer = new StringBuffer("");

        while ( repeat ) {

            word = JOptionPane.showInputDialog(null, "Next word:");

            if ( word.equals("STOP") ) {

                repeat = false;

            } else if ( word.length() % 2 == 0 ) {

                tempStringBuffer.append(word + " ");

            }
        }

        System.out.println( "Output: " + tempStringBuffer );

    }
}
```

Create **StringBuffer** object with an empty string.

Append **word** and a space to **tempStringBuffer.**

We use the append method to append a String or a StringBuffer object to the end of a StringBuffer object. The method append also can take an argument of the primitive data type. For example, all the following statements are valid:

```
int     i  = 12;
float   x  = 12.4f;
char    ch = 'W';

StringBuffer str = new StringBuffer("");
```

```
str.append(i);
str.append(x);
str.append(ch);
```

Any primitive data type argument is converted to a string before it is appended to a StringBuffer object.

Notice that we can write the second example using only String objects. Here's how:

```
boolean repeat = true;
String word, newSentence;

newSentence = ""; //empty string
while ( repeat ) {
    word = JOptionPane.showInputDialog(null, "Next word:");

    if ( word.equals("STOP") )
        repeat = false;
    else if ( word.length() % 2 == 0 )
        newSentence = newSentence + word;
                                //string concatenation
}
```

Although this code does not explicitly use any StringBuffer object, the Java compiler may use StringBuffer when compiling the string concatenation operator. For example, the expression

```
newSentence + word
```

can be compiled as if the expression were

```
new StringBuffer().append(word).toString()
```

Using the append method of StringBuffer is preferable to using the string concatenation operator + because we can avoid creating temporary string objects by using StringBuffer.

In addition to appending a string at the end of StringBuffer, we can insert a string at a specified position by using the insert method. The syntax for this method is

```
<StringBuffer> . insert ( <insertIndex>, <value> ) ;
```

where <insertIndex> must be greater than or equal to 0 and less than or equal to the length of <StringBuffer> and the <value> is an object or a value of the primitive data type. For example, to change the string

```
Java is great
```

to

```
Java is really great
```

we can execute

```
StringBuffer str = new StringBuffer("Java is great");
str.insert(8, "really ");
```

Take my Advice

Java 2 SDK version 1.5 includes a new class called **StringBuilder.** This class be-haves exactly the same as the **StringBuffer** class but has a better performance. In some advanced cases you have to use the **StringBuffer** class, but for the sample programs in this book, you can replace all uses of **StringBuffer** with **StringBuilder** and get a better performance. Of course, to use the **StringBuilder** class, you must be using version 1.5 SDK. You can also continue to use the **StringBuffer** class with version 1.5.

Quick CHECK

1. Determine the value of str after the following statements are executed.

   a.
   ```
   StringBuffer str
         = new StringBuffer( "Caffeine" );
   str.insert(0, "Dr. ");
   ```
   b.
   ```
   String       str  = "Caffeine";
   StringBuffer str1 =
       new StringBuffer( str.substring(1, 3) );
   str1.append('e');
   str = "De" + str1;
   ```

2. Assume a String object str is assigned as a string value. Write a code segment to replace all occurrences of lowercase vowels in a given string to the letter C by using String and StringBuffer objects.

9.7   Sample Development

Building Word Concordance

word con-cordance

One technique to analyze a historical document or literature is to track word occur-rences. A basic form of *word concordance* is a list of all words in a document and the number of times each word appears in the document. Word concordance is useful in revealing the writing style of an author. For example, given a word concordance of a document, we can scan through the list and count the number of nouns, verbs, prepositions, and so forth. If the ratios of these grammatical elements differ signifi-cantly between the two documents, there is a high probability that they are not written by the same person. Another application of word concordance is seen in the indexing of a document, which, for each word, lists the page numbers or line numbers where it appears in the document. In this sample development, we will build a word concordance of a given document, utilizing the string-processing technique we learned in this chapter.

One of the most popular search engine websites on the Internet today is Google (**www.google.com**). At the core of their innovative technology is a concordance of all web pages on the Internet. Every month the company's web crawler software visits 3 billion (and steadily growing) web pages, and from these visits, a concordance is built. When the user enters a query, the Google servers search the concordance for a list of matching web pages and return the list in the order of relevance.

Problem Statement

Write an application that will build a word concordance of a document. The output from the application is an alphabetical list of all words in the given document and the number of times they occur in the document. The documents are a text file (contents of the file are ASCII characters), and the output of the program is saved as an ASCII file also.

Overall Plan

As usual, let's begin the program development by first identifying the major tasks of the program. The first task is to get a text document from a designated file. We will use a helper class called **FileManager** to do this task. File-processing techniques to implement the **FileManager** class will be presented in Chapter 12. The whole content of an ASCII file is represented in the program as a single **String** object. Using a pattern-matching technique, we extract individual words from the document. For each distinct word in the document, we associate a counter and increment it every time the word is repeated. We will use the second helper class called **WordList** for maintaining a word list. An entry in this list has two components—a word and how many times this word occurs in the document. A **WordList** object can handle an unbounded number of entries. Entries in the list are arranged in alphabetical order. We will learn how to implement the **WordList** class in Chapter 10.

We can express the program logic in pseudocode as

program
tasks

```
while ( the user wants to process another file ) {

    Task 1: read the file;

    Task 2: build the word list;

    Task 3: save the word list to a file;

}
```

Let's look at the three tasks and determine objects that will be responsible for handling the tasks. For the first task, we will use the helper class **FileManager.** For the second task of building a word list, we will define the **Ch9WordConcordance** class, whose instance will use the **Pattern** and **Matcher** classes for word extraction, and another helper class **WordList** for maintaining the word list. The last task of saving the result is done by the **FileManager** class also.

Finally, we will define a top-level control object that manages all other objects. We will call this class **Ch9WordConcordanceMain.** This will be our instantiable main class. Here's our working design document:

program classes

Design Document: Ch9WordConcordanceMain	
Class	**Purpose**
Ch9WordConcordanceMain	The instantiable main class of the program that implements the top-level program control.
Ch9WordConcordance	The key class of the program. An instance of this class manages other objects to build the word list.
FileManager	A helper class for opening a file and saving the result to a file. Details of this class can be found in Chapter 12.
WordList	Another helper class for maintaining a word list. Details of this class can be found in Chapter 10.
Pattern/Matcher	Classes for pattern-matching operations.

Figure 9.4 is the working program diagram.

In lieu of the **Pattern** and **Matcher** classes, we could use the **StringTokenizer** class. This class is fairly straightforward to use if the white space (tab, return, blank, etc.) is a word delimiter. However, using this class becomes a little more complicated if we need to include punctuation marks and others as a word delimiter also. Overall, the **Pattern** and **Matcher** classes are more powerful and useful in many types of applications than the **StringTokenizer** class.

We will implement this program in four major steps:

development steps

1. Start with a program skeleton. Define the main class with data members. To test the main class, we will also define a skeleton **Ch9WordConcordance** class with just a default constructor.

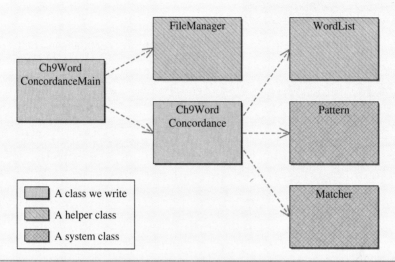

Figure 9.4 The program diagram for the **Ch9WordConcordanceMain** program. Base system classes such as **String** and **JOptionPane** are not shown.

2. Add code to open a file and save the result. Extend the step 1 classes as necessary.

3. Complete the implementation of the **Ch9WordConcordance** class.

4. Finalize the code by removing temporary statements and tying up loose ends.

Step 1 Development: Skeleton

step 1 design

The design of **Ch9WordConcordanceMain** is straightforward, as its structure is very similar to that of other main classes. We will make this an instantiable main class and define the **start** method that implements the top-level control logic. We will define a default constructor to create instances of other classes. A skeleton **Ch9Word-Concordance** class is also defined in this step so we can compile and run the main class. The skeleton **Ch9WordConcordance** class only has an empty default constructor. The working design document for the **Ch9WordConcordanceMain** class is as follows:

Design Document: The Ch9WordConcordanceMain Class		
Method	**Visibility**	**Purpose**
<constructor>	public	Creates the instances of other classes in the program.
start	private	Implements the top-level control logic of the program.

step 1 code

For the skeleton, the **start** method loops (doing nothing inside the loop in this step) until the user selects No on the confirmation dialog. Here's the skeleton:

```java
/*
    Chapter 9 Sample Development: Word Concordance

    File: Step1/Ch9WordConcordanceMain.java
*/

import javax.swing.*;

class Ch9WordConcordanceMain  {

    private FileManager fileManager;
    private Ch9WordConcordance builder;


//-------------------------------
//      Main method
//-------------------------------

    public static void main(String[] args) {
        Ch9WordConcordanceMain main = new Ch9WordConcordanceMain();
        main.start();
    }

    public Ch9WordConcordanceMain() {

        fileManager = new FileManager( );
        builder     = new Ch9WordConcordance( );
    }

    private void start( ) {
        int reply;

        while (true) {

            reply = JOptionPane.showConfirmDialog(null,
                                    "Run the program?",
                                    "Word List Builder",
                                    JOptionPane.YES_NO_OPTION);
            if (reply == JOptionPane.NO_OPTION) {
                break;
            }
        }
```

```
        JOptionPane.showMessageDialog(null,
                                "Thank you for using the program\n"
                                    + "Good-Bye");
    }
}
```

The skeleton **Ch9WordConcordance** class has only an empty default constructor. Here's the skeleton class:

```
class Ch9WordConcordance   {

    public Ch9WordConcordance() {

    }
}
```

step 1 test

We run the program and verify that the constructor is executed correctly and the repetition control in the **start** method works as expected.

Step 2 Development: Open and Save Files

step 2 design

In the second development step, we add routines to handle input and output. The tasks of opening and saving a file are delegated to the service class **FileManager.** We will learn the implementation details of the **FileManager** class in Chapter 12. Our responsibility right now is to use the class correctly. The class provides two key methods: one to open a file and another to save a file. So we can create and view the content easily, the **FileManager** class deals only with text files. To open a text file, we call its **openFile** method. There are two versions. With the first version, we pass the filename. For example, the code

```
FileManager fm  = new FileManager();
String      doc = ...; //assign string data

fm.saveFile("output1.txt", doc);
```

will save the string data **doc** to a file named **output1.txt.** With the second version, we will let the end user select a file using the standard file dialog. A sample file dialog is shown in Figure 9.5. With the second version, we pass only the string data to be saved as

```
fm.saveFile(doc);
```

When there's an error in saving a file, an **IOException** is thrown.

9.7 Sample Development—*continued*

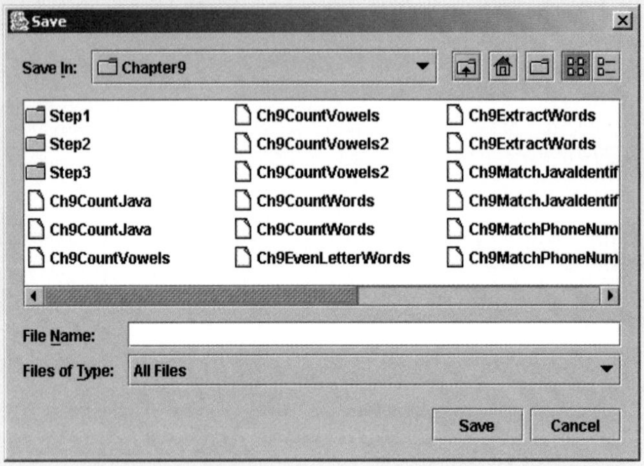

Figure 9.5 A sample file dialog for opening a file.

To open a text file, we use one of the two versions of the **openFile** method. The distinction is identical to the one for the **saveFile** methods. The first version requires the filename to open. The second version allows the end user to select a file to save the data, so we pass no parameter. The **openFile** method will throw a **FileNotFoundException** when the designated file cannot be found and an **IOException** when the designated file cannot be opened correctly.

Here's the summary of the **FileManager** class:

Public Methods of `FileManager`

```
public String openFile(String filename)
                  throws FileNotFoundException, IOException
```
Opens the text file `filename` and returns the content as a `String`.

```
public String openFile( )
                  throws FileNotFoundException, IOException
```
Opens the text file selected by the end user, using the standard file open dialog, and returns the content as a `String`.

```
public String saveFile(String filename, String data)
                       throws IOException
```
Save the string `data` to `filename`.

```
public String saveFile(String data) throws IOException
```
Saves the string `data` to a file selected by the end user, using the standard file save dialog.

We modify the **start** method to open a file, create a word concordance, and then save the generated word concordance to a file. The method is defined as

```
private void start( ) {
    int     reply;
    String document, wordList;

    while (true) {

        reply = ...; //confirmation dialog reply

        if (reply == JOptionPane.NO_OPTION) {
            break;
        }

        document = inputFile(); //open file

        wordList = build(document); //build concordance

        saveFile(wordList); //save the generated concordance
    }
    ... //'Good-bye' message dialog
}
```

Added portion →

The **inputFile** method is defined as

```
private String inputFile( ) {
    String doc = "";

    try {
        doc = fileManager.openFile( );

    } catch (FileNotFoundException e) {
        System.out.println("File not found.");

    } catch (IOException e) {
        System.out.println("Error in opening file: "
                            + e.getMessage());
    }

    System.out.println("Input Document:\n" + doc); //TEMP

    return doc;
}
```

with a temporary output to verify the input routine. Because the **openFile** method of **FileManager** throws exceptions, we handle them here with the **try-catch** block.

The **saveFile** method is defined as

```
private void saveFile(String list) {

    try {
        fileManager.saveFile(list);
```

```
        } catch (IOException e) {
            System.out.println("Error in saving file: "
                                    + e.getMessage());
        }
    }
```

The method is very simple as the hard work of actually saving the text data is done by our **FileManager** helper object.

Finally, the **build** method is defined as

```
private String build(String document) {

    String concordance;

    concordance = builder.build(document);

    return concordance;
}
```

The **Ch9WordConcordanceMain** class is now complete. To run and test this class, we will define a stub **build** method for the **Ch9WordConcordance** class. The method is temporarily defined as

```
public String build(String document) {

    //TEMP
    String list
            = "one 14\ntwo 3\nthree 3\nfour 5\nfive 92\n";

    return list;

    //TEMP
}
```

We will implement the method fully in the next step.

Here's the final **Ch9WordConcordanceMain** class:

step 2 code

```
/*
    Chapter 9 Sample Development: Word Concordance

    File: Step1/Ch9WordConcordanceMain.java
*/
import java.io.*;
import javax.swing.*;

class Ch9WordConcordanceMain   {

    ...
```

```
private String build(String document) {

    String concordance;

    concordance = builder.build(document);

    return concordance;
}

private String inputFile( ) {
    String doc = "";

    try {
        doc = fileManager.openFile( );

    } catch (FileNotFoundException e) {
        System.out.println("File not found.");

    } catch (IOException e) {
      System.out.println("Error in opening file: " + e.getMessage());
    }

    System.out.println("Input Document:\n" + doc); //TEMP

    return doc;
}

private void saveFile(String list) {

    try {
        fileManager.saveFile(list);
    } catch (IOException e) {
      System.out.println("Error in saving file: " + e.getMessage());
    }
}

private void start( ) {
    while (true) {
        ...
        document = inputFile();

        wordList = build(document);

        saveFile(wordList);
    }
    ...
}
}
```

build

inputFile

saveFile

start

The temporary **Ch9WordConcordance** class now has the stub **build** method:

```
class Ch9WordConcordance  {
    ...
    public String build(String document) {

        //TEMP
        String list = "one 14\ntwo 3\nthree 3\nfour 5\nfive 92\n";

        return list;
        //TEMP
    }
}
```

step 2 test

We are ready to run the program. The step 2 directory contains several sample input files. We will open them and verify the file contents are read correctly by checking the temporary echo print output to **System.out.** To verify the output routine, we save to the output (the temporary output created by the **build** method of **Ch9Word-Concordance**) and verify its content. Since the output is a text file, we can use any word processor or text editor to view its contents. (*Note:* If we use NotePad on the Windows platform to view the file, it may not appear correctly. See the box below on how to avoid this problem.)

Take my *Advice*

The control characters used for a line separator are not the same for each platform (Windows, Mac, Unix, etc.) . One platform may use **\n** for a line separator while another platform may use **\r\n** for a line separator. Even on the same platform, different software may not interpret the control characters in the same way. To make our Java code work correctly across all platforms, we do, for example,

```
String newline
    = System.getProperties().getProperty("line.separator");

String output = "line 1" + newline + "line 2" + newline;
```

instead of

```
String output = "line 1\nline 2\n";
```

Step 3 Development: Generate Word Concordance

In the third development step, we finish the program by implementing the **Ch9Word-Concordance** class, specifically, its **build** method. Since we are using another helper class in this step, first we must find out how to use this helper class. The **WordList** class supports the maintenance of a word list. Every time we extract a new word from the document, we enter this word into a word list. If the word is already in the list, its count is incremented by 1. If the word occurs for the first time in the document, then the word is added to the list with its count initialized to 1. When we are done processing the document, we can get the word concordance from a **WordList** by calling its **getConcordance** method. The method returns the list as a single **String** with each line containing a word and its count in the following format:

```
2   Chapter
1   Early
1   However
2   In
1   already
1   also
1   an
7   and
1   are
2   as
1   because
```

Because a single **WordList** object handles multiple documents, there's a method called **reset** to clear the word list before processing the next document. Here's the method summary:

Public Methods of `WordList`

public void `add(String word)`
  Increments the count for the given word. If the word is already in the list, its count is incremented by 1. If the word does not exist in the list, then it is added to the list with its count set to 1.

public `String getConcordance( )`
  Returns the word concordance in alphabetical order of words as a single string. Each line consists of a word and its count.

public void `reset( )`
  Clears the internal data structure so a new word list can be constructed. This method must be called every time before a new document is processed.

The general idea behind the **build** method of the **Ch9WordConcordance** class is straightforward. We need to keep extracting a word from the document,

9.7   Sample Development—*continued*

and for every word found, we add it to the word list. Expressed in pseudocode, we have

```
while (document has more words) {

    word = next word in the document;
    wordList.add(word);
}

String concordance = wordList.getConcordance();
```

The most difficult part here is how to extract words from a document. We can write our own homemade routine to extract words, based on the technique presented in Section 9.2. However, this is too much work to get the task done. Writing a code that detects various kinds of word terminators (in addition to space, punctuation mark, control characters such as tab, new line, etc., all satisfy as the word terminator) is not that easy. Conceptually, it is not that hard, but it can be quite tedious to iron out all the details. Instead, we can use the pattern-matching technique provided by the **Pattern** and **Matcher** classes for a reliable and efficient solution.

The pattern for finding a word can be stated in a regular expression as

```
\b\w+\b
```

Putting it in a string format results in

```
"\\b\\w+\\b"
```

The **Pattern** and **Matcher** objects are thus created as

```
Pattern pattern = Pattern.compile("\\b\\w+\\b");
Matcher matcher = pattern.matcher(document);
```

and the control loop to find and extract words is

```
wordList.reset();

while (matcher.find( )) {

    wordList.add(document.substring(matcher.start(),
                                    matcher.end()));
}
```

step 3 code

Here's the final **Ch9WordConcordance** class:

```
/*
    Chapter 9 Sample Development: Word Concordance

    File: Step3/Ch9WordConcordance.java
*/
```

```
import java.util.regex.*;

class Ch9WordConcordance  {
    private static final String WORD = "\\b\\w+\\b";
    private WordList wordList;
    private Pattern  pattern;

    public Ch9WordConcordance() {
        wordList = new WordList();
        pattern = Pattern.compile(WORD); //pattern is compiled only once
    }

    public String build(String document) {

        Matcher matcher = pattern.matcher(document);

        wordList.reset();

        while (matcher.find()) {
            wordList.add(document.substring(matcher.start(),
                                           matcher.end()));
        }

        return wordList.getConcordance();
    }
}
```

> build

Notice how short the class is, thanks to the power of pattern matching and the helper **WordList** class.

step 3 test

We run the program against varying types of input text files. We can use a long document such as the term paper for the last term's economy class (don't forget to save it as a text file before testing). We should also use some specially created files for testing purposes. One file may contain only one word repeated 7 times, for example. Another file may contain no words at all. We verify that the program works correctly for all types of input files.

Step 4 Development: Finalize

program review

As always, we finalize the program in the last step. We perform a critical review to find any inconsistency or error in the methods, any incomplete methods, places to add more comments, and so forth.

In addition, we may consider possible extensions. One is an integrated user interface where the end user can view both the input document files and the output word list files. Another is the generation of different types of list. In the sample development, we count the number of occurrences of each word. Instead, we can generate a list of positions where each word appears in the document. The **WordList** class itself needs to be modified for such extension.

S u m m a r y

- The char data type represents a single character.
- The char constant is denoted by a single quotation mark, for example, 'a'.
- The character coding scheme used widely today is ASCII (American Standard Code for Information Exchange).
- Java uses Unicode, which is capable of representing characters of diverse languages. ASCII is compatible with Unicode.
- A string is a sequence of characters, and in Java, strings are represented by String objects.
- The Pattern and Matcher classes are introduced in Java 2 SDK 1.4. They provide support for pattern-matching applications.
- Regular expression is used to represent a pattern to match (search) in a given text.
- The String objects are immutable. Once they are created, they cannot be changed.
- To manipulate mutable strings, use StringBuffer.
- Strings are objects in Java, and the rules for comparing objects apply when comparing strings.
- Only one String object is created for the same literal String constants.
- The standard classes described or used in this chapter are

String	Pattern
StringBuffer	Matcher

K e y   C o n c e p t s

characters	pattern matching
strings	character encoding
string processing	String comparison
regular expression	

E x e r c i s e s

1. What is the difference between 'a' and "a"?
2. Discuss the difference between

   ```
   str = str + word; //string concatenation
   ```

   and

   ```
   tempStringBuffer.append(word)
   ```

   where str is a String object and tempStringBuffer is a StringBuffer object.

3. Show that if x and y are String objects and x == y is true, then x.equals(y) is also true, but the reverse is not necessarily true.

4. What will be the output from the following code?

```
StringBuffer word1, word2;
word1 = new StringBuffer("Lisa");
word2 = word1;
word2.insert(0, "Mona ");
System.out.println(word1);
```

5. Show the state of memory after the execution of each statement in the following code:

```
String word1, word2;
word1 = "Hello";
word2 = word1;
word1 = "Java";
```

6. Using a state-of-memory diagram, illustrate the difference between a null string and an empty string—a string that has no characters in it. Show the state-of-memory diagram for the following code. Variable word1 is a null string, while word2 is an empty string.

```
String word1, word2;
word1 = null;
word2 = "";
```

7. Draw a state-of-memory diagram for each of the following groups of statements.

```
String word1, word2;              String word1, word2;

word1 = "French Roast";           word1 = "French Roast";
word2 = word1;                    word2 = "French Roast";
```

8. Write a GUI application that reads in a character and displays the character's ASCII code. The getText method of the JTextField class returns a String object, so you need to extract a char value, as in

```
String inputString = inputField.getText();
char character = inputString.charAt(0);
```

Display an error message if more than one character is entered.

9. Write a method that returns the number of uppercase letters in a String object passed to the method as an argument. Use the class method isUpperCase of the Character class, which returns true if the passed parameter of type char is an uppercase letter. You need to explore the Character class from the java.lang package on your own.

10. Redo Exercise 9 without using the Character class. *Hint:* The ASCII code of any uppercase letter will fall between 65 (code for 'A') and 90 (code for 'Z').

11. Write a program that reads a sentence and prints out the sentence with all uppercase letters changed to lowercase and all lowercase letters changed to uppercase.

12. Write a program that reads a sentence and prints out the sentence in reverse order. For example, the method will display

    ```
    ?uoy era woH
    ```

    for the input

    ```
    How are you?
    ```

13. Write a method that transposes words in a given sentence. For example, given an input sentence

    ```
    The gate to Java nirvana is near
    ```

    the method outputs

    ```
    ehT etag ot avaJ anavrin si raen
    ```

    To simplify the problem, you may assume the input sentence contains no punctuation marks. You may also assume that the input sentence starts with a nonblank character and that there is exactly one blank space between the words.

14. Improve the method in Exercise 13 by removing the assumptions. For example, an input sentence could be

    ```
    Hello, how are you? I use JDK 1.2.2.    Bye-bye.
    ```

    An input sentence may contain punctuation marks and more than one blank space between two words. Transposing the above will result in

    ```
    olleH, woh era uoy? I esu KDJ 1.2.2. eyB-eyb.
    ```

    Notice the position of punctuation marks does not change and only one blank space is inserted between the transposed words.

15. The Ch9CountWords program that counts the number of words in a given sentence has a bug. If the input sentence has one or more blank spaces at the end, the value for wordCount will be 1 more than the actual number of words in the sentence. Correct this bug in two ways: one with the trim method of the String class and another without using this method.

16. The Ch9ExtractWords program for extracting words in a given sentence includes the test

    ```
    if (beginIdx != endIdx) ...
    ```

    Describe the type of input sentences that will result in the variables beginIdx and endIdx becoming equal.

17. Write an application that reads in a sentence and displays the count of individual vowels in the sentence. Use any output routine of your

choice to display the result in this format. Count only the lowercase vowels.

```
Vowel counts for the sentence

        Mary had a little lamb.
# of 'a' : 4
# of 'e' : 1
# of 'i' : 1
# of 'o' : 0
# of 'u' : 0
```

18. Write an application that determines if an input word is a palindrome. A palindrome is a string that reads the same forward and backward, for example, *noon* and *madam*. Ignore the case of the letter. So, for example, *maDaM*, *MadAm*, and *mAdaM* are all palindromes.

19. Write an application that determines if an input sentence is a palindrome, for example, *A man, a plan, a canal, Panama!* You ignore the punctuation marks, blanks, and the case of the letters.

Development Exercises

For the following exercises, use the incremental development methodology to implement the program. For each exercise, identify the program tasks, create a design document with class descriptions, and draw the program diagram. Map out the development steps at the start. Present any design alternatives and justify your selection. Be sure to perform adequate testing at the end of each development step.

20. Write an Eggy-Peggy program. Given a string, convert it to a new string by placing **egg** in front of every vowel. For example, the string

```
I Love Java
```

becomes

```
eggI Leegoveege Jeegaveega
```

21. Write a variation of the Eggy-Peggy program. Implement the following four variations:

- Sha — Add sha to the beginning of every word.
- Na — Add na to the end of every word.
- Sha Na Na — Add sha to the beginning and na na to the end of every word.
- Ava — Move the first letter to the end of the word and add ava to it.

Allow the user to select one of four possible variations. Use JOptionPane for input.

22. Rewrite the Eggy-Peggy program from Exercise 20 by adding GUI. For a frame, use two TextField objects for entering the original text and displaying the encrypted text. When the user presses the ENTER key (while the original text TextField object is active) or clicks the OK button, the frame displays the encrypted text in the second TextField.

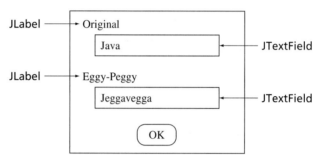

Consider using JTextArea objects instead of TextField objects so the user can enter multiple lines of original text. Do not attempt to implement this program using only one class. Use the supervisor-subordinate design pattern and a logic object to do the Eggy-Peggy string conversion.

23. Redo Exercise 21 with GUI. The choices of encryption are shown by the buttons Sha, Na, and Ava.

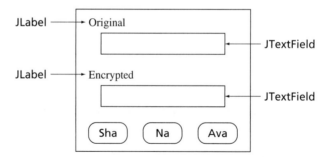

Make sure to design the program using multiple classes.

24. The word game Eggy-Peggy is an example of encryption. Encryption has been used since ancient times to communicate messages secretly. One of the many techniques used for encryption is called a *Caesar cipher*. With this technique, each character in the original message is shifted N positions. For example, if $N = 1$, then the message

        I d r i n k   o n l y   d e c a f

becomes

        J ! e s j o l ! p o m z ! e f d b g

The encrypted message is decrypted to the original message by shifting back every character N positions. Shifting N positions forward and backward is achieved by converting the character to ASCII code and adding or subtracting N. Write an application that reads in the original text and the value for N and displays the encrypted text. Make sure the ASCII value resulting from encryption falls between 32 and 126. For example, if you add 8 (value of N) to 122 (ASCII code for 'z'), you should "wrap around" and get 35.

Write another application that reads the encrypted text and the value for N and displays the original text by using the Caesar cipher technique. Design a suitable user interface.

25. Another encryption technique is called a *Vignere cipher*. This technique is similar to a Caesar cipher in that a key is applied cyclically to the original message. For this exercise a key is composed of uppercase letters only. Encryption is done by adding the code values of the key's characters to the code values of the characters in the original message. Code values for the key characters are assigned as follows: 0 for A, 1 for B, 2 for C, . . . , and 25 for Z. Let's say the key is COFFEE and the original message is I drink only decaf. Encryption works as follows:

Decryption reverses the process to generate the original message. Write an application that reads in a text and displays the encrypted text. Make sure the ASCII value resulting from encryption or decryption falls between 32 and 126. You can get the code for key characters by (int) keyChar - 65.

Write another application that reads the encrypted text and displays the original text, using the Vignere cipher technique.

26. A public-key cryptography allows anyone to encode messages while only people with a secret key can decipher them. In 1977, Ronald Rivest, Adi Shamir, and Leonard Adleman developed a form of public-key cryptography called the *RSA system*.

To encode a message using the RSA system, one needs n and e. The value n is a product of any two prime numbers p and q. The value e is any number less than n that cannot be evenly divided into y (that is, $y \div e$ would have a remainder), where $y = (p - 1) \times (q - 1)$. The values n and e can be published in a newspaper or posted on the Internet, so anybody can encrypt messages. The original character is encoded to a numerical value c by using the formula

$$c = m^e \bmod n$$

where m is a numerical representation of the original character (for example, 1 for A, 2 for B, and so forth).

Now, to decode a message, one needs d. The value d is a number that satisfies the formula

$$e \cdot d \bmod y = 1$$

where e and y are the values defined in the encoding step. The original character m can be derived from the encrypted character c by using the formula

$$m = c^d \bmod n$$

Write a program that encodes and decodes messages using the RSA system. Use large prime numbers for p and q in computing the value for n, because when p and q are small, it is not that difficult to find out the value of d. When p and q are very large, however, it becomes practically impossible to determine the value of d. Use the ASCII codes as appropriate for the numerical representation of characters. Visit http://www.rsasecurity.com for more information on how the RSA system is applied in the real world.

10 Arrays

Objectives

After you have read and studied this chapter, you should be able to

- Manipulate a collection of data values, using an array.

- Declare and use an array of primitive data types in writing a program.

- Declare and use an array of objects in writing a program.

- Define a method that accepts an array as its parameter and a method that returns an array.

- Describe how a two-dimensional array is implemented as an array of arrays.

- Manipulate a collection of objects, using lists and maps.

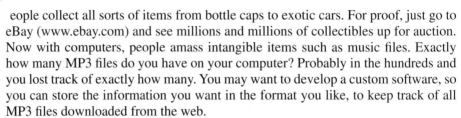

eople collect all sorts of items from bottle caps to exotic cars. For proof, just go to eBay (www.ebay.com) and see millions and millions of collectibles up for auction. Now with computers, people amass intangible items such as music files. Exactly how many MP3 files do you have on your computer? Probably in the hundreds and you lost track of exactly how many. You may want to develop a custom software, so you can store the information you want in the format you like, to keep track of all MP3 files downloaded from the web.

When we write a program to deal with a collection of items, say, 500 Student objects, 200 integers, 300 MP3 files, and so forth, simple variables will not work. It is just not practical or feasible to use 500 variables to process 500 Student objects. In theory, you can, but honestly, do you want to type in identifiers for 500 variables (student1, student2, . . .)? A feature supported by programming languages to manipulate a collection of values is an array.

In this chapter we will learn about Java arrays. In Java, an *array* is an indexed collection of data values of the same type. For example, we can define an array of 10 integers, an array of 15 Student objects, an array of 100 Account objects, and so forth. We are not allowed in Java to create an array of 10 integers and 10 doubles, for example, because the values are of different data types. In this chapter we will learn the basics of array manipulation and how to use different types of arrays properly and effectively.

10.1 | Array Basics

Suppose we want to compute the annual average rainfall from 12 monthly averages. We can use three variables and compute the annual average as

```
double sum, rainfall, annualAverage;

sum = 0.0;

for (int i = 0; i < 12; i++) {
    rainfall = Double.parseDouble(
                 JOptionPane.showInputDialog(null,
                        "Rainfall for month "+ (i+1)));
    sum += rainfall;
}

annualAverage = sum / 12.0;
```

Now suppose we want to compute the difference between the annual and monthly averages for every month and display a table with three columns, similar to the one shown in Figure 10.1.

To compute the difference between the annual and monthly averages, we need to remember the 12 monthly rainfall averages. Without remembering the 12 monthly averages, we won't be able to derive the monthly variations after the annual average

Annual Average Rainfall: 15.03 mm		
Month	Average	Variation
1	13.3	1.73
2	14.9	0.13
3	14.7	0.33
4	23.0	7.97
5	25.8	10.77
6	27.7	12.67
7	12.3	2.73
8	10.0	5.03
9	9.8	5.23
10	8.7	6.33
11	8.0	7.03
12	12.2	2.83

Figure 10.1 Monthly rainfall figures and their variation from the annual average.

is computed. Instead of using 12 variables januaryRainfall, februaryRainfall, and so forth to solve this problem, we use an array.

array

We mentioned that an *array* is a collection of data values of the same type. For example, we may declare an array consisting of double, but not an array consisting of both int and double. The following declares an array of double:

```
double[] rainfall;
```

array declaration

The square brackets indicate the *array declaration*. The brackets may be attached to a variable instead of the data type. For example, the declaration

```
double rainfall[];
```

is equivalent to the previous declaration. In Java, an array is a reference data type. Unlike the primitive data type, the amount of memory allocated to store an array varies, depending on the number and type of values in the array. We use the new operator to allocate the memory to store the values in an array. Although we use the same reserved word new for the array memory allocation as for the creation of a new instance of a class, strictly speaking, an array is not an object.

Helpful Reminder

*In Java, an array is a reference data type. We use the **new** operator to allocate the memory to store the values in an array.*

The following statement allocates the memory to store 12 double values and associates the identifier rainfall to it.

```
rainfall = new double[12]; //create an array of size 12
```

Figure 10.2 shows this array.

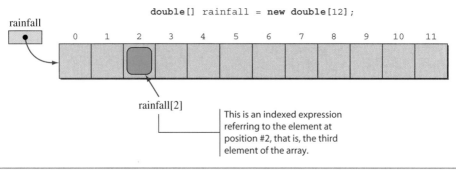

Figure 10.2 An array of 12 **double** values.

We can also declare and allocate memory for an array in one statement, as in

```
double[] rainfall = new double[12];
```

indexed expression

array element

The number 12 designates the size of the array—the number of values the array contains. We use a single identifier to refer to the whole collection and use an *indexed expression* to refer to the individual values of the collection. An individual value in an array is called an *array element*. Zero-based indexing is used to indicate the position of an element in the array. They are numbered 0, 1, 2, . . . , and size – 1, where size is the size of an array. For example, to refer to the third element of the rainfall array, we use the indexed expression

```
rainfall[2]
```

Instead of a literal constant like 2, we can use an expression such as

```
rainfall[i+3]
```

Notice that the index for the first position in an array is zero. As for a String object, Java uses zero-based indexing for an array.

Helpful Reminder

The index of the first position in an array is 0.

Using the rainfall array, we can input 12 monthly averages and compute the annual average as

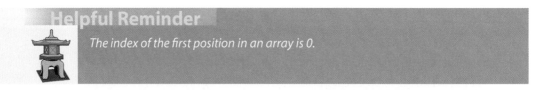

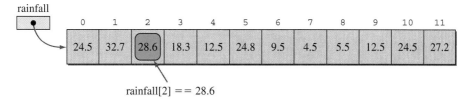

rainfall[2] == 28.6

Figure 10.3 An array of 12 **double** values after all 12 are assigned values.

```
for (int i = 0; i < 12; i++) {

    rainfall[i] = Double.parseDouble(
                    JOptionPane.showInputDialog(null,
                      "Rainfall for month " + (i+1)));
    sum += rainfall[i];
}

annualAverage = sum / 12.0;
```

Figure 10.3 shows how the array will appear after all 12 values are entered.

After the 12 monthly averages are stored in the array, we can print out the table (alignment of the columns is not done).

```
double difference;

for (int i = 0; i < 12; i++) {
    System.out.print(i+1); //month #

    //average rainfall for the month
    System.out.print("  " + rainfall[i]);

    //difference between the monthly and annual averages
    difference = Math.abs( rainfall[i] - annualAverage );
    System.out.println("  " + difference);
}
```

Here's the complete program:

```
/*
    Chapter 10 Sample Program: Compute the annual average rainfall
                               and the variation from monthly average.

    File: Ch10Rainfall.java
*/

import javax.swing.*;

class Ch10Rainfall {
```

```
public static void main (String[] args) {

    double[]  rainfall = new double[12];

    double    annualAverage,
              sum,
              difference;

    sum = 0.0;

    for (int i = 0; i < 12; i++) {

        rainfall[i] = Double.parseDouble(
                            JOptionPane.showInputDialog(null,
                                "Rainfall for month " + (i+1)));
        sum += rainfall[i];
    }

    annualAverage = sum / 12.0;

    System.out.format("Annual Average Rainfall:%5.2f\n\n",
                        annualAverage);

    for (int i = 0; i < 12; i++) {

        System.out.format("%3d", i+1); //month #

        //average rainfall for the month
        System.out.format("%15.2f", rainfall[i]);

        //difference between the monthly and annual averages
        difference = Math.abs( rainfall[i] - annualAverage );
        System.out.format("%15.2f\n", difference);
    }
}
}
```

Notice that the values displayed in the columns are not fully aligned. To do so, you can use the Ch6Format class to pad the varying number of blank spaces before the column values.

length

An array has a public constant **length** for the size of an array. Using this constant, we can rewrite the for loop as

```
for (int i = 0; i < rainfall.length; i++) {
    . . .
}
```

This for loop is more general since we do not have to modify the loop statement when the size of an array is changed. Also, the use of length is necessary when the size of an array is not known in advance. This happens, for example, when we write a method with an array as its parameter. We need to write the method so it can handle an array of any size. We will provide an example of such a method in Section 10.3.

Notice the prompts for getting the values in the previous example are Rainfall for month 1, Rainfall for month 2, and so forth. A better prompt will spell out the month name, for example, Rainfall for January, Rainfall for February, and so forth. We can easily achieve a better prompt by using an array of strings. Here's how:

```
double[] rainfall   = new double[12]; //an array of double

String[] monthName = new String[12]; //an array of String
double    annualAverage,
          sum = 0.0;

monthName[0]  = "January";
monthName[1]  = "February";
monthName[2]  = "March";
monthName[3]  = "April";
monthName[4]  = "May";
monthName[5]  = "June";
monthName[6]  = "July";
monthName[7]  = "August";
monthName[8]  = "September";
monthName[9]  = "October";
monthName[10] = "November";
monthName[11] = "December";

for (int i = 0; i < rainfall.length; i++) {
    rainfall[i] = Double.parseDouble(
                        JOptionPane.showInputDialog(null,
                            "Rainfall for " + monthName[i]));
    sum += rainfall[i];
}

annualAverage = sum / 12.0;
```

Take my *Advice*

It is very easy to mix up the **length** value of an array and the **length** method of a **String** object. The **length** is a method for a **String** object, so we use the syntax for calling a method.

```
String str = "This is a string";
int     size = str.length();
```

But for an array, which is not an object but a reference data type, we do not use the syntax of method calling. We refer to the **length** value as

```
int size = rainfall.length;
```

Instead of assigning array elements individually, we can initialize the array at the time of declaration. We can, for example, initialize the monthName array by

No size is specified

```
String[] monthName = { "January", "February", "March",
                       "April", "May", "June", "July",
                       "August", "September", "October",
                       "November", "December"  };
```

Notice that we do not specify the size of an array if the array elements are initialized at the time of declaration. The size of an array is determined by the number of values in the list. In the above example, there are 12 values in the list, so the size of the array monthName is set to 12.

Let's try some more examples. We assume the rainfall array is declared, and all 12 values are read in. The following code computes the average rainfall for the odd months (January, March, . . .) and the even months (February, April, . . .).

```
double  oddMonthSum, oddMonthAverage,
        evenMonthSum, evenMonthAverage;

oddMonthSum  = 0.0;
evenMonthSum = 0.0;

//compute the average for the odd months
for (int i = 0; i < rainfall.length; i += 2)
    oddMonthSum += rainfall[i];
oddMonthAverage = oddMonthSum / 6.0;

//compute the average for the even months
for (int i = 1; i < rainfall.length; i += 2)
    evenMonthSum += rainfall[i];
evenMonthAverage = evenMonthSum / 6.0;
```

We can compute the same result by using one for loop.

```
for (int i = 0; i < rainfall.length; i += 2 ) {
    oddMonthSum += rainfall[i];
    evenMonthSum += rainfall[i+1];
}

oddMonthAverage  = oddMonthSum / 6.0;
evenMonthAverage = evenMonthSum / 6.0;
```

To compute the average for each quarter (quarter 1 has January, February, and March; quarter 2 has April, May, and June; and so forth), we can write

```
for (int i = 0; i < 3; i++ ) {
    quarter1Sum += rainfall[i];
    quarter2Sum += rainfall[i+3];
    quarter3Sum += rainfall[i+6];
    quarter4Sum += rainfall[i+9];
}
```

```
quarter1Average = quarter1Sum / 3.0;
quarter2Average = quarter2Sum / 3.0;
quarter3Average = quarter3Sum / 3.0;
quarter4Average = quarter4Sum / 3.0;
```

We can use another array to store the quarter averages instead of using four variables:

```
double[] quarterAverage = new double[4];

for (int i = 0; i < 4; i++) {

    sum = 0;

    for (int j = 0; j < 3; j++) { //compute the sum of
        sum += rainfall[3*i + j];  //one quarter
    }

    quarterAverage[i] = sum / 3.0;//average for Quarter i+1

}
```

Notice how the inner for loop is used to compute the sum of one quarter. The following table illustrates how the values for the variables i and j and the expression $3*i + j$ change.

i	j	$3*i + j$
0	0	0
	1	1
	2	2
1	0	3
	1	4
	2	5
2	0	6
	1	7
	2	8
3	0	9
	1	10
	2	11

Here's the complete program:

```
/*

    Chapter 10 Sample Program: Compute different statistics
                            from monthly rainfall averages.

    File: Ch10RainfallStat.java

*/
```

```java
import javax.swing.*;

class Ch10RainfallStat {

    public static void main (String[] args) {

        String[] monthName = { "January", "February", "March",
                               "April", "May", "June", "July",
                               "August", "September", "October",
                               "November", "December"   };

        double[]  rainfall = new double[12];

        double[]  quarterAverage = new double[4];

        double    annualAverage,
                  sum,
                  difference;

        double    oddMonthSum, oddMonthAverage,
                  evenMonthSum, evenMonthAverage;

        sum = 0.0;

        for (int i = 0; i < rainfall.length; i++) {

            rainfall[i] = Double.parseDouble(
                              JOptionPane.showInputDialog(null,
                                  "Rainfall for" + monthName[i]));
            sum += rainfall[i];
        }

        annualAverage = sum / 12.0;

        System.out.format( "Annual Average Rainfall:%6.2f\n\n",
                                              annualAverage );

        oddMonthSum  = 0.0;
        evenMonthSum = 0.0;

        /////////////// Odd and Even Month Averages ///////////////////

        //compute the average for the odd months
        for (int i = 0; i < rainfall.length; i += 2) {

            oddMonthSum += rainfall[i];
        }
```

```
oddMonthAverage = oddMonthSum / 6.0;

//compute the average for the even months
for (int i = 1; i < rainfall.length; i += 2) {

    evenMonthSum += rainfall[i];
}

evenMonthAverage = evenMonthSum / 6.0;

System.out.format( "Odd Month Rainfall Average: %6.2f\n",
                                        oddMonthAverage );

System.out.format( "Even Month Rainfall Average:%6.2f\n\n",
                                        evenMonthAverage );

////////////////// Quarter Averages ///////////////////////

for (int i = 0; i < 4; i++) {

    sum = 0;

    for (int j = 0; j < 3; j++) {       //compute the sum of
        sum += rainfall[3*i + j];       //one quarter
    }

    quarterAverage[i] = sum / 3.0;      //average for Quarter i+1

    System.out.format( "Rainfall Average Qtr %3d:%6.2f\n",
                        i+1, quarterAverage[i] );

    }
  }
}
```

In the previous examples, we used a constant to specify the size of an array, such as the literal constant 12 in the following declaration:

```
double[] rainfall = new double[12];
```

fixed-size array
declaration

Using constants to declare the array sizes does not always lead to efficient space usage. We call the declaration of arrays with constants a *fixed-size array declaration*. There are two potential problems with fixed-size array declarations. Suppose, for example, we declare an integer array of size 100:

```
int[] number = new int[100];
```

The first problem is that the program only can process up to 100 numbers. What if we need to process 101 numbers? We have to modify the program and compile it again. The second problem is a possible underutilization of space. The above declaration allocates 100 spaces whether they are used or not. Suppose the program on the average processes 20 numbers. Then the program's average space usage is only 20 percent of the allocated space. With Java, we are not limited to fixed-size array declaration. We can declare an array of different size every time we run the program. The following code prompts the user for the size of an array and declares an array of designated size:

```
int     size;
int[]   number;

size    = Integer.parseInt(
                  JOptionPane.showInputDialog(null,
                                        "Size of an array:"));
number = new int[size];
```

With this approach, every time the program is executed, only the needed amount of space is allocated for the array. Any valid integer arithmetic expression is allowed for size specification, for example,

```
size = Integer.parseInt(
              JOptionPane.showInputDialog(null,""));
number = new int[size*size + 2* size + 5];
```

variable-size array declaration

We call the declaration of arrays with nonconstant values a *variable-size array declaration*. You will be seeing an example of a variable-size array in Section 10.2.

Take my *Advice*

Notice the first index position of an array is 0. Java adopted this feature from the programming language C. Using the zero-based indexing, the index value of an element indicates the number of elements in front of the element. For example, an index value of 0 for the first element indicates that there are zero elements in front of it; an index value of 4 for the fifth element indicates that there are four elements in front of it. Zero-based indexing allows a simpler formula to compute the actual memory address of array elements.

Quick **CHECK** √

1. Which of the following statements are invalid?

```
a. float    number[23];
b. float    number = { 1.0f, 2.0f, 3.0f };
c. int      number;
   number = new Array[23];
d. int[]    number = [ 1, 2, 3, 4 ];
```

2. Write a code fragment to compute the sum of all positive real numbers stored in the following array.

   ```
   double[] number = new double[25];
   ```

3. Describe the difference between the following two code fragments.

   ```
   //code fragment 1
   for (int i = 0; i < number.length; i++) {
      if ( i % 2 == 0 ) {
         System.out.println( number[i] );
      }
   }

   //code fragment 2
   for (int i = 0; i < number.length; i++) {
      if ( number[i] % 2 == 0 ) {
         System.out.println( number[i] );
      }
   }
   ```

10.2 | Arrays of Objects

Array elements are not limited to primitive data types. Indeed, since a String is an object, we actually have seen an example of an array of objects already in Section 10.1. In this section we will explore arrays of objects. To illustrate the processing of an array of objects, we will use the Person class in the following examples. We will define this Person class later in the chapter to introduce additional object-oriented concepts. Here's the portion of the Person class definition we will use in this section:

Public Methods of the Person **Class**
`public int getAge ( )` Returns the age of a person. Default age of a person is set to 0.
`public char getGender ( )` Returns the gender of a person. The character F stands for female and M for male. Default gender of a person is set to the character U for unknown.
`public String getName ( )` Returns the name of a person. Default name of a person is set to Not Given.
`public void setAge ( int age )` Sets the age of a person.
`public void setGender( char gender )` Sets the gender of a person to the argument gender. The character F stands for female and M for male. The character U designates unknown gender.
`public void setName ( String name )` Sets the name of a person to the argument name.

The following code creates a **Person** object:

```
Person latte;

latte = new Person( );
latte.setName("Ms. Latte");
latte.setAge(20);
latte.setGender('F');

System.out.println( "Name: " + latte.getName()   );
System.out.println( "Age : " + latte.getAge()    );
System.out.println( "Sex : " + latte.getGender() );
```

Now let's study how we can create and manipulate an array of **Person** objects. An array of objects is declared and created just as an array of primitive data types is. The following are a declaration and a creation of an array of **Person** objects.

```
Person[] person;            //declare the person array
person = new Person[20];    //and then create it
```

Execution of the above code will result in a state shown in Figure 10.4.

Notice that the elements, that is, **Person** objects, are not yet created; only the array is created. Array elements are initially null. Since each individual element is an object, it also must be created. To create a **Person** object and set it as the array's first element, we write

```
person[0] = new Person( );
```

Figure 10.5 shows the state after the first **Person** object is added to the array.

Notice that no data values are assigned to the object yet. The object has default values at this point. To assign data values to this object, we can execute

```
person[0].setName  ( "Ms. Latte" );
person[0].setAge   ( 20 );
person[0].setGender( 'F' );
```

The indexed expression

```
person[0]
```

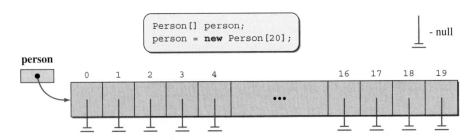

Figure 10.4 An array of **Person** objects after the array is created.

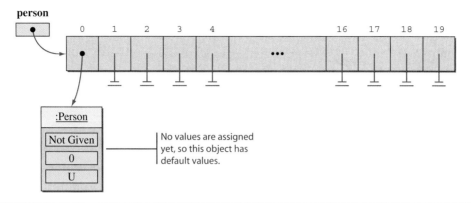

Figure 10.5 The person array with one **Person** object added to it.

is used to refer to the first object in the person array. Since this expression refers to an object, we write

```
person[0].setAge( 20 );
```

to call this **Person** object's **setAge** method, for example. This is the syntax we use to call an object's method. We are just using an indexed expression to refer to an object instead of a simple variable.

Let's go through typical array processing to illustrate the basic operations. The first is to create **Person** objects and set up the **person** array. We assume that the person array is already declared and created.

```
String     name, inpStr;
int        age;
char       gender;

for (int i = 0; i < person.length; i++) {

    //read in data values
    name    = JOptionPane.showInputDialog(null,
                                      "Enter name:");
    age     = Integer.parseInt(
                 JOptionPane.showInputDialog(null,
                                      "Enter age:"));
    inpStr = JOptionPane.showInputDialog(null,
                                      "Enter gender:");
    gender = inpStr.charAt(0);

    //create a new Person and assign values
    person[i] = new Person( );

    person[i].setName  ( name   );
    person[i].setAge   ( age    );
    person[i].setGender( gender );
}
```

Note: To focus on array processing, we used the most simplistic input routine. For instance, we did not perform any input error checking, but this is not to say that input error checking is unimportant. We simply want to focus on array processing.

To find the average age, we execute

find the average age

```
double sum = 0, averageAge;

for (int i = 0; i < person.length; i++) {
    sum += person[i].getAge();
}

averageAge = sum / person.length;
```

To print out the name and age of the youngest and the oldest persons, we can execute

find the youngest and the oldest persons

```
String     nameOfYoungest, nameOfOldest;
int        min, max, age;

nameOfYoungest = nameOfOldest = person[0].getName();
min = max = person[0].getAge();

for (int i = 1; i < person.length; i++) {
    age = person[i].getAge();

    if ( age < min ) {      //found a younger person
        min          = age;
        nameOfYoungest = person[i].getName();

    }else if ( age > max ) { //found an older person
        max          = age;
        nameOfOldest = person[i].getName();
    }
}
System.out.println("Oldest   : " + nameOfOldest + " is "
                                + max + " years old.");

System.out.println("Youngest: " + nameOfYoungest + " is "
                                + min + " years old.");
```

Instead of using separate String and int variables, we can use the index to the youngest and the oldest persons. Here's the code:

```
int  minIdx,      //index to the youngest person
     maxIdx;      //index to the oldest person

minIdx = maxIdx = 0;

for (int i = 1; i < person.length; i++) {

    if ( person[i].getAge() < person[minIdx].getAge() ) {
        //found a younger person
        minIdx     = i;
```

```
        }else if (person[i].getAge() > person[maxIdx.getAge()){
            //found an older person
            maxIdx    = i;
        }
    }

    System.out.println("Oldest   : " + person[maxIdx].getName()
                                     + " is "
                                     + person[maxIdx].getAge()
                                     + " years old.");

    System.out.println("Youngest: " + person[minIdx].getName()
                                     + " is "
                                     + person[minIdx].getAge()
                                     + " years old.");
```

Yet another approach is to use variables for Person objects. Figure 10.6 shows how the Person variables oldest and youngest point to objects in the person array. Here's the code using Person variables:

```
Person    youngest,    //points to the youngest person
          oldest;      //points to the oldest person

youngest = oldest = person[0];

for (int i = 1; i < person.length; i++) {

    if ( person[i].getAge() < youngest.getAge() ) {
        //found a younger person
        youngest   = person[i];
    }
```

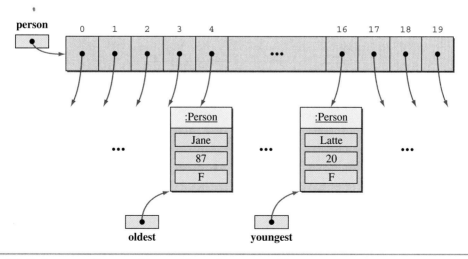

Figure 10.6 An array of **Person** objects with two **Person** variables.

```
        else if ( person[i].getAge() > oldest.getAge() ) {
            //found an older person
            oldest       = person[i];
        }
    }

    System.out.println("Oldest   : " + oldest.getName()
            + " is " +  oldest.getAge() + " years old.");

    System.out.println("Youngest: " + youngest.getName()
            + " is " + youngest.getAge() + " years old.");
```

find a particu-
lar person

Our next example is to search for a particular person. We can scan through the array until the desired person is found. Suppose we want to search for a person whose name is Latte. If we assume the person is in the array, then we can write

```
    int i = 0;
    while ( !person[i].getName().equals("Latte") ) {
        i++;
    }

    System.out.println("Found Ms. Latte at position " + i);
```

The expression

```
    person[i].getName().equals("Latte")
```

is evaluated left to right and is equivalent to

```
    Person p  =   person[i];
    String str=   p.getName();

    str.equals("Latte");
```

In this example, we assume that the person for whom we are searching is in the array. If we cannot assume this, then we need to rewrite the terminating condition to take care of the case when the person is not in the array. Here's how:

```
    int i = 0;

    while ( i < person.length &&//still more persons to search
            !person[i].getName().equals("Latte") ) {
        i++;
    }

    if (i == person.length) {
        //not found - unsuccessful search
        System.out.println("Ms. Latte was not in the array");

    } else {
        //found - successful search
        System.out.println("Found Ms. Latte at position " + i);
    }
```

Here's the complete program that summarizes the topics covered so far in this section:

```
/*
    Chapter 10 Sample Program: Illustrate the processing
                               of an array of Person objects

    File: Ch10ProcessPersonArray.java
*/

import javax.swing.*;

class Ch10ProcessPersonArray {

    public static void main (String[] args) {

        Person[]    person;            //declare the person array
        person = new Person[5];        //and then create it

        //----------- Create person Array ------------------//

        String      name, inpStr;
        int         age;
        char        gender;

        for (int i = 0; i < person.length; i++) {

            //read in data values
            name    = JOptionPane.showInputDialog(null,"Enter name:");
            age     = Integer.parseInt(
                        JOptionPane.showInputDialog(null,"Enter age:"));
            inpStr  = JOptionPane.showInputDialog(null,"Enter gender:");
            gender = inpStr.charAt(0);

            //create a new Person and assign values
            person[i] = new Person( );

            person[i].setName  ( name   );
            person[i].setAge   ( age    );
            person[i].setGender( gender );
        }

        //-------------- Compute Average Age -------------//

        float sum = 0, averageAge;

        for (int i = 0; i < person.length; i++) {

            sum += person[i].getAge();
        }
```

```
        averageAge = sum / (float) person.length;

        System.out.println("Average age: " + averageAge);
        System.out.println("\n");

        //------ Find the youngest and oldest person ----------//
        //------ Approach No. 3: Using person reference -------//

        Person    youngest,         //points to the youngest person
                  oldest;           //points to the oldest person

        youngest = oldest = person[0];

        for (int i = 1; i < person.length; i++) {

            if ( person[i].getAge() < youngest.getAge() ) {
                //found a younger person
                youngest    = person[i];
            }
            else if ( person[i].getAge() > oldest.getAge() ) {
                //found an older person
                oldest      = person[i];
            }
        }

        System.out.println("Oldest   : " + oldest.getName()
                    + " is " +   oldest.getAge() + " years old.");

        System.out.println("Youngest: " + youngest.getName()
                    + " is " + youngest.getAge() + " years old.");

        //----------- Search for a particular person ------------//

        String searchName = JOptionPane.showInputDialog(null,
                                                "Name to search:");

        int i = 0;

        while ( i < person.length &&     //still more persons to search
                !person[i].getName().equals( searchName ) ) {
            i++;
        }

        if (i == person.length) {
            //not found - unsuccessful search
            System.out.println( searchName + " was not in the array" );

        } else {
            //found - successful search
            System.out.println("Found " + searchName + " at position " + i);
        }
    }
}
```

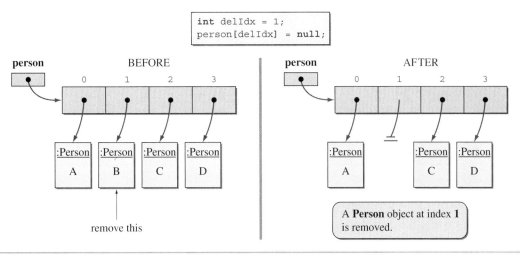

Figure 10.7 Approach 1 deletion: setting a reference to **null.** The array length is 4.

delete a
particular
person

Now let's consider the deletion operation. The deletion operation requires some kind of a search routine to locate the Person object to be removed. To concentrate on the deletion operation, we will assume there's a search method that returns the index of the Person object in the array to be removed. There are two possible ways to remove an object from the array. The first approach is to reset the array element to null. Remember that each element in an array of objects is a reference to an object, so removing an object from an array could be accomplished by setting the reference to null. Figure 10.7 illustrates how the object at position 1 is deleted by using approach 1.

Since any index position can be set to null, there can be "holes," that is, null references, anywhere in the array. Instead of intermixing real and null references, the second approach will pack the elements so the real references occur at the beginning and the null references at the end:

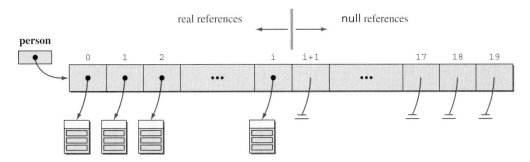

With approach 2, we must fill the hole. There are two possible solutions. The first solution is to pack the elements. If an object at position J is removed (i.e., this position is set to null), then elements from position J+1 up to the last non-null reference are shifted one position lower. And, finally, the last non-null reference is set to null. The second solution is to replace the removed element by the last element in the

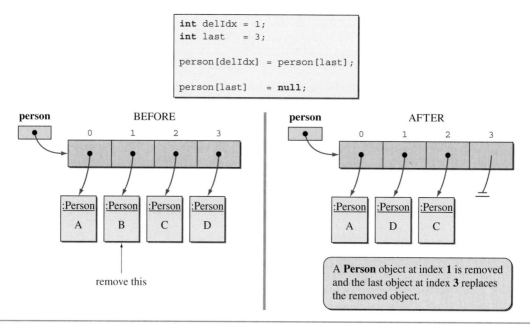

Figure 10.8 Approach 2 deletion: replace the removed element with the last element in the array. The array length is 4.

array. The first solution is necessary if the Person objects are arranged in some order (e.g., in ascending order of age). The second solution is a better one if the Person objects are not arranged in any order. Since we are not arranging them in any order, we will use the second solution. Figure 10.8 illustrates how the object at position 1 is replaced by the last element.

The search routine we presented earlier in this section assumes the full array; that is, all elements are non-null references. With the deletion routine, either approach 1 or 2, given above, an array element could be a null. The search routine must therefore be modified to skip the null references (for approach 1) or to stop the search when the first null reference is encountered (for approach 2).

In both Figures 10.7 and 10.8, we removed the icon for Person B in the diagrams when the array element was set to null as though the object were erased from the memory. Eventually, the object will indeed be erased, but the operation of assigning null to the array element will not erase the object by itself. The operation simply initiates a chain reaction that will eventually erase the object from the memory.

As we have shown several times already, a single object can have multiple references pointing to it. For example, the following code will result in two references pointing to a single Person object:

```
Person p1, p2;

p1 = new Person();
p2 = p1;
```

When an object has no references pointing to it, then the system will erase the object and make the memory space available for other uses. We call the erasing of an object *deallocation* of memory, and the process of deallocating memory is called *garbage collection*. Unlike other programming languages, garbage collection is automatically done in Java, so we do not have to be conscious about it when developing Java programs.

garbage
collection

Quick
CHECK

1. Which of these statements are invalid?

   a. `Person[25] person;`
   b. `Person[ ] person;`
   c. `Person person[] = new Person[25];`
   d. `Person person[25] = new Person[25];`

2. Write a code fragment to print out the names of those who are older than 20. Assume the following declaration and that the array is already set up correctly.

   `Person[ ]  friend = new Person[100];`

10.3 | Passing Arrays to Methods

We discussed the passing of an object to a method by using String objects as illustrations in Chapter 4. Since both an array and an object are a reference data type, the rules for passing an object to a method and returning an object from the method apply to arrays also. However, there are some additional rules we need to remember in passing an array to a method and returning it from a method. We will cover these topics in this section.

Let's define a method that returns the index of the smallest element in an array of real numbers. The array to search for the smallest element is passed to the method. Here's the method:

```
public int searchMinimum(double[] number) {

    int indexOfMinimum = 0;

    for (int i = 1; i < number.length; i++) {
        if (number[i] < number[indexOfMinimum]) { //found a
            indexOfMinimum = i;                    //smaller element
        }
    }

    return indexOfMinimum;
}
```

Notice that we use the square brackets to designate that number is an array. The square brackets may also be attached to the parameter, as in

```
public int searchMinimum(double number[])
```

To call this method (from a method of the same class), we write something like

```
double[] arrayOne, arrayTwo;

//create and assign values to arrayOne and arrayTwo
...
//get the index of the smallest element of arrayOne
int minOne = searchMinimum( arrayOne );

//get the index of the smallest element of arrayTwo
int minTwo = searchMinimum( arrayTwo );

//output the result
System.out.print("Minimum value in Array One is ");
System.out.print(arrayOne[minOne] +" at position "
                                        + minOne);
System.out.print("\n\n");

System.out.print("Minimum value in Array Two is ");
System.out.print(arrayTwo[minTwo] + " at position "
                                        + minTwo);
```

Just like other objects, an array is a reference data type, so we are passing the reference to an array, not the whole array, when we call the searchMinimum method. For example, when the method is called with arrayOne as its argument, the states of memory illustrated in Figures 10.9 and 10.10 will result. There are two references to the same array. The method does not create a separate copy of the array.

Helpful Reminder

When an array is passed to a method, only its reference is passed. A copy of the array is not created in the method.

Now let's try another example in which we return an array (actually the reference to the array) from a method. Suppose we want to define a method that inputs double values and returns the values as an array of double. We can define the method as

```
public double[] readDoubles() {
    double[] number;
    int N = Integer.parseInt(
              JOptionPane.showInputDialog(null,
                             "How many input values?"));

    number = new double[N];

    for (int i = 0; i < N; i++) {
        number[i] = Double.parseDouble(
```

```
                             JOptionPane.showInputDialog(null,
                                            "Number " + i));
        }

        return number;
    }
```

The square brackets beside the method return type double indicate that the method returns an array of double. Because an array is a reference data type, when we say "returns an array of double," we are really saying "returns the reference to an array of double." We will use the shorter expression in general and use the longer expression only when we need to be precise.

The readDoubles method is called in this manner:

```
        double[] arrayOne, arrayTwo;

        //assign values to arrayOne and arrayTwo
        arrayOne = readDoubles();

        arrayTwo = readDoubles();
```

Since a new array is created by the method, we do not have to create an array from the calling side. In other words, we don't have to do this:

```
        double[] arrayOne, arrayTwo;

        arrayOne = new double[30]; //this is NOT necessary

        arrayOne = readDoubles();
```

It won't cause an error if we create an array from the calling side, but we are doing a very wasteful operation. First, it takes up extra memory space. Second, it slows down the whole operation because the computer must garbage-collect the extra memory space that is not being used.

Let's try an alternative approach. This time, instead of creating an array inside the method and returning the array, the calling side creates an array and passes this array to the method:

```
        int[] myIntArray = new int[50];

        readIntegers(myIntArray);
```

The method readIntegers fills the passed array with integers. The method is defined as

```
    public void readIntegers(int[] number) {
        for (int i = 0; i < number.length; i++) {
            number[i] = Integer.parseInt(
                        JOptionPane.showInputDialog(null,
                                    "Number " + i);
        }
    }
```

Notice the return type of readIntegers is void because we are not returning an array. The method modifies the array that is passed to it.

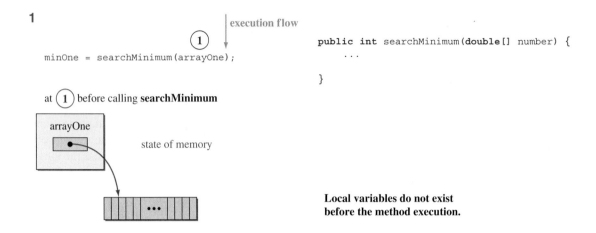

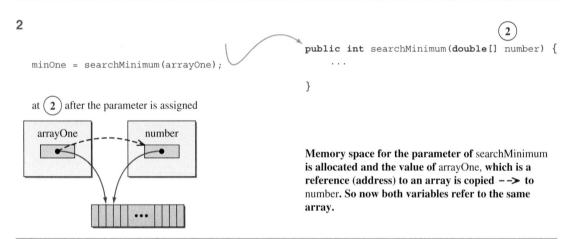

Figure 10.9 Passing an array to a method means we are passing a reference to an array. We are not passing the whole array.

Be careful not to mix the two alternative approaches. The following method will not work:

```
public void badMethod( double[] number ) {
    int N = Integer.parseInt(
                JOptionPane.showInputDialog(null,
                                "How many values?");

    number = new double[N];

    for (int i = 0; i < N; i++) {
        number[i] = Double.parseDouble(
                    JOptionPane.showInputDialog(null,
                                "Number " + i);
    }
}
```

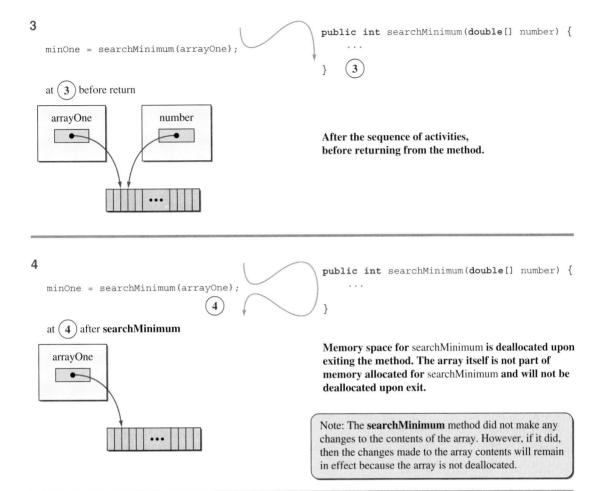

3

```
minOne = searchMinimum(arrayOne);
```

```
public int searchMinimum(double[] number) {
    . . .
}  (3)
```

at (3) before return

arrayOne   number

**After the sequence of activities,
before returning from the method.**

4

```
minOne = searchMinimum(arrayOne);
                        (4)
```

```
public int searchMinimum(double[] number) {
    . . .
}
```

at (4) after **searchMinimum**

arrayOne

Memory space for searchMinimum **is deallocated upon
exiting the method. The array itself is not part of
memory allocated for** searchMinimum **and will not be
deallocated upon exit.**

Note: The **searchMinimum** method did not make any
changes to the contents of the array. However, if it did,
then the changes made to the array contents will remain
in effect because the array is not deallocated.

Figure 10.10 Continuation of Figure 10.9.

Code such as

```
double[] arrayOne = new double[30];
badMethod( arrayOne );
```

will leave **arrayOne** unchanged. Figures 10.11 and 10.12 show the effect of creating
a local array in **badMethod** and not returning it. (*Note:* The return type of bad-
Method is void.)

Quick
CHECK

1. What will be an output from the following code?

```
int[] list = {10, 20, 30, 40 };
myMethod( list );
```

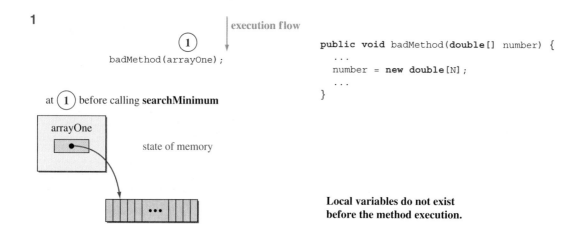

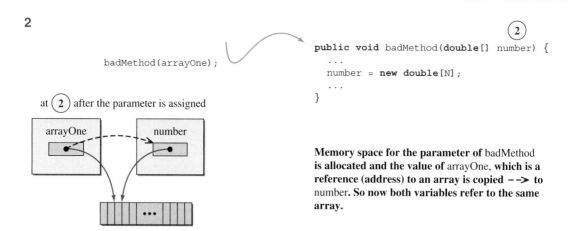

Figure 10.11 Effect of creating a local array and not returning it.

```
    System.out.println( list[1] );
    System.out.println( list[3] );

    . . .
    public void myMethod(int[] intArray)
    {
        for (int i = 0; i < intArray.length; i+=2) {
            intArray[i] = i;
        }
    }
```

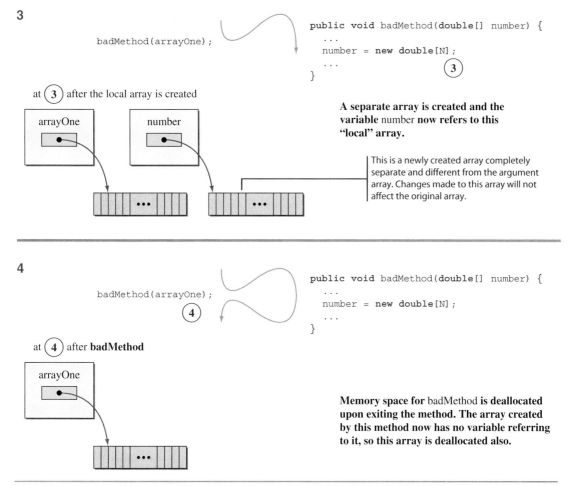

Figure 10.12 Continuation of Figure 10.11.

2. If we replace **myMethod** of question 1 with the following, what will be an output?

```java
public void myMethod(int[] intArray)
{
    int[] local = intArray;
    for (int i = 0; i < local.length; i+=2) {
        local[i] = i;
    }
}
```

The Address Book

In this section, we will design a class called an **AddressBook** to maintain a collection of **Person** objects. The **AddressBook** class is implemented by using an array. We will use the **Person** class defined in Section 10.3. Through the design of the **AddressBook** class, we will reiterate the key principles of object-oriented design.

Notice that we are not developing a complete program here. We are designing only one of the many classes we need for a complete address book program. For the complete program, we need a main window, objects for doing input and output, and so forth. In this section, we will concentrate on one class that is only responsible for maintaining a collection of **Person** objects. This class will not perform, for example, input and output of **Person** objects, following the *single-task object* (STO) principle introduced in Chapter 4. We will discuss the importance of the STO principle while we develop the **AddressBook** class. One objective we have in designing the **AddressBook** class is to make the class reusable in many different programs. Many of the design decisions we will make during the development are based on implementing a reusable class.

Problem Statement

> Write an **AddressBook** *class that manages a collection of* **Person** *objects. An* **AddressBook** *object will allow the programmer to add, delete, or search for a* **Person** *object in the address book.*

Overall Plan

Our first task is to come up with an overall design of the class. Let's begin by first identifying the core operations that an address book object must support. The problem statement indicated three major operations: add, delete, and search. These three operations are pretty much a standard in any collection of data values. For any kind of collections, you will always want to be able to add a new item, delete an old item, and search for an item or items. An address book is no exception as it is a collection of information about people for which you would want to add, delete, and search data.

Our task here is to design a class that will maintain an address book by supporting these three operations. We will define three methods for the class: **add, delete,** and **search.**

Our working design document for the **AddressBook** class is therefore as follows:

Design Document: The Public Methods of the `AddressBook` **Class**	
Method	**Purpose**
`AddressBook`	A constructor to initialize the object. We will include multiple constructors as necessary.
`add`	Adds a new `Person` object to the address book.

Design Document: The Public Methods of the `AddressBook` **Class**
(Continued)

Method	Purpose
`delete`	Deletes a specified `Person` object from the address book.
`search`	Searches for a specified `Person` object in the address book and returns this person if found.

We will implement the class in this order:

develop-
ment steps

1. Implement the constructor(s).

2. Implement the **add** method.

3. Implement the **search** method.

4. Implement the **delete** method.

5. Finalize the class.

This order of development follows a natural sequence. To implement any instance method of a class, we need to be able to create a properly initialized object, so we will begin the class implementation by defining a constructor. As a part of defining a constructor, we will identify necessary data members. We will add more data members as we progress through the development steps. The second step is to implement the add routine, because without being able to add a new **Person** object, we won't be able to test other operations. For the third step, we will implement the search routine. And for the fourth step, we will implement the last routine. Although we could implement the delete routine before the search routine, we need some form of searching to test the correctness of the delete routine. In other words, we delete a person and attempt to search for this person, verifying that the search will not find the deleted person. So we will implement the search routine before the delete routine.

Step 1 Development: Skeleton with Constructors

step 1
design

In step 1, we will identify the data members and define the constructor(s) to initialize them. The main data member for the class is a structure we will use to keep track of a collection of **Person** objects. We will use an array, the only data structure we have learned so far for this purpose. We will create this array in the constructor. At the time we create an array, we must declare its size. Remember that the size of an array is the maximum number of elements this array can hold. The actual number of **Person** objects stored in the array will be anywhere from zero to the size of the array.

We have two possible alternatives for specifying the size of an array. First, we can let the programmer pass the size as an argument to the constructor. Second, we can set the size to a default value. Both alternatives are useful. If the programmer has a good estimate of the number of **Person** objects to manage, she can specify the size in the constructor. Otherwise, she can use the default size by not specifying the size in the constructor. We will define two constructors to support both alternatives. This will give programmers flexibility in creating an **AddressBook** object.

If we are going to provide a constructor in which the programmer can pass the size of an array, then we need to write the constructor so it won't crash when an invalid value is passed as an argument. What would be an invalid argument value? Since we are dealing with a collection of objects and the size of a collection cannot be negative, an argument value of less than zero is invalid. Also, even though a collection whose size is zero may make sense in theory, such a collection makes no sense in practice. Therefore, we will consider zero also as an invalid argument value. We will require an argument to a constructor to be a positive integer. We will throw an **IllegalArgumentException** for an invalid value.

step 1 code

At this point, we have only one data member—an array of objects. We will call it **entry** because a **Person** object is a single entry in an address book. We will set the default size of **entry** to 25. There is no particular reason for selecting this size. We simply picked a number that is not too small or too big. We can change this value later if we need to.

We will define two constructors. The first constructor will call the second constructor with the value 25 (default size) as its argument. The second constructor creates an array of **Person** objects of the size passed as its parameter. Inside the second constructor, we include a temporary test output statement. The class is defined as follows:

```
/**
 * This class is designed to manage an address book that contains
 * Person objects. The user can specify the size of the address book
 * when it is created. If no size is specified, then the default size
 * is set to 25 Person objects.
 *
 * @author Dr. Caffeine
 *
 */
class AddressBook {

    private static final int    DEFAULT_SIZE = 25;
    private Person[]            entry;

    public AddressBook( ) {

        this( DEFAULT_SIZE );
    }
```

Data members

Constructors

```
    public AddressBook( int size ) {

    if (size <= 0 ) { //invalid data value, use default
        throw new IllegalArgumentException("Size must be positive.");
    }
    entry = new Person[size];

    System.out.println("array of "+ size + " is created."); //TEMP
    }
}
```


step 1 test   To test this class, we have included a temporary output statement inside the second constructor. We will write a test program to verify that we can create an **AddressBook** object correctly. The test data are as follows:

Step 1 Test Data	
Data Value	**Purpose**
Negative numbers	Test the invalid data.
0	Test the end case of invalid data.
1	Test the end case of valid data.
>= 1	Test the normal cases.

We will use a very simple test program:

```
/*
    Chapter 10 Sample Program: A test main program for
        verifying the Step 1 AddressBook class.

    File: Person.java
*/
import javax.swing.*;

class TestAddressBook { //Step 1 Test Main

    public static void main(String args[]) {

        AddressBook myBook;
        String      inputStr;
        int         size;
```

```
while (true) {

    inputStr = JOptionPane.showInputDialog(null, "Array size:");

    if (inputStr.equalsIgnoreCase("stop")) {
        break;
    }

    size = Integer.parseInt(inputStr);

    try {
        myBook = new AddressBook(size);
    } catch (IllegalArgumentException e) {
        System.out.println("Exception Thrown: size = " + size);
    }
}
}
}
```

Run the program several times with a different set of test data and verify that we get the correct results.

Step 2 Development: Implement the add Method

step 2 design

In the second development step, we will implement the **add** method. We mentioned in the overall design step that this class will not do any input or output of person data. This decision is based on the STO principle. A single object doing both the input/output routines and maintaining the array will reduce its usability. For example, had the **AddressBook** class used some GUI objects to handle the input and output of person data, the use of this class would dictate or impose the style of input and output routines on the programmers. The programmer will not have an option of using the input and output objects appropriate for his or her uses.

alternative design 1

alternative design 2

Following the STO principle, we will let the programmer decide how she will input and output person data. The task of the **add** method is to accept a **Person** object as its parameter and add the passed **Person** object to the array. Since the array is limited in size, what should we do if there is no more space to add another **Person** object? There are two alternatives. *Alternative design 1* is to return **false** if a new **Person** object cannot be added to the array; that is, the array is full. The method will return **true** otherwise. *Alternative design 2* is to increase the array size. Since the size of an array object cannot be changed once the object is created, we need to create another array with a larger size than the original if we choose to implement the second alternative.

Since the second alternative is more accommodating and less restrictive to the programmer, we will implement this alternative. When the array is full, we will create a new array, copy the objects from the original array to this new array, and finally set the variable **entry** to point to this new array. We will set the size of the new array to 1.5 times larger than the original array. This size increment is just an estimate. Any value between 125 and 200 percent of the old array is reasonable. You don't want to make it too small, say, 105 percent, since that will cause the **enlarge** method to be called too frequently. You don't want to make it too large either, since that will likely result in wasted space. Figure 10.13 illustrates the process of creating a larger array.

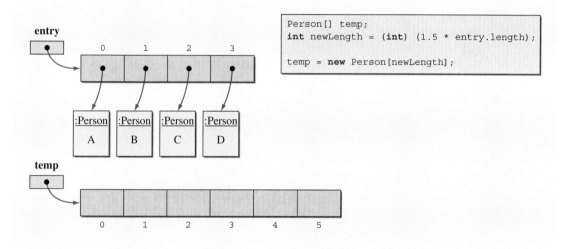

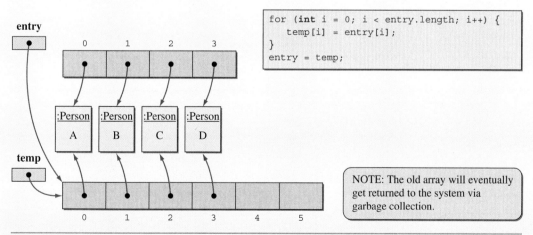

Figure 10.13 How a new array that is 150 percent of the original array is created. The size of the original array is 4.

Now let's think about how to add a **Person** object to the array. To add a new object, we need to locate a position at which to insert the object. Since we are not maintaining **Person** objects in any particular order, we will add a new person at the first available position. If we fill the positions from the low to high indices (**0, 1, 2,** . . .), we can use a variable to remember the index of the next available position. Since we are using an array, the index of the next available position is also the number of **Person** objects currently in the array, so we will call this variable **count.** Figure 10.14 illustrates the **add** operation.

step 2 code

First we add a new instance variable **count** to the class:

```
//---------------------------
//  Data Members
//---------------------------

private int    count; //number of elements in the array,
                      //which is also the position to add
                      //the next Person object
```

We modify the constructor to initialize this data member:

```
public AddressBook( int size ) {

    count = 0;

    //same as before

}
```

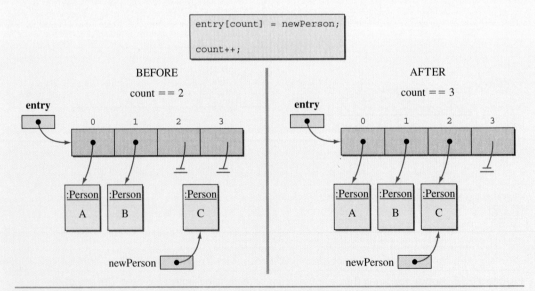

Figure 10.14 Adding a new **Person** object to the next available location. The array length is 4.

(*Note:* Because we defined the first constructor to call the second constructor, we can implement this change by rewriting only one constructor instead of two.) The **add** method is defined as

```
public void add( Person newPerson ) {

    assert count >=0 &&                    Notice the use of the
           count <= entry.length;          assertion feature here.

    if (count == entry.length) { //no more space left,
       enlarge( );                        //create a new larger array
    }

    //at this point, entry refers to a new larger array
    entry[count] = newPerson;
    count++;
}
```

Notice the use of the assertion feature. We place the **assert** statement to make sure the value of **count** is valid. The **enlarge** method is a new private method that creates a new, larger array.

Design Document: The AddressBook **Class**

Method	Visibility	Purpose
...	...	...
enlarge	private	Creates a new array that is 150 percent of the old array.

```
private void enlarge( ) {

    //create a new array whose size is 150% of
    //the current array
    int newLength = (int) (1.5 * entry.length);
    Person[] temp = new Person[newLength];

    //now copy the data to the new array
    for (int i = 0; i < entry.length; i++) {
        temp[i] = entry[i];
    }

    //finally set the variable entry to point to the new array
    entry = temp;

    System.out.println("Inside the method enlarge"); //TEMP
    System.out.println("Size of a new array: "
                                + entry.length); //TEMP
}
```

10.4   Sample Development—*continued*

step 2 test   We will write a test program to verify that a new **Person** object is added to the array correctly. In addition, we need to test that a new array 150 percent larger than the old one is created when there are no more spaces left in the array. The test data are as follows:

Step 2 Test Data	
Test Sequence	**Purpose**
Create the array of size 4	Test that the array is created correctly.
Add four `Person` objects	Test that the `Person` objects are added correctly.
Add the fifth `Person` object	Test that the new array is created and the `Person` object is added correctly (to the new array).

The step 2 test program is as follows:

```
/*
    Chapter 10 Sample Program: A test main program for
            verifying the Step 2 AddressBook class.

    File: TestAddressBook.java
*/

class TestAddressBook {

    public static void main(String[] args) {

        AddressBook    myBook;
        Person         person;

        myBook = new AddressBook( 4 );

        //add four Person objects
        for (int i = 0; i < 4; i++) {
            person = new Person("Ms. X" + i, 10, 'F');
            myBook.add( person );
        }
```

```
            //add the fifth person and see if
            //a new array is created
            person = new Person("fifth one", 10, 'F');
            myBook.add( person );
      }
 }
```

Run the program several times with different sizes for the address book and verify that we get the correct results.

Step 3 Development: Implement the search Method

step 3
design

In the third development step, we implement the **search** method. The method can return one or more **Person** objects that meet the search criteria. We have several options for the search criteria. Since we keep track of name, age, and gender for each person, we can use any one of these values as the search criterion. In this implementation, we will use the person's name. The search routine for the other two criteria will be left as an exercise (see Exercise 14).

To implement the **search** method, we will make an assumption that the name is unique so that there will be at most one matching **Person** object. If the name is not unique, then there are two possibilities. The **search** method can return one **Person** object (among many) that matches the given name or return all **Person** objects that match the given name. We will leave the case when the name is not unique as an exercise (see Exercise 13). Notice that the **add** method we implemented in step 2 does not check the person data. In other words, there is no mechanism to disallow the addition of a **Person** object with a duplicate name. We will leave the implementation of the modified **add** method as an exercise (see Exercise 15).

There are two possible outcomes with the **search** method—a successful or an unsuccessful search. The method has to return a value by which the programmer can verify the result of the search. We will define the **search** method so that it will return a matching **Person** object if it is found and will return **null** otherwise. The search routine will start scanning the array from the first position until the desired **Person** object is found (successful search) or no more **Person** objects are left in the array (unsuccessful search). Expressing the search routine in pseudocode, we have

```
      loc = 0;
      while ( loc < count &&
              name of Person at entry[loc] != searchName ) {
          loc++;
      }
```

```
if (loc == count) {
    foundPerson = null;
}

else {
    foundPerson = entry[loc];
}

return foundPerson;
```

step 3 code

Translating the pseudocode to an actual method will result in the following method:

```
public Person search( String searchName ) {
    Person foundPerson;
    int    loc = 0;

    assert count >= 0 && count <= entry.length;

    while ( loc < count &&
            !searchName.equals( entry[loc].getName() ) ) {
        loc++;
    }

    if (loc == count) {
        foundPerson = null;
    } else {
        foundPerson = entry[loc];
    }

    return foundPerson;
}
```

step 3 test

To test the **search** method, we will build an address book that contains five **Person** objects. We will give names **Ms. X0, Ms. X1,** . . . , and **Ms. X4** to them. After the address book is set up, we test various cases of the search. We test for successful and unsuccessful searches. For the successful searches, we test for the end cases and normal cases. The end cases involve searching for persons stored in the first and last positions of the array. Off-by-1 error (OBOE) is very common in processing an array, so it is very important to test these end cases.

After a successful execution, we will test the class again by changing the size of the array. One test size we should not forget to test is the end case for the array size, which is 1. Also, we need to test the cases where the array is not fully filled, such as an array of size 5 containing only two **Person** objects.

The test data are as follows:

Step 3 Test Data	
Test Sequence	**Purpose**
Create the array of size 5 and add five `Person` objects with unique names.	Test that the array is created and set up correctly. Here, we will test the case where the array is 100 percent filled.
Search for the person in the first position of the array.	Test that the successful search works correctly for the end case.
Search for the person in the last position of the array.	Test another version of the end case.
Search for a person somewhere in the middle of the array.	Test the normal case.
Search for a person not in the array.	Test for the unsuccessful search.
Repeat the above steps with an array of varying sizes, especially the array of size 1.	Test that the routine works correctly for arrays of different sizes.
Repeat the testing with the cases where the array is not fully filled, say, array length is 5 and the number of objects in the array is 0 or 3.	Test that the routine works correctly for other cases.

The step 3 test program is written as follows:

```
/*
    Chapter 10 Sample Program: A test main program for
        verifying the Step 3 AddressBook class.

    File: TestAddressBook.java
*/
class TestAddressBook {

    AddressBook    myBook;
    Person         person;
```

```
public static void main ( String[] args ) {

    TestAddressBook  tester = new TestAddressBook();
    tester.setupArray( 5 );
    tester.testSearch();
}

public void setupArray( int N ) {
    myBook = new AddressBook( N );

    //add N Person objects
    for (int i = 0; i < N; i++) {
        person = new Person("Ms. X"+i, 10, 'F');
        myBook.add( person );
    }
}

public void testSearch( ) {
    //test for the end case
    person = myBook.search("Ms. X2");

    if ( person == null ) {
        System.out.println
            ("Error: Didn't find the person it should");
    } else {
        System.out.println
            (person.getName() + " is found okay.");
    }
}
}
```

Notice the **TestAddressBook** class is now an instantiable main class. Since the code for testing is getting longer, it is not practical anymore to do everything in a single **main** method. For testing, we will modify the method body of **setupArray** and **testSearch** as necessary to test all other cases described in the test data table.

Step 4 Development: Implement the delete **Method**

step 4 design

In the fourth development step, we implement the **delete** method. To delete a **Person** object, the programmer must somehow specify which **Person** object to remove from the address book. Similar to the **search** method, we will use the name of a person to specify which person to delete. Since we assume the name is unique, the **delete** method will remove at most one **Person** object. There are two possible outcomes: the specified person is removed from the address book (successful operation) and the specified person is not removed because he or she is not in the address book (unsuccessful operation). We will define the **delete** method so that it will return **true** if the operation is successful and **false** otherwise.

The removal of an element in an array of objects is done by setting the element to **null**. This will leave a "hole." We will fill this hole by replacing the removed element with the last element, as explained earlier (see Figure 10.8). This filling operation is necessary for other methods, specifically the **add** method, to work correctly.

To fill the hole, we need to know the location of the hole. To find this location, we write a private search method called **findIndex.** The method is very similar to the **search** method. The only difference is that the return value of **findIndex** is an index of an element in the array, whereas the return value of **search** is a **Person** object. By using this **findIndex** method, the **delete** method can be expressed as

```
boolean status;
int     loc;

loc = findIndex( searchName );

if ( loc is not valid) {
   status = false;
} else { //found, pack the hole
   replace the element at index loc+1 by the last element
   at index count;

   status = true;

   count--;  //decrement count,
             //since we now have one less element

   assert 'count' is valid;
}

return status;
```

step 4 code

The private **findIndex** method will look like this:

```
private int findIndex( String searchName ) {
   int loc = 0;

   assert count >=0 && count <= entry.length;

   while ( loc < count &&
          !searchName.equals( entry[loc].getName() ) ) {
      loc++;
   }
```

```
        if (loc == count) {
            loc = NOT_FOUND;
        }

        return loc;
    }
```

The constant **NOT_FOUND** is set in the data member section as

```
//---------------------------
//   Data Members
//---------------------------

private static final int  NOT_FOUND = -1;
```

By using this **findIndex** method, the **delete** method is defined as

```
public boolean delete( String searchName ) {
    boolean   status;
    int       loc;

    loc = findIndex( searchName );

    if (loc == NOT_FOUND) {
        status = false;
    } else { //found, pack the hole

        entry[loc] = entry[count-1];

        status = true;
        count--;        //decrement count,
                        //since we now have one less element

        assert count >= 0 && count <= entry.length;
    }

    return status;
}
```

step 4 test

To test the **delete** method, we will build an address book that contains five **Person** objects, as before. Test cases are to delete the first person in the array, delete the last person in the array, delete someone in the middle (normal case), and try to delete a nonexistent person.

After a successful execution, we will test the class again by changing the size of an array. One test size we should not forget to test is the end case for the array size, which is 1. Also, we need to test the cases where the array is not fully filled, such as an array of size 5 containing only two **Person** objects.

The test data are as follows:

Step 4 Test Data	
Test Sequence	**Purpose**
Create the array of size 5 and add five `Person` objects with unique names.	Test that the array is created and set up correctly. Here, we will test the case where the array is 100 percent filled.
Search for a person to be deleted next.	Verify that the person is in the array before deletion.
Delete the person in the array.	Test that the `delete` method works correctly.
Search for the deleted person.	Test that the `delete` method works correctly by checking that the value `null` is returned by the search.
Attempt to delete a nonexistent person.	Test that the unsuccessful operation works correctly.
Repeat the above steps by deleting persons at the first and last positions.	Test that the routine works correctly for arrays of different sizes.
Repeat testing where the array is not fully filled, say, an array length is 5 and the number of objects in the array is 0 or 3.	Test that the routine works correctly for other cases.

The step 4 test program is written as follows:

```
/*
    Chapter 10 Sample Program: A test main program for
        verifying the Step 4 AddressBook class.

    File: TestAddressBook.java
*/
class TestAddressBook {
    AddressBook      myBook;
    Person           person;

    public static void main ( String[] args ) {
        TestAddressBook tester = new TestAddressBook();
        tester.setupArray( 5 );
        tester.testDelete( );
    }
```

```java
public void setupArray( int N ) {
    myBook = new AddressBook( N );

    //add N Person objects
    for (int i = 0; i < N; i++) {
        person = new Person( "Ms. X" + i, 10, 'F' );
        myBook.add( person );
    }
}

public void testDelete( ) {
    //first make sure the person is in the array

    person = myBook.search( "Ms. X2" );

    if ( person == null ) {
     System.out.println( "Error: Didn't find the person it should" );
    } else {

        System.out.println( person.getName() + " is found okay." );

        boolean success = myBook.delete("Ms. X2" );

        if ( success ) {

            person = myBook.search( "Ms. X2" );

            if (person == null) {

                System.out.println( "Okay: Deletion works" );
            } else {

                System.out.println( "Error: Person is still there" );
            }
        } else {

            System.out.println( "Error: Deletion has a problem" );
        }
    }
}
}
```

Modify the method body of **setupArray** and **testDelete** as necessary to test all other cases described in the step 4 test data table.

Step 5 Development: Finalize

program
review

As always, we finalize the program in the last step. We perform a critical *program review* to find any inconsistency or error in the methods, incomplete methods, places to add more comments, and so forth.

final test

Since the three operations of **add, delete,** and **search** are interrelated, it is critical to test these operations together. The test program should try out various combinations of **add, delete,** and **search** operations to verify that they work together correctly.

After we complete the class implementation and testing, we may consider improvement or extension. In addition to the several alternative designs, it is possible to add other operations. For example, we may want to add an operation to modify a **Person** object. Another common operation that is useful in manipulating a collection of objects is scanning. *Scanning* is an operation to visit all elements in the collection. Scanning is useful in listing all **Person** objects in the address book. The scanning operation is left as Exercise 16.

scanning

10.5 | Two-Dimensional Arrays

two-dimensional array

A table organized in rows and columns is a very effective means for communicating many different types of information. Figure 10.15 shows sample data displayed in a tabular format. In Java, we represent tables as *two-dimensional arrays*. The arrays we have discussed so far are *one-dimensional arrays* because they have only one index. In this section, we describe how two-dimensional arrays are used in Java.

Let's begin with an example. Consider the following table with four rows and five columns. The table contains the hourly rate of programmers based on their skill level. The rows represent the grade levels and the columns represent the steps within a grade level. Reading the table, we know a programmer with skill grade level 2, step 1 earns $36.50 per hour.

| | | **Step** | | | |
	0	**1**	**2**	**3**	**4**
0	10.50	12.00	14.50	16.75	18.00
1	20.50	22.25	24.00	26.25	28.00
2	34.00	36.50	38.00	40.35	43.00
3	50.00	60.00	70.00	80.00	99.99

We declare the pay scale table as

```
double[][] payScaleTable;
```

or

```
double payScaleTable[][];
```

and create the array as

```
payScaleTable = new double[4][5];
```

Distance Table (in miles)

	Los Angeles	San Francisco	San Jose	San Diego	Monterey
Los Angeles	—	600	500	150	450
San Francisco	600	—	100	750	150
San Jose	500	100	—	650	50
San Diego	150	750	650	—	600
Monterey	450	150	50	600	—

Multiplication Table

	1	2	3	4	5	6	7	8	9
1	1	2	3	4	5	6	7	8	9
2	2	4	6	8	10	12	14	16	18
3	3	6	9	12	15	18	21	24	27
4	4	8	12	16	20	24	28	32	36
5	5	10	15	20	25	30	35	40	45
6	6	12	18	24	30	36	42	48	54
7	7	14	21	28	35	42	49	56	63
8	8	16	24	32	40	48	56	64	72
9	9	18	27	36	45	54	63	72	81

Tuition Table

	Day Students	Boarding Students
Grades 1–6	$ 6,000.00	$ 18,000.00
Grades 7–8	$ 9,000.00	$ 21,000.00
Grades 9–12	$ 12,500.00	$ 24,500.00

Figure 10.15 Examples of information represented as tables.

The payScaleTable array is a *two-dimensional array* because two indices—one for the row and another for the column—are used to refer to an array element. For example, to refer to the element at the second column (column 1) of the third row (row 2), we say

```
payScaleTable[2][1]
```

Figure 10.16 illustrates how the two indices are used to access an array element of a two-dimensional array.

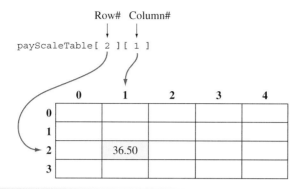

Figure 10.16 Accessing an element of a two-dimensional array.

Let's go over some examples to see how the elements of two-dimensional arrays are manipulated. This code finds the average pay of the grade 2 programmers.

```
double average, sum = 0.0;

for (int j = 0; j < 5; j++) {
    sum += payScaleTable[2][j];
}

average = sum / 5;
```

The next example prints out the pay difference between the lowest and highest steps for each grade level.

```
double difference;

for (int i = 0; i < 4; i++) {
    difference = payScaleTable[i][4] - payScaleTable[i][0];
    System.out.println("Pay difference at Grade Level " +
                        i + " is " + difference);
}
```

This code adds $1.50 to every skill level.

```
for (int i = 0; i < 4; i++) {
    for (int j = 0; j < 5; j++) {
        payScaleTable[i][j] += 1.50;
    }
}
```

In the previous examples, we used literal constants such as 5 and 4 to keep them simple. For real programs, we need to write a loop that will work for two-dimensional arrays of any size, not just with the one with four rows and five columns. We can use the length field of an array to write such a loop. Using the length field, we can rewrite the third example as

```
for (int i = 0; i < payScaleTable.length; i++) {
    for (int j = 0; j < payScaleTable[i].length; j++) {
        payScaleTable[i][j] += 1.50;
    }
}
```

Do you notice a subtle difference in the code? Let's examine the difference between the expressions

```
payScaleTable.length
```

and

```
payScaleTable[i].length
```

First, there is actually no explicit structure called "two-dimensional array" in Java. We only have one-dimensional arrays in Java. However, we can have an array of arrays, and this is how the conceptual two-dimensional array is implemented in Java. The sample array creation

```
payScaleTable = new double[4][5];
```

is really a shorthand for

```
payScaleTable = new double[4][ ];

payScaleTable[0] = new double[5];
payScaleTable[1] = new double[5];
payScaleTable[2] = new double[5];
payScaleTable[3] = new double[5];
```

which is equivalent to

```
payScaleTable = new double[4][ ];

for (int i = 0; i < 4; i++) {
    payScaleTable[i] = new double[5];
}
```

Figure 10.17 shows the effect of executing the five statements. The expression

```
payScaleTable.length
```

refers to the length of the payScaleTable array itself.

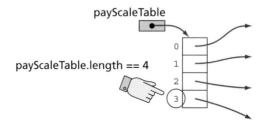

payScaleTable

payScaleTable.length == 4

Executing...   Will result in...

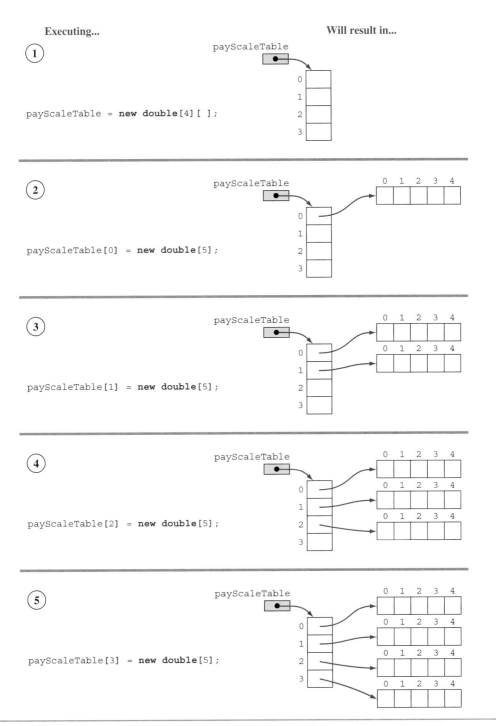

Figure 10.17 Executing the statements on the left in sequence will create the array of arrays shown on the right.

And the expression

```
payScaleTable[1].length
```

refers to the length of an array stored at row 1 of payScaleTable.

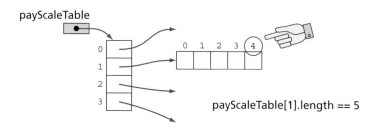

We call an array that is part of another a *subarray*. The payScaleTable has four subarrays of the same length. Since we allocate the subarrays individually, we can create subarrays of different lengths. The following code creates a triangular array whose subarray triangularArray[i] has length i.

```
triangularArray = new double[4][ ];

for (int i = 0; i < 4; i++)
    triangularArray[i] = new double[i+1];
```

The resulting triangularArray looks like this:

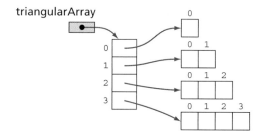

An array of arrays can be initialized at the time of declaration. The following declaration initializes the payScaleTable array:

```
double[][] payScaleTable
       = { {10.50, 12.00, 14.50, 16.75, 18.00},
           {20.50, 22.25, 24.00, 26.25, 28.00},
           {34.00, 36.50, 38.00, 40.35, 43.00},
           {50.00, 60.00, 70.00, 80.00, 99.99}  };
```

Here's the complete sample program:

```
/*
    Chapter 10 Sample Program: Sample program for processing
                          2-D array of double.

    File: Ch10PayScaleTable.java
*/

class Ch10PayScaleTable  {
    public static void main (String[] args) {

        double[][] payScaleTable
                    = {  {10.50, 12.00, 14.50, 16.75, 18.00},
                         {20.50, 22.25, 24.00, 26.25, 28.00},
                         {34.00, 36.50, 38.00, 40.35, 43.00},
                         {50.00, 60.00, 70.00, 80.00, 99.99}  };

        //Find the average pay of Level 2 employees
        double sum = 0.0, average;

        for (int j = 0; j < 5; j++) {
            sum += payScaleTable[2][j];
        }

        average = sum / 5;

        System.out.println(" Average of Level 2 Employees: " + average );
        System.out.println("\n");

        //Display the pay difference at each grade level
        double difference;

        for (int i = 0; i < 4; i++) {
            difference = payScaleTable[i][4] - payScaleTable[i][0];
            System.out.println("Pay difference at Grade Level " +
                                    i + " is " + difference);
        }

        //Print out the pay scale table
        System.out.println("\n");

        for (int i = 0; i < payScaleTable.length; i++) {

            for (int j = 0; j < payScaleTable[i].length; j++) {

                System.out.print( payScaleTable[i][j] + "    " );
            }

            System.out.println("");
        }
```

```
//Increase the pay by 1.50 for every level/step
//and display the resulting table
System.out.println("\n");

for (int i = 0; i < payScaleTable.length; i++) {

    for (int j = 0; j < payScaleTable[i].length; j++) {

        payScaleTable[i][j] += 1.50;

        System.out.print( payScaleTable[i][j] + "    " );
    }

    System.out.println("");
}
}
}
```

There is no limit to the number of dimensions an array can have. We can declare three-dimensional, four-dimensional, and higher-dimensional arrays. However, arrays with dimension higher than 2 are not frequently used in object-oriented languages. For example, data that were represented as a three-dimensional array in a non-object-oriented language can be represented more naturally as a one-dimensional array of objects with each object containing an array or some other form of data structure (see Exercise 12 on page 633).

Quick **CHECK**

1. Write a code fragment to compute the average pay of the pays stored in the payScaleTable array.
2. Write a code fragment that finds the largest integer in this two-dimensional array.

   ```
   int[][] table = new int[10][10];
   ```

3. What is an output from this code?

   ```
   int[][] table = new int[10][5];

   System.out.println(table.length);
   System.out.println(table[4].length);
   ```

10.6 Lists and Maps

In Section 10.4, we defined a method called enlarge that handles the overflow condition. When the original array runs out of space to store additional Person objects, the enlarge method is used to create a new array whose capacity is 150 percent of the original array. If we have to develop many applications that require overflow handling, we can define a class that handles the overflow condition so we don't have to implement the same enlarge method repeatedly in the applications we develop. We might call the new class ExpandableArray. By using this class, we can keep adding a new element without worrying about the overflow condition because the class handles the overflow condition automatically.

java.util

JCF

It turns out there's no need for us to write such an ExpandableArray class because the Java standard library java.util already includes many high-power classes for maintaining a collection of objects. These classes are collectively referred as the *Java Collection Framework* (*JCF*). We will study two of them in this section. We provide an in-depth discussion and analysis of JCF in our data structure textbook, scheduled to be published in 2004.

The first is the List interface. Unlike a class, an interface defines only the behavior, a list of public methods without method bodies. One consequence of this characteristic is that we do not (cannot) create an instance of an interface.

Because the List is an interface, we cannot create an instance of List. The following will result in a compile-time error:

```
List myList = new List ( );
```

What we need is a class that implements the defined behavior of the interface. We have already seen a number of interfaces such as the ActionListener interface. The ActionListener interface defines one method called actionPerformed. A class that implements the ActionListener interface must provide the method body to this method.

There are two classes in JCF that implement the List interface: ArrayList and LinkedList. Because they implement the same interface, they behave exactly the same. That is, there's no difference in using them (as long as we use the methods defined in the List interface). They differ in the internal data structure they use to implement the interface. The ArrayList class uses an array, and the LinkedList class uses a technique called *linked-node representation*. We choose one over the other depending on the nature of application (e.g., choose LinkedList if the application requires frequent insertions and deletions of elements but occasional searching for elements in the list). It is beyond our scope to provide an in-depth comparative analysis, so we will use the ArrayList class here, because we discussed arrays in this chapter. Keep in mind, though, that everything we can do with the ArrayList class, we do with the LinkedList class.

You Might Want to Know

There is another "expandable array" in the JCF called **Vector**. The **Vector** class predates the JCF classes, but from Java 2 SDK 1.2, the class was modified to implement the **List** interface. Because it was designed before the JCF classes, it includes many methods in addition to the **List** methods. In general, the **ArrayList** class is recommended for most situations.

Let's study how we can use the methods of the List interface. Although it is valid to declare and create a list object as

```
ArrayList myList;
...
myList = new ArrayList( );
```

it is more standard to declare the variable as List and assign an instance of the class that implements the List interface to it, as in

```
List myList;
...
myList = new ArrayList( );
```

The same goes for declaring the type of the parameters. This standard will allow a quick way for changing the implementation class. Had we declared variables and parameters in the program as ArrayList, then we would have to replace all occurrences of "ArrayList" in the program to "LinkedList" if we want to change the implementation class. If we declare everything as List, then all we have to change is a single statement to

```
myList = new LinkedList( );
```

Default constructor will create an empty list with the initial capacity of 10 (i.e., enough memory space to hold 10 references is allocated). If we add more than 10 elements, a list object will increase its capacity automatically. We can use the second constructor that accepts the initial capacity as an argument if we want to start with a different initial capacity. Although the increase in capacity is handled automatically by the ArrayList class, it does not mean the operation is free. It costs time to replace the existing internal data array with one bigger in capacity. So if we know beforehand that we will use, say, 500 objects, then we should create a list with 500 as its initial capacity.

Once a list is created properly, we can start adding elements. In the following example, we create a list named friends and add four Person objects to the list:

add

```
import java.util.*;
...
List friends;
Person person;

friends = new ArrayList( );

person = new Person("jane", 10, 'F');
friends.add( person );

person = new Person("jack",  6, 'M');
friends.add( person );

person = new Person("jill",  8, 'F');
friends.add( person );
```

```
person = new Person("john", 14, 'M');
friends.add( person );
```

To find out the number of objects contained in a list, we use its size method. The following code will print out 3:

```
List sample = new ArrayList( );

sample.add( "one java" );
sample.add( "two java" );
sample.add( "three"    );

System.out.println( sample.size( ) );
```

Objects we store in a list can be accessed by giving their index position in the list, much as we did with the array. We use the get method to access an object at index i.

Type casting is
required.

```
Person p = (Person) friends.get( i );
```

Notice that we need to type cast the element to a Person object because the elements inside a list can be an instance of any class. A compile-time error will occur if we forget to type cast the returned element.

Here's a code to display the name of all Person objects in the friends list:

```
Person p;

int limit = friends.size( );

for (int i = 0; i < limit; i++ ) {

    p = (Person) friends.get( i );

    System.out.println( p.getName( ) );
}
```

Another approach to scan the elements inside a list or many other JCF collection classes is to use the iterator method. When we call the iterator method of a list, an **Iterator** object (actually an instance of a class that implements the Iterator interface) that supports two methods hasNext and next is returned. Here's how we print out the name of all Person objects, using the second approach:

Iterator

```
Person p;
Iterator iterator = friends.iterator( );

while ( iterator.hasNext( ) ) {

    p = (Person) iterator.next( );

    System.out.println( p.getName( ) );
}
```

The hasNext method returns true if the iterator has more elements to access. It will be an error to call the next method when there are no more elements to access in the iterator, that is, when the iterator is empty. If we do, then the runtime exception called NoSuchElementException is thrown. It is a safe practice to always call hasNext before calling next.

Using the second approach is restrictive because you can access the elements only in one direction, starting from the first element. With the first approach, you can visit the elements in any order by changing the parameter you pass in the get method. So what is the advantage of the second approach? First, accessing the elements from the first to the last element in a simple linear order is a very commonly used operation for a collection of objects, and the use of iterator is a handy way to do this. Second, although we limit our discussion to the lists and the maps in this section, the Java standard library java.util includes other classes that handle a collection of objects. Most of these collection classes support the iterator method, but only a few support the get method. So the second approach can be used without modification even if we implement friends by using a collection class different from list, while the first approach can be used only when friends is implemented with a collection class that supports the get method.

remove

To remove an element from a list, we can use the remove method with the index of an element to be removed as its parameter. The following code removes the third Person object from friends:

```
friends.remove( 2 ); //the third Person is at index 2
```

All elements after the removed element are moved one position to fill the hole created by the removal of the second element. So the third, fourth, fifth, and other elements before the removal become the second, third, fourth, and so forth, elements after the removal. The size of the list is reduced by 1 after the removal.

Unlike an array, a list cannot include primitive data such as int and double values as its elements. A list element must be an instance of some class. The following code, therefore, will result in a compile-time error:

```
List sample = new ArrayList( );
sample.add( 15 );
sample.add( 30 );
```

If we need to add primitive data values to a list, then we must use wrapper classes such as Integer, Float, and Double. To add integers, we have to do something like this:

```
List intList = new ArrayList( );

intList.add( new Integer( 15 ) );
intList.add( new Integer( 30 ) );
...
```

When we access the elements of intList, they are Integer objects, so we need to use its intValue method to get the integer value. The following code displays the integer values stored in intList:

```
Integer intObject;
Iterator itr = intList.iterator( );

while ( itr.hasNext( ) ) {

    intObject = (Integer) itr.next( );

    System.out.println( intObject.intValue( ) );
}
```

This covers the most basic operations of the List interface. Please refer to the Java API documentation for more information on the List interface.

Let's move on to another useful interface called Map. There are two classes that implement this interface: HashMap and TreeMap. We will describe the TreeMap class in this section because this is the class we used in implementing the helper WordList class in Chapter 9. The TreeMap class actually implements a subinterface of Map called SortedMap, where the entries in the map are sorted.

A map consists of entries, with each entry divided into two parts: key and value. No duplicate keys are allowed in the map. Both key and value can be an instance of any class. The main advantage of a map is its performance in locating an entry, given the key. Consider, for example, we want to maintain a table of course evaluations. For each course offered on campus, we want to keep an evaluation that is summarized from the student opinion poll collected at the end of the term. The course number (e.g., CS0101) is the key, and the evaluation is the value. We would want to store the information as a map because we need to look up the evaluation of a course efficiently, as there are hundreds or thousands of courses. The search would take too long if we used other data structures.

As we know, a Java array allows only integer indices. In some situations we may want to use an array with indices other than integers. For example, a **WordList** from Chapter 9 can be viewed as an array of numbers with words (**String**) as its indices. A map can be characterized as an expandable array with instances of any class as its indices. So whenever we need an array of values with noninteger indices, a map is a possible solution.

We create an instance of a map as

```
Map table;
. . .
table = new TreeMap( );
```

and we add the key-value pairs to the map as

```
table.put("CS0101", "Great Course. Take it");
```

where the first argument is the key and the second argument is a value. To remove an entry from a map, we specify its key as

```
table.remove("CS0233");
```

If there's no matching entry, then nothing happens to the map (the value null is returned). To retrieve the value associated to a key, we call the map's get method.

```
String courseEval = table.get("CS102");
```

We can ask the map if it contains a given key. To check, for example, whether the map contains an evaluation for course number CS0455, we write

```
boolean result = table.containsKey("CS0455");
```

We can retrieve all entries in the map. We use the entrySet method, as in

```
Set entrySet = table.entrySet();
```

where Set is another interface in JCF. The Set interface supports the behavior of mathematical sets, a collection of data with no duplicates. Those interested in using the interface are referred to the Java API documentation. The methods defined in the Set interface are very similar to those defined in the List interface. If we know how to use the List interface, it won't take much additional effort to understand the Set interface.

To access all entries in the map, we get a set of entries with the entrySet method, and then we call the set's iterator method to get an iterator. Once we have the iterator, we access individual entries in the standard way of calling the hasNext and next methods in sequence. An entry of a map is an instance of the class that implements the Map.Entry interface. The dot notation indicates that the Entry interface is defined inside the declaration of the Map interface. Such a nested declaration is useful in avoiding naming conflict. For instance, we can have only one class with the name Entry, but we can have Map.Entry, MyClass.Entry, YourClass.Entry, and so forth.

Two useful methods defined in the Map.Entry interface are the getKey and getValue methods, whose purpose is to retrieve the key and the value of an entry, respectively. For example, to list the course numbers and their evaluations from the table map, we write the code as follows:

```
Iterator itr = table.entrySet().iterator();

while (itr.hasNext()) {
    entry = (Map.Entry) itr.next();

    System.out.println(entry.getKey() + ":");
    System.out.println(entry.getValue() + "\n");
}
```

We are now ready to present the WordList class. It uses a TreeMap object to keep track of distinct words in a document and how many times they occur in the document. Notice the TreeMap class actually implements a more specialized map interface called SortedMap, a subinterface of the Map interface that adds the behavior of sorting the elements in ascending key order. This is exactly the data structure we want to use here because we want to access and display the words and their count in alphabetical order. Here's the definition:

```java
/*
    Chapter 9 Sample Development: Word Concordance

    File: WordList.java
*/

import java.util.*;
import java.text.*;

class WordList  {

    SortedMap table;

    public WordList( ) {
        table = new TreeMap();
    }

    public void add(String word) {
        Integer val;

        if (table.containsKey(word)) {
            val = (Integer) table.get(word);
            val = new Integer(val.intValue()+1);

        } else { //word occurs for the first time
            val = new Integer(1);
        }

        table.put(word, val);
    }

    public String getConcordance( ) {
        String line;
        String lineTerminator
                = System.getProperties().getProperty("line.separator");

        StringBuffer strBuf = new StringBuffer("");

        Map.Entry entry;
        DecimalFormat df = new DecimalFormat("0000");
        Iterator itr = table.entrySet().iterator();

        while (itr.hasNext()) {
            entry = (Map.Entry) itr.next();
```

add

getConcordance

```
        line   =   entry.getValue().toString() + "\t" +
                    entry.getKey() +
                    lineTerminator;

        strBuf.append(line);
    }

    return strBuf.toString();
}

public void reset( ) {
    table.clear(); //remove all entries
}
}
```

reset

Compared to the amount of work the class has to perform, the length of its source code is rather short. This is so because the hard part of maintaining the data structure is done by the TreeMap class. Had we tried to implement the WordList class without using the TreeMap class, the source code would have been much longer. A little effort to study the JCF classes pays handsomely when the time comes for us to implement an efficient data manager class such as the WordList class.

Quick **CHECK**

1. What is the output from the following code?

```
    List list = new ArrayList(  );
    for (int i = 0; i < 6; i++ ) {
        list.add( "element " + i );
        System.out.println( list.capacity( ));
    }
```

2. What is the output from the following code?

```
    List list = new ArrayList( );
    for (int i = 0; i < 6; i++ ) {
        list.add( "element " + i );
    }

    list.remove( 1 );
    list.remove( 3 );

    System.out.println( list.elementAt( 2 ) );
```

3. Identify all errors in the following code.

```
    Map table = new Map( );

    table.put("one", 1);

    System.out.println( table.get("one"));
```

S u m m a r y

- An array is an indexed collection of data values.
- Data values in an array are called array elements.
- Individual elements in an array are accessed by the indexed expression.
- Array elements can be values of primitive data type or objects.
- In Java, an array can only include elements of the same data type.
- A Java array is a reference data type.
- A Java array is created with the new operator.
- An array can have multiple indices.
- When an array is passed to a method as an argument, only a reference to an array is passed. A copy of an array is not created. *Note:* The reference to an array we are passing is a value of an array variable, and therefore, the call-by-value scheme is used here also.
- The standard classes and interfaces described or used in this chapter are

List	Iterator
ArrayList	Map
LinkedList	HashMap
	TreeMap

- The Java Collection Framework includes many data structure classes such as lists and maps.
- The List interface represents a linear ordered collection of objects.
- The ArrayList and LinkedList classes are two implementations of the List interface.
- The Map interface represents a collection of (key, value) pairs.
- The TreeMap and HashMap classes are two implementations of the Map interface.

K e y   C o n c e p t s

arrays	arrays of objects
array elements	multidimensional arrays
index expression	lists
arrays of primitive data type	maps

E x e r c i s e s

1. Identify problems with this code:

```
public int searchAccount( int[25] number ) {
    number = new int[15];
```

```
        for (int i = 0; i < number.length; i++) {
            number[i] = number[i-1] + number[i+1];
        }
        return number;
    }
```

2. Declare an array of double of size 365 to store daily temperatures for one year. Using this data structure, write the code to find

   • The hottest and coldest days of the year.
   • The average temperature of each month.
   • The difference between the hottest and coldest days of every month.
   • The temperature of any given day. The day is specified by two input values: month (1, . . . , 12) and day (1, . . . , 31). Reject invalid input values (e.g., 13 for month and 32 for day).

3. Repeat Exercise 2, using a two-dimensional array of double with 12 rows and each row having 28, 30, or 31 columns.

4. Repeat Exercise 2, using an array of Month objects with each Month object having an array of double of size 28, 30, or 31.

5. For Exercises 2 to 4, the following three data structures are used:

   • One-dimensional array of double of size 365.
   • Two-dimensional array of double with 12 rows. Each row has 28, 30, or 31 columns.
   • An array of Month objects with each Month object having an array of double of size 28, 30, or 31.

   Discuss the pros and cons of each approach.

6. Suppose you want to maintain the highest and lowest temperatures for every day of the year. What kind of data structure would you use? Describe the alternatives and list their pros and cons.

7. If a car dealer's service department wants a program to keep track of customer appointments, which data structure would you choose, an array or a list? If the number of appointments the service department accepts is fixed on any given day, which data structure is appropriate? What are the criteria you use to decide which data structure to use? Explain.

8. In Figure 10.8, the last statement

   ```
   person[last] = null;
   ```

   is significant. Show the state-of-memory diagram when the last statement is not executed.

9. Write an application that computes the standard deviation of N real numbers. The standard deviation s is computed according to

$$s = \sqrt{\frac{(x_1 - \bar{x})^2 + (x_2 - \bar{x})^2 + \cdots + (x_N - \bar{x})^2}{N}}$$

The variable $\bar{x}$ is the average of N input values x_1 through x_N. The program first prompts the user for N and then declares an array of size N.

10. Using the payScaleTable two-dimensional array from Section 10.5, write the code to find

   - The average pay for every grade level.
   - The average pay for every step (i.e., average of every column).

11. Declare a two-dimensional array for the tuition table shown in Figure 10.15.

12. Suppose you want to maintain information on the location where a product is stored in a warehouse. Would you use a three-dimensional array such as location[i][j][k], where i is the warehouse number, j is the aisle number, and k is the bin number? Or would you define three classes Warehouse, Aisle, and Bin? Describe the alternatives and list their pros and cons.

13. The search method of the AddressBook class returns only one Person object. Modify the method so that it will return all Person objects that match the search criteria. You can use an array to return multiple Person objects.

14. Write new search routines for the AddressBook class. The search method given in the chapter finds a person with a given name. Add second and third search methods that find all persons, given an age and a gender, respectively.

15. Modify the add method of the AddressBook class. The method given in the chapter does not check for any duplicate names. Modify the method so that no Person object with a duplicate name is added to the address book.

16. Modify the AddressBook class to allow the programmer to access all Person objects in the address book. Make this modification by adding two methods: getFirstPerson and getNextPerson. The getFirstPerson method returns the first Person object in the book. The getNextPerson method returns the next Person object if there is one. If there is no next person in the book, getNextPerson returns null. The getFirstPerson method must be called before calling the getNextPerson method.

17. In addition to the List and Map interface, the third interface in the Java Collection Framework is Set. A Set is an unordered collection of objects with no duplicates. This interface models, as expected, the mathematical set. Two classes that implement the Set interface in JCF are TreeSet and HashSet. Here's a simple example of using Set:

```
Set set = new HashSet();
set.add("ape");
set.add("bee");
set.add("ape"); //duplicate, so it won't be added
set.add("cat");
set.remove("bee");
set.remove("dog"); //not in the set, nothing happens

System.out.println("Set = " + set);
```

The output from the code will be

```
Set = [ape, cat]
```

To access the individual elements of a set, call the iterator method in the manner identical to the one we used for the List interface.

Modify the Kennel class from Chapter 4, so a Kennel object is capable of tracking a set of Pet objects. The board method of the modified Kennel class adds a new Pet to the set. Include new methods called workoutTime and chowTime. These two methods will iterate through the set and make the pets go through the exercise and feeding routines. Determine your own rule for the exercise and feeding. Please consult the Java API documentation for details on the Set interface.

18. Consider the following Thesaurus class:

```
class Thesaurus {
    //Returns all synonyms of the word as a Set
    //Returns null if there is no such word
    public java.util.Set get (String word){...}

    //Returns all key words in this thesaurus as a Set
    //returns an empty set if there are no keys (if you
    //don't do anything, default behavior of the
    //underlying JCF class will handle it)
    public java.util.Set keys(            ){...}

    //Adds 'synonym' to the synonym set of 'word'
    //Pay close attention to this method.
    public void put (String word, String synonym){...}
}
```

The get method returns a set of all synonyms of a given word. The keys method returns all key words in the thesaurus. The put method adds a new synonym to the given word. Make sure to handle the cases when the word already has a synonym list and when the word is added for the first time. Using this Thesaurus class, we can write, for example, this program:

```
class SampleMain {
    public static void main(String[] args) {
        Thesaurus t = new Thesaurus();
        t.put("fast", "speedy");
        t.put("fast", "swift");
        t.put("slow", "sluggish");

        Set synonyms = t.get("fast");
        System.out.println(synonyms);
        System.out.println(t.keys());
    }
}
```

When the sample program is executed, the output will be

```
C:\WINNT\System32\cmd.exe
[speedy, swift]
[fast, slow]
Press any key to continue . . .
```

Implement the Thesaurus class, using one of the Map classes. The key is the word, and the value is the set of synonyms of this word.

Development Exercises

For the following exercises, use the incremental development methodology to implement the program. For each exercise, identify the program tasks, create a design document with class descriptions, and draw the program diagram. Map out the development steps at the start. Present any design alternatives and justify your selection. Be sure to perform adequate testing at the end of each development step.

19. Write a complete address book maintenance application. The user of the program has four options: add a new person, delete a person, modify the data of a person, and search for a person by giving the name. Use the AddressBook class, either the original one from the chapter or the modified one from the previous exercises. You have to decide how to allow the user to enter the values for a new person, display person information, and so forth.

20. Design a currency converter class whose instance will handle conversion of all currencies. In Chapter 4 we designed a currency converter class where we created one instance for each currency. A single instance of the new currency converter class you design here will handle all currencies. Instead of having specific conversion methods such as toDollar, toYen, and so forth, the new currency converter class supports one generic conversion method called exchange. The method has three arguments: fromCurrency, toCurrency, and amount. The first two arguments are String and give the names of currencies. The third argument is float. To convert $250 to yen, we write

```
yen = converter.exchange( "dollar", "yen", 250.0 );
```

To set the exchange rate for a currency, we use the setRate method. This method takes two arguments: The first argument is the currency name, and the second argument is the rate. For example, if the exchange rate for yen is 140 yen to $1, then we write

```
converter.setRate( "yen", 140.0 );
```

Use an array to keep track of exchange rates.

21. Extend the MyJava Lo-Fat Burgers drive-through ordering system of Exercise 23 on page 313 so the program can output sales figures. For each item on the menu, the program keeps track of the sales. At closing time, the program will output the sales figure in a format similar to the following:

```
Item              Sales Count          Total
Tofu Burger            25           $   87.25
Cajun Chicken          30           $  137.70
...

   Today's Total Sales: $ 2761.20
```

22. Redo the watermelon projectile computing program of Exercise 31 on page 379 to output the average distance covered between each time interval. Use the expression

$$\sqrt{(x_2 - x_1)^2 + (y_2 - y_1)^2}$$

to compute the distance between two coordinate points (x_1, y_1) and (x_2, y_2).

23. Redo the social club program of Exercise 9 of Chapter 8. In the original program, we limit the number of clubs to 5. Remove this restriction by using an array.

24. Redo Exercise 23, but this time use one of the Java Collection Framework classes.

11 Sorting and Searching

After you have read and studied this chapter, you should be able to

- Perform linear and binary search algorithms on arrays.

- Determine whether a linear or binary search is more effective for a given situation.

- Perform selection and bubble sort algorithms.

- Describe the heapsort algorithm and show how its performance is superior to that of the other two algorithms.

- Apply basic sorting algorithms to sort an array of objects, using the **Comparator** interface.

- Define the interface to specify common behavior and provide different versions of classes that implement the interface.

Introduction

n this chapter, we cover searching and sorting. In Chapter 10, we presented a case study of maintaining an address book and described a basic searching method to locate a student given his or her name. In this chapter, we will present a better searching algorithm called *binary search*. To apply binary search, an array must be sorted. *Sorting* is a technique to arrange elements in some order, and it is one of the fundamental operations we study in computer science. We will cover basic sorting algorithms in this chapter and an efficient recursive sorting algorithm in Chapter 15. We will use an array of integers to illustrate searching and sorting algorithms, but all the techniques we present here are equally applicable to any array of objects as well as primitive data types. In the sample development section, we will extend the AddressBook class by adding the capability of sorting an array of **Person** objects.

11.1 | Searching

Let's start with the problem statement for searching:

> *Given a value* X, *return the index of* X *in the array, if such* X *exists. Otherwise, return* NOT_FOUND (−1). *We assume there are no duplicate entries in the array.*

There are two possible outcomes in searching: either we locate an *X* or we don't. We will call the first a *successful search* and the latter an *unsuccessful search*. Figure 11.1 illustrates the successful and unsuccessful searches. As obvious as this may sound, it is critical to differentiate the two because it is possible for one searching algorithm to perform superbly for successful searches, but very poorly for unsuccessful searches. When we analyze the performance of a searching algorithm, we normally derive two separate performances, one for a successful search and another for an unsuccessful search.

successful and unsuccessful searches

Linear Search

linear search

The search technique we used earlier in the book is called a *linear search* because we search the array from the first to the last position in a linear progression. The

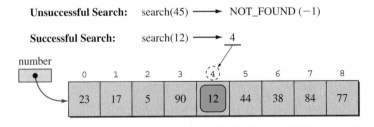

Figure 11.1 Successful and unsuccessful searches.

linear search is also called a *sequential search*. The linear search algorithm can be expressed as

```
public int linearSearch ( int[] number, int searchValue ) {
    int        loc    = 0;
                           More elements
                           to search

    while ( loc < number.length &&
            number[loc] != searchValue ) {

        loc++;                    searchValue is
    }                             not yet found.

    if ( loc == number.length) { //Not found
        return NOT_FOUND;
    } else {
        return loc;                  //Found, return the position
    }
}
```

If the number of entries in the array is *N*, then there will be *N* comparisons for an unsuccessful search (i.e., you search for a value not in the array). In the case of a successful search, there will be a minimum of one comparison and a maximum of *N* comparisons. On the average, there will be approximately *N*/2 comparisons.

Is there a way to improve the linear search? If the array is sorted, then we can improve the search routine by using the binary search technique.

Binary Search

binary search

If the values in the array are arranged in ascending or descending order, then we call the array *sorted*. In the following explanation of the binary search, we assume the array is sorted in ascending order. The crux of *binary search* is the winning strategy you apply for the Hi-Lo game. When you try to guess a secret number, say, between 1 and 100, your first guess will be 50. If your guess is HI, then you know the secret number is between 1 and 49. If your guess is LO, then you know the secret number is between 51 and 100. By guessing once, you eliminated one-half of the possible range of values from further consideration. This is the core idea of binary search.

Consider the following sorted array:

Let's suppose we are searching for 77. We first search the middle position of the array. Since this array has 9 elements, the index of the middle position is **4**, so we search number[4]. The value 77 is not in this position. Since 77 is larger than 38 and

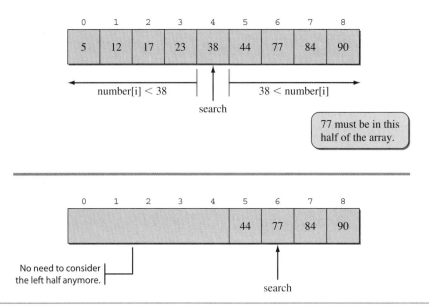

Figure 11.2 Effect of one comparison in binary search.

because the array is sorted, we know that if 77 is in the array, it must be in the right half of the array. So next we search the middle position of the right half of the array, which is position 6. Figure 11.2 illustrates the effect of making one comparison in the binary search.

The search value 77 was found after two comparisons. In contrast, the linear search would take seven comparisons to locate 77. So there is a net reduction of five comparisons. How good is the binary search in general? Let's study the worst-case situation. In the binary search, after we make one comparison, we can eliminate one-half of the array from further consideration. So the number of comparisons in the worst case is the number of times you can divide the array into halves. Suppose the original size of an array is N and the value we are searching for is not in the array. Then after one comparison, we have to search the remaining $N/2$ elements. After two comparisons, we have to search $N/4$ elements, and so on. The following table shows this relationship. The left column is the number of comparisons, and the right column is the number of elements we still need to search after making K comparisons.

Number of Comparisons	Number of Elements
0	N
1	$N/2 = N/2^1$
2	$N/4 = N/2^2$
. . .	. . .
K	$N/2^K$

The maximum number of comparisons K is derived by solving the equation

$$N = 2^K$$

$$\log_2 N = K$$

This is a remarkable improvement. If the size of the original array is 2048, for example, then the unsuccessful binary search takes at most $\log_2 2048 = 10$ comparisons, while the unsuccessful linear search takes 2048 comparisons. The difference between the two algorithms gets larger and larger as the size of an array gets larger.

Now let's write a binary search method. The key point in the method is how to stop the search. If the search value is in the array, we will eventually locate it, so the stopping condition for the successful search is easy. What about the case for an unsuccessful search? How can we detect that there are no more elements in the array to search for? Should we use some kind of a counter? We certainly can use a counter, but we can implement the method without using any counter. To compute the middle location for the next comparison, we need two indexes—low and high. The low and high indexes are initialized to 0 and $N - 1$. The middle location is computed as

```
mid = (low + high) / 2; //the result is truncated
```

If number[mid] is less than the search value, then low is reset to mid+1. If number[mid] is greater than the search value, then high is reset to mid−1, and the search continues. Eventually, we will locate the search value or we will run out of elements to compare. We know that there are no more elements to compare when low becomes larger than high. Figure 11.3 shows how this works.

Here's the binarySearch method:

```java
public int binarySearch ( int[] number, int searchValue ) {
    int        low   = 0,
               high  = number.length - 1,
               mid   = (low + high) / 2;

    while ( low <= high && number[mid] != searchValue ) {

        if (number[mid] < searchValue) {
            low = mid + 1;

        } else { //number[mid] > searchValue
            high = mid - 1;
        }

        mid    = (low + high) / 2;
    }

    if ( low > high) {
        mid = NOT_FOUND;

    }

    return mid;
}
```

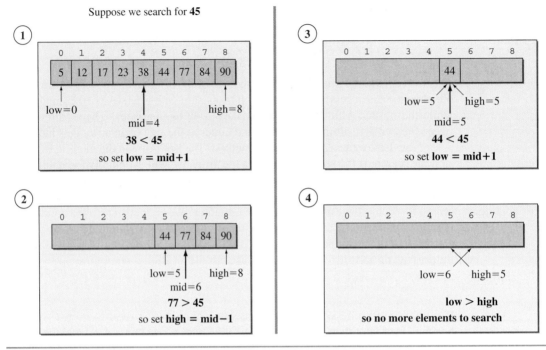

Figure 11.3 How the unsuccessful search is terminated in the binary search routine.

Quick **CHECK**

1. Suppose an array contains 2048 elements. What are the least and the greatest numbers of comparisons for a successful search using linear search?

2. Repeat question 1 with a binary search.

11.2 | Sorting

In this section we will describe two basic sorting algorithms. A more advanced sorting algorithm will be presented in Section 11.3 . Let's start with the problem statement for sorting:

Given an array of N values, arrange the values into ascending order.

Selection Sort

Given a list of integers, how would you sort them? The most natural sorting algorithm for a human looks something like this:

1. Find the smallest integer in the list.
2. Cross out the number from further consideration and copy it to a new (sorted) list.
3. Repeat steps 1 and 2 until all numbers are crossed out in the list.

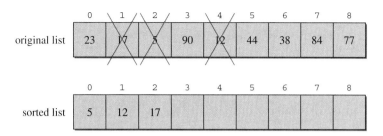

Figure 11.4 Human sorting algorithm after three numbers are moved to the sorted list.

selection sort

sorting passes

Figure 11.4 shows this human sorting algorithm with the first three numbers being copied to the new list.

We can write a real computer program based on this sorting algorithm, but the resulting program will not be a good one. There are two problems. First, we need an extra array to keep the sorted list. This may not sound like much, but when you consider an array of, say, 10,000 elements, using a second array is very wasteful. Second, crossing out numbers is effective for humans only. We humans can see the cross marks and will not consider the numbers once they are crossed out, but in computer programs, we still have to write code to check every element to see whether it is crossed out. We can "cross out" an element by replacing it with a negative number, say, −1, if the numbers are all positive. If not, then we have to use other means to "cross out" an element. So crossing out the numbers does not reduce the number of comparisons in the program.

Although we do not want to implement this human sorting algorithm as is, we can derive an algorithm based on the idea of finding the smallest number in a given list and moving it to the correct position in the list. This sorting algorithm is called *selection sort*.

The selection sort is comprised of *sorting passes*. Figure 11.5 shows the effect of the first pass on a sample array of N (= 9) elements. First we locate the smallest element in the array and set the index min to point to this element. Then we exchange number[start] and number[min]. After the first pass, the smallest element is moved to the correct position. We increment the value of start by 1 and then execute the second pass. We start the first pass with start = 0 and end the last pass with start = N-2. Figure 11.6 shows the sequence of eight passes made to the sample array.

Here's the selectionSort method:

```java
public void selectionSort( int[] number ) {

    int minIndex, length, temp;
    length = number.length;

    for (int startIndex = 0; startIndex <= length-2; startIndex++){
        //each iteration of the for loop is one pass

        minIndex = startIndex;
```

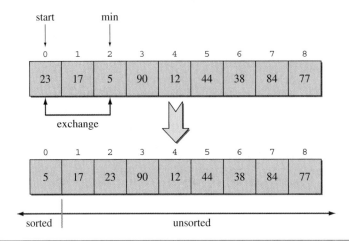

Figure 11.5 Effect of executing the first pass in the selection sort.

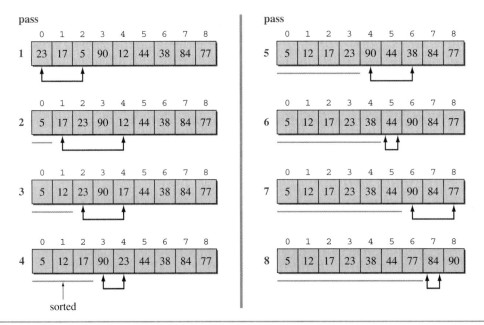

Figure 11.6 Eight passes to sort the sample array of nine elements.

```
//find the smallest in this pass at
//position minIndex
for (int i = startIndex+1; i <= length-1; i++) {
    if (number[i] < number[minIndex]) minIndex = i;
}
```

```
        //exchange number[startIndex] and number[minIndex]
        temp                    = number[startIndex];
        number[startIndex]   = number[minIndex];
        number[minIndex]     = temp;

        assert minStart(number, startIndex):
                "Error: " + number[startIndex] +
                " at position " + startIndex +
                " is not the smallest.";
    }

    assert isSorted(number):
            "Error: the final is not sorted";
}
```

The assertion at the end of one pass confirms that the smallest element in that pass moved to the beginning position of the pass. The minStart method is therefore written as follows:

```
    private boolean minStart(int[] number, int startIndex) {

        for (int i = startIndex+1; i < number.length; i++) {

            if (number[startIndex] > number[i]) {
                return false;
            }
        }
        return true;
    }
```

We put a second assertion at the end of method to verify that no elements are out of place after the sorting is complete. The isSorted method is written as

```
    private boolean isSorted(int[] number) {

        for (int i = 0; i < number.length-1; i++) {

            if (number[i] > number[i+1]) {
                return false;
            }
        }
        return true;
    }
```

Assertion is a very useful tool in a situation such as sorting. While developing the sorting routines, we insert a number of assertion statements to increase our confidence in the program's correctness.

Helpful Reminder

Be sure to compile and run programs with assertions enabled during the development, but disable them during the actual use. Compile the source file that includes assertions with

```
javac -source 1.4 <source file>
```

and run the program with assertions enabled with

```
java -ea <main class>
```

Take my Advice

We use assertions to find coding error. But what will happen when the code we write for assertions, such at the **minStart** method used in the selection sort routine, is wrong? How can we assert that **minStart** is correct? We do not want to write assertions for assertions! One possibility is to create a data set that is correct and run the **minStart** method against these data to test for their validity. The use of assertions is merely an aid, not a fail-safe way to find errors.

Let's analyze the selection sort algorithm. In analyzing different sorting algorithms, we normally count two things: the number of comparisons and the number of data movements (exchanges). We will show you how to count the number of comparisons here. Counting the number of data movements is left as Exercise 4. Keep in mind that the analysis we provide in this chapter is an informal one. A detailed analysis is beyond the scope of this book, so we will give only a taste of the formal analysis.

The selection sort has one comparison (the if statement inside the nested-for loop), so we can easily count the total number of comparisons by counting the number of times the inner loop is executed. For each execution of the outer loop, the inner loop is executed length − start times. The variable start ranges from 0 to length-2. So the total number of comparisons is computed by finding the sum of the right column in the following table:

Start	Number of Comparisons (Length − Start)
0	length
1	length − 1
2	length − 2
. . .	. . .
length − 2	2

The variable length is the size of the array. If we replace length with N, the size of the array, the sum of the right column is

$$N + (N - 1) + (N - 2) + \cdots + 2 = \sum_{i=2}^{N} i = \sum_{i=1}^{N} i - 1$$

$$= \frac{N(N + 1)}{2} - 1 = \frac{N^2 + N - 2}{2} \cong N^2$$

The total number of comparisons is approximately the square of the size of an array. This is a quadratic function, so the number of comparisons grows very rapidly as the size of an array gets larger. Is there a better sorting algorithm? The answer is yes.

Bubble Sort

The effect of one pass of the selection sort is the movement of the smallest element to its correct position. Since an array gets sorted only by moving the elements to their correct position, the whole sorting routine will complete sooner if we increase the number of data movements. In the selection sort, we make one exchange per pass. If we could move more elements toward their correct positions in one pass, we would be able to complete the sorting sooner than the selection sort. The bubble sort is one such algorithm that increases the number of data movements for the same number of comparisons as the selection sort makes.

The key point of the bubble sort is to make pairwise comparisons and exchange the positions of the pair if they are out of order. Figure 11.7 shows the effect of pairwise comparisons in the first past of the bubble sort. After the first pass, the largest element, 90, has moved to its correct position in the array. This is the guaranteed effect of one pass. In addition, we notice that many other elements also have moved toward their correct position, as bubbles move toward the water's surface.

In the worst case, the bubble sort will make $N - 1$ passes, so the worst-case performance is the same as for the selection sort. However, in the average case, we can expect a better performance from the bubble sort. The bubble sort exhibits two properties:

- After one pass through the array, the largest element will be at the end of the array.

- During one pass, if no pair of consecutive entries is out of order, then the array is sorted.

Using these properties, we can express the bubbleSort method in pseudocode:

This **while** loop performs at most $N - 1$ passes for an array with N elements. The loop will terminate when there are no exchanges in one pass.

```
bottom = number.length - 2;
exchanged = true;

while ( exchanged ) { //continue if the exchange is made

    //do one pass of sorting
    exchanged = false; //reset the variable
```

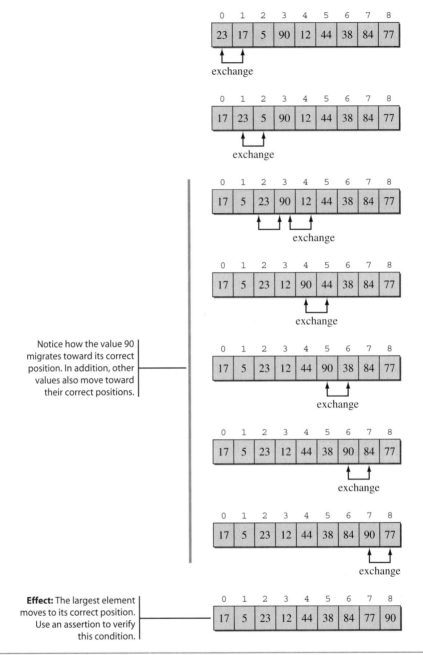

Notice how the value 90 migrates toward its correct position. In addition, other values also move toward their correct positions.

Effect: The largest element moves to its correct position. Use an assertion to verify this condition.

Figure 11.7 Effect of executing the first pass in the bubble sort.

```
        for (int i = 0; i <= bottom; i++) { //pairwise comparison
            if ( number[i] > number[i+1] ) {
                //the pair is out of order
                exchange them;

                exchanged = true; //an exchange is made
            }
            //one pass is done, decrement the bottom index by 1
            bottom--;
        }
```

One pass of
bubble sort

Translating the pseudocode into an actual method, we have

```
public void bubbleSort( int[] number ) {

    int      temp, bottom;
    boolean  exchanged = true;

    bottom = number.length - 2;

    while ( exchanged )  {

        exchanged = false;

        for (int i = 0; i <= bottom; i++) {
            if (number[i] > number[i+1]) {

                temp        = number[i];      //exchange
                number[i]   = number[i+1];
                number[i+1] = temp;

                exchanged   = true; //exchange is made
            }
        }

        assert maxBottom(number, bottom):
                "Error: " + number[bottom] +
                " at position " + bottom +
                " is not the largest.";

        bottom--;
    }

    assert isSorted(number):
            "Error: the final is not sorted";
}
```

Assert the element at position **bottom** is the largest
among elements from
position **0** to **bottom**.

The maxBottom method verifies that the largest element among elements from position 0 to bottom is at position bottom. The method is written as

```
private boolean maxBottom(int[] number, int lastIndex) {

    for (int i = 0; i < lastIndex; i++) {
```

```
            if (number[lastIndex] < number[i]) {
                return false;
            }
        }
        return true;
    }
```

On average, we expect the bubble sort to finish sorting sooner than the selection sort, because there will be more data movements for the same number of comparisons and there is a test to exit the method when the array gets sorted. The worst case of the bubble sort happens when the original array is in descending order. Notice that if the original array is already sorted, the bubble sort will perform only one pass whereas the selection sort will perform $N - 1$ passes.

Quick **CHECK**

1. Show the result of the second pass of bubble sort applied to the array at the bottom of Figure 11.7.

2. For an array with N elements, what is the least number of comparisons the bubble sort will execute?

11.3 | Heapsort

Selection and bubble sorts are two fundamental sorting algorithms that take approximately N^2 comparisons to sort an array of N elements. One interesting sorting algorithm that improves this performance to approximately $1.5N \log_2 N$ is *heapsort*. We will describe the heapsort algorithm and analyze its performance in this section.

heapsort

heap

The heapsort algorithm uses a special data structure called a *heap*. A heap consists of nodes, which contain data values, and edges, which link the nodes. Figure 11.8 shows a sample heap. We use integers as data values for the examples in this section. The topmost node is called the *root node* of a heap. Nodes in a heap

root node

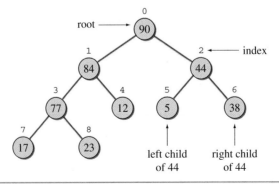

Figure 11.8 A sample heap that includes nine nodes.

are indexed 0, 1, 2, and so forth in the top-to-bottom, left-to-right order, starting from the root. A node in a heap has zero, one, or two *children*. The children of a node are distinguished as the node's *left* and *right children*. If a node has only one child, then it is the left child of the node.

left and right children

A heap must satisfy these two constraints:

heap constraints

1. **Structural constraint:** Nodes in a heap with N nodes must occupy the positions numbered 0, 1, . . . , $N - 1$. Figure 11.9 shows examples of nonheaps that violate the structural constraint.

2. **Value relationship constraint:** A value stored in a node must be larger than the maximum of the values stored in its left and right children. Figure 11.10 shows examples of nonheaps that violate the value relationship constraint.

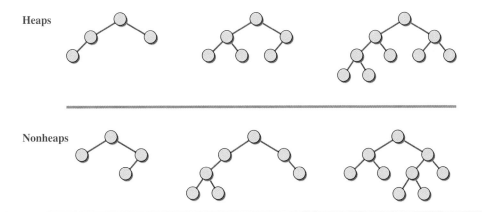

Figure 11.9 Sample heaps and nonheaps that violate the structural constraint.

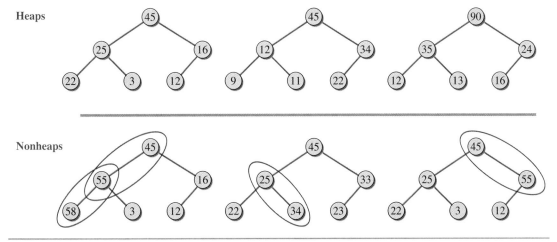

Figure 11.10 Sample heaps and nonheaps that violate the value relationship constraint. Violations are indicated by blue ellipses.

How can we use the heap structure to sort N elements? Heapsort is carried out in two phases:

1. **Construction phase:** Construct a heap given N elements.
2. **Extraction phase:** Pull out the value in the root successively, creating a new heap with one less element after each extraction step.

We will begin the description of heapsort from the extraction phase. Consider the heap shown in Figure 11.8. Since every node in the heap satisfies the value relationship constraint, we can conclude that the value in the root node is the largest among the values stored in the heap. Now, after we remove the value 90 from the heap, we must create a new heap that has one less element. We can build such a heap by first moving the last element (value 23 in the figure) to the root position. With the value 23 in the root position, we have met the structural constraint for the heap with eight elements. However, the value relationship constraint is not met. The violation occurs because 23 is smaller than the larger of its two children. By swapping 84 and 23, the violation is eliminated. Since the value 23 is now at a new location, we must check again if the violation occurs at this position. It does, because 77 is larger than 23, so we swap again. We repeat the process until either there are no more children to consider or the value moved into a new position meets the value relationship

constraint. We will call this process a *rebuild step*. One rebuild step is illustrated in Figure 11.11.

Using a heap with N elements, we can sort the given N elements by performing the rebuild steps $N - 1$ times. Figure 11.12 illustrates the rebuild steps for the sample heap. Notice how the array for the sorted list is filled from the end. All we have to do now is to figure out how to build a heap from a given unsorted list of N elements. Let's study the construction phase of the algorithm.

We will illustrate the construction phase with the following unsorted nine elements:

```
23, 17, 5, 90, 12, 44, 38, 84, 77
```

If we assign the given numbers to a heap structure in ascending index order, we have the heap structure shown in Figure 11.13. This heap structure is not truly a heap because it violates the value relationship constraint. The construction phase will eliminate any violations of the value relationship constraint. The key concept for the construction phase is the rebuild step we used in the extraction phase. We will build a complete heap in a bottom-up fashion. We start out with a small heap and gradually build bigger and bigger heaps until the heap contains all N elements. Figure 11.14 shows the sequence of rebuild steps. The triangles indicate where the rebuild steps are applied. In the extraction step, the rebuild step is always applied to the root node. In the construction step, each rebuild step is applied successively, beginning with the node at index $\lfloor (N - 2)/2 \rfloor$ and ending with the node at index 0 (i.e., the root node).

Now let's consider how we can implement this algorithm in Java. We must first decide how to represent a heap. Among the possible alternatives, the data structure we learned in this book that can be used here very effectively is an array.

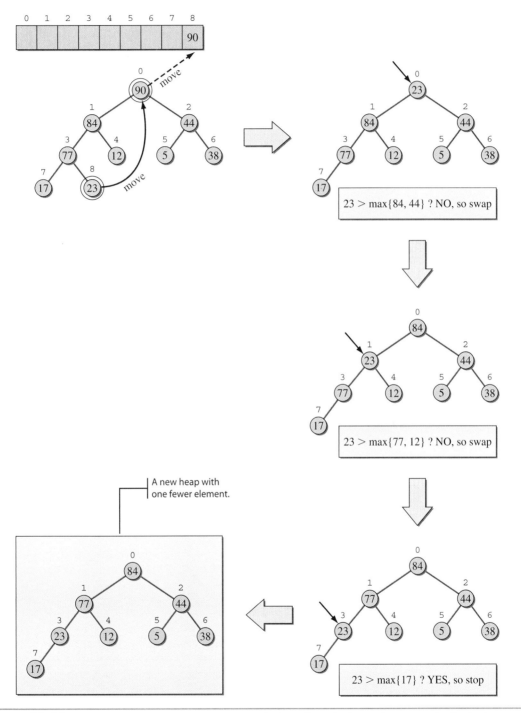

Figure 11.11 One rebuild step after the value 90 is pulled out from the heap. The net result of a single rebuild step is a new heap that contains one fewer element.

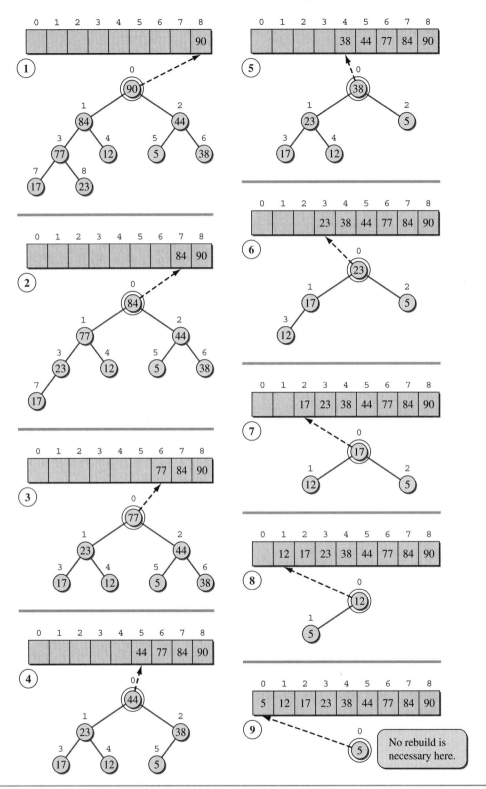

Figure 11.12 Eight rebuild steps to sort a heap with nine elements.

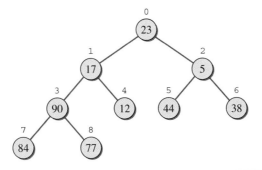

Figure 11.13 A heap structure with given numbers assigned in ascending index order.

Figure 11.15 shows the correspondence between the heap and the array representation. An important aspect in deciding which data structure to use is the ease of locating a given node's left and right children. With an array implementation, we can locate any node's left and right children easily. A node with index I has its left child at index $2I + 1$ and its right child at index $2I + 2$.

Since the heapsort algorithm is more involved than the insertion or bubble sort algorithm, we will put all the necessary code in a single class called Heap to provide a complete picture. To simplify our implementation so we can focus on the algorithm, we will allow only integers. You can modify the class to allow any objects to be sorted; see Exercise 9 at the end of this chapter. The following code illustrates how to use the Heap class:

```
int[ ] number = { 90, 44, 84, 12, 77, 23, 38, 5, 17 };
int[ ] sortedList;

Heap heap = new Heap( );

heap.setData( number );   //assign the original list

sortedList = heap.sort( );//sort the list

for (int i = 0; i < sortedList.length; i++ ) { //print out
    System.out.print("   " + sortedList[i]);   //the sorted
}                                               //list
```

The Heap class will include two arrays as its data members: one to implement a heap and another to store the sorted list.

```
/**
 * This class implements the heapsort algorithm. This class
 * can sort only integers.
 */
class Heap {
```

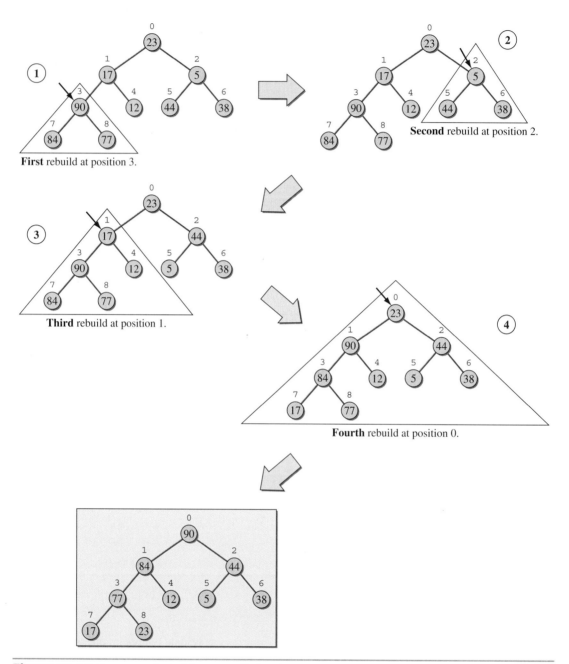

Figure 11.14 Sequence of rebuild steps applied in the construction phase. Rebuild steps are carried out at index positions 3, 2, 1, and 0.

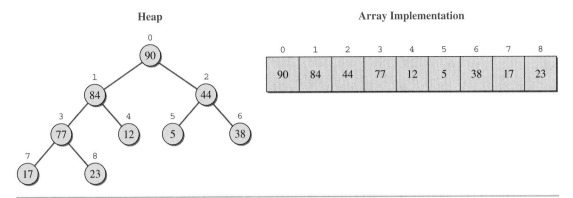

Figure 11.15 A sample heap and the corresponding array implementation.

```
/**
 * Implements the heap
 */
private int[ ] heap;

/**
 * Stores the sorted list
 */
private int[ ] sortedList;

// methods come here
...
}
```

Now let's look at the methods. The setData method initializes the two data members as follows:

```
public void setData( int[ ] data ) {

    heap        = new int[ data.length ];
    sortedList  = new int[ data.length ];

    for (int i = 0; i < data.length; i++ ) {
        heap[i] = data[i];
    }
}
```

Notice that we copy the contents of the data array to the heap array. If we simply assign the parameter to the data member heap as

```
heap = data;
```

then all we are doing is setting two names referring to the same object. Since we do not want to change the original data array, we make a separate copy.

The sort method calls two private methods that implement the two phases of the heapsort algorithm:

```
public int[ ] sort( ) {

    construct( );   //perform the construction phase

    extract( );    //perform the extraction phase

    return sortedList;
}
```

Here's the construct method:

```
private void construct( ) {

    int      current, maxChildIndex;
    boolean done;

    for (int i = (heap.length-2) / 2; i >= 0; i--) {

        current = i;
        done    = false;

        while ( !done ) {//perform one rebuild step
                         //with the node at index i

            if ( 2*current+1 > heap.length-1 ) {

                //current node has no children, so stop
                done = true;

            } else {
                //current node has at least one child,
                //get the index of larger child
                maxChildIndex
                    = maxChild( current, heap.length-1 );

                if ( heap[current] < heap[maxChildIndex] ) {

                    //a child is larger, so swap and continue
                    swap( current, maxChildIndex );
                    current = maxChildIndex;

                } else { //the value relationship constraint
                         //is satisfied, so stop
                    done = true;
                }
            }
        }
    }

    assert isValidHeap(heap, i, heap.length-1):
        "Error: Construction phase is not working " +
        "correctly";
}
```

```
        testPrint( heap.length );   //TEMP
    }
```

The isValidHeap method is used to assert that elements from position start to end form a valid heap structure. Here's the method:

```
    private boolean isValidHeap(int[] heap,
                                int start, int end) {

        for (int i = start; i < end/ 2; i++) {

            if (heap[i] < Math.max(heap[2*i+1], heap[2*i+2])) {
                return false;
            }
        }

        return true;
    }
```

And here's the extract method:

```
    private void extract( ) {

        int     current, maxChildIndex;
        boolean done;

        for (int size = heap.length-1; size >= 0; size--) {

            //remove the root node data
            sortedList[size] = heap[ 0 ];

            //move the last node to the root
            heap[ 0 ] = heap[size];

            //rebuild the heap with one fewer element
            current = 0;
            done    = false;

            while ( !done ) {

                if ( 2*current+1 > size ) {
                    //current node has no children, so stop
                    done = true;

                } else {
                    //current node has at least one child,
                    //get the index of larger child
                    maxChildIndex = maxChild( current, size );

                    if ( heap[current] < heap[maxChildIndex] ) {

                        //a child is larger, so swap and continue
                        swap( current, maxChildIndex );
                        current = maxChildIndex;
```

```
            } else { //value relationship constraint
                   //is satisfied, so stop
               done = true;
            }
         }
      }

      assert isValidHeap(heap, i, heap.length-1):
             "Error: Construction phase is not working " +
             "correctly";
      testPrint( size );   //TEMP

   }
}
```

A number of methods are shared by both methods. The maxChild method returns the index of a node's left or right child, whichever is larger. This method is called only if a node has at least one child. The first parameter is the index of a node, and the second parameter is the index of the last node in a heap. The second parameter is necessary to determine whether a node has a right child. The method is defined as follows:

```
private int maxChild( int location, int end ) {

   int result, leftChildIndex, rightChildIndex;

   rightChildIndex = 2*location + 2;
   leftChildIndex  = 2*location + 1;

   //Precondition:
   //       Node at 'location' has at least one child
   assert leftChildIndex <= end:
          "Error: node at position " + location +
          "has no children.";

   if ( rightChildIndex <= end &&
        heap[leftChildIndex] < heap[rightChildIndex]) {

      result = rightChildIndex;
   } else {
      result = leftChildIndex;
   }

   return result;
}
```

The other two methods shared by the construct and extract methods are swap and testPrint. The swap method interchanges the contents of two array elements, and the testPrint method outputs the heap array for verification and debugging purposes. You can comment out the calls to testPrint from the construct and extract methods after you verify that the algorithm is implemented correctly. Here are the two methods:

```java
private void swap (int loc1, int loc2) {

    int temp;

    temp = heap[loc1];
    heap[loc1] = heap[loc2];
    heap[loc2] = temp;
}

private void testPrint(int limit) {

    for (int i = 0; i < limit; i++) {
        System.out.print( " " + heap[i] );
    }

    System.out.println( "     " );
}
```

There are several improvements we can make to the simple `Heap` class we provided here. These improvements are left as Exercise 9.

Performance

How good is the heapsort? We mentioned in Section 11.2 that the performances of both selection and bubble sort algorithms are approximately N^2 comparisons for sorting N elements. The heapsort algorithm is substantially more complex in design and implementation than the other two basic sorting algorithms. Is the extra complexity worth our effort? The answer is yes. The performance of the heapsort algorithm is approximately $1.5N \log_2 N$ comparisons for sorting N elements. This is a remarkable improvement. Consider the difference between the two performances for large N. For example, to sort 100,000 elements, the selection or bubble sort requires 10,000,000,000 comparisons, while the heapsort requires only $1.5 \cdot 100,000 \log_2 100,000 \approx 2,491,695$ comparisons. If a single comparison takes 1 microsecond (μs) (one millionth second), then the selection or bubble sort takes about 2.8 hours while the heapsort takes only about 2.492 seconds. (*Note:* The sorting operation itself may complete in a few seconds, but printing out the sorted 100,000 elements would take an enormous amount of time.)

Let's study how the performance of $1.5N \log_2 N$ comparisons is derived. What we need to count is the number of comparisons made during the rebuild steps in both the construction and extraction phases. During the extraction phase, the rebuild process is carried for $N - 1$ times. If we let K be the maximum number of comparisons required in one rebuild step, then the total number of comparisons will be $(N - 1)K$. In one rebuild step, we start comparing the value in the root node with the larger of its two children. If the value relationship constraint is not violated, the rebuild step terminates immediately. If there is a violation, we make a swap and

Level #

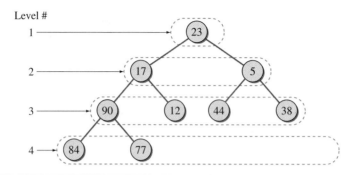

Figure 11.16 A sample heap with depth = 4, which is defined to be the largest level of all nodes in a heap.

continue. This compare-and-swap operation is carried out until either the value relationship constraint is met or there are no more nodes to compare. This means that the maximum number of comparisons K is derived by finding out how many times the value relationship constraint violation can occur before the nodes to compare are exhausted.

level

depth

Consider the heap shown in Figure 11.16. We define the *level* of a node in a heap to be the number of nodes in the path from the root to this node. For example, the level of node 44 in the sample heap is 3. The *depth* of a heap is defined to be the largest level of the nodes in the heap. The depth of the sample heap is therefore 4. Since the compare-and-swap operation starting from the root can never continue comparing beyond the largest level of the nodes, the depth of a heap is the value we seek for K. Thus, the value for K is derived by finding the depth of a heap with N elements.

At level 1, there is one node. At level 2, there are two nodes. Since a node at level i can have at most 2 children, the maximum number of nodes at level $i + 1$ is double the number of nodes at level i. Assuming the maximum number of nodes at all levels, the number of elements at level i is 2^{i-1}, so the maximum total number of nodes in a heap of depth K is

$$\sum_{i=1}^{K} 2^{i-1} = 2^K - 1$$

Because a heap must satisfy the structural constraint, we know the relationships

$$2^{K-1} - 1 < N \leq 2^K - 1$$
$$2^{K-1} < N + 1 \leq 2^K$$

will hold. By applying $\log_2$ to all terms, we have

$$K - 1 < \log_2 (N + 1) \leq K$$

so

$$K = \lceil \log_2 (N + 1) \rceil$$

Finally, the total number of comparisons for the extraction phase is

$$(N - 1)K = N \cdot \lceil \log_2 (N + 1) \rceil \approx N \log_2 N$$

The construction phase will perform approximately $N/2$ rebuild steps. Each rebuild step will take no more than K comparisons, so the total number of comparisons for the construction phase is

$$\frac{N}{2} \log_2 N$$

The total number of comparisons for both phases is therefore

$$1.5N \log_2 N$$

Quick **CHECK**

1. The following structure violates the value relationship constraints. Use the construction phase routine of the heapsort to eliminate the violations.

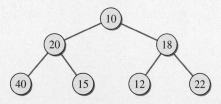

2. Identify all violations on structural and value relationship constraints in the following structure:

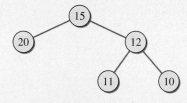

11.4 Sample Program

Sorting an AddressBook

Let's put the our basic knowledge of sorting algorithms into practice. In Chapter 10 we presented the **AddressBook** class that maintains a collection of **Person** objects. We will extend the **AddressBook** class by incorporating a sorting routine. The new **AddressBook** class will include a method that sorts the **Person** objects in alphabetical order of their names or in ascending order of their ages.

Instead of going through the development steps, we will discuss three different implementations to illustrate various techniques of Java programming. The three classes are named **AddressBookVer1, AddressBookVer2,** and **AddressBookVer3.**

We will define an interface and make these three classes implement the defined interface. We have already dealt with interfaces, for example, the **ActionListener** interface in Chapter 7 and the **List** and **Map** interfaces in Chapter 10. As we learned in those chapters, the interface defines a behavior, and if a class implements the interface, we can be certain that the instances of the class will support this behavior. For example, an instance of any class that implements the **ActionListener** interface will support the **actionPerformed** behavior. Making classes implement the same interface is therefore a way to enforce consistency among the implementation classes. Because all three classes **AddressBookVer1, AddressBookVer2,** and **AddressBook3** implement the same interface, they will exhibit the same behavior, and we can therefore use them interchangeably in our programs.

The interface is named **AddressBook,** and we will include the public methods that must be supported by all versions. Collectively these public methods define the behavior common to all implementing classes. All public methods in the interface must not have any method body, only the method prototype followed by a semicolon. Here's the **AddressBook** interface:

```
/*
    Chapter 11 Sample Program: AddressBook Interface

    File: AddressBook.java
*/
interface AddressBook {

    public void      add( Person newPerson );

    public boolean   delete( String searchName );

    public Person    search( String searchName );

    public Person[ ] sort ( int attribute );

}
```

The driver program to test the working of **AddressBook** is defined as follows:

```
/*
        Chapter 11 Sample Program: Test program to verify the
                the AddressBook and Person classes

        File: TestAddressBookSorting.java
*/
```

```java
import javax.swing.*;

class TestAddressBookSorting {

    public static void main(String[] args) {

        TestAddressBookSorting tester = new TestAddressBookSorting();
        tester.start();
    }

    private void start( ) {
        String[] name = {"ape", "cat", "bee", "bat", "eel",
                         "dog", "gnu", "yak", "fox", "cow",
                         "hen", "tic", "man"};

        Person p;

        AddressBook ab;

        int version = Integer.parseInt(
                    JOptionPane.showInputDialog(null,"Version #:"));

        switch (version) {
            case 1:  ab = new AddressBookVer1(); break;
            case 2:  ab = new AddressBookVer2(); break;
            case 3:  ab = new AddressBookVer3(); break;
            default: ab = new AddressBookVer1(); break;
        }

        for (int i = 0; i < name.length; i++) {

            p = new Person(name[i], random(10, 50),
                            random(0,1)==0?'M':'F');

            //note: random(0,1) == 0 ? 'M':'F'
            // means if (random(0,1) == 0) then 'M' else 'F'
                ab.add(p);
        }

        Person[] sortedlist = ab.sort( Person.AGE );

        for (int i = 0; i < sortedlist.length; i++) {
            System.out.println( sortedlist[i].toString( ) );
        }

        System.out.println(" ");

        sortedlist = ab.sort( Person.NAME );
```

start

```
    for (int i = 0; i < sortedlist.length; i++) {
        System.out.println( sortedlist[i].toString( ) );
    }
}

private int random(int low, int high) {                   random

    return (int) Math.floor(Math.random() * (high - low + 1))
                 + low;
}
}
```

Version 1

In describing the basic sorting algorithms, we limit the data values to integers. This makes the comparison test easy. We write something like this:

```
if ( number[i] < number[i+1] ) {
    //do something...
} else {
    //do something else...
}
```

But how do we compare **Person** objects? We cannot say

```
Person p1 = new Person( "Jack", 18, 'M' );
Person p2 = new Person( "Jill", 19, 'F' );
if ( p1 < p2 ) {
    ...
}
```

Cannot compare **Person** objects like this, because it does not make sense. Comparison operators other than equal (==) do not apply for objects.

because the comparison operators such as <, >, and others except the equal operator are meaningful only for comparing primitive data values. To be able to compare **Person** objects, we need to modify the class. Let's suppose that we want to compare two **Person** objects based on either their names or their ages. First we add the following two constants to the **Person** class of Chapter 10:

```
class Person {
    ...
    public static final int NAME = 0;
    public static final int AGE  = 1;
    ...
}
```

Next we add a variable to the **Person** class to set which attribute to use in comparing two objects:

```
private static int compareAttribute = NAME;
```

Notice that the variable is a class variable because this information is not specific to any individual **Person** objects, but applies to the whole class. We initialize it to **NAME** so the **Person** objects will be compared on the name attribute as a default. We define a class method to let the programmer set the comparison attribute. The class method is defined as

```
public static void setCompareAttribute( int attribute ) {

    compareAttribute = attribute;
}
```

Although it is not a syntax error to initialize a class variable inside a constructor, it is a logical error to do so. You cannot define a constructor that includes an initialization of the **compareAttribute** variable as in

```
public Person( ) {

    ...
    compareAttribute = NAME;
}
```

This definition is valid because the class variables can be accessed from the instance methods, but it is wrong to do so here. This constructor will set the class variable **compareAttribute** that is shared by all instances of the **Person** class every time a new **Person** object is created. This is not what we want. We need to initialize it exactly once when the class is loaded into the memory. One way to do this is to initialize at the point the class variable is declared as shown, or to use the *static block* as

static block

```
class Person {
    ...

    static {
        compareAttribute = NAME;
    }
    ...
}
```

Use the **static** block to initialize class variables.

The rule to remember is never to initialize the class variables in the constructor.

Helpful Reminder

*Do not initialize class variables in the constructor. Initialize the class variables in the **static** block.*

Now we are ready to add a method **compareTo** that will compare the designated **Person** objects' names or ages and return the comparison result. The method is used like this:

```
//Persons p1 and p2 are defined and created already

//First set the comparison attribute to NAME
Person.setCompareAttribute( Person.NAME );

int comparisonResult = p1.compareTo( p2 );

if ( comparisonResult < 0 ) {
   //p1's name is lexicographically less than p2's name

} else if ( comparisonResult == 0 ) {
   //p1's name is equal to p2's name

} else { //comparisonResult > 0
   //p1's name is lexicographically larger than p2's name
}
```

To compare two **Person** objects on their ages, we write

```
//Persons p1 and p2 are defined and created already

//First set the comparison attribute to AGE
Person.setCompareAttribute( Person.AGE );

int comparisonResult = p1.compareTo( p2 );

if ( comparisonResult < 0 ) {
   //p1 is younger than p2

} else if ( comparisonResult == 0 ) {
   //p1's age is the same as p2's age

} else { //comparisonResult > 0
   //p1 is older than p2
}
```

Here's the **compareTo** method:

```
public int compareTo( Person person ) {

   int comparisonResult;

   if ( compareAttribute == AGE ) {
      int p2age = person.getAge( );

      if (this.age < p2age) {
         comparisonResult = LESS;

      } else if (this.age == p2age) {
         comparisonResult = EQUAL;
```

```
            } else {
                assert this.age > p2age;
                comparisonResult = MORE;
            }

        } else { //compare names with String's compareTo
            String    p2name = person.getName( );
            comparisonResult = this.name.compareTo(p2name);
        }

        return comparisonResult;
    }
```

The constants **LESS, EQUAL,** and **MORE** are defined in the **Person** class as

```
        private static int LESS  = -1;
        private static int EQUAL =  0;
        private static int MORE  =  1;
```

The **compareTo** method of the **String** class behaves just as our **compareTo** method does. Indeed, our **compareTo** method is modeled after the **String** class's **compareTo** method. The wrapper classes **Integer, Float, Double,** and others also define the analogous **compareTo** method. Having consistent naming and behavior for comparing two objects of the same class allows the implementation of a more general code. See Exercise 9 at the end of the chapter.

Here's the complete **Person** class:

```
/*
    Chapter 11 Sample Program: Person class

    File: Person.java
*/
class Person {

    public static final int NAME = 0;
    public static final int AGE = 1;

    private static final int LESS = -1;
    private static final int EQUAL = 0;
    private static final int MORE  = 1;

    private static int compareAttribute;

    private String  name;
    private int     age;
    private char    gender;
```

Data members

```java
//    Static Initializer
    static {
       compareAttribute = NAME;
    }

    public Person() {                                    Constructors
       this("Not Given", 0, 'U');
    }

    public Person(String name, int age, char gender) {
       this.age    = age;
       this.name   = name;
       this.gender = gender;
    }

    public static void setCompareAttribute(int attribute) {
       compareAttribute = attribute;                   setCompareAttribute
    }

    public int compareTo(Person person, int attribute) {
       int comparisonResult;                           compareTo

       if ( attribute == AGE ) {
          int p2age = person.getAge( );

          if (this.age < p2age) {
             comparisonResult = LESS;
          } else if (this.age == p2age) {
             comparisonResult = EQUAL;
          } else {
             assert this.age > p2age;
             comparisonResult = MORE;
          }

       } else { //compare the name using the String class's
                //compareTo method
          String    p2name = person.getName( );
          comparisonResult = this.name.compareTo(p2name);
       }

       return comparisonResult;
    }

    public int compareTo(Person person) {
       return compareTo(person, compareAttribute);
    }
```

```
public int getAge( ) {
    return age;
}

public char getGender( ) {
    return gender;
}

public String getName( ) {
    return name;
}
```

Accessors

```
public void setAge( int age ) {
    this.age = age;
}

public void setGender( char gender ) {
    this.gender = gender;
}

public void setName( String name ) {
    this.name = name;
}
```

Mutators

```
public String toString( )  {
    return this.name    + "\t\t" +
           this.age     + "\t\t" +
           this.gender;
}
}
```

toString

Now we are ready to add a sorting routine to the **AddressBook** class. The **sort** method accepts one integer parameter that specifies the attribute to compare in sorting the **Person** objects. The method returns an array of **Person** objects sorted on the designated attribute. We use the bubble sort algorithm for the method. Using the heapsort algorithm is left as Exercise 12. Here's the **sort** method.

```
public Person[ ] sort (int attribute) {

    Person[ ] sortedList = new Person[ count ];
    Person p1, p2, temp;

    //copy references to sortedList; see Figure 11.17
    for (int i = 0; i < count; i++) {
        sortedList[i] = entry[i];
    }
```

```
                    //Set the comparison attribute
                    Person.setCompareAttribute(attribute);

                    //begin the bubble sort on sortedList
                    int       bottom, comparisonResult;
                    boolean   exchanged = true;

                    bottom = sortedList.length - 2;

                    while ( exchanged )  {

                        exchanged = false;

                        for (int i = 0; i <= bottom; i++) {
                            p1 = sortedList[i];
                            p2 = sortedList[i+1];

                            comparisonResult = p1.compareTo(p2, attribute);

                            if ( comparisonResult > 0 ) { //p1 is 'larger'
                                sortedList[i]   = p2;      //than p2,so
                                sortedList[i+1] = p1;      //exchange

                                exchanged = true;          //exchange is made
                            }
                        }
                        bottom--;
                    }
                    return sortedList;
                }
```

The **sort** method first creates a temporary array called **sortedList** and copies the references from the **entry** array into this **sortedList.** We do this so we can sort the objects on a specified attribute without affecting the order maintained in the **entry** array. Figure 11.17 illustrates how this **sortedList** array is used in sorting the **Person** objects on the **age** attribute.

Here's the **AddressBookVer1** class:

```
/*
    Chapter 11 Sample Program: Address Book Version 1

    File: AddressBookVer1.java

*/
class AddressBookVer1 implements AddressBook {

    private static final int  DEFAULT_SIZE = 25;
    private static final int  NOT_FOUND    = -1;
```

Data members

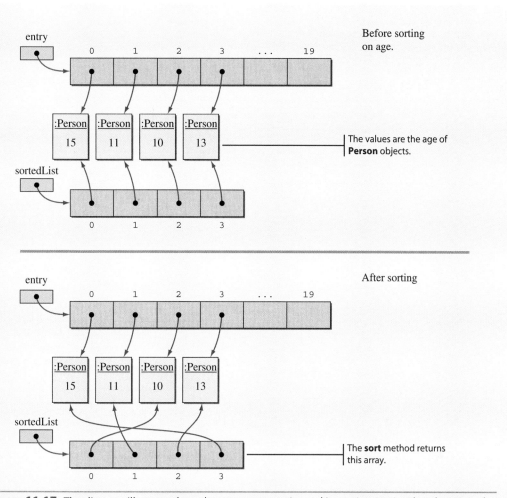

Figure 11.17 The diagram illustrates how the separate array is used in sorting. Notice that the original array is unaffected by the sorting.

```
private Person[]   entry;
private int        count;

public AddressBookVer1( ){
    this( DEFAULT_SIZE );
}

public AddressBookVer1(int size){
    count = 0;
```

Constructors

11.4 **Sample Program**—*continued*

```
        if (size <= 0 ) { //invalid data value, use default
            throw new IllegalArgumentException("Size must be positive");
        }

        entry = new Person[size];

//      System.out.println("array of "+ size + " is created."); //TEMP
    }

    public void add(Person newPerson) {                          add

        if (count == entry.length) {    //no more space left,
            enlarge( );                 //create a new larger array
        }

        //at this point, entry refers to a new larger array
        entry[count] = newPerson;
        count++;
    }

    public boolean delete(String searchName) {                   delete

        boolean    status;
        int        loc;

        loc = findIndex( searchName );

        if (loc == NOT_FOUND) {
            status = false;
        } else { //found, pack the hole

            entry[loc] = entry[count-1];

            status = true;
            count--;            //decrement count,
                                //since we now have one fewer element

        }

        return status;
    }

    public Person search(String searchName) {                    search

        Person foundPerson;
        int        loc = 0;

        while ( loc < count &&
```

```
                     !searchName.equals( entry[loc].getName() ) ) ) {
        loc++;
    }

    if (loc == count) {

        foundPerson = null;
    } else {

        foundPerson = entry[loc];
    }

    return foundPerson;
}

public Person[ ] sort (int attribute) {

    Person[ ] sortedList = new Person[ count ];
    Person p1, p2, temp;
    //copy references to sortedList
    for (int i = 0; i < count; i++) {
        sortedList[i] = entry[i];
    }

    //set the comparison attribute
    entry[0].setCompareAttribute( attribute );

    //begin the bubble sort on sortedList
    int      bottom, comparisonResult;
    boolean   exchanged = true;

    bottom = sortedList.length - 2;

    while ( exchanged )  {

        exchanged = false;

        for (int i = 0; i <= bottom; i++) {
            p1 = sortedList[i];
            p2 = sortedList[i+1];
          // comparisonResult = p1.compareTo( p2, attribute );

            comparisonResult = p1.compareTo( p2 );

            if ( comparisonResult > 0 ) { //p1 is 'larger'
                                          //than p2, so
                sortedList[i]    = p2;    //exchange
                sortedList[i+1]  = p1;
```

sort

11.4 **Sample Program**—*continued*

```
                        exchanged  = true; //exchange is made
                }
            }
            bottom--;
        }
        return sortedList;
    }

    private void enlarge( ) {
        //create a new array whose size is 150% of
        //the current array
        int newLength = (int) (1.5 * entry.length);
        Person[] temp = new Person[newLength];

        //now copy the data to the new array
        for (int i = 0; i < entry.length; i++) {
            temp[i] = entry[i];
        }

        //finally set the variable entry to point to the new array
        entry = temp;
//   System.out.println("Inside the method enlarge");          //TEMP
//   System.out.println("Size of a new array: " + entry.length); //TEMP
    }

    private int findIndex(String searchName) {
        int loc = 0;

        while ( loc < count &&
               !searchName.equals( entry[loc].getName() ) ) {
            loc++;
        }

        if (loc == count) {

            loc = NOT_FOUND;

        }

        return loc;
    }
}
```

enlarge

findIndex

Version 2

In the second implementation of the **AddressBook** interface, we will use the sorting routine provided in the **java.util.Arrays** class, which includes a number of useful methods for handling arrays. To use the **sort** method of the **Arrays** class, we must pass a comparator object as its second argument. A comparator object is an instance of a class that implements the **Comparator** interface. In the first version, we relied on the comparison routines embedded in the **Person** class. We are thus limited to what's provided by the **Person** class, namely, sorting by name or sorting by age. We cannot, for example, sort on gender and then within the same gender sort on age. By providing an implementation class of the **Comparator** interface, we can sort **Person** objects (or any other types of objects) in any manner we want.

To implement the **Comparator** interface, we must implement its **compare** method. The function of the **compare** method is similar to that of the **compareTo** method we define in the **Person** class. Here's the comparator class that compares two **Person** objects based on their age:

```
class AgeComparator implements Comparator {

    private final int LESS = -1;
    private final int EQUAL = 0;
    private final int MORE  = 1;

    public int compare(Object p1, Object p2) {
        int comparisonResult;

        int p1age = ((Person)p1).getAge( );
        int p2age = ((Person)p2).getAge( );

        if (p1age < p2age) {
            comparisonResult = LESS;
        } else if (p1age == p2age) {
            comparisonResult = EQUAL;
        } else {
            assert p1age > p2age;
            comparisonResult = MORE;
        }

        return comparisonResult;
    }
}
```

The data type of the parameters to the **compare** method must be **Object.** Since parameters **p1** and **p2** are actually **Person** objects, we need to type cast them before calling the methods of the **Person** class. Notice the order of type casting; it is

```
((Person) p1).getAge();
```

not

```
(Person) p1.getAge();
```

The bad version attempts to type cast the value returned by **p1.getAge( )**, which is not what we want.

The **NameComparator** is similarly defined. The **AgeComparator** and **Name-Comparator** classes are helper classes specific to the **AddressBookVer2** class, and as such, it is appropriate to define them as the inner classes of **AddressBookVer2**. An

inner class

inner class is a class whose definition is given within the definition of another class, as in

```
class Outer {

    . . .

    class Inner {
       . . .
    } //end of Inner

} //end of Outer
```

We can prefix the inner class definition with the visibility modifier **public** or **private.** The **public** modifier will make the inner class accessible to the client classes outside of the package while the **private** modifier will make the inner class inaccessible to all other classes. Just as the ordinary class definition, a class definition without a visibility modifier is accessible to all other classes within the same package (classes in the same directory are in the same package).

As for the actual sorting task, we will use the **sort** method of the **Arrays** class instead of writing our own sorting algorithm. The **sort** method of the **Address-BookVer2** class is now defined as

```
public Person[ ] sort (int attribute) {

    if (!(attribute == Person.NAME ||
          attribute == Person.AGE) ) {
       throw new IllegalArgumentException( );
    }

    Person[ ] sortedList = new Person[ count ];

    //copy references to sortedList
    for (int i = 0; i < count; i++) {
       sortedList[i] = entry[i];
    }
```

Sorts the list by
using the given
comparator

```
    Arrays.sort(sortedList, getComparator(attribute));

    return sortedList;
}
```

and the private **getComparator** method is defined as

```
private Comparator getComparator(int attribute) {
   Comparator comp = null;

   if (attribute == Person.AGE) {
      comp = new AgeComparator( );
   } else {
      assert attribute == Person.NAME:
            "Attribute not recognized for sorting";

      comp = new NameComparator( );
   }
   return comp;
}
```

The first argument to the **sort** method of the **Arrays** class is an array of objects we want to sort, and the second argument is the comparator to use in comparing array elements. For example, if we want to sort the **Person** objects by gender first and in descending order of age within the same gender, we can define the comparator as

```
class GenAgeComparator implements Comparator {

   private final int LESS = -1;
   private final int EQUAL = 0;
   private final int MORE  = 1;

   public int compare(Object p1, Object p2) {
      int comparisonResult;

      int p1age = ((Person)p1).getAge( );
      int p2age = ((Person)p2).getAge( );

      char p1gender = ((Person)p1).getGender();
      char p2gender = ((Person)p2).getGender();

      if (p1gender < p2gender) {
         comparisonResult = LESS;
      } else if (p1gender == p2gender) {
         if (p2age < p1age) {
            comparisonResult = LESS;
         } else if (p2age == p1age) {
            comparisonResult = EQUAL;
         } else {
            assert p2age > p1age;
            comparisonResult = MORE;
         }
```

Notice that we are switching the position of **p1** and **p2** because we are sorting in descending order.

```
                    } else {
                        assert p1gender > p2gender;
                        comparisonResult = MORE;
                    }

                    return comparisonResult;
                }
            }
```

and we can call the **sort** method as

```
            Arrays.sort(sortedList, new GenAgeComparator());
```

Here's the **AddressBook2** class (only the modified portions are shown):

```
/*
   Chapter 11 Sample Program: Address Book Version 2
   File: AddressBookVer2.java
*/
import java.util.*;

class AddressBookVer2 implements AddressBook {

    public AddressBookVer2( ) {
        this( DEFAULT_SIZE );
    }

    public AddressBookVer2(int size) {
        ...
    }

    ...

    public Person[ ] sort ( int attribute ) {

        if (!(attribute == Person.NAME || attribute == Person.AGE) ) {
            throw new IllegalArgumentException( );
        }

        Person[ ] sortedList = new Person[ count ];

        //copy references to sortedList
        for (int i = 0; i < count; i++) {
            sortedList[i] = entry[i];
        }
```

```
        Arrays.sort(sortedList, getComparator(attribute));

        return sortedList;

    }

    ...

    private Comparator getComparator(int attribute) {
        Comparator comp = null;

        if (attribute == Person.AGE) {
            comp = new AgeComparator( );

        } else {
            assert attribute == Person.NAME:
                    "Attribute not recognized for sorting";

            comp = new NameComparator( );
        }
        return comp;
    }

//    Inner Classes

    //Inner class for comparing age
    class AgeComparator implements Comparator {

        private final int LESS = -1;
        private final int EQUAL = 0;
        private final int MORE  = 1;

        public int compare(Object p1, Object p2) {

            int comparisonResult;

            int p1age = ((Person)p1).getAge( );
            int p2age = ((Person)p2).getAge( );

            if (p1age < p2age) {
                comparisonResult = LESS;
            } else if (p1age == p2age) {
                comparisonResult = EQUAL;
            } else {
                assert p1age > p2age;
                comparisonResult = MORE;
            }

            return comparisonResult;
        }
    }
```

11.4   Sample Program—*continued*

```
//Inner class for comparing name
class NameComparator implements Comparator {

    public int compare(Object p1, Object p2) {

        String p1name = ((Person)p1).getName( );
        String p2name = ((Person)p2).getName( );

        return p1name.compareTo(p2name);
    }
}
}
```

While the main purpose of the **AddressBookVer1** class is pedagogy, the **AddressBookVer2** class, with its use of the efficient **Arrays** class **sort** method based on a high-performance sorting technique called *merge sort* and the generality provided by the **Comparator** interface, is closer to what we would really use in practice. The last version, **AddressBookVer3,** would improve further by using the map from the Java Collection Framework. This eliminates the code to maintain the array in our class.

Version 3

The third implementation of the **AddressBook** interface eliminates the use of an array altogether. Instead of maintaining the array of **Person** objects ourselves, we will rely on the service provided by the **Map** interface from the **java.util** package.

The key for the map is the person's name, and the value is the **Person** object. The **add, delete,** and **search** methods now all just make calls to the map's methods for data management. The **sort** method retrieves a collection of values in the map, converts this collection to an array, and then passes this array to the **sort** method of the **Arrays** class. Here's how we define the **sort** method:

```
public Person[ ] sort ( int attribute ) {

    if (!(attribute == Person.NAME ||
          attribute == Person.AGE) ) {
        throw new IllegalArgumentException( );
    }

    Person[ ] sortedList = new Person[entry.size()];
    entry.values().toArray(sortedList);

    Arrays.sort(sortedList, getComparator(attribute));

    return sortedList;
}
```

Here's the **AddressBookVer3** class:

```
/*
   Chapter 11 Sample Program: Address Book Version 3

   File: AddressBookVer3.java
*/
import java.util.*;

class AddressBookVer3 implements AddressBook {

   private static final int  DEFAULT_SIZE = 25;

   private Map    entry;

   public AddressBookVer3( ) {
       this( DEFAULT_SIZE );
   }

   public AddressBookVer3(int size) {
       entry = new HashMap(size);
   }

   public void add( Person newPerson ) {
       entry.put(newPerson.getName(), newPerson);
   }

   public boolean delete( String searchName ) {

       boolean status;
       Person  p = (Person) entry.remove(searchName);

       if (p == null) {
           status = false;
       } else {
           status = true;
       }

       return status;
   }

   public Person search( String searchName ) {

       return (Person) entry.get(searchName);
   }

   public Person[ ] sort ( int attribute ) {

       if (!(attribute == Person.NAME || attribute == Person.AGE) ) {
           throw new IllegalArgumentException( );
       }
```

Data members

Constructors

add

delete

search

sort

11.4 **Sample Program**—*continued*

```
        Person[ ] sortedList = new Person[entry.size()];
        entry.values().toArray(sortedList);

        Arrays.sort(sortedList, getComparator(attribute));

        return sortedList;
    }

    . . .

}
```

Summary

- Searching and sorting are two of the most basic nonnumeric applications of computer programs.
- Linear search looks for a value in a linear sequence.
- Binary search looks for a value by successively comparing the element in the middle of a sorted list.
- Selection sort is a basic sorting routine that runs in time proportion to N^2, where N is the size of the list to sort.
- Bubble sort is another N^2 performance algorithm, but it runs faster than the selection sort on average.
- Heapsort has a $N \log_2 N$ performance. It uses a special heap data structure to sort the elements.
- Using a class that implements the Comparator interface is convenient and flexible to dictate the manner in which objects of a class are compared.
- The Comparator interface has one method, called compare.
- The standard classes and interfaces described or used in this chapter are

  Comparator   Arrays

Key Concepts

linear search   heapsort
binary search N^2 sorting algorithm
selection sort $N \log_2 N$ sorting algorithm
bubble sort   comparator

Exercises

1. Consider the following array of sorted integers:

0	1	2	3	4	5	6	7	8	9	10	11
10	15	25	30	33	34	46	55	78	84	96	99

   Using the binary search algorithm, search for 23. Show the sequence of array elements that are compared, and for each comparison, indicate the values for low and high.

2. We assumed all elements in an array are distinct; that is, there are no duplicate values in the array. What will be an effect on the linear search algorithm if an array contains duplicate values?

3. Will the sorting algorithms presented in this chapter work if the unsorted array contains any duplicate values?

4. In this chapter we analyzed sorting algorithms by counting the number of comparisons. Another possible method for analyzing the algorithms is to count the number of data exchanges. How many data exchanges do the selection and bubble sort make in the worst case? Regardless of the original list, the selection sort will make the same number of data exchanges. However, the number of data exchanges the bubble sort makes depends on the arrangement of elements in the original list.

5. Another simple sorting algorithm is called an *insertion sort*. Suppose we have a sorted list of N elements and we need to insert a new element X into this list to create a sorted list of $N + 1$ elements. We can insert X at the correct position in the list by comparing it with elements list[$N-1$], list[$N-2$], list[$N-3$], and so forth. Every time we compare X and list[i], we shift list[i] one position to list[i+1] if X is smaller than list[i]. When we find list[i] that is smaller than X, we put X at position $i + 1$ and stop. We can apply this logic to sort an unordered list of N elements. We start with a sorted list of one element and insert the second element to create a sorted list of two elements. Then we add the third element to create a sorted list of three elements. Figure 11.18 illustrates the steps in the insertion sort. Write a method that implements the insertion sort algorithm. You may simplify the method by sorting only integers.

6. Analyze the insertion sort algorithm of Exercise 5 by counting the number of comparisons and data exchanges. Provide the analysis for the worst case.

7. Write a test program to compare the performances of selection sort, bubble sort, and heapsort algorithms experimentally. Use the random method from the Math class to generate 5000 integers and sort the generated integers by using the three sorting algorithms. For each execution, record the time it took to sort the numbers. You can use the

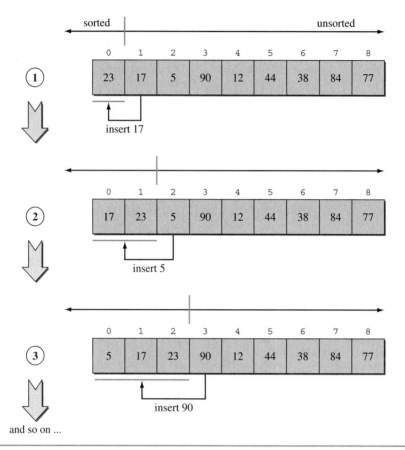

Figure 11.18 Steps in an insertion sort.

java.util.Date class to record the execution time in milliseconds, for example,

```
Date startTime, endTime;
startTime = new Date();
//sort the integers
endTime = new Date();
//record the elapsed time
double elapsedTime
        = endTime.getTime() - startTime.getTime();
```

8. Consider the following property about the bubble sort:

If the last exchange made in some pass occurs at the Jth and (J + 1)st positions, then all elements from the (J + 1)st to the Nth positions are in their correct location.

Rewrite the bubble sort algorithm, using this property.

9. The Heap class given in Section 11.3 sorts only the integers. Improve the class by making it possible to sort any objects that recognize the compareTo method, which is described in Section 11.4, so the new Heap class will be able to sort Person, Integer, Double, and String objects among others. Since the elements in the internal array can be any object, declare an array of Object objects. All Java classes are automatically a subclass of Object, unless they are declared explicitly as a subclass of another class. The declaration of heap will be like

```
private Object[ ] heap;
```

and the setData method will be like

```
public void setData( Object[ ] data ) {
    heap       = new Object[ data.length ];
    sortedList = new Object[ data.length ];

    for (int i = 0; i < data.length; i++ ) {
        heap[i] = data[i];
    }
}
```

10. In the Heap class, we used two separate arrays: one for the heap and another for the sorted list. It turns out we can do everything with just one array. Notice that the heap will decrease in size by one element after every rebuild step. The unused space at the end of the heap array can be used to store the sorted list. Modify the Heap class so it will use only one array.

11. Modify the Heap class by defining a separate method called rebuild, which will be used by both the construct and extract methods.

12. In Section 11.4, we implemented the sorting routine for the AddressBook class with the bubble sort algorithm. Modify the sorting routine by using the Heap class of Exercise 9.

13. Instead of maintaining an unsorted list and returning the sorted list when the sort method is called, modify the AddressBook class so that it maintains the sorted list of Person in alphabetical order. Modify the search routine by using the binary search algorithm.

12 File Input and Output

Objectives

After you have read and studied this chapter, you should be able to

- Include a **JFileChooser** object in your program to let the user specify a file.

- Write bytes to a file and read them back from the file, using **FileOutputStream** and **FileInputStream.**

- Write values of primitive data types to a file and read them back from the file, using **DataOutputStream** and **DataInputStream.**

- Write text data to a file and read them back from the file, using **PrintWriter** and **BufferedReader.**

- Write objects to a file and read them back from the file, using **ObjectOutputStream** and **Object-InputStream.**

Introduction

What is the most important action you should never forget to take while developing programs or writing documents? Saving the data, of course! It's 3 A.M., and you're in the home stretch, applying the finishing touches to the term paper due at 9 A.M. Just as you are ready to select the Print command for the final copy, it happens. The software freezes and it won't response to your commands anymore. You forgot to turn on the Autosave feature, and you have not saved the data for the last hour. There's nothing you can do but reboot the computer.

file output and input

Data not saved will be lost, and if we ever want to work on the data again, we must save the data to a file. We call the action of saving, or writing, data to a file *file output* and the action of reading data from a file *file input*. A program we develop must support some form of file input and output capabilities for it to have practical uses. Suppose we develop a program that keeps track of bicycles owned by the dorm students. The program will allow the user to add, delete, and modify the bicycle information. If the program does not support the file input and output features, every time the program is started, the user must reenter the data.

In this chapter, we will introduce the classes from the java.io and javax.swing packages that are used for file input and output operations Also, we will show how the two helper classes from Chapters 8 and 9—Dorm and FileManager—that provided the file input and output support are implemented.

12.1 | File **and** JFileChooser **Objects**

In this section we introduce two key objects for reading data from or writing data to a file. We use the term *file access* to refer to both read and write operations. If we need to be precise, we write *read access* or *write access*. (We use the terms *save* and *write* interchangeably to refer to file output, but we never say *save access*.) Suppose we want to read the contents of a file sample.data. Before we begin the actual operation of reading data from this file, we must first create a **File** object (from the java.io package) and associate it to the file. We do so by calling a File constructor:

File

```
File inFile = new File("sample.data");
```

current directory

The argument to the constructor designates the name of the file to access. The system assumes the file is located in the *current directory*. For the following examples, we assume the directory structure shown in Figure 12.1, with Ch12 being the current directory. When you run a program whose source file is located in directory X, then the current directory is X. Please refer to Java compiler manuals for other options for designating the current directory.

It is also possible to open a file that is stored in a directory other than the current directory by providing a path name and a filename. Assuming there's a file xyz.data in the JavaPrograms directory, we can open it by executing

```
File inFile = new File("C:/JavaPrograms", "xyz.data");
```

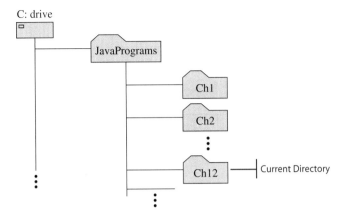

Figure 12.1 Directory structure used for the examples in this section. We assume the Windows environment.

This style of designating the path name is for the Windows platform. The actual path name we want to specify is

        C:\JavaPrograms

but the backslash character is an escape character. So to specify the backslash character itself, we must use double backslashes. For the UNIX platform, we use the forward slash for a delimiter, for example,

        "/JavaPrograms"

For the Mac platform, we also use a forward slash; for example, if the name of a hard disk is MacHD, then we write

        "/MacHD/JavaPrograms"

To maintain the consistency across the platforms, the forward slash character is allowed for the Windows platform also, such as

        "C:/JavaPrograms/Ch12"

The path name could be absolute or relative to the current directory. The absolute path name is the full path name beginning with the disk drive name, for example,

        "C:/JavaPrograms/Ch11"

The relative path name is relative to the current directory. For example, if the current directory is Ch12, then the relative path name

        "../Ch2"

Chapter 12   File Input and Output

is equivalent to the full path name

```
"C:/JavaPrograms/Ch2"
```

where the two dots (. .) in the string mean "one directory above."

We can check if a File object is associated correctly to an existing file by calling its exists method:

```
if ( inFile.exists( ) ) {
    // inFile is associated correctly to an existing file

} else {
    // inFile is not associated to any existing file
}
```

When a valid association is established, we say *the file is opened;* a file must be opened before we can do any input and output to the file.

Helpful Reminder

A file must be opened before executing any file access operations.

A File object can also be associated to a directory. For example, suppose we are interested in listing the content of directory Ch12. We can first create a File object and associate it to the directory. After the association is made, we can list the contents of the directory by calling the object's list method:

```
File   directory  = new File("C:/JavaPrograms/Ch12");
String filename[] = directory.list();

for (int i = 0; i < filename.length; i++) {
    System.out.println(filename[i]);
}
```

We check whether a File object is associated to a file or a directory by calling its boolean method isFile. The following code will print out I am a directory:

```
File file = new File("C:/JavaPrograms/Ch12");

if (file.isFile()) {
    System.out.println("I am a file");

} else {
    System.out.println("I am a directory");
}
```

JFileChooser   We can use a javax.swing.JFileChooser object to let the user select a file. The following statement displays an open file dialog, as shown in Figure 12.2 (the

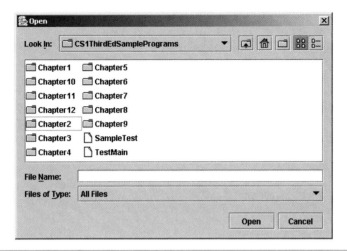

Figure 12.2 A sample **JFileChooser** object displayed with the **showOpenDialog** method. The dialog title and the okay button are labeled **Open.**

actual listing will reflect the content of the machine on which the program is executed):

```
JFileChooser chooser = new JFileChooser( );
...
chooser.showOpenDialog(null);
```

The null argument to the showOpenDialog method has the same semantics as the first argument to the showMessageDialog or showInputDialog method of the JOptionPane class; namely, it indicates that there's no parent frame, and the dialog is displayed at the center of the screen. We pass a frame object if we want to position the file dialog at the center of the frame.

To check whether the user has clicked on the Open or Cancel button, we test the return value from the showOpenDialog method.

```
int status = chooser.showOpenDialog(null);

if (status == JFileChooser.APPROVE_OPTION) {
    JOptionPane.showMessageDialog(null,
                                  "Open is clicked");

} else { //== JFileChooser.CANCEL_OPTION
    JOptionPane.showMessageDialog(null,
                                  "Cancel is clicked");
}
```

Once we determine the Open button is clicked, we can retrieve the selected file as

```
File selectedFile;

selectedFile = chooser.getSelectedFile();
```

and the current directory of the selected file as

```
File currentDirectory;
currentDirectory = chooser.getCurrentDirectory();
```

Notice that a File object is used to represent a directory also. We can use the corresponding setCurrentDirectory method to open the file chooser beginning at the designated directory. Suppose we want to begin the listing from the D:/IntroJava/Programs directory. Then we write

```
File startDir = new File("D:/IntroJava/Programs");
chooser.setCurrentDirectory(startDir);
...
chooser.showOpenDialog(null);
```

To find out the name and the full path name of a selected file, we can use the getName and getAbsolutePath methods of the File class.

```
File file = chooser.getSelectedFile();

System.out.println("Selected File: " +
                                 file.getName());
System.out.println("Full path:     " +
                                 file.getAbsolutePath());
```

To display a JFileChooser with the Save button, we write

```
chooser.showSaveDialog(null);
```

which results in a dialog shown in Figure 12.3 (the actual listing will reflect the content of the machine on which the program is executed).

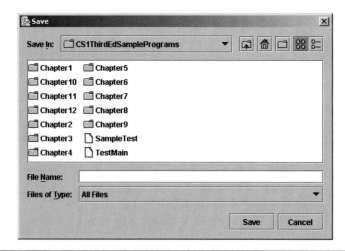

Figure 12.3 A sample **JFileChooser** object displayed with the **showCloseDialog** method. The dialog title and the okay button are labeled **Save.**

The following Ch12TestJFileChooser class summarizes the methods of JFile-Chooser and File classes. Note this sample program does not perform actual file input or output.

```java
/*
    Chapter 12 Sample Program:  Illustrate the use of the
                                JFileChooser and File classes.

    File: TestJFileChooser.java
*/
import java.io.*;
import javax.swing.*;

class Ch12TestJFileChooser {
    public static void main (String[] args) {

        JFileChooser chooser;
        File         file, directory;
        int          status;

        chooser = new JFileChooser( );

        status = chooser.showOpenDialog(null);

        if (status == JFileChooser.APPROVE_OPTION) {
            file      = chooser.getSelectedFile();
            directory = chooser.getCurrentDirectory();

            System.out.println("Directory: " +
                              directory.getName());

            System.out.println("File selected to open: " +
                              file.getName());

            System.out.println("Full path name: " +
                              file.getAbsolutePath());

        } else {
            JOptionPane.showMessageDialog(null,
                                        "Open File dialog canceled");
        }

        System.out.println("\n\n");

        status = chooser.showSaveDialog(null);

        if (status == JFileChooser.APPROVE_OPTION) {
            file      = chooser.getSelectedFile();
            directory = chooser.getCurrentDirectory();

            System.out.println("Directory: " +
                              directory.getName());
```

```
            System.out.println("File selected for saving data: " +
                               file.getName());

            System.out.println("Full path name: " +
                               file.getAbsolutePath());
        } else {
            JOptionPane.showMessageDialog(null,
                                "Save File dialog canceled");
        }
    }
}
```

Figure 12.4 shows a sample output of running the program once.

There is actually no distinction between the Open and Save dialogs created, respectively, by showOpenDialog and showCloseDialog other than the difference in the button label and the dialog title. In fact, they are really a shorthand for calling the showDialog method. Using the showDialog method, we can specify the button label and the dialog title. For example, this code will produce a JFileChooser dialog with the text Compile as its title and label for the okay button:

```
JFileChooser chooser = new JFileChooser();
chooser.showDialog(null, "Compile");
```

file filter

We can use a *file filter* to remove unwanted files from the list. Let's say we want to apply a filter so only the directories and the Java source files (those with the .java extension) are listed in the file chooser. To do so, we must define a subclass of the javax.swing.filechooser.FileFilter class and provide the accept and getDescription methods. The prototypes of these methods are

```
public boolean accept(File file)
public String getDescription( )
```

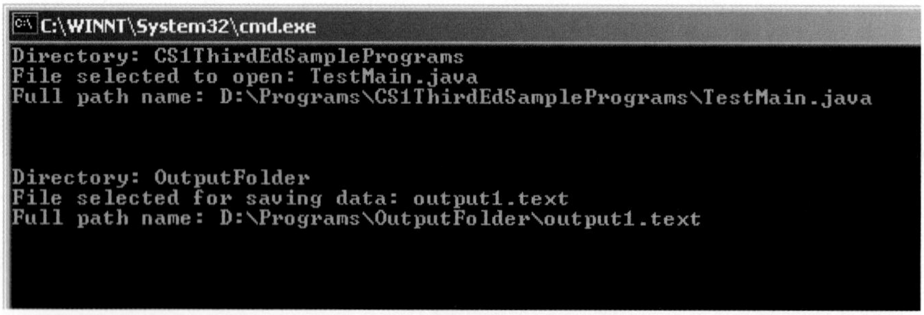

Figure 12.4 A sample output from running the **Ch12TestJFileChooser** program once.

The accept method returns true if the parameter file is a file to be included in the list. The getDescription method returns a text that will be displayed as one of the entries for the "Files of Type:" drop-down list. Here's how the filter subclass is defined:

```java
/*
    Chapter 12 Sample Program: Illustrate how to filter only
                               Java source files
                               for listing in JFileChooser

    File: JavaFilter.java
*/
import java.io.File;
import javax.swing.*;
import javax.swing.filechooser.*;

class JavaFilter extends FileFilter {

    private static final String JAVA  = "java";
    private static final char   DOT   = '.';

    //accepts only directories and
    //files with .java extension only
    public boolean accept(File f) {

        if (f.isDirectory()) {
            return true;
        }

        if (extension(f).equalsIgnoreCase(JAVA)) {
            return true;
        } else {
            return false;
        }
    }

    //description of the filtered files
    public String getDescription( ) {
        return "Java source files (.java)";
    }

    //extracts the extension from the filename
    private String extension(File f) {

        String filename = f.getName();
        int    loc      = filename.lastIndexOf(DOT);

        if (loc > 0 && loc < filename.length() - 1) {
            //make sure the dot is not
            //at the first or the last character position
```

> Notice that we are stating one class in the package explicitly, instead of using the more common form of
> **import java.io.*;**
> to avoid naming conflict. The **java.io** package has the interface named **FileFilter.**

Data members

accept

getDescription

extension

```
            return filename.substring(loc+1);
        } else {
            return "";
        }
    }
}
```

With the filter class JavaFilter in place, we can set to a file chooser

```
JFileChooser chooser = new JFileChooser( );

chooser.setFileFilter(new JavaFilter(());

int status = chooser.showOpenDialog(null);
```

to restrict the listing to directories and Java source files only.

Let's close this section with a Java source file viewer that allows the end user to open a Java source file for viewing. It is left as Exercise 14 to allow the user to edit the source file and save it to a file. Here's the (view-only) class:

```
/*
    Chapter 12 Sample Program: Display a Java source file.

    File: Ch12JavaViewer.java

*/

import javax.swing.*;
import java.io.*;
import java.awt.*;
import java.awt.event.*;

class Ch12JavaViewer extends JFrame implements ActionListener {
    private static final int FRAME_WIDTH    = 450;
    private static final int FRAME_HEIGHT   = 600;              Data members
    private static final int FRAME_X_ORIGIN = 150;
    private static final int FRAME_Y_ORIGIN = 250;

    private JTextArea textArea;

//---------------------------------
//      Main method
//---------------------------------
    public static void main(String[] args) {
        Ch12JavaViewer frame = new Ch12JavaViewer();
```

```java
        frame.setVisible(true);
    }

    public Ch12JavaViewer() {
        Container contentPane;

        //set the frame properties
        setTitle      ("Ch12JavaViewer: Displaying Java Source File");
        setSize       (FRAME_WIDTH, FRAME_HEIGHT);
        setLocation   (FRAME_X_ORIGIN, FRAME_Y_ORIGIN);

        contentPane = getContentPane( );
        contentPane.setBackground( Color.white );

        textArea = new JTextArea();
        textArea.setEditable(false);
        contentPane.add(new JScrollPane(textArea));
        createMenu();

        setDefaultCloseOperation(EXIT_ON_CLOSE);
    }

    public void actionPerformed(ActionEvent event) {
        String  menuName;

        menuName = event.getActionCommand();

        if (menuName.equals("Quit")) {
            System.exit(0);

        } else {
            openFile( );
        }
    }

    private void createMenu( ) {
        JMenuItem    item;
        JMenuBar     menuBar  = new JMenuBar();
        JMenu        fileMenu = new JMenu("File");

        item = new JMenuItem("Open...");    //Open...
        item.addActionListener( this );
        fileMenu.add( item );

        fileMenu.addSeparator();          //add a horizontal separator line

        item = new JMenuItem("Quit");       //Quit
        item.addActionListener( this );
        fileMenu.add( item );
```

Constructor

actionPerformed

createMenu

```
            setJMenuBar(menuBar);
            menuBar.add(fileMenu);
        }

        private void openFile( ) {

            JFileChooser chooser;
            int          status;

            chooser = new JFileChooser( );

            chooser.setFileFilter(new JavaFilter());

            //Modify the sample path "D:/Programs" to fit your environment
        //  chooser.setCurrentDirectory(new File("D:/Programs"));

            status = chooser.showOpenDialog(null);

            if (status == JFileChooser.APPROVE_OPTION) {
                readSource(chooser.getSelectedFile());

            } else {
                JOptionPane.showMessageDialog(null,
                                            "Open File dialog canceled");
            }
        }

        private void readSource(File file) {

            try {
                FileManager fm = new FileManager();
                textArea.setText(fm.openFile(file.getAbsolutePath()));
            } catch (IOException e) {
                JOptionPane.showMessageDialog(null,
                                            "Error in opening a file: \n"
                                            + e.getMessage());        }
        }
    }
```

openFile

readSource

This class was used in the Chapter 9 sample program. We will explain its internal workings in Section 12.3.

Notice the readSource method uses the FileManager class introduced in the Chapter 9 sample program. Its openFile method returns the content of the designated ASCII file as a String. The argument to the method is the filename (String), not a File object. To open a file in any directory, we need to provide a complete path name, which we get by calling the getAbsolutePath method of the File class. We will explain the internal workings of the FileManager class in Section 12.3, specifically, how it reads data from a file and writes data to a file.

1. This question is specific to the Windows platform. Suppose you want to open a file prog1.java inside the directory C:\JavaProjects\Ch11\Step4. What is the actual String value you pass in the constructor for the File class?

2. What is wrong with the following statement?

    ```
    JFileChooser chooser

        = new JFileChooser("Run");

    chooser.showDialog(null);
    ```

3. Which method of the JFileChooser class do you use to get the filename of the selected file? What is returned from the method if the Cancel button is clicked?

12.2 | Low-Level File I/O

Once a file is opened by properly associating a File object to it, the actual file access can commence. In this section, we will introduce basic objects for file operations. To actually read data from or write data to a file, we must create one of the Java stream objects and attach it to the file. A *stream* is simply a sequence of data items, usually 8-bit bytes. Java has two types of streams: an input stream and an output stream. An input stream has a *source* from which the data items come, and an output stream has a *destination* to which the data items are going. To read data items from a file, we attach one of the Java input stream objects to the file. Similarly, to write data items to a file, we attach one of the Java output stream objects to the file.

stream

source

destination

Java comes with a large number of stream objects for file access operations. We will cover only those that are straightforward and easy to learn for beginners. We will study two of them in this section—FileOutputStream and FileInputStream. These two objects provide low-level file access operations. In Section 12.3 we will study other stream objects.

FileOutput-Stream

Let's first study how to write data values to a file by using **FileOutputStream**. Using a FileOutputStream object, we can output only a sequence of bytes, that is, values of data type byte. In this example, we will output an array of bytes to a file named sample1.data. First we create a File object:

```
File outFile = new File( "sample1.data" );
```

Then we associate a new FileOutputStream object to outFile:

```
FileOutputStream outStream
                     = new FileOutputStream( outFile );
```

Now we are ready for output. Consider the following byte array:

```
byte[] byteArray = {10, 20, 30, 40, 50, 60, 70, 80};
```

We write the whole byte array at once to the file by executing

```
outStream.write(byteArray);
```

Notice that we are not dealing with the File object directly, but with outStream. It is also possible to write array elements individually, for example,

```
//output the first and fifth bytes
outStream.write(byteArray[0]);
outStream.write(byteArray[4]);
```

After the values are written to the file, we must close the stream:

```
outStream.close();
```

If the stream object is not closed, then some data may get lost due to data caching. Because of the physical characteristics of secondary memory such as hard disks, the actual process of saving data to a file is a very time-consuming operation, whether you are saving 1 or 100 bytes. So instead of saving bytes individually, we save them in a block of, say, 500 bytes to reduce the overall time it takes to save the whole data. The operation of saving data as a block is called *data caching*. To carry out data caching, a part of memory is reserved as a *data buffer* or *cache,* which is used as a temporary holding place. A typical size for a data buffer is anywhere from 1 KB to 2 KB. Data are first written to a buffer, and when the buffer becomes full, the data in the buffer are actually written to a file. If there are any remaining data in the buffer and the file is not closed, then those data will be lost. Therefore, to avoid losing any data, it is important to close the file at the end of the operations.

data caching

data buffer

Helpful Reminder

To ensure that all data are saved to a file, close the file at the end of file access operations.

Many of the file operations, such as write and close, throw IO exceptions, so we need to handle them. For the short sample programs, we use the propagation approach. Here's the complete program:

```
/*
    Chapter 12 Sample Program:
            A test program to save data to a file using FileOutputStream

    File: TestFileOutputStream.java
*/
import java.io.*;                               Needs this clause because the file
                                                methods throw IO exceptions.
class Ch12TestFileOutputStream {
    public static void main (String[] args) throws IOException {
```

```
        //set up file and stream
        File            outFile   = new File("sample1.data");
        FileOutputStream outStream = new FileOutputStream(outFile);

        //data to output
        byte[] byteArray = {10, 20, 30, 40, 50, 60, 70, 80};

        //write data to the stream
        outStream.write(byteArray);

        //output done, so close the stream
        outStream.close();
    }
}
```

Take my *Advice*

It may be odd at first to have both **File** and **FileStream** objects to input data from a file. Why not have just a **File** to handle everything? **File** represents a physical file that is a source of data. **Stream** objects represent the mechanism we associate to a file to perform input and output routines. **Stream** objects can also be associated to a nonfile data source such as a serial port. So separating the tasks following the STO principle resulted in more than one class to input data from a file.

Now it's true that we can make a shortcut statement such as

```
fileOutputStream outStream
    = new FileOutputStream("input.txt");
```

where we avoid the explicit creation of a **File** object. But this shortcut does not eliminate the fact that the **Stream** object is associated to a file.

**FileInput-
Stream**

To read the data into a program, we reverse the steps in the output routine. We use the read method of **FileInputStream** to read in an array of bytes. First we create a FileInputStream object:

```
        File            inFile   = new File( "sample1.data" );
        FileInputStream inStream = new FileInputStream( inFile );
```

Then we read the data into an array of bytes:

```
        inStream.read(byteArray);
```

Before we call the read method, we must declare and create byteArray:

```
        int    filesize  = (int) inFile.length();
        byte[] byteArray = new byte[filesize];
```

We use the length method of the File class to determine the size of the file, which in this case is the number of bytes in the file. We create an array of bytes whose size is the size of the file.

The following program uses FileInputStream to read in the byte array from the file sample1.data.

```
/*
    Chapter 12 Sample Program:
            A test program to read data from a file using FileInputStream

    File: Ch12TestFileInputStream.java
*/
import java.io.*;

class Ch12TestFileInputStream {
    public static void main (String[] args) throws IOException {

        //set up file and stream
        File            inFile    = new File("sample1.data");
        FileInputStream inStream  = new FileInputStream(inFile);

        //set up an array to read data in
        int fileSize = (int)inFile.length();
        byte[] byteArray = new byte[fileSize];

        //read data in and display them
        inStream.read(byteArray);
        for (int i = 0; i < fileSize; i++) {
            System.out.println(byteArray[i]);
        }

        //input done, so close the stream
        inStream.close();
    }
}
```

It is possible to output data other than bytes if we can convert (i.e., type cast) them into bytes. For example, we can output character data by type casting them to bytes.

```
File             outFile   = new File("sample1.data");
FileOutputStream outStream = new FileOutputStream(outFile);

//data to output
byte[] byteArray = {(byte) 'J',
                    (byte) 'a',
                    (byte) 'v',
                    (byte) 'a' };
```

Type cast characters to bytes.

```
            //write data to the stream
            outStream.write(byteArray);

            //output done, so close the stream
            outStream.close();
```

To read the data back, we use the read method again. If we need to display the bytes in the original character values, we need to type cast byte to char. Without the type casting, numerical values would be displayed. The following code illustrates the type casting of byte to char for display.

```
            File                inFile      = new File("sample1.data");
            FileInputStream inStream  = new FileInputStream(inFile);

            //set up an array to read data in
            int      fileSize  = inFile.length();
            byte[] byteArray = new byte[fileSize];

            //read data in and display them
            inStream.read(byteArray);

            for (int i = 0; i < fileSize; i++) {

                System.out.println( (char) byteArray[i] );
            }

            //input done, so close the stream
            inStream.close();
```

Type cast bytes back to characters.

Type casting char to byte or byte to char is simple because ASCII uses 8 bits. But what if we want to perform file I/O on numerical values such as integers and real numbers? It takes more than simple type casting to output these numerical values to FileOutputStream and read them back from FileInputStream. An integer takes 4 bytes, so we need to break a single integer into 4 bytes and perform file I/O on this 4 bytes. Such a conversion would be too low level and tedious. Java provides stream objects that allow us to read from or write numerical values to a file without doing any conversions ourselves. We will discuss two of them in Section 12.3.

Quick
CHECK

1. What is the method you call at the end of all file I/O operations?
2. What is wrong with the following statements? Assume that outStream is a properly declared and created FileOutputStream object.

```
      byte[ ]  byteArray = { (byte) 'H', (byte) 'i' };
      ...
      outStream.print( byteArray );
      ...
      outStream.close( );
```

12.3 | High-Level File I/O

By using DataOutputStream, we can output Java primitive data type values. A DataOutputStream object will take care of the details of converting the primitive data type values to a sequence of bytes. Let's look at the complete program first. The following program writes out values of various Java primitive data types to a file. The names of the output methods (those preceded with write) should be self-explanatory.

```java
/*
    Chapter 12 Sample Program:
                 A test program to save data to a file using
                 DataOutputStream for high-level I/O.

    File: Ch12TestDataOutputStream.java
*/
import java.io.*;

class Ch12TestDataOutputStream {
   public static void main (String[] args) throws IOException {

      //set up the streams
      File                outFile     = new File("sample2.data");
      FileOutputStream outFileStream = new FileOutputStream(outFile);
      DataOutputStream outDataStream= new DataOutputStream(outFileStream);

      //write values of primitive data types to the stream
      outDataStream.writeInt(987654321);
      outDataStream.writeLong(11111111L);
      outDataStream.writeFloat(22222222F);
      outDataStream.writeDouble(3333333D);
      outDataStream.writeChar('A');
      outDataStream.writeBoolean(true);

      //output done, so close the stream
      outDataStream.close();

   }
}
```

Notice the sequence of statements for creating a DataOutputStream object:

```java
File                outFile     = new File("sample2.data");
FileOutputStream outFileStream= new FileOutputStream(outFile);
DataOutputStream outDataStream
                         = new DataOutputStream(outFileStream);
```

DataOutput-Stream

The argument to the **DataOutputStream** constructor is a FileOutputStream object. A DataOutputStream object does not get connected to a file directly. The diagram

```
File             outFile       = new File("sample2.data");
FileOutputStream outFileStream = new FileOutputStream(outFile);
DataOutputStream outDataStream = new DataOutputStream(outFileStream);
```

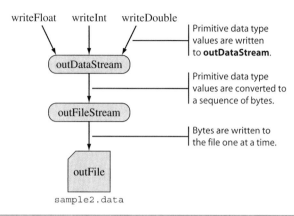

Figure 12.5 A diagram showing how the three objects **outFile, outFileStream,** and **outDataStream** are related.

in Figure 12.5 illustrates the relationships established among the three objects. The role of the DataOutputStream object is to provide high-level access to a file by converting a primitive data value to a sequence of bytes, which are then written to a file via a FileOutputStream object.

DataInput-Stream

To read the data back from the file, we reverse the operation. We use three objects: File, FileInputStream, and **DataInputStream**. The following program reads the data saved by the program Ch12TestDataOutputStream.

```
/*
    Chapter 12 Sample Program:
                A test program to load data from a file using
                DataInputStream for high-level I/O.

    File: Ch12TestDataInputStream.java
*/
import java.io.*;

class Ch12TestDataInputStream {
   public static void main (String[] args) throws IOException {

      //set up file and stream
      File inFile = new File("sample2.data");
      FileInputStream inFileStream = new FileInputStream(inFile);
      DataInputStream inDataStream = new DataInputStream(inFileStream);

      //read values back from the stream and display them
      System.out.println(inDataStream.readInt());
```

```
        System.out.println(inDataStream.readLong());
        System.out.println(inDataStream.readFloat());
        System.out.println(inDataStream.readDouble());
        System.out.println(inDataStream.readChar());
        System.out.println(inDataStream.readBoolean());

        //input done, so close the stream
        inDataStream.close();
    }
}
```

Figure 12.6 shows the relationship among the three objects. Notice that we must read the data back in the precise order. In other words, if we write data in the order of integer, float, and character, then we must read the data back in that order, as illustrated in Figure 12.7. If we don't read the data back in the correct order, the results will be unpredictable.

binary file

Both FileOutputStream and DataOutputStream objects produce a *binary file* in which the contents are stored in the format (called *binary format*) in which they are stored in the main memory. Instead of storing data in binary format, we can store them in ASCII format. With the ASCII format, all data are converted to string data.

text file

A file whose contents are stored in ASCII format is called a *text file*. One major

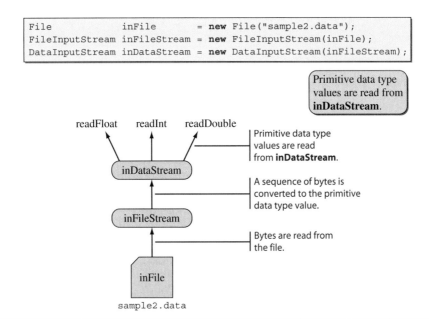

Figure 12.6 A diagram showing how the three objects **inFile, inFileStream,** and **inDataStream** are related.

```
outStream.writeInteger(...);
outStream.writeLong(...);
outStream.writeChar(...);
outStream.writeBoolean(...);
```

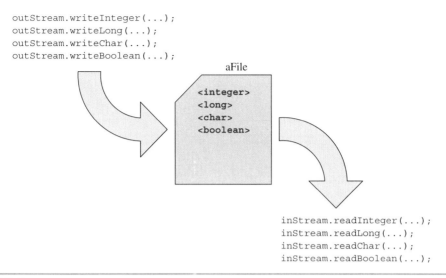

```
                              aFile

                           <integer>
                           <long>
                           <char>
                           <boolean>
```

```
                              inStream.readInteger(...);
                              inStream.readLong(...);
                              inStream.readChar(...);
                              inStream.readBoolean(...);
```

Figure 12.7 The order of write and read operations must match to read the stored data back correctly.

benefit of a text file is that we can easily read and modify the contents of a text file by using any text editor or word processor.

PrintWriter

PrintWriter is an object we use to generate a text file. Unlike DataOutput-Stream, where we have a separate write method for each individual data type, Print-Writer supports only two output methods: print and println (for print line). An argument to the methods can be any primitive data type. The methods convert the parameter to string and output this string value. The constructor of PrintWriter, similar to the one for DataOutputStream, requires an output stream as its argument. In the following program, the parameter is again an instance of FileOutputStream.

```
/*
    Chapter 12 Sample Program:
            A test program to save data to a file using
            PrintWriter for high-level I/O.

    File: Ch12TestPrintWriter.java
*/
import java.io.*;

class Ch12TestPrintWriter {
   public static void main (String[] args) throws IOException {

      //set up file and stream
      File              outFile        = new File("sample3.data");
      FileOutputStream outFileStream   = new FileOutputStream(outFile);
      PrintWriter       outStream      = new PrintWriter(outFileStream);
```

```
        //write values of primitive data types to the stream
        outStream.println(987654321);
        outStream.println(11111111L);
        outStream.println(22222222F);
        outStream.println(33333333D);
        outStream.println('A');
        outStream.println(true);

        //output done, so close the stream
        outStream.close();
    }
}
```

> We use **print** and **println** with **PrintWriter**. The **print** and **println** methods convert primitive data types to strings before writing to a file.

To read the data from a text file, we use the FileReader and BufferedReader objects. The relationship between FileReader and BufferedReader is similar to the one between FileInputStream and DataInputStream. To read data back from a text file, we first need to associate a BufferedReader object to a file. The following sequence of statements associates a BufferedReader object to a file sample3.data:

```
File           inFile    = new File("sample3.data");
FileReader     fileReader = new FileReader(inFile);
BufferedReader bufReader
                         = new BufferedReader(fileReader);
```

Then we read data, using the readLine method of BufferedReader,

```
String str = bufReader.readLine( );
```

and convert the String to a primitive data type as necessary.

Here's the program to read back from sample3.data, which was created by the program Ch12TestPrintWriter:

```
/*
    Chapter 12 Sample Program:
            A test program to load data from a file using the readLine
            method of BufferedReader for high-level String input.

    File: Ch12TestBufferedReader.java
*/
import java.io.*;

class Ch12TestBufferedReader {
    public static void main (String[] args) throws IOException {
```

```
        //set up file and stream
        File           inFile     = new File("sample3.data");
        FileReader     fileReader = new FileReader(inFile);
        BufferedReader bufReader  = new BufferedReader(fileReader);
        String str;

        //get integer
        str = bufReader.readLine();
        int i = Integer.parseInt(str);

        //get long
        str = bufReader.readLine();
        long l = Long.parseLong(str);

        //get float
        str = bufReader.readLine();
        float f = Float.parseFloat(str);

        //get double
        str = bufReader.readLine();
        double d = Double.parseDouble(str);

        //get char
        str = bufReader.readLine();
        char c = str.charAt(0);

        //get boolean
        str = bufReader.readLine();
        Boolean boolObj = new Boolean(str);
        boolean b = boolObj.booleanValue();

        //process data here

        //input done, so close the stream
        bufReader.close();
    }
}
```

> Data are saved in ASCII format, so the conversion to the primitive data format is required.

Take my Advice

Beginning with Java 2 SDK version 1.5, we can use the **Scanner** class introduced in Chapter 3 to input data from a file. Instead of associating a new **Scanner** object to **System.in**, we can associate it to a file. For example,

```
Scanner scanner = Scanner.create(
                    new File("sample3.data"));
```

will associate **scanner** to the file **sample3.data**. Once this association is made, you can use the scanner methods (e.g., **nextInt**, **next**) to input data from the file. The **create** method that takes a **File** as an argument can throw either a **FileNotFoundException** or an **IOException**.

The FileManager Class

In the Chapter 9 sample program and in Section 12.1, we used the helper class File-Manager. A FileManager object provides file IO operations for String data. To refresh our memory, here are the public methods of the class:

Public Methods of FileManager
public String openFile(String filename)   **throws** FileNotFoundException, IOException Opens the text file filename and returns the content as a String.
public String openFile( ) **throws** IOException Opens the text file selected by the end user using the standard file open dialog and returns the content as a String.
public String saveFile(String filename, String data)   **throws** IOException Save the string data to filename.
public String saveFile(String data) **throws** IOException Saves the string data to a file selected by the end user using the standard file save dialog.

The class uses the BufferedReader and PrintWriter classes for text (String) output and input. Notice that all public methods throw an IOException, and only the open-File method that accepts a filename as an argument throws FileNotFoundException also. Here is the class listing:

```java
/*
    Chapter 9 and 12 Helper Class

    File: FileManager.java

*/

import java.io.*;
import javax.swing.*;

class FileManager {

    private static final String EMPTY_STRING = "";
    private static String lineTerminator
                            = System.getProperty("line.separator");

    public FileManager( ) {

    }

    public String openFile( ) throws FileNotFoundException,
                            IOException {
        String filename, doc = EMPTY_STRING;

        JFileChooser chooser = new JFileChooser();
        int reply = chooser.showOpenDialog(null);
```

openFile

```java
        if(reply == JFileChooser.APPROVE_OPTION) {

            doc = openFile(chooser.getSelectedFile().getAbsolutePath());
        }

        return doc;
    }

    public String openFile(String filename)
            throws FileNotFoundException, IOException {

        String          line;
        StringBuffer    document = new StringBuffer(EMPTY_STRING);

        File            inFile    = new File(filename);
        FileReader      fileReader = new FileReader(inFile);
        BufferedReader  bufReader  = new BufferedReader(fileReader);

        while (true) {
            line = bufReader.readLine();

            if (line == null) break;

            document.append(line + lineTerminator);
        }

        return document.toString();
    }

    public void saveFile(String data) throws IOException {
        String filename, doc = EMPTY_STRING;

        JFileChooser chooser = new JFileChooser();
        int reply = chooser.showSaveDialog(null);

        if(reply == JFileChooser.APPROVE_OPTION) {

            saveFile(chooser.getSelectedFile().getAbsolutePath(),
                    data);
        }
    }

    public void saveFile(String filename, String data)
            throws IOException {

        File                outFile       = new File(filename);
        FileOutputStream    outFileStream = new FileOutputStream(outFile);
        PrintWriter         outStream     = new PrintWriter(outFileStream);

        outStream.print(data);

        outStream.close();
    }
}
```

saveFile

1. Which type of files can be opened and viewed by a text editor?
2. Which class is used to save data as a text file? Which class is used to read text files?
3. Assume bufReader, a BufferedReader object, is properly declared and created. What is wrong with the following?

```
double d = bufReader.readDouble( );
```

12.4 | Object I/O

For Java 2 SDK 1.1, we can store objects just as easily as we can store primitive data values. Older versions of Java and many other object-oriented programming languages won't allow programmers to store objects directly. In those programming languages, we must write code to store individual data members of an object separately. For example, if a Person object has data members name (String), age (int), and gender (char), then we have to store the three values individually, using the file I/O techniques explained earlier in the chapter. (*Note:* String is an object, but it can be treated much as any other primitive data types because of its immutability.) Now, if the data members of an object are all primitive data types (or a String), then storing the data members individually is a chore but not that difficult. However, if a data member is a reference to another object or to an array of objects, then storing data can become very tricky. Fortunately with Java 2 SDK 1.1 and newer versions, we don't have to worry about them; we can store objects directly to a file.

ObjectOutputStream

ObjectInputStream

In this section, we will describe various approaches for storing objects. To write objects to a file, we use ObjectOutputStream; and to read objects from a file, we use ObjectInputStream. Let's see how we write Person objects to a file. First we need to modify the definition of the Person class in order for ObjectOutputStream and ObjectInputStream to perform object I/O. We modify the definition by adding the phrase implements Serializable to it.

```
import java.io.*;
class Person implements Serializable {
   //the rest is the same
}
```

◀ Serializable is defined in **java.io.**

Whenever we want to store an object to a file, we modify its class definition by adding the phrase implements Serializable to it. Unlike other interfaces, such as ActionListener, there are no methods for us to define in the implementation class. All we have to do is to add the phrase.

Helpful Reminder

If we want to perform an object I/O, then the class definition must include the phrase **implements Serializable.**

To save objects to a file, we first create an **ObjectOutputStream** object:

```
File                outFile
                         = new File("objects.dat");
FileOutputStream    outFileStream
                         = new FileOutputStream(outFile);
ObjectOutputStream outObjectStream
                         = new ObjectOutputStream
                                      (outFileStream);
```

To save a **Person** object, we write

```
Person person = new Person("Mr. Espresso", 20, 'M');

outObjectStream.writeObject( person );
```

The following sample program saves 10 **Person** objects to a file:

```java
/*
    Chapter 12 Sample Program: Illustrate the use of ObjectOutputStream

    File: Ch12TestObjectOutputStream.java
*/

import java.io.*;

class Ch12TestObjectOutputStream {
    public static void main (String[] args) throws IOException {

        //set up the streams
        File                outFile  = new File("objects.dat");
        FileOutputStream    outFileStream
                                 = new FileOutputStream(outFile);
        ObjectOutputStream outObjectStream
                                 = new ObjectOutputStream(outFileStream);

        //write serializable Person objects one at a time
        Person person;
        for (int i = 0; i < 10; i++) {
            person = new Person("Mr. Espresso" + i, 20+i, 'M');

            outObjectStream.writeObject(person);
        }

        //output done, so close the stream
        outObjectStream.close();
    }
}
```

It is possible to save different types of objects to a single file. Assuming the Account and Bank classes are defined properly, we can save both types of objects to a single file:

```
Account   account1, account2;
Bank      bank1, bank2;

account1 = new Account(); //create objects
account2 = new Account();
bank1    = new Bank();
bank2    = new Bank();

outObjectStream.writeObject( account1 );
outObjectStream.writeObject( account2 );
outObjectStream.writeObject( bank1    );
outObjectStream.writeObject( bank2    );
```

We can even mix objects and primitive data type values, for example,

```
outObjectStream.writeInt    ( 15       );
outObjectStream.writeObject( account1 );
outObjectStream.writeChar   ( 'X'      );
```

To read objects from a file, we use FileInputStream and ObjectInputStream. We use the method readObject to read an object. Since we can store any types of objects to a single file, we need to type cast the object read from the file. Here's an example of reading a Person object we saved in the file objects.data.

```
File              inFile
                     = new File("objects.dat");

FileInputStream   inFileStream
                     = new FileInputStream(inFile);

ObjectInputStream inObjectStream
                     = new ObjectInputStream(inFileStream);

Person person = (Person) inObjectStream.readObject();
```

Need to type cast to the object type we are reading

ClassNot-
Found-
Exception

Because there is a possibility of wrong type casting, the readObject method can throw a **ClassNotFoundException** in addition to an IOException. You can catch or propagate either or both exceptions. If you propagate both exceptions, then the declaration of a method that contains the call to readObject will look like this:

```
public void myMethod( )
              throws IOException, ClassNotFoundException {
   . . .
}
```

The following sample program reads the Person objects from the objects.dat file:

```
/*
    Chapter 12 Sample Program: Illustrate the use of ObjectInputStream

    File: Ch12TestObjectInputStream.java
*/

import java.io.*;

class Ch12TestObjectInputStream {
    public static void main (String[] args) throws ClassNotFoundException,
                                                    IOException {

        //set up file and stream
        File                inFile   = new File("objects.dat");

        FileInputStream     inFileStream
                                = new FileInputStream(inFile);

        ObjectInputStream inObjectStream
                                = new ObjectInputStream(inFileStream);

        //read the Person objects from a file
        Person person;
        for (int i = 0; i < 10; i++) {
            person = (Person) inObjectStream.readObject();

            System.out.println(person.getName() + "     " +
                            person.getAge()   + "     " +
                            person.getGender());
        }

        //input done, so close the stream
        inObjectStream.close();
    }
}
```

If a file contains objects from different classes, we must read them in the correct order and apply the matching type casting. For example, if the file contains two Account and two Bank objects, then we must read them in the correct order:

```
account1 = (Account) inObjectStream.readObject();
account2 = (Account) inObjectStream.readObject();
bank1    = (Bank)    inObjectStream.readObject();
bank2    = (Bank)    inObjectStream.readObject();
```

Now, consider the following array of **Person** objects where **N** represents some integer value:

```
Person[] people = new Person[N];
```

Assuming that all **N** **Person** objects are in the array, we can store them to file as

```
//save the size of an array first
outObjectStream.writeInt( people.length );

//save Person objects next
for (int i = 0; i < people.length; i++ ) {
    outObjectStream.writeObject( people[i] );
}
```

We store the size of an array at the beginning of the file so we know exactly how many **Person** objects to read back:

```
int N = inObjectStream.readInt();

for (int i = 0; i < N; i++) {
    people[i] = (Person) inObjectStream.readObject();
}
```

Since an array itself is an object, we can actually store the whole array with a single **writeObject** method, instead of storing individual elements one at a time, that is, calling the **writeObject** method for each element. The whole **people** array can be stored with a single statement as

```
outObjectStream.writeObject( people );
```

and the whole array is read back with a single statement as

```
people = (Person[]) inObjectStream.readObject( );
```

Notice how the type casting is done. We are reading an array of **Person** objects, so the type casting is (**Person[ ]**). This approach will work with any data structure object such as a list or map.

The Dorm **class**

In the Chapter 8 sample development, we used the helper class **Dorm** to manage a list of **Resident** objects. A **Dorm** object is capable of saving a **Resident** list to a file and reading the list from a file. The class uses object I/O discussed in this section to perform these tasks. A list of **Resident** objects is maintained by using a **HashMap**. Instead of saving **Resident** objects individually, the whole map is saved with a single **writeObject** method and is read by a single **readObject** method. (The map data structure was explained in Chapter 10.) Here's the complete listing:

```
/*
    Chapter 8 Sample Development Helper Class

    File: Dorm.java
*/

import java.io.*;
import java.util.*;

public class Dorm   {

    private Map residentTable;

    public Dorm( ) {                                    Constructors
        residentTable = new HashMap();
    }

    public Dorm(String filename)
                    throws FileNotFoundException,
                           IOException {

        openFile(filename);
    }

    public void add(Resident resident)                  add
                    throws IllegalArgumentException{

        if (residentTable.containsKey(resident.getName())) {
            throw new IllegalArgumentException(
                "Resident with the same name already exists");
        } else {
            residentTable.put(resident.getName(), resident);
        }
    }

    public void delete(String name) {                   delete

        residentTable.remove(name);
    }

    public Resident getResident(String name) {          getResident

        return (Resident) residentTable.get(name);
    }

    public String getResidentList( ) {                  getResidentList
        Resident     res;
        StringBuffer result = new StringBuffer("");
```

```java
        String tab = "\t";
        String lineSeparator = System.getProperty("line.separator");

        Iterator itr = residentTable.values().iterator();

        while (itr.hasNext()) {
            res = (Resident) itr.next();

            result.append(res.getName()     + tab +
                          res.getRoom()      + tab +
                          res.getPassword()  + tab +
                          lineSeparator);
        }

        return result.toString();
    }

    public void openFile(String filename)
                throws FileNotFoundException,
                       IOException {

        File inFile = new File(filename);
        FileInputStream inFileStream =
                new FileInputStream(inFile);
        ObjectInputStream inObjectStream =
                new ObjectInputStream(inFileStream);

        try {
            residentTable = (Map) inObjectStream.readObject();
        } catch (ClassNotFoundException e) {
            throw new IOException(
                        "Unrecognized data in the designated file");
        }

        inObjectStream.close();
    }

    public void saveFile(String filename)
                throws IOException {

        File outFile = new File(filename);
        FileOutputStream outFileStream =
                new FileOutputStream(outFile);
        ObjectOutputStream outObjectStream =
                new ObjectOutputStream(outFileStream);

        outObjectStream.writeObject(residentTable);

        outObjectStream.close();
    }
}
```

openFile

saveFile

Quick **CHECK** √

1. When do you have to include the clause implements Serializable to a class definition?
2. You cannot save the whole array at once—you must save the array elements individually, true or false?

12.5 Sample Development

Saving an AddressBook Object

As an illustration of object I/O, we will write a class that handles the storage of an **AddressBook** object. The class will provide methods to write an **AddressBook** object to a file and to read the object back from the file.

Problem Statement

*Write a class that manages file I/O of an **AddressBook** object.*

Overall Plan

Before we begin to design the class, we must modify the definition of the class that implements the **AddressBook** interface by adding the phrase **implements Serializable,** such as

```
import java.io.*;
class AddressBookVer1 implements AddressBook,
                                 Serializable {
    //same as before
}
```

In the following discussion, we will use the implementation class **AddressBookVers1.** This modification allows us to store instances of the **AddressBookVer1** class. We will use the expression "an **AddressBook** object" to refer to an instance of any class that implements the **AddressBook** interface.

Since the class handles the file I/O operations, we will call the class **AddressBookStorage.** Following the STO (single-task object) principle, this class will be responsible solely for file I/O of an **AddressBook** object. The class will not perform, for instance, any operations that deal with a user interface.

What kinds of core operations should this class support? Since the class handles the file I/O, the class should support two public methods to write and read an **AddressBook** object. Let's call the methods **write** and **read.** The argument will be an **AddressBook** object we want to write or read. If **filer** is an **AddressBookStorage** object, then the calls should be something like

```
filer.write( addressBook );
```

and

```
addressBook = filer.read( );
```

For an **AddressBookStorage** to actually store an **AddressBook** object, it must know the file to which an address book is written or from which it is read. How should we let the programmer specify this file? One possibility is to let the programmer pass the filename to a constructor, such as

```
AddressBookStorage filer
        = new AddressBookStorage("book.data");
```

Another possibility is to define a method to set the file, say, **setFile,** which is called as

```
filer.setFile( "book.data" );
```

Instead of choosing one over the other, we will support both. If we don't provide the **setFile** method, **filer** can input and output to a single file only. By using the **setFile** method, the programmer can change the file if she or he needs to. As for the constructor, we do not want to define a constructor with no argument because we do not want the programmer to create an **AddressBookStorage** object without specifying a filename. Yes, he or she can call the **setFile** method later, but as the **AddressBookStorage** class designer, we cannot ensure the programmer will call the **setFile** method. If the programmer doesn't call the method, then the subsequent calls to the **write** or **read** method will fail. Some may consider assigning a default filename in a no-argument constructor. But what will be the default filename? No matter which filename we choose, there's a possibility that a file with this filename already exists, which will cause the file to be erased. To make our class reliable, we will not provide a no-argument constructor.

We will implement the class in the following order:

develop-
ment steps

1. Implement the constructor and the **setFile** method.

2. Implement the **write** method.

3. Implement the **read** method.

4. Finalize the class.

This order of development follows a natural sequence. We begin with the constructor as usual. Since the constructor and the **setFile** method carry out similar operations, we will implement them together. We will identify necessary data members in this step. The second step is to implement the file output routine, because without being able to write an **AddressBook** object, we won't be able to test the file input routine. For the third step, we will implement the file input routine.

Step 1 Development: Constructor and setFile

step 1
design

In step 1, we will identify the data members and define a constructor to initialize them. We will also implement the **setFile** method, which should be very similar to the constructor.

We need **File, FileInputStream, FileOutputStream, ObjectInputStream,** and **ObjectOutputStream** objects to do object I/O. Should we define a data member for each type of object? This is certainly a possibility, but we should not use any unnecessary data members. We need **ObjectInputStream** and **ObjectOutputStream** objects only at the time the actual read and write operations take place. We can create these objects in the **read** and **write** methods, only when they are needed. Had we used data members for all those objects, we would need to create and assign objects every time the **setFile** method was called. But calling the **setFile** method does not necessarily mean the actual file I/O will take place. Consider the case where the user changes the filename before actually saving an address book to a file. This will result in calling the **setFile** method twice before doing the actual file I/O. To avoid this type of unnecessary repetition, we will use one data member only, a **String** variable **filename** to keep the filename. The **setFile** method simply assigns the parameter to this variable. The constructor can do the same by calling this **setFile** method.

step 1 code

At this point, we have only one data member:

```
//---------------------------
//   Data Members
//---------------------------

private   String   filename; //name of the file to store
                             //an AddressBook object
```

The **setFile** method assigns the parameter to the data member. The class is defined as follows:

```
/*
   Chapter 12 Sample Program: Address Book Storage

   File: AddressBookStorage.java
*/
class AddressBookStorage {

   private String filename;

   public AddressBookStorage ( String filename ) {
      setFile(filename);
   }

   public void setFile(String filename) {
      this.filename = filename;
      System.out.println("Inside setFile. Filename is " + filename);
                                                          //TEMP

   }
}
```

12.5 **Sample Development**—*continued*

step 1 test

To test this class, we have included a temporary output statement inside the **setFile** method. We will write a test program to verify that we can create an **Address-BookStorage** object and use the **setFile** method correctly:

```
/*
    Chapter 12 Sample Program: Driver class to test
                              the skeleton AddressBookStorage

    File: TestAddressBookStorage.java (Step 1)
*/

class TestAddressBookStorage {

    public static void main (String[] args) {

        AddressBookStorage fileManager;

        fileManager = new AddressBookStorage("one.data");
        fileManager.setFile("two.data");
        fileManager.setFile("three.data");
    }
}
```

Step 2 Development: Implement the write Method

step 2
design

In the second development step, we will implement the **write** method. From the data member **filename,** we will create an **ObjectOutputStream** object and write the parameter **AddressBook** object to it. A sequence of method calls to create an **ObjectOutputStream** object can throw an **IOException,** so we must either propagate it or handle it. Following the STO principle, the method will propagate the thrown exception. The responsibility of an **AddressBookStorage** object is to take care of file I/O for others. When there's an exception, the object will inform the caller about the exception and let the caller decide what to do about it.

step 2 code

Here's the step 2 code with the **write** method:

```
/*
    Chapter 12 Sample Program: The class that provides the
                               file I/O for AddressBook

    File: AddressBookStorage.java
*/

import java.io.*;
```

```
class AddressBookStorage {

   ...

   public void write(AddressBook book) throws IOException {
      //first create an ObjectOutputStream
      File outFile = new File(filename);
      FileOutputStream outFileStream =
              new FileOutputStream(outFile);
      ObjectOutputStream outObjectStream =
              new ObjectOutputStream(outFileStream);

      //save the data to it
      outObjectStream.writeObject(book);

      //and close it
      outObjectStream.close();
   }
}
```

step 2 test   We will write a test program to verify that the data are saved to a file. Since we do not have a method to read the file contents yet, we can only verify at this point that the file is created and that this file has something in it. To do so, we run the following step 2 test program first. Then we use whatever tool that is available (e.g., Windows Explorer, DOS command **dir,** UNIX command **ls,** etc.) and check that the specified file exists and that the file size is greater than zero.

The step 2 test program is as follows (**TestAddressBookWrite** is now an instantiable main class):

```
/*
    Chapter 12 Sample Program: Test the write method

    File: TestAddressBookWrite.java
*/

import java.io.*;

class TestAddressBookWrite {

    AddressBook        myBook;
    AddressBookStorage  fileManager;

    public static void main( String[] args )throws IOException {
       TestAddressBookWrite  tester = new TestAddressBookWrite(15);

       tester.write("book.data");
    }
```

```java
public TestAddressBookWrite( int N ) {
    myBook = new AddressBookVer1(N);

    for (int i = 0; i < N; i++) {
        Person person = new Person("Ms. X" + i, 10, 'F');
        myBook.add(person);
    }
}

public void write(String filename) {
    fileManager = new AddressBookStorage(filename);

    try {
        fileManager.write(myBook);
    }
    catch (IOException e) {
        System.out.println("Error: IOException is thrown.");
    }
}
}
```

We run the program several times with different sizes for the address book and verify that the resulting files have different sizes. Notice that we can only verify that the file is created to store an **AddressBook** object. We cannot verify that the object is saved properly until we are able to read the data back, which we will do in the next step.

Step 3 Development: Implement the read Method

step 3 design

In the third development step, we will implement the **read** method. The method reads the **AddressBook** object saved in the file and returns this object to the caller. As with the **write** method, if there's an exception, this method will propagate it back to the caller and let the caller decide what to do to the thrown exception.

step 3 code

Here's the step 3 code with the **read** method:

```java
/*
    Chapter 12 Sample Program: The class that provides the
                               file I/O for AddressBook

    File: AddressBookStorage.java
*/

import java.io.*;
```

```java
class AddressBookStorage {

    . . .

    public AddressBook read() throws IOException {
        AddressBook book;

        //first create an ObjectInputStream
        File inFile = new File(filename);
        FileInputStream inFileStream =
                new FileInputStream(inFile);
        ObjectInputStream inObjectStream =
                new ObjectInputStream(inFileStream);

        try {
            //read the data from it
            book = (AddressBook) inObjectStream.readObject();
        }
        catch (ClassNotFoundException e) {
            book = null;
            System.out.println("Error: AddressBook class not found");
        }

        //and close it
        inObjectStream.close();

        //and return the object
        return book;
    }

    . . .

}
```

step 3 test

We will write a test program to verify that the data can be read back correctly from a file. To test the read operation, the file to read the data from must already exist. Instead of copying the data file created in step 2 to the step 3 folder, we will make this test program to save the data first by using the **TestAddressBookWrite** class. The step 3 test program is as follows:

```java
/*
    Chapter 12 Sample Program: Test the read (and write) method

    File: TestAddressBookRead.java
*/
```

```java
import java.io.*;

class TestAddressBookRead {
    AddressBook         myBook;
    AddressBookStorage  fileManager;

    public static void main( String[] args )throws IOException {
        TestAddressBookWrite writer = new TestAddressBookWrite(15);
        TestAddressBookRead  reader = new TestAddressBookRead( );

        writer.write("book.data");
        reader.read("book.data");

        reader.search("Ms. X5");
    }

    public void search(String name) {
        Person person;

        person = myBook.search(name);

        if (person != null) {
            System.out.print(person.getName() + "    ");
            System.out.print(person.getAge()   + "    ");
            System.out.println(person.getGender() + "\n");
        }
        else {
            System.out.println("Error: object not found");
        }
    }

    public void read( String filename ) {
        fileManager = new AddressBookStorage(filename);

        try {
            myBook = fileManager.read();
        }
        catch (IOException e) {
            System.out.println("Error: IOException is thrown.");
        }
    }
}
```

We run the program several times, changing the method body of **printout** to access different **Person** objects in the address book as necessary, and we verify that we can read the **Person** object in the file correctly. If you did Exercise 16 on page 633, then use the **getFirstPerson** and **getNextPerson** methods to access all **Person** objects in the address book.

Step 4 Development: Finalize

program review

final test

We finalize the program in the last step. We perform a critical review for finding any inconsistency or error in the methods, incomplete methods, places to add more comments, and so forth. And, as always, we will carry out the final test. As the result of the critical review and final testing, we may identify and wish to implement any additional features.

Summary

- A File object represents a file or a directory.
- An instance of the JFileChooser class is a file dialog that lets the user select a file to read data from or to save data to.
- Various input and output stream classes are defined in the java.io package.
- Low-level file input and output read and write data 1 byte at a time.
- FileInputStream and FileOutputStream classes are used for low-level file I/O.
- High-level file input and output read and write data of primitive data type.
- DataInputStream and DataOutputStream classes are used for high-level file I/O.
- With text I/O, data are read and saved as strings.
- PrinterWriter and BufferedReader classes are used for text I/O.
- With object I/O, data are read and saved as objects.
- ObjectInputStream and ObjectOutputStream are used for object I/O.
- To be able to save objects to a file, the class they belong to must implement the Serializable interface.
- The standard classes described or used in this chapter are

File	PrintWriter
JFileChooser	FileReader
FileOutputStream	BufferedReader
FileInputStream	Serializable
DataOutputStream	ObjectOutputStream
DataInputStream	ObjectInputStream

Key Concepts

file	low-level I/O (bytes)
directory	high-level I/O (primitive data types)
file dialog	text I/O (strings)
streams	object I/O (objects)
binary files	Serializable interface
text files	

Exercises

1. What will happen if you forget to close a file?
2. What is the difference between binary files and text files?
3. Using the try–catch block, write code that opens a file default.dat when an attempt to open a user-designated file raises an exception.
4. Using a File object, write code to display files in a user-specified directory.
5. Write code to store and read the contents of the payScaleTable two-dimensional array from Section 10.5 in the following two file formats:
   - A file of double values
   - A file of two-dimensional array
6. Write an application that reads a text file and converts its content to an Eggy-Peggy text (see Exercise 8.20). Save the converted text to another text file. Use JFileChooser to let the user specify the input and output files. Create the input file by using a text editor.
7. Write an application that randomly generates N integers and stores them in a binary file integers.dat. The value for N is input by the user. Open the file with a text editor and see what the contents of a binary file look like.
8. Write an application that reads the data from the file integers.dat generated in Exercise 7. After the data are read, display the smallest, the largest, and the average.
9. Repeat Exercise 7, but this time, store the numbers in a text file integers.txt. Open this file with a text editor and verify that you can read the contents.
10. Repeat Exercise 8 with the text file integers.txt generated in Exercise 9.
11. Extend the AddressBookStorage class by adding import and export capabilities. Add a method export that stores the contents of AddressBook to a text file. Add a second method import that reads the text file back and constructs an AddressBook. This type of import/export feature is a convenient means to move data from one application to another.
12. Extend the encryption application of Exercise 25 of Chapter 9 so that the original text is read from a user-specified text file and the encrypted text is stored to another user-specified text file.

13. Extend the watermelon projectile computation program of Exercise 31 on page 379 so the output is saved to a file. Which file format would you use for the program, a binary file or a text file? Or would you consider using an array to keep the (x, y) coordinates and save this array by using an object I/O?

14. Extend the Ch12JavaViewer class by adding the capabilities to edit and save Java source code. Use JFileChooser to let the user specify the file to save the source code.

Development Exercises

For Exercises 15 through 19, use the incremental development methodology to implement the program. For each exercise, identify the program tasks, create a design document with class descriptions, and draw the program diagram. Map out the development steps at the start. Present any design alternatives and justify your selection. Be sure to perform adequate testing at the end of each development step.

15. Write a currency converter application. Allow the user to specify the from and to currencies and the amount to exchange. Use the interface of your choice to input these three values. When the application starts, read the exchange rates from a text file rate.txt. Use a text editor to create this text file. By using a text file, you can easily update the exchange rates. The format for the text file is

```
<name of currency> <units per dollar>
```

For example, the following shows how much $ 1 is worth in five foreign currencies:

```
French franc               5.95
Indonesian rupiah      12900.0
Japanese yen             123.91
Mexican peso               9.18
Papua New Guinea kina      2.381
```

You can get the exchange rates from various websites, one of which is http://www.oanda.com.

16. Extend any application you have written before by adding a quote-of-the-day dialog. When the user starts the application, a quote of the day is displayed (use JOptionPane). Save the quotes in a text file. Use a random number generator to select the quote to display. Notice the quotes can be about any information (many commercial applications start with a dialog that shows tips on using the software).

17. Extend Exercise 16 by designing a customized frame. Include a TextArea to display a quote and three buttons for control. Clicking the Prev and Next buttons displays the previous and next quote, respectively. Clicking the Close button closes the frame.

18. Write an application that removes extra spaces from a text file. In the days of the typewriter, it was common practice to leave two spaces after periods. We

shouldn't be doing that anymore with the computer, but many people still do. Read an original text file and output an edited version to another text file. The edited version should replace two or more consecutive spaces with one space.

19. Write a mail merge application. You use two files for this program. The first is a text file that contains a template letter in the following style:

```
Dear <<N>>,

Because you are <<A>> years old and <<G>>, we have a
free gift for you. You have absolutely nothing to buy;
just pay the shipping and handling charge of $9.99. To
claim your gift, call us now immediately.

Thank you,
Office of Claims Department
```

The tags <<N>>, <<A>>, and <<G>> are placeholders for the person's name, age, and gender. The second file contains the name, age, and gender information of people to whom you want to send a letter. Use whatever format you wish for the second file. Read two files and print out the letter with the placeholders replaced by the actual values from the second file. Run the program multiple times, each time using a different template file. For this program, output the personalized letter to a customized frame. Add menus to this frame so the user can save personalized letters to files (one personalized letter to a file).

13 Inheritance and Polymorphism

Objectives

After you have read and studied this chapter, you should be able to

- Write programs that are easily extensible and modifiable by applying polymorphism in program design.

- Define reusable classes based on inheritance and abstract classes and abstract methods.

- Differentiate the abstract classes and Java interface.

- Define methods, using the **protected** modifier.

- Parse strings, using a **StringTokenizer** object.

Introduction

In this chapter, we will describe two important and powerful features in object-oriented programming—inheritance and polymorphism. The inheritance feature of object-oriented programming was introduced in Chapter 1, and we used inheritance in defining a subclass of JFrame in Chapter 7. We will provide a more detailed explanation and examples of inheritance in this chapter. Specifically, we will define subclasses of programmer-defined classes, not the subclasses of system classes (e.g., JFrame) as we did in Chapter 7.

polymorphism

The second major topic we cover in this chapter is *polymorphism,* another indispensable feature in object-oriented programming, which allows programmers to send the same message to objects from different classes. Consider the statement

```
account.computeMonthlyFee();
```

where account could be either a SavingsAccount or a CheckingAccount object. If account is a SavingsAccount object, then the method computeMonthlyFee defined for the SavingsAccount class is executed. Likewise, if account is a CheckingAccount object, then the method computeMonthlyFee defined for the CheckingAccount class is executed. Sending the same message therefore could result in executing different methods. The message computeMonthlyFee is called a *polymorphic message* because depending on the receiver object, different methods are executed. Polymorphism helps us write code that is easy to modify and extend. We will explain polymorphism in this chapter.

polymorphic message

13.1 | Defining Classes with Inheritance

In Chapter 7, we defined subclasses of a system class JFrame. We will explain the rules for defining subclasses of programmer-defined classes. Let's start with an example. Suppose we want to maintain a class roster for a class whose enrolled students include both undergraduate and graduate students. For each student, we record her or his name, three test scores, and the final course grade. The final course grade, either pass or no pass, is determined by the following formula:

Type of Student	Grading Scheme
Undergraduate	Pass if (test1 + test2 + test3)/3 >= 70
Graduate	Pass if (test1 + test2 + test3)/3 >= 80

unrelated classes

What kind of objects should we use to model undergraduate and graduate students? There are basically two broad ways to design the classes to model them. The first way is to define two unrelated classes, one for undergraduate students and another for graduate students. We call the two classes *unrelated classes* if they are not connected in an inheritance relationship, that is, if neither one is an ancestor or descendant class of the other nor do they share a common ancestor.[1] The second way is to model undergraduate and graduate students by using classes that are related in an inheritance hierarchy.

Defining two unrelated classes for entities that share common data or behavior would make class definition ineffective because we would end up duplicating code common to both classes. Although different, graduate and undergraduate students do share many common data and behaviors, so we will design these two classes by using inheritance.

We will actually define three classes. The first is the Student class to incorporate behavior and data common to both graduate and undergraduate students. The second and third classes are the GraduateStudent class to incorporate behavior specific to graduate students and the UndergraduateStudent class to incorporate behavior specific to undergraduate students. The Student class is defined as

```java
/*
    Chapter 13 Sample Program: Student.

    File: Student.java

*/

class Student {

    protected    final static int NUM_OF_TESTS = 3;

    protected    String name;
    protected    int[]  test;
    protected    String courseGrade;

    public Student( ) {
        this("No Name");
    }

    public Student(String studentName) {
        name = studentName;
        test = new int[NUM_OF_TESTS];
        courseGrade = "****";
    }

    public String getCourseGrade( ) {
      return courseGrade;
    }
```

Protected fields are visible to the descendant objects.

---

[1]In Java, the class Object is automatically set to be the superclass of a class if the class definition does not include the keyword extends. To be technically precise, we must say that two classes are unrelated if they do not share a common ancestor besides Object.

```
   public String getName( ) {
     return name;
   }

   public int getTestScore(int testNumber) {
     return test[testNumber-1];
   }

   public void setName(String newName) {
     name = newName;
   }

   public void setTestScore(int testNumber, int testScore) {
     test[testNumber-1] = testScore;
   }
}
```

Notice that the modifier for the instance variables is protected, making them visible and accessible to the instances of the class and the descendant classes. If you declare a data member of a class private, then this data member is accessible only to the instances of the class. If you declare a data member public, this data member is accessible to everybody. We declare them protected so they become accessible only to the instances of the class and the descendant classes. We will explore further the protected modifier later in the chapter.

extends

We define the classes UndergraduateStudent and GraduateStudent as subclasses of the Student class. In Java, we say a subclass *extends* its superclass. The difference between the classes GraduateStudent and UndergraduateStudent lies in the way their final course grades are computed. The two subclasses are defined as follows:

```
class GraduateStudent extends Student {

   public void computeCourseGrade() {

      int total = 0;
      for (int i = 0; i < NUM_OF_TESTS; i++) {
         total += test[i];
      }

      if (total/NUM_OF_TESTS >= 80) {
         courseGrade = "Pass";
      } else {
         courseGrade = "No Pass";
      }
   }
}
```

```
class UndergraduateStudent extends Student {

    public void computeCourseGrade() {

        int total = 0;
        for (int i = 0; i < NUM_OF_TESTS; i++) {
            total += test[i];
        }

        if (total/NUM_OF_TESTS >= 70) {
            courseGrade = "Pass";
        } else {
            courseGrade = "No Pass";
        }
    }
}
```

Figure 13.1 shows the class diagram relating the three classes. Notice the use of the pound symbol (#) for the protected modifier. Notice also that we do not show inherited data members and methods in the subclasses. By seeing an inheritance arrow connecting a subclass to its superclass, we know that data members and methods indicated on the superclass are applicable to the subclasses also. We attach methods and data members to the subclasses only if they are defined in the subclasses or if they are overridden in the subclasses (we will discuss overriding in detail later in the chapter). In Figure 13.1, both subclasses have the method computeCourseGrade attached to them because the method is defined in the subclasses.

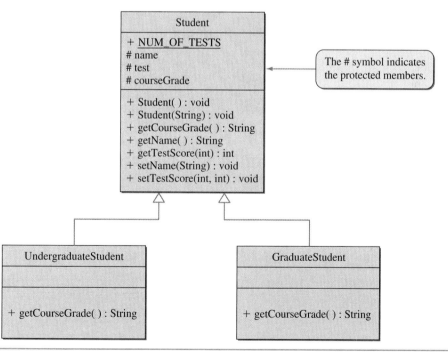

Figure 13.1 A superclass **Student** and its subclasses **GraduateStudent** and **UndergraduateStudent**.

Quick
CHECK

1. Which is the subclass and which is the superclass in this declaration?

```
class X extends Y { ... }
```

2. Which visibility modifier allows the data members of a superclass to be accessible to the instances of subclasses?

13.2 | Using Classes Effectively with Polymorphism

Now let's see how the Student class and its subclasses can be used effectively in the class roster program. Since both undergraduate and graduate students are enrolled in a class, should we declare the two arrays shown below to maintain the class roster?

```
GraduateStudent        gradRoster[20];
UndergraduateStudent   undergradRoster[20];
```

We mentioned in Chapter 11 that an array must contain elements of the same data type. For example, we cannot store integers and real numbers in the same array. To follow this rule, it seems necessary for us to declare two separate arrays, one for graduate students and another for undergraduate students. This rule, however, does not apply when the array elements are objects. We only need to declare a single array, for example,

```
Student roster[40];
```

Elements of the roster array can be instances of either the Student class or any of its descendant GraduateStudent or UndergraduateStudent classes. Figure 13.2 illustrates the array with both types of students as array elements.

Before showing how this array is used in the program, we will explain the concept of polymorphism. In its simplest form, polymorphism allows a single

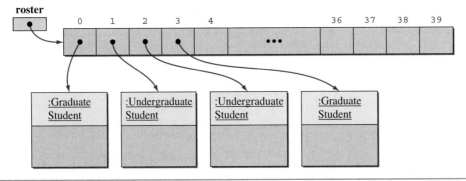

Figure 13.2 The **roster** array with elements referring to instances of **GraduateStudent** or **UndergraduateStudent** classes.

variable to refer to objects from different classes. Consider, for example, the declaration

```
Student student;
```

With this declaration, we can say not only

```
student = new Student( );
```

but also

```
student = new GraduateStudent( );
```

or

```
student = new UndergraduateStudent( );
```

In other words, the single variable **student** is not limited to referring to an object from the **Student** class but can refer to any object from the descendant classes of **Student**. In a similar manner we can say something like

```
roster[0] = new GraduateStudent( );
roster[1] = new UndergraduateStudent( );
roster[2] = new UndergraduateStudent( );
roster[3] = new GraduateStudent( );
...
```

However, you cannot make a variable of class X refer to an object from the superclass or sibling classes of X. *Sibling classes* are those that share the common ancestor class. For example, the following assignment statements are both invalid.

sibling classes

```
GraduateStudent grad1, grad2;
```

X **NOT VALID** →
```
grad1 = new Student( );
grad2 = new UndergraduateStudent( );
```

Now, to compute the course grade using the **roster** array, we execute

```
for (int i = 0; i < numberOfStudents; i++) {
    roster[i].computeCourseGrade();
}
```

If roster[i] refers to a GraduateStudent, then the computeCourseGrade method of the GraduateStudent class is executed; and if it refers to an UndergraduateStudent, then the computeCourseGrade method of UndergraduateStudent is executed. We call the message computeCourseGrade *polymorphic* because the message refers to methods from different classes depending on the object referenced by roster[i]. Polymorphism allows us to maintain the class roster with one array instead of maintaining a separate array for each type of student, and this simplifies the processing tremendously.

Polymorphism makes possible smooth and easy extension and modification of a program. Suppose, for example, we have to add a third type of student, say, audit student, to the class roster program. If we have to define a separate array for each type of student, this extension forces us to define a new class and a third array for audit students. But with polymorphism, we only have to define a new subclass of Student. And as long as this new subclass includes the correct computeCourseGrade method, the for loop to compute the course grade for students remains the same. Without polymorphism, not only do we have to add the new code, but also we have to rewrite existing code to accommodate the change. With polymorphism, on the other hand, we don't have to touch the existing code. Modifying existing code is a tedious and error-prone activity. A slight change to existing code could cause a program to stop working correctly. To be certain that a change in one portion of existing code won't affect other portions of existing code adversely, we must understand the existing code completely. And understanding code, especially one that is long and/or written by somebody else, is a very time-consuming task.

An element of the roster array is a reference to an instance of either the GraduateStudent or the UndergraduateStudent class. Most of the time, we do not have to know which is which. There are times, however, when we need to know the class of a referenced object. For example, we may want to find out the number of undergraduate students who passed the course. To determine the class of an object, we use the instanceof operator. We used this operator in Chapter 7 to determine whether an event source is a JButton or a JTextField object. We can use this operator here; for example,

```
Student x = new UndergraduateStudent( );

if ( x instanceof UndergraduateStudent ) {
    System.out.println("Mr. X is an undergraduate student");
} else {
    System.out.println("Mr. X is a graduate student");
}
```

will print out Mr. X is an undergraduate student. The following code counts the number of undergraduate students in the roster array.

```
int undergradCount = 0;
for (int i = 0; i < numberOfStudents; i++) {
    if ( roster[i] instanceof UndergraduateStudent ) {
        undergradCount++;
    }
}
```

Quick
CHECK

1. Suppose Truck and Motorcycle are subclasses of Vehicle. Which of these declarations are invalid?

```
Truck       t  = new Vehicle();
Vehicle     v  = new Truck();
Motorcycle m1  = new Vehicle();
Motorcycle m2  = new Truck();
```

2. What is the purpose of the instanceof operator?

13.3 | Inheritance and Member Accessibility

We will describe the rules of inheritance in this section and Sections 13.4 and 13.5. In this section, we will explain which members (variables and methods) of a superclass are inherited by a subclass and how these members are accessed. In addition to declaring members private and public, we can declare them protected. The protected modifier is meaningful only if used with inheritance. Consider the following declarations:

```
class Super {                  all lowercase super is a
                               reserved word, so don't use it.

    public    int   public_Super_Field;
    protected int   protected_Super_Field;
    private   int   private_Super_Field;

    public Super() {
        public_Super_Field      = 10;
        protected_Super_Field   = 20;
        private_Super_Field     = 30;
    }
    . . .
}

class Sub extends Super {
    public    int   public_Sub_Field;
    protected int   protected_Sub_Field;
    private   int   private_Sub_Field;

    public Sub() {
        public_Sub_Field        = 100;
        protected_Sub_Field     = 200;
        private_Sub_Field       = 300;
    }
    . . .
}
```

We use instance variables for illustration, but the rules we describe here are equally applicable to other types of members (class variables, class methods, and instance methods). We use the graphical representation shown in Figure 13.3 for the three modifiers.

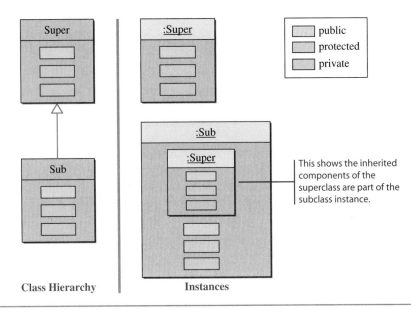

Figure 13.3 A graphical representation of superclasses and subclasses with **public, private,** and **protected** members. (Note: This representation is for illustration purpose only and is not a formal UML diagram.)

You already know the difference between the public and private modifiers. A public member is accessible to any method, but a private member is accessible only to the methods that belong to the same class. Let's illustrate this point. Consider a class that is unrelated to the classes Super and Sub:

```
class Client {
    public void test() {
        Super  mySuper = new Super();
        Sub    mySub = new Sub();

        int i = mySuper.public_Super_Field;

        int j = mySub.public_Super_Field;  //inherited
                                           //by mySub

        int k = mySub.public_Sub_Field;
    }
}
```

✓ VALID →

Public members of a class, whether they are inherited or not, are accessible from any object or class. Private members of a class, on the other hand, are never accessible from any outside object or class. The following statements, if placed in the test method of the Client class, are therefore all invalid:

```
int l = mySuper.private_Super_Field;

int m = mySub.private_Sub_Field;

int n = mySub.private_Super_Field;
```

✗ NOT VALID →

> Private members are not inherited, so this statement is obviously invalid.

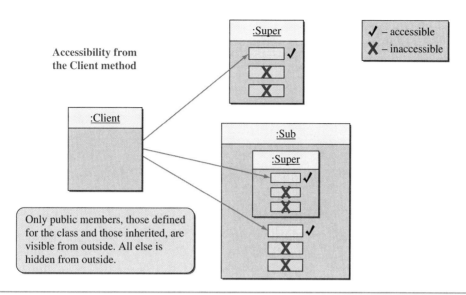

Accessibility from
the Client method

Only public members, those defined
for the class and those inherited, are
visible from outside. All else is
hidden from outside.

Figure 13.4 The difference between **public, private,** and **protected** modifiers. Only public members are visible from outside.

A protected member is accessible only to the methods that belong to the same class or to the descendant classes. It is inaccessible to the methods of an unrelated class. The following statements, if placed in the test method of the Client class, are all invalid:

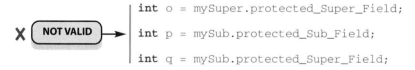

```
int o = mySuper.protected_Super_Field;

int p = mySub.protected_Sub_Field;

int q = mySub.protected_Super_Field;
```

Figure 13.4 summarizes the accessibility of class members from a method of an unrelated class.

Now let's study the accessibility of class members from the methods of a Sub object. A method in the Sub object can access both the protected and public members of Super, but not the private members of Super. Figure 13.5 summarizes the accessibility of members from a method of a Sub object.

Figure 13.5 shows the case where a method of a Sub object is accessing members of itself. Everything except the private members of the Super class is accessible from a method of the Sub class.

What about accessing the members of an object from another object that belongs to the same class? If a member X, whether inherited or defined in a class, is accessible from an instance of the class, then X is also accessible from all instances of the same class. Figure 13.6 illustrates that an instance can access members of other instances of the same class.

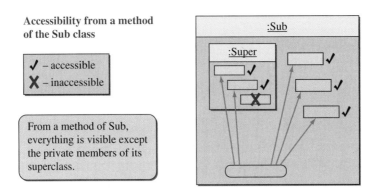

Figure 13.5 The difference between **public, private,** and **protected** modifiers. Everything except the **private** members of the **Super** class is visible from a method of the **Sub** class.

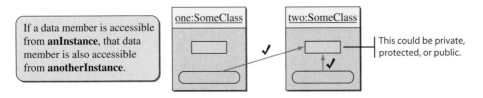

Figure 13.6 Data members accessible from an instance are also accessible from other instances of the same class.

Consider the following two classes:

```
class Super {
    . . .
    public void superToSuper( Super anotherSuper){

        int i = anotherSuper.public_Super_Field;
        int j = anotherSuper.protected_Super_Field;
        int l = anotherSuper.private_Super_Field;
    }
    . . .
}

class Sub extends Super {

    . . .
    public void subToSub( Sub anotherSub){

        int i = anotherSub.public_Sub_Field;
        int j = anotherSub.protected_Sub_Field;
        int k = anotherSub.private_Sub_Field;
```

✓ VALID

✓ VALID

```
✓  VALID     ──▶  │  int l = anotherSub.public_Super_Field;    //inherited
                  │  int m = anotherSub.protected_Super_Field; //members

✗  NOT VALID ──▶     int n = anotherSub.private_Super_Field;
                  }
                     ...
               }
```

All the statements in the two methods, except the last one in subToSub, are valid because members accessible to an object are also accessible from other objects of the same class. Now, consider the following two classes:

```
            class Super {
               ...
               public void superToSub( Sub sub){
✓  VALID     ──▶     int i = sub.public_Sub_Field;

✗  NOT VALID ──▶  │  int j = sub.protected_Sub_Field;
                  │  int k = sub.private_Sub_Field;
                  }
                     ...
               }

            class Sub extends Super {

               ...
               public void subToSuper( Super mySuper){
✓  VALID     ──▶     int i = mySuper.public_Super_Field;

✗  NOT VALID ──▶  │  int j = mySuper.protected_Super_Field;
                  │  int k = mySuper.private_Super_Field;
                  }
                     ...
               }
```

The two methods show that only the public members of an object are accessible from another object if the two objects belong to different classes. Whether one class is a subclass of the other class is irrelevant here.

In addition to the **private, protected,** and **public** modifiers, Java supports the fourth visibility modifier, called *package visibility*. If no explicit modifier (**public, private,** and **protected**) is included in the declaration, then the component is package-visible, which means the component is accessible from any method of a class that belongs to the same package as the component's class. Package visibility is not as critical as the other three visibility modifiers, and therefore, we do not discuss it in the text.

1. If X is a private member of the **Super** class, is X accessible from a subclass of **Super**?
2. If X is a protected member of the **Super** class, is X of one instance accessible from another instance of **Super**? What about from the instances of a subclass of **Super**?

13.4 | Inheritance and Constructors

In this section, we explain how the constructors of a class are affected by inheritance. Unlike other members of a superclass, constructors of a superclass are not inherited by its subclasses. This means that you must define a constructor for a class or use the default constructor added by the compiler. As we mentioned in Chapter 4, a default constructor is added to a class if you do not declare any constructor for the class. A class definition such as

```
class Person {

    public void sayHello( ) {

        System.out.println("Well, hello.");
    }
}
```

is equivalent to

```
class Person {

    public Person( ) {

        super();
    }

    public void sayHello( ) {

        System.out.println("Well, hello.");
    }
}
```

Automatically added to the class by the compiler →

← This statement calls the superclass's constructor.

The statement

```
super();
```

calls the superclass's constructor. Every class has a superclass. If the class declaration does not explicitly designate the superclass with the **extends** clause, then the class's superclass is the **Object** class.

If you declare a constructor, then no default constructor is added to the class. For example, if you define a class as

```
class MyClass {

    public MyClass( int x ) {

        ...
    }
}
```

then a statement such as

```
MyClass test = new MyClass();
```

is invalid because **MyClass** has no matching constructor.

If the constructor you define does not contain an explicit call to a superclass constructor, then the compiler adds the statement

```
super();
```

as the first statement of the constructor. For example, if you define a constructor as

```
class MyClass {

    private int myInt;

    public MyClass( ) {

        myInt = 10;
    }

}
```

then the compiler will rewrite the constructor to

```
public MyClass( ) {

    super();
    myInt = 10;
}
```

Let's look at another example. Consider the following class definitions:

```
class Vehicle {

    private String vin;

    public Vehicle(String vehicleIdNumber) {

        vin = vehicleIdNumber;
    }
```

```
    public String getVIN( ) {

        return vin;
    }
}
```

Since the class has a constructor, no default constructor is added to the class. This means a statement such as

```
Vehicle myCar = new Vehicle();
```

causes a compilation error because the class does not have a matching constructor. This is actually what we want because we do not want to create an instance of Vehicle without a vehicle identification number. Now let's consider a subclass definition for trucks. A Truck object has one additional instance variable called cargoWeightLimit that refers to a maximum weight of cargo the truck can carry. We assume the truck's weight limit for cargo can vary (say, depending on how much the owner pays in fees). Here's our first attempt:

```
class Truck extends Vehicle {
    private int cargoWeightLimit;
    public void setWeightLimit( int newLimit) {
        cargoWeightLimit = newLimit;
    }
    public int getWeightLimit( ) {
        return cargoWeightLimit;
    }
}
```

If we compile this definition, we will get a compiler error. Since no constructor is defined for the class, the compiler adds a default constructor

```
public void Truck() {
    super();
}
```

This constructor calls the superclass's constructor with no arguments, but there's no matching constructor in the superclass. Thus, the compilation error results. Here's a correct definition:

```
class Truck extends Vehicle {
    private int cargoWeightLimit;
    public Truck(int weightLimit, String vin) {
        super(vin);
        cargoWeightLimit = weightLimit;
    }
}
```

> You need to make this call. Otherwise, the compiler will add **super()**, which will result in an error because there is no matching constructor in **Vehicle.**

```
public void setWeightLimit( int newLimit) {

    cargoWeightLimit = newLimit;
}

public int getWeightLimit( ) {

    return cargoWeightLimit;
}
}
```

Now let's apply this knowledge to the design of the UndergraduateStudent and GraduateStudent classes. If we want a constructor that accepts the name, then we need to define such a constructor in both classes because the constructor defined for the Student class is not inherited by these classes. Notice that we can create instances of these classes by

```
student1 = new UndergraduateStudent( );
student2 = new GraduateStudent( );
```

because the default constructor is added by the compiler, not because the one defined in the Student class is inherited by the subclasses. Remember that constructors of a superclass are not inherited by its subclasses.

Here are a rule and a guideline to remember for a subclass constructor:

Helpful Reminder

*If a class has a superclass that is not the **Object** class, then a constructor of the class should make an explicit call to a constructor of the superclass.*

Design Guidelines

Always provide a constructor for every class you define. Don't rely on default constructors.

Quick
CHECK

1. How do you call the superclass's constructor from its subclass?
2. What statement will be added to a constructor of a subclass if it is not included in the constructor explicitly by the programmer?
3. Modify the definition of GraduateStudent and UndergraduateStudent in Section 13.1 so we can create their instances in this way:

```
student1 = new UndergraduateStudent();
student2 = new UndergraduateStudent("Mr. Espresso");
student3 = new GraduateStudent();
student4 = new GraduateStudent("Ms. Latte");
```

13.5 | Abstract Superclasses and Abstract Methods

When we define a superclass, we often do not need to create any instances of the superclass. In Section 13.4, we defined the Student superclass and its two subclasses GraduateStudent and UndergraduateStudent. We gave examples of creating instances of GraduateStudent and UndergraduateStudent, but not of creating instances of Student. Does it make sense to create an instance of the Student class? Depending on whether we need to create instances of Student, we must define the class differently. We will describe different ways of defining a superclass in this section.

Even though we can create an instance of Student if we want to (because of the way the class is currently defined), is there a need to create an instance of Student? If a student can be only a graduate or an undergraduate student, then there is no need to create an instance of Student. In fact, because of the way the class is defined, had we created an instance of Student and stored it in the roster array, the program would crash. Why? Because the Student class does not have a computeCourseGrade method.

In the following discussion, we will consider two cases. In the first case, we assume that a student must be either a graduate or an undergraduate student. In the second case, we assume that a student does not have to be a graduate or an undergraduate student (e.g., the student could be a nonmatriculated auditing student).

Case 1: Student Must Be Undergraduate or Graduate

For the case where a student must be a graduate or an undergraduate student, we only need instances of GraduateStudent and UndergraduateStudent. So we must define the Student class in such a way that no instances of it can be created. One way is to define Student as an abstract class. An *abstract class* is a class defined with the modifier abstract, and no instances can be created from an abstract class. Let's see how the abstract Student class is defined.

abstract class

> The keyword **abstract** here denotes an abstract class.

> The keyword **abstract** here denotes an abstract method.

> Abstract method has no method body, just a semicolon.

```
abstract class Student {

    protected final static int NUM_OF_TESTS = 3;

    protected String   name;
    protected int[]    test;
    protected String   courseGrade;

    public Student( ) {

        this("No name");
    }

    public Student(String studentName) {

        name        = studentName;
        test        = new int[NUM_OF_TESTS];
        courseGrade = "****";
    }

    abstract public void computeCourseGrade();
```

```
        public String getCourseGrade( ) {
            return courseGrade;
        }

        public String getName( ) {
            return name;
        }

        public int getTestScore(int testNumber) {
            return test[testNumber-1];
        }

        public void setName(String newName) {
            name = newName;
        }

        public void setTestScore(int testNumber, int testScore){
            test[testNumber-1] = testScore;
        }
    }
```

abstract method

implementing a method

An *abstract method* is a method with the keyword abstract, and it ends with a semi-colon instead of a method body. A class is *abstract* if the class contains an abstract method or does not provide an implementation of an inherited abstract method. We say a method is *implemented* if it has a method body. If a subclass has no abstract methods and no unimplemented inherited abstract methods (and does not include the keyword abstract in its class definition), then the subclass is no longer abstract, and thus its instances can be created.

abstract superclass

An abstract class must include the keyword abstract in its definition. Notice that the abstract class Student has an incomplete definition because the class includes the abstract method computeCourseGrade that does not have a method body. The intent is to let its subclasses provide the implementation of the compute-CourseGrade method. If a subclass does not provide an implementation of the inherited abstract method, the subclass is also an abstract class, and therefore, no instances of the subclass can be created. Since an abstract class can only make sense when it is a superclass, we frequently use the term *abstract superclass*.

Is the **Math** class an abstract class? It is true that we cannot create an instance of the **Math** class, but it is not an abstract class. If a class is abstract, then you cannot create an instance of the class, but not being able to create an instance does not necessarily imply that the class is abstract. The intent of an abstract class is to define code common to all its subclasses and leave some portions, that is, abstract methods, to be completed by the individual subclasses. We classify the **Math** class as a noninstantiable class, a class for which we cannot create an instance. Notice that an abstract class is a noninstantiable class by definition, but the reverse is not always true. There are noninstantiable classes, for example, the **Math** class, that are not abstract. If you want define a noninstantiable class, then simply declare a private constructor with no arguments and declare no other constructors for the class.

In a program diagram, we represent an abstract class by using the keyword abstract. The Student abstract superclass is drawn as

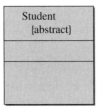

Case 2: Student Does Not Have to Be Undergraduate or Graduate

For the second case, where a student does not have to be a graduate or an undergraduate student, we can design classes in two different ways. The first approach is to make the Student class instantiable. The second approach is to leave the Student class abstract and add a third subclass, say, OtherStudent, to handle a student who is neither a graduate nor an undergraduate student. Let's call students who are neither graduate nor undergraduate students *nonregular students*. Let's assume further that the nonregular students will receive a pass grade if their average test score is greater than or equal to 50. With the first approach, we define the Student class as

Not an abstract class anymore →

```
class Student {

    protected final static int NUM_OF_TESTS = 3;
    protected String           name;
    protected int[]            test;
    protected String           courseGrade;

    public Student( ) {

        this("No name");
    }

    public Student(String studentName) {

        name        = studentName;
        test        = new int[NUM_OF_TESTS];
        courseGrade = "****";
    }
```

Not an abstract method anymore →

```
    public void computeCourseGrade() {

        int total = 0;
        for (int i = 0; i < NUM_OF_TESTS; i++) {
            total += test[i];
        }

        if (total/NUM_OF_TESTS >= 50) {
            courseGrade = "Pass";
        } else {
```

```
            courseGrade = "No Pass";
         }
      }

      public String getCourseGrade( ) {
         return courseGrade;
      }

      public String getName( ) {
         return name;
      }

      public int getTestScore(int testNumber) {
         return test[testNumber-1];
      }

      public void setName(String newName) {
         name = newName;
      }

      public void setTestScore(int testNumber,int testScore){
         test[testNumber-1] = testScore;
      }
   }
```

The class is no longer abstract, and we can create an instance of Student to represent a nonregular student.

With the second approach, we leave the Student class abstract. To represent nonregular students, we define a third subclass called OtherStudent as follows:

```
   class OtherStudent extends Student {

      public void computeCourseGrade() {

         int total = 0;
         for (int i = 0; i < NUM_OF_TESTS; i++) {
            total += test[i];
         }

         if (total/NUM_OF_TESTS >= 50) {
            courseGrade = "Pass";
         } else {
            courseGrade = "No Pass";
         }
      }
   }
```

Figure 13.7 is a program diagram that includes the third subclass.

Which approach is better? There's no easy answer. It all depends on a given situation. To determine which approach is better for a given situation, we can ask ourselves which approach allows easier modification and extension. Consider, for example, which approach will facilitate easier modification if we have to add a new

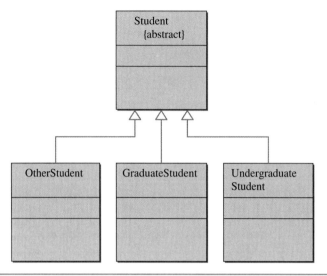

Figure 13.7 A program diagram of the abstract superclass **Student** and its three subclasses.

type of student, say, scholarship students. Or consider the case where the rule for assigning a course grade for the undergraduate and graduate students is modified; say, they become the same.

Finally, not all methods can be declared abstract.

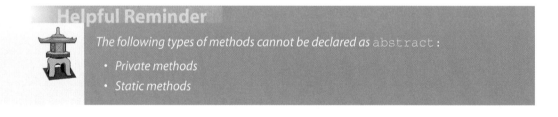

Helpful Reminder

The following types of methods cannot be declared as abstract*:*

- *Private methods*
- *Static methods*

Quick
CHECK

1. Can you create an instance of an abstract class?
2. Must an abstract class include an abstract method?
3. What is wrong with the following declaration?

```
class Vehicle {
    abstract public getVIN();
    ...
}
```

13.6 | Inheritance versus Interface

Java interface and inheritance are language features used to support object-oriented modeling. They are similar because they are both used to model an IS-A relationship. Consider, for example, the following class definitions:

```
class ButtonHandler implements ActionListener {
   . . .
}

class SavingsAccount extends Account {
   . . .
}
```

We say "ButtonHandler is an ActionListener" and "SavingsAccount is an Account." Because of this similarity, beginning programmers often have some difficulty in differentiating the two clearly. Although they are similar, their intended uses are quite different.

We use the Java interface to share common behavior (only method headers) among the instances of different classes. Take the ActionListener interface, for example. Completely unrelated classes (e.g., ButtonHandler and MyMenuFrame) can implement this interface. And one class can implement multiple interfaces. For example, we can define a single Person class that implements multiple interfaces such as Driver, Commuter, and Biker.

We use inheritance, on the hand, to share common code (including both data members and methods) among the instances of related classes. And a single subclass can extend at most one superclass. For example, the GraduateStudent and UndergraduateStudent classes are subclasses of the Student class, the Truck and Motorcycle classes are subclasses of the Vehicle class, and so forth. The superclasses include data members and/or methods that are shared by the subclasses. The IS-A relationship that exists between a subclass and its superclass is a specialization, as Truck is a specialized Vehicle. Such a specialization relationship does not exist with the Java interface.

Design Guidelines

Use the Java interface to share common behavior. Use the inheritance to share common code.

Design Guidelines

If an entity A is a specialized form of another entity B, then model them by using inheritance. Declare A as a subclass of B.

We must be careful not to mix up the use of service class and the inheritance. Beginners often make this mistake. Suppose you want to define a class that maintains a list of music CDs. Which of the following two definitions is a better design?

```
class CDManager extends java.util.ArrayList {
    ...
}

class CDManager {

    private List list;
    ..

}
```

The first version uses inheritance and defines a subclass of ArrayList. The second version defines a data member of type ArrayList. The first version is a misuse of inheritance. When we define a subclass A of superclass B, we must ask ourselves, Is A a B? Can we say CDManager is an ArrayList? No. The CDManager is not a specialized version of the ArrayList. The CDManager class simply needs to reuse the service provided by the ArrayList class. Thus, the second version is the proper design. We call this type of code reuse *code reuse by composition*.

code reuse by composition

Beyond the conceptual problem, defining the CDManager class as a subclass of ArrayList has practical weaknesses. Because it is a subclass, the client of the CDManager class can call any methods defined in the superclass ArrayList. But does it make sense for the client to call the method such as ensureCapacity? Another weakness is the difficulty in changing the implementation of the CDManager class. Suppose we need to modify the data structure class from ArrayList to HashMap for better performance. With the inheritance approach, any client that uses the inherited methods of ArrayList needs to be rewritten. With the composition approach, the client that uses only the methods defined for the CDManager class will continue to work without change. The change made from the ArrayList class to the HashMap class is encapsulated in the CDManager class and does not affect the clients.

13.7 Sample Development

Computing Course Grades

Let's develop a program that illustrates the use of **Student** and its subclasses **GraduateStudent** and **UndergraduateStudent.** The program will input student data from a user-designated text file, compute the course grades, and display the results. We assume the input text file is created by using a text editor or another application. For example, a teacher may have kept his student grades in a notebook. Instead of manually computing the grades with a pencil and calculator, he enters data into a text file and uses this program to compute the course grades. Another possible scenario is that the teacher uses some kind of application software that allows him to maintain student records. Suppose this application does not allow the teacher to use different formulas for computing the course grades of undergraduate and graduate students. In such a case, the teacher can export data to a text file and use our program to compute the course grades for undergraduate and graduate students using the different formulas. Using text files to transfer data from one application to another application is a very common technique used in software applications.

To focus on the data processing aspect of the program, we will keep its user interface very simple and leave it as Exercise 5 to design a better user interface. We will also leave the task of saving the results back to a text file in a different format (e.g., saving only the last name and the final course grade) or to an object-based file as Exercise 4.

Problem Statement

Write an application that reads in a text file organized in the manner shown below and displays the final course grades. The course grades are computed differently for the undergraduate and graduate students based on the formulas listed on page 734. The input text file format is as follows:

- *A single line is used for information on one student.*
- *Each line uses the format*

    <Type> <Name> <Test 1> <Test 2> <Test 3>

    where <Type> designates either a graduate or an undergraduate student, <Name> designates the student's first and last name, and <Test i> designates the ith test score.

- *End of input is designated by the word END. The case of the letters is insignificant.*

Figure 13.8 shows a sample input text file.

<Type>	<Name>	<Test 1>	<Test 2>	<Test 3>
U	John Doe	87	78	90
G	Jill Jones	90	95	87
G	Jack Smith	67	77	68
U	Mary Hines	80	85	80
U	Mick Taylor	76	69	79
END				

Figure 13.8 A sample text file containing student names and test scores. **U** at the beginning of a line designates an undergraduate student, and **G** designates a graduate student.

Overall Plan

We will implement a class that will

1. Read an input text file.

2. Compute the course grades.

3. Print out the result.

To read a text file, we will use the standard file I/O objects **File, FileReader,** and **BufferedReader.** To compute the course grades, we will use the **Student, Undergraduate,** and **Graduate** classes defined earlier in the chapter. The formulas for calculating the course grades are defined in their respective **computeCourseGrades** methods. Since the input file is a text file, we must create either a **Graduate** or an **Undergraduate** object for each line of input, so we will be able to call its **computeCourseGrades** method. To store the created student objects (instances of either **Graduate** or **Undergraduate**), we will use an array of **Student** to gain more practice on using arrays.

To focus on the inheritance and polymorphism topics, we will use two helper classes. The first is the **OutputBox** class which we use to display the course grades and save the result back to a text file. We use its **print** and **println** methods for output and **saveToFile** method to save the data to a text file. The **saveToFile** method saves the complete text in an **OutputBox** to a designated file. If the file already exists, then the original contents of the file will be replaced by the text currently shown in the **OutputBox.** Often, we need the capability to save the text in different format. For example, assuming the student information includes the student ID number, the teacher may want to save only the last four digits of the ID numbers and the final course grades so the results can be posted. If we wish to save the text in a different format, then we have to implement our own method with such capability.

The second helper class is the **MainWindow** class. We will name our main class **ComputeGrades,** and as another example of inheritance, we make it a subclass of **MainWindow.** The **MainWindow** is itself a subclass of **JFrame** and has the functionality of positioning itself at the center of the screen (among other features).

Here's our working design document:

program classes

Design Document: ComputeGrades	
Class	**Purpose**
ComputeGrades	The top-level control object manages other objects in the program. The class is a subclass of `MainWindow` from `javabook`. This class is the instantiable main class.
OutputBox	An `OutputBox` object is used to display the input data and computed course grades.

Design Document: ComputeGrades *(Continued)*	
Class	**Purpose**
Student, Under-graduateStudent, GraduateStudent	These are application logic objects for students. The Student class is an abstract superclass.
File, FileReader, BufferedReader	These are objects necessary for reading data from a text file.

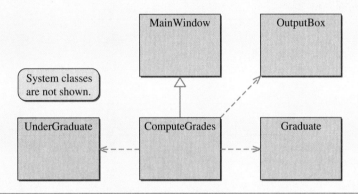

Figure 13.9 An object diagram of the **ComputeGrades** program.

Figure 13.9 is the program diagram.

Now let's think about the methods of **ComputeGrades.** What kinds of public methods should the class support? Since a **ComputeGrades** object is a top-level controller object, we need a single public method to initiate the operations. Let's define a method called **processData** that will carry out the three main tasks. The **main** method of **ComputeGrades** will call this method.

```
public static void main(String[] args) {
    ComputeGrades gradeComputer = new ComputeGrades();
    gradeComputer.processData();
}
```

The **processData** method will look something like this:

```
this.setVisible(true); //display itself, a main window
outputBox.setVisible(true);//and an outputBox

boolean success = readData();

if (success) {
    computeGrade();
    printResult();
```

```
      } else {
          print error message "File Input Error";
      }
```

The **readData** method returns **true** if the input data are read in correctly from a text file and the array of **Student** objects is properly created. Our working design document for the **ComputeGrades** class is as follows:

Design Document: The ComputeGrades Class		
Method	**Visibility**	**Purpose**
<constructor>	public	Creates and initializes the objects used by a ComputeGrades object.
processData	public	Displays itself and carries out three main tasks.
readData	private	Opens and reads data from a text file and creates an array of Student objects from the input data. If the operation is successful, returns true.
computeGrade	private	Scans through the array of Student objects and computes the course grades.
printResult	private	Prints out the student information along with the computed grades to an OutputBox.

We will develop the program in five incremental steps:

1. Start with the program skeleton. Define the skeleton **ComputeGrades** classes.

2. Implement the **printResult** method. Define any other methods necessary to implement **printResult.**

3. Implement the **computeGrade** method. Define any other methods necessary to implement **computeGrade.**

4. Implement the **readData** method. Define any other methods necessary to implement **readData.**

5. Finalize and look for improvements.

We defer the implementation of the hardest method, **readData,** until the last. Some programmers prefer to deal with the hardest aspect of the program first, and there's no strict rule for ordering the implementation steps. You should order the steps in a way with which you are most comfortable. However, this does not mean you can implement the methods at random. You must always plan the implementation steps carefully so the steps follow a logical sequence. For this program, we start with the output routine so we can use the final output routine for testing other methods, instead of defining a temporary output routine for testing purposes.

Step 1 Development: Program Skeleton

step 1
design

Let's begin with the data members and the constructors for the **ComputeGrades** class. We will start with the following data members:

```
private    OutputBox      outputBox;    //for output

private    Student[ ]     roster;       //for maintaining
                                        //student info
```

It is a straightforward operation to create the first four objects, but we need to think a little about the **roster** array. How big should the array be? There are several possibilities:

1. Create an array of an arbitrary size, say, 25.

2. Let the programmer pass the size in the constructor.

3. Do not create it in the constructor. Modify the input text file to include the size of an array in the first line.

Option 3 is not attractive because it will require a change in the problem specification. Moreover, requiring the size information in the input file will put a lot of burden on the user who must go over the text file and count the number of lines the file contains. Such a burdensome task should be left to a computer. So we will implement options 1 and 2. If the data cannot fit into an array of a predesignated size, then we will use the technique discussed in Chapter 9 to expand the array.

We declare a constant

```
private static final int   DEFAULT_SIZE = 25;
```

and declare the two constructors as

```
public ComputeGrades( ) {

   this( DEFAULT_SIZE );

}

public ComputeGrades(int arraySize) {

   super();   //an explicit call to the superclass constructor

   outputBox = new OutputBox( this );
   roster = new Student[arraySize];
}
```

Notice that we can't create **inFile, fileReader,** and **bufReader** until we know the actual file to open. We will create these objects in one of the methods we define later.

13.7 **Sample Development**—*continued*

step 1 code

For the skeleton program, we include temporary output statements in the private methods to verify that they are called correctly in the right order. Here's the skeleton:

```
/*
    Chapter 13 Sample Development: Compute Grades for Undergraduate
                                   and Graduate Students

    File: ComputeGrades.java
*/

import java.io.*;

//---------------------- STEP 1 ----------------------//
class ComputeGrades extends MainWindow {

    private static final int DEFAULT_SIZE = 25;

    private OutputBox    outputBox;

    private Student[]    roster;

    public ComputeGrades() {
        this (DEFAULT_SIZE);
    }

    public ComputeGrades(int arraySize) {
        super();    // an explicit call to the superclass constructor

        outputBox    = new OutputBox(this);

        roster       = new Student[arraySize];
    }

//-------------------------------
// Main
//-------------------------------
    public static void main(String[] args) {
      ComputeGrades gradeComputer = new ComputeGrades();
      gradeComputer.processData();
    }

    public void processData() {
        setVisible(true);
        outputBox.setVisible(true);

        boolean success = readData();
```

```
            if (success) {
                computeGrade();
                printResult();
            } else {
                outputBox.println("File Input Error");
            }
        }

    private void computeGrade() {

        outputBox.println("Inside computeGrade");   //TEMP
    }

    private void printResult() {

        outputBox.println("Inside printResult");   //TEMP
    }

    private boolean readData() {

        outputBox.pristln("Inside readData");   //TEMP
        return true;
    }
}
```

step 1 test

We execute the skeleton main class **ComputeGrades** for verification. When executed, we will see the top-level frame window (**ComputeGrades**) and an **OutputBox** appearing on the screen and the following messages in the **OutputBox:**

```
Inside readData
Inside computeGrade
Inside printResult
```

Step 2 Development: Implement the printResult **Method**

step 2
design

In the second development step, we add a routine that places the result in an **output-Box.** To implement and test this method, we need to create the **roster** array. We will include temporary code inside the **readData** method to build a test **roster** array. We can use **for** loops as in

```
     for (int i = 0; i < 15; i++) {
         roster[i] = new UndergraduateStudent( );
         roster[i].setName( "Undergrad # " + i );

         roster[i].setTestScore(1, 70 + i);
         roster[i].setTestScore(2, 75 + i);
```

The first half of the array is undergraduate students.

```
                    roster[i].setTestScore(3, 80 + i);
            }

            for (int i = 15; i < DEFAULT_SIZE; i++) {
                roster[i] = new GraduateStudent( );
                roster[i].setName( "Grad # " + i );

                roster[i].setTestScore(1, 80 + i);
                roster[i].setTestScore(2, 85 + i);
                roster[i].setTestScore(3, 90 + i);
            }
```

The second half of the array is graduate students.

to create a temporary **roster** for testing purposes.

Now, let's design the **printResult** method. When this method is called, we have the **roster** array built. The method scans through the array and retrieves the student data, using the **getName, getCourseGrade,** and **getTestScore** methods. Expressed in pseudocode, we have the following:

```
for each element i in the roster array {

    output the name of roster[i];

    output the test scores of roster[i];

    output the course grade of roster[i];

    skip to the next line;
}
```

How should we terminate the loop? We should realize first that the **roster** array may or may not be full. For example, its default size is 25, but the actual number of elements may be less than 25, so using the value of **roster.length** will not work. Since **roster** is an array of objects, one possible way to express the loop is as follows:

```
while ( roster[i] != null ) {

    //output roster[i] information
}
```

One problem with this **while** loop is that we must have at least one empty slot in the array for the loop to terminate correctly. We can improve it by using the **length** value as

```
while ( i < roster.length && roster[i] != null ) {
    . . .
}
```

Another possibility is to keep the count, which we set in the **readData** method. This count will be a data member of type **int.** Let's call this count variable

studentCount. Then the processing loop becomes

```
for (int i = 0; i < studentCount; i++) {

    //output roster[i] information
}
```

We will adopt this approach because having this count information is useful for other purposes. For example, if we want to compute the percentage of students passing the course, we can use **studentCount** to compute it. If we don't have this variable, then every time we need to compute the percentage, we have to find out the number of students in the **roster** array.

Finally, to print out student information so the data will align properly, we will output the control character **\t** (for tab). For a simple output like this, sending tabs to output will work fine. For a more elaborate output, we can use the **Ch6Format** class or the **Format** class from the author-provided **javabook** package.

step 2 code   Here's the step 2 code. Notice we add the declaration for a new data member **studentCount,** and this data member is initialized to 0 in the constructor.

```java
/*
    Chapter 13 Sample Development: Compute Grades for Undergraduate
                                    and Graduate Students

    File: ComputeGrades.java

*/

import java.io.*;
import javabook.*;

//---------------------- STEP 2 ------------------------//
class ComputeGrades extends MainWindow {

    ...
    private int         studentCount;

    ...
    public ComputeGrades(int arraySize) {
        ...
        studentCount = 0;
    }
    ...

    private void printResult() {

        for (int i = 0; i < studentCount; i++) {

            //print one student
            outputBox.print (roster[i].getName());
```

```
        for (int testNum = 1; testNum <= Student.NUM_OF_TESTS;
                                                 testNum++) {

            outputBox.print("\t" + roster[i].getTestScore (testNum));
        }

        outputBox.println("\t" + roster[i].getCourseGrade());
    }
}

private boolean readData() {
    outputBox.printLine("Inside readData");   //TEMP

    //TEMP
    //      Create a temporary roster array to
    //      test the printResult method.
    //
    for (int i = 0; i < 15; i++) {
        roster[i] = new UndergraduateStudent();
        roster[i].setName("Undergrad # " + i);

        roster[i].setTestScore(1, 70 + i);
        roster[i].setTestScore(2, 80 + i);
        roster[i].setTestScore(3, 90 + i);

    }
    for (int i = 15; i < DEFAULT_SIZE; i++) {
        roster[i] = new GraduateStudent();
        roster[i].setName("Grad # " + i);

        roster[i].setTestScore(1, 80 + i);
        roster[i].setTestScore(2, 85 + i);
        roster[i].setTestScore(3, 90 + i);

    }

    studentCount = DEFAULT_SIZE;

    return true;
    }
}
```

step 2 test

We verify two items in this step. First, the temporary **readData** method includes creating student objects and calling their methods. Correct execution will verify that we are including the correct student classes and using their methods properly. Second, the **printResult** method should display the output as intended. Since we have not implemented the **computeGrade** method, we will see four asterisks for the course grades. We have to run the program several times and adjust the display format. Also, it is important to try different values for names and test scores before moving to the next step.

Step 3 Development: Implement the computeGrade Method

step 3
design

The functionality of computing the course grades is embedded inside the student classes, specifically, inside the respective **computeCourseGrade** methods of the **GraduateStudent** and **UndergraduateStudent** classes. Therefore, all we need to do in the **computeGrade** method is to scan through the **roster** array and call the element's **computeCourseGrade** method. This simplicity is a direct result of polymorphism.

step 3 code

Here's the listing. The only addition is the **computeGrade** method.

```
/*
    Chapter 13 Sample Development: Compute Grades for Undergraduate
                                 and Graduate Students

    File: ComputeGrades.java

*/

import java.io.*;

//----------------------- STEP 3 -----------------------//
class ComputeGrades extends MainWindow {

    ...

    private void computeGrade() {

        for (int i = 0; i < studentCount; i++) {
            roster[i].computeCourseGrade();
        }
    }
    ...
}
```

step 3 test

We repeat the same testing routines of step 2. Instead of seeing four asterisks for the course grades, we should be seeing correct values. To make the verification easy, we can set the fixed test scores for all students. Make sure you assign test scores that will result in students both passing and not passing. Don't forget to try out end cases such as zero for all three test scores. What about negative test scores? Will the student classes handle them correctly? If we identify serious problems with the **Student** classes at this point, we may have to suspend our development until we correct the **Student** class.

Step 4 Development: Implement the readData **Method**

step 4
design

We will now design the core function of the class, the **readData** method. We can express the overall logic of the method in pseudocode as

```
get the filename from the user;

if (the filename is provided)
    read in data and build the roster array;
else
    output an error message;
```

We will use a **JFileChooser** object from the standard **javax.swing** package to let the user specify the file. If the user cancels this dialog, then **null** is returned. In this case, we print out an error message and stop. If the user specifies a file, then we pass this information to a private method **buildRoster,** which will read data from the designated file and build the **roster** array.

The **buildRoster** method will read one line of data from the designated file at a time, and for each line of data, it creates an appropriate student object (an instance of **GraduateStudent** if the type is **G** and an instance of **UndergraduateStudent** if the type is **U**). The counter **studentCount** is incremented by 1 after each line is processed. When the line contains the terminator **END,** the method completes its execution. If the data in a line do not conform to the designated format, then the line is ignored. The method, expressed in pseudocode, is as follows:

```
try {
    set bufReader for input;

    while ( !done ) {
        line = get next line;

        if (line is END) {
            done = true;
        } else {
            student = createStudent( line );

            if (student != null) {
                roster[studentCount] = student;
                                            //add to roster
                studentCount++;
            }
        }
    }
}
```

createStudent will return **null** if the **line** does not conform to the designated format.

```
catch (IOException e) {
   output an error message;
}
```

We use the **try–catch** block because the creation of the **BufferedReader** object **bufReader** from a given filename could result in an exception. The **createStudent** method accepts a **String** argument, which is one line of the input file, and returns an instance of either **GraduateStudent** or **UndergraduateStudent** depending on the type specified in the line. If there's an error in the input line, then **createStudent** returns **null.** Instead of terminating the whole program, we will simply ignore the lines that do not conform to the specified format.

In a very simplified form, the **createStudent** method looks like this:

```
type = first element of inputLine;

if (type.equals(UNDER_GRAD) || type.equals(GRAD)) {
   student = newStudentWithData( inputLine );
} else { //invalid type is encountered
   student = null;
}
return student;
```

> **newStudentWithData** will return **null** if the **inputLine** contains invalid data.

The top statement requires us to extract the first item in the input line (**String**). How should we do it? The **newStudentWithData** method, which creates an instance of **GraduateStudent** or **UndergraduateStudent** and assigns data to it, also requires an operation to extract individual elements of data from a single line. We can write our own string processing routine to parse a given line and extract data on type, name, and test scores, but there's a better solution. We can use a standard class called **StringTokenizer** from the **java.util** package. We will take a quick detour to explain this class. Instead of using the **StringTokenizer** class, we could use the pattern-matching techniques with the **Pattern** and **Matcher** classes. The **StringTokenizer** class, however, is suitable for a case such as this, where we want to extract tokens from a given string.

String-Tokenizer

A **StringTokenizer** object is used to extract tokens from a given string. A *token* is a string of characters separated by *delimiter characters*, or simply *delimiters*. Any character can be designated as a delimiter, but space is the most commonly used delimiter. By default, a **StringTokenizer** object uses a white space (blank, tab, new line, or return) as its delimiter. Here's an example. The following code

```
String inputString
        = "I drink   100 cups of coffee every morning.";

StringTokenizer parser = new StringTokenizer(inputString);

while ( parser.hasMoreTokens() )  {
   System.out.println( parser.nextToken() );
}
```

will print out

```
I
drink
100
cups
of
coffee
every
morning.
```

The **hasMoreTokens** method returns **true** if there are more tokens remaining in **parser,** and the **nextToken** method returns the next token in **parser.** The **nextToken** method throws a **NoSuchElementException** if there is no token to return. Please refer to a **java.util** reference manual for more information on **StringTokenizer.**

Take my *Advice*

It's great if you already know about **StringTokenizer,** but if you don't, you're out of luck. You would end up programming the functionality of **StringTokenizer** yourself, redoing something that has been done already. That's always a challenge for everybody, not just for beginners. Whenever you encounter a situation that seems to call for a common programming task, first look up the Java API reference manuals. You also can ask your classmates, teaching assistant, or instructor for guidance. They may know something. You should also make a habit of browsing the Java API reference manuals so you will have general knowledge about the standard classes. The key is always to look for the existing classes to reuse.

Now let's get back to the design. Using a **StringTokenizer** object, we can express the **createStudent** method as

```
StringTokenizer parser = new StringTokenizer( line );
String          type;

try {
    type   = parser.nextToken();

    if (type.equals(UNDER_GRAD) || type.equals(GRAD)) {
        student = newStudentWithData(type, parser);
    } else  { //invalid type is encountered
        student = null;
    }

} catch (NoSuchElementException e) { //no token
```

```
        student = null;
    }
    return student;
```

A private **newStudentWithData** method accepts a **String** that specifies the type of student and a **StringTokenizer** object. The method creates an instance of **UndergraduateStudent** or **GraduateStudent** and assigns data to the object by calling the **StringTokenizer** object's **nextToken** method repeatedly:

```
//type and parser are the parameters
try {
    if (type.equals(UNDER_GRAD)) {
        student = new UndergraduateStudent();
    } else {
        student = new GraduateStudent();
    }

    set the student name //use parser.nextToken() to
                         //extract data from a line

    set the student test scores

} catch (Exception e) { //thrown by parser.nextToken() or
    student = null;     //Integer.parseInt(...)
}

return student;
```

Our design document for the **ComputeGrades** class now includes three more private methods:

Design Document: The ComputeGrades Class		
Method	**Visibility**	**Purpose**
. . .	. . .	. . .
buildRoster	private	Reads one line of data from the designated file at a time; and for each line of data, creates an appropriate student object. If the data in a line do not conform to the designated format, then the line is ignored.
createStudent	private	Creates a student object by calling newStudentWithData if the type in the input line is U or G. If successful, returns the created student. Otherwise returns null.
newStudentWithData	private	Creates an instance of UndergraduateStudent or GraduateStudent and assigns data to the object by calling the StringTokenizer object's nextToken method repeatedly.

step 4 code

Here's the complete step 4 code:

```
/*
    Chapter 13 Sample Development: Compute Grades for Undergraduate
                                    and Graduate Students

    File: ComputeGrades.java

*/

import java.io.*;
import java.util.*;
import javax.swing.*;

//------------------------ STEP 4 ---------------------------//
class ComputeGrades extends MainWindow {

    private static final int DEFAULT_SIZE = 25;

    private static final String UNDER_GRAD = "U";
    private static final String GRAD = "G";
    private static final String END_OF_FILE_STR = "END";

    private OutputBox    outputBox;
    private Student[]    roster;
    private int          studentCount;

    public ComputeGrades() {
        this (DEFAULT_SIZE);
    }

    public ComputeGrades(int arraySize) {
        super();    // an explicit call to the superclass constructor

        outputBox    = new OutputBox(this);

        roster       = new Student[arraySize];

        studentCount = 0;
    }


    //-----------------------------------
    // Main
    //-----------------------------------
```

```java
public static void main(String[] args) {
  ComputeGrades gradeComputer = new ComputeGrades();
  gradeComputer.processData();
}

public void processData() {
    setVisible(true);
    outputBox.setVisible(true);

    boolean success = readData();

    if (success) {
       computeGrade();
       printResult();
    } else {
       outputBox.println("File Input Error");
    }
}

private boolean buildRoster(String filename) {
    String   inputLine;
    Student student;

    File           inFile;
    FileReader     fileReader;
    BufferedReader bufReader;

    boolean status  = true;
    boolean done    = false;

    try {
       inFile = new File(filename);
       fileReader = new FileReader(inFile);
       bufReader = new BufferedReader(fileReader);

       while ( !done ) {

          inputLine = bufReader.readLine(); //read one line

          if (inputLine.equalsIgnoreCase(END_OF_FILE_STR)) {
             done = true;
          }
          else {
             student = createStudent(inputLine);

             if (student != null) {
                roster[studentCount] = student;
```

```
                          studentCount++;
                    }
                }
            } // while

        bufReader.close();
    }
    catch (IOException e) {
        status = false;
    }

    return status;
}

private void computeGrade() {
    for (int i = 0; i < studentCount; i++) {
        roster[i].computeCourseGrade();
    }
}

private Student createStudent(String line) {
    Student        student;
    StringTokenizer  parser = new StringTokenizer(line);
    String         type;

    try {
        type = parser.nextToken();

        if (type.equals(UNDER_GRAD) || type.equals(GRAD)) {

            student = newStudentWithData(type, parser);

        } else {

            student = null;
        }
    } catch (NoSuchElementException e) { //no token
        student = null;
    }

    return student;
}

private Student newStudentWithData(String type,
                                   StringTokenizer parser) {
    Student student;
```

```java
    try {
        if (type.equals(UNDER_GRAD)) {

            student = new UndergraduateStudent();

        } else {

            student = new GraduateStudent();
        }

        //set the student name
        String  firstName  = parser.nextToken();
        String  lastName   = parser.nextToken();

        student.setName(firstName + " " + lastName);

        //set the student test scores
        for (int testNum = 1; testNum <= Student.NUM_OF_TESTS;
                                               testNum++) {
            student.setTestScore(testNum, Integer.parseInt(
                                    parser.nextToken()));
        }
    } catch (Exception e) { //either parser.nextToken() or
                            //Integer.parseInt(...)  thrown exception
        student = null;
    }

    return student;

}

private void printResult() {

    for (int i = 0; i < studentCount; i++) {

        //print one student
        outputBox.print (roster[i].getName());

        for (int testNum = 1; testNum <= Student.NUM_OF_TESTS;
                                                testNum++) {

            outputBox.print("\t" + roster[i].getTestScore (testNum));
        }

        outputBox.println("\t" + roster[i].getCourseGrade());
    }
}

private boolean readData() {
    //get file to open
```

13.7 **Sample Development**—*continued*

```
JFileChooser fileChooser = new JFileChooser(".");
                      //start the listing from the current directory

int returnVal = fileChooser.showOpenDialog(this);

boolean result = false;

if(returnVal == JFileChooser.APPROVE_OPTION) {
    String filename
            = fileChooser.getSelectedFile().getAbsolutePath();

    if (filename != null) {

        result = buildRoster(filename);
    }
}

return result;
    }
}
```

step 4 test   We run through a more complete testing routine in this step. We need to run the program for various types of input files. Some of the possible file contents are as follows:

Step 4 Test Data	
Test File File with 5 to 20 entries of student information with all lines in correct format	**Purpose** Test the normal case
File with 5 to 20 entries of student information with some lines in incorrect format	Test that `readData` and supporting methods handle the error case properly
File with no entries	Test that `buildRoster` method handles the error case properly
File with more than 25 entries.	Test that `readData` and supporting methods handle the case where the number of entries is larger than the default size for the `roster` array

Step 5 Development: Finalize and Improve

program
review

As always, we will finalize the program by correcting any remaining errors, inconsistency, or unfinished methods. We also look for improvement in the last step. One improvement we can always look for relates to the length of the methods. Although there are no hard rules for the length, a method should not be any longer than a single page. The **buildRoster** and **newStudentWithData** methods are close to the maximum. If we notice the method is getting longer in the coding stage, we may want to rethink our design. For example, if the **buildRoster** method becomes too big, then we can define a new method that takes care of a portion of the method, such as moving the if–then–else statement in the method to a new method.

One problem that remains (which would have been identified in step 4 testing) is the missing method for expanding the **roster** array when the input file includes more student entries than the set default size of 25. We leave this method as Exercise 3. We also leave some of the possible improvements as exercises.

Summary

- Inheritance and polymorphism are powerful language features to develop extensible and modifiable code.
- Inheritance mechanism is used to share common code among the related classes.
- Inheritance is different from the Java interface, which is used to share common behavior among unrelated classes.
- The third visibility modifier is the protected modifier.
- If no instances are created from a superclass, then define the superclass as an abstract class.
- Polymorphic messages tell us that the method executed in response to the message will vary according to the class to which the object belongs.
- The first statement in a constructor of a subclass must be a call to a constructor of the superclass. If the required statement is not made explicitly, then the statement to call the default constructor of the superclass is inserted automatically by the Java compiler.
- The standard class described or used in this chapter is StringTokenizer.

Key Concepts

superclass and subclass	abstract superclass
inheritance	abstract methods
inheritance and constructors	polymorphism
inheritance and visibility modifiers	inheritance versus interface

1. Consider the following class definitions. Identify invalid statements.

```
class Car {
    public    String    make;
    protected int        weight;
    private   String     color;

    ...
}

class ElectricCar extends Car {
    private   int    rechargeHour;

    public ElectricCar( ) {

       ...
    }

    //copy constructor
    public ElectricCar (ElectricCar car) {
        this.make       = car.make;
        this.weight     = car.weight;
        this.color      = new String( car.color );
        this.rechargeHour= car.rechargeHour;
    }

    ...

}

class TestMain {
    public static void main (String[] args) {
        Car          myCar;
        ElectricCar myElecCar;

        myCar = new Car();
        myCar.make = "Chevy";
        myCar.weight = 1000;
        myCar.color = "Red";

        myElecCar = new ElectricCar();
        myCar.make = "Chevy";
        myCar.weight = 500;
        myCar.color = "Silver";
    }
}
```

2. Consider the following class definitions. Identify which calls to the constructor are invalid.

```
class Car {
    public    String    make;
    protected int        weight;
    private   String     color;
```

```
      private Car (String make, int weight, String color) {
          this.make   = make;
          this.weight = weight;
          this.color  = color;
      }

      public Car ( ) {
          this( "unknown", -1, "white" );
      }

  class ElectricCar extends Car {
      private   int    rechargeHour;

      public ElectricCar( ) {
          this( 10 );
      }

      private ElectricCar(int charge ) {
          super( );
          rechargeHour = charge;
      }
  }

  class TestMain {
      public static void main (String[] args) {

          Car            myCar1,  myCar2;
          ElectricCar myElec1, myElec2;

          myCar1  = new Car();
          myCar2  = new Car("Ford", 1200, "Green");

          myElec1 = new ElectricCar( );
          myElec2 = new ElectricCar(15);
      }
  }
```

3. In the ComputeGrades sample program, we set the default size of the roster array to 25. Modify the program so the size of the array will be increased if the input file contains more than 25 students. You need to add a method that expands the array, say, by 50 percent. The technique to expand an array was discussed in Chapter 10.

4. Extend the ComputeGrades sample program by storing the roster array using ObjectOutputStream. To allow the user to create and read the data using any text editor, add the menu choices Import and Export, which will read in a text file (this is how the original ComputeGrades works) and write out data in ASCII format to a text file.

5. Extend the ComputeGrades sample program to include menu choices Save, Open, and Quit. With the current program, you can open one file for each execution of the program. Extend the program so the user can open more than one file by selecting the menu choice Open repeatedly. Selecting the

menu choice Save will allow the user to save the computed results to a file she or he specifies.

6. How would you modify the ComputeGrades sample program if the formula for computing the course grade is different for freshmen, sophomore, junior, and senior undergraduate students? Would you design four subclasses of UndergraduateStudent? Or would you modify the body of the computeCourseGrade method of UndergraduateStudent? Discuss the pros and cons of each approach.

7. In the Chapter 5 sample development, we defined the DrawableShape class that includes a method to draw one of the three possible shapes—rectangle, rounded rectangle, or ellipse. Modify the DrawableShape class as a super-class of the three subclasses Rectangle, RoundedRectangle, and Ellipse. The actual drawing of a shape is done by the drawShape method defined in each of the three subclasses. Using the DrawingBoard helper class from Chapter 5 and the four classes defined in this exercise, write a screensaver program that draws 10 rectangles, 15 rounded rectangles, and 20 ellipses of various sizes. All shapes will move smoothly across the screen.

Development Exercises

For the following exercises, use the incremental development methodology to implement the program. For each exercise, identify the program tasks, create a design document with class descriptions, and draw the program diagram. Map out the development steps at the start. Present any design alternatives and justify your selection. Be sure to perform adequate testing at the end of each development step.

8. Write a personal finance manager program that maintains information on your bank accounts. Incorporate these rules:

   - For the savings accounts, you can make a maximum of three withdrawals in a month without incurring a fee. The bank charges $1.00 for every withdrawal after the third.

   - For the checking accounts, the bank charges $0.50 for every check you write for the first 20 checks (i.e., withdrawals) in a month. After that, there will be no charge.

   You should be able to open and save account information to a file. You should be able to list all transactions of a given account or of all accounts. Include appropriate menus to select the options supported by the program. Consider using the Date class to record the date of transactions. The Date class is from the java.util package. Please refer to a java.util reference manual for information on this class.

9. Extend the address book sample program from Chapter 9. Instead of managing a single type of Person, incorporate additional types of persons such as PersonalFriend and BusinessAssociate. Define these classes as a subclass of Person. Design carefully to decide whether the Person class will be an abstract class.

10. Consider an asset-tracking program that will track four types of assets: electronic appliances, automobiles, furniture, and compact disks. What classes would you design for the program? Would you define four unrelated classes or one superclass and four subclasses? If you design a superclass, will it be an abstract superclass?

11. Implement the asset-tracking program of Exercise 10. Allow the user to add, modify, and delete electronic appliances, automobiles, furniture, and compact disks. Allow the user to list the assets by category and search for an asset by its serial number.

12. Extend the asset-tracking program of Exercise 11 by adding an object I/O capability.

13. Write an application that reads daily temperatures for 12 months and allows the user to get statistics. Support at least three options: monthly average of a given month, yearly average, and lowest and highest temperatures of a given month. Use a text file to store temperatures. A line in the text file contains daily temperatures for one month. The first line in the text file contains temperatures for January, the second line for February, and so forth. Use StringTokenizer to parse a line into temperatures of type float. For a data structure, consider using either an array of Month or a two-dimensional array of float. Month is a class you define yourself.

14 Advanced GUI

W e introduced graphical user interface objects from the java.awt and javax.swing packages and described event-driven programming in Chapter 7. We will continue the discussion of GUI, introducing more advanced materials in this chapter. Next to the action event, which we introduced in Chapter 7, arguably the most common events to handle in writing GUI-based programs are the mouse (e.g., clicking of a mouse button) and the mouse motion (e.g., moving a mouse) events. We will describe how the mouse-related events are handled in this chapter. In Chapter 7, we used absolute positioning to place GUI objects on a container. Although absolute positioning is acceptable for a simple GUI, for a more manageable and flexible interface, it is more common to use layout managers. We will describe the use of layout managers in this chapter. Finally, we will introduce other GUI objects.

14.1 | Handling Mouse Events

In this section we describe the handling of mouse events. Mouse events include such user interactions as moving the mouse, dragging the mouse (i.e., moving the mouse while the mouse button is being pressed), and clicking the mouse buttons.

Let's look at an example in which we display the x and y pixel coordinates of a location where a mouse button is pressed down. We will define a subclass of JFrame, named Ch14TrackMouseFrame, that handles the left mouse button click events, and we will use System.out to print out the location of mouse clicks. *Note:* For a system with a one-button mouse, we treat this button as the left mouse button.

A Ch14TrackMouseFrame object is an event source of mouse events. We will let this object be a mouse event listener also. For a Ch14TrackMouseFrame object to be a mouse event listener, its class must implement MouseListener. This interface has five abstract methods: mouseClicked, mouseEntered, mouseExited, mousePressed, and mouseReleased. The argument to all five methods is an instance of MouseEvent.

The class declaration for Ch14TrackMouseFrame will look like this:

```
class Ch14TrackMouseFrame extends Frame
                    implements MouseListener {
   ...
}
```

In the constructor we set the frame properties and register this frame as a mouse event listener of itself. The constructor is defined as

```
public Ch14TrackMouseFrame {
   //set the frame properties
   ...

   //set the output for printing out
   //the mouse click points
   output = System.out;
```

```
        //register itself as its mouse event listener
        addMouseListener(this);
    }
```

When the left mouse button is clicked, the mouseClicked method of its mouse event listener is called. In this method, we want to find out the *x* and *y* coordinates of the mouse click point and print out these values in output. To find the *x* and *y* coordinate values, we use the getX and getY methods of MouseEvent. So the mouseClicked method of Ch14TrackMouseFrame is defined as

```
    public void mouseClicked( MouseEvent event ) {
        int x, y;

        x = event.getX(); //return the x and y coordinates
        y = event.getY(); //of a mouse click point

        output.println("[" + x + "," + y + "]");
    }
```

This method is called every time the left mouse button is clicked, that is, the mouse button is pressed down and released. If we want to detect the mouse button press and release separately, then we can provide a method body to the mousePressed and mouseReleased methods. For example, if we define these methods as

```
    public void mousePressed( MouseEvent event ) {
        output.println("Down");
    }
```

and

```
    public void mouseReleased( MouseEvent event ) {
        output.println("Up");
    }
```

instead of empty method bodies, then we will see something like

```
Down
Up
[200,120]
```

when we click a mouse button.

Before we present the complete program, let's extend the mouseClicked method so that when the left mouse button is double-clicked, we will terminate the program. We check the number of button clicks by calling the getClickCount method of MouseEvent. Here's the method that terminates the program when a double-click occurs (a single mouse click will print out the location of a mouse click as before):

```
private static final int DOUBLE_CLICK = 2;

public void mouseClicked( MouseEvent event ) {

    if ( event.getClickCount() == DOUBLE_CLICK) {
        System.exit(0);

    } else {                    //print out mouse click location
        int x, y;

        x = event.getX();
        y = event.getY();

        output.println("[" + x + "," + y + "]");
    }
}
```

Because a double-click is a sequence of two single clicks, this method is called twice when you double-click. The getClickCount method returns 1 for the first call and returns 2 for the second call.

Here's the complete program listing:

```
/*

    Chapter 14 Sample Program: Tracks the mouse movement

    File: Ch14TrackMouseFrame.java

*/

import javax.swing.*;
import java.awt.*;
import java.awt.event.*;
import java.io.*;

class Ch14TrackMouseFrame extends JFrame implements MouseListener {

    private static final int FRAME_WIDTH    = 450;
    private static final int FRAME_HEIGHT   = 300;
    private static final int FRAME_X_ORIGIN = 150;
    private static final int FRAME_Y_ORIGIN = 250;
    private static final int DOUBLE_CLICK = 2;

    private PrintStream output;

    //-----------------------------------
    //     Main method
    //-----------------------------------
    public static void main(String[] args) {
```

```
        Ch14TrackMouseFrame frame = new Ch14TrackMouseFrame();
        frame.setVisible(true);
    }

    public Ch14TrackMouseFrame() {
        //set frame properties
        setTitle      ("TrackMouseFrame");
        setSize       (FRAME_WIDTH, FRAME_HEIGHT);
        setResizable (false);
        setLocation  (FRAME_X_ORIGIN, FRAME_Y_ORIGIN);

        setDefaultCloseOperation(EXIT_ON_CLOSE);

        //create an output for printing out
        //the mouse click points
        output = System.out;

        //register self as a mouse event listener
        addMouseListener( this );
    }

    public void mouseClicked(MouseEvent event) {
        if (event.getClickCount() == DOUBLE_CLICK) {
            System.exit(0);

        } else {
            int x, y;

            x = event.getX(); //get the x and y coordinates of
            y = event.getY(); //the mouse click point

            output.println("[" + x + "," + y + "]");
        }
    }

    public void mouseEntered   ( MouseEvent event ) { }
    public void mouseExited    ( MouseEvent event ) { }
    public void mousePressed   ( MouseEvent event ) {
        output.println("Down");
    }
    public void mouseReleased  ( MouseEvent event ) {
        output.println("Up");
    }
}
```

SketchPad

Let's try another example. This time, let's implement the SketchPad class we've seen in Chapter 2. To distinguish the class we define here from the original, we will call the class `Ch14SketchPad`. The basic idea of `Ch14SketchPad` is to keep track of three events:

1. The left mouse button is pressed down.
2. The right mouse button is pressed down.
3. The mouse is dragged.

Notice that we are processing mouse button presses, not clicks. (*Note:* For the Mac platform, a mouse button press is treated as the left button press, and the Command press is treated as the right button press. For a platform that supports three mouse buttons, the middle mouse button is also treated as the left mouse button.)

To implement this class, we will declare `Ch14SketchPad` to implement two interfaces: MouseListener and MouseMotionListener. Since we want a Ch14SketchPad frame to process mouse button clicks, we must implement the MouseListener interface. In addition, we need to implement the MouseMotionListener interface to track the mouse dragging. The MouseMotionListener interface includes two abstract methods: mouseDragged and mouseMoved. The argument to both methods is an instance of MouseEvent.

When a mouse button, either the left or right button, is pressed, the event listener's mousePressed is called. Let's study how we should implement this method. If the right mouse button is pressed, then we have to erase the current drawing. If the left mouse button is pressed, then it is the start of a new mouse drag, so we have to remember the location where the left button is pressed. To determine which mouse button is pressed inside the mousePressed method, we call the isMetaDown method of MouseEvent as

```
if ( event.isMetaDown() ) {
    //the right button is pressed
    . . .
}
```

The isMetaDown method returns true if the right button is pressed. We don't have a method such as isRightButtonPress in MouseEvent because not all platforms support the right mouse button. The Mac platform, for example, has only one mouse button, and for the Mac, the Command press is treated as the right mouse button press.

The code to erase the contents of the window is

```
if ( event.isMetaDown() ) {
    //the right button is pressed
    //so erase the contents
    Graphics  g = getGraphics();
    Rectangle r = getBounds();
    g.clearRect(0, 0, r.width, r.height);
    g.dispose();
}
```

We erase the contents by drawing a filled rectangle as big as the window itself with the rectangle filled in the background color. The getBounds method returns the size of a window.

If it is not a right mouse button press, then it is a left button press, so we remember the first position to draw a line.

```
if ( event.isMetaDown() ) {
    //the right button is pressed
    ...
} else {
    //remember the starting point of a new mouse drag
    last_x = x;
    last_y = y;
}
```

last_x and **last_y** are instance variables.

The position (*x*, *y*) is computed at the beginning of the mousePressed method as

```
int x = event.getX();
int y = event.getY();
```

The getX and getY methods of the MouseEvent class return the *x* and *y* coordinates, respectively, of the point where the mouse button is pressed.

Now, to process the mouse drag event, we need to define the mouseDragged method. From the argument object MouseEvent, we get a new position (*x*, *y*) and draw a line from the previous position to this new position, using the Graphics object g as follows:

```
g.drawLine(last_x, last_y, x, y);
```

After the drawing is done, we reset the variables

```
last_x = x;
last_y = y;
```

Similar to the mousePressed method, the mouseDragged method is called whether the mouse was dragged with the left or right button. So we need to include the if test

```
if (!event.isMetaDown() ) {
    //it's a left mouse button drag,
    //so draw a line
    ...
}
```

inside the method so the drawing will occur only for the left mouse button drag.

Here's a complete listing of the program:

```
/*
    Chapter 14 Sample Program: My SketchPad

    File: Ch14SketchPad.java

*/
```

```java
import javax.swing.*;
import java.awt.*;
import java.awt.event.*;

class Ch14SketchPad extends JFrame
                    implements MouseListener, MouseMotionListener {

    private static final int FRAME_WIDTH    = 450;
    private static final int FRAME_HEIGHT   = 300;
    private static final int FRAME_X_ORIGIN = 150;
    private static final int FRAME_Y_ORIGIN = 250;

    private int last_x;
    private int last_y;

//-----------------------------------
//    Main method
//-----------------------------------
    public static void main(String[] args) {
        Ch14SketchPad frame = new Ch14SketchPad();
        frame.setVisible(true);
    }

    public Ch14SketchPad( ) {
        //set frame properties
        setTitle   ("Chapter 14 SketchPad");
        setSize    ( FRAME_WIDTH, FRAME_HEIGHT );
        setResizable( false );
        setLocation ( FRAME_X_ORIGIN, FRAME_Y_ORIGIN );

        setDefaultCloseOperation(EXIT_ON_CLOSE);

        last_x = last_y = 0;

        addMouseListener( this );        //adds itself as mouse and
        addMouseMotionListener( this ); //mouse motion listener
    }

//-----------------------------------
// Mouse Event Handling
//-----------------------------------

    public void mousePressed( MouseEvent event ) {
        int x = event.getX();
        int y = event.getY();

        if ( event.isMetaDown() ) {
            //the right mouse button is pressed, so erase the contents
            Graphics    g = getGraphics();
```

```
            Rectangle   r = getBounds();
            g.clearRect(0, 0, r.width, r.height);
            g.dispose();
        } else {
            //the left mouse button is pressed,
            //remember the starting point of a new mouse drag
            last_x = x;
            last_y = y;
        }
    }

    public void mouseClicked ( MouseEvent event ) { }
    public void mouseEntered ( MouseEvent event ) { }
    public void mouseExited  ( MouseEvent event ) { }
    public void mouseReleased( MouseEvent event ) { }

//-----------------------------------
//  Mouse Motion Event Handling
//-----------------------------------

    public void mouseDragged( MouseEvent event ) {
        int x = event.getX();
        int y = event.getY();

        if ( !event.isMetaDown() ) {
            //don't process the right button drag
            Graphics g = getGraphics();

            g.drawLine(last_x, last_y, x, y);
            g.dispose();

            last_x = x;
            last_y = y;
        }
    }

    public void mouseMoved ( MouseEvent event ) { }
}
```

Quick
CHECK
√

1. Which listener object listens to mouse movements? Which listener object listens to mouse button presses and clicks?

2. What is the purpose of the **isMetaDown** method?

3. What is the difference between **mouseClicked** and **mousePressed**?

14.2 | Layout Managers and Panels

layout manager

We used absolute positioning and did not cover the layout managers in Chapter 7 because using a layout manager is advantageous in general, but knowing various layout managers is not indispensable for learning object-oriented and event-driven programming. Absolute positioning may be acceptable while learning object-oriented programming, but for building practical GUI-based Java programs, we must learn how to use layout managers effectively. In this section, we will cover the basic ones, specifically, FlowLayout, BorderLayout, and GridLayout. However basic they may be, combining them with the panels (instances of JPanel) will result in a decent layout acceptable in most applications.

JPanel

Remember that when we placed GUI components on a frame in earlier examples, we were actually placing them on the content pane of the frame. The default content pane of a frame is an instance of JPanel. Since a JPanel object is itself a GUI component, we can place a JPanel inside another JPanel. Each of these nested panels can be assigned a different layout manager. This capability of nesting panels and assigning different layout managers to them leads to an intricate layout of GUI components on a frame. We will first present the three layout managers with sample code and then explain how to use nested panels effectively with the layout managers.

You Might Want to Know

A benefit of using a layout manager is the automatic adjustment of GUI objects when their container (frame, dialog, applet, etc.) is resized. For example, if we place a **JButton** at the center of the container by using some layout manager, then this **JButton** will still be positioned at the center when the size of the container is changed. This automatic adjustment is important also when we consider running your program on different platforms, because by using a layout manager effectively we will get a more consistent look to our frames and dialogs across different platforms. With absolute positioning, a frame that looks nice on one platform may not appear as nice on another platform.

FlowLayout

The most basic layout is java.awt.FlowLayout. In using this layout, GUI components are placed in left-to-right order. When the component does not fit on the same line, left-to-right placement continues on the next line. As a default, components on each line are centered. When the frame containing the component is resized, the placement of components is adjusted accordingly. Figure 14.1 shows the placement of five buttons by using FlowLayout.

Before we add any components, we first assign the desired layout manager to the container, in this case the content pane of a frame, in the frame's constructor.

```
Container contentPane = getContentPane();
...
contentPane.setLayout(new FlowLayout());
```

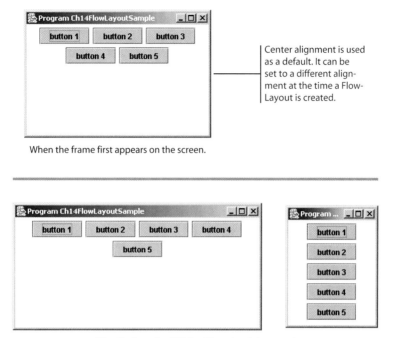

Center alignment is used as a default. It can be set to a different alignment at the time a Flow-Layout is created.

When the frame first appears on the screen.

After the frame's width is widened and shortened.

Figure 14.1 Placement of five buttons by using **FlowLayout** when the frame is first opened and after the frame is resized.

A container has a default layout manager assigned to it, but it is always safer to explicitly assign the desired layout manager ourselves. After the layout manager is set, we create five buttons and add them to the content pane.

```
JButton button1, button2, button3, button4, button5;
...
button1 = new JButton("button1");
//do the same for other buttons

contentPane.add(button1);
contentPane.add(button2);
//and so forth
```

Notice the default is center alignment. We can change it to left or right alignment as

```
contentPane.setLayout(new FlowLayout(FlowLayout.LEFT));
```

or

```
contentPane.setLayout(new FlowLayout(FlowLayout.RIGHT));
```

Here's the complete sample code:

```
/*
    Chapter 14 Sample Program: Illustrates the use of FlowLayout

    File: Ch14FlowLayoutSample.java

*/

import javax.swing.*;
import java.awt.*;
import java.awt.event.*;

class Ch14FlowLayoutSample extends JFrame {

    private static final int FRAME_WIDTH     = 300;
    private static final int FRAME_HEIGHT    = 200;
    private static final int FRAME_X_ORIGIN  = 150;
    private static final int FRAME_Y_ORIGIN  = 250;


//-----------------------------------
//      Main method
//-----------------------------------
    public static void main(String[] args) {
        Ch14FlowLayoutSample frame = new Ch14FlowLayoutSample();
        frame.setVisible(true);
    }

    public Ch14FlowLayoutSample() {
        Container contentPane;
        JButton   button1, button2, button3, button4, button5;

        //set the frame properties
        setSize       (FRAME_WIDTH, FRAME_HEIGHT);
        setTitle      ("Program Ch14FlowLayoutSample");
        setLocation   (FRAME_X_ORIGIN, FRAME_Y_ORIGIN);

        contentPane = getContentPane( );
        contentPane.setBackground( Color.white );
        contentPane.setLayout(new FlowLayout());

        //create and place four buttons on the content pane
        button1 = new JButton("button 1");
        button2 = new JButton("button 2");
        button3 = new JButton("button 3");
        button4 = new JButton("button 4");
        button5 = new JButton("button 5");
```

```
            contentPane.add(button1);
            contentPane.add(button2);
            contentPane.add(button3);
            contentPane.add(button4);
            contentPane.add(button5);

            //register 'Exit upon closing' as a default close operation
            setDefaultCloseOperation( EXIT_ON_CLOSE );
        }
    }
```

BorderLayout

The second layout manager is java.awt.BorderLayout. This layout manager divides the container into five regions: center, north, south, east, and west. Figure 14.2 shows five buttons placed in these five regions. The right frame in the figure is the state after it is resized. The north and south regions expand or shrink in height only, the east and west regions expand or shrink in width only, and the center region expands or shrinks on both height and width. Not all regions have to be occupied. Figure 14.3 shows the frame with only the center and east regions occupied with buttons.

We set the BorderLayout analogously as

```
            contentPane.setLayout(new BorderLayout());
```

When the frame first appears on the screen.

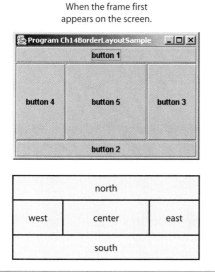

After the frame is resized.

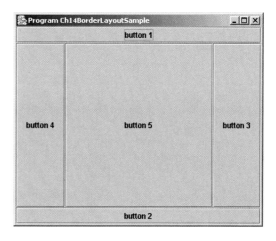

Figure 14.2 Placement of five buttons by using **BorderLayout** when the frame is first opened and after the frame is resized.

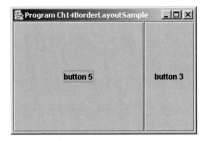

Figure 14.3 Placement of two buttons by using **BorderLayout.** Buttons are placed on the center and east regions.

and then we place the GUI components, in this case, buttons, with the second argument specifying the region.

```
contentPane.add(button1, BorderLayout.NORTH);
contentPane.add(button2, BorderLayout.SOUTH);
contentPane.add(button3, BorderLayout.EAST);
contentPane.add(button4, BorderLayout.WEST);
contentPane.add(button5, BorderLayout.CENTER);
```

The BorderLayout used in Figures 14.2 and 14.3 has no gaps between the regions, which is the default. We can specify the amount of vertical and horizontal gaps between the regions in pixels. For example, to leave 10-pixel-wide gaps and 20-pixel-high gaps between the regions, we create a BorderLayout object by passing these values as arguments to the constructor.

```
contentPane.setLayout(new BorderLayout(10, 20));
```

Here's the complete sample program:

```
/*
    Chapter 14 Sample Program: Illustrates the use of BorderLayout

    File: Ch14BorderLayoutSample.java

*/

import javax.swing.*;
import java.awt.*;
import java.awt.event.*;

class Ch14BorderLayoutSample extends JFrame {

    private static final int FRAME_WIDTH    = 300;
    private static final int FRAME_HEIGHT   = 200;
```

```
    private static final int FRAME_X_ORIGIN = 150;
    private static final int FRAME_Y_ORIGIN = 250;

//----------------------------------
//      Main method
//----------------------------------
    public static void main(String[] args) {
        Ch14BorderLayoutSample frame = new Ch14BorderLayoutSample();
        frame.setVisible(true);
    }

    public Ch14BorderLayoutSample() {
        Container contentPane;
        JButton   button1, button2, button3, button4, button5;

        //set the frame properties
        setSize     (FRAME_WIDTH, FRAME_HEIGHT);
        setTitle    ("Program Ch14BorderLayoutSample");
        setLocation (FRAME_X_ORIGIN, FRAME_Y_ORIGIN);

        contentPane = getContentPane( );
        contentPane.setBackground( Color.white );
        contentPane.setLayout(new BorderLayout());

        //contentPane.setLayout(new BorderLayout(/*hgap*/10, /*vgap*/10));

        //create and place four buttons on the content pane
        button1 = new JButton("button 1");
        button2 = new JButton("button 2");
        button3 = new JButton("button 3");
        button4 = new JButton("button 4");
        button5 = new JButton("button 5");

        contentPane.add(button1, BorderLayout.NORTH);
        contentPane.add(button2, BorderLayout.SOUTH);
        contentPane.add(button3, BorderLayout.EAST);
        contentPane.add(button4, BorderLayout.WEST);
        contentPane.add(button5, BorderLayout.CENTER);

        //register 'Exit upon closing' as a default close operation
        setDefaultCloseOperation( EXIT_ON_CLOSE );
    }
}
```

GridLayout   The third layout manager is java.awt.GridLayout. This layout manager places GUI components on equal-size $N \times M$ grids. Figure 14.4 shows five buttons placed on 2×3 grids. Components are placed in top-to-bottom, left-to-right order. The frame

When the frame first appears on the screen.

After the frame is resized.

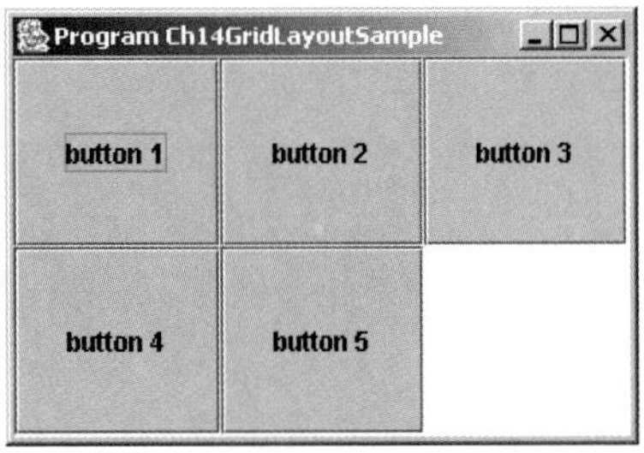

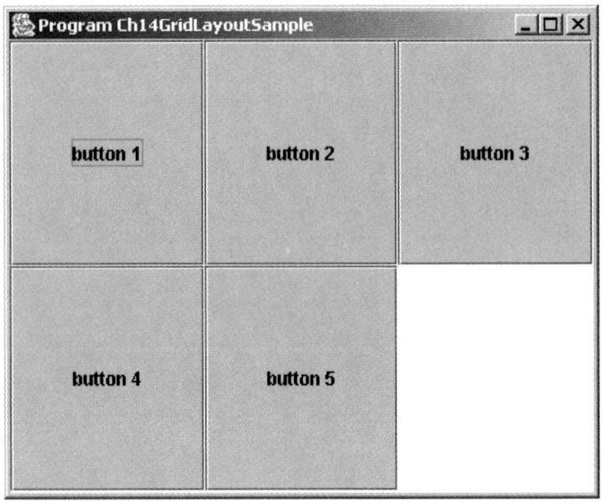

Figure 14.4 Placement of five buttons by using **GridLayout** of two rows and three columns when the frame is first opened and after the frame is resized.

on the right in Figure 14.4 is the state after it is resized. Notice the number of rows and columns remains the same, but the width and height of each region are changed.

To create a GridLayout object, we pass two arguments: number of rows and number of columns.

```
contentPane.setLayout(new GridLayout(2, 3));
```

We then place GUI components in the manner analogous to the one used for FlowLayout. If the value provided for the number of rows is nonzero, then the value we specify for the number of columns is actually irrelevant. The layout will create the designated number of rows and adjust the number of columns so that all components will fit in the designated number of rows. For example, placing the five buttons with any one of the following three statements will result in the same layout, namely, two rows of grids:

```
contentPane.setLayout(new GridLayout(2, 0));
contentPane.setLayout(new GridLayout(2, 1));
contentPane.setLayout(new GridLayout(2, 5));
```

Here's the complete program listing for Ch14GridLayoutSample:

```
/*
    Chapter 14 Sample Program: Illustrates the use of GridLayout

    File: Ch14GridLayoutSample.java

*/
```

```java
import javax.swing.*;
import java.awt.*;
import java.awt.event.*;

class Ch14GridLayoutSample extends JFrame {

    private static final int FRAME_WIDTH    = 300;
    private static final int FRAME_HEIGHT   = 200;
    private static final int FRAME_X_ORIGIN = 150;
    private static final int FRAME_Y_ORIGIN = 250;

//---------------------------------
//      Main method
//---------------------------------
    public static void main(String[] args) {
        Ch14GridLayoutSample frame = new Ch14GridLayoutSample();
        frame.setVisible(true);
    }

    public Ch14GridLayoutSample() {
        Container contentPane;
        JButton    button1, button2, button3, button4, button5;

        //set the frame properties
        setSize      (FRAME_WIDTH, FRAME_HEIGHT);
        setTitle     ("Program Ch14GridLayoutSample");
        setLocation  (FRAME_X_ORIGIN, FRAME_Y_ORIGIN);

        contentPane = getContentPane( );
        contentPane.setBackground( Color.white );
        contentPane.setLayout(new GridLayout(2,3));

        //create and place four buttons on the content pane
        button1 = new JButton("button 1");
        button2 = new JButton("button 2");
        button3 = new JButton("button 3");
        button4 = new JButton("button 4");
        button5 = new JButton("button 5");

        contentPane.add(button1);
        contentPane.add(button2);
        contentPane.add(button3);
        contentPane.add(button4);
        contentPane.add(button5);

        //register 'Exit upon closing' as a default close operation
        setDefaultCloseOperation( EXIT_ON_CLOSE );
    }
}
```

1. How does the flow layout place the components?
2. Which layout manager divides the container into grids of equal size?
3. Write a statement to create a border layout with 20-pixel gaps in both horizontal and vertical directions.

14.3 | Effective Use of Nested Panels

In this section, we will discuss how to nest panels effectively to get a desired layout of GUI components. It is possible, but very difficult, to place all GUI components on a single JPanel or other types of containers. A better approach is to use multiple panels, placing panels inside other panels. To illustrate this technique, we will create two sample frames that contain nested panels. The first sample, shown in Figure 14.5, provides the user interface for playing Tic Tac Toe. And the second sample, shown in Figure 14.6, provides the user interface for playing HiLo. Note that we only illustrate the visual layout using nested panels. The sample frames do not include any code for actually playing the games.

The frame shown in Figure 14.5 has four panels. The topmost JPanel, the content pane of the frame, has a border layout. The content pane's center region is occupied by an instance of Ch14TicTacToePanel named gamePanel. Ch14TicTac-ToePanel is itself a nested panel. We will design and implement this panel in Section 14.4. The content pane's east region is occupied by an instance of another JPanel named controlPanel. A border layout is used for this panel. The north region of controlPanel is occupied by another JPanel named scorePanel, and the south region is occupied by a JButton. The layout for scorePanel is set to a grid layout with four grids, each occupied by a JLabel object. The nesting relationship is shown in Figure 14.7.

Figure 14.5 A sample frame that contains nested panels. Four **JPanel** objects are used in this frame.

Figure 14.6 Another sample frame that contains nested panels. Five **JPanel** objects are used in this frame.

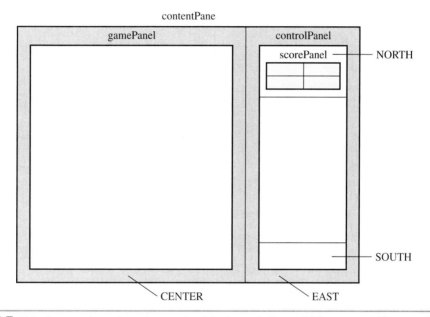

Figure 14.7 This diagram shows how the panels of the frame in Figure 14.5 are nested. There are four **JPanel** objects. We associate a border layout to both **contentPane** and **controlPanel** and grid layout to **scorePanel.** The **gamePanel** is a specialized **JPanel** (it's a subclass of **JPanel**) that uses a grid layout.

When we nest panels, it is often very useful to mark their borders. In this sample frame, we use a titled border for scorePanel and a lowered bevel border for gamePanel. A titled border draws a rectangle around the panel and displays a designated title. We create a titled border by calling the class method createTitledBorder of the BorderFactory class and assign to a panel by calling the setBorder method. Here's the statement:

```
scorePanel.setBorder(
        BorderFactory.createTitledBorder("Scores:"));
```

A lowered bevel border gives an illusion of the panel being recessed into the frame. Here's the statement to create and set the lowered bevel border to gamePanel:

```
gamePanel.setBorder(
                BorderFactory.createLoweredBevelBorder());
```

Additional types of borders, such as line border, matte border, and raised bevel border, are available. For more information, please consult the documentation for the BorderFactory class.

Here's the complete listing of the program:

```java
/*
    Chapter 14 Sample Program: Illustrates the use of
                        nested panels

    File: Ch14NestedPanels1.java
*/
import javax.swing.*;
import java.awt.*;
import java.awt.event.*;

class Ch14NestedPanels1 extends JFrame {

    private static final int FRAME_WIDTH    = 500;
    private static final int FRAME_HEIGHT   = 350;
    private static final int FRAME_X_ORIGIN = 150;
    private static final int FRAME_Y_ORIGIN = 250;

    public static void main(String[] args) {
        Ch14NestedPanels1 frame = new Ch14NestedPanels1();
        frame.setVisible(true);
    }

    public Ch14NestedPanels1() {
        Container           contentPane;
        Ch14TicTacToePanel  gamePanel;
        JPanel              controlPanel;
        JPanel              scorePanel;

        //set the frame properties
        setSize       (FRAME_WIDTH, FRAME_HEIGHT);
        setTitle      ("Program Ch14NestedPanels1");
        setLocation   (FRAME_X_ORIGIN, FRAME_Y_ORIGIN);

        contentPane = getContentPane( );
        contentPane.setLayout(new BorderLayout(10, 0));

        gamePanel = new Ch14TicTacToePanel();
        gamePanel.setBorder(BorderFactory.createLoweredBevelBorder());
        controlPanel = new JPanel();
        controlPanel.setLayout(new BorderLayout( ));
```

```
contentPane.add(gamePanel, BorderLayout.CENTER);
contentPane.add(controlPanel, BorderLayout.EAST);

scorePanel = new JPanel();
scorePanel.setBorder(BorderFactory.createTitledBorder("Scores:"));
scorePanel.setLayout(new GridLayout(2, 2));
scorePanel.add(new JLabel("Player 1:"));
scorePanel.add(new JLabel("      0"));
scorePanel.add(new JLabel("Player 2:"));
scorePanel.add(new JLabel("      0"));

controlPanel.add(scorePanel, BorderLayout.NORTH);
controlPanel.add(new JButton("New Game"), BorderLayout.SOUTH);

//register 'Exit upon closing' as a default close operation
setDefaultCloseOperation( EXIT_ON_CLOSE );
    }
}
```

Remember that this class illustrates only the visual aspect of the program. There is no code for handling events or actually playing the game. We will discuss how to handle the logic of playing the game of Tic Tac Toe in the sample development in Section 14.5.

Now let's move on to the second sample frame. For this frame, we will use nested panels shown in Figure 14.8. Notice the panel that has a BorderLayout. This

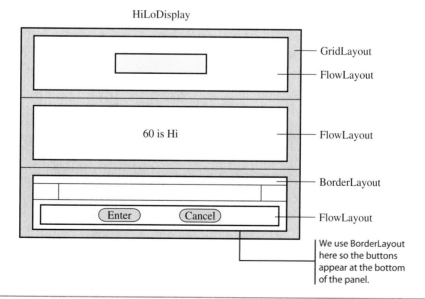

Figure 14.8 The nested panels and associated layout managers for **HiLoDisplay.**

panel seems extra, but without it, the buttons will appear away from the bottom, closer to the response label. We feel it is more appealing visually when the buttons are placed at the bottom.

Here's the Ch14NestedPanels2 class:

```
/*
    Chapter 14 Sample Program: Illustration of Nested Panels

    File: Ch14NestedPanels2.java
*/

import javax.swing.*;
import java.awt.*;
import java.awt.event.*;

class Ch14NestedPanels2 extends JFrame {

    private static final int FRAME_WIDTH    = 250;
    private static final int FRAME_HEIGHT   = 270;
    private static final int FRAME_X_ORIGIN = 150;
    private static final int FRAME_Y_ORIGIN = 250;

    private final String ENTER = "Enter";
    private final String CANCEL = "Cancel";
    private final String BLANK = "";

    private JTextField guessEntry;
    private JLabel     hint;

    public static void main(String[] args) {
        Ch14NestedPanels2 frame = new Ch14NestedPanels2();
        frame.setVisible(true);
    }

    public Ch14NestedPanels2( ) {
        JPanel  guessPanel, hintPanel,
                controlPanel, buttonPanel;

        JButton enterBtn, cancelBtn;

        Container contentPane;

        //set the frame properties
        setSize        (FRAME_WIDTH, FRAME_HEIGHT);
        setTitle       ("Program Ch14NestedPanels2");
        setLocation    (FRAME_X_ORIGIN, FRAME_Y_ORIGIN);

        contentPane = getContentPane( );

        contentPane.setLayout(new GridLayout(3, 1));
```

```
        guessPanel = new JPanel();
        guessPanel.setBorder(BorderFactory.createTitledBorder(
                                              "Your Guess"));
        guessPanel.add(guessEntry = new JTextField(10));

        hintPanel = new JPanel();
        hintPanel.setBorder(BorderFactory.createTitledBorder("Hint"));
        hintPanel.add(hint = new JLabel("Let's Play HiLo"));

        controlPanel = new JPanel(new BorderLayout());
        buttonPanel  = new JPanel();
        buttonPanel.add(enterBtn = new JButton(ENTER));
        buttonPanel.add(cancelBtn = new JButton(CANCEL));
        controlPanel.add(buttonPanel, BorderLayout.SOUTH);

        contentPane.add(guessPanel);
        contentPane.add(hintPanel);
        contentPane.add(controlPanel);
    }
}
```

Tic Tac Toe Panel

As promised, let's design and implement a panel specialized in displaying the Tic Tac Toe board of $N \times N = N^2$ cells (default is $3 \times 3 = 9$ cells). Figure 14.5 shows this Tic Tac Toe panel placed on a frame. The panel handles the mouse click events, so every time the player clicks on the cell, the circle or cross is displayed. However, this code for handling mouse click events is only for demonstration. There's no logic of actually playing the game of Tic Tac Toe. For instance, when we click on the cell that already has a cross or circle, a new mark replaces the current one. In the real game, this should not happen. The demonstration code simply alternates between the cross and circle. When we click the panel for the first time, the circle is placed, then the cross, then the circle, and so forth.

How shall we implement this panel? There are two approaches. The first approach is to compute the origin point—the top left corner—of each cell based on the dimension of the panel and the number of cells in the panel. When we know the origin point of a cell, then we can draw a circle or cross by using the drawLine and drawOval methods. Figure 14.9 illustrates how this is done. When a cell is clicked, we get the x and y coordinates of the mouse click location and determine in which cell the mouse click event has occurred. Once we know the cell, we use its origin point to draw a circle or cross at the correct position and size. This approach requires a fair amount of coding to determine the cell and the correct position to draw lines and circles. We can avoid all these computations by using the second approach.

The second approach, the one which we will adopt here, uses the nested panels. We will define two classes—Ch14TicTacToePanel and Ch14TicTacToeCell—both subclasses of JPanel. An instance of Ch14TicTacToePanel will contain N^2 instances

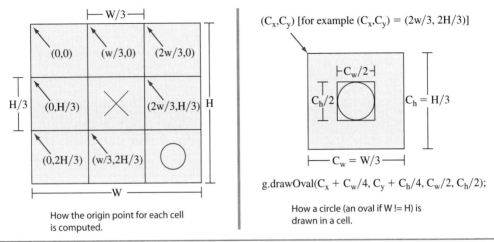

How the origin point for each cell is computed.

How a circle (an oval if W != H) is drawn in a cell.

Figure 14.9 The approach not adopted here. This approach is left as Exercise 11. The panel is divided into equal-size cells. A circle or cross can be drawn using the **drawOval** or **drawLine** method at the position slightly offset from the origin point of the cell.

of Ch14TicTacToeCell, each instance representing a single cell in the tic tac toe board. A Ch14TicTacToeCell object contains one component, namely, an instance of JLabel. Instead of a text, we assign an image icon to this JLabel object. We have three image files: the first one for the circle, the second for the cross, and the last one for a blank cell. These files are named circle.gif, cross.gif, and blank.gif, respectively. All three images have a transparent background so the background color of the Ch14TicTac-ToeCell will be visible. Notice that these image files must be put in the same folder as the class files Ch14TicTacToePanel.class and Ch14TicTacToeCell.class. Initially, all cells are assigned the blank.gif image. And we set a line border for each cell so the boundary lines are visible. Without such boundary lines, we wouldn't be able to tell how many cells the board had and where each cell began and ended. When a cell is clicked, Ch14TicTacToePanel will set it to a cross or a circle by calling the cell's setContent method.

The class includes one data member called location, a Point object, to record the cell's position on the tic tac toe board. This information is not used in this sample. We need to process the location information when we develop the complete Tic Tac Toe playing program.

Here's the complete listing of the Ch14TicTacToeCell class:

```
/*
    Chapter 14 Sample Program: Tic Tac Toe

    File: Ch14TicTacToeCell.java
*/
```

```java
import java.awt.*;
import java.awt.event.*;
import javax.swing.*;

public class Ch14TicTacToeCell extends JPanel   {

    public static final int BLANK  = 0;
    public static final int CIRCLE = 1;
    public static final int CROSS  = 2;

    private static final String CROSS_IMAGE_FILE = "cross.gif";
    private static final String CIRCLE_IMAGE_FILE = "circle.gif";
    private static final String BLANK_IMAGE_FILE  = "blank.gif";

    private JLabel content;
    private Point location;

    public Ch14TicTacToeCell( ) {
        this(null);
    }

    public Ch14TicTacToeCell(Point pt ) {

        ImageIcon initImage = new ImageIcon("blank.gif");

        setLayout(new BorderLayout());
        setBackground(Color.white);
        setBorder(BorderFactory.createLineBorder(Color.black));

        content = new JLabel(initImage);
        add(content);

        location = pt;
    }

    public Point getPosition( ) {
        return location;
    }

    public void setContent(int image) {

        switch (image) {

            case CIRCLE: content.setIcon(new ImageIcon(CIRCLE_IMAGE_FILE));
                         break;

            case CROSS:  content.setIcon(new ImageIcon(CROSS_IMAGE_FILE));
                         break;

            default:     //do nothing
                         break;
        }
    }
}
```

The main tasks for the Ch14TicTacToePanel to handle are the layout of N^2 Ch7TicTacToeCell objects and the mouse click events. Since the board is divided into equal-size cells, the grid layout is the perfect layout manager to use here. By using the grid layout manager, the images will stay at the center of the cells even when the panel is resized.

Each cell is the source of mouse events, and the container of these cells, that is, an instance of Ch14TicTacToePanel, is designated as the listener of the mouse events. Again, the event-handling code for this class is temporary. We will set an image of a circle or a cross to the clicked cell. There's no logic here to actually play the game, for example, to determine the winner. The actual game-playing logic will be added to the class in Section 14.5. Here's the complete listing of the Ch14TicTacToePanel class:

```
/*
    Chapter 14 Sample Program: Tic Tac Toe Board

    File: Ch14TicTacToePanel.java
*/

import java.awt.*;
import javax.swing.*;
import java.awt.event.*;

public class Ch14TicTacToePanel extends JPanel implements MouseListener {

    private boolean circle;

    public Ch14TicTacToePanel() {
        this(3);
    }

    public Ch14TicTacToePanel(int size) {

        Ch14TicTacToeCell cell;

        setLayout(new GridLayout(size, size));

        for (int row = 0; row < size; row++) {
            for (int col = 0; col < size; col++) {
                cell = new Ch14TicTacToeCell( );

                cell.addMouseListener(this);
                add(cell);
            }
        }

        circle = true;
    }

    public void mouseClicked(MouseEvent event) {

        Ch14TicTacToeCell cell = (Ch14TicTacToeCell) event.getSource();
```

```
        if (circle) {
            cell.setContent(Ch14TicTacToeCell.CIRCLE);
        } else {
            cell.setContent(Ch14TicTacToeCell.CROSS);
        }

        circle = !circle;
    }

    public void mouseEntered    ( MouseEvent event ) { }
    public void mouseExited     ( MouseEvent event ) { }
    public void mousePressed    ( MouseEvent event ) { }
    public void mouseReleased   ( MouseEvent event ) { }
}
```

14.4 | Other GUI Components

In Chapter 7, we introduced a number of Swing components such as JButton and JTextField. We will introduce other useful Swing components in this section. Please keep in mind that we limit the discussion to the most basic use of these components. They are actually far more capable than what we present here. However, the materials presented in this section should be enough to let you use them in most common situations and should serve as a good starting point from which you can explore more advanced uses of these components on your own.

JCheckBox

The JButton class represents a type of button called a *pushbutton*. Two other common types of buttons are called *check-box* and *radio buttons*. We will explain the check-box buttons in this subsection and the radio buttons in the next subsection.

The JCheckBox class is used to represent check-box buttons. Figure 14.10 shows a frame with four check-box buttons and one pushbutton. Check-box buttons

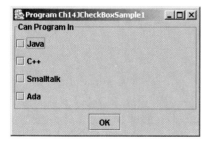
The state when the frame first appeared on the screen.

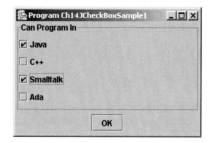
The state after the two check-box buttons are clicked.

Figure 14.10 A frame with four check-box buttons and one pushbutton.

are useful in presenting a collection of binary (yes/no, true/false) options. The frame shown in Figure 14.10 gives the user the option to select the programming languages he or she can program with by clicking on the appropriate check-box button.

We deal with the JCheckBox class in a manner very similar to that for the JButton class. To create a check-box button with a text Java, we write

```
JCheckBox cbBtn = new JCheckBox("Java");
```

To check if a check-box button is selected (i.e., has a check mark) or deselected, we call its isSelected method. For example,

```
if (cbBtn.isSelected()) {
    System.out.println("You can program in "
                            + cbBtn.getText());

} else {
    System.out.println("You cannot program in "
                            + cbBtn.getText());
}
```

Just as with a pushbutton, we can retrieve the text associated to a check-box button by calling its getText method. We can use the corresponding setText method to change the button text.

The following Ch14JCheckBoxSample1 class displays the frame shown in Figure 14.10. When the OK pushbutton is clicked, we respond by opening a message dialog with a list of selected programming languages. In the program, notice the use of an array of string btnText in creating an array of JCheckBox buttons. We can easily list any number of names by simply including all names when btnText is initialized, for example,

```
String[] btnText = {"Java", "C++", "Smalltalk", "Ada",
                    "COBOL", "Algol", "Pascal", "BASIC"};
```

There's no need to modify the program code. The ease of achieving this generality is a direct benefit of using panels and layout managers instead of absolute positioning. (You still can do it, but it would be a lot more tedious work to code the same capability with absolute positioning.)

Here's the class:

```
/*
    Chapter 14 Sample Program: Illustrates the use of JCheckBox

    File: Ch14JCheckBoxSample1.java
*/

import javax.swing.*;
import java.awt.*;
import java.awt.event.*;
```

```java
class Ch14JCheckBoxSample1 extends JFrame implements ActionListener {

    private static final int FRAME_WIDTH    = 300;
    private static final int FRAME_HEIGHT   = 200;
    private static final int FRAME_X_ORIGIN = 150;
    private static final int FRAME_Y_ORIGIN = 250;

    private JCheckBox[] checkBox;

    public static void main(String[] args) {
        Ch14JCheckBoxSample1 frame = new Ch14JCheckBoxSample1();
        frame.setVisible(true);
    }

    public Ch14JCheckBoxSample1() {
        Container    contentPane;
        JPanel       checkPanel, okPanel;

        JButton      okButton;
        String[]     btnText = {"Java", "C++", "Smalltalk", "Ada"};

        //set the frame properties
        setSize      (FRAME_WIDTH, FRAME_HEIGHT);
        setTitle     ("Program Ch14JCheckBoxSample1");
        setLocation  (FRAME_X_ORIGIN, FRAME_Y_ORIGIN);

        contentPane = getContentPane( );
        contentPane.setBackground(Color.white);
        contentPane.setLayout(new BorderLayout());

        //create and place four checkboxes
        checkPanel = new JPanel(new GridLayout(0,1));
        checkPanel.setBorder(BorderFactory.createTitledBorder(
                                          "Can Program In"));

        checkBox = new JCheckBox[btnText.length];

        for (int i = 0; i < checkBox.length; i++) {
            checkBox[i] = new JCheckBox(btnText[i]);
            checkPanel.add(checkBox[i]);
        }

        //create and place the OK button
        okPanel = new JPanel(new FlowLayout());
        okButton = new JButton("OK");
        okButton.addActionListener(this);
        okPanel.add(okButton);

        contentPane.add(checkPanel, BorderLayout.CENTER);
        contentPane.add(okPanel, BorderLayout.SOUTH);

        //register 'Exit upon closing' as a default close operation
        setDefaultCloseOperation( EXIT_ON_CLOSE );
    }
```

```
public void actionPerformed(ActionEvent event) {

    StringBuffer skill = new StringBuffer("You can program in\n");
    for (int i = 0; i < checkBox.length; i++) {
        if (checkBox[i].isSelected()) {
            skill.append(checkBox[i].getText() + "\n");
        }
    }

    JOptionPane.showMessageDialog(this, skill.toString());
}
}
```

Although we did not process them in the Ch14JCheckBoxSample1 program, a JCheckBox object generates action events just as any other buttons do. So we can associate an action listener to JCheckBox objects, but it is not that common to process action events generated by JCheckBox objects. In addition, a JCheckBox object generates another type of event called *item events*. An item event is generated when the state (selected or deselected) of a check-box button changes. We can register an instance of a class that implements the ItemListener interface as an item listener of a JCheckBox object. When an item event is generated, its itemStateChanged method is called. Inside the method, we can check the state of change by calling the getStateChange method. Here's a sample itemStateChanged method:

item events

```
public void itemStateChanged(ItemEvent event) {

    if (event.getStateChange() == ItemEvent.SELECTED) {
        System.out.println("You checked the box");
    } else {
        System.out.println("You unchecked the box");
    }
}
```

Here's the Ch14JCheckBoxSample2 class that adds the item event handling to the Ch14JCheckBoxSample1 class (pay attention to the portions with white background):

```
/*
    Chapter 14 Sample Program: Illustrates the use of JCheckBox

    File: Ch14JCheckBoxSample2.java
*/
```

```
import javax.swing.*;
import java.awt.*;
import java.awt.event.*;

class Ch14JCheckBoxSample2 extends JFrame
                           implements ActionListener,
                                      ItemListener     {

    private static final int FRAME_WIDTH    = 300;
    private static final int FRAME_HEIGHT   = 200;
    private static final int FRAME_X_ORIGIN = 150;
    private static final int FRAME_Y_ORIGIN = 250;

    private JCheckBox[] checkBox;

    public static void main(String[] args) {
        Ch14JCheckBoxSample2 frame = new Ch14JCheckBoxSample2();
        frame.setVisible(true);
    }

    public Ch14JCheckBoxSample2() {
        Container    contentPane;
        JPanel       checkPanel, okPanel;

        JButton      okButton;
        String[]     btnText = {"Java", "C++", "Smalltalk", "Ada"};

        //set the frame properties
        setSize       (FRAME_WIDTH, FRAME_HEIGHT);
        setTitle      ("Program Ch14JCheckBoxSample2");
        setLocation   (FRAME_X_ORIGIN, FRAME_Y_ORIGIN);

        contentPane = getContentPane( );
        contentPane.setBackground(Color.white);
        contentPane.setLayout(new BorderLayout());

        //create and place four checkboxes
        checkPanel = new JPanel(new GridLayout(0,1));
        checkPanel.setBorder(BorderFactory.createTitledBorder(
                                        "Can Program In"));

        checkBox = new JCheckBox[btnText.length];

        for (int i = 0; i < checkBox.length; i++) {
            checkBox[i] = new JCheckBox(btnText[i]);
            checkPanel.add(checkBox[i]);

            checkBox[i].addItemListener(this);
        }

        //create and place the OK button
        okPanel = new JPanel(new FlowLayout());
```

```java
        okButton = new JButton("OK");
        okButton.addActionListener(this);
        okPanel.add(okButton);

        contentPane.add(checkPanel, BorderLayout.CENTER);
        contentPane.add(okPanel, BorderLayout.SOUTH);

        //register 'Exit upon closing' as a default close operation
        setDefaultCloseOperation( EXIT_ON_CLOSE );
    }

    public void actionPerformed(ActionEvent event) {

        StringBuffer skill = new StringBuffer("You can program in\n");

        for (int i = 0; i < checkBox.length; i++) {

            if (checkBox[i].isSelected()) {
                skill.append(checkBox[i].getText() + "\n");
            }
        }

        JOptionPane.showMessageDialog(this, skill.toString());
    }

    public void itemStateChanged(ItemEvent event) {

        JCheckBox source = (JCheckBox) event.getSource();

        String state;

        if (event.getStateChange() == ItemEvent.SELECTED) {
            state = "is selected";
        } else {
            state = "is deselected";
        }

        JOptionPane.showMessageDialog(this, "JCheckBox '" +
                                            source.getText() +
                                            "' " + state);

    }
}
```

JRadioButton

The **JRadioButton** class is used to represent a type of button called a *radio button*. Similar to a check-box button, you can select or deselect a radio button. But unlike with a check-box button, you can only select one of the radio buttons that belong to the same group. Figure 14.11 shows a frame with four radio buttons and one push-button. We can select exactly one of the four radio buttons at a time because they

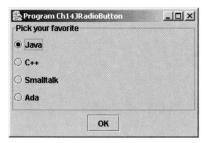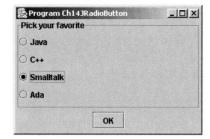

The state when the frame first appeared on the screen.

The state after the third radio button is clicked. Previous selection gets deselected.

Figure 14.11 A frame with four radio buttons and one pushbutton.

belong to the same group. When we select a new one, then the currently selected radio button will get deselected. Radio buttons are useful in allowing the user to select one from a list of possible choices. The sample frame in Figure 14.11 allows the user to select the favorite programming language.

We can use the JRadioButton class in almost an identical manner as that for the JCheckBox class. Like JCheckBox, JRadioButton generates both action events and item events. The key difference is the requirement to add JRadioButton objects to a button group, in addition to adding them to a container. Notice that the addition of radio buttons to a group is a logical operation (only one radio button in a group can be selected at a time), and the addition of radio buttons to a container is a visual layout operation. Here's a portion that creates radio buttons and adds them to a group (an instance of a ButtonGroup) and a container (an instance of a JPanel):

```
ButtonGroup languageGroup = new ButtonGroup( );
JPanel      radioPanel    = new JPanel(...);

for (int i = 0; i < radioButton.length; i++) {
    radioButton[i] = new JRadioButton(...);
    ...
    languageGroup.add(radioButton[i]);
    radioPanel.add(radioButton[i]);
}
```

(Three dots . . . represent a piece of actual code not directly relevant here.)
Here's the Ch14JRadioButtonSample class:

```
/*

    Chapter 14 Sample Program: Illustrates the use of JRadioButton

    File: Ch14JRadioButtonSample.java

*/
```

```java
import javax.swing.*;
import java.awt.*;
import java.awt.event.*;

class Ch14JRadioButtonSample extends JFrame
                             implements ActionListener,
                                        ItemListener    {

    private static final int FRAME_WIDTH    = 300;
    private static final int FRAME_HEIGHT   = 200;
    private static final int FRAME_X_ORIGIN = 150;
    private static final int FRAME_Y_ORIGIN = 250;

    private JRadioButton[] radioButton;

    public static void main(String[] args) {
        Ch14JRadioButtonSample frame = new Ch14JRadioButtonSample();
        frame.setVisible(true);
    }

    public Ch14JRadioButtonSample() {
        Container   contentPane;
        JPanel      radioPanel, okPanel;
        ButtonGroup languageGroup;

        JButton     okButton;
        String[]    btnText = {"Java", "C++", "Smalltalk", "Ada"};

        //set the frame properties
        setSize      (FRAME_WIDTH, FRAME_HEIGHT);
        setTitle     ("Program Ch14JRadioButton");
        setLocation  (FRAME_X_ORIGIN, FRAME_Y_ORIGIN);

        contentPane = getContentPane( );
        contentPane.setBackground(Color.white);
        contentPane.setLayout(new BorderLayout());

        //create and place four radio buttons
        radioPanel = new JPanel(new GridLayout(0,1));
        radioPanel.setBorder(BorderFactory.createTitledBorder(
                                        "Pick your favorite"));

        languageGroup = new ButtonGroup();
        radioButton = new JRadioButton[btnText.length];

        for (int i = 0; i < radioButton.length; i++) {
            radioButton[i] = new JRadioButton(btnText[i]);
            radioButton[i].addItemListener(this);
            languageGroup.add(radioButton[i]);
            radioPanel.add(radioButton[i]);
        }
```

```
        radioButton[0].setSelected(true); //selects the first choice

        //create and place the OK button
        okPanel = new JPanel(new FlowLayout());
        okButton = new JButton("OK");
        okButton.addActionListener(this);
        okPanel.add(okButton);

        contentPane.add(radioPanel, BorderLayout.CENTER);
        contentPane.add(okPanel, BorderLayout.SOUTH);

        //register 'Exit upon closing' as a default close operation
        setDefaultCloseOperation( EXIT_ON_CLOSE );
    }

    public void actionPerformed(ActionEvent event) {

        String favorite = null;

        int i = 0;
        while (favorite == null) {
            if (radioButton[i].isSelected()) {
                favorite = radioButton[i].getText();
            }

            i++;
        }

        JOptionPane.showMessageDialog(this, "Your favorite language is "
                                            + favorite);
    }

    public void itemStateChanged(ItemEvent event) {

        JRadioButton source = (JRadioButton) event.getSource();

        String state;

        if (event.getStateChange() == ItemEvent.SELECTED) {
            state = "is selected";
        } else {
            state = "is deselected";
        }

        JOptionPane.showMessageDialog(this, "JRadioButton '" +
                                            source.getText() +
                                            "' " + state);
    }
}
```

Every time a radio button is selected, the itemStateChanged method is called twice. The first time is for the deselection of the currently selected item, and the second is for the selection of the new item. Also notice the statement

```
radioButton[0].setSelected(true);
```

in the constructor. If we don't include this statement, then no item will be selected when the frame is first opened. For radio buttons, it is more common to start with one preselected when they first appear on the screen.

JComboBox

The JComboBox class presents a combo box. This class is similar to the JRadio-Button class in that it also allows the user to select one item from a list of possible choices. The difference between the two lies in how the choices are presented to the user. Another name for a combo box is a *drop-down list,* which is more descriptive of its interaction style. Figure 14.12 shows a frame with one combo box and one pushbutton.

We can construct a new JComboBox by passing an array of String objects, for example,

```
String[] comboBoxItem
           = {"Java", "C++", "Smalltalk", "Ada"};

JComboBox comboBox = new JComboBox(comboBoxItem);
```

A JComboBox object generates both action events and item events. An action event is generated every time a JComboBox is clicked (note it is not that common to process action events of JComboBox). Every time an item different from the currently selected item is selected, an item event is generated and the itemState-Changed method is called twice. The first time is for the deselection of the currently selected item, and the second is for the selection of the new item. Notice that when the same item is selected again, no item event is generated.

The state when the frame first appeared on the screen.

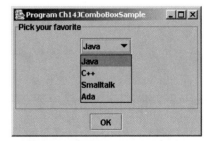

The state after the items in the combo box are revealed by clicking on the down arrow.

Figure 14.12 A frame with one combo box (drop-down list) and one pushbutton.

To find out the currently selected item, we call the getSelectedItem method of JComboBox. Because the return type of this method is Object, we must type cast to the correct type. For this example, items are String objects, so we write

```
String selection = (String) comboBox.getSelectedItem();
```

Also, we can call the getSelectedIndex method to retrieve the position of the selected item. The first item in the list is at position 0.

Here's the Ch14JComboBoxSample class:

```
/*
    Chapter 14 Sample Program: Illustrates the use of JComboBox

    File: Ch14JComboBoxSample.java
*/

import javax.swing.*;
import java.awt.*;
import java.awt.event.*;

class Ch14JComboBoxSample extends JFrame
                          implements ActionListener,
                                     ItemListener   {

    private static final int FRAME_WIDTH    = 300;
    private static final int FRAME_HEIGHT   = 200;
    private static final int FRAME_X_ORIGIN = 150;
    private static final int FRAME_Y_ORIGIN = 250;

    private JComboBox comboBox;

    public static void main(String[] args) {
        Ch14JComboBoxSample frame = new Ch14JComboBoxSample();
        frame.setVisible(true);
    }

    public Ch14JComboBoxSample() {
        Container   contentPane;
        JPanel      comboPanel, okPanel;

        JButton     okButton;
        String[]    comboBoxItem = {"Java", "C++", "Smalltalk", "Ada"};

        //set the frame properties
        setSize     (FRAME_WIDTH, FRAME_HEIGHT);
        setTitle    ("Program Ch14JComboBoxSample");
        setLocation (FRAME_X_ORIGIN, FRAME_Y_ORIGIN);

        contentPane = getContentPane( );
        contentPane.setBackground(Color.white);
        contentPane.setLayout(new BorderLayout());
```

```java
        //create and place a combo box
        comboPanel = new JPanel(new FlowLayout());
        comboPanel.setBorder(BorderFactory.createTitledBorder(
                                        "Pick your favorite"));

        comboBox = new JComboBox(comboBoxItem);
        comboBox.addItemListener(this);
        comboPanel.add(comboBox);

        //create and place the OK button
        okPanel = new JPanel(new FlowLayout());
        okButton = new JButton("OK");
        okButton.addActionListener(this);
        okPanel.add(okButton);

        contentPane.add(comboPanel, BorderLayout.CENTER);
        contentPane.add(okPanel, BorderLayout.SOUTH);

        //register 'Exit upon closing' as a default close operation
        setDefaultCloseOperation( EXIT_ON_CLOSE );
    }

    public void actionPerformed(ActionEvent event) {

        String favorite;
        int    loc;

        favorite = (String) comboBox.getSelectedItem();
        loc      = comboBox.getSelectedIndex();

        JOptionPane.showMessageDialog(this, "Currently selected item '" +
                        favorite + "' is at index position " + loc);
    }

    public void itemStateChanged(ItemEvent event) {

        String state;

        if (event.getStateChange() == ItemEvent.SELECTED) {
            state = "is selected";
        } else {
            state = "is deselected";
        }

        JOptionPane.showMessageDialog(this, "JComboBox Item '" +
                                        event.getItem() +
                                        "' " + state);
    }
}
```

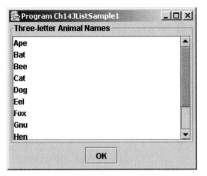
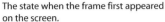

The state when the frame first appeared
on the screen.

The state after the item Gnu is selected.

Figure 14.13 A frame with one list and one pushbutton.

JList

The JList class is useful when we need to display a list of items, for example, a list
of students, a list of files, and so forth. Figure 14.13 shows a frame with one JList
listing animals with three-letter names and one pushbutton.

We can construct a JList object in a manner identical to the way we construct
a JComboBox object, that is, by passing an array of String, such as

```
String[]    names = {"Ape", "Bat", "Bee", "Cat",
                     "Dog", "Eel", "Fox", "Gnu",
                     "Hen", "Man", "Sow", "Yak"};
JList list = new JList(names);
```

With JList, we have an option of specifying one of the three selection modes:
single-selection, single-interval, and multiple-interval. The single-selection mode
allows the user to select only one item at a time. The single-interval mode allows the
user to select a single contiguous interval. And the multiple-interval mode allows
the user to select multiple contiguous intervals (each interval will include one or
more items). The multiple-interval mode is the default mode. The following three
statements show how to set the three selection modes:

```
list.setSelectionMode(
        ListSelectionModel.SINGLE_SELECTION);

list.setSelectionMode(
        ListSelectionModel.SINGLE_INTERVAL_SELECTION);

list.setSelectionMode(
        ListSelectionModel.MULTIPLE_INTERVAL_SELECTION);
```

Because multiple items can be selected, we use getSelectedValues and get-
SelectedIndices to retrieve an array of selected items and an array of the indices of

the selected items, respectively. The following code will display the selected items and their index positions:

```
Object[] name;
int[]    loc;

name = list.getSelectedValues();
loc  = list.getSelectedIndices();

for (int i = 0; i < name.length; i++) {
   System.out.println((String)name[i] +
                  " at position " + loc[i]);
}
```

Notice the return type of getSelectedValues is an array of Object, so we type cast the items in the name array to String before printing it on System.out. If we know the selection mode is single selection, then we can use getSelectedValue and get-SelectedIndex instead. Also notice in the code that we are not adding a JList object directly to a panel. Instead, we wrap it in a JScrollPane and add this JScrollPane to a panel because JList itself does not include scrollbars.

Here's the Ch14JListSample class:

```
/*
    Chapter 14 Sample Program: Illustrates the use of JList

    File: Ch14JListSample.java
*/

import javax.swing.event.*;
import javax.swing.*;
import java.awt.*;
import java.awt.event.*;

class Ch14JListSample extends JFrame
                      implements ActionListener {

    private static final int FRAME_WIDTH    = 300;
    private static final int FRAME_HEIGHT   = 250;
    private static final int FRAME_X_ORIGIN = 150;
    private static final int FRAME_Y_ORIGIN = 250;

    private JList list;

    public static void main(String[] args) {
        Ch14JListSample frame = new Ch14JListSample();
        frame.setVisible(true);
    }

    public Ch14JListSample() {
        Container    contentPane;
        JPanel       listPanel, okPanel;
```

```
        JButton      okButton;
        String[]     names = {"Ape", "Bat", "Bee", "Cat",
                              "Dog", "Eel", "Fox", "Gnu",
                              "Hen", "Man", "Sow", "Yak"};

        //set the frame properties
        setSize      (FRAME_WIDTH, FRAME_HEIGHT);
        setTitle     ("Program Ch14JListSample2");
        setLocation  (FRAME_X_ORIGIN, FRAME_Y_ORIGIN);

        contentPane = getContentPane( );
        contentPane.setBackground(Color.white);
        contentPane.setLayout(new BorderLayout());

        //create and place a JList
        listPanel = new JPanel(new GridLayout(0,1));
        listPanel.setBorder(BorderFactory.createTitledBorder(
                                    "Three-letter Animal Names"));

        list = new JList(names);
        listPanel.add(new JScrollPane(list));
        list.setSelectionMode(
                    ListSelectionModel.MULTIPLE_INTERVAL_SELECTION);
            //this is default, so the explicit call is not necessary

        //create and place the OK button
        okPanel = new JPanel(new FlowLayout());
        okButton = new JButton("OK");
        okButton.addActionListener(this);
        okPanel.add(okButton);

        contentPane.add(listPanel, BorderLayout.CENTER);
        contentPane.add(okPanel, BorderLayout.SOUTH);

        //register 'Exit upon closing' as a default close operation
        setDefaultCloseOperation( EXIT_ON_CLOSE );
    }

    public void actionPerformed(ActionEvent event) {

        Object[] name;
        int[]    loc;

        name = list.getSelectedValues();
        loc  = list.getSelectedIndices();

        System.out.println("Currently selected animal names are ");
        for (int i = 0; i < name.length; i++) {
            System.out.println((String)name[i] + " at position " + loc[i]);
        }
    }
}
```

JSlider

The JSlider class represents a slider in which the user can move a nob to a desired position. The position of the nob on a slider determines the selected value. Figure 14.14 shows a frame with three sliders. This is a classic example of sliders where the user moves the three nobs to set the red, green, blue (RGB) value in selecting a color. Values for the R, G, and B range from 0 to 255, inclusive. Some of properties we can set for a JSlider object are the minimum and maximum range of values, whether to display the tick marks, the spacing of major and minor tick marks, whether to display the label for the major tick marks, and the placement orientation (either vertical or horizontal).

The sliders in the sample program are created and initialized in the following manner:

```
JSlider slider = new JSlider();

slider.setOrientation(JSlider.VERTICAL);
slider.setPaintLabels(true); //show tick mark labels
slider.setPaintTicks(true);  //show tick marks
slider.setMinimum(MIN_COLOR);
slider.setMaximum(MAX_COLOR);
```

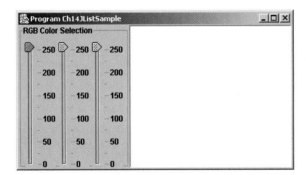

The state when the frame first appeared on the screen.

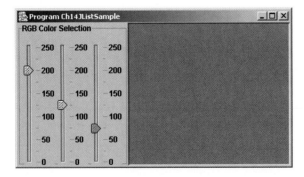

The state after three nobs are moved.

Figure 14.14 A frame with three vertical sliders for setting an RGB value.

```
slider.setValue(MAX_COLOR); //initial position of a nob
slider.setMajorTickSpacing(50);
slider.setMinorTickSpacing(25);
```

When a nob is moved, a JSlider object generates a change event (this event occurs when there's a change in the event source, such as the nob is moved). To process change events, we must register change event listeners to a JSlider event source object. The class that implements the ChangeListener interface must define a method called stateChanged, whose parameter is an instance of ChangeEvent. For this program, whenever a change event is generated, we read the value from each slider and set the background of a panel to a designated color. Here's the body of the stateChanged method:

```
int R, G, B;

R = redSlider.getValue();
G = greenSlider.getValue();
B = blueSlider.getValue();

colorPanel.setBackground(new Color(R, G, B));
```

Here's the Ch14JSliderSample class:

```
/*
    Chapter 14 Sample Program: Illustrates the use of JSlider

    File: Ch14JSliderSample.java
*/

import javax.swing.event.*;
import javax.swing.*;
import java.awt.*;
import java.awt.event.*;

class Ch14JSliderSample extends JFrame
                        implements ChangeListener {

    private static final int FRAME_WIDTH    = 450;
    private static final int FRAME_HEIGHT   = 250;
    private static final int FRAME_X_ORIGIN = 150;
    private static final int FRAME_Y_ORIGIN = 250;

    private static final int MIN_COLOR = 0;
    private static final int MAX_COLOR = 255;

    private JSlider redSlider;
    private JSlider greenSlider;
    private JSlider blueSlider;

    private JPanel colorPanel;
```

```java
public static void main(String[] args) {
    Ch14JSliderSample frame = new Ch14JSliderSample();
    frame.setVisible(true);
}

public Ch14JSliderSample() {
    Container   contentPane;
    JPanel      sliderPanel;

    //set the frame properties
    setSize       (FRAME_WIDTH, FRAME_HEIGHT);
    setTitle      ("Program Ch14JListSample");
    setLocation   (FRAME_X_ORIGIN, FRAME_Y_ORIGIN);

    contentPane = getContentPane( );
    contentPane.setBackground(Color.white);
    contentPane.setLayout(new BorderLayout());

    //create and place a JList
    sliderPanel = new JPanel(new FlowLayout());
    sliderPanel.setBorder(BorderFactory.createTitledBorder(
                                        "RGB Color Selection"));

    redSlider = createSlider(MAX_COLOR);
    greenSlider = createSlider(MAX_COLOR);
    blueSlider = createSlider(MAX_COLOR);

    sliderPanel.add(redSlider);
    sliderPanel.add(greenSlider);
    sliderPanel.add(blueSlider);

    colorPanel = new JPanel( );
    colorPanel.setBackground(Color.white);
    colorPanel.setBorder(BorderFactory.createLoweredBevelBorder());
    contentPane.add(colorPanel, BorderLayout.CENTER);
    contentPane.add(sliderPanel, BorderLayout.WEST);

    //register 'Exit upon closing' as a default close operation
    setDefaultCloseOperation( EXIT_ON_CLOSE );
}

public void stateChanged(ChangeEvent event) {

    int R, G, B;

    R = redSlider.getValue();
    G = greenSlider.getValue();
    B = blueSlider.getValue();

    colorPanel.setBackground(new Color(R, G, B));
}
```

```
private JSlider createSlider(int value ) {

    JSlider slider = new JSlider();

    slider.setOrientation(JSlider.VERTICAL);
    slider.setPaintLabels(true);
    slider.setPaintTicks(true);
    slider.setMinimum(MIN_COLOR);
    slider.setMaximum(MAX_COLOR);
    slider.setValue(value);
    slider.setMajorTickSpacing(50);
    slider.setMinorTickSpacing(25);

    slider.addChangeListener(this);

    return slider;
}
}
```

TicTacToe

In Section 14.3, we programmed only the user interface aspect of the Tic Tac Toe game and deferred the implementation of the full program. Specifically, we left out the logic of playing the game. We will complete the full program in this section by defining an object that keeps track of the board configuration and determines the winner of a game. For this program, the game is played by two human players. If we want a computer to play against a human, further modification is necessary. This extension is left as Exercise 10.

Problem Statement

Write a game-playing program that lets two human players play Tic Tac Toe.

Overall Plan

We already built the user interface objects **Ch14TicTacToePanel** and **Ch14TicTacToe-Cell.** We will reuse the **Ch14TicTacToeCell** class as is, but we will have to modify the **Ch14TicTacToePanel** class so its instance can be integrated with a game-playing logic object. Remember that the **Ch14TicTacToePanel** class includes only a temporary (and simplistic) code just for switching the images of cross and circle alternately. We need to add the code that lets the players really play the game.

What are the types of objects we need for this program? As usual, we need an interface object that handles user interaction, a logic object that handles the logic of playing a game, and a supervisor object that manages other objects in the program. We have been using a supervisor-subordinate design pattern to connect these types of objects. For this program, we will use another design pattern called *model-view-controller, or **MVC***. This design pattern is suitable for building a flexible GUI-based application in which we can easily mix and match the user interface and logic objects. Using the MVC terminology, we call the user interface objects ***views*** and the logic objects ***models***. A model object handles the logic of a given task. A view object handles the visual display of a given task. In addition, there is a controller object in MVC that handles the user input. In Java, Swing objects assume the roles of both view and controller, so our design here is actually an adaptation of MVC.

> MVC

> view and model

Using the MVC pattern, we envision four classes in the program. The first is a logic class whose instance will maintain the board configuration by using a two-dimensional array of integers. A two-dimensional array is the perfect data structure to keep track of the board configuration. Each cell in the Tic Tac Toe board can be identified uniquely by its row and column numbers. The content of a cell can be a blank, a circle, or a cross. The second is the GUI class for visually displaying a cell. Its instance will handle the task of displaying an image for cross and circle. The third is another GUI class for holding $N \times N$ cells. Its instance will handle the mouse click events. The last is the top-level supervisor class whose instance will control other objects in the program. These classes are named as follows:

Design Document: Classes for the `TicTacToe` **Program**

Class	Role
`Ch14TicTacToeCell`	Visually represents a single cell on the game board. The class is a subclass of the `JPanel` class.
`Ch14TicTacToeView`	Visually represents a game board that consists of N^2 cell objects. It handles the mouse click events. This class is also a subclass of the `JPanel` class. Although we use the word *view* here, this class assumes the MVC's view and controller.
`Ch14TicTacToeModel`	Handles the game-playing logic. It keeps track of the board configuration, tracks the player's turn, and determines the winner. It uses a two-dimensional array of integers to represent a board. The games are played by two human players.
`Ch14TicTacToeFrame`	Supervises other objects in the program. It is an instantiable main class and is a subclass of `JFrame`.

The big design question is, How can we make these objects talk to each other? We have two key players—a user interface object and a logic object. When the user interface object detects an event, such as the mouse click on a cell, it notifies the logic object. Upon receiving this notification, the logic object updates its internal state. For example, the Tic Tac Toe model object will update the board configuration after receiving a notification. Once its internal state is adjusted, it tells the user interface object to reflect this internal change visually by updating the view. For example, if the Tic Tac Toe model determines a cell will now contain a cross, it tells the view object to update the visual representation of the game board. Figure 14.15 shows the dependencies among the classes. And if we remove the calls to the constructors, public constants, or the methods to set the cross references between the view and model objects, we are left with the key method calls. These calls are identified in Figure 14.16.

We will implement the program in this order:

development steps

1. Implement the visual layout aspect of the user interface. Start with **Ch14TicTac-ToeView** and **Ch14TicTacToeCell.** Use a stub **Ch14TicTacToeFrame.**

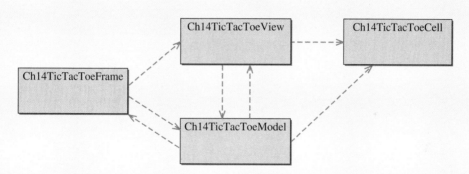

Figure 14.15 The working program diagram for the **TicTacToe** program. This program maintains the MVC communication pattern where the **notify–update** cycles exist between the view controller and model.

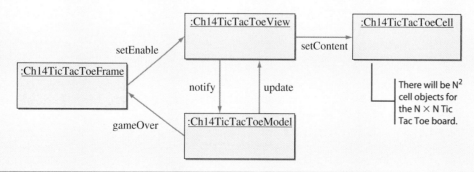

Figure 14.16 The key method calls among objects in the **TicTacToe** program.

2. Add event-handling routines to **Ch14TicTacToView** and integrate it with the stub **Ch14TicTacToeModel** class. Modify the **Ch14TicTacToeFrame** class as necessary.

3. Fully implement the **Ch14TicTacToeModel** class. Modify the **Ch14TicTacToeFrame** class as necessary.

4. Finalize the program.

Step 1 Development: Visual Layout

step 1
design

In step 1, we will develop the visual aspect of the program. Specifically, we will implement the two classes—**Ch14TicTacToeView** and **Ch14TicTacToeCell**—for the user interface. We already discussed the alternative designs for the **Ch14TicTacToeView** class in Section 14.4 (we called the class **Ch14TicTacToePanel**), so we will not repeat the discussion here. As we decided in Section 14.4, we will use nested panels to implement the **Ch14TicTacToeView** class.

The **Ch14TicTacToeView** class is a subclass of **JPanel,** and the class implements the **MouseListener** interface. At this step, all we want to verify is that the mouse click is detected correctly. This can be done easily by accessing the location information of the clicked cell. The stub **mouseClicked** is implemented as follows:

```
public void mouseClicked(MouseEvent event) {

    currentCell = (Ch14TicTacToeCell) event.getSource();

    Point pt = currentCell.getPosition();

    System.out.println("[" + pt.x + "," + pt.y + "]");
}
```

The location of a cell on the Tic Tac Toe board is identified in the following manner:

	0	1	2
0	[0,0]	[0,1]	[0,2]
1	[1,0]	[1,1]	[1,2]
2	[2,0]	[2,1]	[2,2]

Notice the value **pt.x** refers to the row number and **pt.y** to the column number.

Cells are created and their locations are set in the **Ch14TicTacToeView** constructor as follows:

```
public Ch14TicTacToeView(int size) {

    Ch14TicTacToeCell cell;

    setLayout(new GridLayout(size, size));

    for (int row = 0; row < size; row++) {
        for (int col = 0; col < size; col++) {
            cell = new Ch14TicTacToeCell(
                                new Point(row, col));

            cell.addMouseListener(this);
            add(cell);
        }
    }
}
```

To test the user interface classes, we will begin with a skeleton **Ch14TicTacToeFrame** class. All we do at this step is to set an instance of **Ch14TicTacToeView** as the content pane of the frame.

step 1 code

We are now ready for the step 1 code. **Ch14TicTacToeCell** is the same, so we will not list it here again. The **Ch14TicTacToeView** is as follows:

```
/*
    Chapter 14 Sample Program: Tic Tac Toe

    File: Step1/Ch14TicTacToeView.java

*/

import java.awt.*;
import javax.swing.*;
import java.awt.event.*;

public class Ch14TicTacToeView extends JPanel implements MouseListener {

    Ch14TicTacToeCell  currentCell;

    public Ch14TicTacToeView(int size) {

        Ch14TicTacToeCell cell;

        setLayout(new GridLayout(size, size));

        for (int row = 0; row < size; row++) {
            for (int col = 0; col < size; col++) {
                cell = new Ch14TicTacToeCell(new Point(row, col));
```

14.5 **Sample Development**—*continued*

```
                cell.addMouseListener(this);
                add(cell);
            }
        }

    }

    public void mouseClicked(MouseEvent event) {

        currentCell = (Ch14TicTacToeCell) event.getSource();

        Point pt = currentCell.getPosition();

        System.out.println("[" + pt.x + "," + pt.y + "]");
    }

    public void mouseEntered   ( MouseEvent event ) { }
    public void mouseExited    ( MouseEvent event ) { }
    public void mousePressed   ( MouseEvent event ) { }
    public void mouseReleased  ( MouseEvent event ) { }
}
```

And here's the listing of a skeleton **Ch14TicTacToeFrame:**

```
/*
    Chapter 14 Sample Development: Tic Tac Toe

    File: Step1/Ch14TicTacToeFrame.java

*/

import java.awt.*;
import javax.swing.*;

public class Ch14TicTacToeFrame extends JFrame  {

    private static final int DEFAULT_BOARD_SIZE = 3;
    private Ch14TicTacToeView gameView;

    public static void main(String[] arg) {

        Ch14TicTacToeFrame frame = new Ch14TicTacToeFrame();
        frame.setVisible(true);
    }
```

```
public Ch14TicTacToeFrame() {

    gameView    = new Ch14TicTacToeView(DEFAULT_BOARD_SIZE);

    setSize(400, 400);
    setTitle("Let's Play Tic Tac Toe");

    setContentPane(gameView);

    setDefaultCloseOperation(EXIT_ON_CLOSE);
}
}
```

step 1 test

To test step 1, we run the program and click on the cells to verify the correct de-tection of the mouse click events. Figure 14.17 shows the state after all nine cells are clicked.

Step 2 Development: Implement the Event-Handling Routine

step 2
design

In the second development step, we will replace the stub **mouseClicked** method with the real one. The focus of this step is to establish the necessary mutual references between the model and view objects so they can call each other's methods. The task of the **mouseClicked** method is simply to notify the model of which cell was clicked. The model will then check whether the click is valid and will inform the view object accordingly. In this step, the model object is basically a stub. It just alternates the image to display between the circle and the cross. The real logic will be implemented in step 3.

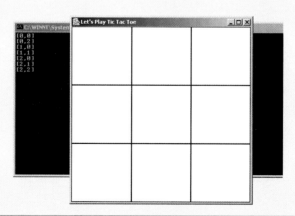

Figure 14.17 The state after seven cells are clicked.

The **mouseClicked** method is very simple because all the work is done by the model object. We implement the method as

```
public void mouseClicked(MouseEvent event) {

    currentCell = (Ch14TicTacToeCell) event.getSource();

    model.notify(currentCell.getPosition());
}
```

where model is a data member of type **Ch14TicTacToeModel.** The **notify** method of **Ch14TicTacToeModel** at this point is a stub and is defined as follows:

```
public void notify(Point loc) {

    int state;

    int row = loc.x;
    int col = loc.y;

    if (circle) {
        state = Ch14TicTacToeCell.CIRCLE;
    } else {
        state = Ch14TicTacToeCell.CROSS;
    }

    view.update(state);

    circle = !circle;
}
```

As already mentioned, all it does is to alternate the image between the cross and the circle. The boolean data member **circle** is used to keep track of which image to display next.

Notice the method calls the **update** method of the view object. The view object remembers which cell is most recently clicked, so the **update** method can display the designated image on this cell simply by calling the appropriate cell's **setContent** method. The **update** method is defined as

```
public void update(int mark) {
    currentCell.setContent(mark);
}
```

Figure 14.18 illustrates a sequence of calls made after a mouse click occurs. Here's the sequence:

1. A cell is clicked.

2. The **actionPerformed** method of the listener **Ch14TicTacToeView** is called.

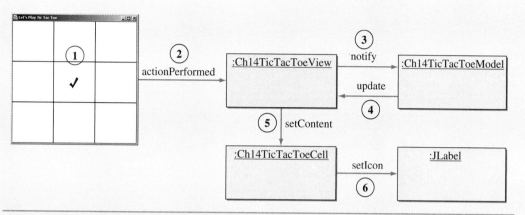

Figure 14.18 A sequence of calls after a mouse click occurs on the Tic Tac Toe board.

3. The view object notifies the model object by calling its **notify** method.

4. The model object verifies the move and informs the view object by calling its **update** method.

5. The view object tells the corresponding cell to display the designated image by calling its **setContent** method.

6. Finally, the cell object commands its data member **JLabel** object to display the image by calling the **setIcon** method of **JLabel.**

To make such a sequence of calls possible, the view and model must have mutual references. They are established by defining the **setView** and **setModel** methods to the model and view, respectively. Here are the methods:

```
public void setView(Ch14TicTacToeView view) {
    this.view = view;
}

public void setModel(Ch14TicTacToeModel model) {
    this.model = model;
}
```

These methods are called from the supervisor **Ch14TicTacToeFrame** constructor

```
gameView  = new Ch14TicTacToeView(DEFAULT_BOARD_SIZE);
gameModel = new Ch14TicTacToeModel(DEFAULT_BOARD_SIZE);

gameView.setModel(gameModel);
gameModel.setView(gameView);
```

where **gameView** and **gameModel** are data members of **Ch14TicTacToeFrame.** After the constructor is executed, the mutual references between the model and view are set as shown in Figure 14.19.

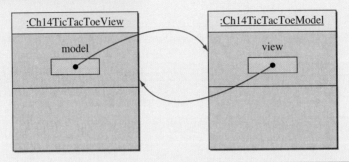

Figure 14.19 Mutual references between the two objects so they can "talk" to each other.

step 2 code

The step 2 **Ch14TicTacToeView** is now modified to the following:

```
/*
    Chapter 14 Sample Program: Tic Tac Toe

    File: Step2/Ch14TicTacToeView.java

*/

import java.awt.*;
import javax.swing.*;
import java.awt.event.*;

public class Ch14TicTacToeView extends JPanel implements MouseListener {

    ...

    Ch14TicTacToeModel model;

    ...

    public void setModel(Ch14TicTacToeModel model) {

        this.model = model;
    }

    public void update(int mark) {
        currentCell.setContent(mark);
    }

    public void mouseClicked(MouseEvent event) {

        currentCell = (Ch14TicTacToeCell) event.getSource();
```

```
            model.notify(currentCell.getPosition());
        }
        ...
}
```

Here's the stub **Ch14TicTacToeModel** class:

```
/*
    Chapter 14 Sample Program: Tic Tac Toe

    File: Step2/Ch14TicTacToeModel.java
*/

import java.awt.*;

public class Ch14TicTacToeModel {

    private Ch14TicTacToeView view;
    private boolean circle;

    public Ch14TicTacToeModel(int size) {

        circle    = true;
    }

    public void setView(Ch14TicTacToeView view) {

        this.view = view;
    }

    public void notify(Point loc) {

        int state;

        int row = loc.x;
        int col = loc.y;

        if (circle) {
            state = Ch14TicTacToeCell.CIRCLE;
        } else {
            state = Ch14TicTacToeCell.CROSS;
        }

        view.update(state);

        circle = !circle;
    }
}
```

Last, the supervisor **Ch14TicTacToeFrame** is modified as follows:

```
/*
    Chapter 14 Sample Development: Tic Tac Toe

    File: Step2/Ch14TicTacToeFrame.java

*/

import java.awt.*;
import javax.swing.*;

public class Ch14TicTacToeFrame extends JFrame  {

    private static final int DEFAULT_BOARD_SIZE = 3;

    private Ch14TicTacToeView gameView;
    private Ch14TicTacToeModel gameModel;

    public static void main(String[] arg) {

        Ch14TicTacToeFrame frame = new Ch14TicTacToeFrame();
        frame.setVisible(true);
    }

    public Ch14TicTacToeFrame() {

        gameView  = new Ch14TicTacToeView(DEFAULT_BOARD_SIZE);
        gameModel = new Ch14TicTacToeModel(DEFAULT_BOARD_SIZE);

        gameView.setModel(gameModel);
        gameModel.setView(gameView);

        setSize(400, 400);
        setTitle("Let's Play Tic Tac Toe");

        setContentPane(gameView);

        setDefaultCloseOperation(EXIT_ON_CLOSE);
    }
}
```

step 2 test

We run the program and verify that the circle and cross images are displayed alternately as we click on the cells. Once we confirm this behavior, we move on to the next step.

Step 3 Development: Complete the Model

In the third development step, we will complete the model class **Ch14TicTacToe-Model** and make any necessary changes to the other classes. The main tasks of the **Ch14TicTacToeModel** class are to

1. Check whether the move is valid. For example, click on a cell that already contains a cross or circle is invalid.

2. Check whether a given valid move results in a win.

Both of these tasks are done in the **notify** method. We use a two-dimensional array of **int** to keep track of the board configuration. Figure 14.20 illustrates the relationship between the display and the internal representation. We create and initialize the two-dimensional array named **board** in the **Ch14TicTacToeModel** constructor (**size** is an argument to the constructor).

```
board = new int[size][size];

for (int row = 0; row < size; row++) {
    for (int col = 0; col < size; col++) {
        board[row][col] = Ch14TicTacToeCell.BLANK;
    }
}
```

The argument to the **notify** method is a **Point** object that identifies the clicked cell. We consult the **board** array to see if the cell is blank. If it is, then we assign either a cross or a circle, depending on whose turn it is, to the cell. If the cell is not blank, then the mouse click is ignored. After the internal two-dimensional array is updated, we call the **update** method of **Ch14TicTacToeView** to reflect the change visually. The **update** method of **Ch14TicTacToeView** sets the content of the clicked cell with the

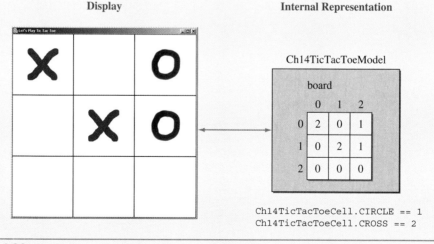

Figure 14.20 A two-dimensional array of **int** is used to keep track of the board configuration.

designated mark (an image of a circle or a cross). At the end of the **notify** method, we check the **board** array to see if there's a winner. Here's the method:

```
public void notify(Point loc) {

    int row = loc.x;
    int col = loc.y;
    int state;

    if (board[row][col] == Ch14TicTacToeCell.BLANK) {

        if (circle) {
            state = Ch14TicTacToeCell.CIRCLE;

        } else {
            state = Ch14TicTacToeCell.CROSS;
        }

        board[row][col] = state;
        view.update(state);

        circle = !circle; //switch turn

        checkWin(row, col);
    }
}
```

We check the board for a win by looking at *N* consecutive cells with the same mark in the horizontal, vertical, and diagonal directions. Which row and column to check and whether to check the diagonal or the inverse diagonal direction are determined by the cell that was clicked. For example, if the clicked cell is at position [1,2] in the 3 × 3 board, then we check the second row and the third column, but not the diagonals, as illustrated in Figure 14.21. If there's a win, then we inform the supervisor that the game is over by calling the **gameOver** method. The programmer who implements the supervisor class can decide what to do in the **gameOver** method. In this sample program, the supervisor simply displays the message and stops. It is left as Exercise 8 to extend the supervisor so the players can play multiple games. Here's the **checkWin** method:

```
public void checkWin(int row, int col) {

    if (checkRow(row, col) ||
        checkCol(row, col) ||
        checkDiagonal(row, col) ||
        checkInvDiagonal(row, col) ) {

            supervisor.gameOver(board[row][col]);
    }
}
```

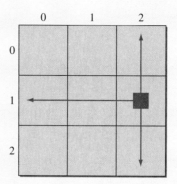

Figure 14.21 The position of the clicked cell determines which row and column to check and whether to check the diagonal and inverse diagonal directions. For example, if cell [1,2] is clicked, then row 1 and column 2 are checked.

Notice the argument we pass to the **gameOver** method. The content of the board cell identifies the winning player (either the cross or the circle). There are four private methods for checking the horizontal, vertical, diagonal, and inverse diagonal directions. The following is the **checkRow** method. The other methods are very similar to it.

```java
public boolean checkRow(int row, int col) {

    for (int i = 0; i < boardSize; i++) {

        if (board[row][i] != board[row][col]) {
            return false;
        }
    }

    return true;
}
```

step 3 code   Only two classes are modified in this step. Here's the step 3 **Ch14TicTacToe-Model** class in its entirety:

```java
/*
    Chapter 14 Sample Program: Tic Tac Toe

    File: Step3/Ch14TicTacToeModel.java

*/

import java.awt.*;
```

```java
public class Ch14TicTacToeModel {

    private Ch14TicTacToeFrame supervisor;
    private Ch14TicTacToeView  view;
    private int[][]            board;
    private int                boardSize;
    private boolean            circle;

    public Ch14TicTacToeModel(int size) {

        board = new int[size][size];

        for (int row = 0; row < size; row++) {
            for (int col = 0; col < size; col++) {
                board[row][col] = Ch14TicTacToeCell.BLANK;
            }
        }

        boardSize = size;
        circle    = true;
    }

    public void setView(Ch14TicTacToeView view) {

        this.view = view;
    }

    public void setSupervisor(Ch14TicTacToeFrame supervisor) {

        this.supervisor = supervisor;
    }

    public void notify(Point loc) {

        int row = loc.x;
        int col = loc.y;
        int state;

        if (board[row][col] == Ch14TicTacToeCell.BLANK) {

            if (circle) {
                state = Ch14TicTacToeCell.CIRCLE;

            } else {
                state = Ch14TicTacToeCell.CROSS;
            }

            board[row][col] = state;
            view.update(state);
```

```
                circle = !circle;

                checkWin(row, col);
        }
    }

    private void checkWin(int row, int col) {

        if (checkRow          (row, col) ||
            checkCol          (row, col) ||
            checkDiagonal     (row, col) ||
            checkInvDiagonal(row, col) ) {

                supervisor.gameOver(board[row][col]);
        }
    }

    private boolean checkRow(int row, int col) {

        for (int i = 0; i < boardSize; i++) {

            if (board[row][i] != board[row][col]) {
                return false;
            }
        }

        return true;
    }

    private boolean checkCol(int row, int col) {

        for (int i = 0; i < boardSize; i++) {

            if (board[i][col] != board[row][col]) {
                return false;
            }
        }

        return true;
    }

    private boolean checkDiagonal(int row, int col) {

        if (row != col) return false;

        for (int i = 0; i < boardSize; i++) {

            if (board[i][i] != board[row][col]) {
                return false;
            }
        }
```

```
            return true;
        }

    private boolean checkInvDiagonal(int row, int col) {

        if (row + col != boardSize - 1) return false;

        for (int i = 0; i < boardSize; i++) {

            if (board[i][boardSize-i-1] != board[row][col]) {
                return false;
            }
        }

        return true;
    }
}
```

And here's the top-level supervisor class:

```
/*
    Chapter 14 Sample Development: Tic Tac Toe

    File: Step3/Ch14TicTacToeFrame.java
*/

import java.awt.*;
import javax.swing.*;

public class Ch14TicTacToeFrame extends JFrame  {

    private static final int DEFAULT_BOARD_SIZE = 3;

    private Ch14TicTacToeView  gameView;

    private Ch14TicTacToeModel gameModel;

    public static void main(String[] arg) {

        Ch14TicTacToeFrame frame = new Ch14TicTacToeFrame();
        frame.setVisible(true);
    }

    public Ch14TicTacToeFrame() {
```

```
        gameView  = new Ch14TicTacToeView(DEFAULT_BOARD_SIZE);
        gameModel = new Ch14TicTacToeModel(DEFAULT_BOARD_SIZE);

        gameView.setModel(gameModel);
        gameModel.setView(gameView);
        gameModel.setSupervisor(this);

        setSize(400, 400);
        setTitle("Let's Play Tic Tac Toe");

        setContentPane(gameView);

        setDefaultCloseOperation(EXIT_ON_CLOSE);
    }

    public void gameOver(int winner) {
        String winnerName;

        if (winner == Ch14TicTacToeCell.CIRCLE) {
            winnerName = "Circle";
        } else {
            winnerName = "Cross";
        }

        JOptionPane.showMessageDialog(this, winnerName + " WON");
    }
}
```

We keep the supervisor class very simple to keep focus on the other classes. By adding more bells and whistles to the supervisor class (and without making any changes to other classes) a more realistic program can be developed. See the chapter exercises for suggestions.

step 3 test

For this step, we run the program and play games. We test both legal and illegal moves and confirm that the program handles both cases correctly. We check all types of wins (horizontal, vertical, etc.). Wins are detected correctly, but since the event handling is not disabled after a win, the players can continue to click on the empty cells, which results in an awkward user interface. We will correct this bug in the next step.

Step 4 Development: Finalize

We finalize the program in the last step by finding any inconsistency or error in the methods, incomplete methods, places to add more comments, and so forth. We noticed a bug in the step 3 test. When a game is won by a player, clicking on a cell should be disabled, but this was not done. We will correct this problem here. Disabling of event handling can be done easily by keeping a boolean variable. We initialize this variable to **true** when a game is started and set it to **false** when a win is detected. We

14.5 Sample Development—*continued*

add a boolean variable **active** and a method named **setEnable** to the **Ch14TicTac-ToeView** class. The method is defined as

```
public void setEnable(boolean state) {
    active = state;
}
```

The constructor of **Ch14TicTacToeView** calls the **setEnable** method with **true** as an argument. At the end of the **gameOver** method of the **Ch14TicTacToeFrame** class, we call the **setEnable** method with **false** as an argument. Finally, we rewrite the **actionPerformed** method of **Ch14TicTacToeModel** as

```
public void mouseClicked(MouseEvent event) {

    if (active) {
        currentCell = (Ch14TicTacToeCell) event.getSource();

        model.notify(currentCell.getPosition());
    }
}
```

Since the changes made are minimal, we will skip the listing of the source code here.

Summary

- User actions such as moving or dragging the mouse and clicking the mouse buttons will result in the generation of mouse events.
- By using layout managers, absolute positioning of GUI components on a container becomes unnecessary.
- Effective layout of GUI components is achieved by nesting panels and applying different layout managers to the panels.
- There are many different kinds of GUI components, each suitable for a particular type of application.
- The standard classes and interfaces described or used in this chapter are

MouseListener	GridLayout
MouseMotionListener	JCheckBox
MouseEvent	ItemListener
JPanel	ItemEvent
FlowLayout	JRadioButton
BorderLayout	ButtonGroup

JComboBox	JSlider
JList	ChangeListener
JScrollPane	ChangeEvent

- **MouseListener** handles the button actions, and **MouseMotionListener** handles the mouse movements.

- **JPanel** is a container for GUI components. **JPanel** itself is a GUI component, and therefore, we can nest **JPanel** objects.

- The **FlowLayout** manager places components in left-to-right, top-to-bottom order.

- The **BorderLayout** manager places components in one of the five regions: north, south, east, west, and center.

- The **GridLayout** manager places components in one of the equal-size $N \times M$ grids.

- The **JCheckBox** class is used for check-box buttons. An instance of the class generates action and item events.

- **ItemEvent** is generated when the state (selected/deselected) of an item changes.

- **ItemEvent** is handled by an instance of a class that implements the **ItemListener** interface.

- The **JRadioButton** class is used for radio buttons. An instance of the class generates action and item events.

- The **JComboBox** class is used for combo boxes, also known as drop-down lists. An instance of the class generates action and item events.

- The **JList** class is used for displaying a list of items. (*Note:* A JList object generates action and list events. To keep the examples brief and at the introductory level, we did not give any sample code that deals with events generated by a JList object.)

- The **JSlider** class is used for sliders. An instance of the class generates change events.

- **ChangeEvent** is handled by an instance of a class that implements the **ChangeListener** interface.

Key Concepts

mouse events	layout managers
mouse listeners	nested panels
item events	radio and check-box buttons
item listeners	combo boxes (drop-down lists)
change events	lists
change listeners	sliders

Exercises

Some of these exercises were already given in the earlier chapters. For these exercises, redo them by designing the user interface with the techniques learned in this chapter.

1. Write a program that teaches arithmetic to children. Design a user interface similar to the one shown here. When the user presses the ENTER key (while the JTextField object is active) or clicks the OK button, the frame displays a message stating whether the given entry is correct. Consider using a larger font for the JLabel and TextField text. Also, consider using images for the reply.

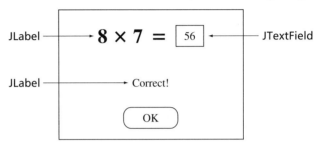

2. Write a GUI interface for the Eggy-Peggy program. When the user presses the ENTER key (while the top JTextField is active) or clicks the OK button, display the encrypted text in the bottom JTextField.

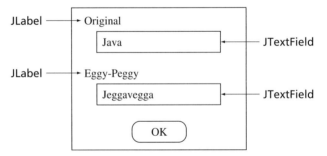

3. Modify the user interface of the HiLo program to include the listing of guesses made by the user. Use a JList object to list the user's guesses.

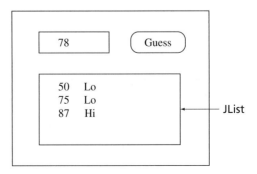

4. (Challenge) Write a calculator program.

Use nested panels and various layout managers for placing the buttons and text field. On the logic side, these are some of the issues you need to consider:

- How to determine whether the user is entering a left operand or a right operand.
- How to handle the entering of multiple decimal points. A typical calculator accepts the first decimal point and ignores the rest. For example, if you press 1 . 4 . 3 . , the number entered is 1.43.
- When the display is 0 and the user enters 0, the display will not change. However, if the display is nonzero and the user enters 0, the 0 is appended to the number currently displayed.
- How to handle the operator precedence. For example, what will be the result if the user enters 4 + 3 × 2? Will it be 14 or 10? It is easier to treat all operators as having equal precedence and process them from left to right.

Study any real four-function calculator and try to implement a software calculator that simulates the real calculator as faithfully as possible, but feel free to make any reasonable changes.

5. Write an application that draws a circle every time the mouse button is clicked. The position where the mouse is clicked will become the center of the circle. Set the radius of the circle to 100 pixels.

6. Extend Exercise 15 by adding the following menu to let the user select the shape to draw every time the mouse button is clicked. The clicked point will be the center of the selected shape. Choose appropriate values for the dimensions of the three shapes.

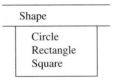

7. Modify the mortgage table program of Exercise 30 on page 378 by adding a new user interface. The left side of a frame is used to enter the loan amount, interest rate, and loan period. The right side of a frame displays the mortgage table for given input values. The following layout is merely a suggestion. Feel free to use other GUI components as you see fit. For example, consider using JComboBox for entering interest rates and loan periods.

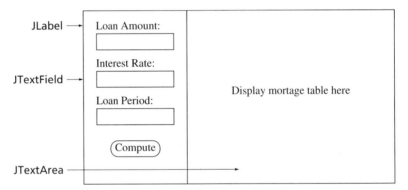

8. Modify the Ch14TicTacToeFrame class by adding a menu item New Game under a File menu so the players can play multiple games. Prompt the players for confirmation to start a new game if the current game is not yet finished.

9. Extend Exercise 8 further by keeping track of scores (the number of wins by each player) and modifying the user interface of the TicTacToe program to something similar to the following:

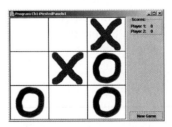

10. Modify the TicTacToe program so it plays the game against the human player. You can start with a very simple algorithm. For example, when it is a computer's turn to play, randomly select one from a number of valid moves. After the program works correctly, you can then improve the algorithm. One

possibility is to choose the one that will result in occupying three adjacent positions (in other words, the computer wins). If there's no such move, then select the one that will result in occupying two adjacent positions.

11. Rewrite the Ch14TicTacToePanel class by using the approach illustrated in Figure 14.9.

Development Exercises

For Exercises 12 through 19, use the incremental development methodology to implement the program. Design a visually appealing GUI with Swing components and layout managers. For each exercise, identify the program tasks, create a design document with class descriptions, and draw the program diagram. Map out the development steps at the start. Present any design alternatives and justify your selection. Be sure to perform adequate testing at the end of each development step.

12. Latte Gallery in Carmel, California, is a small gallery that specializes in selling contemporary fine art, especially lithographs and photographs. All items sold in the gallery are signed and numbered. Write an application that keeps track of

    • Customers and their art purchases.

    • Artists and their works that have appeared in the gallery.

    • Current inventory.

    Allow the user to add, delete, or modify the customer, artist, and artwork information. An inventory will include the purchase prices of the artwork and the selling price when sold. Give the user an option to list all customers or one customer. The user will specify the customer to display by entering the customer's last name and phone number.

    Define at least four data members for each type of information. For customers, include the name, phone number, address, and artwork and artist preferences. For artists, include the name, speciality, whether alive or deceased, and price ranges of artwork. For artwork, include the title, date purchased, date sold, and artist. Feel free to add more data members as you see fit.

    Design appropriate GUI for entering and editing customers, artists, and artwork.

13. Improve the Latte Gallery Information Manager application by adding the following capabilities:

    • List all customers who bought artwork by a given artist.

    • List all artists who are still alive (so you can buy their artwork while the price is still reasonable).

    • List all artwork in the inventory that did not sell for over 3 months. (This requires the use of the Date class from the java.util package.)

    Adjust the GUI accordingly.

14. Improve the Latte Gallery Information Manager application by adding a feature that allows the user to select a customer from the list of all customers

by clicking on the customer that he or she wants to see. The listing of all customers will include their names. When the user clicks on a name, the full information of the selected customer will appear on the right side of the frame.

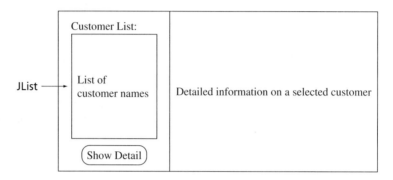

15. Write a program that plays the game of Fermi. The program generates three distinct random digits between 0 and 9. These digits are assigned to positions 1, 2, and 3. The goal of the game is for the player to guess the digits in three positions correctly in the least number of tries. For each guess, the player provides three digits for positions 1, 2, and 3. The program replies with a hint consisting of Fermi, Pico, or Nano. If the digit guessed for a given position is correct, then the reply is Fermi. If the digit guessed for a given position is in a different position, the reply is Pico. If the digit guessed for a given position does not match any of the three digits, then the reply is Nano. Here are sample replies for the three secret digits 6, 5, and 8 at positions 1, 2, and 3, respectively.

Guess	Hint	Explanation
1 2 5	Nano Nano Pico	The value 5 matches but at the wrong position.
8 5 3	Pico Fermi Nano	The value 5 matches at the correct position. The value 8 matches but at the wrong position.
5 8 6	Pico Pico Pico	All match at the wrong positions.

Notice that if the hints like the above are given, the player can tell which number did not match. For example, given the hint for the second guess, we can tell that 3 is not one of the secret numbers. To avoid this, provide hints in a random order or in alphabetical order (e.g., it will be Fermi Nano Pico instead of Pico Fermi Nano for the second reply). Implement the program with an attractive and elegant GUI.

16. Extend the Fermi playing program by allowing the player to

   • Select the number of secret digits.
   • Select alphabets instead of digits.
   • Include duplicate secret digits.

Adjust the GUI accordingly.

17. Write a personal scheduler application. Each entry in the scheduler is an appointment, a to-do item, or a memo. Each entry has the date and the time it is entered. An entry can be locked, and if it is locked, the user cannot modify it. For an appointment entry, include the person and the place of meeting. For a to-do entry, include a short description of a task and the due date. For a memo, include a text. Implement the program with an attractive and elegant GUI.

18. Write a rental point-tracking system for an up-and-coming Espresso's Dynamo Mopeds in Monterey, California. To compete against Ms. Latte's Mopeds R Us, Espresso's Dynamo Mopeds decided to install an automated points-tracking system. When a customer first rents a moped, his or her information is entered into a database. For each rental, a customer receives points, and when the total points reach 100, the customer can rent a moped free for 3 h or redeem a free movie rental coupon from Espresso's Majestic Movies. The points are earned in the following scheme:

Renter	Type	Points
College student	50cc Moppi	15
	150cc Magnum	20
Adult	50cc Moppi	10
	150cc Magnum	15
Senior	50cc Moppi	20
	150cc Magnum	30

In addition to the basic operations of updating the point information for every rental, include an operation to list all customers who earned over 100 points. Also, support an operation to edit the customer information. Implement the program with an attractive and elegant GUI.

19. Update the rental point-tracking system to support a new rental system and point-awarding rules for Espresso's Dynamo Mopeds. Now the customers can rent only on an hourly basis, and the points are awarded accordingly. Upon rental, the customer will state the number of hours he or she will rent in increments of 1 hour with a maximum of 10 hours. The rental fee is based on the following formula:

Renter	Type	Total Rental ≤ 5 hours	Total Rental > 5 hours
College student	50cc Moppi	$3.50 per hour	$2.50 per hour
	150cc Magnum	$4.50 per hour	$3.50 per hour
Adult	50cc Moppi	$5.00 per hour	$4.00 per hour
	150cc Magnum	$6.50 per hour	$5.00 per hour
Senior	50cc Moppi	$4.00 per hour	$3.00 per hour
	150cc Magnum	$5.25 per hour	$4.00 per hour

15 Recursive Algorithms

Objectives

After you have read and studied this chapter, you should be able to

- Write recursive algorithms for mathematical functions and nonnumerical operations.

- Decide when to use recursion and when not to.

- Describe the recursive quicksort algorithm and explain how its performance is better than that of selection and bubble sort algorithms.

Introduction

e introduced recursion in Chapter 6 and showed how to write recursive methods to implement mathematical functions. We used mathematical functions in Chapter 6 because it is easier to see how the recursion works with mathematical functions. However, recursive methods are not limited to implementing mathematical functions, and we will present several nonnumerical recursive algorithms in this chapter. We will also discuss some criteria for deciding when to use recursion and when not to. All the recursive algorithms we provide in this chapter, other than those we use for explanation, are algorithms that should be written recursively.

15.1 | Basic Elements of Recursion

recursive method

A *recursive method* is a method that contains a statement (or statements) that makes a call to itself. In Chapter 7, we implemented three mathematical functions using recursion. In this chapter, we will present recursive algorithms for nonnumerical operations. But before we introduce new examples, let's review one of the recursive algorithms we presented in Chapter 7.

The *factorial* of N is the product of the first N positive integers, denoted mathematically as

```
N! = N * (N-1) * (N-2) * ... * 2 * 1
```

We can define the factorial of N recursively as

$$\text{factorial(N)} = \begin{cases} 1 & \text{if N = 1} \\ \\ \text{N * factorial(N-1)} & \text{otherwise} \end{cases}$$

We mentioned in Chapter 6 that any recursive method will include the following three basic elements:

1. A test to stop or continue the recursion.
2. An end case that terminates the recursion.
3. A recursive call(s) that continues the recursion.

These three elements are included in the following recursive factorial method.

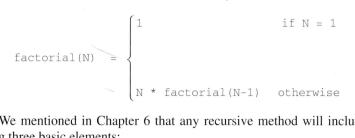

```
public int factorial(int N)
{
    if (N == 1) {          ← Test to stop or continue.

        return 1;          ← End case: recursion stops.
    }
```

```
    else {
        return N * factorial(N-1);
    }
}
```

Recursive case: recursion
continues with a
recursive call.

15.2 | Directory Listing

Let's try some recursive algorithms for nonnumerical applications. A first nonnumerical recursive algorithm will list the filename of all files in a given directory (or
folder) of a hard disk and its subdirectories. We will use a File object from the java.io
package to implement the method. Assuming a Windows platform, we create a File
object by passing the name of a file or a directory, as in

```
File file = new File("D:/Java/Projects");
```

Notice that we pass the full path name. If a File object represents a directory,
then the boolean method isDirectory returns true. To get an array of names of files
and subdirectories in a directory, we use the list method.

```
String[] fileList = file.list();
```

Let's call the method directoryListing. The argument to the method will be a
File object that represents a directory. The basic idea can be expressed as follows:

```
public void directoryListing(File dir) {

    //assumption: dir represents a directory

    fileList = an array of names of files and
               subdirectories in the directory dir;

    for (each element in fileList) {

        if (an element is a file) {
            output the element's filename;  //end case: it's
                                            //a file.
        } else { //recursive case: it's a directory
            call directoryListing with element as
            an argument;
        }
    }
}
```

The complete method is as follows:

```
public void directoryListing(File dir) {

    //assumption: dir represents a directory

    String[] fileList = dir.list();  //get the contents
    String dirPath = dir.getAbsolutePath();
```

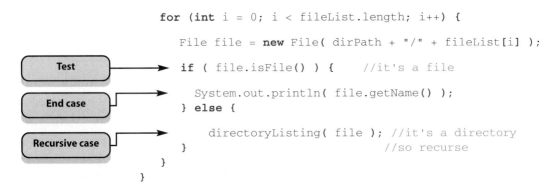

```
        for (int i = 0; i < fileList.length; i++) {

            File file = new File( dirPath + "/" + fileList[i] );

            if ( file.isFile() ) {      //it's a file

                System.out.println( file.getName() );
            } else {

                directoryListing( file ); //it's a directory
            }                                      //so recurse
        }
    }
```

Notice the argument we pass to create a new File object inside the for loop is

```
    File file = new File(dirPath + File.separator
                            + fileList[i] );
```

where dirPath is set as

```
    String dirPath   = dir.getAbsolutePath();
```

and File.separator is a class constant for the system-dependent character used as the file separator.

The getAbsolutePath method returns the full path name for the directory, and we need to prepend it to the name (fileList[i]) of a file or a subdirectory in this directory in order to make the testing

```
    if ( file.isFile() ) ...
```

work correctly.

To give you more practice in reading recursive methods, we will remove the assumption that the argument File represents a directory and rewrite the method. If the argument File object to directoryListing can be either a file or a directory, then we need to check this first. If the argument object is a file, then we list its filename and stop the recursion. If the argument object is a directory, then we get the list of contents in the directory and make recursive calls. Here's the second version:

```
    public void directoryListing(File file) {
        //'file' may be a directory or a file

        String[] fileList;
        String   pathname = file.getAbsolutePath();

        if ( file.isFile() ) {
                                            //it's a file so
            System.out.println( file.getName() );   //print it out

        } else { //it's a directory, so recurse
```

```
                           │  fileList = file.list();
                           │  for (int i = 0; i < fileList.length; i++) {
  ┌──────────────────┐     │     File nextFile = new File(pathname+ File.separator
  │ Recursive case   │────▶│                                    + fileList[i]);
  └──────────────────┘     │     directoryListing(nextFile); //recursive call
                           │  }
                      }    │
                   }       │
```

15.3 | Anagram

anagram

Our second example of a nonnumerical recursive method is to derive all anagrams of a given word. An *anagram* is a word or phrase formed by reordering the letters of another word or phrase. If the word is CAT, for example, then its anagrams are

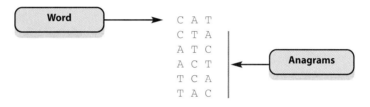

Figure 15.1 illustrates the basic idea of using recursion to list all anagrams of a word.

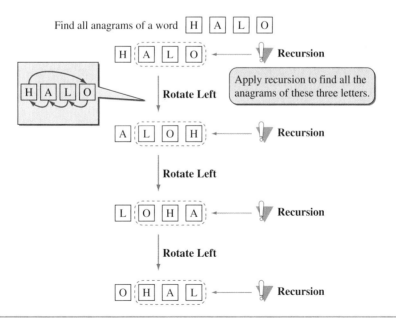

Figure 15.1 How to generate all the anagrams of a word by using recursion.

Expressing the basic idea, we have something like this:

```java
public void anagram( String word ) {
    int numOfChars = word.length();

    if (numOfChars == 1) {
        //End case: there's only one character left,
        //          so we can't recurse anymore
    } else {
        for (int i = 1; i <= numOfChars; i++ ) {

            char firstLetter = word.charAt(0);

            suffix = word.substring(1, numOfChars);

            anagram( suffix );  //recurse with the remaining
                                //letters in the word

            //rotate left
            word = suffix + firstLetter;
        }
    }
}
```

This **for** loop is illustrated in Figure 15.1.

To derive the real method that executes correctly, we must finalize a number of things. First, what will we do when the recursion stops? Hitting upon the end case means that we have found one anagram, so we will print it out. Now, this is the tricky part. When we call the method recursively, we are passing a word that has the first letter chopped off. This means the words being passed to successive recursive calls are getting shorter and shorter. But we need to access all letters in a word to print it out. We can solve this problem by passing two parameters: the prefix and the suffix of a word. In each successive call, the prefix becomes one letter more and the suffix becomes one letter less. When the suffix becomes one letter only, then the recursion stops. Using this idea, we see the method now looks like this:

```java
public void anagram( String prefix, String suffix ) {
    int numOfChars = suffix.length();

    if (numOfChars == 1) {
        //End case: print out one anagram
        System.out.println( prefix + suffix );
    } else {
        ...
    }
}
```

and this method is initially set with an empty **prefix** and the word being the **suffix**, as in

```java
anagram( "", "HALO" );
```

Now, by using the two parameters prefix and suffix, the for loop is written as

```
for (int i = 1; i <=numOfChars; i++ ) {

    newSuffix = suffix.substring(1, numOfChars);
    newPrefix = prefix + suffix.charAt(0);

    anagram( newPrefix, newSuffix ); //recursive case

    //rotate left to create a rearranged suffix
    suffix = newSuffix + suffix.charAt(0);
}
```

Putting everything together, we have the final anagram method:

```
public void anagram( String prefix, String suffix ) {
    String newPrefix, newSuffix;
    int numOfChars = suffix.length();

    if (numOfChars == 1) {
        //End case: print out one anagram
        System.out.println( prefix + suffix );
    } else {
        for (int i = 1; i <= numOfChars; i++ ) {
            newSuffix = suffix.substring(1, numOfChars);
            newPrefix = prefix + suffix.charAt(0);

            anagram( newPrefix, newSuffix );
                                        //recursive call

            //rotate left to create a rearranged suffix
            suffix = newSuffix + suffix.charAt(0);
        }
    }
}
```

Test → (points to `if (numOfChars == 1) {`)

End case → (points to `System.out.println( prefix + suffix );`)

Recursive case → (points to the for loop block)

Because the ending condition for recursion is tricky, let's study carefully the test to stop the recursion. We set the test to

```
if (numOfChars == 1 ) ...
```

Is there any assumption we must make about the parameters so that this method will work correctly? We mentioned earlier that the initial call to the recursive method is something like

```
anagram( "", "HALO" );
```

What would happen if we made the call initially like

```
String str = inputBox.getString();
anagram( "", str );
```

and the user entered an empty string? This is left as Exercise 8.

1. Determine the output of these calls without actually running the method.

    a. `anagram( "", "DOG" );`
    b. `anagram( "", "CAFE");`

15.4 | Towers of Hanoi

The objective of a puzzle called the *Towers of Hanoi* is deceptively simple, but find-ing a solution is another matter. The goal of the puzzle is to move *N* disks from peg 1 to peg 3 by moving one disk at a time and never placing a larger disk on top of a smaller disk. See Figure 15.2.

    The Towers of Hanoi puzzle can be solved very nicely by using recursion. The Aha! moment to this puzzle occurs when you realize that you can solve the puzzle if somehow you can move the top *N* − 1 disks to peg 2. After the top *N* − 1 disks are moved to peg 2 temporarily, you move the largest disk from peg 1 to peg 3 and finally move the *N* − 1 disks from peg 2 to peg 3. Figure 15.3 illustrates these three steps. The first and the third steps are, of course, the same puzzle with one fewer disk and the destination peg changed. So you apply the same logic recursively to the first and third steps. When the number of disks becomes 1, then the recursion stops. Applying this recursive thinking, we can write the method as

```
public void towersOfHanoi( int N,        //number of disks
                           int from,      //origin peg
                           int to,        //destination peg
                           int spare )  //"middle" peg
{
    if ( N == 1 ) {
        moveOne( from, to );
    } else {
        towersOfHanoi( N-1, from, spare, to );
```

Figure 15.2 Towers of Hanoi with *N* = 4 disks.

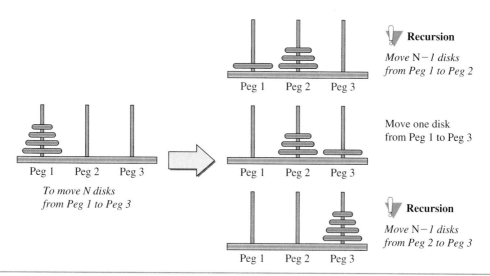

Figure 15.3 Recursive solution to the Towers of Hanoi puzzle.

```
            moveOne( from, to );
            towersOfHanoi( N-1, spare, to, from );
        }
    }
```

The moveOne is the method that actually moves the disk. Here we will define the method to print out the move, using System.out

```java
private void moveOne( int from, int to ) {
    System.out.println( from + " ---> " + to );
}
```

When we run this method with $N = 4$, we get the following output:

```
1 ---> 2
1 ---> 3
2 ---> 3
1 ---> 2
3 ---> 1
3 ---> 2
1 ---> 2
1 ---> 3
2 ---> 3
2 ---> 1
3 ---> 1
2 ---> 3
1 ---> 2
1 ---> 3
2 ---> 3
```

The output is very difficult to read. We can improve the output considerably by padding a varying number of blank spaces to show the level of recursion. We can change the output to

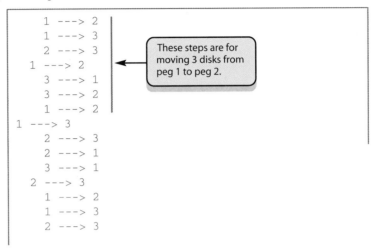

```
          1 ---> 2
          1 ---> 3
          2 ---> 3
      1 ---> 2
          3 ---> 1
          3 ---> 2
          1 ---> 2
  1 ---> 3
          2 ---> 3
          2 ---> 1
          3 ---> 1
      2 ---> 3
          1 ---> 2
          1 ---> 3
          2 ---> 3
```

These steps are for moving 3 disks from peg 1 to peg 2.

by rewriting the methods as follows:

```
public void towersOfHanoi( int N,      //number of disks
                           int from,   //origin peg
                           int to,     //destination peg
                           int spare,  //"middle" peg
                           int indent )//# of leading spaces
{
    if (N == 1) {
        moveOne(from, to, indent);

    } else {
        towersOfHanoi(N-1, from, spare, to, indent+2);

        moveOne( from, to, indent+2 );

        towersOfHanoi(N-1, spare, to, from, indent+2);
    }
}

private void moveOne(int from, int to, int indent) {
    System.out.println(Ch6Format.pad(indent) +
                       from + " ---> " + to );
}
```

15.5 | Quicksort

We will present a third sorting algorithm that uses recursion in this section. This sorting algorithm is called *quicksort,* and we will compare the performance of quicksort against that of the previous two sorting algorithms at the end of this section, to verify that quicksort deserves its name.

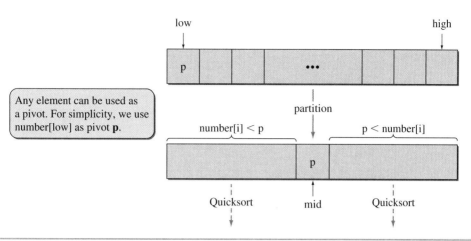

Figure 15.4 The core idea of the quicksort algorithm.

Figure 15.4 illustrates the core thinking of quicksort. To sort an array from index low to high, we first select a pivot element p. We can select any element in the array as a pivot, but for simplicity, we choose number[low] as the pivot. Using p as the pivot, we scan through the array and move all elements smaller than p to the lower half (left half in the figure) and all elements larger than p to the upper half. Then we sort the lower and upper halves recursively, using quicksort. The variable mid points to the position where the pivot is placed. So the lower half of the array is from index low to mid-1, and the upper half of the array is from index mid+1 to high. The recursion stops when the condition low >= high becomes true.

Here's the quicksort algorithm:

```
public void quickSort( int[] number, int low, int high ) {
    if ( low < high ) {

        int mid = partition( number, low, high );

        quickSort( number,   low, mid-1 );
        quickSort( number, mid+1, high  );
    }
}
```

The partition method splits the array elements number[low] to number[high] into two halves, as shown in Figure 15.4. We use number[low] as the pivot element. The method returns the position where the pivot element is placed. Figure 15.5 shows the result of partitioning the array by using the element 23 as a pivot.

We first set the pivot to number[low]. Then we start looking for a number smaller than the pivot from position high, high-1, and so forth. Let's say the number is found at position J. Since this number is smaller than the pivot, we move it to position low. Now we start looking for a number larger than the pivot from low+1, low+2, and so forth. Let's say the number is found at position I. We move it to position J. We then repeat the process, this time looking for a number smaller than the pivot from J-1, J-2, and so forth. Figure 15.6 shows the details of the partitioning process.

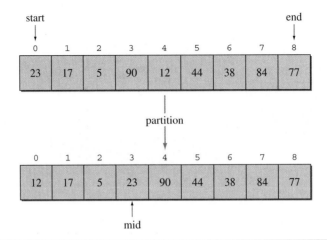

Figure 15.5 Result of partitioning using **23** as a pivot.

Here's the partition method:

```
private int partition(int[] number, int start, int end) {
    //set the pivot
    int pivot = number[start];

    do {
        //look for a number smaller than pivot from the end
        while ( start < end && number[end] >= pivot) {
            end--;
        }

        if ( start < end ) { //found a smaller number
            number[start] = number[end];

            //now find a number larger than pivot
            //from the start
            while ( start < end && number[start] <= pivot) {
                start++;
            }

            if (start < end) { //found a larger number
                number[end] = number[start];
            }
        }

    } while (start < end);

    //done, move the pivot back to the array
    number[start] = pivot;

    return start;
}
```

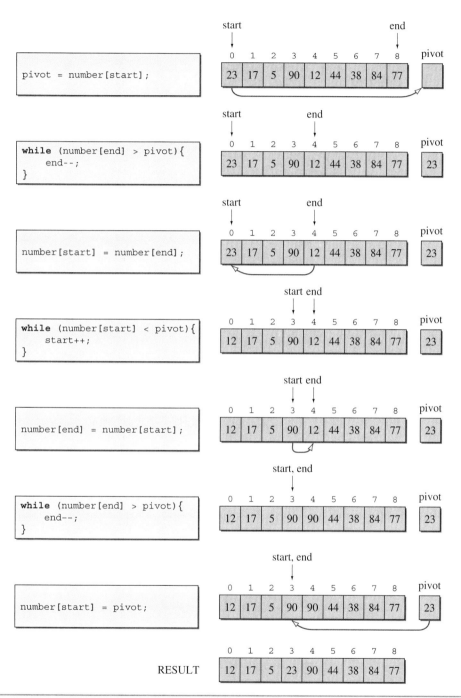

Figure 15.6 Details of one partitioning.

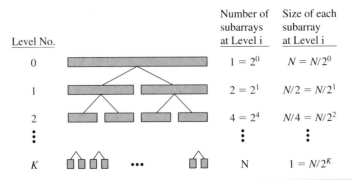

	Level No.		Number of subarrays at Level i	Size of each subarray at Level i
	0		$1 = 2^0$	$N = N/2^0$
	1		$2 = 2^1$	$N/2 = N/2^1$
	2		$4 = 2^4$	$N/4 = N/2^2$
	$\vdots$		$\vdots$	$\vdots$
	K		N	$1 = N/2^K$

Figure 15.7 A hierarchy of partitioning an array into smaller and smaller arrays in the quicksort.

How good is quicksort? Does the algorithm execute a fewer number of comparisons than the selection or bubble sort? The answer is no in the worst case. Quicksort executes roughly the same number of comparisons as the selection sort and bubble sort in the worst case. When the original list is either already sorted or in descending order, then after a partition process, either the lower half or the upper half has $N - 1$ elements. The effect is the same as that of the previous two sorting algorithms; that is, either the smallest or the largest number moves to its correct position. The worst situation can be improved somewhat if we select the median of three numbers, say, number[low], number[high], and number[(low+high)/2], as the pivot element. Even with this improvement, the number of comparisons in the worst case is still approximately the square of the size of the array.

Is the name quicksort a kind of false advertisement? Not really. On the average, we can expect a partition process to split the array into two subarrays of roughly equal size. Figure 15.7 shows how the original array is partitioned into smaller subarrays. When the size of all subarrays becomes 1, then the array becomes sorted. At level i, there are 2^i subarrays of size $N/2^i$. So there will be $N/2^i$ partition processes at level i. The total number of comparisons of all those partition processes at level i is therefore $2^i \cdot N/2^i = N$. Since there are K levels, the total number of comparisons for sorting the whole array is

$$K \cdot N$$

but

$$N = 2^K$$

$$\log_2 N = K$$

so

$$KN = N \log_2 N$$

The total number of comparisons is proportional to $N \log_2 N$, which is a great improvement over N^2. A more rigorous mathematical analysis will show that the quicksort on the average requires approximately $2N \log_2 N$ comparisons.

Quick
CHECK

1. Partition the following arrays, using the partition method.

   a.

0	1	2	3	4	5	6	7	8
18	19	5	77	12	14	13	84	45

   b.

0	1	2	3	4	5	6	7	8
98	19	15	86	12	44	13	24	45

15.6 | When Not to Use Recursion

Recursion is a powerful tool to express complex algorithms succinctly. For example, writing a nonrecursive algorithm for the Towers of Hanoi is unexpectedly difficult. Likewise, a recursive quicksort algorithm is easier to understand than its nonrecursive counterpart. For both problems, we prefer recursive algorithms because recursion is the most natural way to express their solution. However, just being natural is not the criterion for selecting a recursive solution over a nonrecursive one.

Consider a solution for computing the Nth Fibonacci number. A Fibonacci number is defined recursively as

$$\text{fibonacci}(N) \ = \ \begin{cases} 1 & \text{if N = 0 or N = 1} \\ \\ \begin{array}{l}\text{fibonacci}(N\text{-}1) \\ \ + \ \text{fibonacci}(N\text{-}2)\end{array} & \text{otherwise} \end{cases}$$

Because the function is defined recursively, it is natural to implement the function by using a recursive method.

```
public int fibonacci( int N ) {
   if (N == 0 || N == 1) {

      return 1;       //end case

   } else {//recursive case

      return fibonacci(N-1) + fibonacci(N-2);

   }
}
```

This recursive method is succinct, easy to understand, and elegant. But is this the way to implement it? The answer is no, because the recursive method is grossly inefficient and a nonrecursive version is just as easy to understand. The method is inefficient because the same value is computed over and over. Figure 15.8 shows the recursive calls for computing the fifth Fibonacci number. Notice that the same value, for example, fibonacci(2), is computed repeatedly.

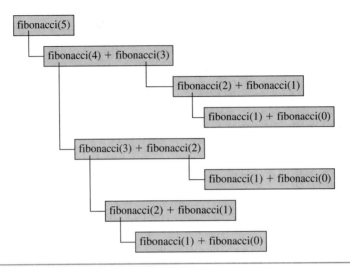

Figure 15.8 Recursive calls to compute **fibonacci(5).**

The Nth Fibonacci number can be computed by using a nonrecursive method.

```
public int fibonacci( int N ) {

    int fibN, fibN1, fibN2, cnt;

    if (N == 0 || N == 1 ) {
        return 1;
    } else {

        fibN1 = fibN2 = 1;
        cnt = 2;

        while ( cnt <= N ) {
            fibN = fibN1 + fibN2; //get the next Fib no.

            fibN1 = fibN2;
            fibN2 = fibN;

            cnt ++;
        }
        return fibN;
    }
}
```

$$
\begin{array}{ccccc}
F_0 & & F_1 & & F_2 \\
1 & + & 1 & = & 2 \\[4pt]
F_1 & & F_2 & & F_3 \\
1 & + & 2 & = & 3 \\[4pt]
F_2 & & F_3 & & F_4 \\
2 & + & 3 & = & 5
\end{array}
$$

The nonrecursive method is not as succinct as the recursive version, but at the same time, it is not that difficult to understand either. The nonrecursive version is much more efficient, and it is the one that should be used. This nonrecursive version is written in such a way that its structure parallels the structure of the recursive version, so we can compare the two easily. It is possible to rewrite the nonrecursive version with a simple for loop as

```java
public int fibonacci (int N)  {

    int fibN1, fibN2, fibN;

    fibN = fibN1 = fibN2 = 1;

    for (int i = 1; i < N; i++)  {

        fibN = fibN1 + fibN2;

        fibN1 = fibN2;
        fibN2 = fibN;
    }

    return fibN;
}
```

There is no clearcut rule to determine whether a routine should be implemented recursively or nonrecursively. In general, we should always search for a nonrecursive solution first. We should use recursion only when a recursive solution is more natural and easier to understand and the resulting method is not too inefficient. We repeat the guideline for using recursive methods we mentioned in Chapter 6.

Design Guidelines

Use recursion if

1. A recursive solution is natural and easy to understand.
2. A recursive solution does not result in excessive duplicate computation.
3. The equivalent iterative solution is too complex.

Summary

- Recursion is a special type of repetition control.
- A recursive method is a method that calls itself.
- A recursive method consists of a test to stop the recursion, the end case that gets executed at the end of recursion, and the recursive case that makes a recursive call to continue the recursion.
- The use of recursion should be avoided if a suitable nonrecursive looping statement can be developed.

K e y   C o n c e p t s

recursive methods   recursive cases

end cases

E x e r c i s e s

1. Write a recursive method to find the smallest element in an array. *Note:* This is strictly an exercise. You should not write the real method recursively.

2. Write a recursive method to compute the average of the elements in an array. *Note:* This is strictly an exercise. You should not write the real method recursively.

3. Write a recursive method to determine whether a given string is a palindrome. A string is a palindrome if it reads the same both forward and backward. Ignore the case of the letters and punctuation marks.

4. Write a recursive binary search method. Should this method be written recursively or nonrecursively in practice?

5. Write a recursive method to compute the greatest common divisor of two integer values. The greatest common divisor (GCD) of two integers is derived by using the following rules:

$$
GCD(i, j) = \begin{cases} i & \text{if } j = 0 \\ GCD(j, i \bmod j) & \text{if } j \ != 0 \end{cases}
$$

6. Write a nonrecursive version of GCD in Exercise 5, and compare the two solutions. Which version is the one you should use in practice?

7. The partition method of the quicksort selects the first element as its pivot. Improve the method by using the median of the values in the first, the middle, and the last element of an array. If an array number to partition has 8 elements indexed from 0 to 7, then the first element is number[0], the middle element is number[4], and the last element is number[7]. If these elements are 55, 34, and 89, for example, then the median is 55.

8. What would happen if the anagram method were called initially by passing an empty string as the second parameter as

    ```
    anagram( "", "" );
    ```

    Will the method work? Why or why not? If not, correct the problem. If yes, then would it be logical to leave it as is or should the method be corrected to make it more logical?

9. Another recursive sorting algorithm is called *merge sort*. The merge sort divides the array into two halves, sorts the two halves recursively using mergesort, and finally merges the two sorted halves into a sorted list. In diagram, the process of merge sort looks like this:

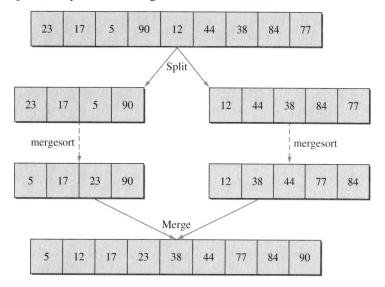

Write the mergesort method.

10. You can visualize the growth of a tree recursively. First you start with a trunk of a set length:

From this trunk, two branches grow out:

Now if you consider the two branches as the trunks of their respective subtrees, you have another growth, resulting in

Continue this recursive growth, and you will end up with a tree that looks something like this:

The length of the branch will get shorter and shorter. Once the length becomes shorter than some preset value, the recursion stops. Also, as you can see from the tree above, you should use some form of probability whether the branch will continue to grow or not. Try first the fixed probability of 0.9. Experiment with others, such as the probability of growth as a function based on the length of the branch.

Appendix A
How to Run Java Programs

One can master programming only by writing and running programs, no[t] reading the sample programs in the text. All sample programs (plus some mor[e] provided in a source file format so you can actually compile and run them and s[ee] how they work. This appendix is intended for those who need to install necessary tools on their computer. Those who have an access to a computer lab with the necessary tools already installed may still want to read this appendix for general information.

In this appendix, we will explain a number of different ways of running Java programs. They can be divided broadly into three categories: minimalist, enhanced editor, and full *integrated development environment* (IDE). For the beginning programmers, we recommend the enhanced editor approach. You can find additional information, such as detailed step-by-step instructions, on using some of the tools mentioned in this appendix from our website at www.drcaffeine.com.

Helpful Reminder

Please read Chapter 2 before this appendix.

At the end of this appendix, we will describe how to use classes from programmer-defined packages, such as the author-provided javabook package, in running your programs.

The Minimalist Approach

In this approach we use the absolute minimum to compile and run Java programs. We need to download a necessary compiler and other tools for compiling and running Java programs from the Sun Microsystems website at http://java.sun.com. A collection of tools for compiling and running Java programs is called a *Java 2 SDK (Software Development Kit)*. Sun Microsystems provides three versions for SDK: enterprise edition (J2EE SDK), standard edition (J2SE SDK), and micro edition (J2ME SDK). The one you need to download is the standard edition. We describe the steps for the MS Windows platform here.

as MyFirstProgram.java.txt. Make sure there's no txt suffix appended to the filename. To avoid the automatic appending of the txt suffix, don't forget to set the value for Save as type to All Files.

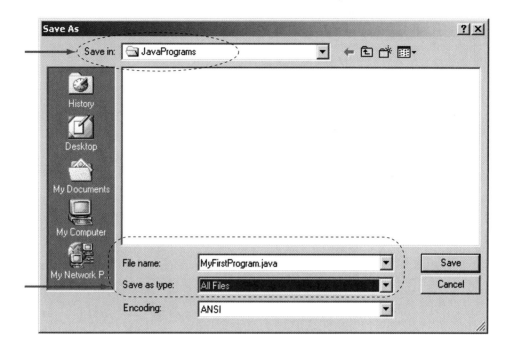

4. **Open a Command Prompt Window**
   After the source file is created and saved properly, we are ready to compile and run it. We use a command prompt window to enter the commands for compiling and running Java programs. Open a command prompt window by selecting the Start/Run... option

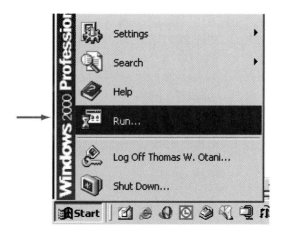

and entering the text cmd in the text field of the Run dialog box (if cmd does not work, try command):

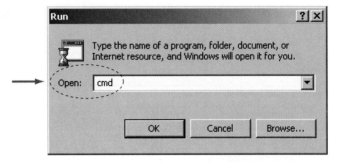

Click the OK button. A command prompt window appears on the screen:

From this point on, all commands are entered in this window.

5. **Set the Environment**

   Before we can actually compile and run the program, we must set the environment. First change to the JavaPrograms directory where the source file is stored by entering the command cd JavaPrograms (and pressing the Enter key):

Note: It is beyond the scope of this appendix to explain DOS commands. Please consult other sources if you need to learn DOS commands.

Enter the following two commands in sequence to set the environment:

```
set path=c:\j2sdk1.4.0_01\bin
set classpath=.
```

Enter the commands exactly as shown. Do not introduce any spaces between the equals symbols (=), for example. The first command sets the PATH environment variable so we can refer to the executable files in the bin subdirectory of C:\j2sdk1.4.0_01. The second command tells the Java compiler and interpreter where to find the source files. The period (.) indicates the current directory. You need to enter the two commands only once.

6. **Compile the Program**

   Finally we are ready to compile the program. To compile a Java source file, use the javac command followed by the filename of the source file. Enter the following command exactly, that is, in a case-sensitive manner:

```
javac MyFirstProgram.java
```

After a moment of pause, when there's no error in the program, the prompt to enter the next command appears. An error message will appear if there's an error. If that happens, go back to Notepad and check the program. Make any necessary changes and save it again. Then enter the javac command again. As explained in Chapter 2, successful compilation will result in a creation of a bytecode file.

7. **Run the Program**

   After the successful compilation of the program, we are finally ready to run the program by executing its bytecode file. To run the program, we use the java command followed by the name of the bytecode file (with no suffix). Enter the command

   ```
   java MyFirstProgram
   ```

   and press the Enter key. The program starts and a message dialog appears on the screen:

Close this message dialog by clicking its OK button. The program terminates, and another prompt appears on the command prompt window:

Congratulations! You have successfully executed your first Java program.

The Significance of the System.exit **Statement**
The last statement of the sample program was

```
System.exit(0);
```

which caused the program to terminate. If you adopt the minimalist approach of using Notepad (or another simple text editor) and a command prompt window, you must include the exit statement to terminate the sample MyFirstProgram program. If you don't, then the program will not terminate. The message dialog disappears from the screen when you click its OK button, but the program is still active. When this happens, you will not get another prompt in the command prompt window. And, of course, without getting a command prompt, you can't enter another command anymore. Not all programs behave in this way. Specifically, a program that uses console-based standard input and output does not require the exit statement, while a program that uses GUI-based input and output (such as MyFirstProgram that uses the GUI-based JOptionPane for output) requires the exit statement. When you are using the minimalist approach, the easiest thing to do is to include the exit statement for all programs.

The Enhanced Editor Approach

For a very simple program, the minimalist approach may be an acceptable alternative. However, when the programs we develop become larger, the minimalist approach becomes cumbersome. Unlike with the minimalist approach in which we have to deal with separate tools for editing (Notepad) and running (command prompt) programs, with the enhanced editor approach, we interact with a single tool that will let us edit, compile, and run Java programs. For the beginning programmers, we recommend the enhanced editor approach.

There are a number of good software tools that fall under this category. Some of the more well-known ones are

- TextPad (www.textpad.com)
- jEdit (www.jedit.org)
- JCreator (www.jcreator.com)
- BlueJ (www.bluej.org)
- jGrasp (www.eng.auburn.edu/grasp)

You can look for other enhanced editors by visiting Google and entering the search text "Java editors." Most of these tools are available free or for a nominal fee. For a list of 10 free Java editors and IDEs, visit http://java.about.com/cs/ides/tp/top10javeditors.htm. The enhanced Java editors are diverse in user interface style and the options they support, but they share two key features:

1. Support of color syntax highlighting. Different portions of the code are displayed in different colors (reserved words in blue, comments in green, string constants in cyan, and so forth).

2. Use of Java 2 SDK. The enhanced editors provide us with an environment where we can enter, compile, and run Java programs, but the actual compilation and execution of programs are done by Java 2 SDK tools (javac, java, etc.). In other words, instead of dealing with Java 2 SDK tools directly by entering commands in the command prompt window, we deal with them by selecting corresponding menu choices of the enhanced editor.

Since we cannot describe the enhanced editors adequately in a limited space, we refer you to their respective websites for instructions on how to use them. Also, brief how-to documents on most of the enhanced editors listed here can be found at our website (www.drcaffeine.com).

The IDE Approach

Tools in the IDE approach are geared toward serious programmers developing large-scale programs. Borland JBuilder, IBM VisualAge, Metrowerks CodeWarrior, and Sun Forte are some of the well-known full IDEs. In addition to many features, they typically include a visual editor that lets programmers design the user interface of a program visually by dragging and dropping GUI objects from the component palettes. They are complicated, and it takes time to master and use the various features supported by them properly. For this reason, this approach is not recommend for beginning programmers.

Using Programmer-Defined Packages

When we are using classes from the system packages such as javax.swing, java.util, and others, all we do is to include appropriate import statements in the program. This is not enough when we are using classes from programmer-defined packages. We must also set the environment correctly. How we set the environment is dependent on the development tools we use. We will describe how to set the environment to use programmer-defined packages with the minimalist approach. Please visit our website (www.drcaffeine.com) for information on using programmer-defined packages with the enhanced editor approach.

We will use the author-provided javabook package as an example to illustrate the procedure. You can download this package and its documentation from the textbook website. We assume you have downloaded and installed the javabook classes under the C:\JavaPrograms\javabook directory. Notice that the name of the package is javabook, and the directory that contains the classes in this package is also named javabook. This is the requirement. The classes in the package xyz must be placed in the directory named xyz. The directory xyz, however, can be placed anywhere you want. In this example, we put the javabook directory under C:\JavaPrograms. When the installation is done correctly, you should see the source and bytecode files of the javabook classes such as MainWindow.java, MainWindow.class, OutputBox.java, OutputBox.class, and others in the C:\JavaPrograms\javabook directory.

Helpful Reminder

For this example, we assume that the classes from the author-provided **javabook** *package are placed in the directory.*

`C:\JavaPrograms\javabook`

All you have to do is to change the setting for the class path as follows:

`set classpath=.;c:\JavaPrograms`

Notice that we specify the directory that contains the javabook directory. We do specify the full path name to the javabook directory itself.

Helpful Reminder

To use the **javabook** *classes stored in the directory* **C:\Javaprograms\javabook**, *set the class path by entering the command.*

`set classpath=.;c:\JavaPrograms`

Here's how we set both path and class path environment variables at the beginning of a session:

```
C:\WINNT\System32\cmd.exe
Microsoft Windows 2000 [Version 5.00.2195]
(C) Copyright 1985-2000 Microsoft Corp.

C:\>set path=c:\j2sdk1.4.0_01

C:\>set classpath=.;c:\JavaPrograms

C:\>
```

Appendix B

Sample Programs

In this appendix, we provide a chapter-by-chapter list of all sample classes (programs). For each sample class, we provide a brief description, the page number where the class is listed or discussed, and a list of system classes used by this class. You can download the source files of all sample classes (programs) from our website at http://www.drcaffeine.com.

Chapter-by-Chapter List

The single asterisk means only the fragment of the program is listed in the main text. The double asterisks mean the program is not listed in the main text. Such programs are provided as additional examples or variations on the programs listed in the main text.

<chapter #>		
Name	**Page #**	**Standard Classes**
<class name>	<page # where the class is listed>	<list of standard classes or interfaces used or referred to in the class> *Note:* Unless the String class is the major focus of a program, it will not be listed in this column.
<A brief description of the class>		
<class used in the sample development>		

Chapter 2		
Class Name	**Page #**	**Standard Classes**
Ch2Sample1	33	JFrame
This program opens a simple JFrame window.		
Ch2FunTime	51	
Structurally this (optional) program is identical to Ch2Sample1. The only difference lies in the use of the javabook.SketchPad class instead of JFrame. This program reinforces the idea of using an object in a program.		

Chapter 2 *(Continued)*

Class Name	Page #	Standard Classes
Ch2MyWebBrowser	53	

Structurally this (optional) program is identical to Ch2Sample1. The only difference lies in the use of the javabook.SketchPad class instead of JFrame. Like Ch2FunTime, this program reinforces the idea of using an object in a program.

Class Name	Page #	Standard Classes
Ch2ShowMessageDialog	59	JFrame JOptionPane

This program illustrates the use of the showMessageDialog class method of JOptionPane.

Class Name	Page #	Standard Classes
Ch2StringProcessing	64	String JOptionPane

This program illustrates string processing with the substring, indexof, and length methods of the String class.

Class Name	Page #	Standard Classes
Ch2StringProcessing2 **	N/A	

This is the same as Ch2StringProcessing but accepts input. It uses the showInput-Dialog class method of JOptionPane for input.

Class Name	Page #	Standard Classes
Ch2DateDisplay	68	Date SimpleDateFormat JOptionPane

It creates and displays today's date in two different styles: one in the format 1/12/03 9:25AM and another in the format Sunday January 12, 2003.

Class Name	Page #	Standard Classes
Ch2Greetings	70	String JOptionPane

It accepts a name as a string input and replies with a greeting.

Class Name	Page #	Standard Classes
Ch2Monogram	74, 76	String JOptionPane

This class in the Chapter 2 sample development program accepts a full name as a string input and displays the monogram of the input name. It uses the showInputDialog class method of JOptionPane for input.

Chapter 3

Class Name	Page #	Standard Classes
Ch3Circle	101	String JOptionPane Double

This program accepts a radius as an input and displays the circle's area and circumference. The program shows how to convert a string input to a double value with the parseDouble class method of the Double class.

Chapter 3 *(Continued)*

Class Name	Page #	Standard Classes
Ch3Circle2 **	N/A	String JOptionPane Double DecimalFormat

It is the same as Ch3Circle, but restricts the fractional values to three decimal places when displaying the area and circumference. Formatting of the double values is done by using the DecimalFormat class.

Class Name	Page #	Standard Classes
Ch3SystemOut *	106	System

It illustrates the use of System.out for console output.

Class Name	Page #	Standard Classes
Ch3Circle3	107	String JOptionPane Double DecimalFormat System

This is the same as Ch3Circle2, but the output is sent to System.out.

Class Name	Page #	Standard Classes
Ch3SystemIn *	110	BufferedReader InputStreamReader System String

It illustrates the use of System.in for console input.

Class Name	Page #	Standard Classes
Ch3Circle4	112	BufferedReader InputStreamReader System String

This is the same as Ch2Circle2, but the input and output are done exclusively with System.in and System.out.

Class Name	Page #	Standard Classes
Ch3StatueHeight	116	JOptionPane DecimalFormat Double Math

This program computes the height of a given statue. It illustrates mathematical computation by using the class methods of the Math class.

Class Name	Page #	Standard Classes
Ch3TestCalendar	119	GregorianCalendar System

It illustrates how to use the GregorianCalendar class for date manipulation.

Class Name	Page #	Standard Classes
Ch3IndependenceDay	121	GregorianCalendar SimpleDateFormat JOptionPane

This program displays the day of the week of a designed date (in this example, we chose Independence Day). The date is specified in the program by changing the arguments in the GregorianCalendar constructor.

Chapter 3 *(Continued)*

Class Name	Page #	Standard Classes
Ch3FindDayOfWeek	121	GregorianCalendar SimpleDateFormat BufferedReader InputStreamReader System Integer

This is the same as Ch3IndependenceDay, but this program accepts year, month, and day as input and displays the day of the week of the given date.

Ch3LoanCalculator	126, 128, 130, 132	System Integer Double DecimalFormat Math

It computes and displays the monthly and total payments for a given loan amount, loan period, and interest rate.

Chapter 4

Class Name	Page #	Standard Classes
CurrencyConverter	160	

This is the first instantiable class we designed in the book. The class is designed to perform conversion between the U.S. dollar and a foreign currency.

CurrencyConverter2 *	168	JOptionPane, Double, Float, Integer, Long, String

This is a modified CurrencyConverter class that automatically charges a fee and deducts it from the converted amount.

Weight	186	Math

This class is an encapsulaion of weight information. The weight can be accessed in grams or in pounds and ounces.

Ch4TestWeight	188	

This is a test program to verify the Weight class.

Kennel	192	

This class models a kennel for housing virtual online pets.

Pet	191	

This class models a virtual pet that can eat, sleep, and walk.

Ch4TestKennel	193	

This is a test program to verify the Kennel class.

Chapter 4 *(Continued)*		
Class Name	**Page #**	**Standard Classes**
InputHandler *	201	JOptionPane, Double, Float, Integer, Long, String
This service class provides convenience methods for getting int, long, float, double, and String data.		
Ch4TestInputHandler **	N/A	
This is a simple program to test the methods of the InputHandler class.		
Loan	211, 215, 219	Math
An instance of this class maintains three pieces of loan information: amount, period, and interest rate.		
LoanCalculator	210, 214, 217	JOptionPane System Double
This is the top-level controller class for the loan program.		
LoanCalculatorMain	210	
This is the main class of the loan program. Its main method creates and starts a LoanCalculator object.		

Chapter 5		
Class Name	**Page #**	**Standard Classes**
Ch5Circle	241	
This class illustrates the use of if statements. An instance of this class can compute the area and circumference of a circle, given the radius.		
Ch5Sample1	242	JOptionPane System
This is a program to test the operations of the Ch5Circle class.		
Ch5Triangle	250	
This class illustrates the use of if statements. An instance of this class can compute the area and perimeter of a triangle, given its three sides.		
Ch5Sample2	252	BufferedReader, InputStreamReader, Double, System
This is a program to test the operations of the Ch5Triangle class. It uses the console input and output, and the main method may throw IOException.		
Ch5LetterGrader	260	
This class illustrates the use of if–else–if statements. The class includes methods to compute letter grades.		

Chapter 5 *(Continued)*

Class Name	Page #	Standard Classes
Ch5Sample3	260	System

This program tests the operations of the Ch5LetterGrader class.

| Ch5Weight * | 266 | |

This class is a modified version of the Weight class from Chapter 4. This class includes comparison methods for comparing two Weight objects.

| Ch5TestWeight ** | N/A | |

This program tests the operations of the Ch5Weight class.

| Ch5SampleGraphics | 275 | JFrame Graphics |

This class illustrates how a Graphics object is used by drawing a rectangle and filled rectangle on a frame window.

| Ch5SampleGraphics2 | 279 | JFrame Graphics Color |

This class is the same as the Ch5SampleGraphics class, but it draws the rectangles in blue and red.

| DrawableShape | 286, 288, 295, 301 | Point, Dimension, Color, Graphics |

The class encapsulates the functionalities of a shape that can be drawn.

| Ch5DrawShape | 289, 293, 299, 302 | Point, Dimension, JOptionPane |

This is the instantiable main class of the sample development program.

Chapter 6

Class Name	Page #	Standard Classes
Ch6SleepStatistics	319	DecimalFormat Double JOptionPane

This program computes the average sleeping time of dorm residents. This program uses a while loop.

| Ch6DroppingWaterMelon | 335 | BufferedReader, InputStreamReader, Double, Math, System |

This program inputs the initial height and computes the position of a watermelon every second until it touches the ground. This program illustrates the use of the for loop.

Chapter 6 *(Continued)*		
Class Name	**Page #**	**Standard Classes**
Ch6ComplexForLoops *	337	
This program illustrates the use of complex `for` loops.		
Ch6CarpetPriceTable *	340	System
This program illustrates the use of nested `for` loops. The program outputs the price of a carpet ranging in size from 5 by 11 to 25 by 20.		
Ch6Format	342	String
This class includes methods that return a specified number of blank space characters or a specified number of designated characters. It is useful in formatting output values.		
Ch6CarpetPriceTablewithFormat	344	System
This class modifies the Ch6CarpetPriceTable class by formatting the output values. The format is done by using Ch6Format.		
Ch6SampleConfirmDialog **	N/A	JOptionPane
A simple program to illustrate the use of the showConfirmDialog method of JOptionPane.		
Ch6TestRandomGenerator	350	Math, Long, Date, JOptionPane
This is a test program that generates *N* random numbers and tracks the time it takes to generate them.		
Ch6HiLo	357	
This sample development program plays the HiLo game.		

Chapter 7		
Class Name	**Page #**	**Standard Classes**
Ch7DefaultJFrame	384	JFrame
This is a test program to check the default properties of a JFrame object.		
Ch7JFrameSubclass1	386	JFrame
This simple subclass of JFrame illustrates the basics of inheritance.		
Ch7TestJFrameSubclass	387	
This is a test main class that creates an instance of Ch7JFrameSubclass1.		
Ch7JFrameSubclass2	388	JFrame
This is the same as the Ch7JFrameSubclass1, but this class sets the background of a frame to white.		

Chapter 7 *(Continued)*

Class Name	Page #	Standard Classes
Ch7JButtonFrame	390	JFrame JButton

This is a subclass of JFrame with two JButton objects. This class only does the layout; no events are processed.

Ch7JButtonEvents	396	JFrame JButton

This class is an extension of Ch7JButtonFrame by adding event-handling routines. The event handler is an instance of ButtonHandler (see below).

ButtonHandler	396	JRootPane JButton ActionListener

An instance of this class is registered as an action event listener for two buttons in the Ch7JButtonEvents frame.

Ch7JButtonFrameHandler	398	JFrame JButton ActionListener

This class places two JButton objects on its frame and handles the action events of the buttons. This class combines the functionalities of Ch7ButtonEvents and ButtonHandler.

Ch7TextFrame1	401	JFrame JButton JTextField ActionListener

This class places two buttons (JButton) and one text field (JTextField) and handles actions events generated by these three GUI components.

Ch7TextFrame2	404	JFrame, JLabel, JButton, JTextField, ImageIcon, ActionListener

This is similar to Ch7TextFrame1, but adds JLabel objects. How an image is added to a JLabel is demonstrated in this class.

Ch7TextFrame3	407	JFrame, JButton, JTextField, JTextArea, BorderFactory, ActionListener

This class places two buttons, one text field, and one text area. String data entered in the text field are added to the strings in the text area when an action event is generated.

Ch7JMenuFrame	413	JFrame, JMenuBar, JMenu, JMenuItem, ActionListener

This is a frame class with menus that illustrates the menu action processing.

Chapter 7 *(Continued)*		
Class Name	**Page #**	**Standard Classes**
Ch7HiLo	431, 438	Math

This is a logic class for handling the playing of HiLo games.

Ch7HiLoFrame	418, 423, 433, 439, 442, 446	JFrame, JButton, JLabel, JTextField, ImageIcon, JMenuBar, JMenu, JMenuItem, ActionListener

This is the top-level frame with menus for the HiLo program. This class uses the service of Ch7HiLo for playing HiLo games.

Chapter 8		
Class Name	**Page #**	**Standard Classes**
Ch8Sample1 **	N/A	JOptionPane Integer

This sample program illustrates the throwing of NumberFormatException when an input cannot be converted to an int.

AgeInputVer1	461	JOptionPane Integer

This is the first version of a class that provides methods to input ages. This class includes no exception-handling routines; that is, the system will handle any thrown exceptions.

Ch8AgeInputMain	462	GregorianCalendar JOptionPane

This is a test program to illustrate the behavior of different versions of the age input class. The program asks for the user's age and replies with the year in which the user was born.

AgeInputVer2 *	465	JOptionPane Integer NumberFormatException

This is the second version of the age input class with the try-catch exception handling. Its getAge method will not return until a valid integer is entered. The method includes a while loop that repeats until a valid integer is entered. The loop continues while there's a number format exception.

AgeInputVer3 *	467	

This is the third version of the age input class that improves the second version by throwing an exception when the input is a negative integer.

Chapter 8 *(Continued)*		
Class Name	**Page #**	**Standard Classes**
AgeInputVer4	477	JOptionPane, Integer, NumberFormatException, IllegalArgumentException, Exception
In this fourth version of the age input class, a client programmer can set the lower and upper bounds of the acceptable input age values. An exception is thrown if the input value is not an integer (as in previous versions) or violates the specified bounds.		
Ch8TestAgeInputVer4 **	N/A	JOptionPane System
This driver program tests the behavior of the AgeInputVer4 class.		
AgeInputException	482	Exception IllegalArgumentException
This is a programmer-defined exception class that includes the designated lower and upper bounds and the input value that violates the specified bounds.		
AgeInputVer5 **	N/A	JOptionPane, Integer, NumberFormatException, IllegalArgumentException
The fifth version of the age input class is similar to the fourth version. The key difference is in the throwing of programmer-defined exception AgeInputException when the input value is outside the range of specified bounds.		
Ch8TestAgeInputVer5	483	JOptionPane
This driver program tests the behavior of the AgeInputVer5 class.		
CurrencyConverter *	485	IllegalArgumentException
This is the currency converter class with assertion statements added to the conversion methods.		
Ch8TestAssertMain **	N/A	JOptionPane Double
This is a driver program to test the behavior of the CurrencyConverter class.		
Resident	498	
An instance of this class represents a dorm resident. A Resident object has a name, room number, and password.		
InputFrame	503	JFrame JTextField JPasswordField JButton
This is a user interface of the program that accepts name, room number, and password.		

Chapter 8 *(Continued)*

Class Name	Page #	Standard Classes
Ch8EntranceMonitor	499, 506	JOptionPane

This is the main class of the program.

| SampleCreateResidentFile | 500 | IOException |

This is a simple (self-contained) program to create sample test data for the Ch8EntranceMonitor program.

Chapter 9

Class Name	Page #	Standard Classes
Ch9TestChar *	516	JOptionPane

This program is a simple illustration of conversion between char and int.

| Ch9CountVowels | 519 | JOptionPane String |

It illustrates basic string processing. The program counts the number of vowels in a given string.

| Ch9CountVowels2 | 520 | JOptionPane String |

This is the same as Ch9CountVowels but uses the toUpperCase method to simplify the testing.

| Ch9CountWords | 522 | JOptionPane String System |

This program counts the number of words in a given string. This program has a minor bug of counting one more than the actual number of words if there are one or more spaces at the end.

| Ch9CountJava | 524 | JOptionPane String System |

This program inputs words (one word at a time) and counts the number of times the word *java* occurs in input (case-insensitive comparison). The program terminates when the word *STOP* (case-sensitive) is entered.

| Ch9ExtractWords | 526 | JOptionPane String System |

This programs extracts words from a given string and displays them one word per line.

| Ch9PatternMatch1   ** | N/A | String System |

This is a simple illustration of the matches method, a pattern-matching method of the String class. It requires Java 2 SDK 1.4 or later to use this method.

Chapter 9 *(Continued)*

Class Name	Page #	Standard Classes
Ch9MatchJavaIdentifier	530	JOptionPane String

This program illustrates the basic pattern-matching technique by showing how to determine whether a given input word is a valid Java identifier.

Class Name	Page #	Standard Classes
Ch9MatchPhoneNumber	531	JOptionPane String

This program illustrates the basic pattern-matching technique by showing how to determine whether a given input is a valid phone number.

Class Name	Page #	Standard Classes
Ch9MatchPhoneNumber2 **	N/A	JOptionPane String Matcher Pattern

It performs the same task as Ch9MatchPhoneNumber but uses the Matcher and Pattern classes.

Class Name	Page #	Standard Classes
Ch9MatchJavaIdentifier2	536	JOptionPane String Matcher Pattern

It performs the same task as Ch9MatchJavaIdentifier but uses the Matcher and Pattern classes.

Class Name	Page #	Standard Classes
Ch9PMCountJava	537	JOptionPane String Matcher Pattern

It performs the same task as Ch9CountJava but uses the pattern-matching technique with the Matcher and Pattern classes.

Class Name	Page #	Standard Classes
Ch9PMCountJava2	538	JOptionPane String Matcher Pattern

This is similar to Ch9PMCountJava, but instead of counting the number of occurrences, this program displays the locations in the string where the word java is found.

Class Name	Page #	Standard Classes
Ch9ReplaceVowelWithX	542	JOptionPane String StringBuffer System

This program illustrates the use of the StringBuffer class by showing how the vowels in a given string are replaced by character X.

Chapter 9 *(Continued)*

Class Name	Page #	Standard Classes
Ch9EvenLetterWords	544	JOptionPane String StringBuffer System

This is another sample program illustrating the use of the StringBuffer class. This program extracts words with an even number of letters from a given string and creates a new string with these words.

Ch9WordConcordance	551, 556	Matcher Pattern

This class creates a word concordance for a given document. For each word in the document, the number of times the word occurs in the document is kept.

Ch9WordConcordanceMain	550, 554, 558	JOptionPane String FileNotFoundException IOException

This is the instantiable main class of the program.

Chapter 10

Class Name	Page #	Standard Classes
Ch10RainFall	571	DecimalFormat Double JOptionPane System

This is the first sample program that illustrates the use of a one-dimensional array of numbers. The program computes the annual average rainfall and the variation from the monthly averages.

Ch10RainFall2 *	573	DecimalFormat Double JOptionPane System

This is the variation of Ch10RainFall that uses an array of String so the month name is used to prompt the user when inputting monthly rainfall averages. The original Ch10RainFall uses month number (1, 2, etc.) instead of month names (January, February, etc.).

Ch10RainFallStat	575	DecimalFormat Double JOptionPane System

This program illustrates more examples of using arrays to compute various statistics from given monthly rainfall averages.

Chapter 10 *(Continued)*

Class Name	Page #	Standard Classes
Person *	579	

This simple class is used by Ch10ProcessPersonArray to illustrate how an array of objects is processed.

| Ch10ProcessPersonArray | 585 | JOptionPane |
| | | System |

This class illustrates the processing of an array of Person objects.

| Ch10TestArrayParameter * | 589 | |

This class is a collection of methods to show how an array is passed to a method.

| Ch10PayScaleTable | 619 | |

This sample program maintains a pay scale table by using a two-dimensional array of double.

| Ch10FriendsList * | 623 | List |
| | | ArrayList |

This simple program shows how a list of Person objects can be manipulated with an ArrayList.

| WordList | 627 | SortedMap |
| | | TreeMap |

This is the helper class for the Chapter 9 sample development program. This class maintains a word list to track the number of times each word in the list occurs in a given document.

| Person ** | N/A | |

This logical class represents a person. This class is the same as the Person class used in the regular sample programs.

| AddressBook | 598, 602, 606 | |

This class implements the functionalities of an address book for keeping track of persons. The class supports insertion, deletion, and search operations. Assertion statements are used in this class.

| TestAddressBook | 600, 604, 607, 611 | System |

This is a test program to check the operations of AddressBook.

Chapter 11

Class Name	Page #	Standard Classes
SearchRoutines *	637, 639	

The class defines two search methods—linear and binary search.

| Ch11TestLinearSearch | | System |

This is a driver program to test the linear search method defined in SearchRoutines.

Chapter 11 *(Continued)*

Class Name	Page #	Standard Classes
`Ch11TestBinarySearch **`	N/A	`System`

This driver program tests the binary search method defined in `SearchRoutines`.

`SortingRoutines *`	641, 643, 647	

The class defines two sorting methods—selection and bubble sort.

`Ch11TestSelectionSort **`	N/A	

This is a driver program to test the selection sort method defined in `SortingRoutines`.

`Ch11TestBubbleSort **`	N/A	

This is a driver program to test the bubble sort method defined in `SortingRoutines`.

`Heap *`	656, 657, 658	

This class implements the heapsort sorting method.

`Ch11TestHeapSort **`	N/A	

This driver program tests the sorting method defined in `Heap`.

`Person`	667	

This is a logical class that represents a person. The class includes methods to compare its instances.

`AddressBook (interface)`	662	

This interface defines the behavior of an address book that maintains a collection of `Person` objects. An address book is capable of adding and removing objects and sorting objects by name or age.

`AddressBookVer1`	670	

This class implements the `AddressBook` interface by using an array of `Person` objects. Bubble sort is used to sort the objects.

`AddressBookVer2`	678	`Arrays`

This class implements the `AddressBook` interface by using an array of `Person` objects. For sorting, it uses the generic sorting method included in the `Arrays` class.

`AddressBookVer3`	681	`Map`
		`HashMap`
		`Arrays`

This class implements the `AddressBook` interface by using an array of `Person` objects. The `HashMap` class is used for managing `Person` objects and the `Arrays` class for sorting `Person` objects.

`AgeComparator` (inner class)	679	

This is the inner class of `AddressBookVer2` and `AddressBookVer3` that compares two Person objects on their ages.

Chapter 11 *(Continued)*

Class Name	Page #	Standard Classes
NameComparator (inner class)	680	

The inner class of `AddressBookVer2` and `AddressBookVer3` that compares two `Person` objects on their names.

| TestAddressBookSorting | 663 | Integer
JOptionPane
System |

This driver program tests the sorting routine of the address book.

Chapter 12

Class Name	Page #	Standard Classes
Ch12TestJFileChooser	693	JFileChooser File

It is a simple program that shows how to use `JFileChooser` and `File` classes.

| JavaFilter | 695 | FileFilter
File |

This simple program illustrates the use of file filter to list only Java source files in a `JFileChooser`.

| Ch12JavaViewer | 696 | JFrame, ActionListener,
JTextArea, ActionEvent,
JMenuBar, JMenu, JMenuItem,
JFileChooser |

This program provides a frame that lets the user view Java source files. Only viewing is supported; no editing is allowed.

| Ch12TestFileOutputStream | 700 | IOException
File
FileOutputStream |

This is a test program to save data to a file using `FileOutputStream`.

| Ch12TestFileInputStream | 702 | IOException
File
FileInputStream |

This test program reads data from a file using `FileInputStream`.

Chapter 12 *(Continued)*

Class Name	Page #	Standard Classes
Ch12TestDataOutputStream	704	IOException File FileOutputStream DataOutputStream

It is a test program to save data to a file using DataOutputStream.

| Ch12TestDataInputStream | 705 | IOException
File
FileInputStream
DataInputStream |

This test program reads data from a file using DataInputStream.

| Ch12TestPrintWriter | 707 | IOException
File
FileOutputStream
PrintWriter |

It is a test program to save data to a text file using PrintWriter.

| Ch12TestBufferedReader | 708 | IOException
File
FileReader
BufferedReader |

This is a test program to read text data from a text file using BufferedReader.

| FileManager
(Chapter 9 helper class) | 710 | FileNotFoundException,
IOException, File,
FileReader, BufferedReader,
FileOutputStream,
PrintWriter, JOptionPane |

This helper class for Chapter 9 sample development is used for saving to and reading data from a text file.

| Person * | 712 | |

The serializable class used to illustrate the object I/O.

| Ch12TestObjectOutputStream | 713 | IOException
File
FileOutputStream
ObjectOutputStream |

This is a test program to save objects to a file using ObjectOutputStream.

| Ch13TestObjectInputStream | 715 | ClassNotFoundException,
File, FileInputStream,
ObjectInputStream |

This test program reads objects from a file using ObjectInputStream.

Chapter 12 *(Continued)*

Class Name	Page #	Standard Classes
Dorm (Chapter 8 helper class)	717	FileNotFoundException, IOException, IllegalArgumentException, ClassNotFoundException, File, FileInputStream, ObjectIn- putStream, FileOutputStream, ObjectOutputStream, StringBuffer

This helper class for Chapter 8 sample development maintains a list of Resident objects. In addition, the class supports file input and output operations.

Person **	N/A	Serializable

This is the same class from Chapter 11, but modified to implement the Serializable interface so its instances can be saved to a file.

AddressBook (interface) **	N/A	

This is the same interface from Chapter 11.

AddressBookVer1 **	N/A	

This is the same class from Chapter 11.

AddressBookStorage	721, 723, 725	IOException, File, FileOutputStream, ObjectOutputStream, FileInputStream, ObjectInputStream

This class provides file input and output services to save to and read AddressBook objects from a file.

TestAddressBookRead	725	IOException System

This class tests the read and search operations.

TestAddressBookWrite	723	IOException System

This class tests the write operation.

TestAddressBookFinal**	N/A	IOException

This class tests the read and write operations.

Chapter 13		
Class Name	**Page #**	**Standard Classes**
Student	733	
This class models a student entity.		
GraduateStudent	734	
This is a subclass of Student to model a graduate student entity.		
UndergraduateStudent	735	
It is a subclass of Student used to model an undergraduate student entity.		
Student **	N/A	
This is a slightly different version of the Student class used in the sample development program. This version is declared as an abstract class.		
GraduateStudent **	N/A	
This is a slightly different version of the GraduateStudent subclass used in the sample development program.		
UndergraduateStudent **	N/A	
It is a slightly different version of the UndergraduateStudent subclass used in the sample development program.		
ComputeGrades	760, 763, 765, 770	File, FileReader, BufferedReader, StringTokenizer, JFileChooser
This is the main class of the grading program that determines the course grade for graduate and undergraduate students by using different formulas. Standard use of inheritance and polymorphism is illustrated.		

Chapter 14		
Class Name	**Page #**	**Standard Classes**
Ch14TrackMouseFrame	784	JFrame MouseListener System
This program tracks the mouse click events. When a mouse button is clicked, the location where the mouse button is clicked is displayed.		
Ch14SketchPad	787	JFrame MouseListener MouseMotionListener
This program implements the SketchPad class introduced in Chapter 2.		

Chapter 14 *(Continued)*		
Class Name	**Page #**	**Standard Classes**
Ch14FlowLayoutSample	792	JFrame FlowLayout JButton
This sample frame illustrates the placing of GUI objects with the `FlowLayout` manager.		
Ch14BorderLayoutSample	794	JFrame BorderLayout JButton
This is a sample frame to illustrate the placing of GUI objects with the `BorderLayout` manager.		
Ch14GridLayoutSample	796	JFrame BorderLayout JButton
It is a sample frame to illustrate the placing of GUI objects with the `GridLayout` manager.		
Ch14NestedPanels1	800	JFrame, JPanel, BorderFactory, GridLayout, BorderLayout, JButton
This sample frame illustrates the placing of nested panels with each panel having a different layout manager.		
Ch14NestedPanels2	802	JFrame, JPanel, BorderFactory, GridLayout, BorderLayout, JButton, JTextField, JLabel
This is a redesigned GUI for the HiLo game using nested panels.		
Ch14TicTacToePanel	806	JPanel MouseListener
It is a panel for displaying the Tic Tac Toe gameboard. This sample class illustrates the use of nested panels.		
Ch14TicTacToeCell	804	JPanel, JLabel, ImageIcon, BorderLayout, BorderFactory, Point
An instance of this class represents a single cell in the Tic Tac Toe gameboard. A standard game is 3 × 3, so there are 9 cells.		
Ch14JCheckBoxSample1	809	JFrame, ActionListener, ActionEvent, JPanel, JButton, BorderLayout, GridLayout, FlowLayout, BorderFactory, JCheckBox
This is a sample frame to illustrate the use of `JCheckBox`.		

Chapter 14 *(Continued)*

Class Name	Page #	Standard Classes
Ch14JCheckBoxSample2	810	JFrame, ActionListener, ActionEvent, ItemListener, ItemAction, JPanel, JButton, BorderLayout, GridLayout, FlowLayout, BorderFactory, JCheckBox

This is an extended version of Ch14JCheckBoxSample1 that processes item events in addition to action events.

| Ch14JRadioButtonSample | 813 | JFrame, ActionListener, ActionEvent, ItemListener, ItemAction, JPanel, JButton, BorderLayout, GridLayout, FlowLayout, BorderFactory, JRadioButton |

This is a sample frame to illustrate the use of JRadioButton.

| Ch14JComboBoxSample | 817 | JFrame, ActionListener, ActionEvent, ItemListener, ItemAction, JPanel, JButton, BorderLayout, GridLayout, BorderFactory, JRadioButton |

This sample frame illustrates the use of JComboBox.

| Ch14ListSample | 820 | JFrame, ActionListener, ActionEvent, JPanel, JButton, BorderLayout, GridLayout, FlowLayout, BorderFactory, JScrollPane, JList |

It is a sample frame to illustrate the use of JList.

| Ch14JSliderSample | 823 | JFrame, ChangeListener, ChangeEvent, JPanel, JButton, BorderLayout, BorderFactory, JSlider |

It is a sample frame to illustrate the use of JSlider.

| Ch14TicTacToeCell | 804 | JPanel, JLabel, ImageIcon, BorderLayout, BorderFactory, Point |

An instance of this class represents a single cell in the Tic Tac Toe gameboard. A standard game is 3 × 3, so there are 9 cells. This is the same class as listed above.

Chapter 14 *(Continued)*

Class Name	Page #	Standard Classes
`Ch14TicTacToeView`	829,834	`JPanel` `MouseListener`

This class is similar to `Ch14TicTacToePanel` listed above, but this class adopts the model-view-controller design pattern.

Class Name	Page #	Standard Classes
`Ch14TicTacToeModel`	835,840	

This is the logic class of the program that keeps track of the gameboard.

Class Name	Page #	Standard Classes
`Ch14TicTacToeFrame`	830,836,842	`JFrame`

This is the main class of the program. The game is played by two human players.

Chapter 15

Class Name	Page #	Standard Classes
`Ch15Algorithms`	854–864	

This class includes a collection of recursive algorithms discussed in Chapter 15.

Class Name	Page #	Standard Classes
`TestCh15Algorithms **`	N/A	

This is a driver program for testing algorithms in `Ch15Algorithms`.

Appendix C

Standard Classes and Interfaces

In this appendix, we provide a list of standard Java classes and interfaces used in the textbook's sample programs. Many of these classes and interfaces are discussed fully in the book and used extensively in the sample programs, while some are mentioned briefly and used only in a few sample programs. For a subset of these classes and interfaces, we provide a brief summary and a list of key methods.

Alphabetical List

Standard Java classes and interfaces mentioned in this book are listed alphabetically. The interfaces are shown in italic font.

Alphabetical List		
ActionEvent	Double	InputStreamReader
ActionListener	Exception	Integer
ArrayList	File	IOException
Arrays	FileFilter	ItemEvent
BorderFactory	FileInputStream	*ItemListener*
BorderLayout	FileNotFoundException	JButton
BufferedReader	FileOutputStream	JCheckBox
ChangeEvent	FileReader	JFileChooser
ChangeListener	Float	JFrame
ClassNotFoundException	FlowLayout	JLabel
Color	Graphics	JList
DataInputStream	GregorianCalendar	JMenu
DataOutputStream	GridLayout	JMenuBar
Date	HashMap	JMenuItem
DecimalFormat	IllegalArgumentException	JOptionPane
Dimension	ImageIcon	JPanel

Alphabetical List *(Continued)*

JPasswordField	Matcher	PrintWriter
JRadioButton	Math	*Serializable*
JRootPane	MouseEvent	SimpleDateFormat
JScrollPane	*MouseListener*	*SortedMap*
JSlider	*MouseMotionListener*	StringBuffer
JTextArea	NumberFormatException	String
JTextField	ObjectInputStream	StringTokenizer
LinkedList	ObjectOutputStream	System
List	Pattern	TreeMap
Long	Point	
Map	PrintStream	

Logical List

The following list organizes the standard classes and interfaces from the alphabetical list in logical groups.

Logical List

	Drawing	
Color	Dimension	Graphics
Point		
	Events	
ActionEvent	*ActionListener*	ChangeEvent
ChangeListener	ItemEvent	*ItemListener*
MouseEvent	*MouseListener*	*MouseMotionListener*
	Exceptions	
ClassNotFoundException	Exception	FileNotFoundException
IllegalArgumentException	IOException	NumberFormatException
	File Input and Output	
BufferedReader	DataInputStream	DataOutputStream
File	FileFilter	FileInputStream

Logical List *(Continued)*

FileOutputStream	FileReader	InputStreamReader
ObjectInputStream	ObjectOutputStream	PrintStream
PrintWriter	*Serializable*	

GUI

BorderFactory	BorderLayout	FlowLayout
GridLayout	ImageIcon	JButton
JCheckBox	JFileChooser	JFrame
JLabel	JList	JMenu
JMenuBar	JMenuItem	JOptionPane
JPanel	JPasswordField	JRadioButton
JRootPane	JScrollPane	JSlider
JTextArea	JTextField	

Java Collection Framework

ArrayList	HashMap	LinkedList
List	*Map*	*SortedMap*
TreeMap		

Utility

Arrays	Date	DecimalFormat
GregorianCalendar	Matcher	Math
Pattern	SimpleDateFormat	StringBuffer
String	StringTokenizer	System

Wrapper

Double	Float	Integer
Long		

Class Hierarchy for Swing Components

Many of the methods we use for various Swing-based components are defined in the common superclass. Instead of repeating the same information in individual classes, we will list the methods in the class in which they are defined. Here is the inheritance hierarchy for the Swing components mentioned in the book (classes summarized in the next section are shown in blue):

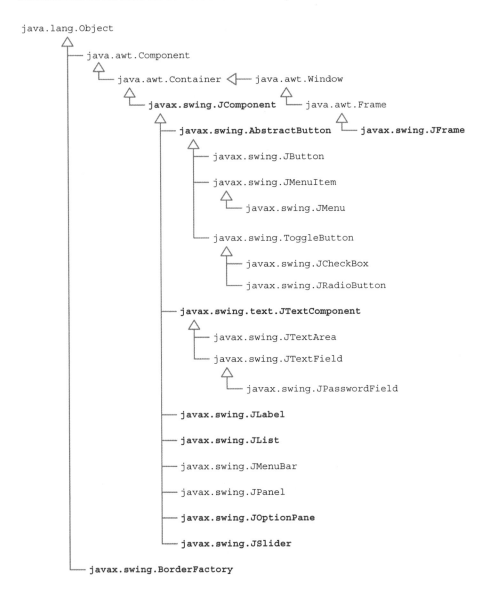

Summary of Selected Classes and Interfaces

In this section, we summarize a subset of standard classes and interfaces mentioned in the book. The classes and interfaces are listed in alphabetical order. For each class and interface we summarize, we include a brief description and some of its methods. The summary is intended as a quick reference. It is not a substitute for the API documentation. For a complete list of methods and full description, please consult the API documentation.

Class: `javax.swing.`**`AbstractButton`**

Purpose:	This is the base class of button and menu objects. Methods defined here are applicable to all subclasses.
Hierarchy:	`java.lang.Object` ◁— `java.awt.Component` ◁— `java.awt.Container` ◁— `javax.swing.JComponent` ◁— `javax.swing.AbstractButton`
Subclasses:	`JButton, JCheckBox, JRadioButton, JMenuItem, JMenu`

Public Methods:

`void ActionListener (ActionListener listener)`

> Adds `listener` as an action listener of this button.

`String getText ( )`

> Returns the text of this button.

`void setText (string text)`

> Sets the text of this button.

Class: `java.awt.event.`**`ActionEvent`**

Purpose:	An instance of this class represents an action event such as clicking a pushbutton or pressing the `Enter` key while the text field has a focus.
Hierarchy:	`java.lang.Object` ◁— `java.util.EventObject` ◁— `java.awt.AWTEvent` ◁— `java.awt.event.ActionEvent`

Public Methods:

`String getActionCommand( )`

> Returns a string associated with the event source.

`Object getSource( )`

> Returns the source object that generated an action event.

Interface: `java.awt.event.`**`ActionListener`**

Purpose:	An instance of this class represents an action event such as clicking a pushbutton or pressing the `Enter` key while the text field has a focus.
Hierarchy:	`java.util.EventListener` ◁— `java.awt.event.ActionListener`

Public Methods:

`void actionPerformed(ActionEvent event)`

> This method is called when the event source generates an action event. A class that implements this interface must define the `actionPerformed` method.

Class: `javax.swing.`**`BorderFactory`**

Purpose:	This factory class produces various types of borders for GUI components
Hierarchy:	`java.lang.Object` ◁— `javax.swing.BorderFactory`

Public Methods:

```
static Border createBevelBorder (int type, Color highlight,
                                            Color shadow)
```

> Creates a beveled border object of a specified type and colors for highlighting and shadowing. The value for `type` can be either `BevelBorder.LOWERED` or `BevelBorder.RAISED`.

```
static Border createEtchedBorder (int type, Color highlight,
                                            Color shadow)
```

> Creates an etched border object of a specified type and colors for highlighting and shadowing. The value for `type` can be either `EtchedBorder.LOWERED` or `EtchedBorder.RAISED`.

```
static Border createLineBorder (Color color)
```

> Creates a line border object in a specified color and default line thickness.

```
static Border createLineBorder (Color color, int thickness)
```

> Creates a line border object in a specified color and line thickness.

Class: `java.util.`**`Date`**

Purpose:	This class represents a specific instance in time with millisecond precision.
Hierarchy:	`java.lang.Object` ◁— `java.util.Date`

Constructors:

`Date ( )`

> Creates a new `Date` whose value is set to the time instance when it is created.

Public Methods:

`boolean after (Date date)`

> Returns `true` if this date is after the argument `date`.

`boolean before (Date date)`

> Returns `true` if this date is before the argument `date`.

`long getTime ( )`

> Returns the elapsed time in milliseconds since the epoch, which is designated as January 1, 1970, 00:00:00 GMT.

Class: `java.text.`**`DecimalFormat`**

Purpose:	This class is used to format decimal numbers.
Hierarchy:	`java.lang.Object` ◁— `java.text.Format` ◁— `java.text.NumberFormat` ◁— `java.text.DecimalFormat`

Constructors:

`DecimalFormat (String pattern)`

> Creates a new `DecimalFormat` initialized to a given `pattern`.

Public Methods:

`String format (long number)`
`String format (double number)`

> Return the formatted string of a given `number`.

Class: `java.io.`**`File`**

Purpose:	An instance of this class represents a file or a directory.
Hierarchy:	`java.lang.Object` ◁— `java.io.File`

Public Constants:

`String pathSeparator`

> This system-dependent path separator symbol is represented as a string. A path separator for Windows is the semicolon. This value can be retrieved by the statement `System.getProperty("path.separator")` also.

`String separator`

> This system-dependent file separator symbol is represented as a string. A file separator for Windows is the backslash. This value can be retrieved by the statement `System.getProperty("file.separator")` also.

Constructors:

`File (String filename)`

> Creates a `File` object for a given filename. The filename can be a full path name or a name relative to the current directory.

Public Methods:

`String getAbsolutePath (   )`

> Returns the full path name of this file.

`boolean isDirectory(   )`

> Returns `true` if this `File` object represents a directory.

`boolean isFile(   )`

> Returns `true` if this `File` object represents a file.

`String[] list(   )`

> Returns an array of file and subdirectory names of this `File` object representing a directory.

Class: `java.awt.`**`Graphics`**

Purpose:	This class supports drawing functionality.
Hierarchy:	`java.lang.Object` ◁— `java.awt.Graphics`

Class: `java.awt.Graphics` *(Continued)*

Public Methods:

`void drawLine(int x1, int y1, int x2, int y2)`

> Draws a line between (`x1`, `y1`) and (`x2`, `y2`).

`void drawOval(int x, int y, int width, int height)`

> Draws an oval.

`void drawRect(int x, int y, int width, int height)`

> Draws a rectangle.

`void drawRoundRect(int x, int y, int width, int height,`
`                    int arcWidth, int arcHeight)`

> Draws a rectangle with rounded corners

`void drawString(String text, int x, int y)`

> Draws a given text at position (*x, y*).

`void fillOval(int x, int y, int width, int height)`

> Draws a filled oval.

`void fillRect(int x, int y, int width, int height)`

> Draws a filled rectangle.

`void fillRoundRect(int x, int y, int width, int height,`
`                    int arcWidth, int arcHeight)`

> Draws a filled rectangle with rounded corners.

`void setColor(Color  color)`

> Sets the pen color to `color`.

`void setFont(Font font)`

> Sets the font to `font`.

Class: `java.util.`**`GregorianCalendar`**

Purpose:	This class represents a specific instance in time using the Gregorian calendar.
Hierarchy:	`java.lang.Object` ◁— `java.util.Calendar` ◁— `java.util.GregorianCalendar`

Public Constants: A partial list of constants defined in the `Calendar` class.

    int DAY_OF_MONTH

    int DAY_OF_WEEK

    int DAY_OF_WEEK_IN_MONTH

    int DAY_OF_YEAR

    int HOUR

    int HOUR_OF_DAY

    int MINUTE

    int SECOND

See the `Ch3TestCalendar` class for the sample uses of these constants.

Constructors:

`GregorianCalendar ( )`

> Creates a new `GregorianCalendar` set to the time and date of the system clock when this object is created.

`GregorianCalendar (int year, int month, int day)`

> Creates a new `GregorianCalendar` set to the argument year, month, and day. Notice the month ranges from 0 to 11.

`GregorianCalendar (int year, int month, int day,`
`                int hour, int minute)`

> Creates a new `GregorianCalendar` set to the argument values.

`GregorianCalendar (int year, int month, int day,`
`                int hour, int minute, int second)`

> Creates a new `GregorianCalendar` set to the argument values.

Public Methods:

`int get (int field)`

> Returns the specified field's value. See the class constants for the possible fields.

Class: `java.util.`**`GregorianCalendar`** *(Continued)*

`Date getTime (  )`

> Returns this object represented as a `Date`.

`long getTime (  )`

> Returns the elapsed time in milliseconds since the epoch, which is designated as January 1, 1970, 00:00:00 GMT.

Class: `javax.swing.`**`JComponent`**

Purpose:	This is the base class of all Swing GUI components such as buttons, text fields, menus, and others. Methods defined here are applicable to all subclasses.
Hierarchy:	`java.lang.Object` ⟵ `java.awt.Component` ⟵ `java.awt.Container` ⟵ `javax.swing.JComponent`

Public Methods:

`JRootPane getRootPane (  )`

> Returns the root pane that contains this component.

`void setBackground (Color color)`

> Sets the background of this component to `color`.

`void setBorder (Border border)`

> Sets the border of this component to `border`.

`void setEnabled (boolean state)`

> Enables this component if `state` is `true` and disables it if `state` is `false`.

`void setFont (Font font)`

> Sets the font used for this component to `font`.

Class: `javax.swing.JComponent`   *(Continued)*

`void setForeground (Color color)`

> Sets the foreground of this component to `color`. This is how you change the text color of a component.

`void setVisible (boolean state)`

> Makes this component visible if `state` is `true` and invisible if `state` is `false`.

Class: `javax.swing.JFrame`

Purpose:	This class is the extended version of `java.awt.Frame` that works as a container for Swing GUI components.
Hierarchy:	`java.lang.Object` ◁— `java.awt.Component` ◁— `java.awt.Container` ◁— `java.awt.Window` ◁— `java.awt.Frame` ◁— `javax.swing.JFrame`

Constructors:

`JFrame (   )`

> Creates a new `JFrame` initialized to default properties.

`JFrame (String title)`

> Creates a new `JFrame` with a specified title and default values for other properties.

Public Methods:

`Container getContentPane (   )`

> Returns the content pane of this frame.

`void resizable (boolean state)`

> Enables the resizing of this frame if `state` is `true` and disables the resizing if `state` is `false`.

`void setContentPane (Container pane)`

> Sets the content pane of this frame. You can pass an instance of `JPanel` as an argument.

Class: `javax.swing.`**`JFrame`** *(Continued)*

`void setJMenuBar (JMenuBar menubar)`

> Sets the menu bar of this frame.

`void setBounds (int x, int y, int width, int height)`

> Sets the origin point of this frame to (*x, y*), width to `width`, and height to `height`.

`void setLocation (int x, int y)`

> Sets the origin point of this frame to (*x, y*).

`void setSize (int width, int height)`

> Sets the width to `width` and height to `height`.

`void setTitle (String title)`

> Sets the title of this frame.

`void setVisible (boolean state)`

> Makes this frame visible if `state` is `true` and invisible if `state` is `false`.

Class: `javax.swing.`**`JLabel`**

Purpose:	An instance of this class is used to display uneditable text or image (or both).
Hierarchy:	`java.lang.Object` ⟵ `java.awt.Component` ⟵ `java.awt.Container` ⟵ `javax.swing.JComponent` ⟵ `javax.swing.JLabel`

Constructors:

`JLabel (    )`

> Creates a new `JLabel` initialized to an empty image and text.

`JLabel (Icon icon)`

> Creates a new `JLabel` with the specified image. Note that `Icon` is an interface, and the `ImageIcon` class implements this interface, so you can pass an `ImageIcon` object as an argument.

Class: `javax.swing.`**`JLabel`** *(Continued)*

`JLabel (String text)`

      Creates a new `JLabel` with the specified text.

Public Methods:

`Icon getIcon (  )`

      Returns the icon of this label.

`String getText (  )`

      Returns the text of this label.

`void setIcon (Icon icon)`

      Sets the icon of this label.

`void setText (String text)`

      Sets the text of this label. The argument should be a single line of text. Any text after the new-line character is ignored.

Class: `javax.swing.`**`JList`**

Purpose:	This component represents a list box.
Hierarchy:	`java.lang.Object` ⟵ `java.awt.Component` ⟵ `java.awt.Container` ⟵ `javax.swing.JComponent` ⟵ `javax.swing.JList`

Constructors:

`JList (Object[] list)`

      Creates a new `JList` with its items set to the passed array elements.

Public Methods:

`int getSelectedIndex (  )`

      Returns the index of the first selected items. If no item is selected, then -1 is returned.

`int[] getSelectedIndices (  )`

      Returns an array of indices of all selected items.

Class: `javax.swing.`**`JList`** *(Continued)*

`void setSelectionMode (int mode)`

> Sets the selection mode of this list to `mode`. The three possible values for mode are `List-SelectionModel.SINGLE_SELECTION`, `ListSelectionModel.SINGLE_INTERVAL_SELECTION`, and `ListSelectionModel.MULTIPLE_INTERVAL_SELECTION`. The default mode is `ListSelectionModel.MULTIPLE_INTERVAL_SELECTION`.

Class: `javax.swing.`**`JOptionPane`**

Purpose:	This is a convenience class that supports a quick and easy way to deal with a standard dialog box for displaying short messages or getting an input value.
Hierarchy:	`java.lang.Object` ◁— `java.awt.Component` ◁— `java.awt.Container` ◁— `javax.swing.JComponent` ◁— `javax.swing.JOptionPane`

Public Constants:	This is a partial list.
	
	`int YES_OPTION`
	`int NO_OPTION`
	`int CANCEL_OPTION`
	`int OK_OPTION`
	`int YES_NO_CANCEL_OPTION`

Public Methods:	Note the listed methods are all class methods.

`static int showConfirmDialog (Component parent, Object message)`

> Displays a standard confirmation dialog and returns the value to indicate which button (`Yes`, `No`, or `Cancel`) is clicked.

`static int showConfirmDialog (Component parent, Object message, String title, int optionType)`

> Displays a confirmation dialog with `message` as its prompt and `title` as the dialog title. The value of `optionType` determines which buttons are shown in the dialog.

`static String showInputDialog (Component parent, Object message)`

> Displays a standard input dialog and returns the entered value as a `String`.

`static void showMessageDialog (Component parent, Object message)`

> Displays a standard message dialog with the text `message`.

Class: `javax.swing.JSlider`

Purpose:	This component represents a slider.
Hierarchy:	`java.lang.Object` ◁— `java.awt.Component` ◁— `java.awt.Container` ◁— `javax.swing.JComponent` ◁— `javax.swing.JSlider`

Constructors:

`JSlider ( )`

Creates a new horizontal slider ranging from 0 to 100. The initial position of the slider knob is set to 50.

`JSlider (int min, int max)`

Creates a new horizontal slider ranging from `min` to `max`. The initial position of the slider knob is set to the average of `min` and `max`.

`JSlider (int orientation, int min, int max, int value)`

Creates a new slider ranging in values from `min` to `max`. The initial position of the slider knob is set to `value`, and the orientation to `orientation` (`JSlider.VERTICAL` or `JSlider.HORIZONTAL`).

Public Methods:

`int getValue ( )`

Returns the current value of this slider.

`void setMajorTickSpacing (int spacing)`

Sets the major tick spacing to `spacing`.

`void setMaximum (int max)`

Sets the maximum to `max`.

`void setMinimum (int min)`

Sets the minimum to `min`.

`void setMinorTickSpacing (int spacing)`

Sets the minor tick spacing to `spacing`.

`void setPaintLabels (boolean state)`

Draws the labels if `state` is `true`.

Class: `javax.swing.`**`JSlider`** *(Continued)*

`void setPaintTicks (boolean state)`

> Draws the tick marks if `state` is `true`.

`void setValue (int value)`

> Sets the current value of this slider to `value`.

Class: `javax.swing.`**`JTextComponent`**

Purpose:	An instance of this class is used to display uneditable text or image (or both).
Hierarchy:	`java.lang.Object` ⟵ `java.awt.Component` ⟵ `java.awt.Container` ⟵ `javax.swing.JComponent` ⟵ `javax.swing.JTextComponent`
Constructors:	They use the constructors of the subclasses `JTextArea` and `JTextField`.

Public Methods:

`String getSelectedText ( )`

> Returns the selected text of this text component.

`String getText ( )`

> Returns the text of this text component.

`void setEditable (boolean state)`

> Makes this text component editable if `state` is `true` and an editable if `state` is `false`.

`void setText (String str)`

> Sets the text of this text component to a specified `str`.

Class: `java.lang.`**`Math`**

Purpose:	This class supports mathematical functions.
Hierarchy:	`java.lang.Object` ⟵ `java.awt.Graphics`

Class: `java.lang.`**Math** *(Continued)*

Public Constants:

`double PI`

The value of pi.

`double E`

The value of natural number *e*.

Public Methods: Please refer to Table 3.6 for a list of methods.

Class: `java.text.`**SimpleDateFormat**

Purpose:	This class is used to format dates.
Hierarchy:	`java.lang.Object` ◁— `java.text.Format` ◁— `java.text.DateFormat` ◁— `java.text.SimpleDateFormat`

Constructors:

`SimpleDateFormat (   )`

Creates a new `SimpleDateFormat` initialized to a default format.

`SimpleDateFormat (String format)`

Creates a new `SimpleDateFormat` initialized to the specified format. See Table 2.1 for the symbols you can use to specify the format.

Public Methods:

`String format (Date date)`

Returns the formatted string of a given `date`.

Class: `java.lang.`**String**

Purpose:	This class represents an immutable sequence of characters.
Hierarchy:	`java.lang.Object` ◁— `java.lang.String`

Class: `java.lang.`**`String`** *(Continued)*

Constructors:

`String ( )`

Creates a new empty `String`.

`String (String str)`

Creates a new `String` from a given `str`.

Public Methods:

`char chatAt (int index)`

Returns a character at position `index`. The first character in a string is at position 0.

`String concat(String str)`

Returns a new string that is a concatenation of this string and the argument `str`. The concatenation operator + is equivalent to this method.

`boolean equals(String str)`

Returns `true` if this string has the same sequence of characters as the argument `str`. Comparison is done in a case-sensitive manner.

`boolean equalsIgnoreCase(String str)`

Is the same as `equals` but in a case-insensitive manner.

`int length()`

Returns the number of characters in this string.

`boolean matches(String regex)`

Returns `true` if this string matches the given regular expression `regex`.

`String substring(int start)`

Returns a substring of this string from index position `start` to the last character of this string.

`String substring(int start, int end)`

Returns a substring of this string from index position `start` to `end-1`.

Class: `java.lang.`**`String`** *(Continued)*

`String toLowerCase(    )`

>   Converts this string to all lowercase characters.

`String toUpperCase(    )`

>   Converts this string to all uppercase characters.

`String trim(    )`

>   Removes the leading and trailing whitespaces (e.g., blank spaces, tabs, new lines).

Class: `java.lang.`**`StringBuffer`**

Purpose:	This class represents a mutable sequence of characters.
Hierarchy:	`java.lang.Object` ◁— `java.lang.StringBuffer`

Constructors:

`StringBuffer ( )`

>   Creates a new empty `StringBuffer` with the initial capacity of 16 characters.

`StringBuffer (String str)`

>   Creates a new `SringBuffer` whose content is initialized to a given `str`.

Public Methods:

`StringBuffer append (char ch)`
`StringBuffer append (String str)`

>   Appends an argument to this string buffer.

`char charAt(int index)`

>   Returns a character at position `index`. The first character in a string is at position 0.

`StringBuffer deleteCharAt(int index)`

>   Removes the character at position `index` from this string buffer.

Class: `java.lang.`**`StringBuffer`** *(Continued)*

```
StringBuffer insert (int index, char ch)
StringBuffer insert (int index, String str)
```

  Inserts an argument to this string buffer at position `index`.

```
int length()
```

  Returns the number of characters in this string.

```
StringBuffer reverse(  )
```

  Reverses this string buffer.

```
String substring(int start)
```

  Returns a substring of this string buffer from index position `start` to the last character of this string.

```
String substring(int start, int end)
```

  Returns a substring of this string buffer from index position `start` to `end-1`.

Appendix D
UML Diagrams

What is UML?

The unified modeling language (UML) provides graphical notation that can be used to model computer systems developed using object-oriented software engineering (OOSE). The focus of OOSE is identifying the problem elements that produce or consume information and describing the relationships among these elements. In OOSE, objects are defined to represent these elements during the system analysis and design process. UML diagrams allow software engineers to indicate the relationships among the objects used to define the system. Most of these objects will need to be implemented using software in the final system. UML is particularly useful when the plan is to implement the system in an object-oriented language like Java.

Software engineers use several types of models during the analysis and design phases of the software development process. Data models describe object attributes and relationships with each other. Functional models show how data is transformed as it flows through the system. Behavioral models depict the actions taken by the system in response to events. Architectural diagrams show the relationships among the hardware and software components needed to implement the complete system. UML provides several types of diagrams to support the modeling needs of software engineers. The author has made use of a subset of the UML class diagram notation to describe class content throughout this text.

This appendix will describe the use of UML diagrams to model the attributes, behavior, and architecture of a simple vending machine. This vending machine accepts a single coin and dispenses a single product. The machine does not give change. If a bad coin is inserted, or if the machine has no product to dispense, the coin will be returned to the customer. A merchant owns the machine and adds products to it. The merchant also removes the coins from the coin box.

Class Diagram

Class diagrams were introduced in the first two chapters of this text. Class diagrams are one of the most important UML diagrams used by software engineers. Class diagrams are used to create logical models of computer-based systems. A class diagram shows class structure, contents, and the static relationships among the classes used to model a system. These relationships are known as associations and are drawn as lines connecting the related graph nodes. Each node in a class diagram is

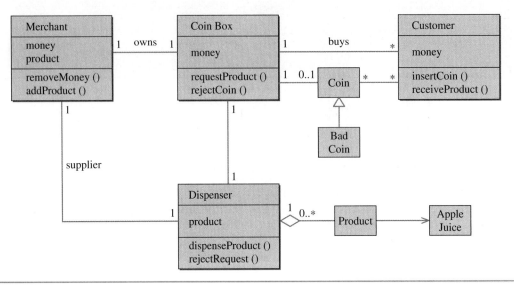

Figure 1 Class diagram.

labeled with its class name. The class node may also contain lists of data attributes and method prototypes. The visibility of attributes or methods can be indicated by prefixing their names with a + (public) or − (private).

An association line indicates that there is a linkage between two classes. Some associations may be labeled with a string indicating the type of relationship between the classes. Each end of the association is labeled with a number, *, or range to describe the multiplicity of the link (e.g. 1..* designates a multiplicity that ranges from 1 to many). Part whole relationships (known as aggregations in UML) are indicated using an open diamond at one end of the link. Inheritance relationships (known as generalizations in UML) are indicated using an open triangle to point to the appropriate super class. Class instances are shown drawing an arrowhead pointing to a class instance node.

Use Case Diagram

Use case diagrams are used to model system functional requirements. These diagrams show how users interact with the system. They are drawn to be independent of the specific user interface design that will be used in the final system. Use cases summarize several scenarios for a user task or goal. A scenario is an instance of an instance of use case for a particular actor, at a specific time, with specific data. Each scenario would be described using text description and shown graphically with a sequence diagram. Use case diagrams assist software engineers to develop test cases.

Users are called actors and are represented in use case diagrams by labeled stick figures. Use case nodes are labeled with user goals or tasks. Actors are connected to the appropriate nodes using lines. Links may be labeled with the string

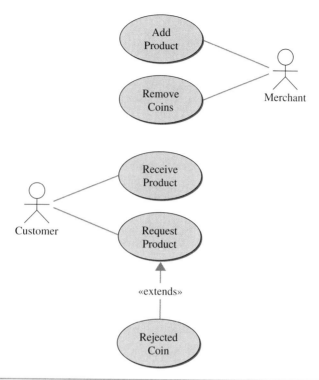

Figure 2 Use case diagram.

«extends» to show explicitly optional actor interactions or handling of exceptional uses. The string «uses» may be used to label links to existing use cases being used as subsystems in the current use case. Each path through a use case diagram represents a separate use case.

Sequence Diagram

Sequence diagrams model system behavior for use cases by showing the necessary class interactions. Sequence diagrams depict workflow from a use case graphically. They show the temporal sequence of message exchanges among a collection of objects as they communicate to achieve a specific task. In particular they show how the user (actor) interacts with a system to get work done (i.e. what messages get sent and when are they sent). The events modeled in sequence diagrams are external events initiated by an actor.

The actors and objects are arranged horizontally across the top of the diagram. The vertical dimension represents time. A vertical line called a lifeline is attached to each actor or object. The lifeline becomes an activation box to show the live activation period of the object or actor. A message is represented using an arrow labeled with a message. The message label may contain an argument list and a return type. Dashed arrows may be used to indicate object flow. If an object's

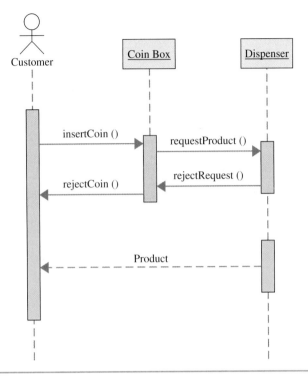

Figure 3 Sequence diagram.

life ends during the execution of the use case an X is placed at the bottom of its lifeline.

Collaboration Diagram

Collaboration diagrams show the message passing structure of the system. The focus is on the roles of the objects as they interact to realize a system function. They can be used to represent portions of a design pattern and are useful for validating class diagrams.

A collaboration diagram is a directed graph with the objects and actors as vertices. Directional links are used to indicate communication between objects. These

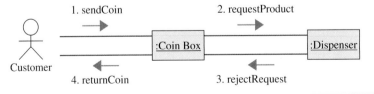

Figure 4 Return coin collaboration diagram.

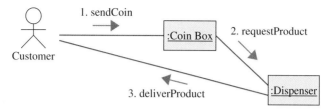

Figure 5 Product delivery collaboration diagram.

links are labeled using appropriate messages. Each message is prefixed with a sequence number to indicate the time ordering required to complete the system function. As you can see in Figure 5, not every collaboration diagram can be drawn horizontally or vertically.

State Diagram

State diagrams describe the behavior of a system, subsystem, or an individual object. The system state is determined by the values assigned to object attributes. A system is assumed to remain in its current state until some new event occurs. State diagrams show changes in system state or object attributes in response to external

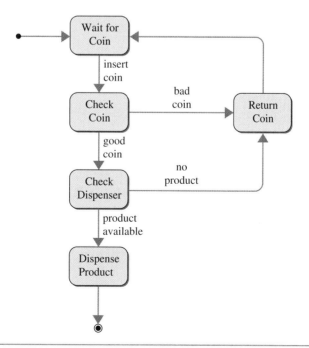

Figure 6 State diagram.

events or triggers. They can display the sequence of states an object goes through in response to potential triggers.

A state diagram is a directed graph whose nodes are labeled with state names. The nodes in a state diagram are drawn as rectangles with rounded corners. The links between the nodes are called transitions and are labeled with the name of the triggering event. A small black circle is used to represent the start state. A small back circle with a ring around it is used to represent the end state. Enclosing a group of nodes in the state diagram with a rectangle having rounded corners can be done to identify a substate.

Activity Diagram

Activity diagrams show the workflow that an object or system component performs. They can show both data flow (information exchange) and control flow (operation ordering). Activities are states representing the execution of a set of operations or thread needed to realize a system function. The transitions to new activities are triggered by the completion of the current activity. Activity diagrams are similar to state

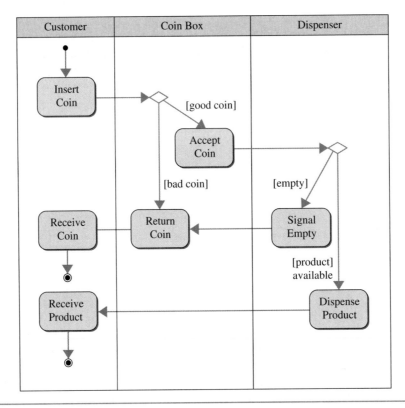

Figure 7 Activity diagram.

diagrams except that transitions are triggered by internal events. Internal events are not visible to the system user. Activity diagrams can be used to visualize the inter-relations and interactions between different use cases. Activity diagrams are usually associated with several classes.

Object responsibilities can be shown in an activity diagram by drawing swim lanes labeled with object names. Activity nodes are drawn using rectangles having semicircles on each end. The start and end state symbols are the same as those used in state diagrams. Links may be labeled with conditions that are the result of com-pleting an activity. Decision points may be represented using unlabeled diamonds. Activity diagrams can be used to show concurrent operations like fork, join, and rendezvous.

Component Diagram

The component diagram shows the relationships (i.e. dependencies, communica-tion, location, and interfaces) among the software building blocks or components in a system. The component diagram might be described as a physical analog of the system class diagram. It is typically made up of several classes and shows the high level code structure of the system.

Each system component is represented as a rectangle with tabs. A component interface is represented using a small round circle connected to a component by a line. An interface describes a group of operations used or created by a component. Arrows can be used to show the direction of information flow. Dashed lines can be used to indicate dependencies among components.

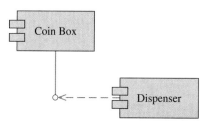

Figure 8 Component diagram.

Deployment Diagram

Deployment diagrams depict the physical resources for a system including nodes, components, and connections. Deployment diagrams show the relationships among both hardware and software components. They can also show the config-uration or deployment of run-time elements, software components, processes, and objects. Often component diagrams are combined in a single system deploy-ment diagram.

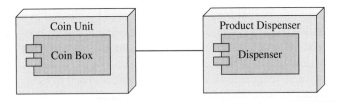

Figure 9 Deployment diagram.

Nodes in a deployment diagram are typically capable of executing code components and are represented by 3D drawings of boxes. Associations between two nodes are drawn as lines to represent physical connections (e.g. Ethernet) between the nodes.

Index